W0084764

Media competence

Auf den neuen **Media-competence-**Seiten trainierst du den Umgang mit Medien – von gedruckt bis digital.

Unit task

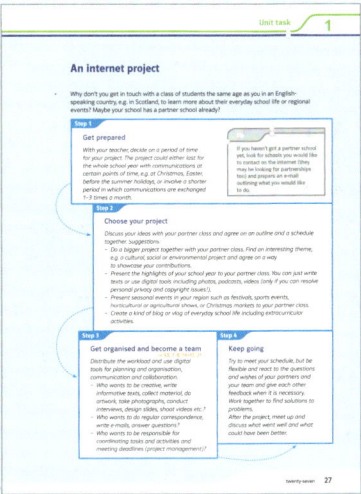

In den **Unit tasks** kannst du deine neu erworbenen Fähigkeiten überprüfen und kreativ einsetzen.

⟨ Texts ⟩

Die fakultativen ⟨**Texts**⟩-Seiten sind nicht verpflichtend. Hier erwarten dich Texte und Übungen, mit denen du Themen aus der *Unit* vertiefen oder weitere Aspekte kennenlernen kannst.

Skills

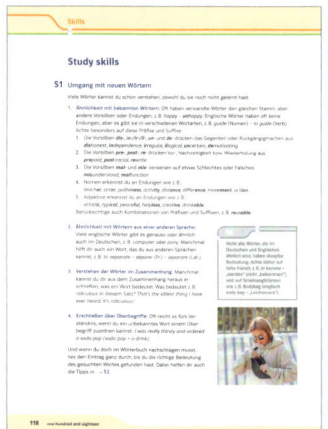

Im **Skills**-Anhang findest du allerlei Lernhilfen und Methodentipps.

Grammar

Im **Grammar**-Anhang findest du die wichtigsten Grammatikregeln, gegliedert nach ihrer Funktion, sowie Übungen zur Selbsteinschätzung und Wiederholung.

Und im Anhang findest du auch das Vokabular, eine alphabetische Wortliste (E→D) und vieles mehr ...

Find more online:
e9x67r

Auf einigen Seiten im Buch findest du Green-Line-Codes. Diese führen dich zu weiteren Übungsmaterialien im Internet. Gib den Code einfach in das Suchfeld auf schueler.klett.de ein.

Symbole

→ △ 90/1	zusätzliche / leichtere Aufgabe im Practice pool
→ ▲ 90/2	anspruchsvollere Aufgabe im Practice pool
→ WB 7/3	Übung im Workbook
→ G2	Grammatik im Anhang
→ TS	*Text smart* im Anhang
→ S3	Arbeitsmethode *(Skill)* im Anhang
👥	Partnerarbeit
👥👥	Gruppenarbeit
📱	Produkt für dein Portfolio
A1 🔊	Schüler-Audio
A1/33 ◎	Lehrer-Audio
V1 🎞	Lehrer-Video

Alle Schüler-Audios sind im Workbook und im Green Line eBook verfügbar.

Green Line 5
2. Fremdsprache
für Gymnasien

Zusatzmaterial für Schülerinnen und Schüler zu diesem Band:

Workbook mit Mediensammlung und Übungssoftware
978-3-12-813056-9

Workbook mit Mediensammlung
978-3-12-813055-2

Trainingsbuch Standard- und Schulaufgaben mit Lösungsheft und Mediensammlung
978-3-12-813051-4

1. Auflage   1 5 4 3 2 1 | 2026 25 24 23 22

Alle Drucke dieser Auflage sind unverändert und können im Unterricht nebeneinander verwendet werden.
Die letzte Zahl bezeichnet das Jahr des Druckes.

Das Werk und seine Teile sind urheberrechtlich geschützt. Jede Nutzung in anderen als den gesetzlich zugelassenen Fällen bedarf der vorherigen schriftlichen Einwilligung des Verlages. Hinweis § 60a UrhG: Weder das Werk noch seine Teile dürfen ohne eine solche Einwilligung eingescannt und in ein Netzwerk eingestellt werden. Dies gilt auch für Intranets von Schulen und sonstigen Bildungseinrichtungen. Fotomechanische oder andere Wiedergabeverfahren nur mit Genehmigung des Verlages.
Nutzungsvorbehalt: Die Nutzung für Text und Data Mining (§ 44b UrhG) ist vorbehalten. Dies betrifft nicht Text und Data Mining für Zwecke der wissenschaftlichen Forschung (§ 60d UrhG).

Hinweis: Die enthaltenen Links verweisen auf digitale Inhalte, die der Verlag bei verlagsseitigen Angeboten in eigener Verantwortung zur Verfügung stellt. Links auf Angebote Dritter wurden nach den gleichen Qualitätskriterien wie die verlagsseitigen Angebote ausgewählt und bei Erstellung des Lernmittels sorgfältig geprüft. Für spätere Änderungen der verknüpften Inhalte kann keine Verantwortung übernommen werden.

© Ernst Klett Verlag GmbH, Stuttgart 2022. Alle Rechte vorbehalten. www.klett.de
Das vorliegende Material dient ausschließlich gemäß § 60b UrhG dem Einsatz im Unterricht an Schulen.

Autorinnen und Autoren: Jennifer Baer-Engel, Göppingen; Louise Carleton-Gertsch, München; Melissa Keller, Iphofen; Jon Marks, Ventnor; Alison Wooder, Ventnor; sowie Rosemary Hellyer-Jones, Ehingen (Donau) und Peter Lampater, Ehingen (Donau)
Beratung: Dr. Thomas Becker, Nürnberg; Christel Beck-Zangenberg, Erlangen; Elmar Beyersdörfer, Gräfelfing; Wolfgang Funk, Bamberg; Michael Kleis, Geltendorf; Berit Möckel, Nürnberg; Uli Nürnberger, München; Wolfram Scharrer, Laaber

Entstanden in Zusammenarbeit mit dem Projektteam des Verlages.

Redaktion: Lektorat editoria: Cornelia Schaller *(Vokabular)*
Gestaltung: Petra Michel, Essen
Umschlaggestaltung: know idea, Freiburg; Koma Amok, Stuttgart
Titelbild: 1. Getty Images Plus, München (Nathan Bilow);
2. Alamy stock photo, Abingdon (robertharding/Chris Hepburn)
Druck: Mohn Media Mohndruck GmbH, Gütersloh

Printed in Germany
ISBN 978-3-12-813050-7

Green Line 5

2. Fremdsprache

Sarah Blanchard
10a

von
Jennifer Baer-Engel
Louise Carleton-Gertsch
Melissa Keller
Jon Marks
Alison Wooder
Rosemary Hellyer-Jones
Peter Lampater

Ernst Klett Verlag
Stuttgart · Leipzig

Inhalt

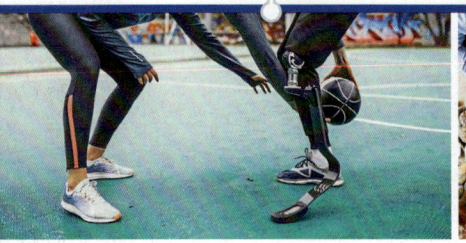  

| Lektionsteil / Thema | Kompetenzen / Medien / Inhalte |

Legende

‹ › Fakultativ

Welcome to Scotland
Fàilte gu Alba

Legende

‹ › Fakultativ

Legende

⟨⟩ Fakultativ

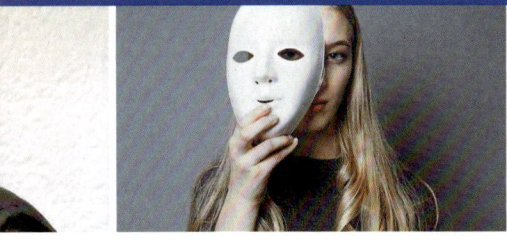  

Der Verlag orientiert sich bei der Bezeichnung von Minderheiten an Begrifflichkeiten, die sich zum Zeitpunkt des Erscheinens als Selbstbezeichnungen mit breiter Akzeptanz durchgesetzt haben. Dabei respektieren wir ausdrücklich die Belange der Betroffenen und die Vielfalt der Positionen in der Diskussion um korrekte bzw. präferierte Bezeichnungen. Konkret werden in diesem Band die Bezeichnungen „African-Americans" und großgeschriebenes „Black" bzw. „Schwarz" verwendet; Originaltexte wurden diesbezüglich nicht verändert. Im Hinblick auf geschlechtergerechte Schreibung im Deutschen wird gemäß der aktuellen Empfehlungen des Rats für deutsche Rechtschreibung verfahren. Für den Fall, dass sich der akzeptierte Sprachgebrauch über die Laufzeit des Lehrwerks verändert, weisen wir ausdrücklich darauf hin, dass zu keiner Zeit eine Diskriminierung von Menschen durch die verwendeten Begriffe intendiert war und ist.

"Same same but different?"

A Freedom of religion is a basic human right

B The rainbow has become an LGBTQIA+ symbol

C You are what you eat

D Inclusion means participation

SPEAKING **1 Working with the pictures**

Talk about the photos and the captions. Relate them to basic needs and aspects of human life. Identify similarities and differences between the people and the activities in the pictures.

SPEAKING **2 Talking about the title**

"Same same but different" is a phrase in Tinglish, a pidgin spoken in Thailand. Pidgins often develop where two or more languages come into contact. A pidgin is a simplified version of a language containing features of another language and usually serves as a lingua franca for special purposes. The words in this case are English, but there are no articles in Thai, and repeating a word for emphasis is a typical feature of Thai grammar. Explain what it could mean and discuss whether it's a good title for the material collected here. Give reasons for your opinion.

SPEAKING **3 Multiculturalism and diversity** → WB 3/1

a) *Work with the terms:* **multicultural, diverse, pluralistic, parallel society, discrimination, segregation, integration, inclusion.** *First, say what you associate with them, then look them up and write a definition for each one. Add example sentences.*

b) *What do you associate with the term 'culture'? Discuss if there can be one uniform culture in one country. How can people from different cultural backgrounds interact in a mutually beneficial way?*

E Globally, over 30 % of the people in cities live in slums

F Shopping can be a free time activity

G Feeling part of a group

H All humans are created equal

BLACK LIVES MATTER

SPEAKING

4 Changing societies

a) *Migration can change societies. What reasons for migration are there? Think of different periods in the past and at present and give examples.*

b) *In most countries, people from different ethnic backgrounds live together. There are different opinions on how this can work out.*

1. Remember and discuss historical examples of groups of people suppressing other groups and forcing them to assimilate.
2. Read the first five articles of the *Universal Declaration of Human Rights* proclaimed in 1948 and try to explain in your own words what they mean. Find current examples of places and situations in which these rights are not granted to everyone and talk about possible reasons.

LISTENING

5 Encounters → WB 3/2

A1/1–3

Listen to three situations with open endings. Think of a solution for each one and present it.

WRITING

6 A song: 'People are people' by Depeche Mode

→ S2, 6

Find the song and the lyrics on the internet and look up the words you don't know. Write a short summary and interpretation (about 100 words).

Scottish history

READING/SPEAKING **1** **Scottish clans** → WB 4/1

→ S17 **a)** *Describe the picture and say what you associate with it.*

→ S4–5 **b)** *Read the reference article and outline how the clan system worked.*

Scotland is famous for its clans, and there are many films
and books about their heroes. Clans are said to have formed
in Scotland around 1100 AD and to have descended from
kings. The word 'clan' comes from a Gaelic word meaning
5 'children'. It describes a group of relatives with a very strong
bond. But anyone who pledged their allegiance to the chief
of the clan could belong. The most important chiefs were
very powerful and had the roles of king, protector and
judge. The clanspeople were farmers but fiercely protected
10 their lands against other clans – and the English. They were
exceptional fighters known for their bravery and great loyalty
to their chief and the other clan members.

Across cultures

When people started using **surnames** in the 16th century, many Scots used the name of their clan
leader, such as Campbell, Mackintosh or MacGregor. Some people's names showed their profession,
e.g. Baxter (baker) or Webster (weaver). Others reflect where people lived, like Murray from Moray,
which is in the northeast of Scotland. The "Mac" or "Mc" often found in Scottish surnames is a Celtic
prefix meaning "son".

Find out and talk about surnames in your class or region.

READING/SPEAKING **2** **The historical background of a play**

*Read the following part of a programme flyer for the play 'Mary Queen of Scots got her head chopped
off' by Liz Lochhead. Say what you expect the play to be about.*

Although England and Scotland were finally
united in 1707, relations between the two
countries have often been problematic. The
kingdom of Scotland was founded in 843
5 and reigned by Scottish monarchs until 1290,
when the Scottish heiress to the throne died.
Edward I of England then declared the Scot
John of Balliol the next Scottish king. But when
the English asked Scotland to help defeat the
10 French, the Scottish leaders decided to help
the French instead, beginning Scotland's 260-
year alliance with England's enemy. So, Edward
took Balliol prisoner and declared himself king
of Scotland. Over the years, the Scots fought

back, led by famous rebels including William   15
Wallace and Robert the Bruce. Eventually,
in 1328, Edward III recognised Scotland's
independence.

Yet the countries continued fighting over
the next two centuries, even when James IV of   20
Scotland married the daughter of Henry VII of
England in 1503. Then in 1542, after the death
of James V, his daughter Mary Stuart became
the new Scottish queen. She was half-French
and was sent to France to marry the future   25
king Francis. They claimed the English crown
too. After her husband's early death, she
returns to Scotland in 1561 …

LISTENING **3** **Elizabeth I and Mary Stuart** → WB 4/2

A 1/4 ◉
→ S13

a) *Listen to the opening of the play 'Mary Queen of Scots got her head chopped off' by Liz Lochhead. It is partly written in Scots, a language which isn't easy to understand, but you should be able to answer these questions:*

1. Name the city which is described. *One green island*
2. Compare the two queens and their kingdoms (2–3 aspects) and try to guess why there was a conflict between them.

Elizabeth I
(1533–1603)

Mary Queen of Scots
(1542–1587)

b) *Think of what you know about British history and match the two queens with these contrasts in a grid:*

Scottish – English | Catholic – Protestant | unmarried – married three times | queen at age 25 – queen at six days old | was executed – reigned very successfully | her son became king of England and Scotland – had no children | gave her name to an era – became a romanticised character in literature and films

WRITING/SPEAKING **4** **Scottish contributions to modern life** → WB 5/3

→ S7–10

a) *Here is the beginning of an essay about the ideas and innovations which were brought forward by Scottish people in the 18th and 19th centuries and which are essential to our modern life. The author has made some notes in the yellow box. Complete the essay (about 280 words) by doing research and using some of the notes for the main part. Choose 2–3 aspects you find especially important. Then write an ending to sum up the impact of Scottish ideas and inventions on your life.*

> The Scottish Enlightenment was one of the most influential and innovative periods in Scottish history. Not only was the Industrial Revolution underway, but it was a time
> 5 when the emphasis moved from religion to reason, and some of the greatest thinkers, writers, artists, engineers and scientists were challenging old ideas. Much of what was happening was centred around
>
> Scotland's capital, Edinburgh. It was here 10 that the philosopher David Hume and the philosopher and economist Adam Smith debated important ideas. The 18th-century French philosopher Voltaire said, "We look to Scotland for all our ideas of civilization." 15
> Who were some of the other famous Scots who advanced science and technology as well as arts and literature?

> **James Watt**: engineer / Industrial Revolution / steam engine | **Charles Macintosh**: waterproof fabrics | **John Logie Baird**: television | **Alexander Graham Bell**: telephone | **William Cullen**: refrigerator | **James Clerk Maxwell**: mathematician / electromagnetic fields | **Alexander Fleming**: biologist / penicillin | **Robert Burns** / **Arthur Conan Doyle**: literature | **Robert Adam** / **Charles Rennie Mackintosh**: architecture | *Underestimated women:* **Williamina Fleming** / **Mary Somerville** / **Maria Gordon** / **Elizabeth Blackwell** / **Victoria Drummond** | . . .

👥👥
→ S14, 20

b) *You are going to hold a balloon debate. In groups, decide which person from Ex. 4a) you are going to be and prepare 2–3 arguments as to why you think your person is so important that he / she should remain in the balloon. One of you will represent your group, while the others will be part of the audience and ask questions. At the end of the debate, the audience should vote on who stays in the balloon.*

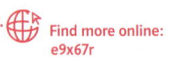

Find more online:
e9x67r

Unit 1
Scotland

| A | A view of Edinburgh, the capital of Scotland |

| B | Urquhart Castle with Loch Ness in the background |

SPEAKING **1 Pictures of Scotland**

→ △ 90/1

Which aspects of Scotland do these photos represent? Find out more about one of them and use pictures, text and pieces of oral presentation to create a short video (3–5 minutes) to attract tourists to Scotland.

VIEWING **2 A road trip into the Highlands on the NC 500**

V1 **a)** *While you are watching, make notes on the following points.*

1. the landscape people see when they travel along the road | 2. Tom Campbell's reasons for creating the new road | 3. its benefits | 4. Rob Mack's business idea | 5. the difficulties drivers face when they are going to Applecross | 6. what Applecross inhabitants think of the NC500

b) *Watch the film again and talk about it. What was new to you? What did you like?*

LISTENING **3 Living in Scotland**

A 1/5–8 **a)** *Listen to four people talking about life in Scotland. Make a grid with the headings Edinburgh, Glasgow, Aberdeen and Inverness. Note down what each person says about the city they live in.*

→ ▲ 90/2

b) *Say which city is the most attractive to you, and why.*

| C | Celtic football fans in a stadium |

| D | Scottish dancers in a Highland Fling competition |

READING **4** **A poem: Scottish traditions** → WB 6/1–2 → TS Poetry

A1
A1/9 ⊙

Use a dictionary and other sources to find and note down information about the cultural features of Scotland mentioned in the text. Comment on the image of Scotland presented in the poem.

→ S1–3
→ △ 90/3
→ ▲ 90/4

The Scottish Prince by Carol Ann Duffy

Every summer, I visit the Scottish Prince
at his castle high on a hill outside Crieff.
We dine on haggis and tatties and neeps –
I drink water with mine and the Prince sips

5 at a peaty peppery dram. Then it's time
    for the dance.
O Scottish Prince, the heathery air sweetens
    the night. Bats hang upside down
    in the pines like lamps waiting for light.

10 *Ask me, ask me to dance to the skirl*
    o' the pipes.
All the girls are in dresses. The boys are in
    kilts, but no boy's so fine as the Prince
    in his tartan pleats.

15 I wait for a glance from the Prince, for the
    chance to prance or flounce by his side,

to bounce hand in hand
down the Gay Gordon line.
Och, the pleasure's a' mine!
O Scottish Prince, the heathery air sweetens … 20
Ask me, ask me to dance to the skirl …
At the end of summer, I say goodbye to the
    Scottish Prince and catch a train
    to the South, over the border,
    the other side of the purple hills, 25
    far from the blue and white flag,
    waving farewell from the castle roof.
The Prince will expect me back again
next year – here's a sprig of heather
    pressed in my hand as proof. 30
O Scottish Prince, the heathery air sweetens …
Ask me, ask me to dance to the skirl …

Highlands

READING **1** **Leaving city life behind** → WB 7/3, 8/4 → G5–6, 10–11

A2 ◁))
A 1/10 ⊙

Sunshine on buildings and handbag departments, glamorous restaurants and stylish new clothes … these are definitely a few of my favourite things. I was born and
5 bred in Manchester, and until very recently, believed that without regular injections of indie[1] cinema, cocktails and art galleries, I might disintegrate helplessly into a pile of dust. But that was before I met my partner,
10 Andy, who lives 300 miles away in the West Highlands of Scotland.

Andy's two-bedroom cottage is between a loch and a forest, there's a river running through the garden and from the hill behind
15 his house you can see snow-crowned Ben Cruachan towering over the water. When I open the bedroom curtains in the morning, there are sheep staring in, often through a swathe[2] of soft rain, and beyond them, the
20 misty loch.

It is very beautiful – and very, very isolated. You'd wait a long time for a casual visitor to travel 14 miles up the single-track road and pop in for a cup of tea. There is no local pub.
25 There was one once, but it shut down due to lack of customers. The same goes for any kind of village shop. If we want supplies, we have to drive 40 minutes to the nearest town – which is actually not much more than a high street
30 and post office that inexplicably sells fancy dress wigs – and stock up for several days.

Any ideas I had of growing my own vegetables were quickly destroyed. "It's too exposed," said Andy. "My dad spent three years

35 preparing the soil before he could grow an onion." It would be faster to drive to France and buy them from a street market.

I'm also aware that while I hope to make one or two friends – and persuade the mobile
40 library to visit – I will desperately miss my social circle. Of course, they've promised to come and stay, and I'm sure they will, in high summer, when it doesn't get dark until 2 am, everything's in jaunty leaf[3] and red deer jump
45 around playfully through the forest. In winter, however, when gales are lashing[4] the house ("the roof's only ever blown off once," Andy reassures me) and the rain is, to quote Terry Pratchett, "a vertical sea with slots", it's less
50 likely they'll be making the six-hour pilgrimage.

I'm also going to have to stop locking the door. In urban Manchester, if you don't lock your front door at night, you're crazy. In rural Scotland, if you do, you're a paranoid
55 madwoman. There, it's not the burglars you have to worry about, it's the midges. In warm, still weather, they form an evil curtain it's impossible to walk through without getting them in your hair, up your nose and between
60 your teeth.

Then there are the power cuts when storms come, the patchy[5] internet, the lack of mobile signal … it's a rather different world from the one I'm used to. I hope I'm ready for
65 it – because if I can cope with the downsides, the upsides are worth any amount of urban convenience.

Flic Everett, The Telegraph, 2016 (adapted)

→ S5 a) *In two columns, collect the differences between life in Manchester and life in the Highlands mentioned in the text. Say which of the things the author left behind she misses most. Why does she want to stay nevertheless?*

b) *How does she adapt to the situation? Come up with more suggestions for her.*

→ S6 c) *What imagery does the author use to bring her new home to life for the readers? How does she use humour to describe the downsides of life in the cottage? Find examples.*

1 indie *(slang)* ['ɪndi] unabhängig | **2 swathe** [sweɪð] breiter Streifen | **3 in jaunty leaf** [ɪn ˌdʒɔːnti 'liːf] in unbeschwertem Grün | **4 to lash** [læʃ] peitschen | **5 patchy** ['pætʃi] lückenhaft

READING / WRITING **2** **A land of myths and legends** → WB 8/5

Scotland's breathtaking lochs, misty mountains and enchanted woodlands have inspired countless myths and legends. They contain many mythical creatures, including kelpies,
5 glaistigs, brownies, monsters and fairies. But what exactly are they?

The **kelpie** is a water spirit that is said to be found in lochs, rivers and streams. It usually takes the form of a horse and can be identified
10 by its dripping mane, although it can also assume human form. According to legend, it gets humans to ride on its back, takes them to the water and eats them.

Selkies are mythical creatures that live
15 under the sea. They transform themselves into seals to swim to the shore. Once there, they can take off their seal skin and assume human form (they are very beautiful!). But if they lose their seal skin, they are not able to return to
20 the sea.

Glaistigs are thin little grey women with long yellow hair who often wear green. Despite their size, they are said to be very strong. They haunt fields and houses, where they sometimes do chores at night. But if they get 25 upset, they do mischievous or nasty things.

Brownies on the other hand are usually male. Like glaistigs, they help around the home or farm at night. But if they are given clothes, they put them on and never return again. 30

Some Scottish lochs are said to be home to **monsters**. The most famous is the Loch Ness Monster, also known as Nessie. She is said to be like a dinosaur, with a long neck, small head and humps that can be seen above the water. 35 Although many people say they have caught sight of her, no one has managed to prove her existence. At least, not yet …

→ ▲ 91/5
a) *You want to play a fantasy game set in medieval Scotland. You can choose avatars from several mythical creatures. Read this short introduction to a book about Scotland's mythical creatures and discuss which avatars you would choose and why / why not. Think of how useful their individual powers and characteristics could be in a game.*

→ S7–8

b) *Create a fairy tale containing human characters as well as one or two of the mythical creatures. Write about 250 words or use digital storytelling methods.*

VIEWING **3** **Another lake monster**

V 2
→ S19
a) *Watch the video about Loch Morag (or Morar). Make a note of when the monster is supposed to appear, and how people can tell if it is there.*

b) *Explain when and how humour / a scary atmosphere is created in the film (think of music, visual effects, the speaker, the actor).*

c) *What do you think of the film?*

READING / WRITING
4   **The lonely campsite** → G2, 10–12

A 3–9 🔊
A 1/11–17 ◉

The novel 'Sea Change' is set in a remote part of the Scottish Highlands. Sixteen-year-old Alex lives with his mother in a small cottage. After his father's death, he is struggling to look after her and continue school at the same time. He regularly goes out fishing in the boat his father left him to help earn money to pay the bills. During the summer holidays, Alex and his best friend Daniel got to know Chuck, a mysterious young stranger, hiding on a campsite near an abandoned cottage. Chuck told them he was being traced by some bad people because he had witnessed a crime. He persuaded the boys to help him and kept challenging them to take risks. They secretly provided him with food and spent time at the campsite with him.

On his way to school with Daniel, Alex goes down to the beach to check on his boat and finds a dead body with a smashed face. The body is dressed in a pullover he gave to Chuck. Alex tells Daniel that he found Chuck's body and persuades him not to tell anyone. After arriving at school, Alex returns to make sure nobody recognises the pullover, but it is too late: Somebody else has found the body. Later that day, he goes out in his boat with his cousin Moth, who knows nothing about the events.

A   Dragging the creel[1] over the side of the boat, Alex was grateful for the monotony of the routine. He could work on autopilot: examine the catch and carefully remove any lobster that
5   had crept in; clear out the old bait[2]; then set the creel aside, ready to be re-baited and dropped back into the sea. The blue rubber gloves he'd given Moth to wear were far too big, but she quickly learned how to tie the
10   lobster's claws together once he'd measured it up to check the size. He was pleased and surprised at how much help Moth was and they landed his catch in record time.

"I want to look at a few more possible sites
15   while we're out," he said as Moth, obviously content with her efforts, slumped[3] amid the ropes.

In her nest, Moth nodded an okay before closing her eyes and turning her face to catch the sun's rays.   20

B   It was a pull against the wind to get to the part of the peninsula[4] where Chuck had his campsite by the Keeper's Cottage. As they drew closer and closer to the shore, there were no obvious signs of recent activity. But Chuck's   25
tent was set up in the lee of a ravine[5] where a fresh water spring erupted from the rock face.

Alex manoeuvred the boat into a nearby narrow inlet. After nudging[6] Moth's toes to wake her up, he jumped out and pulled the   30
boat onto a strip of sandy beach.

"I won't be long. Will you stay with the boat?"

Moth opened her eyes a fraction[7] to indicate that she'd be fine before wriggling[8]   35
deeper into the pile of ropes.

C   Viewed from the shore the cottage looked unchanged, despite having had its guts[9] ripped out and burned.

The circle of rocks that had bordered their   40
fire looked smaller in bright daylight. It was only eight or ten paces[10] across, yet it had seemed like a flickering ocean of flame when Alex had stepped onto the plank. The only remains were a few half-charred[11] sticks beside   45
some grey ash. The plank had been mostly consumed, but Alex could still make out its

---

1 creel [kriːl] Hummerkorb | **2 bait** [beɪt] Köder | **3 to slump** [slʌmp] zusammensacken | **4 peninsula** [penˈɪnsjələ] Halbinsel | **5 ravine** [rəˈviːn] Klamm | **6 to nudge** [nʌdʒ] anstupsen | **7 fraction** [ˈfrækʃn] Bruchteil | **8 to wriggle** [ˈrɪɡl] sich winden | **9 guts** [ɡʌts] Eingeweide | **10 pace** [peɪs] Schritt | **11 charred** [tʃɑːd] verkohlt

straight edges as he tossed pebbles[1] into the centre and watched puffs of ash fly out.

50 How many times had they each crossed the fire? Chuck challenging them to take crazier turns. Alex had chickened out[2] at being blindfolded[3] but Daniel had taken it on with a shrug. He'd almost reached the other end, too,
55 before the plank had given away and he'd fallen into the embers[4].

Alex had screamed at Chuck to help him get Daniel off, but Chuck had said, calmly, "That's the consequence of taking a risk,"
60 before stalking off to his tent, game over. There was no doubt. Chuck had proved himself to be a complete arsehole.

D Alex moved away from the fire pit and crouched on the cottage doorstep. A spider
65 dropped into the back of his hand and he let it run over his fingers before flicking it off. A pair of butterflies whirled over the nearby flowers.

Finally, he got up and walked on, beyond the Keeper's Cottage, towards Chuck's tent.
70 Chuck's tent. Ha! For all his fancy gadgets – his iPhone that he couldn't charge and his diver's watch – the tent was nothing but a camouflage tarpaulin[5] thrown over some branches.
75 When they'd first met, Alex had assumed Chuck was another wild camper – admittedly more adventurous than the ones who only made it a few hundred metres from the road. He'd even tolerated Chuck's seemingly crazy

story of being a runaway. And Alex hadn't 80 minded getting the provisions Chuck had asked for, and dropping them at the remote campsite when he was out fishing anyway.

Chuck's 'kitchen' was still intact: the gas bottle and burner still balanced on a 85 construction made of wood and corrugated roofing, the fishing rod[6] leaning against a corner. A plastic box in the branches of an oak tree contained an assortment of cutlery and tools. 90

E Alex picked out the penknife he'd lent to Chuck when the tin opener had broken. "Call that a knife? You'd have a job skinning rabbits with that blunt thing," Chuck had mocked; then he'd shown Alex the hunting knife he kept in 95 his kitbag[7].

It was a great setup[8] and, for a moment, Alex could see himself living there, away from the constant hassles of school and his lack of money. But beside the stove was the stack of 100 tins Alex had been encouraged to "borrow" when Chuck's cash had run out – they might as well have had "shame" stamped on every one.

Had Chuck been telling the truth about 105 the blokes he'd said were searching for him? Had they found him? Alex felt panic rise up in him again. All he needed to do was to make sure there was nothing more of his or Daniel's lying around and get out quick. 110

F His search over, he gave the site of the fateful fire a wider berth[9] on his return to the boat. He was hurrying along now, keeping his head down. His eye was caught by a soft glint[10] in the sand. He brushed the sand aside and 115 picked up a pound coin. It could have been dropped by any of them, at any time, yet Alex knew it was the one Chuck had kept in his shorts' pocket. The one he took out whenever there was a decision to be made. 120

Alex tossed the coin and caught it in his hand. Well, there were no decisions to be made now. It was all over. He'd been stupid to get involved in the first place but he wasn't going

---

1 pebble ['pebl] Kieselstein | **2 to chicken out** *(coll.)* [ˌtʃɪkn̩ˈaʊt] kneifen | **3 blindfolded** ['blaɪndfəʊldɪd] mit verbundenen Augen | **4 embers** ['embəz] Glut | **5 camouflage tarpaulin** [ˌkæməflɑːʒ tɑːˈpɔːlɪn] Tarnplane | **6 fishing rod** ['fɪʃɪŋ ˌrɒd] Angelrute | **7 kitbag** ['kɪtbæg] Seesack | **8 setup** ['setʌp] Aufbau | **9 *to give sth a wide berth** [ˌgɪv ə ˌwaɪd ˈbɜːθ] einen großen Bogen um etw. machen | **10 glint** [glɪnt] Glitzern

125 to get dragged into the aftermath[1].
Moth wasn't aware of the rising tide
lapping[2] at the boat when he got back. Alex let

her sleep on as he pushed the boat out to sea
and rowed back to the village.

From: Sylvia Hehir, *Sea Change* (adapted)

→ △ 91/6
→ S1, 4–5

a) *While you read, guess the meanings of new words (think of similar words and context).*

b) *Sum up what happens in sections A and B and explain why Alex goes back to the campsite.*

c) *Examine section C and collect words, phrases and ideas connected with the fire in a mind map. Think of how it is described and what Alex associates with it (e.g. danger).*

→ S6

d) *Look at lines 37–49. The author uses a simile and a metaphor when she describes the scene. Identify them and say what effect they have on the reader.*

→ S12

e) *Write a short characterisation of Alex, the main character (about 150 words). Think of what we learn about him through his thoughts and actions and by comparing him with Chuck.*

READING / WRITING   **5**   **Daniel's perspective**   → G4, 11

A 10–11 🔊
A 1/18–19 ⊙

At school, Daniel has been waiting for Alex, who hasn't turned up again.

A "No Alex today?"
Daniel, leaning against the fence, looked up at
the girl speaking to him. "Seems not."
The girl, Caitlin, was in sixth year, but Daniel
5 had seen her in his physics class earlier in the
day. She tipped[3] her head.
"Sorry, that came out wrong," he said. "He
was here first thing." Daniel hadn't seen Alex
since then and despite sending several texts
10 during the day, Alex hadn't answered any of
them. "You missed your bus?" he asked, putting
away his phone.
"No." She laughed. "I'm staying back to help
out at youth club. Volunteering. For my CV."
15 "Oh. I should do something like that,
I suppose."
"You won't have time in fifth year. It's crazy
how much work you're expected to do in –
what? – nine months."
20 "I believe you!" Daniel said.
"You going to the shop?" Caitlin asked.
Daniel nodded. "Yeah. It's hot. I'll get a coke."

B The line of customers waiting at the
counter was made up of a mixture of tourists
and locals and apart from a few polite phrases 25
exchanged between them there was nothing
of importance being chatted about. Still,
Daniel knew the big story of the day would
be circulating around the village and what
wasn't known for fact would be filled in along 30
the way. He had to keep reminding himself
that he'd done nothing wrong, and trust that
whatever Alex was doing wouldn't cause them
any further problems.
Daniel managed to avoid getting involved 35
in conversation with anybody, keeping his
head down, not looking at anyone, until they
reached the counter. But as he was passing
over money to pay for his drink, Halves came
behind him to join the queue. His words were 40
slurred[4] but Daniel could tell what he was
saying as he leaned in close. "They think it was
a teenager. Nobody we know."

From: Sylvia Hehir, *Sea Change* (adapted)

a) *Point out how Daniel and Caitlin interact with each other and what could be the reason.*

b) *Write Daniel's diary entry for that day (about 150 words). Include his worries as well as positive thoughts. Exchange texts with a partner and peer-edit each other's work.*

→ S7–9

c) *Guess how the plot of the novel could develop further. Discuss if you would like to read on.*

1 aftermath [ˈɑːftəmɑːθ] Auswirkungen | **2 to lap** [læp] schlagen | **3 to tip** [tɪp] senken | **4 slurred** [slɜːd] undeutlich

DIATION / VIEWING **6** **A film about Scotland** → WB 10/6–7

→ S16 **a)** *Your Scottish friend Fraser has found the description of a German documentary about Scotland on the internet. He asks you what the title of the film is about, what topics are dealt with in the film and what image of Scottish people is presented in the text. Write an English e-mail to him and answer his questions (about 180 words).*

V3 📹 **b)** *Watch the beginning of the film (up to 01:50) and make notes. Imagine you want to show it to an exchange class from Britain. Divide into groups and write English subtitles for the film. Compare your results in class and give each other constructive feedback.*

TV Programm	Sender	Beschreibung

Schottland – Rebellen im Rock
Ein Film von Alexander Stenzel

Schotten sind anders und darauf legen sie Wert.
Nicht nur der Kilt unterscheidet sie vom Rest der
Insulaner. Zu ihren Traditionen gehören genauso der
Hang zur Rebellion und die Lust auf neue Wege. Der
5 Earl von Glasgow wagte ein Experiment, das anderen
Adelsfamilien das Blut in den Adern gefrieren ließ.
Er engagierte brasilianische Straßenkünstler, um sein
Schloss mit Fantasiefiguren zu bemalen. Schloss
Kunterbunt ist mittlerweile ein Publikumsmagnet.

10 Rebellische Kreativität findet sich überall in
Schottland. So gibt es zwar ziemlich viele Wanderer
in Schottland, aber nicht wirklich hohe Gipfel. Sehr
viele erreichen gerade mal die 1.000-Meter-Marke.
Egal, sagen sich die Schotten: Wenn es schon keine
15 hohen Berge gibt, dann werden einfach möglichst
viele kleine bestiegen. Inzwischen ist das „Sammeln"
von Tausendern ein Volkssport. Die Schotten sind
wahre Meister, wenn es darum geht, aus der Not
eine Tugend zu machen.

20 Das sagten sich auch die Einwohner der
Hebrideninsel Eigg. Abgeschnitten vom Stromnetz
des Festlandes haben sie einfach die Insel gekauft
und eine eigene Energieversorgung aufgebaut. Was
auf der Insel politisch passiert, bestimmt die Basis.
25 Eigg ist eine Art „Freie Republik".

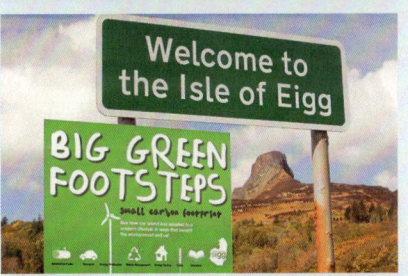

Eine Rebellin der ganz besonderen Art ist Evelyn
Glennie. Sie hat gewissermaßen die Naturgesetze
überwunden. In früher Jugend verlor sie ihr Gehör
bis auf einen winzigen Rest und studierte trotzdem
30 gegen alle Widerstände Musik. Nun ist Evelyn Glennie
eine der berühmtesten Percussion-Künstlerinnen der
Welt.

**Sendung vom Mo., 13.9.2021 13:15 Uhr,
Website des SWR, 2015 (adaptiert)**

Lowlands

READING **1** **Glasgow's miles better than this portrayal of a hopeless, dying city** → WB 11/8

A12 🔊
A 1/20 ⊙

There is much more to Scotland's largest urban economy than ill health and desolation, writes Gavin Moffat.

→ △ 91/7

While I am glad that the recent photo essay on Glasgow's excess mortality blamed it on the
5 city's housing policy and not its people, I was saddened to see how the piece presented a wholly negative view of the city (The Glasgow Effect: examining the city's life expectancy gap – a photo essay, 26 February).
10 For the vast majority, life in Glasgow is not a grim death sentence. The city is Scotland's largest urban economy and its base for arts and media. Glasgow is home to three universities, one of the world's most
15 prestigious art schools and – in the west and south – some of the UK's most culturally vibrant and bourgeois districts outside London. This does not detract from Glasgow's appalling social inequalities, but it is far from the
20 hopeless, dying city portrayed in the article.
It must be noted that while Glasgow city council area has Scotland's lowest life expectancies, Scotland's two council areas with highest life expectancy, East Renfrewshire and
25 East Dunbartonshire, both fall within Greater

Glasgow. They are home to 203,000 people and both begin just a couple of miles from the city centre yet are excluded from Glasgow's demographic data. This counterpoint rarely
30 makes its way into media portrayals of the city.
Lastly, there is the loaded term of the "Glasgow effect" itself. The Glasgow Centre for Population Health, who used the phrase in the title of a 2010 report, now discourages its use
35 as the mystery surrounding excess mortality has been solved. There is no "Glasgow effect", only a policy effect that has left long-lasting damage.↲
Glasgow is undergoing an unprecedented
40 level of development, socially and commercially. The article's lopsided portrayal of the city will only add to the social apartheid it discusses and deter tourism and investment. There is much more to Glasgow than ill
45 health and desolation. I hope future Guardian coverage of the city reflects this.
Gavin Moffat, Cumbernauld, North Lanarkshire
The Guardian, 2021 (adapted)

a) *Find the expressions in the text with the following meanings:*

1. a state without hope or confidence, **2.** the fact that more than an average number of people die, **3.** to hold sb responsible for sth, **4.** to make sb unhappy, **5.** a number of people that is higher compared to others, **6.** harsh, cruel, **7.** lively, dynamic, **8.** middle-class, **9.** to reduce the importance of sth, **10.** horrible, **11.** contrast, **12.** to not support any longer, **13.** never having existed before, **14.** unbalanced, **15.** to prevent, **16.** news about sth

Modern architecture on the Clyde Waterfront

b) *Explain what type of text it is and why the author wrote it.*

c) *Sum up what Moffat says about Glasgow and the Glaswegians. What arguments does he give to support his views? What are his hopes for the future?*

d) *Find the text online, explain the purpose of each of the links and sum up what further information they provide.*

e) *Do more research about Glasgow and discuss what you would like to see there on a visit.*

2   A song and a podcast about Glasgow → WB 12/9 → TS Poetry

The Dear Green Place

It was by the clear Molendinar Burn
Where it meets and runs with the River Clyde,
And they tell the tale of the holy one
Who was fishing down by the riverside.
5   A holy man, from Fife he came,
His name, they say, was Kentigern,
And by the spot where the fish was caught
The Dear Green Place was born.

Now the salmon ran through the river stream,
10 And they salted them by the Banks o' Clyde,
And the faces glowed as the silver flowed,
And the place arose by the riverside.
There was cloth to dye and hose to buy
The traders came from all around
15 And they raised a glass to the Dear Green
    Place,
The place that was a town.

Chorus: There is a town that once was green,
And the river flowed to the sea.
20 *The river flows forever on,*
But the Dear Green Place is gone.

When the furnaces came to fire the iron,
And the folk were thrown from the farmland,
Then the Irishman, and the Highland man,
25 And the hungry man came with willing hands.
They wanted work, a place to live,
Their empty bellies needed filled,
And the farmyard was another world
From the dirty, overcrowded mill.

Now, you may have heard of the foreign trade,   30
And fortunes made by tobacco lords,
But the working man slaved his life away
And an early grave was his sole reward.
A dreary room, a crowded slum,
Disease and hunger everywhere,   35
And the price to pay was another day
To fight the anger and despair.

Chorus

A thousand years have been here and gone
Since Kentigern saw the Banks of Clyde.   40
How many dreams and how many tears
In a thousand years of a city's life.
A city hard, a city proud,
And no mean city it has been.
Perhaps tomorrow it yet may be   45
The Dear Green Place again.
There is a town that once was green,
And the river flowed to the sea.
The river flows forever on,
But the Dear Green Place is gone.   50

Words: Alan Reid

a) *Find the song performed by the* Battlefield Band *and listen to it. Describe the kind of music and the instruments you can hear. How would you visualise what comes to your mind?*

A 1/21 ◉
→ △ 91/8
→ S13

b) *Listen to a podcast, in which the young US host, Joe Pearson, interviews a Scottish historian about the history of Glasgow. Make notes on the following:*
St Kentigern | St Kentigern and the fish | Trade | Industry | Living & working conditions

c) *Using your notes, look at the lyrics and explain what each verse is about. Listen to the song again and say how the music underlines the words (changes in vocals, voices, tempo, dynamics, tension).*

→ △ 91/8
→ S3, 7–10

d) *The song was written in the 1980s. Find out about the situation in Glasgow at that time and its development since 1990. Interpret the line "The Dear Green Place is gone" and comment on it from today's perspective. Write about 200 words.*

READING   **3**   **The Edinburgh Fringe Festival** → WB 12/10 → G7–8, 12

A 13
A 1/22
→ △ 92/9

The Edinburgh Fringe has so much going on that to try to sum it up quickly is virtually impossible – there's theatre, dance, cabaret, comedy, exhibitions, events, musicals, opera,
5 children's shows, music and more! Put it this way – the brochure is over 400 pages long, is on A4 paper, and has fairly small and closely packed type[1]. What we're trying to say is that it's huge. Really huge. In fact, the Edinburgh
10 Fringe is unquestionably the biggest arts festival in the world.

The Fringe is open to everyone – anyone can put on a show here, and so every year up-and-coming artists flock to Edinburgh to
15 try out new material, hoping to follow in the footsteps of famous artists who got their big break here, while established names return again and again to enjoy the artistic vibrancy[2] of this incredible festival.
20 With its gigantic size, the Edinburgh Fringe can seem a bit daunting at first, but as you leaf through the programme remember this is a wonderful and (almost) endless collection of opportunities – there really is something for
25 everyone at the Fringe, and the best way is often just to plunge in headfirst and see what takes your fancy[3].

The Festival Fringe story dates back to 1947, back when the Edinburgh International
30 Festival was still in its infancy[4]. Even though they hadn't been invited to perform in the International Festival, eight theatre groups came up to Edinburgh anyway and put on

their own productions outside the regular programme. These shows became known as 35 the "Fringe" of the festival – and the name stuck.

Over the next few years more performers followed their example and in 1958 the Festival Fringe Society was formed. The Society doesn't 40 select or censor any performances. Anyone who wants to put on a show and secure a venue is welcome to perform at the Edinburgh Festival Fringe.

If you are in Edinburgh city centre during 45 the month of August, the Edinburgh Festival Fringe is pretty hard to miss. From fences and walls plastered with posters, flyers being offered at every corner and intriguing street performers popping up everywhere, it feels like 50 the Fringe takes over the city.

Indeed the spread of the Fringe is far and wide across Edinburgh, with over 300 venues ranging from grand theatres to small basements. 55

From: Forever Edinburgh website (adapted)

→ S5   **a)** *Read the text and briefly sum up what is on offer at the festival, where it all began, who can take part, and where the events take place.*

→ S11   **b)** *Say what purpose the text was written for. Give examples of the language that is used to support your opinion. What effect does the text have on you?*

VIEWING   **4**   **An insider's guide to Edinburgh**

V 4
→ S19

a) *Watch the video by health and lifestyle blogger Claudia and describe how she presents her city. What impression of Edinburgh do you get? Comment on her vlog.*

b) *What does Claudia say about the differences between Glasgow and Edinburgh?*

1 type [taɪp] Schrift | **2 vibrancy** [ˈvaɪbrnsi] Lebendigkeit | **3 what takes your fancy** [wɒt ˌteɪks jə ˈfænsi] woran man Gefallen findet | **4 in its infancy** [ɪn ɪtsˌˈɪnfənsi] in den Kinderschuhen

Young people's issues

→ WB 15/11   → G3–4, 12–13

SPEAKING **1** What young people want

a) *Look at this extract about the topic of education from the SYP's manifesto for the years 2021–2026 called "From Scotland's Young People". It aims to give decision-makers information about the changes young people in Scotland want. What are your first impressions?*

EDUCATION AND LIFELONG LEARNING

The Scottish Government and Councils should invest in more support for and awareness of learners with Additional Support Needs.

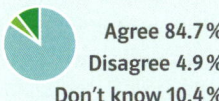

Agree 84.7 %
Disagree 4.9 %
Don't know 10.4 %

> There's been a lot in my life that's happened and I've not really been able to focus on school. With my dad passing away, (I didn't find) the school very supportive (…) They gave me one and a half days off. I was in a really bad place and I didn't want to be in school, and they were forcing me (to attend).
>
> **A young person whose family is affected by alcohol or drugs**

There should be more investment in college and university welfare services, such as mental health support, pastoral care, advice services, and housing support.

Agree 85.5 %
Disagree 4.2 %
Don't know 10.3 %

There should be a dedicated fund for initatives to educate, prevent and address LGBT bullying and discrimination in schools.

Agree 73.8 %
Disagree 12.9 %
Don't know 13.3 %

> I experienced some harassment from students that went largely ignored. When I came out (as a transgender man) at school, another pupil stood up to declare that he couldn't just "come in tomorrow and say I'm a girl." (…) He was told to be quiet but nothing was done beyond that – no actual challenge was made to the lack of tolerance his comments showed.
>
> **A transgender young person**

From: The Scottish Youth Parliament's Manifesto, 2021 (adapted)

→ S4–5

b) *The content presented here is based on a survey conducted by the SYP in Scotland in 2020. Summarise the results in your own words.*

c) *Identify the different elements used and say what effect they have on the readers.*

d) *Say if you would want to improve the design and how. What else would you expect to have been asked?*

e) *Try to explain the reactions to the transgender person's coming out. What could the teacher / the other pupils / the school have done about them?*
→ S14

Across cultures

The Scottish Youth Parliament (SYP) represents and is led by young people in Scotland between the ages of 14 and 25. It aims to give them an opportunity to discuss issues that are important to them. At the same time, it wants decision-makers in Scotland to actively listen to young people and uphold their rights. The SYP organises projects and runs national campaigns (e.g. for 16-year-olds to be able to vote in all Scottish parliamentary elections).

The SYP is politically impartial. Elections are held every two years and anyone who lives in Scotland between the ages of 12 and 25 is allowed to vote. Discuss the idea of youth parliaments and find out about the situation in your country.

READING / WRITING   **2**   **Issues that matter to young voters** → G2, 8, 11

→ △ 92/10   *Almost 19 out of 20 people felt it was important to vote in Scotland in the 2019 elections, an increase of 15 % since 2004 – and this increase is partly due to young people. But what issues matter to them? The BBC asked young people before the 2021 elections.*

David, 20, Edinburgh

David, a second year maths and physics student, said there was only one issue that mattered. "It's the NHS by quite a mile," he said. "To me right now, all the other issues seem very insignificant compared to the health crisis that's looming. Currently I've got a nerve issue with

5   my leg which is undiagnosed and I first spoke to a doctor in November – it's a bit stressful, I have to be honest. I feel like one of the lucky ones. I know someone with an eating disorder who collapsed the other day, and the mental health backlog is ridiculous."

Betty, 16, Cairndow

In the midst of studying, Betty has her sights on one day working for an international

10   organisation such as Amnesty International. With her eye on issues that affect people around the world, Betty has been struck by the exposure of disadvantaged countries to climate hazards. She said: "Climate change affects everyone but what really gets me is that the countries that suffer most are the ones that contributed the least emissions. Scotland could be really good at helping the climate with resources like solar panels and wind turbines. Improving

15   public transport would also cut emissions by so much."

   Over the past year, Betty's main focus has been on her education – an area she would like to see significantly improved by the next parliament. "I think young people should be a lot more involved in deciding what goes into education," she said. "I think they should reform the curriculum and exam diet – a single exam is a really unfair way of basing results on and it puts

20   so much stress on young people."

Kate, 23, Banchory

Politics graduate Kate teaches gymnastics to children. "I feel responsible in a way to make sure that they're getting a good education and that their lives are good outside gymnastics."

   Kate has considered this responsibility when deciding how to cast her vote. One issue she

25   believes has been neglected in the election campaign has been the criminal justice system and how it affects children. She said: "Children who haven't been convicted of any crime can be held on remand – I don't know what possible benefit that can have. Also the Black Lives Matter movement has shone a light on the justice system as whole and prompted me to look into it. Afro-Caribbean and black people in the UK are more likely to spend more time in prison.

30   If you think that something is unfair, you feel a responsibility to say something about it."

From: Mary McCool, BBC website, 2021 (adapted)

a) *Sum up the issues that the young people are concerned about and give their reasons.*

→ ▲ 92/11   **b)** *Do you agree with what Betty says, "I think young people should be a lot more involved into deciding what goes into education"? Discuss what you would want to improve.*

→ S8–10, 21   **c)** *Agree on 6–8 main topics that are important to young people. Your aim is to design a manifesto in English for EU decision-makers with one page for each topic. Divide the class into groups, one for each topic. Agree on two propositions for your topic. Discuss which elements you are going to include and create your page.*

READING / SPEAKING   3   Year of Young People in Scotland → G1–3, 9

The Scottish government made 2018 the Year of Young People (YoYP). It was the first time that this happened in the world. The aim was to celebrate the achievements, talents and contributions of young people in Scotland and to give them the chance to get involved in planning and co-designing events around the country. Sports, science and technology, art, music, writing and theatre events were created, and the contributions of young people have had a lasting impact. Here is an interview with Craig (17) from Inverness, one of 500 young people who volunteered to become one of the Year of Young People ambassadors in 2018.

Tell us about the type of activity you have been doing?

Craig: In my role as Year of Young People Ambassador I have been trying to
5   champion the work done by young people on a local and regional level through the use of social media, which has meant that the good work of people in the Highlands is being noticed more often!

10   ***Why did you want to get involved?***

Craig: I got involved with the Year of Young People in order to complement the work I have been doing as a Member of the Scottish Youth Parliament (MSYP). This
15   means that I have been able to build on my work as an MSYP and represent the area I grew up in on a national level.

What skills have you learnt so far?

Craig: I feel like I have gained two key skills
20   while being a YoYP Ambassador, the first one being public speaking and the second being the use of social media. Being a

YoYP Ambassador has meant that I have spoken to many Highland Councillors as well as some MSPs. This has allowed me   25
to develop my public speaking skills, which I have transferred to my work being an MSYP. Through YoYP I have also developed my skills in social media, I have tried to make tweets more engaging for young   30
people, which has enabled me to reach more young people with my MSYP tweets and has provided me with the skills to capture more voices in consultations.

Do you think there's a gap between young   35
people and older generations?

Craig: I do believe there is a gap between young people and some people in older generations. This may be due to the fact that they may not take on the ideas of   40
young people and ignore what they say – this could mean that the voices of young people can be completely ignored.

Scottish Government website, 2019 (adapted)

→ S3   **a)**   *Comment on the idea of the YoYP. (You can find out more about it on the internet.)*

b)   *Sum up why Craig became a YoYP Ambassador, what he wanted to achieve and what he has learned.*

c)   *Which tense is used most often? Explain why (simple and progressive form).*

→ S20–21   **d)**   *Imagine there was going to be a Year of Young People in Germany. Choose one of the following tasks and collect information to present to the rest of the class:*

1.   Whom would you invite to take part, and why?
2.   Whose achievements and contributions would you want to showcase?
3.   What events would you have, and why?
4.   Whom would you invite to be YoYP Ambassadors and what tasks would they have?

Online vocabulary research

The internet offers more possibilities to find out about words than just online dictionaries.

1 Warm up: Talking about dictionaries

Compare print vs. online and monolingual vs. bilingual dictionaries. List the pros and cons of each type and say which you prefer a) for looking up words to understand a text and b) for looking up words to write a text. Give reasons.

> **Tip**
>
> **Tips for working with online resources**
> 1. You want to look up a word that is not standard British or American English.
>   → Look for **specialised dictionaries** or **websites**, e.g. for slang, technical terms, idioms, Scots, etymology, pronunciation …
> 2. You want to avoid using a word too often. Is there a similar word you can use instead?
>   → Look for a **thesaurus** (a dictionary for synonyms).
> 3. You aren't sure how to use a word in a particular context.
>   → Look for a **dictionary of collocations**. Or: Look for the word in a **corpus** (a set of different kinds of authentic texts), e.g. the British National Corpus. Or: Type the complete phrase you want to use in inverted commas into the search box of a **search engine** and check **how many** results you get, if the examples are from **native speakers** of English (you can change the settings of the search engine accordingly) and if they are from **similar contexts**. These criteria help you to judge how the word is used correctly.

2 Using dictionaries and other resources

→ WB 16/12–13

You know how to find translations or definitions in standard dictionaries using standard abbreviations (→ S2). To check if a word fits a given context, check if it is the right word category (or part of speech), if its meaning makes sense within the context and if it belongs to the appropriate register. Cross-check with other sources to be sure.
Do the following exercises (try out the tips in the box). Afterwards, discuss which tools were most helpful to you.

1. Decide which translations of German *"umgehen"* fit these sentences.

   There's a ghost that `1` the castle for 300 years. He got up extremely early to `2` rush hour. She knows how to `3` difficult situations.

   | to avoid | to deal with | to handle | to treat | to walk |

2. Can you use these words in the plural? If yes, in what kind of context?

   | communication | fish | information | status | water |

   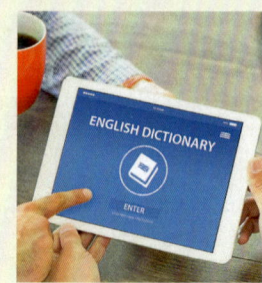

3. What are the past participles of these verbs?

   | to dive | to get | to glide | to heave | to knead |
   | to lead | to leave | to slide | to sink | to sting |

4. What is the right translation in each of these contexts?
   They went for frequent <u>walks</u> with their dog. They came from all <u>walks</u> of life.

5. How are these words pronounced?

   | angel | angelic | buoyant | cushion | fragile | privacy | router | tear | tier | weary |

An internet project

Why don't you get in touch with a class of students the same age as you in an English-speaking country, e.g. in Scotland, to learn more about their everyday school life or regional events? Maybe your school has a partner school already?

Step 1

Get prepared

With your teacher, decide on a period of time for your project. The project could either last for the whole school year with communications at certain points of time, e.g. at Christmas, Easter, before the summer holidays, or involve a shorter period in which communications are exchanged 1–3 times a month.

Tip

If you haven't got a partner school yet, look for schools you would like to contact on the internet (they may be looking for partnerships too) and prepare an e-mail outlining what you would like to do.

Step 2

Choose your project

Discuss your ideas with your partner class and agree on an outline and a schedule together. Suggestions:
- *Do a bigger project together with your partner class. Find an interesting theme, e.g. a cultural, social or environmental project and agree on a way to showcase your contributions.*
- *Present the highlights of your school year to your partner class. You can just write texts or use digital tools including photos, podcasts, videos (only if you can resolve personal privacy and copyright issues!).*
- *Present seasonal events in your region such as festivals, sports events, horticultural or agricultural shows, or Christmas markets to your partner class.*
- *Create a kind of blog or vlog of everyday school life including extracurricular activities.*

Step 3

Get organised and become a team
 → S3, 7–8, 14–15, 21

Distribute the workload and use digital tools for planning and organisation, communication and collaboration.
- *Who wants to be creative, write informative texts, collect material, do artwork, take photographs, conduct interviews, design slides, shoot videos etc.?*
- *Who wants to do regular correspondence, write e-mails, answer questions?*
- *Who wants to be responsible for coordinating tasks and activities and meeting deadlines (project management)?*

Step 4

Keep going

Try to meet your schedule, but be flexible and react to the questions and wishes of your partners and your team and give each other feedback when it is necessary. Work together to find solutions to problems.
After the project, meet up and discuss what went well and what could have been better.

Green Scotland

READING / WRITING **1** Scotland's Young People's Forest → WB 17/14

Hannah is a member of Young Scot. Read her blog entry and sum up what you learn about the Young People's Forest. Imagine you want to join the project. Write an e-mail to Hannah, introduce yourself and say why you are interested (about 150 words).

> **HANNAH'S BLOG**   **12 Jan 2022**
>
> Scotland's Young People's Forest is a flagship project calling on young people to act against the climate crisis by sustaining and designing forests and woodlands in Scotland. I joined
> 5 the project last year because I want to help protect forests and save animal species. We are supported by organisations like Young Scot and YouthLink Scotland and a range of other funds
> 10 and foundations. I've learned a lot about eco-systems and different kinds of trees already, but to join you don't need experience in forest design. Mentors educate us on sustainable planting strategies and forest management, while we,
>
> the young people, get to decide what work will be 15 done and then do it. I'd like to see more young people join because we are the next generation of adults, and we will be dealing with the climate crisis soon. We are making a difference already. Just look at the numbers: We have created 20 around 33,000 hectares of new forest by planting around 66 million trees in the last three years! Our goal is to cover 21 % of Scotland in woodland by 2032 (we're at 19 % now). We might even be able to recreate an ancient rainforest in the 25 Scottish Highlands, the Caledonian Forest, that is facing extinction. If you want to make a difference too, please get in touch.

SPEAKING **2** Creating green cities

> In 2019, a study by The First Mile (a recycling company) compared 21 UK cities according to criteria such as green spaces, air pollution, recycling rates and electric charging points. They identified Edinburgh, Glasgow and Aberdeen as the three greenest cities. A study by NatWest (a banking enterprise) in 2021 ranked Edinburgh second after Sheffield as one of the greenest places among the UK's 25 biggest cities. London came in 11th place.

→ S15, 20 *Work in groups. Think of measures to make your home town greener. Agree on one proposal for the town council and collect facts to support your arguments. Present your proposal in class (about three minutes). Take a vote in class to decide on the three most convincing proposals.*

VIEWING **3** Wind energy in Caithness → WB 17/15

a) *Find Thurso on the map. Say why it is probably a good place for wind turbines.*

V 5
→ S19 **b)** *The blind reporter Ian Hamilton travelled across Scotland before the 2021 elections to find out what issues people were concerned with. Watch the interview he did in Caithness and answer the following questions.*

1. Who benefits from the wind farm and how? | 2. What is the problem for the local people? | 3. What would the interviewee like the future government to do?

c) *Compare what you know about wind energy in Germany with what you have learned from the video.*

Scottish tales

ADING / WRITING **1** **Taming¹ the kelpie** → WB 18–22/16–21

A 14–21 ◁))
A 1/23–30 ⊙

I heard this story from Ian Stephen, a fabulous storyteller, author and poet from the Isle of Lewis. I decided to set it in the Northwest as there was something in the story that evoked² that incredible, primeval³ landscape for me. The kelpies have returned to Scotland in a striking way. A monument formed of two thirty-metre-high horse heads, named "The Kelpies", was completed in 2013 and towers over the land around Falkirk.

A Up in the far Northwest of Scotland, where jagged⁴ mountains rise over rain-soaked moors, a young man named John once lived with his parents on their croft. They had a few fields
5 for crops, a herd of milking goats and a horse to drag the plough. John grew up on the croft and never dreamed of going anywhere else. It was a hard life, for crops didn't grow well in the thin soil, but they got by and were happy
10 enough.

As John grew older, his parents grew older. He grew stronger, and they grew weaker and frailer⁵. The crofting work became too much for them, so John took over everything. He did
15 so gratefully, as his parents had cared for him, and he was proud to do the same for them. But they couldn't go on forever, and in time they both died, leaving John alone on the croft.

A few years went by. John worked hard
20 and managed to keep the croft going until tragedy struck. His horse took ill and died. John was truly alone now, for the horse had been a friend and companion to him. He was frightened, too. He couldn't afford another
25 horse, and how was he to plough the stony fields without it?

Winter came. After winter passed, it would be ploughing season. John kept warm by the fire, telling himself old stories as he sharpened
30 knives and axes. He tried not to worry, but he couldn't help it. One day, he tired of his fire and went out for a walk.

He wandered over the moors and among the lochs. The low winter sun shone out from
35 among the clouds, lighting up the landscape

in shades of burnished⁶ gold. John was in no mind to appreciate the beauty of it all. What was he going to do? How could he manage without his horse?

He was so caught up in his thoughts 40
that he paid no attention to where he went. Suddenly he came to his senses.

B He had come to a loch where no one ever dared to walk. It was said that a kelpie, a water horse, lived in the loch. If anyone saw that 45
horse and got up on its back, it would carry them under the water and drown them.

John stood there, searching the shore for any sign of such a creature. As he stood there, an old woman, a cailleach as they are called 50
in the Gaelic language, came walking past.

"Good afternoon," she called to him.

"It's not so good," said John, shaking his head. He reached into his pocket and pulled out a bannock: a cake made from oats⁷ that he 55
grew on his croft. "Would you like a bannock?" he asked her.

"Well, yes, I would," she said, hirpling⁸ over to him and taking the bannock he offered.

---

1 to tame [teɪm] zähmen | **2 to evoke** [ɪˈvəʊk] heraufbeschwören | **3 primeval** [praɪˈmiːvl] urzeitlich |
4 jagged [ˈdʒægɪd] gezackt | **5 frail** [freɪl] gebrechlich | **6 to burnish** [ˈbɜːnɪʃ] polieren | **7 oats** [əʊts] Hafer |
8 to hirple [ˈhɜːpl] humpeln

60 They ate and talked until the old woman said, "Well, I'll be getting home before dark, and so should you. But you gave me something, so I'll give you something in return."

She took from her pocket a woollen shawl[1].

65 "You take that," she said, "and remember, it can cover more than skin."

They parted ways. John went home and remained there as the winter deepened. More than ever, he fretted[2] over what he would do

70 come the ploughing season.

C   One day, he decided to go out walking again. The sky was clear, the air was sharp and the mountains wore their white winter cloak. John walked without caring where he went.

75 Just as before, he came to the loch where the kelpie was said to live.

This time he walked along its shore, remembering the stories his father used to tell about kelpies. They looked like horses,

80 but with dark, curly[3] beards. A kelpie would walk up to someone on a lochside and lower its hindquarters[4], looking expectantly at that person as if offering a ride. When the poor, unsuspecting[5] soul sat upon the kelpie, it

85 would race for the water. The rider would try to leap or climb off, but they would find themselves stuck to the kelpie's back. Into the water they went, never to be seen again.

As John walked, he saw coming towards

90 him the old cailleach.

"Good afternoon," she said. "It's good to see you again."

"It's good to see you too."

"You looked like you were deep in thought,

95 just now," she said.

"I was only telling myself a story."

"It's a while since anyone told me a story," said the old cailleach.

"Well," said the young man, "I'll tell you

100 a story." So he told her the story he had been thinking of, and she told him one, and he told her another.

"Thank you for sharing your stories with me," she said. "I'll be getting home now, but let

105 me give you something first."

From her pocket she took a little pot, which she gave to John. It was full of salt.

"Remember," she said to him, "salt can harm as well as heal."

D   Midwinter came and went. The wheel of   110 the seasons spun towards spring, and the first snowdrops had broken free when John next went out walking. Patches of melting snow dotted[6] the moor, and the sun felt warm on his face. Winter would be over soon. Ploughing   115 season would come with the spring, and he was without a horse.

Once more, John walked here and there until he found himself at the edge of the kelpie's loch. He saw the old woman there.   120 As he drew closer, he saw she was carrying an armful of creels: woven baskets for trapping lobsters. She seemed to be struggling to carry them.

John greeted the old woman and said,   125 "Where are you taking those creels?"

"I'm taking them home."

"Would you like some help?"

"Thank you. I would."

John took a couple of the creels from her.   130 Together they walked over the moors until they came to the little house in which the old woman lived.

"Thank you," she said. "You've made my day easier. Now, there's something I'd like to give   135 you." She bent over an old chest, rummaged[7] around inside and drew out a tangled[8] web of leather and iron. It was a horse's bridle[9].

"You take that," she said. "It can harness[10] more than a horse."   140

John walked home.

That night, he sat by his fire, the old woman's gifts laid out before him. The shawl, the pot of salt and the bridle.

He knew what he must do; but he was   145 afraid to do it.

E   In spite of his fear, John walked to the loch the next day. This time, he had the shawl in his left pocket, the pot of salt in his right pocket and the bridle slung over his shoulder.   150

He reached the loch. Against a stunted[11]

---

1 shawl [ʃɔːl] Tuch | **2 to fret** [fret] sich Sorgen machen | **3 curly** [ˈkɜːli] lockig | **4 hindquarters** [ˈhaɪndˌkwɔːtəz] Hinterhand | **5 unsuspecting** [ˌʌnsəsˈpektɪŋ] arglos | **6 to dot** [dɒt] mit Punkten verzieren | **7 to rummage** [ˈrʌmɪdʒ] kramen, stöbern | **8 tangled** [ˈtæŋgld] verheddert | **9 bridle** [ˈbraɪdl] Zaum | **10 to harness** [ˈhɑːnəs] aufzäumen, anschirren | **11 stunted** [ˈstʌntɪd] verkrüppelt

little hawthorn[1] tree he sat, humming tunes to himself, waiting.

The sun sank into the mouth of the West. The birds of night spread their wings across the sky. John closed his eyes. He waited.

Drifting in and out of sleep, he was awoken by a gentle whinny[2]. John opened his eyes. Stood a little way away from him, its dark fur glistening in the moonlight, was the kelpie. It looked him in the eye and whinnied again. Still looking at John, it lowered its hindquarters. John got to his feet.

"Oh my," he said, "what a beautiful horse you are. Would it be alright if I took a ride on you?"

F　The kelpie whinnied again. It seemed to nod its head, ever so slightly. John walked over to it. He stood beside it, ready to climb on. The kelpie tensed. John pulled the shawl from his pocket. He threw it over the kelpie's back and leapt atop it.

The kelpie shot to its feet. It tossed its head and neighed[3] at John. The sound was full of anger: for though John was upon its back, the shawl was between him and the kelpie, so he wasn't stuck to it.

The kelpie was furious. It cantered[4] then galloped towards the loch, twisting and bucking as it tried to throw John off. He held on tightly and managed to stay on its back. The kelpie tried something else.

Before Johns eyes, the kelpie's mane turned from hair into a writhing[5] mass of snakes. The snakes reared up, hissing, spitting and striking at John. He leaned back, reached into his pocket and pulled out the pot of salt. John threw the salt all over the snakes and they became hair again.

The kelpie was almost at the water now. It thundered over the grass, determined to take John under the water and drown him. But before they reached the water, John took the bridle from over his shoulder.

The kelpie reared up high, roaring its anger to the night. John threw the bridle over its head and pulled hard. The bit[6] went between the kelpie's teeth.

The creature instantly calmed. It stood still upon the bank, heaving[7] for breath, waiting for an instruction from John. He had harnessed the kelpie, and it was his to command. John rode the kelpie home. He put it in his horse's old stable and went to bed.

G　Spring came. The last of the snow had melted away and the land was humming with life. It was time to plough.

John led the kelpie to his fields and set the plough upon its back. It powered through the fields, breaking up the soil beautifully, and John was overjoyed[8]. He sowed his crop, knowing in his heart that this year's harvest would be a good one.

As for the kelpie? One day, soon after the ploughing was done, John took it out to the moor at the edge of the croft. He gave it a last affectionate stroke and removed its bridle.

The kelpie didn't hesitate. It shot away from him, over the moor, heading for its underwater home.

How did John get by without it? I don't know. But I think he did the right thing in letting it go. A power like the kelpie can be harnessed for a while, but it can never truly be tamed.

From: Daniel Allison, *Scottish Myths and Legends*
(adapted)

a) *Sum up the situation John and his family are in at the beginning of the story. Then make notes about the plot and visualise the actions in a diagram.*

→ S11

b) *Analyse the structure of the story, the characters and their behaviour as well as the way the story is told. Which text type you already know is very similar? Find another example of that text type and write a comparison of the two stories (about 200 words). Exchange texts with a partner and peer-edit each other's work.*

1 **hawthorn** ['hɔːθɔːn] Weißdorn | 2 **whinny** ['wɪnɪ] Wiehern | 3 **to neigh** [neɪ] wiehern | 4 **to canter** ['kæntə] leicht galoppieren | 5 **to writhe** [raɪð] sich winden | 6 **bit** [bɪt] Gebiss | 7 °**to heave** [hiːv] hier: tief einatmen | 8 **overjoyed** [ˌəʊvəˈdʒɔɪd] überglücklich

Find more online:
ag636x

Scottish identity

SPEAKING **1** **Symbols of Scottish identity**

→ S17 *Describe and comment on the pictures. Match each of the pictures with an aspect of Scottish identity. What else do you associate with Scotland?*

A

B

C

D

SPEAKING **2** **Language and identity**

Besides English, Gaelic and Scots are official languages in Scotland. Scots is similar to English, but it has a lot of words that are completely different. Gaelic on the other hand is a Celtic language closely related to Irish and used to be spoken throughout Scotland.

Talk about the distribution of languages in Scotland today (see the map at the back) and possible reasons for the decline of Gaelic. Discuss if languages should be kept from dying out by political measures.

READING / SPEAKING **3** **A poem partly written in Scots** → TS Poetry

→ S6 **a)** *Robert Burns (1759–1796), the Scottish national poet wrote in English and in Scots. Read the first two stanzas of 'To a mouse' and compare them. What do we learn about the situation and the speaker's attitude towards the mouse?*

A 22 🔊
A 1/31 ⊙

To a Mouse
On Turning Her Up in Her Nest with the Plough, November, 1785
Wee[1], sleekit[2], cowrin[3], tim'rous[4] beastie,
O, what a panic's in thy[5] breastie!
5   Thou need na[6] start awa[7] sae[8] hasty,
Wi' bickering brattle[9]!
I wad be laith[10] to rin[11] an' chase thee[12],
Wi' murdering pattle[13]!

I'm truly sorry Man's dominion
Has broken Nature's social union,   10
An' justifies that ill opinion
Which makes thee startle
At me, thy poor, earth-born companion
An' fellow-mortal!   15

Robert Burns

1 wee = little | **2 sleekit** = smooth-skinned | **3 cowrin** = cowering | **4 tim'rous** = timorous | **5 thy** = your |
6 na = not | **7 awa** = away | **8 sae** = so | **9 brattle** = clattering noise | **10 I wad be laith** = I'd hate | **11 rin** = run |
12 thee = you | **13 pattle** = an old tool with a blade

→ S14 **b)** *Role play: Imagine one of you dislikes poetry, the other wants to convince his / her friend to read Burns. Act out a short dialogue.*

SPEAKING / WRITING **4** **Scotland as part of the UK**

a) *Comment on the following statistics:*

The 2011 census showed that about 62 % of Scottish citizens see themselves as Scottish only, about 18 % feel they are Scottish and British at the same time, 8 % feel they are rather British than Scottish, 2 % identify as Scottish and another identity, and 10 % feel they are neither Scottish nor British.

> **Across cultures**
>
> What about **Scotland's role** in the UK? The country belongs to the "Celtic fringe" of the UK, like Wales and Northern Ireland, but it has been closely linked with England for centuries. It is a country of strong traditions, but also very modern. With Brexit, Scotland needs to redefine its place in the UK and in Europe. The Scottish Nationalist Party (SNP) as its strongest political force would prefer the country to be an independent country within the European Union.
>
> Discuss the pros and cons of a union of states (like the Federal Republic of Germany or the USA) in an argumentative essay of about 220 words.

→ S18 b) *Find out how strongly students in your class identify with your region. Do an anonymous survey in class and compare the results with the Scottish figures.*

VIEWING **5** **A (fairly bloody) history of democracy in Scotland**

V6 *A student took notes on a video about the history of democracy in Scotland, but he didn't get everything right. Watch the video and correct the wrong statements.*

The Tolbooth in Glasgow was the first meeting place of the Scottish parliament and also a prison. Later the members of parliament met in Parliament House. The Act of Union
5 was signed there in 1630. Scottish politicians had to move to London afterwards. There is a monument in Calton graveyard for the five million men who were deported to New Zealand because they demanded that workers
10 get the right to vote. At the beginning of the 20th century, women still weren't allowed to vote. The suffragettes were against the right to vote for women. They protested by chaining themselves to rails and slashing pictures of the king. In 1918 the suffragettes in Calton prison 15 went on hunger strike. At last, women were allowed to vote in 1997. The Democracy Cairn on Calton Hill reminds people of the time when Scotland fought for its own parliament. The transfer of power from the UK government to 20 the Scottish parliament started in 1979 and is called devolution. Scotland has a very modern proportional electoral system today. People who have the right to remain in Scotland can vote from the age of 18, even if they are not of 25 Scottish nationality.

VIEWING **6** **Scotland and Brexit**  → WB 24/1 → TS Speech

a) *According to the Brexit referendum in 2016, 62 % of the people in Scotland would have preferred to stay in the EU. Can you imagine why?*

V7
→ S19 b) *Watch the speech given in 2018 by Nicola Sturgeon (SNP), First Minister of Scotland. She argues for staying in the European market by referring to a forecast by the fiscal commission. Make notes about the three areas where losses are expected, the three factors that should be boosted, the four areas of protection granted by the EU and the four areas in which Scotland is excellent.*

Find more online:
hb94xv

Folk and folk-inspired music

A   Traditional music session in a pub, Ireland   **B**   Red Hot Chilli Pipers

SPEAKING

1   Characteristics of folk music

a) *Talk about traditional folk music. What do you associate with it? When and where is it played? What typical instruments are there (use a dictionary)? Compare it with pop music and classical music. Collect your results in a mind map.*

b) *Folk music and folk-inspired music have always been popular. Talk about reasons why.*

READING

2   The impact of folk music   → WB 25/1

Folk music has constantly influenced other musical genres, including classical music, and there are a lot of popular crossover styles like folk rock, folk rap or folk metal.

5   Almost everyone knows Celtic folk music as it is still played in Ireland or Scotland but also in other countries. While bands like the *Dubliners*, *Clannad* or the *Battlefield Band* played more traditional arrangements of
10   folk music, other artists have incorporated folk music elements into popular music and created a variety of new pieces and genres.

The *Red Hot Chilli Pipers* from Scotland, for example, use traditional instruments in
15   their arrangements of modern rock songs from *Queen* or *AC/DC*, the *Dropkick Murphys* from Massachusetts or *Flogging Molly* from Los Angeles play a hard and fast punk version of Irish folk, the former *Clannad* singer Enya became a pop star with her folk-inspired
20   ballads and contributed to the "Lord of the Rings" soundtrack, French rappers *Manau* combined French rap with traditional folk tunes from Brittany and *Celtas Cortos* uphold the Celtic tradition of Galicia by playing
25   Spanish folk rock.

Not only is the Celtic influence important, but Oriental and Latino as well as Eastern European styles have had a notable impact on pop music too, and social media made it
30   possible in 2021 that an old a cappella shanty called "Wellerman" performed by Scottish postman Nathan Evans shot to the top of the international charts. In Germany, young and old people alike party to the sounds of bands
35   like *LaBrassBanda* or *Santiano*.

→ S5, 7–10   *Read the text and sum up the main point of each part. Say where you would expect to find this kind of text. Think of a more interesting title and finish the text with another paragraph (50–80 words) giving more information about the situation in Germany.*

READING / WRITING **3** **A traditional theme** → TS Poetry

→ S5–6

Find a recording of the following song on the internet. Also look for a recording and the words of the song "Deifedanz" by Dreivviertelblut. *Listen to both songs (there may be different versions). Then analyse and compare them (words and music). Write about 200 words.*

The Devil Went Down To Georgia

The Devil went down to Georgia. He was lookin' for a soul to steal. He was in a bind[1] 'cause he was way behind[2] and he was willing to make a deal when he came across
5 this young man sawin'[3] on a fiddle and playin' it hot. And the Devil jumped upon a hickory[4] stump and said, "Boy, let me tell you what."

"I guess you didn't know it, but I'm a fiddle player, too. And if you'd care to take a dare I'll
10 make a bet with you. Now you play a pretty good fiddle, boy, but give the Devil his due[5]. I'll bet a fiddle of gold against your soul 'cause I think I'm better than you."

The boy said, "My name's Johnny, and it might
15 be a sin, but I'll take your bet; you're gonna regret 'cause I'm the best there's ever been."

Johnny, rosin up[6] your bow and play your fiddle hard. 'Cause Hell's broke loose in Georgia and the Devil deals[7] the cards. And
20 if you win you get this shiny fiddle made of gold, but if you lose the Devil gets your soul.

The Devil opened up his case and he said, "I'll start this show." And fire flew from his fingertips as he rosined up his bow. And he
25 pulled the bow across the strings and it made an evil hiss. And a band of demons[8] joined in and it sounded something like this.

When the Devil finished, Johnny said, "Well, you're pretty good, old son, but sit down in that chair right there, let me show you how 30 it's done."

"Fire on the Mountain". Run, boys, run!
The Devil's in the house of the rising sun;
Chicken in the bread pan picking out dough.
Granny, does your dog bite? No, child, no.[9] 35

The Devil bowed his head because he knew that he'd been beat. And he laid that golden fiddle on the ground at Johnny's feet. Johnny said, "Devil, just come on back, if you ever wanna try again, I done told you once, you 40 son of a bitch[10], I'm the best there's ever been."
And he played:
"Fire on the Mountain". Run, boys, run! …

Words: J. T. Crain, C. Daniels, J. W. Marshall,
J. Di Gregorio, F. L. Edwards, C. F. Hayward

SPEAKING **4** **A presentation** → WB 25/2

→ S3, 15

Do some research on a folk-inspired artist or band of your choice and present it to the class (about ten minutes, including audio examples).

1 bind [baɪnd] Zwickmühle | **2 way behind** [ˈweɪ bɪˌhaɪnd] weit zurück | **3 to saw** [sɔː] sägen | **4 hickory** [ˈhɪkri] Walnussbaum | **5 his due** [hɪz ˈdjuː] was ihm gebührt | **6 to rosin up** [ˈrəʊzɪnˌʌp] mit Kolophonium (Geigenharz) behandeln | **7 *to deal** [diːl] geben | **8 demon** [ˈdiːmən] Dämon | **9** *Anspielungen auf bekannte Lieder* | **10 bitch** [bɪtʃ] *Schimpfwort*

Find more online:
2yz3uf

Slavery and the Civil War

READING / SPEAKING **1** The triangular slave trade

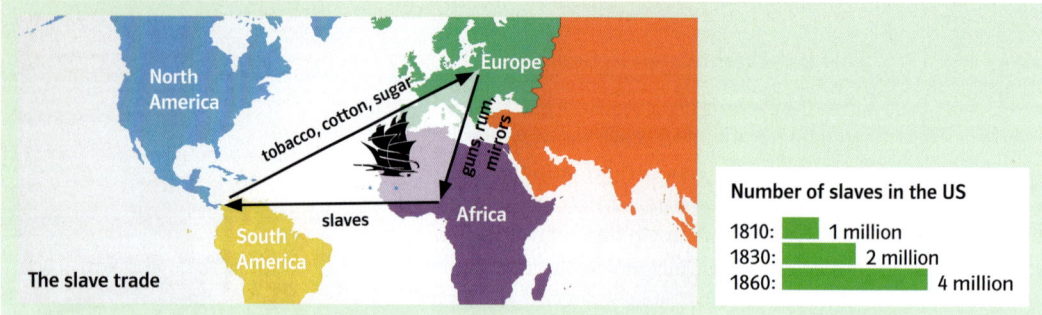

North America

Europe

tobacco, cotton, sugar

guns, rum, mirrors

slaves

Africa

South America

The slave trade

Number of slaves in the US

1810: 1 million
1830: 2 million
1860: 4 million

From the 16th to the 19th century, shipping routes for slave trade ran between Europe, Africa and the Americas, forming a triangle. Soon after the first colonies were established
5 in the so-called New World, the European powers needed a cheap labor force to make them profitable. Large agricultural enterprises, like cotton, sugarcane and tobacco plantations, couldn't have thrived without slavery.
10 Slaves were absolutely essential for these labor-intensive businesses and enabled the landowners to gather wealth and power.
Portugal and Spain were soon joined by Britain in capturing people especially in
15 western Africa. At the time, this practice of kidnapping children and adults and enslaving them wasn't questioned much. There was an accepted belief, which was backed by 'scientific theories', that people with darker
20 skin were not even to be considered people but rather an inferior species.
The Europeans cleverly got local chiefs to help capture people. In raids against enemy tribes, people were captured and sold to the

Europeans, who in turn sold the people to 25 shipping companies. The ships had arrived in Africa carrying guns, cloth or iron, for example. The goods were then traded in for slaves.
After loading the ships with human cargo, they set sail for the Americas – South America, 30 the West Indies and North America. The traders had little interest in providing comfortable passage and in their calculations they included losses, throwing the dead overboard. The lack of proper food and water, untreated diseases, 35 close quarters and beatings were the main causes of death. Whoever managed to survive the journey was sold a third time at an auction, where a trader might receive up to three times more than what he had paid in Africa. 40
On the final voyage back to Europe, the ships were filled with goods from the Americas. There was a growing demand in Britain and other European countries for agricultural products like sugar and cotton, 45 so the traders made a good profit again. The triangular slave trade was a lucrative business on every part of the journey.

→ S5 a) *Use the reference article and the graph to describe how the triangular slave trade worked.*

b) *Explain which people profited from the slave trade and in what way. Think of possible reasons for Europe's growing demand for sugar and cotton.*

→ S14 c) *Imagine it's around 1790 and a journalist (partner A) is interviewing one of the slave traders (partner B). Think of questions you would like to ask and answers you could give. Use digital storytelling tools to present the interview.*

2 **A slave's life**

Jobah (Adam) Hayes spent the first years of his life as a house slave and playmate for his master's son. This is how he was able to learn to read and write, but when his master discovered he had learned these skills, Jobah was banned from the house and sent to work in the fields. Although this account is fictional, many enslaved people had similar experiences.

I do carry my master's name, Hayes. This was common practice, as were the brands with our master's initials we bear on our backs. We slaves were often known by one name to our
5 master, a name the master had chosen, and by our real name to the other slaves. Master Hayes named me Adam, from the Bible, but among the slaves I was called Jobah.

I was born in Rockland, Louisiana, but
10 I know neither the exact date of my birth nor who my father was. In fact, I barely knew my mother. As was the custom among plantation owners, she and I were separated when I was still very young. I was put in the care of some
15 women who were too old to work in the fields. My mother was sold and I never saw or heard from her again. I never knew what a real family was. While all the slaves did help each other, we learned not to become too attached
20 because a person you loved could be sold and you would never see them again. It was easier for the master to keep control over us if we didn't form strong bonds.

All of the slaves lived in primitive cabins
25 within sight of the master's house. Every month each adult slave was given eight pounds of pork, the pieces not good enough for the master's house, and a sack of cornmeal. Work in the fields was from dawn to dusk,
30 meaning that in the summer months we spent more time in the fields than in our cabins. On a sugarcane plantation the hardest time of the year is October until Christmas. After the sugarcane is harvested, it must be processed
35 immediately. Even in Louisiana it is cold during these months, but we worked outside, wearing few clothes. The men had the job of tending to the large kettles of boiling juice, scooping the sticky juice from one kettle to the next, always
40 in danger of getting burned. This went on 24 hours a day for one month until the sugar was ready. But worse than the work and the danger was the overseer, Mr. Butler, a brutal beast who always carried a weapon with him – a whip, a
45 club, or an iron poker. Slaves were punished for working too slowly, stealing or talking back to the overseer. By far the worst time was when Mingo, who had worked at the kettles with me, was burned alive before our eyes for trying to
50 run away.

a) *Describe your first reaction after reading Jobah's account.*

b) *Sum up what the everyday life of an enslaved person was like. Why do you think enslaved people were used to process the sugarcane?*

c) *Think-pair-share: Think about these questions: What does family life normally mean? What are the advantages of having a family? In what way was this different for enslaved people? Share your ideas with a partner and then with the class.*

→ S20

Slave cabins and kettles for making sugar
at the historic site of Whitney Plantation in Louisiana,
which is a museum today

LISTENING **3 A presentation on some very strange ideas** → WB 26/1

A 1/32–34 ⊙
→ S13

a) *Listen to a presentation on the ideas of race and slavery and do the following tasks.*

1. **Parts 1+2:** Make a grid to collect the different ideas and 'theories' about race mentioned. For each, add who 'invented' the idea and for what reason(s).
2. **Part 3:** Describe the Quakers' motives for fighting these ideas and explain what the Underground Railroad is.

→ S14 **b)** *Discuss: What were the motives for creating these 'theories' about race and slavery? How do these ideas fit in with a Christian way of living?*

SPEAKING **4 Abraham Lincoln: US president 1861–1865**

A Lincoln declares slaves to be free (1863)

FREEDOM FOR ALL, BOTH BLACK AND WHITE!

B A cartoon

"DO YOU HAVE ANOTHER FORM OF PHOTO I.D. ?"

→ S17 **a)** *Describe the picture and the cartoon. What place do you think Abraham Lincoln holds in US history? Do some research to find out more about his achievements.*

b) *Collect examples of illustrations on banknotes in different countries. Discuss the reasons for (not) showing people.*

READING / WRITING **5 The great emancipator?** → WB 27/2–3 → G1–2, 9, 13

A 23–24 ◁)) **A** Lincoln started to preach that slavery needed
A 2/1–2 ⊙ to end – but not because of the human horror.
Because if labor was free, what exactly were
poor White people expected to do to make
5 money? Because he'd taken an antislavery
approach, the Republicans were labeled "Black
Republicans," which was the worst thing to be
called, obviously. There were still racists in the
North. Still racists everywhere. And why would

racists want to vote for the party "in support" 10
of Black people? So, Lincoln changed his tune.
Lincoln was against Black voting.
Lincoln was against racial *equality*.
Lincoln and the party pledged *not* to
challenge Southern slavery. 15
And Lincoln won.
But with the sixteenth president of the
United States in place, slaveholders broke

into panic. Panic that the economic institution
20 that kept them living like kings would be in
jeopardy[1]. Panic that they wouldn't be able
to stop slave revolts. So, they did what most
people, well … most bullies do when they've
been bested[2] on the playground. They – the
25 South – took their ball and left.

The *secession*, which just means to
withdraw from being a member of, started
with South Carolina. They left the Union. Which
means they were starting their own territory,
30 where they could make up their own rules and
live their lives as racist as they wanted. Shortly
thereafter, the rest of the South joined in on
the disjoining. This was a big deal, because to
lose an entire region meant the other states
35 lost that region's resources. The split-offs called
themselves the Confederacy. They voted in
their own president, Jefferson Davis, who had
declared that Black people should never and
would never be equal to Whites. There were
40 now two governments, like rival gangs. And
what have gangs always done when one gang
feels their turf[3] is being threatened?

FIGHT!

Welcome to the Civil War.
45 The biggest change agent[4] in the war was
that slaves wanted to fight against their slave
owners. They wanted the chance to fight
against the thing that had been beating them,
raping them, killing them. So, the first chance
50 they got, they ran north to join the Union army.

Anything for freedom.

And then got sent back.

Anything for slavery.

Union soldiers were enforcing the Fugitive
55 Slave Act, returning runaways to their owners.

However, a year later, the slave act had been
repealed[5] and a new bill by Lincoln declared
"All persons held as slaves within any state
shall then and forever, be free."

Just like that. 60

B Lincoln was labeled the Great
Emancipator[6], but really, Black people were
emancipating themselves. By the end of 1863,
four hundred thousand Black people had
escaped their plantations and found freedom. 65
Or at least the potential for it. Because let's not
pretend that life in the North was immediately
sweet. The Union believed most of the same
hype about Black people as the Confederacy.
Their feelings toward Black people – that they 70
were lazy and savage[7] and blah, blah, blah –
were the same. On top of that, there were
many Black people who feared that freedom
would be nothing without land. What good
was it to be free if they had nowhere to go 75
and no way to build a life for themselves?
And what about voting? These were a couple
of the questions at hand, a few of the issues
Lincoln was trying to work through. What he
was comfortable with, however, was the way 80
Black people praised him. They'd run up to him
in the street, drop to their knees, and kiss his
hands. And when the Civil War finally ended
in April 1865, Lincoln delivered his plans for
reconstruction. And in that plan, he said what 85
no president had ever said before him – that
Blacks (the intelligent ones) should have the
right to vote.

No wonder three days later he was shot in
the back of the head. 90

From: Jason Reynolds, Ibram X. Kendi, *Stamped: Racism,
Antiracism and you* (adapted)

a) *Compare the different reasons for the American Civil War given in the extract.
What do you think of Lincoln's and the North's attitude towards Black people and slavery?*

→ S11   b) *The excerpt deals with a historical event. What do you think are the authors' main
intentions? How do they manage to keep the reader interested? Give examples.*

→ S4, 7–10   c) *Up until today, Abraham Lincoln ranks among the top three presidents in the US
and is known as the "Great Emancipator". Use what you've learned so far to write an
argumentative essay (about 250 words) discussing if Lincoln deserves this title.*

1 **in jeopardy** [ɪn ˈdʒepədi] in Gefahr | 2 **to best** [best] besiegen | 3 **turf** [tɜːf] Revier |
4 **change agent** [ˈtʃeɪndʒ ˌeɪdʒənt] Motor der Veränderung | 5 **to repeal** [rɪˈpiːl] (Gesetz) aufheben |
6 **emancipator** [ɪˈmænsɪpeɪtə] *hier:* Befreier | 7 **savage** [ˈsævɪdʒ] wild; primitiv

Unit 2
Black in America

Find more online:
i9i5xw

A Juneteenth, a day to celebrate the end of slavery in 1865

B A memorial for African-Americans killed by police

SPEAKING **1 Different realities**

→ S17 *Black people are a historically relevant minority in the US. Describe the pictures A–D and say which impression you get of the situation of African-Americans in the US today.*

SPEAKING **2 A changing population** → WB 28/1–2

a) *With a partner, talk about the image you have of American society: What different ethnic groups are there and how big are they? Which groups play an important role in politics and economy?*

→ S18 b) *Compare your ideas from a) with the information given in the graph on the composition of the US population. What was new/surprising to you?*

Across cultures

Living in a **diverse society** requires mutual respect and sensitivity. When talking about groups of people, it's a sign of respect to use politically correct language. Terms for indigenous populations and minority groups which were coined by conquerors from Europe are widely considered inappropriate today. In the US, people with African ancestry are currently often referred to as **African-Americans**, **Blacks** or **People of Color**. It's always best to use the terms the groups themselves prefer. 'Race' as a term referring to people has become increasingly problematic, especially in German. However, in English-speaking countries it is still used to differentiate between outside characteristics (e.g. skin colour) and ethnic factors (e.g. culture, religion etc.), often in statistical contexts.

Find statistics on how ethnic diversity has changed in your society and present your findings.

C A protest for voting rights

D A high school basketball team

The US population

	White	Black	Hispanic*	Asian	Native populations	Other
2010	72.4	12.6	16.3	4.8	1.1	9.1
2020	61.6	12.4	18.7	6	1.3	18.6

* In current statistics, 'Hispanic' is usually considered an ethnicity and includes people of any race.

Source: U.S. Census Bureau (2020)

E

The **diversity index** measured by the US census shows the probability that two randomly chosen people will be from different racial and ethnic groups. In 2020 the diversity index was 61.6 %, compared to 54.9 % in 2010.

F

SPEAKING **3 Equality and diversity**

Choose one of the quotes and explain it in your own words. (Use a dictionary if necessary.) Include an everyday example that illustrates the main idea of the quote.

"Rightful liberty is unobstructed action according to our will within limits drawn around us by the equal rights of others."

Thomas Jefferson, third US president

"Equality is not in regarding different things similarly, equality is in regarding different things differently."

Tom Robbins, writer

"In diversity there is beauty and strength."

Maya Angelou, writer

LISTENING **4 Equal opportunities?**

A 2/3–4

→ S13

Listen to the podcast "Historically Atlanta" about education in the US and do these tasks.

Part 1:
Take notes on these points:
1. history of Spelman College
2. reasons for founding HBCUs (historically black colleges and universities)
3. importance of HBCUs today

Part 2:
1. Explain why, according to Professor Mellon, the US still has to deal with the repercussions of slavery today.
2. Describe how, according to her, income, education and success are related.
3. Give examples of how HBCUs are "giving back" to society and why this is important.

Growing up Black

READING / WRITING **1** **Living in two worlds** → WB 28/3 → G1, 5, 11–12

A 25–30 ◁))
A 2/5–10 ◉
→ ▲ 93/1

Starr lives in the fictitious urban neighborhood of Garden Heights, which is predominantly Black and lower-income. She's a student at Williamson, a predominantly white, posh private school outside of her neighborhood, where she met her white boyfriend, Chris. However, Starr finds it difficult to completely fit in in either place. One evening, she's at a party in Garden Heights, where she accidentally meets her childhood friend Khalil.

A **Part 1: The party**

People glance over at me with that "who is this chick[1], standing against the wall by herself like an idiot?" look. I slip my hands into my pockets. As long as I play it cool and keep to myself,
5 I should be fine. The ironic thing is though, at Williamson I don't have to "play it cool" – I'm cool by default because I'm one of the only black kids there. I have to earn coolness in Garden Heights, and that's more difficult than
10 buying retro Jordans on release day.

Funny how it works with white kids though. It's dope[2] to be black until it's hard to be black.

"Starr!" a familiar voice says.

The sea of people parts for him like he's a
15 brown-skinned Moses. Guys give him daps[3], and girls crane[4] their necks to look at him.

Khalil is fine, no other way of putting it. And I used to take baths with him. Not like *that*, but way back in the day when we would giggle
20 because he had a wee-wee and I had what his grandma called wee-ha. I swear it wasn't perverted though.

He hugs me, smelling like soap and baby powder. "What's up, girl? Ain't seen you in a
25 minute." He lets me go. "You don't text nobody, nothing. Where you been?"

"School and the basketball team keep me busy," I say. "But I'm always at the store. You're the one nobody sees anymore."
30 His dimples[5] disappear. He wipes his nose like he always does before a lie. "I been busy."

Obviously. The brand-new Jordans, the crisp[6] white tee[7], the diamonds in his ears. When you grow up in Garden Heights, you

know what "busy" really means. 35

Fuck. I wish *he* wasn't that kind of busy though. I don't know if I wanna tear up[8] or smack[9] him.

But the way Khalil looks at me with those brown eyes makes it hard to be upset. I feel 40 like I'm ten again, having my first kiss with him at Vacation Bible School. Suddenly I remember I'm in a hoodie, looking a mess … and that I actually *have* a boyfriend.

B "How's your grandma?" I ask. "And 45 Cameron?"

"They a'ight. Grandma's sick though." Khalil sips from his cup. "Doctors say she got cancer or whatever."

"Damn. Sorry, K." 50

"Yeah, she taking chemo. She only worried 'bout getting a wig though." He gives a weak laugh that doesn't show his dimples.

The music changes, and Drake raps from the speakers. I nod to the beat and rap along 55 under my breath. Everybody on the dance floor yells out the "started from the bottom, now we're here" part. Some days, we *are* at the

---

1 chick *(infml)* [tʃɪk] junge Frau | **2 dope** *(sl)* [dəʊp] cool | **3** *°***to give sb daps** [ˌɡɪv ˈdæps] jmdn. abklatschen *(Begrüßungsgeste)* | **4 to crane** [kreɪn] (Hals) recken | **5 dimple** [ˈdɪmpl] Grübchen | **6 crisp** [krɪsp] makellos | **7 tee** *(AE, infml)* [tiː] T-Shirt | **8 to tear up** [ˌtɪərˈʌp] den Tränen nahe sein | **9 to smack** [smæk] schlagen

bottom in Garden Heights, but we still share
60 the feeling that damn, it could be worse.

Khalil is watching me. "Can't believe you still love whiny-ass[1] Drake. 'Baby, you my everything, you all I ever wanted,'" Khalil sings in a whiny voice.

65 I flip him off[2]. He puckers[3] his lips and makes a kissing sound. All these months apart, and we've fallen back into normal like it's nothing.

A noise comes from the middle of the
70 dance floor. Voices argue louder than the music. Cuss words[4] fly left and right.

Pop! A shot rings out. I duck.

Pop! A second shot. The crowd runs toward the door, which leads to more cussing and
75 fighting since it's impossible for everybody to get out at once.

Khalil grabs my hand. "C'mon."

Cars speed away outside, and people run into the night in any direction where shots
80 aren't firing off. Khalil leads me to a Chevy Impala parked under a weak streetlight. He pushes me in through the driver's side, and I climb into the passenger seat. We screech off[5], leaving chaos in the rearview mirror[6].

85 "Always some shit," he mumbles. "Can't have a party without somebody getting shot."

Stop and think:
Comment on Khalil's last statement.
What does he mean by saying it?
What effect does it have on you?

C *When Starr and Khalil are pulled over by the police, things get out of control and Khalil, who is unarmed, is shot and killed by the police officer. Starr is the only witness.*

Part 2: A few days later, at Williamson
Khalil's funeral is Friday. Tomorrow. Exactly one week since he died.

I'm at school, trying not to think about
90 what he'll look like in the coffin, how many people will be there, what he'll look like in the coffin, if other people will know I was with him when he died … what he'll look like in the coffin.

I'm failing at not thinking about it. 95

On the Monday night news, they finally gave Khalil's name in the story about the shooting, but with a title added to it – Khalil Harris, a Suspected Drug Dealer. They didn't mention he was unarmed. They said that an 100 "unidentified witness" had been questioned and that the police were still investigating.

After what I told the cops, I'm not sure what's left to "investigate".

D *After eating fried chicken for lunch, Starr and her friends Hailey, a white girl, and half-Asian Maya play a game of basketball against Chris and his friends in the gym. At first, the game goes well for the girls, but Starr is worried by her thoughts of Khalil and of Chris, so she makes some mistakes.*

"Dammit, Starr!" Hailey yells, recovering the 105 ball. She passes it to me. "Hustle![7] Pretend the ball is some fried chicken. Bet you'll stay on it then."

What.

The. 110

Actual.

Fuck?

The world surges forward[8] without me. I hold the ball and stare at Hailey as she jogs away, blue-streaked hair bouncing behind her. 115

I can't believe she said … She couldn't have. No way.

The ball falls out of my hands. I walk off the court. I'm breathing hard, and my eyes burn.

The smell of sweat hangs in the girls' locker 120 room. I pace from one side of the lockers to the other.

Hailey and Maya rush in, out of breath. "What's up with you?" Hailey asks.

"Me?" I say, my voice bouncing off the 125 lockers. "What the hell was that comment?"

"Calm down! It was only game talk."

---

1 whiny-ass ['waɪni ˌæs] weinerliche Person | **2 to flip sb off** *(infml)* [ˌflɪp ˈɒf] jmdm. den Stinkefinger zeigen | **3 to pucker** ['pʌkə] (Lippen) spitzen | **4 cuss word** *(infml)* ['kʌs wɜːd] Schimpfwort | **5 to screech off** [ˌskriːtʃ ˈɒf] mit quietschenden Reifen losfahren | **6 rearview mirror** [ˌrɪəvjuː ˈmɪrə] Rückspiegel | **7 Hustle!** ['hʌsl] Los!; Mach schon! | **8 to surge forward** [ˌsɜːdʒ ˈfɔːwəd] vorwärts stürzen

"A fried chicken joke[1] was only game talk? Really?" I ask.

130 "It's fried chicken day!" she says. "You and Maya were just joking about it. What are you trying to say?"

I keep pacing.

Her eyes widen. "Oh my God. You think 135 I was being *racist*?"

I look at her. "You made a fried chicken comment to the only black girl in the room. What do you think?"

"Ho-ly shit, Starr! Seriously? After 140 everything we've been through, you think I'm a racist? Really?"

"You can say something racist and not be a racist!"

E   "Is something else going on, Starr?" Maya 145 says.

"Why does everyone keep asking me that?" I snap.

"Because you're acting so weird lately!" Hailey snaps back. She looks at me and asks, 150 "Does this have something to do with the police shooting that drug dealer in your neighborhood? I heard about it on the news. And then they said the drug dealer's name was Khalil."

"We've wanted to ask if it was the Khalil 155 who used to come to your birthday parties," Maya adds. "We didn't know how, though."

The drug dealer. That's how they see him. It doesn't matter that he's suspected of doing it. "Drug dealer" is louder than "suspected" ever 160 will be.

If it's revealed that I was in the car, what will that make me? The thug ghetto girl with the drug dealer? What will my teachers think about me? My friends? The whole fucking 165 world, possibly?

"I –"

I close my eyes. Khalil stares at the sky. *"Mind your business, Starr,"* he says.

I swallow and whisper, "I don't know 170 that Khalil."

From: Angie Thomas, *The Hate U Give* (adapted)

a) *Describe your first reactions after reading: What did / didn't you like? Would you like to read the whole novel? Give reasons.*

→ △ 93/2
→ ▲ 93/3
b) *Describe what the party in part 1 tells you about life in Garden Heights. Then read until l. 88 and go back to Khalil's comment (ll. 85–86). What do you think of it now?*

→ S6, 11, 12
c) *Have a closer look at part 2 and do these tasks.*

1. Explain why Starr feels hurt by Hailey's comment. What does Starr mean by saying "You can say something racist and not be a racist" (l. 142)?
2. Compare how Starr, the media and her friends see Khalil.
3. Examine the relationship between Starr and Khalil in parts 1 and 2 and write a characterisation (about 150 words) of Starr.

d) *Many African-Americans speak "Black English", which is different from Standard English in several ways. Typical features are: 1. using double negatives; 2. building verb forms differently; 3. leaving out 'to be'; 4. slang expressions. Find examples in part 1.*

e) *Choose one of these tasks.*

→ S7–8
👤👤👤
→ S14
1. In a diary entry, Starr describes her feelings after denying Khalil. Write about 150 words.
2. Create an alternative ending with Starr admitting that she knows Khalil. In groups of three, act out the conversation between Starr and her two friends (or use digital storytelling tools).

1 fried chicken joke *„Fried chicken" wird häufig abwertend gebraucht in Bezug auf Afroamerikaner/-innen, vgl. Üb. 3*

SPEAKING   → S3, 18

2 Violence and crime

a) *Find up-to-date figures about police killings in the US concerning different ethnic groups and use digital tools to visualise and compare your figures with the ones in the text.*

b) *The text describes some aspects of the justice system in the US: prison sentences for small crimes, the bail system, possible loss of voting rights. Find out about the situation in Germany and discuss the pros and cons of each system.*

→ S14
→ △ 93/4
→ ▲ 94/5

c) *There are several ideas to solve the problems mentioned in the text, e.g. improving education, gun control or crime prevention. In groups, compare the approaches and discuss which is the most effective one.*

> According to various statistics, African-Americans suffer disproportionately from the **criminal justice system** in the US. In relation to their actual share of the population (around 12 % in 2020), African-Americans are unproportionally often targets of stop-and-search practices by the police, they make up the biggest share of the prison population (around 33 % in 2018) and they are also
> 5 more often the victims of police killings than other racial groups (37 Black, 28 Hispanic, but only 15 white people per million inhabitants in 2021).
> This is certainly in part due to racist individuals in the justice system, but there are also other factors: In the US, you usually get a prison sentence even for small crimes. The bail system additionally disadvantages poor people – many of whom are Black – because they can't afford to
> 10 pay the bail and have to stay in prison until their trial takes place. Moreover, after being sentenced for certain crimes, you may be prohibited from voting for a certain period of time. These voting bans, which even come with smaller crimes such as stealing or breaking into houses, statistically affect Black people four times more often than other ethnicities. Another issue across all ethnic groups are street gangs, which are usually located in urban low-income neighbourhoods and often
> 15 involved in serious crimes.

SPEAKING   → S3, 15

3 Just a joke?

Do some research and give a short presentation on typical African-American soul food dishes.

Across cultures 🇺🇸

In the excerpt from *The Hate U Give*, Hailey makes a 'joke' involving fried chicken which Starr considers racist. However, it wouldn't be uncommon to hear African-Americans making the same kind of joke among themselves. This is an example of **reclaiming**: adopting negative terms or features for positive self-empowerment. Collect similar examples and give your opinion on this issue.

Fried chicken is considered typical African-American food, which is often called **soul food**. Soul food is home-made food that originated in the rural South. The term was coined in the 1960s, however, many soul food dishes go back to a time when African-Americans were enslaved. Enslaved people made use of what their white owners gave to them, i.e. cheap ingredients such as beans, greens, cornmeal and parts of the pig that you wouldn't necessarily find in a butcher shop today, e.g. feet, legs, ears, intestines. Originally meant to nourish people who did hard physical work, soul food typically contains lots of fat, salt and sugar. Today, this is one of the reasons for people to have a higher risk of developing health problems like obesity and heart disease. Talk about 'soul food' from your region and say what you think about it.

READING / WRITING   **4**   **School experiences** → WB 31/4 → G1–2, 4

A 31 🔊
A 2/11 ◎

As their previously mostly Black neighborhood is changing with people from other ethnic groups and trendy businesses moving in, so do the lives of Maya (the narrator of the story) and her twin sister Nikki. While their best friend Essence had to move away because her mother couldn't afford the rent in the newly renovated house, a (white) family with the children Kate and Tony moved in next door. The teenagers all go to Richmond High, a school known for low tests scores and problems with alcohol and drugs. Earlier that day, the new principal, who seems to be more interested in the school's reputation than the students' actual achievements and problems, gave a pep talk calling for change.

So far, the first day of school has been full of ice-breaker activities and free writes about what we did over summer break. It's lunch now, and sitting here in the cafeteria, I notice
5   there are more white and Latino students here than last year. My freshman year, Richmond was mostly black, but in the past two years our student body has changed.

Kate and Tony are sitting with Nikki. As
10 Essence and I walk up to our table, I hear Nikki saying, "Things at Richmond are never going to change. That assembly was a waste of time." She sips her flavored water. She's bringing her lunch to school now because she believes
15 the food in the cafeteria is oppressive and damaging our bodies with each bite.
"It wasn't a waste," I say. "Well, we could have done without Principal Green's fake pep talk at the end. But he kind of had a good point about
20 being one another's keeper."
"I don't have time to worry about nobody else," Essence says. "I got enough problems of my own." She eats a handful of fries.
Nikki says, "If people don't want to change,
25 you can't make them. I'm here to get my education." Her eyes survey the room. She sighs. "If they don't want to get theirs, that's on them."

Kate wipes her lips with her napkin. "What do you think the problem is?" she asks.   30
Something inside me begins to crumble when everyone at the table starts listing everything that's wrong with Richmond and nothing that is right – as if a place can't be bad and good at the same time.   35
Kate joins in on what's wrong with Richmond (feeling comfortable, I guess, since everyone else is complaining). And I am wondering how it can be that a girl who has spent one day in a place can all of a sudden be   40
an expert. "St. Francis has a multimedia literacy room with iPads and laptops that we could check out. We had a garden on our rooftop that our school lunches were made from. I don't understand why Richmond can't have   45
those things," she says. "My math teacher told me today that I couldn't take my book home because she needed it for her other classes. I –"
"We know how bad it is," I say.
Kate's shoulders shrink. "I know you do,   50
I just, I think –"
"Do you know why St. Francis is able to have all those things? Do you have any suggestions on how to make things better here?" I ask.   55

From: Renée Watson, *This Side of Home* (adapted)

a) *Sum up what you learn about the situation at Richmond High School.*

b) *Describe the characters' different reactions to the situation at the school and explain what this tells the reader about their attitudes.*

→ S8–10
→ △ 94/6

c) *Maya is a member of the student council. They make a list of suggestions on how to improve things at Richmond for Principal Green. Write this list, including reasons for your suggestions (about 170 words).*

READING / WRITING **5** **Feeling at home** → WB 32/5–6 → TS Poetry

a) *Read the title of the poem and talk about what "heart" can stand for. Then explain the saying "Home is where the heart is". Do you agree with it? Give reasons.*

A 32 ◁))
A 2/12 ⦾

The Heart of Harlem

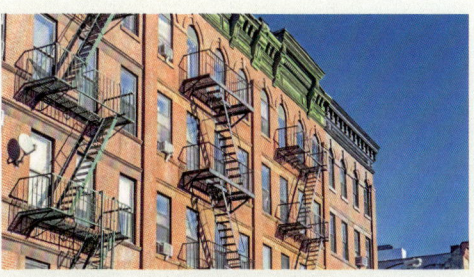

The buildings in Harlem are brick and stone
And the streets are long and wide,
But Harlem's much more than these alone,
Harlem is what's inside –
5 It's a song with a minor¹ refrain,
It's a dream you keep dreaming again.
It's a tear you turn into a smile.
It's the sunrise you know is coming after a
   while.
10 It's the shoe that you get half-soled twice.
It's the kid you hope will grow up nice.
It's the hand that's working all day long.
It's a prayer that keeps you going along –
That's the Heart of Harlem!

15 It's the pride all Americans know.
It's the faith God gave us long ago.
It's the strength to make our dreams come
   true.
It's a feeling warm and friendly given to you.
20 It's that girl with the rhythmical walk.

It's my boy with the jive² in his talk.
It's the man with muscles of steel.
It's the right to be free a people never will
   yield.
A dream … a song … half-soled shoes …   25
   dancing shoes
A tear … a smile … the blues … sometimes
   the blues
Mixed with the memory … and forgiveness
   … of our wrong.   30
But more than that, it's freedom –
Guarded for the kids who came along –
Folks, that's the Heart of Harlem!

by Langston Hughes, 1951 (abridged)

b) *Read the poem out loud. In 2–3 sentences, sum up the impression you get of Harlem in the mid-20th century.*

→ S6 c) *Have a closer look at the poem and do these tasks.*

1. Identify the three main parts and briefly sum them up.
2. Choose three of the metaphors Hughes uses ("It's a / the …") and explain them. Then say which one you like best and why.
3. The poem combines rhyming poetry and prose. Use examples from the text to illustrate the effect on the reader.
4. Describe your overall impression: What mood are you in after reading? What makes the poem special? Give examples from the text.

> **Useful phrases**
>
> The rhyme scheme in part 1 is … |
> The repetition of … / The (flowing / slow) rhythm / The combination of … emphasises / intensifies the feeling of / creates an atmosphere of … |
> song-like / dream-like / reflective |
> warm / safe / confident / affectionate

→ ▲ 94/7 d) *Choose one of these tasks.*
→ S7–10

1. Write your own short poem with the title "The Heart of *(name of your home town)*".
2. In about 180 words, comment on the statement "Where you live determines everything."

1 minor [ˈmaɪnə] Moll | **2 jive (talk)** [dʒaɪv] *afroamerikanischer Slang, entstanden in Harlem*

Proud to be Black

READING / WRITING **1** Five things to know about black culture now → WB 33/7, 34/8 → G9, 11–13

A 33–38 🔊
A 2/13–18 ⊙
→ △ 94/8
→ △ 95/9

There's a scene in my satirical film "Dear White People" in which social misfit[1] Lionel Higgins is asked to write a black culture piece by the editor of a campus newspaper staffed
5 with mostly white people. Lionel accepts the assignment with some anxiety. Despite the benefit of being black, large Afro and all, he feels underqualified, because he has yet to find a pocket of culture he identifies with at the
10 fictional Winchester University.

Lionel's dilemma is one many black Americans share: a deep desire to have an identity rooted in black culture coupled with the knowledge that what's seen as
15 "authentically black" in popular culture doesn't reflect our actual experience.

Here are five things I've come to know about black culture now:

1. There is a difference between
20   **black culture and "Black Culture"**
Black culture, without quotes, is the sum total of cultural contributions to the mainstream by the black subculture. It's a fluid and a diverse often contradictory thing.
25   Meanwhile "Black Culture" is a lifestyle standard made of assumptions about black identity, often used successfully by marketers, studio heads, fashion brands and music labels to make money. It can be the "cool factor" that
30 makes kids line up for hours to spend their last dime[2] on brand new Michael Jordan sneakers. Or the thing that makes white people call me "brotha" and blast[3] 2 Chainz[4] when I hop in the car. It's what people assume about black
35 people and how they should sound, live and act.

Black culture may have been born in black communities, or created by black Americans. But when appropriated for commerce, there
is a danger of mistaking "Black Culture" for   40
actual cultural EXPERIENCE. That's where the myth begins, and it can devalue real human experiences.

2. "Black Culture" oftentimes employs, but is
not always defined by, actual black people   45
Often by the time "Black Culture" is being used to sell a product or idea, it's already been reinterpreted by white people. This isn't necessarily malicious, but it's something to note. We are often told what being black is by   50
people who aren't. Up and coming black hip hop artists are formed to attract the masses by white label executives. Television shows with black characters might have no black writers or directors.   55

3. Black culture is multicultural
Black culture draws from a variety of influences born both in and outside black communities. Being black in America involves a process of moving through and adopting   60
from many different cultures. To define what's authentically black is virtually impossible, as there are as many ways to be black as there are black people.

4. Black culture is not proprietary   65
to black people
Many observers had a tough time when rapper Macklemore & Ryan Lewis[5] won the Grammy for best rap album over Kendrick Lamar[6]. There is similar discontent over the lack of black   70
artists being recognized or rotated on radio in categories once "owned" by black musicians, like R&B or hip hop. But this is not new. Once communities of black artists birth something to the mass culture, in many ways it is no   75
longer ours. For every Dizzy Gillespie[7] there is a Dave Brubeck[8].

---

1 misfit [ˈmɪsfɪt] Außenseiter/-in | **2 dime** (AE) [daɪm] Dime (Zehncentstück) | **3 blast** [blɑːst] dröhnen |
4 2 Chainz [ˌtuː ˈtʃeɪnz] Rapper | **5 Macklemore & Ryan Lewis** [ˌmæklmɔːr ənd ˌraɪən ˈluːɪs] weißes Hip-Hop-Duo |
6 Kendrick Lamar [ˌkendrɪk lʌˈmɑː] Schwarzer Rapper | **7 Dizzy Gillespie** [ˌdɪzi ɡɪˈlespi] Schwarzer Jazzmusiker |
8 Dave Brubeck [ˌdeɪv ˈbruːbek] weißer Jazzmusiker

It can be a tough pill to swallow.
Particularly when a culture we feel ownership
80 over reaches new heights of success in
more mainstream, i.e. whiter, hands. There is
something alarming about the fact that black
artists doing things associated with "Black
Culture" (rapping, twerking) doesn't seem to
85 capture the mainstream's attention as strongly
as when white artists do it. (See: Miley Cyrus).
Personally, I don't define my black
experience in something as transient as music
or fashion. I get much angrier when presented
90 with an overtly defined and limited image of
what being black represents. Like being told I
"talk white" in school.

5. Black culture is a starting point
Culture of any kind can be grounding[1] and
95 comforting. But at a certain point a cultural
identity too tightly defined keeps us from
growing. I'm grounded in, but not limited by,
my blackness.
When I began trying to get my film made,

the confines[2] of "Black Culture" seemed to   100
suggest that if a black movie wasn't broadly
comedic, a historical epic tragedy or a street
story, there would be no audience for it. But
I made it anyway.
And that is really the genesis of any   105
culture: Ultimately, it's created by individuals
and communities with the courage to do
something different and unexpected. Like be
themselves.   Justin Simien, CNN, 2014 (adapted)

a) *Give a short summary of the five points the author addresses and explain the difference between black culture and "Black Culture" in your own words.*

→ S5, 11   b) *Explain the author's ideas on appropriation and ownership of a culture and the examples he gives. In your opinion, is there a difference between using other people's ideas because you like them and using them to make money? Explain why / why not.*

c) *In the last paragraph, Simien describes what culture means to him. Explain his idea and discuss whether you agree with it or not.*

→ S3, 15   d) *Find more examples of cultural appropriation in your peer group or your society. Think about fashion, music, food, costumes, slang, accents. Use digital tools to give a short presentation.*

> **Useful phrases**
>
> to be influenced / created / defined by |
> to be based on (actual / own) experiences |
> to belong to | to use / exploit sth (to do
> sth) | a fixed / constantly changing concept |
> complex / simple | authentic / unique /
> mainstream | to enter / to be adopted by
> the mainstream | creativity | collaboration
> | profit

LISTENING   **2 A podcast: Who has inspired you?** → WB 34/9

A 2/19–23   a) *Listen to a podcast about people who have inspired others: Alice Walker, Toni Morrison, Marley Dias, Spike Lee and David Adjaye. Collect more information on them in a grid with these headings:* name | profession | aims | achievements

b) *Find out more about a book, film or project made by one of the people from a). Prepare a two-minute talk.*

1 to ground [graʊnd] erden; eine Grundlage bieten | **2 confines** (pl) [kənˈfaɪnz] enge Grenzen

READING **3**   **A human computer** → WB 35/10 → G3, 9

→ △ 96/10

| October 25, 2022 | Topic: Science | previous post | next post |

Dorothy Johnson Vaughan became a well-known name after the 2016 release of the film "Hidden Figures", which tells the story of three African-American women – including Vaughan – who worked for NASA (National Aeronautics and Space Administration) as 'human computers'.

Ms. Vaughan had always had a passion for math and after receiving her college degree in it, she went on to teach at high schools in Virginia, which were still segregated. In the 1930s this was considered the top of the career ladder for an African-American woman, even though their pay was only half as much as their white counterparts'.

Dorothy Vaughan was ambitious though and when the opportunity came up to apply for a position at the US space agency at the height of World War II, Vaughan jumped at the chance. Because of the shortage of male workers due to the war, women with a mathematical background were being recruited. However, even though Vaughan and others like her were highly sought after, segregation was still an accepted everyday practice at NASA. The African-American women had to work in a separate area, called "West Area Computing". They were also not allowed to use the same dining or bathroom facilities as their white co-workers.

As a 'human computer' before the computer age, Vaughan did complex calculations for aerospace engineers conducting flight experiments. After the war, Vaughan and other women worked on calculations for satellite launch vehicles. The Space Race between Americans and Soviets was on and these women were at the starting line to ensure a successful finish for the US.

NASA didn't officially desegregate until 1958. Despite this, in 1949 the determined Vaughan, who knew her skills were of great

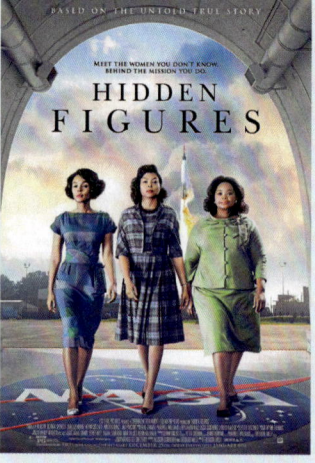

value to NASA, was promoted to the position of supervisor of West Area Computing. This was quite a milestone for her as one of the few women – and the first Black person at all – in such a position.

Vaughan was a quiet and a fair fighter. Throughout her very successful career at NASA, she advocated fair treatment of and appropriate pay raises and promotions for women (Black and white) and for African-Americans. When she noticed that soon manual computing would be replaced by machines (i.e. by computers as we know them today), she took the initiative to learn programming languages on her own and teach them to the women she supervised, ensuring they would continue to be valuable employees at NASA.

Of her time at NASA Vaughan said, "I changed what I could, and what I couldn't, I endured." In recognition of her contributions to the US space program, a crater on the Moon was named after her. She retired from NASA in 1971 and died in 2008 at the age of 98.

a) *Talk about your reactions to the text. What information was most interesting to you?*

→ S5   b) *Describe the most important milestones in Dorothy Vaughan's career and the difficulties she had to face.*

c) *Explain what 'human computers' did and why women were chosen for this type of work.*

d) *Describe the role Vaughan played for her female and African-American co-workers.*

Towards a post-racial society

ADING / SPEAKING **1 Bringing about change** → WB 36/11

→ ⚠ 96/11

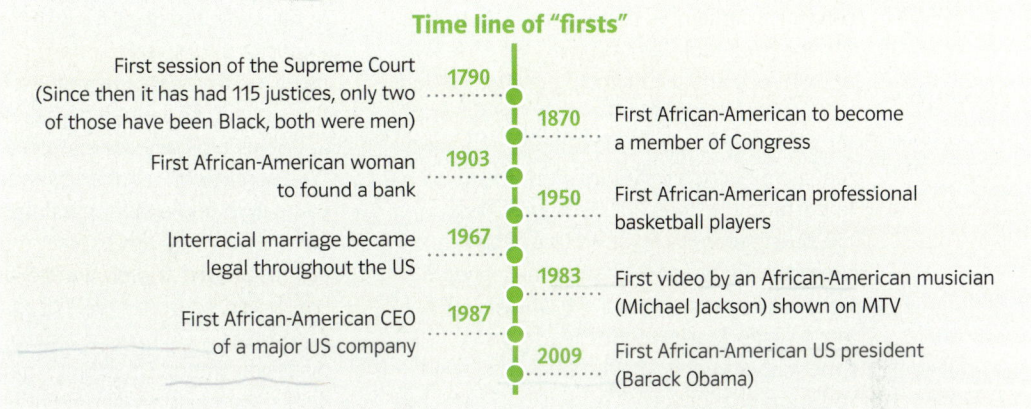

Time line of "firsts"

First session of the Supreme Court (Since then it has had 115 justices, only two of those have been Black, both were men) — **1790**

1870 First African-American to become a member of Congress

First African-American woman to found a bank — **1903**

1950 First African-American professional basketball players

Interracial marriage became legal throughout the US — **1967**

1983 First video by an African-American musician (Michael Jackson) shown on MTV

First African-American CEO of a major US company — **1987**

2009 First African-American US president (Barack Obama)

A 39 🔊
A 2/24 ⊙

Why Kamala Harris and 'Firsts' Matter

Kamala Harris will forever have "first" attached to her name – the first woman, the first Black American and the first person of South Asian descent to serve as vice president of the
5 United States.

People celebrate firsts because they are momentous, and they signal progress and representation for people who have not had power before. Yet the obligation to represent
10 an entire community – or, in Ms. Harris's case, multiple overlapping communities – can also be an impossible burden. Members of a group never all feel the same way, and any single representative is bound to disappoint some of
15 them. This happened with President Obama and African-Americans, Professor Dawuni [a political scientist at Howard University] said, and Ms. Harris has come under similar pressure. "That is why it's important to have
20 more than one. There has to be a certain number of people for change to happen."

The focus on someone's identity can also overshadow the qualifications that earned the job in the first place. "There were other things about who I was, what I cared about, how I'd 25 done leadership roles that were much more significant in reality than that I was a woman," said Barbara Roberts, who in 1990 was elected the first female governor of Oregon. "We want to recognize the first, but we don't think that's 30 all they have to offer," she said.

Claire Cain Miller, The New York Times, 2021 (adapted)

a) *Talk about which information from the time line and the article surprised you most. Then discuss what criteria are most important for becoming a role model: being the first, a person's identity, their qualifications, …?*

👥 **b)** *Work with a partner. Choose an area (science, education, sports, …) and find out to what*
→ S3, 15 *extent African-Americans are represented in this area and if their share has changed over time. Use statistics or visuals to present your results in a short talk.*

READING/VIEWING **2** Barack Obama – yes, he tried? → WB 36/12 → G4 → TS Speech

A savior of politics *Obama: A big dissapointement?*

A 40–42
A 2/25–27

A The rest of the world fell as hard for Barack Obama as Americans did. Back in 2008, the same qualities in the 47-year-old senator from Illinois that excited U.S. voters fascinated people around the globe. He was a fresh face and a convincing orator. He had spent his childhood in the Asia-Pacific, and his skin color alone made billions of people feel a connection with him. Perhaps most importantly, he was not George W. Bush, the president who invaded Iraq. Obama promised "hope" and "change" and people believed he could deliver – that he would end wars in Muslim countries, improve America's standing on human rights, even reduce global poverty. "Yes we can!" shouted The Age, an Australian newspaper, when he won office. Just months later, the rookie[1] president was awarded the Nobel Peace Prize, a nod more to his promise than to anything he had accomplished.

Obama's overseas poll numbers were stratospheric in those early days. In countries like France and Germany, more than 90 percent of people surveyed by the Pew Research Center expressed confidence that Obama would "do the right thing regarding world affairs." Even in some Middle Eastern countries, where U.S. presidents are rarely liked, nearly half of the population had high expectations for Obama. But peace did not arrive in Obama's time.

Nahal Toosi, Politico, 2016 (adapted)

B Obama swept into office with a reputation as an intellectual politician with vision. Obama said that the subject of race was too important to ignore and implicitly promised to confront it if he won the presidency. He has not. He has avoided the subject. And when he has addressed it, he has typically done so only obliquely[2]. "Trayvon Martin[3] could have been me 35 years ago" and similar musings[4] over the Obama years do not explain much, do not promise much and do not tell us where we should go from here. For many African-Americans, he has been a hero – but also a disappointment. On critical matters of racial justice, he has provided no agenda, unveiled[5] no vision, set no overarching[6] mission to be accomplished.

Some critics note that according to key indicators of material well-being – employment, income, incarceration rates, educational outcomes and homeownership rates – blacks as a whole have fared badly during Obama's presidency. Obama loyalists point to the benefits black poor and working-class people have profited disproportionately from the rescue of the automobile industry, the jobs generated by the American Recovery and Reinvestment Act, the expansion of Medicaid and the Affordable Care Act enabling millions of blacks to receive health insurance.

Randall Kennedy, Politico, 2014 (adapted)

a) *In groups, choose one of the articles **A**, **B** or **C**. Do the following tasks and present your results in a short talk to the class.*

1. **A, B, C:** Note down important key words and find a suitable title for your article.
2. **A, B, C:** In a grid, collect information on the expectations people (in the US or around the globe) had of Obama, the reasons for these expectations, and his actual achievements/failures.
3. **C:** Sum up what makes Obama 'unusual'.

1 **rookie** ['rʊki] Neuling | 2 **oblique** [əʊ'bliːk] indirekt | 3 **Trayvon Martin** *von einem Wachmann getöteter Schwarzer* | 4 **musing** ['mjuːzɪŋ] Überlegung | 5 **to unveil** [ʌn'veɪl] enthüllen | 6 **overarching** [ˌəʊvr'ɑːtʃɪŋ] übergreifend

C Symbols are important. Let's talk about the exceptionalism of President Barack Obama. First, his name: Barack Hussein Obama. If a writer gave that name to a
5 character in a political novel, readers might bristle at[1] its implausibility. But beyond his name, so much of Obama's life veers away[2] from the experiences of most black Americans. He is the son of an African man,
10 from Kenya, and was raised by a white Kansan mother and white grandparents in Hawaii – one of the most non-black places in America.

He attended an elite college preparatory
15 high school, Punahou, in Honolulu, very selective colleges and then an even more selective law school. He was the first black editor-in-chief of the Harvard Law Review. He married a black woman who attended
20 Princeton University and Harvard Law School. In 1993 he became a homeowner.

Though he and his wife had $120,000 of student debt, he was able to pay off their student loans with proceeds[3] from a book advance[4]. He became a millionaire as a result 25
of his best-selling books. His taxable income in 2005 was roughly $1.5 million.

In 2008, America elected our first black President. Immediately after the election we started hearing commentators discussing 30
our entry into a post-racial era. Because a black man had been elected president, they argued that racism was a thing of the past. Except John McCain got 55% of the white vote in 2008 and Mitt Romney got 59% in 35
2012. The majority of white voters each time voted for the white guy. How can racism be over when most white voters rejected the black guy? We were not then nor have we ever been post-racial. 40

Dorothy A. Brown, CNN, 2017 (adapted)

b) *State the purpose of your text (A, B, C). Then comment on the author's opinion of Obama's key slogan "Yes we can". Give examples from the text that show his / her attitude.*
→ S4, 11

V8 **c)** *Watch the excerpt from Obama's farewell speech in Chicago. Describe the impression you get of Obama's personality (consider the tone, his choice of words, body language, the atmosphere). Then try to sum up the spirit of the speech in one word.*

SPEAKING **3** **Sports and politics** → WB 37/13

→ S17 **a)** *In 2016, NFL players started protesting police brutality against African-Americans by kneeling during the US national anthem (instead of remaining standing as required). Describe the picture and try to imagine what the atmosphere in the stadium was like.*

→ △ 96/12
→ ▲ 96/13 **b)** *Many sports leagues around the world, right to the IOC (International Olympic Committee), don't allow athletes to voice their opinions on political topics while representing their sport. Discuss whether you agree with this practice or not.*

NFL players protesting before a football game

1 to bristle (at) ['brɪsl] sich empören (über) | **2 to veer away** [ˌvɪərˌə'weɪ] abweichen | **3 proceeds** *(pl)* [prəʊ'siːdz] Einnahmen | **4 book advance** ['bʊkˌəd̩ˌvɑːns] Honorarvorschuss für ein Buch

MEDIATION **4** Everyday racism

→ S16

For an international youth project on racism you're going to present the situation in Germany. Based on the following text write a short essay (about 190 words). Give examples of everyday racism, describe typical reactions of people who are affected by racism and ones who aren't, and explain what can be done against racism.

Als ich noch in Nippes gewohnt habe, habe ich mich dort, an der Kaffeebude, oft mit meiner Freundin Luise getroffen. Der Kaffeeladen wird von zwei Frauen betrieben. Eines Tages, als Lu-
5 ise ihren Kaffee bezahlte und Trinkgeld geben wollte, stellte eine der Frauen eine Spardose vor uns. „Hier kannst du es reinschmeißen", sagte sie vergnügt. Es war eine antike Spardo-se: der Oberkörper eines Schwarzen Mannes.
10 Rote Lippen, breit zu einem absurden Lächeln geformt, große Augen und Nase. Vor seinem Mund eine Hand, in die man die Münze hinein-legen konnte. Als die Frau einen Hebel betätig-te, hob sich die Hand. Die Augen des Mannes
15 rollten nach hinten, die Münze verschwand in seinem Mund und landete scheppernd im Inneren der Spardose.

Hier war ich nun auf dem rummeligen Marktplatz vor der netten Kaffeeverkäuferin
20 und der rassistischen Spardose, die gerade Luises Trinkgeld verschluckt hatte. Offensicht-lich kannte oder erkannte die Frau den histo-rischen Zusammenhang nicht. Vielleicht fand sie das witzig. Eine Sekunde lang überlegte ich,
25 einfach nichts zu sagen. Das machte ich oft. Ich wusste, wenn ich das „R-Wort" aussprechen würde, wäre die Stimmung dahin.

Weiße Menschen haben so wenig Übung darin, mit ihrem eigenen Rassismus konfron-
30 tiert zu werden, dass sie meist wütend darauf reagieren, anfangen zu weinen oder einfach gehen. Wenn ich jemanden rassistisch nenne, dann hört dieser Mensch meist nicht, was ich ihm oder ihr sage. Was er oder sie hört, ist:
35 „Du bist ein schlechter Mensch. Du bist böse. Du bist ein Nazi."

Wenn man Rassismus als Denkweise begreift, die ausschließlich bewusst und mit böser Absicht erfolgt, dann ist die Kaffee-
40 budenbesitzerin keine Rassistin. Die Spardose, die sie hat, bleibt allerdings rassistisch. Rassis-mus ist in unserem System. So sehr, dass er oft unbewusst geschieht. Es kann zum Beispiel

sein, dass man am Tag gegen Rassismus demonstriert – und trotzdem Angst bekommt, 45 wenn ein Schwarzer Mann einem nachts über den Weg läuft. Oder dass man kurz überrascht ist, wenn eine Frau mit Hijab perfekt Deutsch spricht. Auch wenn diejenigen, die auf die an-dere Straßenseite wechseln oder kurz verdutzt 50 sind, glauben, diese eine harmlose Handlung würde keinen großen Unterschied machen, tut sie es doch. Und zwar für die Betroffenen. Eine deutsche Hijabi bekommt täglich ver-dutzte Blicke, wenn sie den Mund aufmacht. 55 Ein Schwarzer Mann sieht in seinem Leben Hunderte verängstigte Gesichter, wenn er durch die Straßen läuft. Diese kleinen Momen-te, sie wirken wie Mückenstiche. Kaum sichtbar, im Einzelnen auszuhalten, doch in schierer 60 Summe wird der Schmerz unerträglich.

Ich stand also vor der Kaffeebudenbesitze-rin und versuchte, möglichst nett zu sagen: „Na ja, das ist doch ein wenig rassistisch, oder?" Die Frau blickte verunsichert auf die Dose. 65 Weil ich befürchtete, dass sie gleich zu einer Rechtfertigung ansetzen könnte, nahm ich den Kaffee und ging zu meinem Platz. Mehr brach-te ich nicht übers Herz.

Ich glaube, dass man rassistisches Verhal- 70 ten nur durch bewusste Konfrontation ändern kann. Das ist nicht leicht. Wer wirklich etwas gegen Diskriminierung tun möchte, sollte bei sich selbst anfangen. Damit meine ich wirklich alle, auch mich. Allerdings müssen vor allem 75 diejenigen, die nicht betroffen sind, sich mal bewegen. Sich den eigenen Vorurteilen zu stel-len, verlangt Veränderung. Und Verantwortung. Klingt erst einmal nicht so toll. Klingt aber auch wie Therapie. Und danach geht es einem 80 bekanntlich meist besser.

Als ich ein paar Wochen später wieder an der Kaffeebude stand, war die Spardose übrigens weg.

Aus: Alice Hasters, *Was weiße Menschen nicht über Rassismus hören wollen aber wissen sollten* (adaptiert)

Dealing with (online) sources

You've already done lots of research and know that the internet can be a great source of information, but its biggest advantage – that anyone can contribute to it – can also turn into a problem: Distinguishing fact from fiction or individual opinion isn't always easy.

1 Finding and assessing information → WB 38/14

→ S3

a) *With a partner, make a list of 4–5 tips for how to get good results using a search engine. Share your results with the class.*

b) *Compare the news headlines (use a dictionary if necessary): What language do they use? Where is the emphasis? Then find out more about the newspapers (type of newspaper, where from, audience).*

> **China building more than 100 'nuclear' missile silos in desert**
> (The Guardian, 01.07.21)

> **WATCH THIS SPACE** *China's 'Area 51' being built in remote desert site in race with West to produce 'secret weapons', satellite pics show*
> (The Sun, 12.07.21)

2 Would you have believed it? → WB 38/15

a) *Fake news, i.e. information that is presented as news but is not true, is a serious problem. Discuss why people would create and share fake news.*

→ S7–10

b) *Divide up in groups and find a website to create your own 'fake news'. Each group chooses a topic (e.g. "crazy pets" or "an unusual discovery in your region") and creates either a serious or a fake news article. Exchange articles with another group. Explain what type of article they created and if it is convincing. Give reasons.*

→ S3, 15

c) *Find out what you can do to prevent fake news from spreading. Present your results.*

> **Tip**
>
> **Typical features of fake news**
> 1. Sensational headlines (exaggerations, capital letters, …)
> 2. Persuasive style (often simplified, one-sided or sensational messages)
> 3. Shocking pictures that are manipulated or used out of context
> 4. Facts, statistics, quotes etc. used out of context or cannot be verified (no sources given; other reliable sources don't confirm content)
> 5. Dubious source (no imprint; sources known for having a certain (political) agenda; rather new account with little followers; lots of spelling mistakes)

3 The whole picture → WB 38/16

→ S20

a) *Create a poster or a digital information sheet with tips for doing research. Use criteria such as **number of sources, origin** (reliability, different countries/languages), **relevance** (up-to-date/outdated), **intention** (informing, influencing, …), **text type, audience, language/style**.*

b) *When researching a historical event, would you prefer to use a student's book or an internet source? Think of aspects like author (e.g. government official/ordinary citizen/journalist), his/her knowledge and perspective to compare the pros and cons of both types of sources.*

A poetry slam

Moving poetry out of the academic world and into pop culture was the motivation for the birth of poetry slams in Chicago in the 1980s. For this type of contest you need poems, performers, an audience and judges. Here is one way to organise a poetry slam.

Step 1

Get ready → S6

The basic rules: Poems must be the original work of the people performing them. For poetry slams, they don't (have to) follow the rules of traditional poetry. Decide who is going to be a performer and who part of the audience.

Step 2

Collect ideas (performers)

Choose one of these topics: **My next journey | My worst day at school | The best party ever** *and collect vocabulary for your topic (e.g. in a grid, list or mind map). Think about how to turn your ideas into a poem:*

- Note down alliterations and rhyming words.
- Find metaphors, similes or symbols to illustrate key ideas / emotions.
- Write 2–3 lines of your poem. Read them out loud, snapping your fingers to determine their rhythm. Change the words or the sentence structure to create a more regular / an irregular rhythm.
→ TS Poetry, Speech

Step 3

📖 Write and rehearse your poem (performers)

Use your ideas from Step 2 to write your poem. Think about the mood or emotions in it and perform accordingly. Not only your words, but also your performance must convince the judges! → Texts A, p. 47, Extra line pp. 104–105

> **Tip**
>
> Use vivid descriptions and rhythm to convey emotions, e.g. excitement: short, choppy lines; calm: flowing, long lines; thought-provoking: rhetorical questions.

Step 4

Hold your slam

You can recite the poem from memory or read off a piece of paper / your phone. The use of music, costumes or props is not allowed, but you can sing or beatbox. The time limit is three minutes.

Step 5

Give scores

Five judges are randomly chosen from the audience. They give scores from 0 to 10 for each poem based on the following criteria: Topic, style (rhyme, rhythm, use of imagery, …) and performance. The audience may try to influence the judges, e.g. by snapping their fingers, booing or laughing.

Of dreams and heroes

READING / WRITING **1** **On the come up** → WB 39–44/17–22

A 43–47 🔊
A 2/28–32 ⊙

Sixteen-year-old Bri Jackson lives in the fictitious urban neighborhood of Garden Heights and dreams of making it as a rapper. Her father was a hip hop star who died just as his career was starting to take off. Bri, however, simply needs to make some money to help her family – her mom Jay and her brother Trey – survive. The previous night, she took part in a rap battle in the Ring, a place that can help start her rap career. While she won, her opponent Milez is getting lots of attention for one of his songs. Bri looks for her aunt Pooh to speak about the family situation and her frustration. She finds her sitting on a car in front of her housing block with Scrap, a friend.

A She tugs my hoodie so it covers my eyes. "Thought so. How you get over here anyway? Your momma drop you off on her way back to work? Should've told me I was gon' be
5 babysitting your hardheaded¹ ass."

Oh.

I forgot the reason I came over here in the first place. I stare at my Not-Timbs². "Jay got laid off."

10 "Oh, shit," Aunt Pooh says. "For real?"

"Yep. The church let her go so they could pay for repairs to the daycare."

"Shit, man." Aunt Pooh wipes her face. "You a'ight?"

15 Jacksons can't cry, but we can tell the truth. "No."

Aunt Pooh pulls me into her arms. As much of a hard-ass³ as my aunt is, her hugs are the best. They somehow say "I love you" and "I'll do
20 whatever for you" all at once.

"It'll be a'ight," Aunt Pooh murmurs. "I'm gon' help y'all out, okay?"

"You know Jay won't let you." Jay never takes money from Aunt Pooh, since she knows
25 where she gets it from. I understand. If drugs almost destroyed me, I wouldn't take money that's made from them either.

"Her stubborn ass," Aunt Pooh mumbles, "I know this shit is probably scary as hell right
30 now, but one day you gon' look back, and this gon' feel like a lifetime ago. This a temporary setback for a major comeback. We ain't letting it stop the come up."

That's what we call our goal, the come up. It's when we finally make it with this rap
35 stuff. I'm talking get-out-the-Garden-and-have-enough-money-to-never-worry-again make it.

"I gotta do something, Aunty," I say. "I know Jay's looking for a job, and Trey's working, but I don't wanna be deadweight⁴."
40

"What you talking 'bout? You ain't deadweight."

Yeah, I am. My mom and my brother bust their butts⁵ so I can eat and have somewhere to lay my head, and what do I do? Absolutely
45 nothing. Jay doesn't want me to get a job – she wants me fully focused on school.

I need to do more, and the only thing I know to do is rap.

Now, let me be real: I know not every
50 rapper out there is rich. A whole lot of them fake for the cameras, but even the fakers have more money than me. Then you got folks like Dee-Nice who don't have to fake thanks to that million-dollar deal. He played his cards right
55 and got his come up.

B "We gotta make this rap stuff happen," I tell Aunt Pooh. "Like now."

"I got you, okay? I was gon' call you anyway. I've had all kinds of folks hitting me
60 up⁶ because of the battle. I made some stuff happen for you a li'l while ago."

"For real?"

"Uh-huh. For one, we getting you back in the Ring. That'll help make a name for you."
65

A name? "Yeah, but it won't make me any money."

"Just trust me, a'ight?" she says. "Besides,

---

1 hardheaded [ˌhɑːdˈhedɪd] dickköpfig | **2 Timbs** *(infml)* [tɪmz] Timberlands *(Schuhmarke)* | **3 hard-ass** [ˈhɑːdæs] knallhart (sein) | **4 deadweight** [ˈdedweɪt] Belastung | **5 to bust one's butt** *(infml)* [ˌbʌst wʌnz ˈbʌt] sich abrackern | **6 *to hit sb up** [ˌhɪt ˈʌp] jmdn. kontaktieren

that ain't the only thing I arranged."

70 "What else then?"

She rubs her chin. "I don't know if you can handle this one yet."

Oh my God. This is not the time to drag me along[1]. "Just tell me, dang[2]!"

75 Aunt Pooh laughs. "A'ight, a'ight. Last night, a producer came up to me after the battle and gave me his card. I called him earlier, and we arranged for him to make a beat[3] and for you to go into his studio tomorrow."

80 I blink. "I … I'm going in a studio?"

Aunt Pooh grins. "Yep."

"And I'm making a song?"

"You damn right."

"Yoooooooo!" I put my fist at my mouth.

85 "For real? For real?"

"Hell yeah! Told you I was gon' make something happen!"

Damn. I've dreamed of going into a studio since I was like ten. I would stand in front of 90 my bathroom mirror with my headphones on my ears and a brush in my hand like it was a mic, as I rapped along with Nicki Minaj. Now I'm gonna make my own song.

C "Shit." There's a slight problem. "Which song 95 will I do though?"

I've got tons in my notebook. Plus, a hell of a lot more ideas that I haven't written down. But this is my first real song. It's gotta be the right one.

"Look, whatever you do is gon' be a 100 banger[4]," Aunt Pooh says. "Don't sweat it.[5]"

Scrap shoves a spoonful of cereal into his mouth. "You need to do something like that song ol' boy you battled got."

"That 'Swagerific[6]' trash?" Aunt Pooh asks. 105 "Man, get outta here! That shit ain't got no substance."

"It ain't gotta have substance," Scrap says. "Milez lost last night, yet that song so catchy, he got even more folks talking 'bout it. Shit 110 was trending this morning."

"Hold up," I say. "You mean to tell me that I won the battle, am *clearly* the better rapper, and yet he's getting all the buzz?"

"So basically," Scrap says, "you won the 115 popular vote 'cause everybody loved you in the Ring, but you still lost the election since he the one getting fame?"

I shake my head.

"Look, don't worry 'bout that, Bri," Aunt 120 Pooh says. "If that fool can blow up[7] 'cause of some garbage, I know you can –"

"Pooh!" This skinny older man zigzags across the courtyard. "Lemme holla at you![8]"

"Goddamn, Tony!" Aunt Pooh groans. "I'm in 125 the middle of an important conversation."

It's not *that* important. She goes over to him.

I bite my lip. I don't know how she does it. I don't mean the actual selling drugs part. She 130 hands them the product, they hand her the money. Simple. I mean I don't know how she can do it, knowing that at one time somebody else was the dealer and my mom, *her sister*, was the junkie. 135

But if I make this rap stuff happen, hopefully she'll give all that up. "Real talk, Bri," Scrap says. "Although Milez getting all the attention, you oughta be proud. You got skills. I mean, he blowing up, and I don't know what 140 the hell gon' happen for you, but yeah, you got skills."

What kinda shady-ass[9] compliment is this? "Thanks?"

D

1 **to drag sb along** [ˌdræɡ_əˈlɒŋ] jmdn. hinhalten | 2 **dang** [dæŋ] verdammt | 3 ***to make a beat** [ˌmeɪk_ə ˈbiːt] einen Beat *(Basis für Rapsong)* produzieren | 4 **banger** [ˈbæŋə] Kracher | 5 **Don't sweat it.** [ˌdəʊnt ˈswet_ɪt] Keine Panik. | 6 **swag(-erific)** [ˌswæɡəˈrɪfɪk] cool *(Anspielung auf eine Stelle in Milez' Song)* | 7 ***to blow up** [ˌbləʊ_ˈʌp] groß rauskommen | 8 **Lemme holla at you.** *(infml)* [ˌlemi ˈhɒlər_ət juː] Ich muss mit dir reden. | 9 **shady-ass** *(infml)* [ˈʃeɪdiæs] fragwürdig

145 "The Garden need you, for real," he says. "I remember when your pops[1] was on the come up. Every time he made a music video around the neighborhood, my li'l ass tried to get in it. Just wanted to be in his presence. He gave us 150 hope. Hardly anything good ever come from around here, you know?"

I watch Aunt Pooh slip something into Tony's shaky hand. "Yeah, I know."

"But *you* could be the something good," says Scrap. 155

I hadn't thought about it like that. Or the fact that so many people looked up to my dad. Enjoyed his music? Yeah. But he gave them hope? It's not like he was the "cleanest" rapper.

But in the Garden, we make our own 160 heroes. The kids in the projects love Aunt Pooh because she gives them money. They don't care how she gets it. My dad talked about foul[2] shit, yeah, but it's shit that happens around here. That makes him a hero. 165

Maybe I can be one, too.

Scrap slurps the rest of the milk from his bowl. "Swag-erific, so call me terrific," he raps with a little shoulder bounce. "Swag-erific. Swag-erific … Swag, swag, swag …" 170

From: Angie Thomas, *On the Come Up* (adapted)

→ S1–2 **a)** *While reading, collect words connected with making (rap) music. Use a dictionary if necessary.*

b) *Sum up what you learn about the situation Bri and her family live in and explain what "the come up" (l. 33 ff) means to her and Aunt Pooh.*

c) *Take notes on what happens in the extract: the surprise Aunt Pooh has for Bri, what Scrap and Bri talk about, why Tony comes to visit Aunt Pooh.*

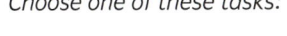

→ S6, 11, 12 **d)** *In groups, choose one of these tasks. Present your results to the class in a short talk.*

1. Describe the role (rap) music plays in Bri's life and why she dreams of becoming a famous rapper. Give examples from the text.
2. What role does Aunt Pooh play for her family and the people in Garden Heights? Write a characterisation of her.
3. Examine how the characters talk to each other. What effect does this create?

> **Useful phrases**
>
> a way out (of sth) | to pursue a goal | to care for | to rely on | to cheer sb up | to help / to support | warm / friendly / confident / generous | no-nonsense / tough / strong / cool / easy-going | humour / irony

→ S7–10 **e)** *Choose one of these tasks:*

1. Bri has just learned that she will make her own song in a studio the next day. She messages her best friend about it. Write their chat dialogue (about 150 words).
2. Comment on Bri's statement "In the Garden, we make our own heroes" (ll. 160–161). To do so, choose a hero / heroine from a book or a film you've read / seen or an 'everyday hero' you know (a nurse, a neighbour helping others, …) and think about these questions: What qualities make people heroes? Is it essential for a hero to have only positive qualities? Write about 200 words.

1 pops *(AE, infml)* [pɒps] Papa | **2 foul** [faʊl] übel, verdorben

Find more online:
nt4948

Fight for your rights!

SPEAKING **1** **Two pictures**

→ S17 *Compare these two pictures from 1963 and 2020. Describe and explain the differences and similarities.*

A

B

READING / WRITING **2** **It has happened again – a comment by Nicole B.** → G1, 4, 13

It has happened again. A case of mistaken identity. A case of being in the wrong place at the wrong time. A case of overt racism. It all depends on how you look at it. When
5 15-year-old Ramone Kendall was walking home from a birthday party last Friday night, he was wearing what he always wore – jeans and a hoodie. Ramone was walking through his own neighborhood. He was exactly where
10 he belonged. The color of Ramone's skin and the skin color of the man who shot him are very different. The shooter thought Ramone was a burglar, that he couldn't possibly belong in this middle-class, predominantly white
15 neighborhood. So he shot. At Ramone. And killed him.

We have laws that are supposed to protect us, protect everyone. Remember the Thirteenth (1865), Fourteenth (1868) and
20 Fifteenth Amendments (1870), which abolished slavery, strengthened the legal rights of newly freed slaves and further strengthened their voting rights? Apparently segregation and discrimination are not as far away as we would like to think. Perhaps in the mind of Ramone's
25 killer, Jim Crow laws, introduced in the late 19th century, are still in place today. (They stated that all citizens were equal and at the same time prohibited Blacks from riding the same buses, going to the same schools or using the
30 same public facilities as whites.) Perhaps he didn't understand Rosa Parks' act of defiance in 1955 when she refused to move to the part of the bus 'reserved' for Blacks, which advanced the civil rights movement.
35

In 1954, the National Association for the Advancement of Colored People (NAACP), an organization that has fought for racial equality since 1909, achieved a big success: In the revolutionary case Brown vs. Board of
40 Education, the Supreme Court decided that it was indeed unconstitutional for schools to be segregated. So, did Ramone's murderer think the neighborhood should be segregated? Did he think it was reserved only for people of his
45 own skin color?

Despite all the advancements that have been made regarding racial equality, there are times that I wonder if we've really come
50 that far at all. How can it be, for example, that the Ku Klux Klan, a white supremacist group founded in 1865 by six former army officers of the Confederacy, still exists today? How does a group with the goal of repressing the rights
55 and freedoms of not only African-Americans but also of Catholics, Jews, and foreign-born minorities exist in a country proud of its democracy and constitution? Did the man who shot Ramone feel superior based on his race?
60 I wish I knew what happened to the dream that civil rights icon Dr Martin Luther King, Jr. evoked in his speech at the end of the March on Washington in 1963. It was a dream of a society in which Black and white children
65 knew no discrimination, no death based on prejudices and xenophobia. But neither Dr King's dream nor the dream that came true for many African-Americans when Barack Obama became the first Black president of the US in 2008 could end racism in the land of the free 70 and home of the brave.

Just like protesters marched in Selma, Alabama in 1965 to advocate voting rights for African-Americans and to protest the death of a civil rights youth leader at the hands of law 75 enforcement, people of all ages and skin colors have joined together in the Black Lives Matter movement to protest police brutality against people of color. And they will remember Ramone Kendall, who died at the hands of 80 a racist. The protest in 1965 became known as Bloody Sunday because the non-violent protesters were met with tear gas and clubs after they refused to leave. Later that year the Voting Rights Act was passed. A small success. 85 I hope that the current BLM protests remain peaceful, draw attention to the problems that haven't gone away, and result in more understanding between all of us. And I hope that Ramone's story doesn't happen again. 90

a) *Create a time line of the civil rights movement, describing the milestones from the 1950s and '60s mentioned in the comment. Add more information as you work on these Focus pages.*

→ S11   b) *Analyse the stylistic devices the author uses to make the text convincing. Explain how the structure and the perspective add to the effect. Give examples from the text.*

VIEWING   **3**   **The real story of Rosa Parks**

V9
→ S19

a) *Watch the first part of David Ikard's talk about Rosa Parks and history myths (until 05:08). In one sentence, sum up what Rosa Parks became famous for. Then compare what Mr. Ikard's son Elijah learns at school about Rosa Parks and what is said in the talk about her real motives.*

b) *Watch the second part and do the following tasks.*

1. *Sum up the reasons why Rosa Parks wrote her autobiography. How do the pictures shown in the background support this part of the talk?*
2. *Explain what David Ikard means when he says that it's easier for people "to digest an old grandmother with tired feet".*

c) *Mr. Ikard quotes the famous Black author Toni Morrison as follows: "If in order for you to be tall, I have to be on my knees, you have a serious problem." Explain the statement in your own words and discuss whether you agree with it or not.*

SPEAKING **4** ## Making history

→ S20

With a partner, choose one historical event or person you've learned about in your English classes. Discuss these questions: Why is this event/person included in the curriculum (and others aren't)? Do you think textbooks or reference articles give all the relevant facts about the event/person? How could you get a more accurate picture? Share your ideas in class.

LISTENING / SPEAKING **5** ## Two famous leaders → WB 46/1 → TS Speech

a) *You're going to deal with excerpts from the speeches "I have a dream" by Dr Martin Luther King, Jr. and "The ballot or the bullet" by Malcolm X. Look at the information about the two activists. Then sum up in one sentence what you expect from each speech.*

When **Martin Luther King, Jr.** started college at the age of 15, he was rather
5 unmotivated and somewhat of a rebel. However, being a deeply religious person, he became a Baptist minister and soon played an
10 important role in the civil rights movement. Believing in non-violent protest, he led actions like the Montgomery Bus Boycott in 1955, which lasted for 382 days. King was known as an excellent orator. His most
15 famous speech ("I have a dream") is from the March on Washington in 1963. In 1964, he received the Nobel Peace Prize. Four years later, he was assassinated.

Malcolm X (born Malcolm Little) grew up in a family of civil rights activists.
5 However, after his father died he dropped out of school at 15 and became involved with selling drugs. In
10 1946 he was sent to prison, where he converted to Islam. After his release, he became a Muslim minister and human rights activist criticising Dr. King's methods and advocating Black
15 empowerment. He changed his 'slave name' (Little) to X to symbolise that he didn't know about his African roots. In 1965, he was assassinated.

→ S7, 13

b) *In your group, choose one speech excerpt: A "I have a dream" ("I am not unmindful" – "this must become true") or B "The ballot or the bullet" ("Whether you are" – "to back that up"; "I'm not a Republican – "born in jail"). Find an audio of your excerpt online and do these tasks.*

1. Make sure you understand these words: **A**: jail, persecution, redemptive, despair, creed; **B**: to swing (at sb), Cassius Clay (later Muhammad Ali, boxer), pattern, hypocrisy.
2. Sum up the speaker's main points.
3. Examine the tone and style. Give examples of rhetorical devices that make the speech convincing.
4. Explain how the speaker wants to deal with racial inequality. What are his main reasons for this kind of approach? Give examples from the speech.

c) *Present your results to the other groups. Then exchange your ideas about these points:*

1. Both speakers use the metaphor of the dream. Explain this metaphor and compare the speakers' attitudes towards it.

→ S4, 15
2. Both speakers suggest different ways to achieve political aims. Assess the pros and cons of both approaches. Visualise and present your results (e.g. in a grid, word cloud, …).

EAKING / WRITING **6 Black Lives Matter** → WB 46/2

In 2012, George Zimmerman, member of a neighborhood watch, shot 17-year-old Trayvon Martin, an unarmed African-American high school student. Although there were doubts
5 about Zimmerman's version of the events, he was found not guilty of murder by a jury in 2013. This was not the first such incident, but it prompted three African-American women to start a grassroots movement, Black Lives
10 Matter (BLM), aimed at raising awareness of police brutality and racially motivated violence against African-Americans.

→ S3, 15 **a)** *Exchange your ideas to what extent "Black Lives Matter" is similar or different to the civil rights movement from the 1950s and '60s. Focus on these points: how the movement is organised, forms of activism (non-violent, rather militant, other?), main goals. Then do some research to check whether your ideas about BLM were right and present your results in a suitable way.*

→ S7–10 **b)** *What do you think of the name of the movement? Write a short comment (about 150 words) explaining the slogan "Black Lives Matter" in your own words and giving your opinion on it.*

SPEAKING **7 A song: Black and white America**

a) *Find the song and the lyrics by Lenny Kravitz. Sum up the speaker's view on equality and civil rights in the US.*

b) *Find other songs dealing with the same topic. Choose one and present it to the class.*

SPEAKING **8 There will come a time ...** → WB 47/3

And an antiracist America is sure to come. No power lasts forever. There will come a time when Americans will *realize* that the only thing wrong with Black people is that they think something is wrong with Black people. There will come a time when we will gain the courage to fight for an equitable[1] society for our beloved humanity, knowing, that when we fight for humanity, we are fighting for ourselves. There will come a time. Maybe, just maybe, that time is now.

From: Jason Reynolds, Ibram X. Kendi, *Stamped: Racism, Antiracism and you* (adapted)

→ S5, 11 **a)** *Compare this short text from author Ibram X. Kendi to the excerpt from Martin Luther King's speech "I have a dream" from Ex. 5 and highlight the similarities.*

b) *Sum up the different views on the current state of civil rights expressed by BLM activists, in the song and in Mr. Kendi's text. Then discuss how far the US has come in your opinion. Try to come up with ideas for what could be done to achieve true equality.*

1 equitable [ˈɛkwɪtəbl] gerecht

Find more online:
6a259k

The Black roots of pop music

Today, music is available to every taste and for every occasion, pop music being commercially the most successful kind. It started to spread and become commercialised around the middle of the 20th century and has developed into numerous different genres and subgenres, most of which can be traced back to the African-American experience in some way.

SPEAKING

1 My favourite kind of music

a) *Do an anonymous survey in class to find out about your preferences:*

1. What is your favourite genre of music? (open question)
2. Do you know anything about its origin? (yes / no)
3. When and where do you listen to it? (multiple choice)
4. Do you enjoy dancing or going to live concerts? (yes / no)
5. Do you play music yourself and what kind? (open question)

→ S15, 18

b) *Each group summarises and visualises in a diagram the answers to one question and presents them (in 3–5 minutes). Discuss the results in class.*

READING / WRITING

2 Examples of influential music genres → WB 48/1

a) *Choose one of the fact boxes below. Make up three multiple choice questions for your partner. Then read the other box and answer your partner's questions. Find more artists for each box.*

→ S3, 7–8

b) *Identify the five most popular genres from your survey in Ex. 1. Divide into groups, each choosing one of them. Do research and design your own fact box.*

Blues

Slavery ended in the US in 1865. Around that time, blues developed in the Southeast of the US out of musical styles which were created by enslaved people. 'To feel blue' or 'to have the blues' means 'to feel sad', and the lyrics of many blues songs deal with topics such as broken relationships, poverty and oppression. The earliest blues was for voice only, but as it developed, it started to use musical instruments too, especially the piano and the guitar. Blues led to jazz, and rock and roll, and much of Western popular music is based on blues.

Artist profile: Bessie Smith
Bessie Smith (1894–1937) was one of the best-known blues singers of her time. Many of her songs deal with her experiences as a working-class, African-American woman. Other songs focus on social issues and are seen as an early form of protest music.
Key tracks: "Downhearted Blues" (1923), "Nobody Knows You When You're Down and Out" (1929)

Rock and roll

Rock and roll (or rock 'n' roll) took elements from blues and other forms of American music to make fast, simple pop songs mainly aimed at young people. Rhythm and blues (or R&B), the popular music of African-Americans in the late 1940s and early 1950s, was essential in its development. It spread to a wider audience and became commercially successful when it was promoted under its new name by white record companies. "Rock Around the Clock" by Bill Haley & His Comets (1954) was one of the first big rock 'n' roll hits. Black and white audiences in the USA danced to it alike though they were still segregated in its early days. Influential Black artists like Chuck Berry and Little Richard also inspired white musicians in Europe, like the Beatles and the Rolling Stones, who further contributed to the genre's world-wide success.

Artist profile: Elvis Presley

Elvis Presley (1935–1977) is often called the 'King of Rock and Roll'. His career began because record producer Sam Phillips wanted to bring African-American music to a bigger audience. Presley became one of the most successful musical artists of all time.

Key tracks: "That's All Right" (1954), "Heartbreak Hotel" (1956)

VIEWING **3** **Music and history** → WB 48/2

V10

a) *Work with the video Dr Mark Naison, professor of African American Studies and History at Fordham University, uses to introduce his course "From rock and roll to hip hop". Watch up until 00:52. What impression do you get of Dr Naison and his course?*

b) *Watch the three parts of the video and deal with the questions.*

Part 1 (00:52–02:42):
1. What does Dr Naison say about music and history?
2. Explain what he calls "the big bang".
3. Why did rock and roll upset the country?

Part 2 (02:42–04:49):
4. What happened when rock and roll was "sanitized" (made less erotic)?
5. Why does Dr Naison call rock and roll a "subtext" of the civil rights movement?

6. What does he say about the differences between rock and roll and hip hop?

Part 3 (04:49–07:55):
7. Where did hip hop start and what was new about it?
8. How does Dr Naison illustrate the reason why it isn't so easy for white people to appropriate hip hop?
9. Sum up Dr Naison's conclusion.

c) *Say if you would like to join Dr Naison's course and why / why not.*

EAKING / WRITING **4** **The most popular music genres today**

a) *Find out how commercially successful the music genres you chose in Ex. 1 are in the US and compare the figures with the results from your survey. Make a list of the ten most successful artists of all time and say what you know about them and if you like their music.*

→ S7–10

b) *Experts agree that most popular music genres are based on or have been strongly influenced by Black culture in some way. Write an essay supporting this view with arguments and examples (about 200 words). Exchange texts with a partner and peer-edit each other's work.*

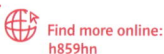
Find more online:
h859hn

My generation?

A | Fans at a Beatles concert in London, 1964

B | Hippies at the Isle of Wight Festival, 1970

C | Punks at a demonstration in London, 2006

D | Gamers at a gaming convention, 2018

SPEAKING **1** **Generation gap?** → WB 49/1

→ S15, 20

What do you associate with being young and with being old? What are the differences between younger and older people today and what do both have in common? Discuss what growing up means to you. Give a three-minute talk to present your results in class.

> **Useful phrases**
>
> belonging | to share common values | distinct | role model | ambition | goals | to fit in | to confront | to become mature | to settle | to try out | curious | open-minded | courage | to take risks | permission | age limit | drugs | overprotective | career | to marry | to start a family | sexual orientation | responsibility

WRITING **2** **Youth then and now**

→ S17

a) *Describe and compare the pictures above. Try to explain the behaviour of the people shown in the pictures and point out what is the same / different today.*

b) *Find out about the historical context of each photo. Choose one of them and write a short text (about 100 words) to relate it to its contemporary society and explain what it tells you about the mindsets of the people in the pictures.*

SPEAKING **3** **Dying to be different** → TS Poetry

a) *Hippies, punks, rappers, metalheads, emos and gamers are examples of people belonging to so-called subcultures. How would you define the term 'subculture' as opposed to 'mainstream culture'?*

→ S4, 6 b) *Analyse and compare these two excerpts from song lyrics. Find out when they were written and which subculture they belong to. Say if you think there is still a need for young people to unite and change society.*

The Who: My generation

People try to put us down (talkin' 'bout my generation)
Just because we get around (talkin' 'bout my generation)
Things they do look awful cold (talkin' 'bout my generation)
I hope I die before I get old (talkin' 'bout my generation)
5 This is my generation
This is my generation, baby
Why don't you all fade away (talkin' 'bout my generation)
Don't try to dig what we all say (talkin' 'bout my generation)
I'm not trying to cause a big sensation (talkin' 'bout my generation)
10 I'm just talkin' 'bout my generation (talkin' 'bout my generation)

Words and music: Pete Townshend

Generation X: Your generation

I'm trying to forget your generation
Using any way I see!
Well, the end must justify the means
I said, your generation don't mean a thing to me!
5 It might take a bit of violence
But only violence ain't our stance
It might make our friends enemies
But we've gotta take that chance!

There ain't no time for substitutes!
There ain't no time for idle threats!   10
Actions are rather hard to place
'cos what you give is what you get!
It's your generation!
Well, it's your generation!
It's time your generation's gotta end!   15

Words and music: William Michael Broad, Anthony Eric James

LISTENING **4** **Finding and defining your tribe** → WB 49/2

a) *Name the advantages and disadvantages of belonging to a group with common values.*

A 3/1–3
→ S13 b) *Listen to three parts of an interview with an expert on youth subcultures. Make notes and report her opinion on these aspects:*

Part 1: 1. The attractiveness of subcultures to young people | 2. Political conflicts which influenced youth subcultures in the 1960s, 70s and 80s | 3. Similarities and differences between punks and hippies | 4. What has become of the hippie and punk cultures

Part 2: 1. Hippies and punks creating music and fashion styles | 2. Differences between gaming and earlier subcultures
Part 3: 1. Media influence on youth culture since the 1980s | 2. Differences between finding and defining your tribe then and now

Find more online:
p359bz

Unit 3
Youth (and) culture

A

SPEAKING **1** **Quotes** → WB 50/1–2

> "Buy less, choose well and do it yourself."
>
> Vivienne Westwood, fashion designer who became famous in the punk era

> "Do everything you can to make it around the system, over the system, or out the system."
>
> Tupac Shakur, hip hop artist

> "If someone pauses their game just to text you back, marry them."
>
> Common gamers' quote

a) *Compare the three quotes, interpret them and say what they tell you about the youth subcultures they are related to. Give your own opinion on the quotes.*

→ S14, 20
→ 97/1

b) *Think of ways subcultures have influenced our society (lifestyles, values, rights), e.g. flower power in the 1960s, punk in the 1980s, video gaming in the 1990s, and discuss them.*

Useful phrases

to reject | to identify with | consumerism | to provide opportunities | role model | creativity | equality | diversity | self-esteem | to adapt to | to set yourself apart from | to emancipate yourself | to establish your own … | to have an impact / to leave its mark on … | to be appropriated / absorbed by mainstream culture | to replace

VIEWING **2** An exhibition at the Metropolitan Museum of Art in New York

V 11 📽
→ S19

Watch the video and complete the curator's statements about the exhibition.

The purpose of the exhibition is to show ⬛1⬛ . According to the curator, the main ideas of the punk movement were ⬛2⬛ and ⬛3⬛ as well as a ⬛4⬛ attitude towards the state of society. Therefore, he defines it not only as an aesthetical, but also a ⬛5⬛ movement. Historically, it originated in ⬛6⬛ and ⬛7⬛ during a ⬛8⬛ of economic depression and dissatisfaction, and in his opinion it ⬛9⬛ emerged if the ⬛10⬛ had been different. He appreciates that punks were ⬛11⬛ individuals who didn't ⬛12⬛ other people's opinions and wants to highlight a ⬛13⬛ that was all about creativity and about ⬛14⬛ the conventions of ⬛15⬛ and fashion.

LISTENING **3** A closer look at hip hop culture

A 3/4–5 ⊙
→ S13

a) *Listen to part 1, make notes and sum up the basic facts about these aspects of hip hop culture: its five elements, its background and its commercial success. Then listen to part 2 and explain why some people love hip hop while others dislike it.*

b) *Discuss the pros and cons of hip hop. What do you think of it compared with other kinds of youth subcultures you know? Give reasons.*

Teenage lifestyles

READING / WRITING
1   Two worlds colliding → WB 51/3–4 → G1–2, 5–6

A 48–53
A 3/6–11

Capricorn Anderson is a teenage boy growing up with his grandmother, Rain, in what is left of a former hippie community. He has never been in contact with any girls or boys outside and doesn't know about the average US teenager's school experiences and everyday activities. When his grandmother has an accident, his life is about to change fundamentally.

A   I was thirteen the first time I saw a police officer up close. He was arresting me for driving without a license. At the time, I didn't even know what a license was. I wasn't too
5   clear on what being arrested meant either. But by then they were loading Rain onto a stretcher to rush her in for X-rays. So I barely noticed the handcuffs the officer slapped on my wrists.

10   "Who's the owner of this pickup?"

"It belongs to the community," I told him. He made a note on a ring-bound pad.

"What community? Golf club? Condo deal[1]?"

"Garland Farm." He frowned.

15   "Never heard of that one." Rain would have been pleased. That was the whole point of the community – to allow us to escape the money-hungry rat race[2] of modern society. If people didn't know us, they couldn't find us, and we
20   could live our lives in peace.

"It's an alternative farm commune," I explained. The officer goggled[3] at me.

"Alternative – you mean like *hippies*?"

"Rain used to be one, back in the sixties.
25   There were fourteen families at Garland then. Now it's just Rain and me." I tried to edge my way toward the nursing station. "I have to make sure she's okay." He was unmoved.

"Who is this Rain? According to her Social
30   Security card, the patient's name is Rachel Esther Rosenblatt."

"Her name is Rain, and she's my grandmother," I said stiffly. "She fell out of a tree." He stared at his notes.

35   "What was a sixty-seven-year-old woman doing up a tree?"

"Picking plums," I replied defensively. "She slipped."

"So you drove her here. At thirteen."

"I drive all the time," I informed him. "Rain   40
taught me when I was eight." Sweat appeared on his upper lip.

"And you never thought of just dialing 911?" I regarded him blankly.

"What's nine-one-one?"   45

"The emergency number! On the telephone!" I told him the truth.

"I've talked on a telephone a couple of times. In town. But we don't have one." He looked at me for what seemed like forever.   50

"What's your name, son?"

"Cap. It's short for Capricorn." He unlocked my handcuffs. I was un-arrested.

B   How could an able-bodied teenager allow his grandmother to scale[4] a plum tree? Simple.   55
She wasn't my grandmother at the time. She was my teacher. I was homeschooled. That was the law. Even on a tiny farm like ours, you

---

1 condo deal [ˈkɒndəʊ ˌdiːl] Wohnungseigentümergemeinschaft | **2 rat race** [ˈræt ˌreɪs] Hamsterrad, Konkurrenzkampf | **3 to goggle** [ˈɡɒɡl] starren | **4 to scale** [skeɪl] hochklettern

had to get an education. No school bus could
60 ever make it up the rutted[1], snaking dirt road
that led to Garland. But transportation wasn't
the only problem. If we'd been serviced by
an eight-lane highway, Rain still would have
handled my schooling personally. We wanted
65 to avoid the low standards and cultural poison
of a world that had lost its way.

So that's what I was doing when Rain fell –
working on a vocabulary lesson. Most of the list
came from the state eighth grade curriculum:
70 *barometer, decagon[2], perpendicular[3]* … I could
always spot the extra words Rain threw in:
nonviolence, Zen Buddhism, psychedelic …
Microprocessor? I frowned at the paper on the
unpainted wooden table. Was that Rain or the
75 state? I'd never heard that term before.

I stepped out of the house, careful not
to disturb my science project – the Foucault
pendulum suspended from the porch roof.
The tester from the education department
80 thought it was good enough to enter in the
county science fair. Too bad we didn't believe
in competition – all that emphasis on trophies[4]
and medals, the shiny symbols of an empty
soul. Anyway, Rain said the whole thing was a
85 trick to get me to go to regular school.

"If your project is excellent, it only proves
that you're getting a superior education right
here with me" had been her reasoning.

I spotted her up in the tree, reaching across
90 a limb[5] to pick a plum.

C "Rain," I called, "there's a word I don't
under…" And it happened. One minute she
was on the branch; the next she was on the
ground. I don't even recall seeing her fall. Just
the faint cry followed by the dull clunk.   95

"Aaah!" *Whump.*

"Rain!" She was lying on her side amid
the scattered plums when I pounded onto
the scene. Her face was very pale. She
wasn't moving. My terror was total. Rain was   100
everything to me – my teacher, my family, my
whole universe. Garland was a community, but
we were the community – the two of us!

I knelt beside her. "Rain – are you okay?
Please be okay!"   105

Her eyes fluttered open and focused on me.
She tried to smile, but the pain contorted her
expression into a grimace.

"Cap …" she began faintly. I leaped back to
my feet.   110

"I'll get Doc Cafferty!" Doc Cafferty lived
a few miles away. He was technically a
veterinarian. But he was used to working on
humans, since he had six kids. He'd given me
stitches[6] once when I was eight. She reached   115
up a tremulous[7] hand and gripped my arm.

"We need a real doctor this time. A people
doctor."

I stared at her like she was speaking a
foreign language. Doc Cafferty had filled all   120
of Garland's medical needs as long as I could
remember. She spelled it out.

"You're going to have to take me to the
hospital."

D Rain always said that anger upsets the   125
balance inside a person. So when you yell at
somebody, you're attacking yourself more
than whoever it is you're yelling at. Falling out
of the tree must have made her forget this.
Because when the nurses finally let me in to   130
see her, she was screaming at the doctor at top
volume.

"I can't do eight weeks of rehab! I can't do
eight days!"

"You've got no choice," the doctor said   135
matter-of-factly. "You have a broken hip. It has

1 rutted [ˈrʌtɪd] zerwühlt | **2 decagon** [ˈdekəgən] Zehneck | **3 perpendicular** [ˌpɜːpenˈdɪkjələ] lotrecht | **4 trophy**
[ˈtrəʊfi] Trophäe; Preis | **5 limb** [lɪm] Ast | **6** *to give stitches** [ˌɡɪv ˈstɪtʃɪz] eine Wunde nähen | **7 tremulous** [ˈtremjələs]
zittrig

to be pinned. After that you'll need extensive physical therapy. It's a long process, and you can't ignore it just because it doesn't fit in with
140 your plans."

"You're not listening!" Rain shrilled. "I'm the caregiver to my grandson! The *only* caregiver!"

"What about the parents?" the doctor asked. "Where are they?" She shook her head.
145 "Long dead. Malaria. They were with the Peace Corps in Namibia. They gave their lives for what they believed in."

That sounds worse than it is. But I never knew my parents except from old pictures.
150 They left when I was little. Besides, the rule at Garland back then was that we all belonged to each other, and it didn't matter who was related by blood. I have a few vague recollections of other people in the community
155 when I was really young. But whether they were my parents or not, I can't tell. Anyway, it's impossible to miss what you never had.

E   I rushed to my grandmother's bedside. "Are you okay? Is your leg all fixed up?"
160 She looked grave.

"We've got a problem, Cap. And you know what we do with problems."

"We talk it out, think it out, work it out," I said readily. It had been that way since the very beginning of Garland in 1967, long before 165
I was born. Now that there were only two of us, Rain still gave me a full vote. She never treated me like I was just a kid. The doctor was growing impatient.

"How about cousins? Or maybe a close 170
friend from school?"

"I'm homeschooled," I supplied. The doctor sighed.

"Mrs. Rosenblatt –"

"That name hasn't applied to me for 175
decades. You can call me Rain."

"All right. Rain. I'm admitting you now. We'll operate in the morning. And I'll call social services to see what arrangements can be made for your grandson." 180

That was when I started to worry about what was going to happen to me.

From: Gordon Korman, *Schooled* (adapted)

→ S5–6   **a)** *Describe the narrative perspective and the setting.*

b) *Sum up the plot and comment on it. (Say whether you find it funny, exciting, interesting etc. and if you would like to read the entire novel. Give reasons.)*

→ △ 97/2   **c)** *With the help of a grid, compare and contrast the 'two worlds' presented in the excerpt and explain the conflict between them.*

→ S6, 11, 15   **d)** *Divide into groups and choose one of the following tasks. Visualise your results, present and discuss them in class.*

1. Analyse the characters and their dialogues. What are their roles in the excerpt?
2. In what way is the state represented in the text? What are the roles of its institutions?
3. Why does Rain want to keep away from the outside world? What are her fears?
4. Say which parts of the text you find funny and why.
5. Compare and contrast the concept of family presented in the text with the concept that is common in your society.

Across cultures

Hippie communities in the 1960s lived an alternative lifestyle. They shared values like love, peace, freedom, collective property and care for humans and nature. Groups like the **Amish** in the US have been living apart from mainstream society and institutions since the 1700s in a similar way. They strictly follow their religious rules and maintain their own language and schools. They live on agriculture, some groups refusing to use modern technology. Discuss the pros and cons of such communities.

→ S7–8   **e)** *What do you expect to happen next? Write a follow-up scene (about 220 words). You may also act it out or use digital storytelling tools to present it.*

2 The importance of music → WB 52/5–6, 53/7 → G6, 9, 11

A 54–59
A 3/12–17
→ △ 97/3

Brian Oswald is a teenager growing up in the 1990s. He realises that he is falling in love with his best friend Gretchen, a punk rocker who often gets into trouble because she becomes very aggressive when someone insults her. Music plays a very important part in their lives.

A Mostly all Rod and I did was listen to records. Sometimes we'd go to the mall or video arcade, but mostly we went to different record stores looking for old vinyl. On Saturdays,
5 we'd go to the flea market and he'd search for some obscure soul album like Curtis Mayfield or some ABKCO[1] Rolling Stones title and I'd go there to try out the Chinese stars[2] and butterfly knives. Rod was very into music, all
10 kinds: pop, R&B, rock, even jazz – which, for a high school kid, was weird. I mean, I always figured it had to do with his dad, who had this immense record collection. You saw it as soon as you walked into their living room – the
15 living room which looked like it belonged on a television show, with white curtains and yellow furniture and all of it was perfectly clean with plastic on the sofa cushions and lace coasters[3] under everything – and there, set inside wood
20 shelves all around the room like a library, were hundreds and hundreds of vinyl records – blues, ragtime, modern jazz, bebop, soul – and his dad would be sitting in his soft red chair with a cardigan sweater and black slippers on,
25 smoking his pipe and nodding his head and listening to Don Cherry.
And Rod would walk in and say he'd found some B-side of a Marvin Gaye song and his dad and him would high-five each other, and
30 then gently, like parents of a newborn baby, they'd lift the record out of its paper sleeve[4] and place it on the hi-fi to play. Rod would take a seat on the couch and I'd just stand there, wondering, *Who exactly are these people?* and
35 then the music would come on – a song like "Underdog" or "Living for the City" – music I had never heard before in my life, and yet after just a few notes, they were songs so simple and pure and full of joy that they'd make their way
40 into my heart.
Me, a dumb white kid humming Motown[5]

and not caring, and I'd sing them all, one after the other, on the bus ride home, maybe.
B Once we walked into the house and Rod's
45 dad, who insisted I call him Burt, was sitting in his red chair with his black slippers on, and said, "Boys, boys, listen to this one," and just then the needle met the small vinyl grooves[6] of the record and "Time After Time" by Chet Baker
50 began playing, the strange haunting voice of a man that to me sounded like a woman, so that I asked, "Wow, who's this lady?" and Rod's dad nodded and laughed and said, "That's Chet Baker, son, the trumpet player," and I said, "He
55 sounds spooky," and Rod's dad said to Rod, "This was the first song your mother and I ever made love to," and I thought that was a little strange for him to say, but I didn't say anything. I just listened, and the more I heard
60 that ghostly, quiet, nighttime voice rising, the more I was thinking about Gretchen and kissing her to a song like that, and then it was over and we were all standing around silent and Rod's dad said, "That's how you should feel
65 after you hear a good song. Like a brand new man," and I said, "Burt, I know what you mean," and we walked off into Rod's room, still kind of listening.
C The only record I could listen to straight
70 through was Guns 'n' Roses' *Appetite for Destruction*. When everything else was wrong, that record made it right. I could go back to it, always. No matter what, that record would make me feel all right. *Appetite for Destruction.*
75 Guns 'n' Roses. That was it. That was my record. "It's So Easy," "Nightrain," "Out ta Get Me," then classics like "Paradise City," "Welcome to the Jungle," and probably the greatest song ever, of all time:
80 "Sweet Child o' Mine." What was it about that song? I loved that song so much it sometimes made me want to kick a hole in the wall.

1 **ABKCO** *eine Plattenfirma* | 2 **Chinese star** [ˌtʃaɪniːz ˈstɑː] Wurfstern | 3 **lace coaster** [ˈleɪs ˌkəʊstə] Spitzenuntersetzer | 4 **sleeve** [sliːv] Hülle | 5 **Motown** [ˈməʊtaʊn] *eine Plattenfirma* | 6 **groove** [gruːv] Rille

If Gretchen and I were driving and if her stereo was working – which it did once every ten million years – and if that song happened to come on, I'd have to get her to pull over so I could listen to it, without having to hear the engine running or traffic going by. She always pulled over; she understood, I guess. That one part, where the song kind of slows down – "Where do we go now? Where do we go now? Where do we go now?" – I didn't even know what Axl[1] was talking about, but if I was in the car with Gretchen, or better, at home alone in the basement where my room was, I would have to stop and crank[2] it or just stand there and do the air guitar parts. In the car, I'd try to get Gretchen to sing along, but since it wasn't punk, she wasn't having it, though one time she did do the "Where do we go? Where do we go now" parts, but to get her to do anything else was almost impossible where GNR was concerned.

D   When I brought the record over to Rod's to try to get him to listen, all he did was roll his eyes and shake his head. It was the first time I had played a record of mine for him and he just folded his arms over his chest, raising his eyebrows, and laughed.

"Lame[3]," was all he said.

"What? How can you not like this?" I asked.

"It's just so lame," he said.

"Lame? Stevie Wonder is lame."

"Seriously. I'll take Stevie over this any day," he muttered[4], getting up to switch it off.

"Dude[5], you've got to listen to the whole thing. At the end. It gets all quiet and pretty and everything."

He stood up and walked beside the deep mahogany[6] record player, his hand on the record arm, and I thought, *If he touches that needle, I am going to kick his ass* and *Maybe white kids and black kids can't be friends* and *If he turns this fucking record off, I am never going to talk to him again,* and just then Slash[7] began his solo and the song began to build and Rod waited, closing his eyes, and listened, and sat back down on the bed. We listened to the whole song together and then when it was over, he nodded and said, "That was a jam[8]. I was wrong. That really was a jam."

E   "Like I said." He handed me back the LP[9], gently sliding it into its paper sleeve.

"Hey, man, I need to put a mix-tape[10] together for this girl. Can you help me pick out some cool songs she's never heard before?" I asked.

"Why do you want to put songs she's never heard on it?"

"Because she does that for me. Plays songs I've never heard, you know." Rod frowned, crossing his arms in front of his chest.

"Don't be lame, man," he said. "That would be like writing somebody else's love letter."

"No it isn't," I said.

"I'm not helping you out. If you like this girl, you should be able to pick the songs out you want her to hear yourself."

"But I'll pick fucking rock songs. I need sexy songs like that shit your dad listens to. Like Chet Baker and shit."

"Man, forget it. I'm not doing it."

"You're screwing me here, Rod," I said. "You're blowing my chance with love."

"No, man, you are," he said, and I knew I was on my own from there.

From: Joe Meno, *Hairstyles of the Damned* (adapted)

→ S12   **a)** *Describe the characters in the excerpt and their relationships with each other.*

→ S4   **b)** *Examine what types of music are mentioned and what music means to each of the characters. Compare the results to your own experiences with music.*

c) *Comment on Rod's refusal to help Brian with a tape for Gretchen.*

d) *Create a music playlist for your best friend. Talk about your choices.*

1 **Axl** *Sänger der* Guns 'n' Roses | 2 **to crank** [kræŋk] aufdrehen | 3 **lame** [leɪm] lahm, uncool | 4 **to mutter** [ˈmʌtə] brummeln | 5 **Dude!** (AE coll) [duːd] Alter! | 6 **mahogany** [məˈhɒɡni] Mahagoni (Holz) | 7 **Slash** *Gitarrist der* Guns 'n' Roses | 8 **a jam** [ə ˈdʒæm] *hier etwa:* erste Sahne | 9 **LP** [ˌelˈpiː] Langspielplatte | 10 **tape** [teɪp] Musikkassette

Rap and hip hop

READING / WRITING **1** ## Parts of an interview with 2Pac (Tupac Shakur) → WB 54/8

Hip hop journalist Davey D conducted this interview with 2Pac in 1991.

*What's the concept behind your album
'2Pacalypse Now'?*
The concept is the young Black male. Everybody's
been talkin' about it but now it's not important.
5 It's like we just skipped over it. It's no longer
a fad¹ to be down for² the young Black male.
Everybody wants to go past. Like the gangster
stuff, it just got exploited. Now everybody's doing
rap songs with the singing in it. I'm still down
10 for the young Black male. I'm gonna stay until
things get better. So it's all about addressing the
problems that we face in everyday society.

What are those problems?
Police brutality, poverty, unemployment,
15 insufficient education, disunity and violence,
black on black crime, teenage pregnancy, crack
addiction. Do you want me to go on?

*How do you address these problems? Are you
pointing them out or are you offering solutions?*
20 I do both. In some situations, I show us having
the power, and in some situations, I show how
it's more apt to happen with the police or power
structure having the ultimate power. I show both
ways. I show how it really happens and I show
25 how I wish it would happen.

*You refer to yourself as the 'Rebel of the
Underground'. Why so?*
Cause, as if Digital Underground³ wasn't diverse
enough with enough crazy things in it, I'm even

that crazier. I'm the rebel totally going against the 30
grain⁴ … I'm the lunatic⁵ that everyone refers to.
I always want to do the extreme. I want to get as
many people looking as possible.

*Can [we] talk about your recent encounter with
police brutality at the hands of the Oakland* 35
PD⁶?
We're letting the law do its job. It's making its
way through the court system. We filed a claim …

Recount the incident for those who don't know.
For everyone who doesn't know, I, an innocent 40
young black male was walking down the streets
of Oakland minding my own business and the
police department saw fit⁷ for me to be trained
or snapped back into my place⁸. So they asked for
my I-D and sweated⁹ me about my name because 45
my name is 'Tupac'. My final words to them was
'f--- y'all'. Next thing I know I was in a choke
hold¹⁰ passing out with cuffs on headed for jail
for resisting arrest. Yes, you heard right – I was
arrested for resisting arrest. 50

Where is all this now?
We're in the midst of having a ten million dollar
law suit against the Oakland Police Department.
If I win and get the money, then the Oakland
Police Department is going to buy a boys home, 55
me a house, my family a house and a 'Stop Police
Brutality Center' and other little odd things like
that.   From: Davey D website (adapted)

→  98/4   a)   *Tupac Shakur was one of the most successful figures in hip hop culture
and one of the first rappers to address social issues. Make notes of
what you learn about him from the interview extracts.*

→ S3, 7–10   b)   *Find out more about his biography and write a short article (about 180
words) about him and his impact on hip hop culture.*

1 fad [fæd] Mode | **2 *to be down for** [bɪ ˈdaʊn fə] stehen auf | **3 Digital Underground**
ein Musikprojekt | **4 against the grain** [əˌɡenst ðə ˈɡreɪn] gegen den Strich | **5 lunatic**
[ˈluːnətɪk] Irre/-r | **6 PD** *Polizeibehörde* | **7 *to see fit** [ˌsiː ˈfɪt] für richtig halten |
8 to snap sb back into place [snæp ˌbæk ˌɪntə ˈpleɪs] einrasten lassen, *hier:* jmdn. wieder
auf den ihm zustehenden Platz verweisen | **9 to sweat** *(slang)* [swet] nerven |
10 choke hold [ˈtʃəʊk həʊld] Schwitzkasten

READING / WRITING
2 Artist, Icon, Billionaire: How Jay-Z created his $1 billion fortune → WB 55/9

A 60
A 3/18

Forbes is a magazine that publishes a list of the 400 wealthiest US citizens every year. In 2010 Forbes journalists interviewed the billionaire Warren Buffett and the increasingly successful rapper Jay-Z together. In 2019 the following article was published.

Nine years ago, two unlikely lunch partners sat down at the Hollywood Diner in Omaha, Nebraska. One, Warren Buffett, was a regular there. The other, Jay-Z, was not. The billionaire
5 and the rapper ordered strawberry malts[1] and chatted amiably[2], continuing the conversation back at Buffett's Berkshire Hathaway offices.

   Buffett, then 80, walked away impressed with the artist 40 years his junior[3]: "Jay is
10 teaching in a lot bigger classroom than I'll ever teach in. For a young person growing up, he's the guy to learn from." This moment made it clear that Jay-Z already had a blueprint for his own ten-figure fortune. "Hip-hop from the
15 beginning has always been aspirational[4]," he said.

   Less than a decade later, it's clear that Jay-Z has accumulated a fortune that conservatively totals $1 billion, making him one of only
20 a handful of entertainers to become a billionaire – and the first hip-hop artist to do so. Jay-Z's steadily growing kingdom is expansive, encompassing liquor, art, real estate (homes in Los Angeles, the Hamptons, Tribeca)
25 and stakes in companies like Uber. His journey is all the more impressive given its start: Brooklyn's notorious Marcy housing projects. He was a drug dealer before becoming a musician, starting his own label, Roc-A-Fella
30 Records, to release his 1996 debut, *Reasonable Doubt*. Since then he's amassed 14 No. 1

Jay Z and Warren Buffet, 2012

albums, 22 Grammy awards and over $500 million in pretax earnings in a decade.

   Crucially, he realized that he should build his own brands rather than promote someone 35 else's: the clothing line Rocawear, started in 1999 (sold for $204 million to Iconix in 2007); D'Ussé, a cognac he co-owns with Bacardi; and Tidal, a music-streaming service.

   Kasseem "Swizz Beatz" Dean, the 40 superproducer behind some of Jay-Z's biggest hits ("On To The Next One," Beyoncé's "Upgrade U"), looks at Jay-Z as something others can model: "It's bigger than hip-hop … it's the blueprint for our culture. A guy that looks 45 like us, sounds like us, loves us, made it to something that we always felt that was above us."

   "If he's a billionaire now, imagine what he's about to be," Swizz Beatz says. "Because he's 50 only just starting."

   Zack O'Malley Greenburg, Forbes, 2019 (adapted)

a) *Find information about the names mentioned in the article to help you understand it better.*

→ S2

→ ▲ 98/5

b) *Collect economy-related words from the text with possible collocations in a mind map.*

c) *Give reasons why Warren Buffett and Jay-Z were "unlikely lunch partners" nine years before and what has changed since then.*

→ S3, 8–11

d) *Choose one of these topics and write 150–200 words:*

1. Do research on the two men's biographies and compare their stories of success explaining Buffett's "classroom" metaphor referring to Jay-Z.
2. Interpret Kasseem Dean's statement: "… it's the blueprint for our culture."

1 malt [mɔːlt] Milchshake | **2 amiable** [ˈeɪmɪəbl] freundlich | **3 his junior** [hɪz ˈdʒuːniə] jünger als er |
4 °to be aspirational [bi ˌæsprˈeɪʃnl] nach Höherem streben

MEDIATION   **3**   **Rap music and sexism** → WB 56/10, 57/11

→ S16
→ ▲ 98/6

Ella from Wisconsin has a blog about hip hop. She wants to write an essay about sexism in rap songs and has asked her readers from other countries to share their knowledge and experiences with her. You have found an interview with social scientist Heidi Süß on the internet and write an e-mail to Ella. Summarise for her what Süß says about the following issues. Write 1–2 sentences about each aspect.

1. how widespread sexism in rap music is
2. reasons for the popularity of music with violent and misogynist lyrics
3. how rap plays with different personas
4. the psychological background of misogynist lyrics (male fears, weak points)
5. artistic licence
6. what effects sexist lyrics can have

Der Hashtag #UnhateWomen soll auf Sexismus im Rap aufmerksam machen. Forscherin Heidi Süß spricht im Interview darüber, ob es noch Kunst ist, wenn Frauen „Hoes" genannt werden.

Frau Süß, hat Deutschrap ein „Sexismusproblem", wie gern geschrieben wird?

5 Heidi Süß: Ich würde sagen: Die ganze Gesellschaft hat ein Sexismusproblem. Es ist nicht so, dass Sexismus in das Normen- und Wertesystem des Rap eingeschrieben wäre.

Ist Rap ein Spiegel der Gesellschaft?

10 Heidi Süß: Nein, aber Rap spiegelt gesellschaftliche Probleme. Im Rap findet nichts statt, was es nicht auch woanders gibt. Rap hat natürlich eine eigene Sprachtradition, einen eigenen Wortschatz, eine bestimmte
15 Dringlichkeit, mit der er auf Probleme, auf Ungleichheit verweist. Und gerappt wird oft aus Sicht von einem Mann, der einerseits sozial benachteiligt ist, andererseits aber auch selbst auf andere runterblickt.

20 *Musik, die zwar oft von sozial Benachteiligten gemacht, aber auch von Gymnasiasten gehört wird.*

Heidi Süß: Ich denke, das ist eine Art sozialer Voyeurismus: Die Lust an dem, was man

selber nicht ist und wovon man sich dann 25 abgrenzen kann. So in der Art: „Wir beleidigen unsere Frauen nicht, wir nennen die auch nicht Bitches." Was natürlich so auch nicht stimmt. Und, klar, es ist natürlich auch die Lust an der Provokation, die Abgren- 30 zung von den Eltern.

Der Tabubruch gehört zur Jugendkultur; früher verkörpert vom Outlaw im Rock, vom Anarchisten im Punk, vom Hedonisten im Techno. Sind sexistische Tabubrüche in Zeiten, in denen 35 #MeToo ein wichtiges Stichwort ist, besonders reizvoll für Rapper?

Heidi Süß: Ja. Es ist ein gesamtgesellschaftliches Phänomen, dass Frauen gerade in viele Bereiche eindringen, die vorher 40 weitestgehend männlich dominiert waren, und dort Machtpositionen besetzen. Und viele Männer reagieren darauf mit Verunsicherung, fühlen sich bedroht, weil sie der Auffassung sind, ihnen würde irgendwas 45 weggenommen, was ihnen qua Penis zusteht; ein verqueres Denken. Es ist eine neue Situation, auch im Rap. Und Rapper

50 existieren ja auch in der Gesellschaft und
sind da nun von selbstbewussten Frauen
umgeben. Wenn einem da die Mittel fehlen,
sich anderweitig zu positionieren, greift
man auf solche Diskriminierungsstrategi-
55 en wie sexistische Zeilen zurück. Oder gar
Gewalt.

*Fler rappt Zeilen wie die von der Kampagne
#UnhateWomen angeprangerte „Will keine
Frauen, will Hoes / Sie müssen b*** wie Pros",
und er droht Frauen auch im echten Leben.*

60 Heidi Süß: Ähnliches hatten wir ja auch schon
bei Gzuz. Eine Besonderheit am Rap ist
auch, dass eine sehr geringe Rollendistanz
herrscht zwischen realer Persona und Rap-
Persona. Darin liegt auch ein gewisser Un-
65 terhaltungswert und Spannungsmoment:
Meint der das jetzt ernst? Und im Rap spielt
Authentizität eine wichtige Rolle, die von
dem Rapper eigentlich sogar verlangt, dass
er das, was er sagt, auch tut. Dass dann,
70 wenn er das wirklich tut, der Aufschrei groß
ist, ist eigentlich merkwürdig.

*Fler postete auf Instagram ein Bild der Kampa-
gne mit dem Zitat aus seinem Song „Fame" und
schrieb darunter: „Die Bezeichnung Hoe gilt im
75 Rap-Jargon für das perfekte Schönheitsideal.
In dieser Zeile wird nicht nur die Frau, sondern
auch der männliche Interpret auf seine Sexualität reduziert. Wenn sie ‚b*** kann wie ein Pro'
gilt dies als Kompliment." Was sagen Sie zu der
80 Interpretation?*

Heidi Süß: Das ist Nonsens. Natürlich gibt es so
etwas wie Rap-Jargon. Aber „Hoe" bedeutet
meiner Ansicht nach im Rap-Jargon genau
das, was es auch sonst heißt, nämlich
85 „Hure" oder „Schlampe". Eigentlich müsste
man solche Texte ganz anders lesen, mit
einer gewissen Entspanntheit. Die Message in so einer Zeile ist ja: Fler kann nicht
lieben. Oder er fürchtet einen Männlich-
90 keitsverlust, wenn er sich zu so etwas wie
Liebe oder Emotionen bekennt. Also will er
keine Frauen und tritt hypermännlich auf,
indem er die Frau zur sexuellen Dienstleis-
terin erniedrigt. Wenn er wüsste, dass die
95 Überbetonung von Männlichkeit immer auf

einen Bruch verweist oder auf eine Fragili-
tät, dann würde er das wahrscheinlich nicht
rappen.

*Ist es überhaupt berechtigt, dass „Terre des
100 Femmes" solche Zeilen im Kontext von* Hate
Speech *anprangert – oder fallen Rap-Texte
schlicht unter Kunstfreiheit?*

Heidi Süß: Natürlich ist das berechtigt, das
ist ja auch eine Form von Hate Speech.
105 Ich finde die Kampagne auch sehr wichtig
und sehr gut gemacht. Klar, Rap ist Kunst,
und Kunstfreiheit ist eine schützenswerte
Errungenschaft der Demokratie, aber kein
Freifahrtschein. Es gibt einige Männer im
110 Rap, und das sind tatsächlich immer Männer, denen schon seit Jahrzehnten aufgrund
irgendwelcher vermeintlicher Dienste für
die Kultur eine sagenumwobene Aura der
Unantastbarkeit anhaftet. Und Fler ist so je-
115 mand, weil: Fler ist ja schon so lange dabei.
Und Fler kommt aus dem Graffiti. Und Fler
hat ja den Trap in Deutschland etabliert.
Was passieren kann auf der Grundlage so
einer männlichen, verklärten, nie kritisier-
120 ten Machtposition, haben wir beim Rapper
Taktloss gesehen: Der hat die Rap-Journalis-
tin Jule Wasabi gewürgt.

*Trägt Sexismus im Deutschrap zu einer Nor-
malisierung alltäglicher, verbaler Hassgewalt
gegenüber Frauen bei?* • 125

Heidi Süß: Mir sind keine Studien bekannt, die
eine kausale Beziehung herstellen zwischen Hörgewohnheit und tatsächlichem
Handeln. Ich finde aber auch nicht, dass
130 das ganz fern liegt. Da ärgert es mich allerdings, dass der Gangsta-Rapper immer so
als böser Bube dasteht: Wir haben genug
andere Genres und Medien, die uns nicht
minder gewalttätige oder sexistische Bilder
135 präsentieren. Aber im Fall von Gangsta-Rap
haben wir auch eine sehr junge Zielgrup-
pe. Und über die Rezeption von Popkultur
bildet sich natürlich auch Geschlechts-
identität heraus. Insofern, so viel kann
140 man sagen, sind Rapper als Popstars ganz
einflussreiche Menschen.

Jurek Skrobala, Der Spiegel, 2020 (adaptiert)

The digital age

SPEAKING **1** **Video killed the radio star** → WB 57/12 → TS Speech

→ S4–6 *Find the music video for this song online. It was the first music video shown on MTV when the channel started in 1980. Analyse and interpret it. What has changed in the digital age? Discuss the role media have played in spreading youth culture.*

I heard you on my wireless[1] back in '52
Lying awake, intent at tuning in on[2] you
If I was young, it didn't stop you coming through
They took the credit for your second symphony
5 Rewritten by machine and new technology
And now I understand the problems you can see
I met your children
What did you tell them?
Video killed the radio star
10 Pictures came and broke your heart
And now we meet in an abandoned studio
We hear the playback and it seems so long ago
And you remember the jingles[3] used to go
You were the first one

You are the last one 15
Video killed the radio star
In my mind and in my car
We can't rewind[4], we've gone too far
Video killed the radio star
In my mind and in my car 20
We can't rewind, we've gone too far
Pictures came and broke your heart
Put the blame on VCR[5]
You are a radio star
You are a radio star 25
Video killed the radio star

Words: Geoffrey Downes,
Bruce Woolley, Trevor Horn

LISTENING/WRITING **2** **Gaming culture** → WB 58/13

A 3/19 ◎
→ S13
a) *Listen to the dialogue between two teenagers and make notes of the pros and cons of gaming. What suggestions do they have for gamers to improve their gaming experience?*

b) *Do you agree that video games have become more important to young people than music and that gaming is a subculture of its own? Give reasons.*

→ S17 **c)** *Which aspects of gaming do the cartoons deal with? Analyse and interpret them.*

👥
→ S7–10 **d)** *Write a short argumentative essay on the pros and cons of video gaming (about 200 words). Exchange texts with a partner and peer-edit each other's work.*

"These online fantasy worlds are great fun. I can be 'Dave the Accountant' from Birmingham."

1 wireless ['waɪələs] Radio | **2 to tune in on** [ˌtjuːn ˈɪn ɒn] einen Sender einstellen | **3 jingle** ['dʒɪŋgl] Erkennungsmelodie | **4 to rewind** [riːˈwaɪnd] zurückspulen | **5 VCR** [ˌviːsiːˈɑː] Videoaufzeichnung

READING/WRITING   **3**   **Teenage girls show the scary effects of editing apps** → WB 60/14 → G8–9

A 61 ◁))
A 3/20 ⊙

British photographer Rankin asked teens to edit their own portraits until they were "social media ready." The results are fascinating.

→ △ 98/7

Photo editing has become an open secret in the land of social media. Apps have made it
5 so easy for us to change the way we look – through filters, retouching or a combination of both – that it's becoming harder to determine what's real and what's not. We'd also argue that these apps are enabling us to perpetuate[1]
10 a homogenized expression of beauty, as opposed to celebrating true individuality.

British photographer Rankin (born John Rankin Waddell) explored these apps and their potentially harmful effects in a recent photo
15 series titled, "Selfie Harm." For the project, Rankin photographed a group of teenagers and then asked them to edit their own portrait until it was "social media ready."

The before and after images offered a
20 striking look at what these apps can do with just a few taps of a finger.

Rankin had been noticing people on social media retouching their own photos for the past few years. So, he came up with
25 the idea of using photography to show the ways individuals, particularly young people, use these [photo editing] tools to alter their appearances.

"What I was particularly scared by on that
30 was how much like a game it is to do it," he said. "You take a picture of yourself and, as you're changing it, you can look at a before and after very easily. It also makes you feel very inadequate about what you look like in
35 this game-y way." Photo editing apps, Rankin noted, are increasingly easy to use. So easy, in fact, that he edited a selfie I sent him in under an hour. The photographer, whose photography subjects have included David Bowie and Queen
40 Elizabeth II, took portraits of 15 individuals

wearing minimal makeup. Some of the girls were models, and others were scouted from a local school. The only precondition was that they didn't use retouching apps regularly.

"I didn't want it to be about what people   45
do personally but how you can use the app to change yourself even if you don't know much about it," Rankin said.

As he witnessed the girls edit their photos, he realized that they all seemed to do the   50
same things – enlarge their eyes and plump[2] their lips, for example – which he felt was a reflection on how people see beauty at the moment. Interestingly, he said, the individuals didn't really like the altered versions of   55
themselves, but they did feel like the edited images would warrant more likes on social media.

Rankin's goal for the project wasn't to blame apps or the people who created them.   60
Instead, he wanted to raise awareness that these apps exist and people are using them to alter their faces to fit an ideal that has become extremely homogenous.

In his opinion, being the better version   65
of yourself is about looking like yourself, not someone else.   Huffington Post, 2019 (adapted)

a) *Describe Rankin's project and its goal. Sum up the results and his evaluation.*

b) *Write a letter to the editor with reference to the article, giving your own opinion on the subject*
→ S7–10 *(about 120 words). Exchange texts with a partner and peer-edit each other's work.*

1 to perpetuate [pəˈpetʃʊeɪt] verewigen | **2 to plump** [plʌmp] fülliger machen

READING / WRITING **4 Youth subcultures: what are they now?** → WB 60/15 → G8, 10, 13

Mod-style scooters

A goth boy

Hippie campers

A 62–66 🔊))
A 4/1–5 ⊚

Mods, punks, soulboys, metallers, goths, hippies: there was a time when young people made it clear what tribe and music they were into by the way they dressed. Not any more.

A Down the phone, Helina is explaining what a haul girl is to me. "Basically, you go out
5 shopping for clothes or beauty products," she says, "then you make a haul video and show viewers on YouTube what you got. You go through the items of clothing one by one. I guess what people get out of them is not
10 showing off, like, how much money you've got or anything, but lifestyle: you get to see how one person lives, what their taste is."

If you're likely to sneer at a youth cult that involves making videos about your shopping,
15 then Helina has a pretty intriguing counter-argument. "It's not just about showing what you've got," she says. "It's a whole creative process behind the videos as well, which is what I enjoy about it. Choosing the right
20 music, going from the filming to the editing. Sometimes I even storyboard things, because I want certain shots, how I can present different items and things like that." Besides, she says, it's a genuine community. She thinks a lot of
25 haul girls "turn the camera on because it's a way to talk to people without having to go outside and face their fears. I know that was the case with me: I turned on my camera because I was at home, signed off work,
30 sick, and really bored. And it helped with my confidence in a way. There's this community where you can talk to like-minded people."

You hardly need a degree in sociology to realise that something fairly dramatic has
35 happened to youth subcultures over the past couple of decades; you just need a functioning pair of eyes. When I arrived at secondary

school in the mid-80s, the fifth and sixth forms, where uniform requirements were relaxed,
40 looked like a mass of different tribes, all of them defined by the music they liked, all of them more or less wearing their tastes on their sleeves[1]. There were goths. There were metallers. There were punks. There were
45 soulboys. There were Morrissey acolytes, and even a couple of ersatz hippies. It was fairly obvious who was who and what was what.

B In 2014, however, the only real teenage cults visible to an outsider, displaying their
50 allegiances by the way they dress, seem to be metalheads and emos.

Something has clearly changed, and over the past week, I've listened to a lot of hypotheses as to why, of varying degrees of
55 plausibility. A sociologist at the University of Sussex, Dr Kevin White, tells me he thinks it has something to do with Britain's changing class structure. Elsewhere, there's a rather grumpy[2] "tsk[3]-kids-today" theory that teenagers are now
60 so satiated[4] by the plethora[5] of entertainment on offer that they don't feel the need to rebel through dress or ritual – and a deeply depressing one that people are too worried about their futures in the current financial
65 climate to be creative. And I've had a long and fascinating conversation with historian David Fowler, author of the acclaimed[6] book Youth Culture in Modern Britain, who has an intriguing, if controversial, theory that
70 subcultures such as hippy and punk had very little to do with the actual teenagers who participated in them – "They were

---

1 *to wear ... on your sleeve** [ˌweər ˈɒn jə ˈsliːv] sich offen zu etw. bekennen | **2 grumpy** [ˈɡrʌmpi] mürrisch | **3 tsk**
Zungenschnalzen | **4 satiated** [ˈseɪʃieɪtɪd] übersättigt | **5 plethora** [ˈpleθərə] Fülle | **6 acclaimed** [əˈkleɪmd] hochgelobt

consumers … they were sort of puppets[1]" – and were instead informed and controlled by a slightly older, university-educated generation. "Youth culture as a kind of transformative, counter-cultural philosophy, it has to be shaped by older people and invariably[2] it's by students," he says. Meanwhile, Dr Ruth Adams of King's College London thinks it might be linked to the speed at which "the cycle of production and consumption" now moves. "Fashion and music, they're much cheaper and they're much faster today," she says. "When I was a teenager, you had to make more commitment to music and fashion, because it took more of a financial investment.

C   But the most straightforward theory is that, as with virtually every area of popular culture, it's been radically altered by the advent of the internet: that we now live in a world where teenagers are more interested in constructing an identity online than they are in making an outward show of their allegiances and interests.

"It's not necessarily happening on street corners any more, but it's certainly happening online," says Adams. "It's a lot easier to adopt personas[3] online that cost you absolutely nothing apart from demonstrating certain types of arcane[4] knowledge, what Sarah Thornton called subcultural capital."

Once you start examining subcultures online, things become blurred and confusing. In search of latterday[5] youth subcultures, I'm pointed in various directions by various people, but I invariably can't work out whether what I'm looking at is meant to be serious or a joke: never really a problem in the days

when members of different youth cults were prepared to thump[6] each other. There's plenty of stuff that seems weird and striking and creative out there, but there's something oddly self-conscious and non-committal about it: perhaps that's the result of living in a world dominated by social media, where you're under constant surveillance by your peers.

D   And then there's seapunk, a movement that started out as a joke on social media, then gained traction[7] to the point where it became a real-life scene, with a seapunk 'look' that involved dyeing your hair turquoise, seapunk club nights and seapunk music. it's perhaps worth noting that seapunk genuinely appeared to make an impact on mainstream pop: the seapunk look was variously appropriated by rapper Azealia Banks, Lady Gaga, Rihanna and Taylor Swift. In any case, I'm too late. One of seapunk's supposed core members, Zombelle, apparently declared the movement dead when pop stars started cottoning on to[8] it, which perhaps tells you something about subcultures in 2014. They catch people's imagination, get appropriated by mainstream culture then die away: it was ever thus, but now it happens at warp-speed[9].

It's hard not to be struck by the impression that, emos and metalheads aside, what you might call the 20th-century idea of a youth subculture is now just outmoded[10]. The internet doesn't spawn[11] mass movements, bonded together by a shared taste in music, fashion and ownership of subcultural capital: it spawns brief, microcosmic ones.

Alexis Petridis, The Guardian, 2014 (adapted)

a) *Divide the article into meaningful sections and find suitable headings for each one.*

→ S11
→ 98/8

b) *Analyse how the author compares youth culture in the past and in the present, explain the differences and sum up the five possible reasons on why there has been a change.*

c) *Say which reason the author finds most plausible and discuss his opinion in class.*

→ S7–10
→ 99/9

d) *Comment on the development of youth culture as presented in the article from your point of view, giving examples. Write about 200 words.*

1 **puppet** ['pʌpɪt] Marionette | 2 **invariably** [ɪn'veəriəbli] ausnahmslos | 3 **persona** [pə'səʊnə] Rolle | 4 **arcane** [ɑːˈkeɪn] geheim | 5 **latterday** ['lætə deɪ] heutig | 6 **to thump** [θʌmp] verhauen | 7 **to gain traction** [ˌɡeɪn 'trækʃn] an Zugkraft gewinnen | 8 **to cotton on to** (coll) [ˌkɒtn̩ˈɒn] spitzkriegen | 9 **at warp speed** [ət ˈwɔːp ˌspiːd] rasend schnell | 10 **outmoded** [ˌaʊtˈməʊdɪd] überholt | 11 **to spawn** [spɔːn] hervorbringen

Social media

Social media have become part of (young) people's lives. Obviously, they have their pros and cons. They can be of great help, but you need to be aware of how to use them. And remember that it is impossible to take anything back that has been uploaded to the internet! As experienced users, you can probably give good advice. In this media task, you will work in groups to make a list of important tips.

1 Teens' social media habits → WB 61/16

Look at the survey results. Discuss if they represent your own experiences and add any important aspects that may be missing.

> **Teens say social media helps strengthen friendships, provide emotional support, but can also lead to drama, feeling pressure to post certain types of content**
> % of U.S. teens who say the following about social media
>
> **POSITIVE**
>
> **81 %** feel more connected to their friends
>
> **69 %** think it helps teens interact with a more diverse group of people
>
> **68 %** feel as if they have people who will support them through tough times
>
> **NEGATIVE**
>
> **45 %** feel overwhelmed by all of the drama there
>
> **43 %** feel pressure to only post content that makes them look good to others
>
> **37 %** feel pressure to post content that will get a lot of likes and comments
>
> Note: Respondents who did not give an answer or gave other responses are not shown.
> Source: Pew Research Center (2018)

2 Your social media wish list → WB 61/17

→ S20

Talk about what you expect of social media. What do you hope to gain? How would you want people to interact? Collect your ideas and try to sum them up in about five statements.

> **Useful phrases**
> keeping in touch with … | sharing … | getting help / information / new ideas … | no hate speech | no lies | no pressure from …

3 Your tips → WB 61/18

a) *Discuss your results from Ex. 2 in class and how these requirements can be implemented.*

→ S14

b) *Agree on a list of no more than ten important tips for using social media. Think of a good way to present your results (e.g. design a poster or a digital product).*

> **Tip**
> **Don't forget to think of:**
> privacy | technology, settings | copyright, intellectual property | social behaviour | explicit language | cooperation | honesty | freedom | reporting hate speech | taking a break

Girl power – a digital collaborative project

In this group project, you will use collaborative methods provided by digital tools.

Male artists are often known as the main representatives of youth subcultures. Yet the contributions by girls and women must not be overlooked. They are just as creative and powerful as their male counterparts. Your task is to show how women have succeeded in bringing about change. Choose an influential female artist, examine her career and her achievements and do a presentation of about 10–15 minutes. Do not only concentrate on commercial success, but on her impact. Use text, audio and visual material and a form of presentation that suits your topic. Be creative!

Step 1

Get prepared

Get together in groups and choose your topic (suggestions: Patti Smith, Debbie Harry, Siouxsie Sioux, Nina Hagen, Madonna, Beyoncé, Lauryn Hill).

Madonna, 1990

Step 2

Make a plan → S21

Do a brainstorming session and make a plan: Assign roles and work packages, agree on a time schedule with milestone meetings.

Step 3

Finish your presentation → S15

Collect material and put it together. Prepare your presentation and a handout.

Step 4

Present your results

Rehearse and finally give your presentation.

Tip

Suggestions for digital / collaborative tools:
• Use search engines for internet research.
• Use digital communication tools to plan meetings.
• Use online conference tools for meetings outside the classroom.
• Use an online noticeboard, a mindmapping tool, and / or a pad for collaborative writing, editing and proof-reading in the actual writing process.
• Use digital presentation tools and include a variety of media.

Two poems

READING **1** **Two poems by 2Pac** → WB 62/19 → TS Poetry

A 67–68 🔊
A 4/6–7 ◉
→ S5–6

a) *Examine the language (sounds, rhythm, words) of each poem. From what you know about poetry, say what is typical and what strikes you as unusual.*

b) *Poem 1: Use your knowledge about 2Pac and hip hop culture to explain what the rose stands for and who could identify with it. Give reasons for your opinion.*

→ S12

c) *Poem 2: Characterise the speaker and describe what issues are referred to in the poem. Use your knowledge about 2Pac and hip hop culture to explain who the speaker is addressing and what the speaker wants to achieve.*

The rose that grew from concrete

Did you hear about the rose that grew
from a crack in the concrete?
Proving nature's law is wrong it
learned to walk with out[1] having feet.
5 Funny it seems, but by keeping its dreams,
it learned to breathe fresh air.
Long live the rose that grew from concrete
when no one else ever cared.

And 2Morrow

Today is filled with anger
fueled[2] with hidden hate
scared of being outcast[3]
afraid of common fate[4]

Today is built on tragedies   5
which no one wants 2 face
nightmares 2 humanities
and morally disgraced[5]

Tonight is filled with rage
violence in the air   10
children bred with ruthlessness[6]
because no one at home cares

Tonight I lay my head down
but the pressure never stops
knawing[7] at my sanity[8]   15
content[9] when I am dropped

But 2morrow I c change
a chance 2 build a new[10]
Built on spirit intent of[11] Heart
and ideals based on truth   20

and tomorrow I wake with second wind[12]
and strong because of pride
2 know I fought with all my heart
2 keep my dream alive

---

1 with out = without | **2 to fuel** [ˈfjuːəl] antreiben | **3 outcast** [ˈaʊtkɑːst] ausgestoßen | **4 fate** [feɪt] Schicksal | **5 disgraced** [dɪsˈɡreɪst] geschändet | **6 ruthlessness** [ˈruːθləsnəs] Rücksichtslosigkeit | **7 knawing = gnawing** [ˈnɔːɪŋ] nagend | **8 sanity** [ˈsænəti] geistige Gesundheit | **9 content** [kənˈtent] zufrieden | **10 a new = anew** [əˈnjuː] von Neuem | **11 intent of** [ɪnˈtent ˌəv] *hier:* aufmerksam / bedacht auf | **12 with second wind** [wɪð ˌseknd ˈwɪnd] mit frischem Auftrieb

Female images

READING **1** **Role models?** → WB 63/20

A 69 🔊)
A 4/8 ⊙

A group of Brooklyn girls are playing cards and talking about their female rap idols.

"Aye yo, Jasmine," Tamika says, throwing out a ten of clubs[1]. "Who's your favorite? Lil' Kim or Foxy Brown?"

I say it extra fast.

5   "None of them." The table glares[2] at me.

"You serious?" La'Tasha asks, seeming hurt. "What you got against Kim?"

"Or Foxy?" Tamika snaps. I shrug, taking another long sip. The alcohol has me talking
10   reckless.

"I mean, they only getting all this attention 'cause they dressing half-naked and rapping about sex. They'd be nothing if they covered themselves up for a change." Ronnie cocks[3] her
15   head to the side.

"So what? You rather them dress in kente cloth[4], grow dreadlocks, and rap about herbs?"

"Nah, but … what kind of message are they sending us women? That the only way to get
20   ahead in the game is to play into man's porn fantasy?" Ronnie sighs, throwing out an ace of spades[5].

"My daddy taught me that anything a man can do, a woman can do too. So if a man can
25   rap about sex, why can't a woman?"

"Yeah, but …"

"But nothing. And if you can't see how you wrong for judging them, then you a hypocrite." My back straightens.

30   "I ain't no hypocrite."

"Who are you or anyone to judge the way they want to live their lives? No one judging you for living yours." She glances at my medallion. "To me, when they talk about sex,
35   they just sound … powerful."

"Powerful? You bugging[6]." She smirks.

"You know how gully[7] you gotta be to break the mold[8] everybody tries to bake you in? How I see it, Kim and Foxy took all the shit that guys throw at us – calling us bitches, hoes,   40
I pay your bills, blah blah blah – and started using it on themselves. It's like they took men's weapons and used it against them. 'Cause once you let someone know they weak-ass words can't hurt you, that you don't need them,   45
that you got your own, they no longer have any power over you. And you can be, do, say whatever you want."

"And so what they talking about sex?" Tamika says, her neck rolling. "Men talk about   50
sex in songs all damn day! How it makes them feel good. So what, chicks[9] can't *feel* good?" Ronnie chuckles[10], throwing down a four of hearts.

"Word. Like, how *dare* ladies enjoy sex,   55
too?" They clap each other up, laughing. I'll be honest, I never expected they'd have such feminist views. Maybe I really am too … judgmental.

"A'ight, I feel you," I say with a smile. "Guess   60
I never really looked at it like that. But … If taking back your power means you can be whoever you want to be … how about be a teacher and help children to read. A doctor and help cure cancer. A humanitarian and help   65
feed the world's poor. A social worker and help kids in the hood[11]. If your only goal is a selfish one … if your looks is only thing you care about … what does that say about you?"

From: Tiffany D. Jackson, *Let me hear a rhyme* (adapted)

→ S5–6, 11   **a)** *Examine the language the girls use and what they talk about. Say what it tells you about their social background.*

b) *Analyse the girls' different views and comment on them. Discuss if boys have similar issues.*

1 clubs [klʌbz] Kreuz | **2 to glare** [gleə] starren | **3 to cock** [kɒk] neigen | **4 kente cloth** [ˈkentə ˌklɒθ] *afrikanischer Stoff* | **5 spades** [speɪdz] Pik | **6 to bug** *(coll)* [bʌg] nerven | **7 gully** *(slang)* [ˈgʌli] mutig | **8 mold** [məʊld] Form | **9 chick** *(coll)* [tʃɪk] junge Frau | **10 to chuckle** [ˈtʃʌkl] glucksen | **11 in the hood** = in the neighborhood

The world of online games

1 Pushing buttons: Gaming is culture　→ WB 63–67/21–26

A 70 ◁))
A 4/9 ⊙

In the first edition of our gaming newsletter: Why games, like all art, have the power to connect, entertain and cause change.

I want to use this first issue to tell you what to expect from this newsletter. The gaming world
5　is fast-moving, and it can be hard to keep up with while also living a busy real life. I want to be a friendly guide to what's interesting and relevant, and what games are worth your valuable time and attention.
10　　But this won't just be a news rundown[1]. Video games don't exist in cultural vacuum, and they're not just products that appear and are quickly forgotten. For anyone who plays them – which, increasingly, is pretty
15　much everyone – games are a part of life, not something separate from it. I want to talk about them in a way that reflects that.
　　Ask any anthropologist and they'll tell you that we can learn a lot about people by
20　looking at how we play. I find that games that break through to become popular often reflect some interesting aspect of our culture and the world we live in: whether that's the *Sims'* potent mixture of ultracapitalist fantasy and
25　soothing control over human affairs, or space-skullduggery[2] hit *Among Us'* undercurrent of anxiety, instability and mistrust. Even a game that apparently has nothing much to say – *Fortnite*, for instance – can tell us a lot when
30　we look at how people play it. Teenagers use it as a place to hang out; their generation's equivalent of loitering pointlessly around the local park with your mates, though possibly without the hidden cans of cider.
35　　And gaming culture – because it is young, because it is technologically cutting-edge – can give us an insight into what's on the cards for the world as a whole. There's the sad example of Gamergate, the 2014 harassment campaign that foreshadowed[3] the Trump campaign　40 and the seductive tactics of the alt-right[4]; but gamers were also early representatives of the internet's ability to connect and empower people, with our newsgroups and online lobbies. People were creating and taking good　45 care of new selves and friendship circles in video game worlds long before they were doing the same on social media.
　　I say all this to support the notion that games matter. They're not some secret　50 pleasure, some pointless waste of time. Like all art and culture, they have power. Games connect and entertain and, sometimes, bring about change. The people who make and play them can be fascinating. I love video games in　55 all their forms, from the sublime[5] to the very, very ridiculous, and that is exactly why I take them seriously. The right game at the right time can change your life. Or it can give you something fun and wonderfully escapist to　60 do in between working long days, raising your kids, or navigating the everyday sufferings of life. That's good, too.
　　I've been a games journalist for 16 years, and I still find them endlessly fascinating. I'm　65 excited to share the games and stories that make my brain happy with all of you.

Keza MacDonald, The Guardian, 2021 (adapted)

a)　*Summarise what the author tells the readers about herself and what she intends to do. Point out where you have found this information in the text.*

→ S7–10　b)　*Outline what she says about the impact of video games and how she illustrates her point. Then write a comment of about 200 words to explain if you agree or not.*

1 **rundown** [ˈrʌndaʊn] Kurzüberblick | 2 **space-skullduggery** [ˌspeɪs skʌlˈdʌɡri] Weltraum-Betrügerei | 3 **to foreshadow** [fɔːˈʃædəʊ] ahnen lassen | 4 **alt-right** *(AE)* [ɔːltˈraɪt] rechtsextrem | 5 **sublime** [səˈblaɪm] erhaben

Find more online:
zy965r

The soundtrack to history

A

B

READING **1** **Music as a vehicle of expressing opposition and criticism** → WB 69/1

a) *Read this wiki article and match the pictures A–E with the topics mentioned in the text.*

→ S3, 7–10

b) *You were asked to contribute to the article. Do some research and make suggestions on how to expand it with more aspects, examples and pictures. Use a digital version of the text and expand it by at least 1/3 with your additions.*

The tradition of protest songs in English is very long. It is said to date back to 14th-century England when feudal lords owned all the land and poor serfs had to do all the
5 work. The first songs to be acknowledged as protest songs emerged in England in the 17th century, when people who were not part of the gentry demanded more rights, e.g. to participate in the government.
10 In the 19th-century US, protest songs were mainly about the Civil War, the abolition of slavery and women's suffrage.
Protest songs became very popular in the 20th century, especially when pop
15 culture grew more politicised in the 1960s with the civil rights movement and protests against the Vietnam war. Joan Baez has been one of the most prominent political activists and musicians representing the
20 protest song genre.
The 1980s saw British miners fighting against structural change in Britain in the form of extensive pit closures, which were to cause massive unemployment. This kind
25 of social hardship has been one of the main themes of English singer-songwriter Billy Bragg since 1977.

Conflicts between Catholics and Protestants in Ireland originated in the 17th century, when British settlers and other
30 Protestants were given land in the north of the island. These so-called 'Troubles' peaked in a horrible period of civil war and terrorism in the 20th century and were dealt with in a number of well-known songs like "Sunday Bloody
35 Sunday" by U2 or the Cranberries' "Zombie".
Starting in the US, countless rap songs have been telling of racial conflicts and accusing politics and society of still denying Black people equal chances, and also of
40 women fighting against sexism and abuse.
Songs expressing political or social criticism can be found all across musical genres, although there has obviously been an especially high number of protest songs
45 in periods dominated by political conflict or economic recession and these songs have been realised according to the musical styles popular at the time, e.g. the folk style of the 1960s or the hard and aggressive punk, metal
50 or hip hop styles that developed later.

C

D

E

SPEAKING

→ S3, 6, 15, 21

2 A song project → WB 69/2

a) *One of the most frequently sung about political issues is war. Sadly, wars have been going on all over the world. Thus, there are a lot of anti-war songs of all kinds of musical genres. Do a group project: Choose an anti-war song. Do research on its background, its words and music and discuss what you think of it. Prepare a presentation on the song and relate it to the time it was created, making use of short audio and / or video clips, visualisation techniques and a handout. Here are some suggestions from very different genres:*

Barry McGuire: Eve of destruction (1965)
John Lennon: Imagine (1971)
Status Quo: In the army now (1981)
Fischer Z: Red skies over paradise (1981)
New Model Army: Spirit of the Falklands (1984)
Slayer: Skeletons of society (1990)
Guns 'n' Roses: Civil war (1990)
Black Eyed Peas: Where is the love? (2003)
Drive-By Truckers: That man I shot (2008)
Green Day: 21 guns (2009)
Avenged Sevenfold: Danger Line (2010)
Muse: Psycho (2015)

…

Joan Baez

Green Day

b) *Alternatively, do a project on another political song, e.g. about social injustice or racism.*

SPEAKING / WRITING

3 Social and historical developments reflected in culture

Cultural evidence in the form of literature or works of art, e.g. anti-war films, can also help you understand social and historical developments better. Find some examples, discuss them in class and / or write an argumentative essay of about 220 words.

Legende

Diese Symbole und Erklärungen zeigen dir,
wie du mit den Hilfen, Aufgaben und Aktivitäten
auf den *Practice-pool*-Seiten arbeiten kannst.

△ Hilfe zur Unit-Aufgabe | oder eine
zusätzliche Aufgabe

▲ eine zusätzliche Herausforderung

Unit 1

△ **1 Describing a country** → Help with Introduction, p. 12/1

*Use a dictionary (e.g. for synonyms) to
collect more synonyms or phrases with
a similar meaning for each mind map.
They can help you prepare your film about
Scotland's attractions.*

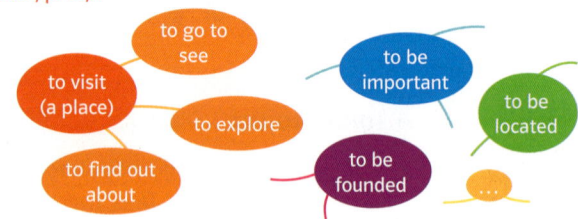

▲ **2 Our town's best** → After Introduction, p. 12/3

*Prepare a presentation of your home town like the ones you've heard.
Record your own "Living in …" (about two minutes).*

△ **3 Typically Scottish** → Help with Introduction, p. 13/4

a) *The poem mentions Scottish **food / drinks**, **music / dance**, **clothing**, **wildlife**, **landscape**
and **(national) symbols**. Match the six categories with the following words / phrases
and find out what they mean.*

> castle | haggis | tatties | neeps | a peaty peppery dram | heath(ery) | bats | pines |
> the pipes | kilt | tartan pleat | Gay Gordon | the purple hills | the blue and white flag

b) *You can use these phrases to talk about the importance of the items in a) in Scotland today.*

> A typical meal / drink / country dance is … | … is often used for celebrations. | … is a
> symbol of Scottish history / traditions. | … is / are a defining feature of the landscape. |
> … can be found in | … are worn for special festivities. | Traditional Scottish music is often
> played by … |

c) *Find a recipe and prepare a meal with tatties and neeps. Bring your dish to class (or take photos)
and talk about it.*

▲ **4 The Highland-Lowland divide** → After Introduction, p. 13/4

*Historically, Scotland was divided into the Highlands and the Lowlands. Do some quick research and
present the main characteristics of each region in a two-minute talk. Think of traditions and economy.
Don't forget to mention the islands.*

▲ **5** **Mythical creatures** → After Texts A, p. 15/2a)

Write a similar text (ca. 200 words) to introduce 3–4 mythical creatures typical of your country.

△ **6** **A closer look at the text** → Help with Texts A, p. 18/4a)–d)

a) *Find related English or German words that help you to guess the meanings of these words:*

catch (l. 4) | sandy (l. 31) | remains (l. 45) | to consume (l. 46) | ash (l. 49) | butterfly (l. 67) | admittedly (l. 76) | balanced (l. 85) | intact (l. 84) | roofing (l. 87) | cutlery (l. 89)

b) *The context (summed up in blue) will help you to find the meanings of these words:*

to drag (l. 1): what Alex does to the creel with his hands | to measure (l. 10): to check the size | to be content (l. 16): Moth can relax because the result of her actions seems OK | to flicker (l. 43): what flames do | to stalk (l. 60): a way of walking | to crouch (l. 64): the opposite of to get up (l. 68) | blunt (l. 94): not sharp | hassle (l. 99): what gives Alex stress | fateful (l. 112): with important consequences for the future

c) *Use these ideas to explain why Alex goes back to the campsite.*

to be upset / nervous / scared / worried | to wonder | to make sure | to keep secret | a bad conscience | to feel ashamed | to regret | to risk | to avoid | to be held responsible | to get questioned | to get in trouble | to protect | dangerous | criminal | murder

d) *Look at the examples and decide if they are metaphors or similes.*

You were as brave as a lion. | They say love is like a rose. | Time is money. | Watching the show was like watching grass grow. | She's the black sheep of our family.

△ **7** **Mediation: A trip to St Andrews** → After Texts B, p. 20/1

A 4/10 ⊚

Your family and the family of your younger cousin Lukas are on holiday in Scotland. Today you're visiting St Andrews, a small town on Scotland's east coast. In the morning, the adults asked you and Lukas to collect information about sights and activities at the tourist information office. Interpret between Lukas, who doesn't speak much English, and the assistant.

△ **8** **Rebuilding Glasgow** → Help with Texts B, p. 21/2b), d)

Make sure you understand these words and phrases (use a dictionary if necessary). They can help you understand the podcast in Ex. 2 b) and write your comment in d).

> **Glasgow's history** missionary | founder | monk | miracle | salmon | knight | port | goods | Industrial Revolution | weaving | dyeing | steam power | iron works | slum
>
> **Going down and rebuilding of Glasgow**
> **before WWII:** decline of the heavy industries and shipbuilding / increase in unemployment / fear of youth gangs | **during WWII:** many houses bombed | **1950s:** city was redesigned to rebuild houses and construct new roads | **1980s:** new sectors in finance, manufacturing and service start to replace heavy industries | **1990s – now:** was designated 'European Capital of Culture' in 1990 / new image as hotspot for culture, arts and architecture

△ **9** **Mixed bag: Belladrum Tartan Heart Festival** → After Texts B, p. 22/3

Read this blog post by a festival visitor and put in the missing words or phrases.

Hi guys! Guess **1** : I **2** (just) from my first weekend at the Belladrum Festival near Inverness. That's a music and arts festival with performers from around the world, but mostly Scottish **3** . The nearly 20,000 people **4** this year created a great atmosphere. To be **5** , at first I wasn't sure if I **6** at all. Before I went, I **7** stories about festivals with too **8** people and poor security, but Belladrum is family-friendly, so many parents **9** their children. Most youngsters had ear defenders – they're headphones **10** reduce outside noise – **11** their hearing. I found a store on-site and got a pair for **12** ! When I met people who **13** (already) the festival in previous years, I asked about their experiences. **14** they all recommended the festival, they made me aware **15** its problems too, like people **16** their waste behind and not taking home their tents after the festival. If you **17** this happen, please speak up! Another thing I **18** about for a while now is this: What would change if less people **19** by car? There'd be much more space for visitors and definitely less pollution! The festival strives **20** more eco-conscious, for example by **21** a 'green campsite' and tents to rent. As usual, the drinks were expensive, and going to the toilet took hours (of course, jumping the **22** wasn't an option). I still had an amazing time and **23** back next year!

△ **10** **Find the mistakes: Mental health problems** → After Texts C, p. 24/2

Read this newspaper article by a teenager in Scotland who fights mental health stigmas. Check the marked words and phrases and decide if they are correct or not. Correct the mistakes in your exercise book.

I **1** have be suffered of depression since I **2** have lost my father some years ago, but back then **3** no of my friends **4** can understand why I was cancelling meetings, why I **5** have often been late for school, or why I **6** have stopped going out, even after some time **7** has passed. Luckily, I got therapy and could fully recover. But this post **8** wasn't on me.

If you **9** had ever searched for "mental health" online, you may have noticed the results increased over the past few years. **10** Obvious mental issues **11** are being taken **12** more serious and more people **13** want learn about their causes and how to help. **14** After my opinion this is a great development. I learned a lot in my therapy sessions, but my friends didn't learn about mental health at all. **15** Scared from be stigmatised, I initially only posted some information about mental health online – my blog **16** became popular; **17** I'm posting for four years now. I have received many comments saying it's been a trusted **18** surce for informations. In recent years, the internet **19** have became a starting point for finding helpful contacts, giving tips on how to be there **20** for anyone and contacting specialists. **21** Wile I'm sure an online search can never replace therapy, it **22** is bringing together people who have the same goal: ending the stigma around mental health issues. If you **23** were interested to find out more, check out my blog.

▲ **11** **Education: What matters to me** → After Texts C, p. 24/2b)

Make a concrete suggestion and describe it in detail (about 80 words), e.g.:

Make a timetable for your Year 6. | Write an outline of your Year 6 English curriculum. | List social / cultural / … activities and explain why they should be included in the curriculum.

Unit 2

▲ 1 Us and them → Before Texts A, p. 42/1

a) *Imagine your school introduced a new rule set. Read the rules thoroughly.*

> Students with blue and green eyes must not leave the classroom during breaks, chat with anyone or eat food while in school. Those who don't follow the rules are suspended for a week.

> Students with other eye colours receive a bag of crisps and a free beverage every day, may leave the classroom at any time without asking for permission and can chat with each other.

b) *Do the following tasks.*

1. Take notes on how people from each group may act and react and how the members of each group might feel.
2. Analyse possible behaviour: How does discrimination work? Which kind of behaviour reinforces discrimination? How can you break free from discrimination?
3. Discuss possible consequences: Would you give up part of your identity (clothing, language, religion) in exchange for not being discriminated against? How far would you go?

△ 2 Life in Garden Heights → Help with Texts A, p. 44/1b)–c)

a) *Use these points to describe life in Garden Heights:* **ways to be cool | music | shootings**

b) *These ideas can help you examine Khalil and Starr's relationship and to characterise Starr.*

Part 1: common childhood memories, his grandma, Drake's role, how they act after not having seen each other for a long time
Part 2: Khalil in a coffin, Starr snapping at Hailey and Maya, Starr denies Khalil

▲ 3 Thug life → After Texts A, p. 44/1b)–c)

In the context of the novel, 'thug' has two meanings.

a) *The everyday usage describes a violent or cruel, sometimes criminal person. Explain why Starr is afraid of being seen as "thug ghetto girl" (l. 163).*

b) *The title of the novel is based on an acronym invented by rapper Tupac. He said that "thug life" stands for "The hate u give little infants fucks everyone." Explain the meaning of this statement.*

△ 4 Approaches to reduce violence and crime → Help with Texts A, p. 45/2

This information can help you to compare and discuss the different approaches.

- improving education: give schools better equipment; improves social status
- gun control: easy to get hold of weapons in the US; many weapons available lead to many shootings (police, school massacres); stricter laws could help
- crime prevention: free-time activities to keep young people from joining gangs; support with finding a job; support people in need (better social care / health care / free meals)

▲ **5 Police and minorities** → After Texts A, p. 45/2

Do you think minorities are discriminated against by German police too, e.g. by more stops or searches? Do some research and discuss your findings in class.

△ **6 Schools in the US** → Help with Texts A, p. 46/4c)

Read the educational leaflet and discuss which problem(s) high school students could help to solve. Think of specific ways that they could make improvements.

Standardised tests show that Black students are academically about two years behind white students. This is partly due to school location: Public schools in wealthier districts receive more tax money and can equip the schools better (e.g. with healthier lunches, technical equipment, libraries) and pay the teachers more, which generally attracts higher-qualified teachers. There are usually less extra-curricular activities offered at poorer schools so that Black students more often miss out on opportunities such as team sports, drama lessons, or exchanges. In addition, non-white students often lack role models in school as less than 10 % of teachers are Black or represent other minorities. Ignoring these issues over time has led to higher rates of drug and alcohol abuse among Black students.

▲ **7 People of Harlem** → After Texts A, p. 47/5

Read this stanza from "The Heart of Harlem". In your group, choose three people or places mentioned in the stanza and research them. Interpret their meaning in the poem.

It's Joe Louis and Dr. W. E. B.,
A stevedore, a porter, Marian Anderson, and
  me.
It's Father Divine and the music of Earl Hines,
Adam Powell in Congress, our drives on bus
  lines.
It's Dorothy Maynor and it's Billie Holiday,
The lectures at the Schomburg and Apollo
  down the way.

It's Father Shelton Bishop and shouting
  Mother Horne.
It's the Rennie and the Savoy where new
  dances are born.
It's Canada Lee's penthouse at Five-Fifty-Five.
It's Small's Paradise and Jimmy's little dive.
It's 409 Edgecombe or a cold-water walk-up
  flat –
But it's where I live and it's where my love is at
Deep in the Heart of Harlem!

△ **8 Working with words** → Help with Texts B, p. 48/1

While reading, work with the vocabulary.

1. A lot of the new words are related to words you already know. Make a list of the new words and their word family 'partners'.
2. Match these definitions with words from the text.

> 1. hairstyle with strong curls | 2. with many different aspects | 3. someone who advertises things | 4. to have less worth than before | 5. with bad intentions | 6. being at the start of a career | 7. to take from somewhere | 8. belonging to only one group / person | 9. a trial, a tough time | 10. momentary, quickly changing | 11. origin, source

⚠ **9** **Mediation: How racist is Hollywood?** → After Texts B, p. 48/1

You need to give a two-minute talk on racism in Hollywood in your English class. Read the article and prepare a handout for your talk. Include why and how Black people are disadvantaged in Hollywood's film industry and what is done against discrimination. Write about 150 words.

Die Oscars sind zu weiß, Afroamerikaner haben in Hollywood das Nachsehen, es mangelt an Vielfalt. Diese Vorwürfe sind nicht neu, doch die Rassismusdebatte feuert die Kritik wieder an.

Regisseur
Spike Lee

Auch nach Meisterwerken wie „Malcom X", „Do the Right Thing" und „BlacKkKlansman"
5 muss Oscar-Preisträger Spike Lee (63) um seine Projekte hart kämpfen. „Wir haben den neuen Film beinahe nicht machen können", erzählt der schwarze Filmemacher über seinen 25. Spielfilm „Da 5 Bloods". „Wir sind zu
10 jedem Studio gegangen, aber alle lehnten ab." Am Ende brachte Lee seinen Film über vier schwarze Vietnam-Veteranen bei Netflix unter.

In Hollywoods langer, von weißen Stu-diobossen dominierter Geschichte, hatten es
15 afroamerikanische Themen oder Filme mit schwarzen Hauptdarstellern immer schwer. Doch mit dem Hashtag #OscarsSoWhite kocht die Kontroverse um die mangelnde Vielfalt und die Anerkennung schwarzer Talente in
20 Hollywoods Filmgeschäft seit Jahren immer wieder hoch. Als 2016 zum zweiten Mal hintereinander keine Schwarzen in den vier begehrten Schauspielerkategorien nominiert wurden, reagierte die Oscar-Akademie auf
25 die massive Kritik und kündigte „historische Maßnahmen" an. Im Zuge der Rassismusde-batte reagierte der Filmverband jetzt wieder mit Selbstkritik und Maßnahmen, die Vielfalt und Gleichstellung zu fördern. Es sollen mehr
30 Schwarze, Latinos und Asiaten als neue Mit-glieder in die mehrheitlich weiße Academy aufgenommen werden. Es soll Kurse und Ge-sprächsrunden geben, um Voreingenommen-heit abzubauen und Themen wie Diskrimi nie-
35 rung wegen der Ethnie anzusprechen.

Abgesehen von einigen Megahits wie „Black Panther" und „Get Out" gibt es in Hollywood auch eine endlose Debatte, ob Filme von, für und mit Schwarzen überhaupt
40 kommerziell erfolgreich sind. Hartnäckig hält sich die Vorstellung, es sei besonders schwer, diese ins Ausland zu verkaufen. „Obwohl wir an den Kinokassen besser abschneiden als eine ganze Runde weißer Filme, sagen die Verleiher, dass ‚Black movies' international
45 nicht gut funktionieren", beschwerte sich Regisseur Boots Riley. Vor allem auf Produzen-tenseite gibt es kaum Schwarze, die Geld für Filme zur Verfügung stellen oder zusammen-trommeln können. Das Online-Magazin Black
50 Enterprise schreibt zudem, dass sie häufig Filme mit deutlich kleinerem Budget an den Start bringen.

Ein weiteres Beispiel für schwarz-weiße Hollywood-Unterhaltung ist „The Help" über
55 Schicksale schwarzer Dienstboten in den Südstaaten. Regisseur Tate Taylor erzählt die Geschichte aus der Sicht einer weißen Frau. Die Afroamerikanerin Viola Davis in der Hauptrolle eines Kindermädchens bedauerte
60 2018 ihre Teilnahme an dem Film. Am Ende sei es nicht wirklich um die Perspektive der Dienstboten gegangen, sagte Davis.

Hat sich also kaum etwas verändert, seitdem 1976 Bürgerrechtsautor James
65 Baldwin schrieb, dass kein Schwarzer je auf der Leinwand sein volles Potenzial hat zeigen können? Immerhin vorsichtige Initiativen gründen sich gerade. Der Think Tank For Inclusion and Equity (TTIE) hat in einem
70 offenen Brief gefordert, Schwarze nicht nur als Autoren anzustellen, wenn es um ihre eigenen Themen oder um afroamerikanische Charaktere geht. **dpa, 2020 (adaptiert)**

△ 10 Mixed bag: Just Mercy → After Texts B, p. 50/3

Read this film review and put in the missing words or phrases.

The movie *Just Mercy* (2019) **1** a true story that **2** place in the late 1980s. Bryan Stevenson, a young lawyer who **3** (just) from Harvard, moves to Alabama to defend people on death row[1]. Walter McMillian is **4** Stevenson's first defendants[2]. In 1987, the real McMillian **5** (accuse of) and **6** (arrest for) the murder of an 18-year-old white girl. Since McMillian **7** in 2013, Jamie Foxx, the actor **8** played his character, **9** (not) talk to him about the story and his role. However, Foxx said that **10** (grow up) as a Black man in Texas and experiencing racism first-hand helped **11** him for the role. In the movie, McMillian says to Stevenson that if you **12** Black, you are guilty from the moment you **13** (be born). The movie **14** after McMillian is freed. Stevenson continued **15** for justice by founding the Equal Justice Initiative and freeing over 130 prisoners who had also been **16** convicted.

△ 11 Find the mistakes: Eric Adams for NYC → After Texts C, p. 51/1

Read this article about the mayor of New York City. Check the marked words and phrases and decide if they are correct or not. Correct the mistakes in your exercise book.

Eric Adams won the 2021 mayoral election of New York City, **1** to become its second Black mayor **2** at the age from 61. **3** Adams start wasn't easy, though, as he **4** facing Covid, crime and a suffering economy all at the same time. **5** Serving the New York Police Department for two decades as well as **6** being elected for various political positions before, however, he has faced troubles and hardship throughout his career. After decades of public service, Adams promised that **7** as a mayor he **8** would continue to work for the people and help struggling New Yorkers. **9** During his career is certainly impressive, his personal life **10** isn't always easy. He **11** growed up in Queens and Brooklyn as **12** the fourth of the sixth children in a family that struggled **13** financial. It was after **14** experiencing police brutality when he was 15 that Adams **15** decided starting his career in law enforcement in order to change the department from within. But first he **16** has to get through high school, where he had trouble with his grades. To pay for his college tuition, he worked **17** like mechanic after school. It was during this time that he **18** had been diagnosed with dyslexia[3]. After **19** receiving help, he became an **20** excellently student. In the end, his **21** comittment allowed him **22** to turn his life into a success story.

△ 12 Voicing your opinion → Help with Texts C, p. 53/3b)

Consider arguments for and against voicing one's opinion as an athlete in your discussion.

> direct attention towards injustice / issues | show support | not mixing politics and sports |
> freedom of speech | considering fans' opinions

▲ 13 Addressing political issues → After Texts C, p. 53/3

Discuss other actions that the athletes could have taken to address the problem.

1 death row [deθ ˈrəʊ] Todeszelle | **2 defendant** [dɪˈfɛndənt] Angeklagte/-r | **3 dyslexia** [dɪˈslɛksɪə] Dyslexie, Leserechtschreibschwäche

Unit 3

▲ **1** **A presentation on subcultures** → After Introduction, p. 68/1b

Do some research on one of these subcultures: flower power, punk, video-gaming. Find out about the time it started, special features and values, and its famous people. Give a 5-minute presentation with the help of digital tools.

△ **2** **Different worldviews** → Help with Texts A, p. 72/1c

Explain in your own words what is meant by these words and phrases. Say what concepts they are contrasted with in the text.

> license (l. 3) | the community (l. 11) | the money hungry rat race of modern society (ll. 17–18) | 911 (l. 43) | the low standards and cultural poison of a world that had lost its way (ll. 65–66) | state curriculum (l. 69) | education department (l. 79) | shiny symbols of an empty soul (ll. 83–84) | hospital (l. 124) | Rain still gave me a full vote. (l. 167) | Social Services (ll. 178–179)

△ **3** **Mixed bag: The benefits of music** → After Texts A, p. 73/2

Musician and researcher Carol Smith was interviewed about the role music plays in her life. Put in the missing words and phrases to complete the article.

Carol Smith is a young pianist and researcher **1** can talk at length **2** the advantages of **3** music a part of your life. She **4** with us last week about how music has influenced her everyday life. Smith remembered that when she was nervous **5** child, she would practice **6** piano and that would make her **7** . She said, "Especially in their teenage years, people are often confused **8** emotions. But I **9** (already) control my emotions well, **10** I attribute to my musical training." Smith moreover claimed that **11** an instrument made her **12** stressed as a teenager. That's when she asked herself **13** making music had other positive **14** on people. She enjoyed **15** about this topic so much that she went into behavioural research. General findings suggest that, firstly, singing in groups **16** stress and raises one's spirit. **17** , students **18** (perform) on stage do **19** on tests, are usually more

self-confident and **20** coordinate well. **21** , making music can even **22** a positive impact on your heart. Even though Smith makes **23** researching the benefits of music, she can't get enough of music in her free time **24** . She explained that after a long day, she still **25** the piano for a while before **26** to bed. "I feel music **27** (vibrate) in my body," said the prize-winning pianist, "music is my medicine – I can't **28** without it."

△ 4 Tupac's language → Help with Texts B, p. 75/1a)

Examine Tupac's language: Make a list of elements which are standard / formal and elements which are informal. What does his language tell you about him?

▲ 5 The success of rap music → After Texts B, p. 76/2b)

Do some research on the revenue of the global music industry and the share rap music has in it. Use the vocabulary from Ex. 2b) to write a short summary of what you found out (about 150 words).

▲ 6 The language of rap songs → After Texts B, p. 77/3

What is your opinion on rap lyrics and the influence they have on young listeners? Write an argumentative essay of about 200 words.

△ 7 Find the mistakes: Ideas about beauty → After Texts C, p. 80/3

Read this article from a beauty magazine. Check the marked words and phrases and decide if they are correct or not. Correct the mistakes in your exercise book.

Social media nowadays **1** bombards us constant with pictures often **2** show unrealistic body and beauty standards. What we **3** easy forget, however, is that these standards are different **4** in the world and **5** changed frequently throughout history until today. **6** For exemple, **7** as plump[1] women **8** are considered attractive in Ancient Greece and Victorian England, the 1920s **9** called for a boyish **10** figur in Europe and the US. **11** Chinas standards considered small **12** feets beautiful for **13** hundreds years. **14** Tough it may seem like beauty ideals only **15** effect women, they **16** apply for male bodies as well. A currently popular look **17** under American men requires them to grow a beard, wear shirts, and have a muscular shape. In Nigerian culture, men shouldn't be **18** to tall – a contrast to Scandinavian **19** ideals. The expectation **20** that people look a certain way comes with side effects. Research has shown that individuals **21** considered pretty profit from a 'beauty bias'[2] due to **22** be attributed with more positive traits such as higher intelligence. When **23** compare salaries, pretty people earn **24** average 5% more **25** then less-attractive co-workers. Social media users often unknowingly support these trends by uploading **26** heavily editing pictures for more likes. However, social movements **27** advocate **28** the acceptence of all body shapes and sizes.

△ 8 Changes in youth culture → Help with Texts C, p. 82/4b)

In the section where possible reasons for a change in youth culture are presented, different theories are mentioned. Find the ones that are presented together with the names of experts. One of the experts has a theory that doesn't actually give a reason for the change. Sum up each theory in your own words.

1 plump [plʌmp] mollig | **2 bias** [ˈbaɪəs] Voreingenommenheit

△ **9** Mediation: A gamer's life insurance → After Texts C, p. 82/4

Your friend from England is interested in e-sports. She found a German article about the topic, but has problems understanding everything. She is confused why a fitness trainer works with gamers, and wants to know which clichés there are about them and if they are true. Read the interview and answer her questions in an English e-mail (about 150 words).

Fabian Broich, 30, war Fußballprofi – jetzt arbeitet er als Fitness- und Mentaltrainer im E-Sport. Der Head of Performance sagt, er sei eine Art Lebensversicherung für die
5 Gamerinnen und Gamer.

Mit welchen Vorurteilen haben Sie es zu tun?
Fabian Broich: Es gibt das Klischee, dass man die Gamer aus dem Keller holen muss, wo sie sich nur von Tiefkühlpizza und
10 Energydrinks ernähren. Und dass alle richtig ungenießbare Charaktere sind. Und diese Typen gibt es auch.

Die Klischees stimmen?
Broich: Manchmal habe ich den Eindruck,
15 dass die Gamer wenig von der „Schule des Lebens" mitbekommen haben. Meine Aufgabe ist es – um im Bild zu bleiben –, sie aus dem Keller zu holen. Manche haben wirklich kaum oder gar kein Bewusstsein
20 für ihren Körper und wie das mit der Leistung zusammenhängt. Viele glauben zum Beispiel, sie müssten immer mehr zocken, um mit den Besten mitzuhalten. Das führt aber langfristig zum Burn-out.

25 *Was macht man als Head of Performance?*
Broich: Wenn ich als *Head of Performance* dazukomme, ist die Frage: Bin ich krank, wenn ich einen Mentalcoach habe? Nein. Es geht um Optimierung. Ich bin eine Art
30 Lebensversicherung für die Spieler. Wenn die Leistung nicht stimmt, kann das schnell zum Karriereende führen. Ich möchte ihnen dabei helfen, ihre Leistung konstant abzurufen.

35 *Können Sie das konkretisieren?*
Broich: Nehmen wir zum Beispiel Manuel Neuer. Der hat 99 Prozent seiner maximalen Leistung erreicht. Er ist psychisch so fit, dass er selbst an einem schlechten Tag
40 70 bis 80 Prozent dieser Leistung abrufen

kann. Bei E-Sportlern ist das oft nicht so. Sie sind weder an ihrer Leistungsgrenze noch sind sie mental so gefestigt, um auch unter Druck ihre Leistung abzurufen.

45 *Wie können Sie helfen?*
Broich: Es gibt vier Säulen, die ich meinen Spielern beibringen möchte: Schlafen, Ernährung, Bewegung und mentale Gesundheit. Meistens fange ich beim Thema Schlafen an. Aus meiner Erfahrung
50 haben 70 Prozent der E-Sportler Schlafprobleme.

Auch so ein Klischee.
Broich: Viele gehen zu spät ins Bett und schlafen zu wenig. Ich zeige ihnen,
55 wie positiv sich gesunder Schlaf auf die Leistung auswirkt. Vor Mitternacht ins Bett gehen und mindestens acht Stunden schlafen – das ist wichtig für die Leistungsfähigkeit. Die professionellen
60 Gamer merken einen schnellen Effekt, was sehr wichtig ist, denn das kennen sie schon vom Spielen: direkte und schnelle Belohnungen für gute Leistungen. Bei den anderen drei Säulen muss ich länger
65 dranbleiben, bis sich ein positiver Effekt einstellt.

Wie gehen Sie da vor?
Broich: Ich will wissen, was die Spielenden für Ziele haben und was sie bereits wissen.
70 Danach erstelle ich Ernährungs-, Tages- und Wochenpläne. Vorher haben die Spieler oft sechs Stunden am Stück trainiert. Ich sage dann: Vielleicht ist es sinnvoller dreimal zwei Stunden zu spielen. Ich kenne
75 die Situation der Spieler, bin selbst mit 21 Jahren von zu Hause ausgezogen, um professioneller Fußballer zu werden. Von daher versuche ich, für die Spieler wie ein großer Bruder zu sein.
80

Fabian Held, Die Zeit, 2021 (adaptiert)

A 71–77 🔊
A 4/11–17 ◉

Secrets

Alex comes to Daniel's place, the Manse, late in the evening. Daniel has just talked to Eva, the housekeeper, about the food he wants the next day. Then he and Alex go outside.

A "Still waited on[1] hand and foot, heh?" Alex said, aiming for a casual tone as they passed the woodlands behind the Manse.

Daniel shrugged, obviously saving himself
5 until they were out of earshot.

"So where the fuck have you been all day?" he spat out when they'd reached their usual tree stump a little way up the hill.

There'd been a bench way back, but as
10 bits had dropped off, kids had used the wood to keep their poor attempts at fires going. The oak[2] stump was wide enough for the two of them to sit side by side. Initials had been carved[3] into all available surfaces along with
15 comments on some of the locals.

"There's no need for –"

"What? It was you that insisted we had to get to school." Daniel spat out the words.

"'Give me till the end of the day,' you said.
20 Then you disappear, leaving me wondering what the hell's going on."

"I know … Sorry. But it was like I said."

"Like what? And why am I having to ask you now?"

"I went back to the clifftop. All right? Mrs 25 MacKinnon was on the beach. She … she found him."

"Yeah. I heard something about that," Daniel responded in a calmer tone.

"What? At school?" 30

"Don't panic. I kept well away from the gossip[4]." Daniel stretched out his leg. "But *that* didn't take you all day."

Alex really didn't want to argue. And Daniel deserved some explanation. "I went to the 35 campsite. I wanted to make sure there was nothing of ours lying around."

"That was your big plan? And I would have been a liability[5]?"

"No. Well yes, I suppose you would have, 40 like that." Alex pointed at Daniel's leg. "But I think you should stay out of it."

"Fine by me."

"And for your information, everything was just as we left it." 45

They sat in silence for a while until Daniel said, "I can't believe he's dead."

"No." Alex took a deep breath.

"It could have been one of us."

"He must have had an accident. Chuck 50 pushed things too far."

Daniel gave him a sideways look. "And we knew when to stop, did we?"

"Leave it, will you. We were stupid too. But there's no need for us to get involved from 55 now on."

B "We pretend nothing happened," Daniel said, making a point of putting his leg in a better position to ease[6] the pain.

"How is the leg now, anyway?" Alex asked. 60

Daniel hitched[7] up his jeans and prodded at the edge of a dressing[8] on his shin[9]. "Shit sore."

Alex recognised a thawing[10] in Daniel's

---

1 to wait on sb [ˌweɪt ˈɒn] jmdn. bedienen | **2 oak** [əʊk] Eiche | **3 to carve** [kɑːv] schnitzen |
4 gossip [ˈɡɒsɪp] Klatsch | **5 liability** [ˌlaɪəˈbɪləti] Bürde | **6 to ease** [iːz] lindern | **7 to hitch up** [ˌhɪtʃ ˈʌp] hochziehen |
8 dressing [ˈdresɪŋ] Verband | **9 shin** [ʃɪn] Schienbein | **10 to thaw** [θɔː] auftauen

voice. The beginnings of a truce¹? "Nothing's
65 been said at home?" he said in a quieter voice.

"Eva has given me a few funny looks."
Daniel twisted his leg to get a view of the
blister² at the back of his knee that wasn't
covered by a dressing.

70 "It doesn't look infected or anything," Alex
said.

"And you would know, how?"

"Well, you can hardly waltz into the doctor's
with it, can you?"

75 Daniel didn't reply.

"We agreed." Alex stood up and kicked the
side of the tree stump. "We tell nobody."

Daniel straightened his jeans and stood
next to Alex; together they took in the view
80 over the loch.

"But what about when the police come
round? What will we tell them?"

"We tell them nothing … and they might
not come."

85 "You what? They've got a dead body on
their hands. Even with an accident they'll make
enquiries³. A boy a bit older than us." Daniel
paused before adding. "They'll come all right."

Alex found a stick⁴ and started to beat⁵ the
90 fronds⁶ of bracken⁷ growing nearby. "They'll
work out who he is without us telling them.
They don't need us. We can keep quiet." They
could get through this if they stuck together.

"And if they ask what we were doing over
the summer …?" 95

"We'll get our stories straight. Like I said. No
way can my mum find out." The wind dropped
and midges began to ditz around them. Daniel
pulled up his hood. "What did he look like?"

"What? You mean … his body?" 100
Daniel nodded.

Alex stuffed his hands in his jacket pockets.
"Horrible. His legs all stuck out. And … all the
flesh on his face was gone … like something
had been eating at him or he'd smashed 105
against the rocks … and the stink."

"No face?"
Alex shook his head.
"But it was Chuck?"
"Oh, it was Chuck all right," Alex said. 110

🙢 🙠

C *The next day, Daniel is on his own.*

From his window Daniel watched Alex climb
over the fence⁸ and head up the hill towards
the croft⁹. Back at his desk and safe in his
seclusion Daniel opened his email account, 115
tapping in his password. A dark bold entry
showed there was a new message from Ellie.
Emailing was the only way Daniel had ever
communicated with her. He preferred it that
way. The other occasional¹⁰ emails he received 120
were mostly from the librarian, so it felt like his
and Ellie's own private forum.

Over the last month since she'd first
contacted him, she'd shared a lot of her life
story. She'd had a rough time moving from 125
one set of foster carers to another. Daniel was
luckier. He'd been a baby when the reverend¹¹
and his wife adopted him.

He'd spent hours re-reading her messages
several times over to try and understand what 130
she'd had to cope with¹² – was coping with still.
He didn't open the new mail immediately but
scrolled up the screen to the message she'd
sent yesterday.   →

---

1 truce [truːs] Waffenstillstand | **2 blister** ['blɪstə] Brandblase | **3 enquiry** [ɪnˈkwaɪri] Untersuchung |
4 stick [stɪk] Stock | **5 °to beat** [biːt] schlagen | **6 frond** [frɒnd] Wedel | **7 bracken** ['brækn] Farn |
8 fence [fens] Zaun | **9 croft** [krɒft] kleiner Bauernhof | **10 occasional** [əˈkeɪʒnl] gelegentlich |
11 reverend ['revrnd] Pfarrer | **12 to cope with sth** ['kəʊp wɪð] fertigwerden mit

135 Hi Danny,
You sound so clever – all those science
subjects you're taking! Not like me. I wasn't too
bad at art, but you could say school and me
didn't agree. LOL I'm a poet and didn't know
140 it. My foster parents tried to get me to study.
You know, bribed[1] me, or grounded me when
I didn't come home at night. They try harder at
things like that, don't you think? Making out[2]
they're really strict. Or maybe it's just mine.
145 Yours sound a bit more normal. Oh though,
sorry. I forgot about your mum. Bet she was
lovely. Not like the old biddy[3] I'm with. I'll have
to sign off[4] now, got to sign on[5] tomoz[6]. LOL
Need to be up early.
150 Ellie

His replies to her messages were only
ever a couple of lines but that didn't stop her
rambling on to him. He felt ready to open her
new message.

155 Hi Danny,
Guess what. I'm going to Perth tomorrow.
Clothes shopping. Don't get too excited. It's
only with Mum. And not for proper clothes –
not things I can wear going out. She's got
160 me an interview. It's only in a cafe. Probably
washing up. Have to look willing though to keep
getting my Magners vouchers.
I looked up that shinty[7] on the internet. It looks
mental[8]. Some fit fellas though. I've got brown
165 eyes. What about you?
Ellie

Ellie had suggested exchanging
photographs earlier on, but Daniel hadn't
answered that message and she hadn't
170 mentioned it again. He hit 'Reply' and started
his message:

Hi Ellie,
Yes, brown eyes. Dark brown hair.

He deleted the 'Dark brown hair' and
continued: 175

I'm a bit of a fraud[9] at shinty. I scored a lucky
goal one day from half way up the pitch. That
bought me some kudos.

He deleted 'kudos' and replaced it with
'respect'. 180

We've got a match on Saturday but I'm not
sure I'll be able to play. I hurt my leg a few
days ago, which makes running a bit difficult.
Hope your interview goes well. That is if you
want the job. 185
Daniel

He read through his reply. He wanted to tell
her about meeting Caitlin. About how good it
was to have someone to go over homework
with – and how he secretly thought Caitlin 190
might like him. But there was no way he could
have told her about Chuck's body turning up on
the beach and all the problems that promised.
Even though he hadn't seen the body, he
couldn't bring himself to talk about it – not 195
even to his twin sister.

☙   ❧

D *Another day later, Alex comes home after an
argument with Daniel.*

Up in his bedroom Alex switched on his
computer, logged in to his PayPal account 200
and checked his balance[10]. He opened a
bookmarked favourite in another tab and

---

1 to bribe [braɪb] bestechen | **2 *to make out** (coll) [ˌmeɪkˈaʊt] so tun, als ob | **3 old biddy** (pej) [ˌəʊld ˈbɪdi] alte
Schachtel | **4 to sign off** [ˌsaɪnˈɒf] sich abmelden | **5 to sign on** (coll) [ˌsaɪnˈɒn] sich arbeitslos melden | **6 tomoz**
(slang) [təˈmɒz] morgen | **7 shinty** [ˈʃɪnti] eine Art Hockey | **8 mental** (coll) [ˈmentl̩] irre | **9 *to be a fraud** [bɪˌəˈfrɔːd]
ein/-e Betrüger/-in, ein/-e Schwindler/-in sein | **10 balance** [ˈbæləns] Kontostand

scrolled down the page, reciting the spec[1] of the new outboard motor he dreamed of
205 buying: *Recoil start with 6 amp charging coil; 4-stroke OHC – 2 cylinders; 222cm³ displacement; 8 hp @ 5000 rpm.* Over a grand[2], even second-hand. There was no chance of getting it when he couldn't even afford to pay
210 the household bills. He shrugged the tension out of his shoulders and closed the tab.

Stretching to the top of the bedroom doorframe[3], he let his fingertips find the desk drawer[4] key then opened the drawer and took
215 out the webcam. Even before Dad's accident they hadn't been rolling in cash, but Mum had insisted that Alex needed a computer for his homework. It was the lowest spec model, even back then, but he could plug in a webcam.

220 Next he took a curly[5] black wig out of the drawer. Chuck had looked at him in disbelief when Alex voiced his wonder[6] at why Chuck should own a wig. Didn't Alex know anything about how protected witnesses were moved
225 around the country? In a safe place now, Chuck wouldn't need it until he appeared in court next. Alex could borrow it, Chuck had said, passing it over to Alex with the list of websites.

E Alex went through to Mum's bedroom to
230 get what he needed there before going into the bathroom.

The sun superheated the small space and Alex fought with the metal catch[7] to open the window. Pulling the hand towel off the rickety[8]
235 chair, he swatted[9] at a lone bluebottle[10]. It hit the windowsill[11] and whizzed around on its back amidst the bodies of its smaller cousins.

Moving to the sink[12] to look into the tiny mirror Alex felt his stomach tighten, heard
240 it grumble in complaint about what he was going to do. Still, best not to think too much.

He stripped off his t-shirt, threw it in the bath and set to work. It didn't usually take long

and if he could keep his five-star rating he'd be
245 able to increase his fee. He held out his hand until the trembling[13] reduced then carefully applied the black eyeliner and mascara before pulling the wig over his close-cropped ginger stubble[14] – until he was completely
250 unrecognisable as Alex Cameron. He searched in the cupboard under the sink for Mum's lavender body oil, squelched a bit into one hand and rubbed his palms[15] together before massaging the oil into his upper arms, making
255 his biceps glisten[16].

He'd used tweezers[17] the first time, on Chuck's recommendation, to remove the few hairs from his chest. He wasn't going to do that again in a hurry. And on the webcam the few
260 hairs that had since corkscrewed out between his pectorals[18] didn't show up anyway. Twenty minutes later, after a thorough shower, he checked that his PayPal account was £20 up.

F He was in the kitchen making soup when
265 he heard a vehicle on the track. It was the right time for Mum to be getting back but he could tell from the rattle of the vehicle over the rough stones that it wasn't the Corsa van. A look out of the window confirmed it. Going
270 through the back door he picked up one of Mum's rag dolls[19] that lay next to an empty plant pot. How had he missed that when he'd come home, with its bright dress and rosy cheeks?
275

The police van changed its tone to a low rumble as it reached the drive leading to the back door. The policewoman behind the wheel had only been in the area for a short while. As she stepped out of the van there was no hint
280 of a smile. This wasn't a 'getting to know you' call.

From: Sylvia Hehir, *Sea Change* (adapted)

---

1 spec *(coll)* [spek] technische Daten | **2 grand** *(coll)* [grænd] tausend | **3 doorframe** [ˈdɔːˌfreɪm] Türrahmen | **4 drawer** [ˈdrɔːə] Schublade | **5 curly** [ˈkɜːli] lockig | **6 wonder** [ˈwʌndə] Verwunderung | **7 catch** [kætʃ] Haken | **8 rickety** [ˈrɪkəti] wacklig | **9 to swat** [swɒt] schlagen | **10 bluebottle** [ˈbluːbɒtl] Schmeißfliege | **11 windowsill** [ˈwɪndəʊˌsɪl] Fensterbrett | **12 sink** [sɪŋk] Spülbecken | **13 to tremble** [ˈtrembl] zittern | **14 ginger stubble** [ˌdʒɪndʒə ˈstʌbl] rote Stoppeln | **15 palm** [pɑːm] Handfläche | **16 to glisten** [ˈɡlɪsn] glänzen | **17 tweezers** [ˈtwiːzəz] Pinzette | **18 pectoral** [ˈpektrl] Brustmuskel | **19 rag doll** [ˈræɡ dɒl] Stoffpuppe

A 78–81 🔊
A 4/18–21 ⊙

Poems by Black Americans

"I'm Rooting for Everybody Black"

Everybody Black is my hometown team. Everybody Black dropped the hottest album of the year, easy. Everybody Black is in this show, so I'm watching. Everybody Black is in this movie, so I'm watching. Everybody Black wore it better, tell the truth. Everybody
5   Black's new book was beautiful. How you don't know about Everybody Black?! Everybody Black mad underrated. Everybody Black remind me of someone I know. I love seeing Everybody Black succeed. I hope Everybody Black get elected. Everybody Black deserves the promotion[1] more than anybody. I want Everybody Black to find somebody special. Everybody Black is good peoples. Everybody Black been through
10 some things. Everybody Black don't get the credit[2] they're due[3]. I met Everybody Black once and they were super chill and down-to-earth. I believe in Everybody Black. There's *something* about Everybody Black.   Cortney Lamar Charleston (*1991)

I, too

I, too, sing America.

I am the darker brother.
They send me to eat in the kitchen
5   When company comes,
But I laugh,
And eat well,
And grow strong.

Tomorrow,
10 I'll be at the table
When company comes.
Nobody'll dare
Say to me,
"Eat in the kitchen,"
15 Then.

Besides,
They'll see how beautiful I am
And be ashamed[4] –

I, too, am America.
                    Langston Hughes (1902–1967)

Malcolm X, February 1965

i will die this month. how
i do not know. still there
is much work to be done. i
am afraid not for myself but
5   for betty and the girls. some
nights i stay awake looking
out the window, a gun in my
hand. i know how cruel people
can be. i have known hatred[5] and
10 blindness. there are brothers
waiting to do me harm[6]. i will
die for them. i will love them
as only i can. may allah be my
15 witness.   E. Ethelbert Miller (*1950)

---

1 promotion [prəˈməʊʃn] Beförderung | **2 credit** [ˈkredɪt] Anerkennung | **3 °to be due to sb** [bi ˈdjuː] jmdm. zustehen | **4 °to be ashamed** [bi ˌəˈʃeɪmd] sich schämen | **5 hatred** [ˈheɪtrɪd] Hass | **6 °to do sb harm** [duː ˈhɑːm] jmdm. Leid zufügen

Dear Basketball

Dear Basketball,

From the moment
I started rolling my dad's tube socks
5   And shooting imaginary
Game-winning shots
In the Great Western Forum[1]
I knew one thing was real:

I fell in love with you.

10 A love so deep I gave you my all
From my mind & body
To my spirit & soul.

As a six-year-old boy
Deeply in love with you
15 I never saw the end of the tunnel.
I only saw myself
Running out of one.

And so I ran.
I ran up and down every court
20 After every loose ball for you.
You asked for my hustle[2]
I gave you my heart
Because it came with so much more.

I played through the sweat and hurt
25 Not because challenge called me
But because YOU called me.
I did everything for YOU
Because that's what you do
When someone makes you feel as
30 Alive as you've made me feel.

You gave a six-year-old boy his Laker[3] dream
And I'll always love you for it.
But I can't love you obsessively[4] for much longer.

35 This season is all I have left to give.
My heart can take the pounding[5]
My mind can handle the grind[6]
But my body knows it's time to say goodbye.

And that's OK.
I'm ready to let you go.   40
I want you to know now
So we both can savor[7] every moment we
have left together.
The good and the bad.
We have given each other   45
All that we have.

And we both know, no matter what I do next
I'll always be that kid
With the rolled up socks
Garbage can in the corner   50
:05 seconds on the clock
Ball in my hands.
5 … 4 … 3 … 2 … 1
Love you always,
Kobe   Kobe Bryant (1978–2020)   55

---

1 Great Western Forum [ˌɡreɪt westən ˈfɔːrəm] *Stadion in Kalifornien* | **2 hustle** *(AE)* [ˈhʌsl] Anstrengung, Einsatz |
3 Lakers [ˈleɪkəz] *Basketballmannschaft in Los Angeles* | **4 obsessive** [əbˈsesɪv] besessen | **5 to pound** [paʊnd]
schlagen, pochen | **6 grind** [ɡraɪnd] gleichförmige Routine | **7 to savor** *(AE)* [ˈseɪvə] auskosten

A 82–84 🔊
A 4/22–24 ⊙

Two unlikely friends

Troy Billings and Curt McCrae meet for the first time at a subway train station in New York.

A I'm a sweating fat kid standing on the edge of the subway platform staring at the tracks. I'm seventeen years old, weigh 296 pounds, and I'm six-foot-one. I have a crew cut[1], *yes a crew cut*, yellowish skin, and the kind of mouth that puckers[2] when I breathe. I'm wearing a shirt that reads MIAMI BEACH – SPRING BREAK 1997, and huge, boring brown pants – the only kind of pants I own. Eight pairs, all brown.

It's Sunday afternoon and I'm standing just over the yellow line trying to decide whether people would laugh if I jumped. *Would it be funny if the Fat Kid got splattered by a subway train? Is that funny?* Seriously, I really want to know. Like it or not, apparently there's something funny about fat people. Something unpredictable. Like when I put on my jacket and everyone in the hallway tries not to laugh. Or when I stand up after sitting in the cafeteria and Jennifer Maraday, Brooke Rodriguez, and Amy Glover all kill themselves laughing. I don't get angry. I just think, *What was funny about that? Did my butt[3] jiggle[4]? Did I make the bench creak[5] so that it sounded like a fart[6]? Did I leave an indentation[7]?* There's got to be something, right? *Right?*

So it's not very unlikely to be standing on the wrong side of the yellow line giving serious thought to whether people would laugh if I threw myself in front of the F train. And that's the one thing that can't happen. People can't laugh. Even *I* deserve a decent[8] suicide.

That's why I'm standing here. Because I can't decide.

I'm thinking about what Dayle said. *Go ahead[9]. I wouldn't miss you. Go ahead … Go ahead …* I'm telling myself my brother didn't mean it, but even I know that's a lie.

Meanwhile it's hot and I've been standing too long. … I close my eyes and imagine the whole scene as it might play out.

First, the train is coming, its single headlight illuminates the dark tracks. I hear its deep rumble and take the fateful[10] step forward. I want to picture myself flying dramatically through the air but realize I wouldn't have the muscle power to move my body. Instead, I would drop straight down. Maybe I wouldn't even get my other leg off the platform – my weight would pull me down like an anchor. That's how I see it. The train crashes into me; my fat splashes apart, covering the train window and the tunnel walls. I'm splattered. Except for my left leg, which is lying on the platform untouched – a fat, bleeding piece of raw meat.

FAT KID MESSES UP – coming soon to a theater near you.

I start to laugh. Suddenly there's something funny about it. I swear to God. There really is.

B "You laughing at me?" The ghostly voice is clearly addressing me.

"Huh …?!" I turn away from the tracks.

"You're laughing at me?"

"No …"

Who the hell is talking to me? I have to scan the entire subway platform before I find the voice. Twisted staircase, black gum-covered tile walls, infested concrete pit … and then, ah, the source of the paranoid voice. He's right beside me, but he's sitting on the floor, which is why I didn't see him.

He looks like a blond ferret[11]. Stringy[12] unwashed hair and huge eyes, jeans that are barely recognizable, discolored white T-shirt, huge red overshirt, worn old sweater … The sneakers, one Converse and one Nike, are both untied and the layers are all partially buttoned[13] even though it's got to be one

---

1 crew cut [ˌkruː kʌt] Bürstenschnitt | **2 to pucker** [ˈpʌkə] kräuseln | **3 butt** *(slang)* [bʌt] Hintern |
4 to jiggle [ˈdʒɪɡl] wackeln | **5 to creak** [kriːk] knarren | **6 fart** *(coll)* [fɑːt] Furz | **7 indentation** [ˌɪndenˈteɪʃn]
Delle | **8 decent** [ˈdiːsnt] anständig | **9 Go ahead!** [ˌɡəʊ əˈhed] Nur zu! | **10 fateful** [ˈfeɪtfl] verhängnisvoll |
11 ferret [ˈferɪt] Frettchen | **12 stringy** [ˈstrɪŋi] strähnig | **13 buttoned** [ˈbʌtnd] zugeknöpft

80 hundred degrees in the subway. The guy is
so dirty I can hardly look at him. I mean, he's
covered in dirt – looks like an old war victim
from some black-and-white film.

There's one more thing I notice – and if I'm
85 telling the truth, I should admit that I noticed
it first. He's the skinniest person I've ever seen.
Even in all those layers, the kid is skinny.

"You making fun of me?" I say, angry. I want
to say it threateningly, but a little puff of air
90 escapes despite my best intentions and I end
up sounding like an overweight dog farting.
I'm getting nervous and I think, *Did that sound
funny?*

The kid laughs. His face wrinkles[1] and he
95 looks even more like a ferret. He says, "Now
that was funny." Except he doesn't hold his
nonexistent stomach and howl, and he doesn't
try to keep a straight face to be nice while
obviously trying not to break into hysterical
100 laughter. He says it straight-out. Makes me
think. A little puff of air while I was trying to be
tough? I guess it is funny. The dirty, skinny kid
got it right.

I'm ready to give him full credit[2] and be
105 on my way, wander off to think of some new
nonfunny form of suicide (FAT KID GETS HIT
BY A BUS?), but the blond ferret stands up and
extends[3] a dirty hand.

"Curt MacCrae," he says. That's when I just
110 about piss my pants.

C   Curt MacCrae is a legend at our high school.
He's the only truly homeless, sometimes
student, sometimes dropout[4], punk rock, artist
god among us. He's the only one who's ever
115 played a concert at The Dump. The only one
that bands like the Trees and King-Pin *invite* to
hang with them. He's the only one to get into
five fights in one day, get beaten up[5] in all five,
and still have everyone's respect. He's the only
120 fucking genius guitar player I've ever met. And,
of course, he's the only one to get up in the
middle of class on a Tuesday and disappear

permanently. Kids at school loved that.

Since then, no one's actually *seen* Curt
MacCrae, and that was last year. The school   125
newspaper asked the students their opinion
and three-quarters think he's dead. And I just
shook his hand.

"Troy," I say. "Troy Billings." It comes out
enthusiastic and I frown a little to compensate.   130
"I know your music. I mean, I heard a bootleg[6]
of a show you played. It was so great. Really
great. Really, really great."

Curt makes a face, then looks at the tracks.
He walks sideways two steps and looks as   135
if he's thinking hard. The F train speeds into
the station and the Sunday afternoon crowd
climbs into the empty train. I should've thrown
myself in front of it, but now I'm left standing
there, awkward.   140

"That's my train," I say. I need to leave
before I do anything stupid. Anything *else*
stupid.

Curt grins. "Hell it is."

"What?"   145

"You owe[7] me lunch."

"What?" This, the only word in my
vocabulary.

"I just saved your life. It's the least you
could do."   150

He says it straight-out and I'm confused.
I'm standing there sweating and I wonder if
I smell. God knows he does. He stinks.

"I owe you lunch?" I say, further confirming
the impression that I am an idiot incapable[8] of   155
conversation.

"Yeah. *Mmm-hmm.* Handicapped[9] elevator's
this way." I'm insulted about the elevator
comment and he's completely wrong about
saving my life, but I'm hungry and by some   160
unpredictable coincidence in the universe Curt
MacCrae appears to want to have lunch with
me. So, I go.

From: K. L. Going, *Fat kid rules the world* (adapted)

1 to wrinkle ['rɪŋkl] in Falten legen | **2 credit** ['kredɪt] Anerkennung | **3 to extend** [ɪk'stend] ausstrecken | **4 dropout**
['drɒpaʊt] Schulabbrecher- | **5 °to beat up** [bi:t ˌ'ʌp] zusammenschlagen | **6 bootleg** ['bu:tleg] illegale Aufnahme |
7 to owe [əʊ] schulden | **8 incapable** [ɪn'keɪpəbl] unfähig | **9 handicapped** ['hændɪkæpt] Behinderten-

Text smart
Poetry

SPEAKING **1** **Warm-up: Poetry and I**

a) *Talk about your experiences: On what occasions do you read, hear or recite poetry? Do you enjoy it? Have you ever written a poem yourself? If yes, did you show it to anyone?*

b) *Make sure you know how to use the words in the word bank to analyse and interpret poetry. Collect them in a mind map.*

> **Word bank**
>
> speaker | voice | to address | to create | to express | to associate | atmosphere | emotion | effect | pattern | letter | sound | syllable | line | stanza | to stress | rhythm | metre | alliteration | rhyme | metaphor | simile | imagery

READING **2** **Identifying patterns – Poem A**

→ S6   *Read the first of three poems by Carol Ann Duffy and do these tasks.*

1. What is the main theme? How can you tell? Say what you like about it and why.
2. What pattern can you identify? Think of words, lines, stressed syllables, rhymes, imagery.
3. What other words could you use to replace "the look"?
4. Think of more examples and write an extra stanza before the last one.

> **Tip**
>
> **Poetry** is a kind of artistically designed language. Usually, poems are rather short, but there are also epic poems that tell a story and may be much longer. The way a poem is printed can be significant, but mostly it helps to read it out loud to find out how it works and what effect it has.

A 85 🔊
A 4/25 ⊙

The Look

A

The heron's[1] the look of the river.
The moon's the look of the night.
The sky's the look of forever.
Snow is the look of white.

5 The bees are the look of the honey.
The wasp[2] is the look of pain.
The clown is the look of funny.
Puddles[3] are the look of rain.

The whale is the look of the ocean.
10 The grave is the look of the dead.
The wheel is the look of motion.
Blood is the look of red.

The rose is the look of the garden.
The girl is the look of the school.
The snake is the look of the Gorgon[4].   15
Ice is the look of cool.

The clouds are the look of the weather.
The hand is the look of the glove.
The bird is the look of the feather.
You are the look of love.   20

1 heron ['herən] Reiher | **2 wasp** [wɒsp] Wespe | **3 puddle** ['pʌdl] Pfütze | **4 Gorgon** ['gɔːgn] Gorgone (*schreckliche Sagengestalt mit Schlangenhaaren*)

READING / WRITING 3 Different realities – Poem B

→ S2–3 **a)** *Find out about the process of enlarging photos in a dark room before photography became digital and research the places named in poem B and what they stand for. Work with a dictionary.*

b) *Sum up what you learn about the war photographer and his work and how the poem makes you relate to his experiences.*

→ S7–8 **c)** *Imagine what he would write in a diary entry (about 150 words) about his job, his feelings and the people who look at his pictures.*

READING / WRITING 4 A poem about poems – Poem C

a) *Work with a dictionary. Analyse what poem C says about poetry. Think of more examples to illustrate the point and write another stanza.*

b) *Write an analysis and interpretation of one of the three poems (about 200 words).*

B

A 86–87
A 4/26–27

War photographer

In his dark room he is finally alone
with spools[1] of suffering set out in ordered rows.
The only light is red and softly glows,
as though this were a church and he
5 a priest preparing to intone a Mass[2].
Belfast. Beirut. Phnom Penh. All flesh is grass.

He has a job to do. Solutions slop[3] in trays[4]
beneath[5] his hands, which did not tremble then
though seem to now. Rural England. Home again
10 to ordinary pain which simple weather can dispel[6],
to fields which don't explode beneath the feet
of running children in a nightmare heat.

Something is happening. A stranger's features
faintly[7] start to twist before his eyes,
15 a half-formed ghost. He remembers the cries
of this man's wife, how he sought approval[8]
without words to do what someone must
and how the blood stained into foreign dust.

A hundred agonies[9] in black and white
20 from which his editor[10] will pick out five or six
for Sunday's supplement[11]. The reader's eyeballs
     prick[12]
with tears between the bath and pre-lunch beers.
From the aeroplane he stares impassively at where
25 he earns his living and they do not care.

1 spool [spuːl] Filmrolle | **2 Mass** [mɑːs] Messe |
3 to slop [slɒp] schwappen | **4 tray** [treɪ] Schale |
5 beneath [bɪˈniːθ] unter | **6 to dispel** [dɪˈspel] vertreiben |
7 faint [feɪnt] undeutlich | **8 approval** [əˈpruːvl]
Einverständnis | **9 agony** [ˈægəni] Todesqual |
10 editor [ˈedɪtə] Redakteur/-in | **11 supplement** [ˈsʌplɪmənt]
Beilage | **12 to prick** [prɪk] stechen

C

The words of poems

The words of poems are nails
which tack the wind to a page,
so that the gone hour
when your kite pulled you over the field
5 blows in your hair.
They're hand-mirrors, a poem's words,
holding the wept tears on your face,
like a purse holds small change, or the breath
that said things.

10 They're fishing-nets,
scooping sprats and tiddlers out of a stream
or the gleaming trout that startled the air
when you threw it back. The words of poems

are stars, dot-to-dots of the Great Bear,
15 the Milky Way your telescope caught; or breves
filled with the light of the full moon you saw
from your bedroom window; or little flames
like the tongues of Hallowe'en candles.

The words of poems are spells, dropping
20 like pennies into a wishing-well, remember
the far splash? They're sparklers,
scrawling their silver loops and hoops
on the night, again in your gloved fist
on November the Fifth.

25 They're goldfish
in their sad plastic bags at the fair,
you stood there. The words of poems
are coins in a poor man's hat; the claws of a lost
     cat.
The words of poems are who you were. 30

Drama

→ S6

SPEAKING **1** **Warm-up: Features of a play**

a) *Talk about a play you've seen (live in a theatre or in film): How did you learn about the setting, plot and characters? (Think of actors' voices and body language, costumes, props, sounds etc.) Was it a modern / traditional production? Which elements did you find most / less convincing? What was the atmosphere like? Use your experiences to compare plays to other forms of storytelling like novels or poems.*

Useful phrases

comedy / tragedy / short play | act / scene | scenery / stage directions / props | to be set indoors / outdoors / in *(time)* | hero / heroine / antihero / extra | to enter / exit the stage | dialogue / monologue / crowd scene | … gives a clue about XY's feelings / plans / character. | … shows a conflict between … | … is used to move the action forward.

b) *In pairs, put the following situation into a short dramatic scene (it can be serious, funny or exaggerated). Decide if you need any material (props etc.) and if you want to make a written 'script'. Act out and record your mini-drama (or use digital storytelling tools) and present it to the class.*

You and your friend wanted to meet up. Because of a misunderstanding, both of you are waiting in different places.

READING / WRITING **2** **Analysing a scene from a play**

A 88 🔊
A 4/28 ⊙

Mary Stuart, the Scottish queen whose claim to the English throne was supported by many Catholics, was one of the biggest threats to Elizabeth I's position as Queen of England. No wonder Elizabeth had her cousin Mary arrested when she got the chance and kept her prisoner for over 18 years. Still, Elizabeth was always torn between supporting and fighting Mary.

Scene Seven

ELIZABETH. Why me? Why? Why help her? Why does she come here, throwing herself on my mercy? Merciful God, I cannot afford to be merciful.

5 **ADVISER 1.** Kill her now.

ADVISER 2. It were a kindness.

ELIZABETH. I cannot welcome her here at court. I cannot help restore her to her throne in Scotland. I cannot be seen to condone[1]

10 rebellion against a rightful prince.

ADVISER 2. Exactly.

ADVISER 1. And you cannot keep her in prison indefinitely.

ELIZABETH. She is my honoured guest.

ADVISER 1. Yes, and some day she'll escape. 15

ADVISER 2. The focus of every Catholic hope, of every anti-Elizabeth faction[2] in England.

ELIZABETH. Is she a witch?

ADVISERS 1 and 2. Ask the Scotch.

They fall back into the shadows, leaving her 20
isolated and alone.

ELIZABETH. They split her from her Bothwell[3], drive him from their shores, they

---

1 to condone [kənˈdəʊn] dulden | **2 faction** [ˈfækʃn] Gruppe | **3 Bothwell** [ˈbɔθwəl] *Marys dritter Ehemann*

25 seize her infant son, strip her of[1] her crown, lock her in a castle in the middle of an island and throw away the key.
And still she can charm[2] some man into helping her escape.
30 God help me, why does she come to England when she could have sailed to bloody France!

ADVISERS advance again, mill around **ELIZABETH** –

ADVISER 2. Three years …
35 **ADVISER 1.** You really cannot keep her in prison indefinitely. Seven … Eight …
ADVISER 2. – And some day she'll escape … thirteen, fift-

– and then, audibly counting the passing
40 *years, they fall back again into the shadows. With steely[3] determination –*

ELIZABETH. My subjects love me! I am the Virgin Queen! I love my good cousin Queen Mary and will continue to keep her my most honoured guest in all luxury in the lavish[4]
45 hospitality of my proudest castle. For her own safety.
And my so-called 'wise advisers' would have to trick me before I would consent[5] to sign a warrant[6] for her death.
50 Would have to trick me. Trick me. Trick me!

Her manic repetitions increase in volume, turn into obvious instructions. Thus summoned[7], **ADVISERS** *reappear by her side*
55 *complete with a document. Without looking at it or them, she signs it. One of these absolutely impassive[8]* **ADVISERS** *blots[9] it, picks it up and blows on the signature.*

Careful! We do not want a blot[10]!

The **ADVISER** *puts it inside his jacket. Both*
60 *of them melt away.* **ELIZABETH** *stands alone, breathing, then exits in the other direction.*

From: Liz Lochhead, *Mary Queen of Scots Got Her Head Chopped Off* (adapted)

→ S5 a) *Sum up Elizabeth's dilemma and the arguments she puts forward in the excerpt.*

b) *In groups of three, read the excerpt out loud or act it out. First think about the following points:*

1. How would you feel in Elizabeth's situation?
2. How does Elizabeth reach her decision (development, at which point is it made, how)?
3. What are the adviser's arguments and motives?

> **Tip**
>
> Think of appropriate positions, movements, gestures and experiment with your voice: loud / low, quick / slow, stressing words / phrases. Don't forget to consider the information in the stage directions.

PEAKING / WRITING **3** ## It's your turn!

 Choose one of these tasks.

1. If you were Elizabeth, how would you have decided? Write an alternative ending for the scene and act it out.
→ S6, 11–12 2. Write a full analysis of the excerpt (about 200 words). In the main part describe the role of each character and the effects setting, atmosphere and language have. Exchange texts with a partner and peer-edit each other's work.

1 to strip sb of sth [strɪp] jmdn. einer Sache berauben | **2 to charm sb into doing sth** [tʃɑːm] jmdn. dazu bringen, etw. zu tun | **3 steely** [ˈstiːli] eisern | **4 lavish** [ˈlævɪʃ] großzügig | **5 to consent** [kənˈsent] einwilligen | **6 warrant** [ˈwɒrɪnt] Vollstreckungsbefehl | **7 to summon** [ˈsʌmən] herbeirufen | **8 impassive** [ɪmˈpæsɪv] teilnahmslos | **9 to blot** [blɒt] (Tinte) ablöschen | **10 blot** [blɒt] Klecks

Short film

SPEAKING / WRITING **1** **Warm-up: Talking about films**

→ S2, 20

a) *Look at the word cluster for 'film set' below. Then divide up into groups of 5–6. Each group chooses one of the five categories on the other card. Make a word cluster for your category, as a poster. Use words in the yellow box below and other words you might know too. (Some words belong to more than one category.) Put all the posters up on the wall for a classroom vocabulary display.*

– genres	– audio / visual
– camera	elements
– actors / acting	– plot

action | appearance | background noises | body language | camera shots | cast |
characters | climax | close-up shot | comedy | conflict | costume | dialogue | director |
facial expression | first-person narrator | horror | humour | location | main role | make-up |
medium shot | music | mystery | plot | props | roles | romance | scene | science-fiction |
setting | shot sizes | sound effects | special effects | stage directions | supporting role |
third-person narrator | turning point | use of voice | wide shot | to zoom in on sb / sth

 b) *Start a glossary of film terms by writing down short definitions for all the words on your posters.*

SPEAKING **2** **Before you watch: A first look at Penny**

→ S17

In the following exercises, you're going to deal with the short film College Romance – The Musical *(by Isabelle Sieb). Learn about the film's content, characters and key features and the effect they achieve together. In the still below, the girl on the right is Penny, the film's main character. Exchange ideas with a partner as you answer these questions:*

1. **People:** Describe the emotions Penny and the other girl are feeling at the moment.
2. **Plot:** Say what you think might have happened to cause a reaction like this in public.
3. **Location:** Say where you think the action might take place.

VIEWING **3** **Getting from picture A to picture B**

V 12
→ S19

a) *Watch until 00:55. Describe what happens to make the boy's mood change from A to B.*

b) *How would you have reacted if you were the boy or Penny?*

c) *Your turn: In small groups, think of situations you think are equally embarrassing (e.g. sweat stains / walking around with toilet paper on shoe / stains on shirt). They can be real or invented. Then decide which situation is the most embarrassing!*

VIEWING **4** **Penny's problem**

a) *Go back to the beginning of the film and watch until 03:13. Sum up the action in the three scenes which involve Penny and a different college boy.*

b) *Now describe Penny's overall problem. Refer to these words and phrases Penny uses:*

| booboo | ouchie | misery | uncomfortable | true love | | the tears I try to fight | I let myself go | I can't hold back | someone who understands | I did it again |

→ S20

c) *Think – pair – share: Exaggeration is a key element in this comedy. But do you feel the film is too exaggerated in showing teenagers' lives and problems? If yes, what is being exaggerated, and why?*

VIEWING **5** **Penny as master of her own fate?**

Watch from 03:14 till 03:56, the scene in which Penny says the following key lines: "Now I've had enough. I'm the master of my own fate." Explain what Penny means with her statement. What is her new approach to her old problem? Name the key line that tells you exactly what her new approach is.

VIEWING **6** **The ending**

a) *Now watch from 03:14 till the end. Describe the action. Point out what is similar to the previous scenes with the three college boys and what is very different this time.*

b) *Sum up the overall message of the film. In your explanation, give the words and lines from Penny's first song (00:56–01:56) which you feel are the most important for understanding the message.*

SPEAKING / VIEWING **7** **Understanding genre: The musical teen comedy**

a) *In class, talk about musical films. Give some examples – e.g.* La La Land *(2016) or* West Side Story *(1961/2021) – and name typical elements of this genre. Say why you enjoy watching such films or why not.*

b) *Read the skills box. Before you watch the film again, divide up into groups. Each group chooses element 1, 2 or 3 from the box.*

While viewing, think of these questions:
- When is your element used? Give 1–2 examples.
- How effectively do you think your element is featured? Share your results with the class.

> **Film skills**
>
> Most teen comedies feature serious topics, but packaged in a way that can be considered 'light entertainment'. Typical elements:
> 1. **humour**
> 2. **exaggeration**
> 3. **romance and dating**
>
> And if it's a *musical* teen comedy, there will of course be music, singing and dancing.

VIEWING **8** **A closer look at the music: Comparing two scenes**

a) *Compare the library scene (02:30–02:45) and the basketball scene (02:46–03:13):*

1. Describe how the lines below reflect a difference in Penny's mood and actions in the two scenes:

> **A** And now I'm dancing with books in the library! What's become of me?

> **B** Maybe it's not too late. Maybe he's worth the wait.

2. Do you think Penny's style of singing and her movements match the scenes well? Explain.
3. What do you like / dislike in each scene?

b) *Use a copy of the film script and read the lines from the two scenes aloud. What sounds better to you: the spoken or the sung lines? Give your opinion.*

SPEAKING **9**   **Facial expressions**

a) *Describe the emotions that are shown in stills A–E. What situations cause people to make faces like that? Take turns to describe the situations.*

b) *A facial expression can show lots of things: a small change in the action, or maybe even a major turning point in the plot. Which moments below tell you that something is changing? Describe those moments.*

 A   02:29
 B   03:03
 C   02:20
 D   01:10
 E   02:56

SPEAKING **10**   **Camera shots and their functions**

a) *Read the skills box and find examples of each camera shot on the previous pages. Now read the notes on their functions and match them with the shots.*

- often used to start or end a film
- shows the entire person, groups of people and objects in the context of their complete surroundings
- often used to establish main characters
- often used in sequences where a small group of people are acting
- gives information about the setting by showing some of the background
- important for showing detail, like a character's emotions

> **Film skills**
>
> Films, whether short clips or full-length cinema films, depend on a mix of different **camera shots** for dramatic effect.
> The most common three are the **close-up**, the **medium shot**, and the **wide shot** (also called 'long shot').

b) *Look at the film stills of* College Romance – The Musical *again. Say why you think each shot was chosen for that particular moment.*

c) *A good film needs a mix of different camera shots. Discuss what would happen if there were **only** close-ups in a film, with no medium or wide shots.*

EAKING / WRITING **11**   **Musical film classics**

→ S15

Grease *(1978) and* West Side Story *(1961/2021) are two of the biggest-selling musical films ever. In a group, watch one of the films. Prepare a handout and give a presentation about the film in class. Include these points:*

plot summary | typical 'teen' elements that are featured | examples of effective / interesting camera shots | facial expressions / body language | use of music and dance

Speech

SPEAKING **1 Warm-up: Public speaking**

→ S17   **a)** *Describe the cartoon and explain its message.*

b) *Talk about a speech you've heard. Where and by whom was it given? What was the speaker's main aim and what effect did the speech have on you? Share your experiences in class.*

> **Useful phrases**
>
> **Context:** a political / birthday / farewell speech | given by a political leader / an expert in (history) / an (environmental) activist / our head teacher / … | in parliament / at a demonstration / at school / …
>
> **Aims:** to inform about sth | to educate / to explain | to outline an idea / a plan | to persuade the audience to take action | to warn sb of sth | to congratulate sb on sth | …
>
> **Style and effect:** serious / entertaining / boring / long / short / to the point | to put forward convincing arguments / examples | lots of empty talk / promises | … touched me / made me rethink / was new to me.

"People! You must think for yourselves and I'm going to tell you how!"

LISTENING / SPEAKING **2 Understanding a speech: Yes, we can**

a) *You're going to work with excerpts from the speech Barack Obama gave after he was elected president in 2008. Talk about your expectations of the speech: What topics will he cover? What kind of style / tone (serious, humorous, …) do you expect?*

→ S13   **b)** *Find an audio of the speech online and read/listen to the beginning (part 1). Describe what audience Obama addresses and why.*

Hello Chicago!
If there is anyone out there who still doubts that America is a place where all things are possible; who still wonders if the dream
5 of our founders is alive in our time; who still questions the power of our democracy, tonight is your answer.
   It's the answer told by lines that stretched around schools and churches in
10 numbers this nation has never seen; by people who waited three hours and four hours, many for the very first time in their lives, because they believed that this time must be different; that their voices could be
15 that difference.
   It's the answer spoken by young and old, rich and poor, Democrat and

Republican, Black, white, Hispanic, Asian, Native American, gay, straight, disabled and not disabled – Americans who sent a message 20 to the world that we have never been a collection of red states and blue states; we are, and always will be, the United States of America.
   It's the answer that led those who have 25 been told for so long by so many to be cynical, and fearful, and doubtful of what we can achieve to put their hands on the arc of history and bend it once more toward the hope of a better day. 30
   It's been a long time coming, but tonight, because of what we did on this day, in this election, at this defining moment, change has come to America.

c) *Listen to part 2 ("The road ahead" – "people will get there"; "This election had" to the end). Explain what topics Obama wants to highlight by mentioning various historical events / developments in his speech. Use the following information for help.*

> **1.** 1930s: A series of droughts and dust storms forced farmers to leave the "Dust Bowl" (part of the Great Plains); the "Great Depression", a terrible economic crisis, hit the US, and was fought with reforms called the "New Deal" | **2.** 1941: Japan bombed Pearl Harbor, which led to the US entering WWII | **3.** 1954 ff: Protests by African-Americans, like the Montgomery Bus Boycott and the Children's March in Birmingham, which were led among others by the "preacher" Martin Luther King, jr. | **4.** 1969: "a man on the moon" (Neil Armstrong) | **5.** 1989: "a wall came down" (Berlin) | **6.** up to now: "a world connected by science and imagination"

d) *Find key words to describe Obama's message and explain the slogan "Yes, we can".*

LISTENING **3** **A closer look at the speech**

→ S7, 11 *Listen to both parts again and do the following tasks.*

1. Match the rhetorical devices with the examples from the speech and describe their effect.

1. despair in the Dust Bowl and depression across the land | **2.** spoken by Black, white, Hispanic, Asian, Native American | **3.** What progress will we have made? | **4.** This is our chance. This is our moment. This is our time. | **5.** If there is anyone out there who still doubts … tonight is your answer. | **6.** through the best of times and the darkest of hours | **7.** When the bombs fell … she was there to witness a generation rise. | **8.** a New Deal, new jobs and a new sense of common purpose	**A** direct address | **B** anaphora | **C** alliteration | **D** contrast | **E** enumeration | **F** repetition | **G** rhetorical question | **H** personalising events

2. Obama also uses pauses, word stress and repeats elements three times for emphasis. Find examples in the text.
3. Examine how he uses Ann Nixon Cooper to personalise events from US history. Also think about how active and passive voice are used.
4. Analyse the vision presented at the end of the speech and the effect it creates.

SPEAKING / WRITING **4** **Dear audience, my fellow students …**

a) *Imagine you had to give a speech on one of these topics. In pairs, collect ideas (e.g. an anecdote, statistics, …) for an introduction that catches your listeners' interest.*

staying safe online | a more sustainable lifestyle | celebrating classmates winning an award

→ S6, 8 **b)** *Change the following text using rhetorical devices to make it more convincing.*

I believe that having a sustainable lifestyle is important for saving our planet. That's why I want to help you reduce your carbon footprint. For example, you can eat less meat, buy regional products or drink tap water instead of bottled water. In the mobility sector flying and driving your car are problematic, so take your bike or the bus. It also helps to plan your trips, that's how you save time and fuel. Turning off lights when leaving a room, heating cleverly or using biological cleaning products will help you to save the environment from home.

Study skills

S1 Umgang mit neuen Wörtern

Viele Wörter kannst du schon verstehen, obwohl du sie noch nicht gelernt hast.

1. **Ähnlichkeit mit bekannten Wörtern:** Oft haben verwandte Wörter den gleichen Stamm, aber andere Vorsilben oder Endungen, z.B. *happy* – *unhappy*. Englische Wörter haben oft keine Endungen, aber es gibt sie in verschiedenen Wortarten, z.B. *guide* (Nomen) – *to guide* (Verb). Achte besonders auf diese Präfixe und Suffixe:
   1. Die Vorsilben ***dis-*, *in-/ir-/il-*, *un-*** und ***de-*** drücken das Gegenteil oder Rückgängigmachen aus: ***dis****honest,* ***in****dependence,* ***ir****regular,* ***il****logical,* ***un****certain,* ***de****motivating*
   2. Die Vorsilben ***pre-*, *post-*, *re-*** drücken Vor-, Nachzeitigkeit bzw. Wiederholung aus: ***pre****paid,* ***post****-racial,* ***re****write*
   3. Die Vorsilben ***mal-*** und ***mis-*** verweisen auf etwas Schlechtes oder Falsches: ***mis****understood,* ***mal****function*
   4. Nomen erkennst du an Endungen wie z.B.: *teach**er**, act**or**, polite**ness**, activ**ity**, dist**ance**, differ**ence**, move**ment**, act**ion**.*
   5. Adjektive erkennst du an Endungen wie z.B.: *artist**ic**, typ**ical**, peace**ful**, help**less**, creat**ive**, drink**able**.*

   Berücksichtige auch Kombinationen von Präfixen und Suffixen, z.B. ***re****us**able**.*

2. **Ähnlichkeit mit Wörtern aus einer anderen Sprache:** Viele englische Wörter gibt es genauso oder ähnlich auch im Deutschen, z.B. *computer* oder *pony*. Manchmal hilft dir auch ein Wort, das du aus anderen Sprachen kennst, z.B. *to separate* – *séparer* (Fr.) – *separare* (Lat.).

3. **Verstehen der Wörter im Zusammenhang:** Manchmal kannst du dir aus dem Zusammenhang heraus erschließen, was ein Wort bedeutet. Was bedeutet z.B. *ridiculous* in diesem Satz? *That's the silliest thing I have ever heard. It's ridiculous!*

4. **Erschließen über Oberbegriffe:** Oft reicht es fürs Verständnis, wenn du ein unbekanntes Wort einem Oberbegriff zuordnen kannst: *I was really thirsty and ordered a soda pop (soda pop = a drink).*

Und wenn du doch im Wörterbuch nachschlagen musst, lies den Eintrag ganz durch, bis du die richtige Bedeutung des gesuchten Wortes gefunden hast. Dabei helfen dir auch die Tipps in → **S2**.

> **Tip**
> Nicht alle Wörter, die im Deutschen und Englischen ähnlich sind, haben dieselbe Bedeutung. Achte daher auf *false friends*, z.B. *to become* = „werden" (nicht „bekommen"), und auf Scheinanglizismen wie z.B. Bodybag (englisch *body bag* = „Leichensack").

S2 Umgang mit dem Wörterbuch

Es gibt verschiedene Arten von Wörterbüchern: ein- oder zweisprachige, gedruckte oder digitale. Beachte die grundsätzlichen Unterschiede zwischen digitalen und gedruckten Wörterbüchern: So haben digitale Wörterbücher z. B. den Vorteil, dass du nicht blättern, sondern das gesuchte Stichwort nur richtig eingeben musst. Zum Verstehen der Aussprache musst du bei einem gedruckten Wörterbuch die Lautschrift beherrschen; bei einem digitalen kannst du dir die Aussprache anhören. Bei jeder Art von Wörterbuch musst du darauf achten, aus den vielen zusätzlichen Informationen genau diejenigen herauszufiltern, die gerade wichtig sind.

1. **Zweisprachiges Wörterbuch:** Dieses hilft dir vor allem, wenn du die Bedeutung eines unbekannten Wortes herausfinden willst.

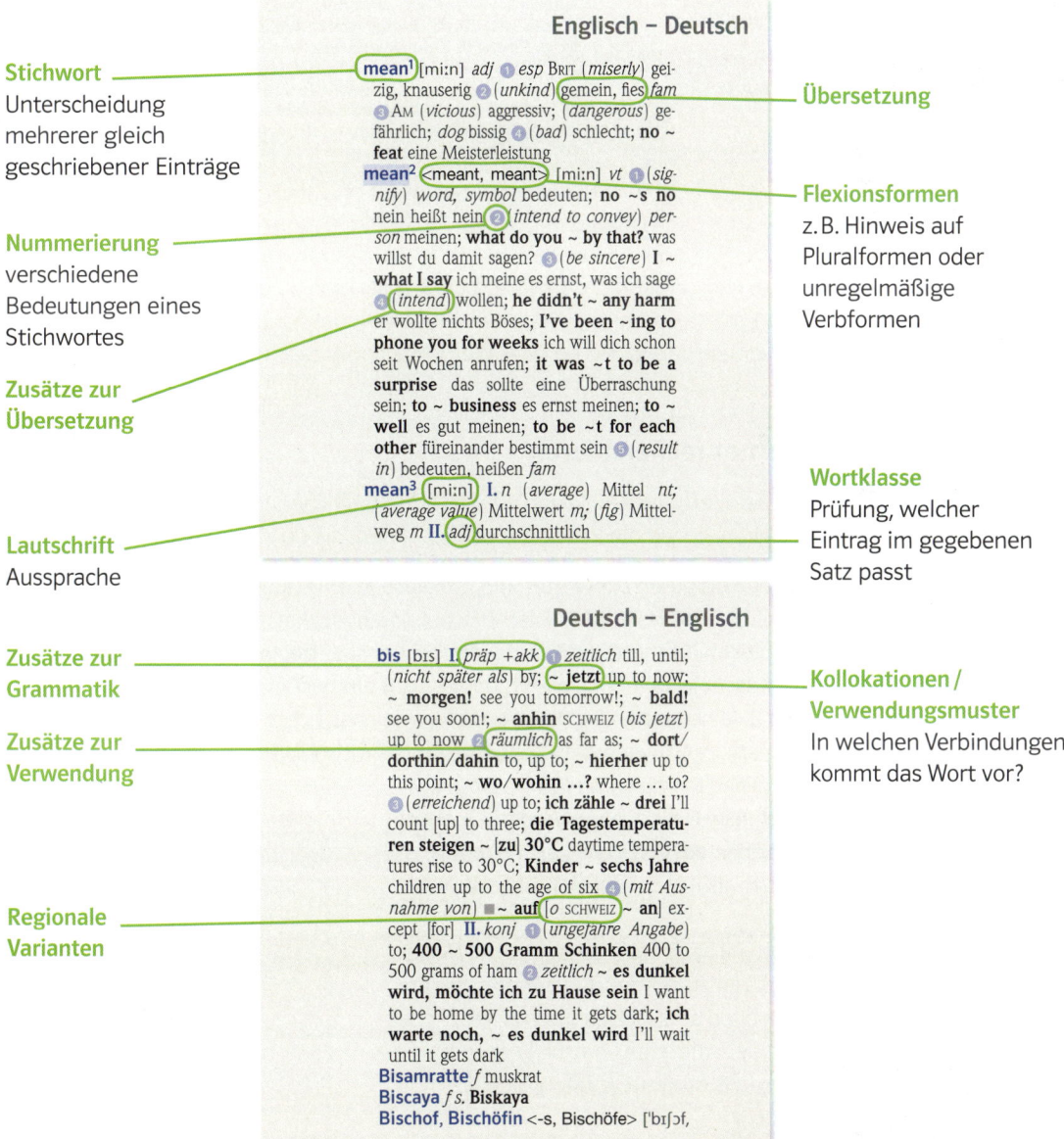

one hundred and nineteen **119**

2. **Einsprachiges Wörterbuch:** Ein einsprachiges Wörterbuch hilft dir, englische Wörter korrekt zu verwenden, da es Definitionen, Beispiele und andere Informationen zum Gebrauch eines Wortes enthält. Vergiss nicht, dich mit Aufbau und Struktur deines Wörterbuchs vertraut zu machen, damit du vor allem bei Schulaufgaben und Prüfungen schnell nachschlagen kannst.

Lautschrift
Aussprache

Wortklasse

Zusätze zur Verwendung

Nummerierung
verschiedene Bedeutungen eines Stichworts mit Definition und Anwendungsbeispiel

Redewendungen

decline /dɪˈklaɪn/ verb; noun
► verb GO DOWN ► 1 B2 [I] to gradually become less, worse, or lower: *His interest in the project declined after his wife died.* ○ *The party's popularity has declined in the opinion polls.* ○ formal *The land declines sharply away from the house.* REFUSE ► 2 B2 [I or T] formal to refuse: *I invited him to the meeting but he declined.* ○ *He declined my offer.* ○ [+ to infinitive] *They declined to tell me how they had got my address.* GRAMMAR ► 2 [I or T] specialized If a noun, PRONOUN, or adjective declines, it has different forms to show if it is the subject or object, etc. of a verb or if it is singular or plural, etc. If you decline such a word, you list its various forms: *In Latin we learned how to decline nouns.* IDIOM sb's declining years the last years of someone's life: *He became very forgetful in his declining years.*
► noun [S or U] B2 when something becomes less in amount, importance, quality or strength: *industrial decline* ○ *Home cooking seems to be on the/in decline* (= not so many people are doing it). ○ *a decline in the number of unemployed* ○ *She seemed to be recovering and then she went into a decline.*

Zusätze zur Grammatik (z.B. [I] = intransitives Verb)

Frequenz (Wichtigkeit des Wortes laut dem Gemeinsamen europäischen Referenzrahmen)

Kollokationen / Verwendungsmuster

Für ein- und zweisprachige Wörterbücher gilt: Falls du ein Wort nachschlagen willst und es nicht sofort findest, überprüfe, ob du es korrekt gebildet hast, z.B. ~~unexperienced~~ statt *inexperienced*. Achte online darauf, ein seriöses Wörterbuch mit geprüften Einträgen zu verwenden.

S3 Im Internet recherchieren

Das Internet bietet eine Fülle von meist frei zugänglichen Informationen. Die folgenden Tipps können dir helfen, genau die Informationen zu finden, die du z.B. für eine Präsentation brauchst:

1. Überlege dir gute Stichwörter und gib diese in eine Suchmaschine ein. Wenn du z.B. eine Übersicht über das amerikanische Schulsystem suchst, nimm als Stichwort *US school system*. Je mehr Stichwörter du eingibst, desto genauer sind deine Ergebnisse. Über die Einstellungen der Suchmaschine kannst du die Ergebnisse auf ein bestimmtes Land oder eine Sprache eingrenzen.

2. Wenn du eine passende Webseite gefunden hast, achte darauf, wer sie erstellt hat. Sind die Informationen zuverlässig (Online-Lexikon, seriöse Zeitung usw.) oder handelt es sich eher um persönliche Meinungen (Forum, Blog, Kommentar usw.)? Sind glaubwürdige Quellen angegeben oder ist etwas als Werbung oder gar als Falschinformation gekennzeichnet?

3. Kopiere nicht einfach ganze Artikel. Mache dir Notizen zu den wichtigsten Informationen und gib sie mit eigenen Worten wieder.

4. Ordne dein Material und suche gezielt weiter, falls du weitere Informationen brauchst.

> **Tip**
>
> **Fakten und Inhalte überprüfen**
> - Nutze stets mehrere Quellen.
> - Prüfe wie aktuell die Quelle ist. Sind die Informationen ggf. veraltet?
> - Gib einen Satz aus dem gefundenen Text in eine Suchmaschine ein. So kannst du herausfinden, ob der Inhalt bereits verwendet wurde, also ggf. „abgeschrieben" wurde.

S4 Operatoren verstehen

Bestimmte Verben werden in Aufgaben als „Operatoren" verwendet. Operatoren helfen dir zu verstehen, was in einer Aufgabe erwartet wird. Zugleich erlauben sie eine Messung beim Erreichen von Kompetenzzielen und geben damit eine Bewertungsgrundlage für Schulaufgaben und Prüfungen. Hier findest du einige wichtige Operatoren für schriftliche und mündliche Aufgabenstellungen.

Operator	Erläuterung	Beispiel
analyse	Beschreibe und erkläre im Detail.	*Analyse the girls' views.*
assess	Schildere Vor- und Nachteile, bevor du deine (begründete) Meinung darlegst.	*Assess the pros and cons of both approaches.*
characterise	Beschreibe und untersuche, wie eine Figur präsentiert wird.	*Characterise (name).*
comment (on)	Gib deine Meinung zum Thema anhand von Belegen wieder.	*Comment on the plot of the story.*
compare	Beschreibe Unterschiede und Gemeinsamkeiten.	*Compare the three quotes.*
describe	Beschreibe eine Person / einen Sachverhalt detailliert.	*Describe the narrative perspective.*
discuss	Beleuchte ein Thema von verschiedenen Seiten anhand von Argumenten und gib ein begründetes Urteil ab.	*Discuss how subcultures influence society.*
examine	Beschreibe und erkläre im Detail.	*Examine Tupac's language.*
explain	Beschreibe einen Sachverhalt mit Hilfe von Beispielen / Begründungen.	*Explain what the speaker wants to achieve.*
illustrate	Erkläre einen Sachverhalt anhand von Beispielen.	*Illustrate the effect on the reader.*
interpret	Analysiere Form und Inhalt einer Statistik / eines Cartoons / ... und erkläre die Bedeutung im Kontext.	*Interpret the song.*
outline	Beschreibe wesentliche Elemente, Funktionsweisen oder Prinzipien.	*Outline how the clan system worked.*
state	Benenne die wichtigsten Aspekte.	*State the purpose of the text.*
summarise / sum up	Gib kurz die wichtigsten Punkte mit eignen Worten wieder.	*Sum up the plot of the story.*
write a ...	Verfasse einen Text, der die Kriterien der genannten Textsorte erfüllt.	*Write a letter to the editor.*

Hörverstehen wird häufig mit standardisierten Aufgabenformaten abgeprüft. Wichtige Operatoren sind hier ***tick*** (ankreuzen), ***match*** (zuordnen), ***complete / fill in*** (vervollständigen).

Reading skills

S5 Wichtige Inhalte von Texten herausfinden

Um den Inhalt und die Besonderheiten eines Textes zu verstehen, helfen dir die folgenden Tipps: Wende Schnelllesetechniken *(Skimming* und *Scanning)* an, markiere wichtige Textstellen und mache dir Notizen, z.B. Schlüsselwörter *(key words)*, Fragen oder Anmerkungen. Um deine Ergebnisse belegen zu können, notiere die Fundstelle (Seite, Zeilennummer).

Skimming („den Rahm abschöpfen")	Scanning („maschinell durchsuchen")
Wenn du das Wichtigste *(gist)* aus einem Text wiedergeben sollst, dann musst du den Text zusammenfassen und nicht einfach nacherzählen. Überfliege den Text und achte darauf, ob bestimmte Wörter *(key words)* oder Personen häufiger vorkommen. Überschriften oder Bilder können dir helfen einzuschätzen, was wichtig ist und was nicht. Diese Art des Schnelllesens nennt man *skimming*.	Wenn du nach bestimmten Einzelheiten *(details)* in einem Text gefragt wirst, überfliege ihn und finde die Stellen mit der wichtigen Information. Dazu suchst du gezielt nach passenden Stichwörtern *(key words)*. Sie zeigen an, welche Teile du genauer lesen solltest, um die gesuchte Information zu bekommen. Diese Art des Überfliegens nennt man auch *scanning*.

S6 Wichtige Merkmale von Texten erkennen

1. Erzähltexte

Wenn du eine Geschichte genauer liest oder analysierst, solltest du nicht nur über die Handlung *(plot)* selbst nachdenken, sondern auch darüber, wie die Geschichte erzählt wird. Zu den wichtigsten Erzähltechniken *(narrative techniques)* gehören:

Climax	Der Höhepunkt *(climax)* ist der Hauptwendepunkt in einer Geschichte. Die Spannung ist hier am höchsten. Die Hauptfigur befindet sich oft in einer schwierigen Situation und macht Veränderungen durch, sie wird z.B. stärker oder selbstbewusster. (Siehe auch *turning point*.)
Flashback	Eine Rückblende *(flashback)* erzählt Ereignisse, die vor einem bestimmten Zeitpunkt in der Geschichte stattgefunden haben, z.B. wird die Erinnerung einer Figur an etwas Vergangenes beschrieben.
Language / Style	Die Art, wie eine Geschichte erzählt wird – über bestimmte Wörter und Beschreibungen – erzeugt eine gewisse Stimmung *(atmosphere* oder *mood)*. Häufig werden z.B. die fünf Sinne *(five senses)* angesprochen: Wenn man liest, was die Figuren sehen, hören, riechen, schmecken und fühlen, ist es leichter, sich in sie hineinzuversetzen. Ebenso können sprachliche Bilder, z.B. Vergleiche *(similes)* und Metaphern *(metaphors)*, sowie Humor *(humor)* und Ironie *(irony)* zur besonderen Atmosphäre einer Geschichte beitragen.

Narrative perspective	Die Wirkung, die eine Geschichte auf den Leser/die Leserin hat, wird stark von der Erzählperspektive (*narrative perspective*) beeinflusst. Wer ist der Erzähler/die Erzählerin und wie ist seine/ihre Einstellung zu den Figuren der Geschichte? Was erzählt er/sie und wann? Die häufigsten Erzählperspektiven sind: 1. **Ich-Erzähler/-in** *(first-person narrator)* Der Ich-Erzähler/die Ich-Erzählerin erzählt die Geschichte aus seiner/ihrer Perspektive. Oft (aber nicht immer) ist der Ich-Erzähler/die Ich-Erzählerin die Hauptfigur der Geschichte. Der Leser/die Leserin und der Ich-Erzähler/die Ich-Erzählerin erleben die Geschichte sozusagen „gemeinsam". 2. **Erzähler/-in, der/die in der 3. Person erzählt** *(third-person narrator)* Dieser Erzähler/diese Erzählerin erzählt die Geschichte „von außen". Die Sichtweise ist nicht unbedingt immer die der Hauptfigur.
Suspense	Spannung (*suspense*) ist eine wichtige Erzähltechnik, um den Leser/die Leserin in die Geschichte hineinzuziehen. Spannung kann direkt in den ersten Zeilen der Geschichte aufgebaut werden oder aber langsam im Verlauf der Geschichte. Sie wird z.B. durch starke, dramatische Sprache erzeugt oder durch das Zurückhalten von Informationen.
Turning point	Ein Wendepunkt ist der Punkt in einer Geschichte, an dem eine entscheidende, oft unerwartete, Wendung in der Handlung eintritt. Diese Wendung beeinflusst den weiteren Verlauf der Geschichte. Sie kann durch eine Entscheidung, eine neue Information oder ein bestimmtes Ereignis eintreten und für die Hauptfigur und die anderen Figuren gut oder schlecht sein. (Siehe auch *climax*.)

2. Kurzgeschichten

Kurzgeschichten (*short stories*) beschränken sich meist auf wenige Elemente: eine oder zwei Hauptfiguren, einen Schauplatz und ein zentrales Thema/einen zentralen Konflikt. Typisch für den Aufbau sind ein direkter Einstieg ins Thema (d.h. keine oder nur eine sehr kurze Einleitung) sowie ein meist überraschender Wendepunkt (*turning point*) kurz vor Ende der Geschichte. Durch die Knappheit der Schilderung und das überraschende bzw. häufig auch offene Ende werden die Leser/-innen angeregt, weiterzudenken und eigene Schlüsse zu ziehen.

3. Drama

Theaterstücke (*plays*) sind in Akte (*acts*) und Szenen (*scenes*) unterteilt. Es gibt in der Regel keinen Erzähler/keine Erzählerin, der/die die Figuren genauer beschreibt. Stattdessen wird die Handlung direkt durch die gesprochene Sprache und durch die Darstellung der Figuren vermittelt. Deshalb ist es bei der Interpretation von Theaterstücken besonders wichtig, neben dem Text auch auf die Sprechweise, Gestik und Mimik zu achten. So kannst du Rückschlüsse auf Charaktereigenschaften, Gedanken und Gefühle der Figuren ziehen.

Characters	Die Figuren (*characters*) stellen oft klassische Typen oder Rollen dar, so gibt es z. B. einen Helden (*hero*) / eine Heldin (*heroine*), dem / der ein Gegen-spieler (*antihero*) / eine Gegenspielerin (*antiheroine*) gegenübersteht. Bei der Beschreibung der Figuren hilft dir → **S12**.
Language	In Theaterstücken wird die Handlung durch gesprochene Sprache vermit-telt. Die Figuren sprechen in Dialogen miteinander.
Stage directions	Alles, was nicht durch gesprochene Sprache vermittelt werden kann, wird in Regieanweisungen (*stage directions*) vorgegeben. Hier werden auch Angaben zu Requisiten (*props*), Bühnenbild und Licht gemacht. Beim Lesen eines Theaterstücks können die Regieanweisungen wichtige Hinweise z. B. auf die Stimmung der Szene und die Gefühle der Figuren geben. In einer Bühnenaufführung wird die Handlung und Stimmung des Stückes durch Körpersprache, Bewegungen, Bühnenbild, Licht, Musik usw. getragen.

4. Lyrische Texte

Bei der Interpretation von **Gedichten** (*poems*) gibt es nicht die eine „richtige" Bedeutung. Wichtig ist aber, dass du deine Lesart am Text belegen kannst. Dazu ist es hilfreich, auch formale Merkmale zu untersuchen und mit dem Inhalt in Verbindung zu bringen.

Rhyme scheme	Gedichte, die sich reimen, folgen immer einem bestimmten Reimschema (*rhyme scheme*). Typische Reimschemata sind: **AABB** und **ABAB** sowie **ABCB**. Es gibt aber auch Gedichte, die sich nicht reimen, sogenannte *free verse poems*.
Rhythm / Stress	Ein Gedicht funktioniert nur mit dem richtigen Rhythmus (*rhythm*). Er bestimmt, welche Stelle in jeder Zeile betont wird. Die Betonung (*stress*) liegt dann immer an der gleichen Stelle. Bei Gedichten, die sich nicht rei-men, ist es wichtig, dass du selbst entscheidest, wo die Betonung liegt oder wo eine Pause gemacht werden sollte.
Symbol / Simile / Metaphor	In Gedichten spielt die Bildsprache (*imagery*) eine wichtige Rolle. Dazu gehören **Symbole** (*symbols*), also Begriffe, die stellvertretend für etwas anderes (Gefühle, Ideen, Handlungen usw.) stehen, z. B. das Herz für die Liebe. Bei einem **Vergleich** (*simile*) werden Dinge oder Personen mit etwas anderem verglichen, um auszudrücken, dass sie die gleichen Eigenschaften besitzen. Dabei wird *like* oder *as* verwendet, z. B. *happy as a rainbow*. Eine **Metapher** (*metaphor*) ist ein verkürzter Vergleich ohne *like* oder *as*, z. B. *I'll be the light to guide you*.
Stylistic devices	Stilmittel werden in Gedichten – und auch anderen Texten – eingesetzt, um eine bestimmte Wirkung zu erzeugen. Dazu gehören u.a.: Alliteration (*alliteration*), z. B. *the look of love*; Gegensatz (*contrast*), z. B. *the good and the bad*; Aufzählung (*enumeration*) z. B. *Belfast. Beirut. Phnom Penh.*; Wie-derholung (*repetition*), z. B. *Everybody Black is … Everybody Black dropped … about Everybody Black*.

Achte bei **Liedern** (*songs*) zusätzlich darauf, wie Musikstil, Melodie, Gesang und Instrumente den Inhalt unterstützen.

5. Sachtexte

Sachtexte informieren über ein bestimmtes Thema oder einen Sachverhalt. Dabei ist es wichtig zu erkennen, was mit dem Text bezweckt wird. Es werden meist diese Grundtypen unterschieden:

- informierende Texte (z.B. *newspaper article, report*)
- darstellende Texte (z.B. *feature, biography*)
- argumentierende / kommentierende Texte (z.B. *argumentative essay, comment*)
- appellierende / auffordernde Texte (z.B. *flyer, brochure, speech*)
- instruierende Texte (z.B. *recipe, instructions*)

Beachte auch die typischen Merkmale der einzelnen Textsorten (→ **S7**). Insbesondere bei informierenden Texten wie Nachrichten (in der Zeitung, im Fernsehen und im Internet) ist es wichtig darauf zu achten, ob der Urheber tatsächlich in neutraler Weise informieren möchte – wie dies seriöse Quellen wie z.B. staatliche Institutionen, große Tageszeitungen oder der öffentlich-rechtliche Rundfunk tun – oder ob das Publikum in eine bestimmte Richtung gelenkt werden soll. Nachrichten aus nicht seriösen Quellen sind u.a. durch folgende Elemente gekennzeichnet: Reißerische Überschriften, schockierende Bilder, einseitige Darstellung des Themas, emotionaler Stil, Zahlen und Fakten sind aus dem Zusammenhang gerissen oder gar nicht durch Quellen belegt. Immer häufiger sind auch *fake news* anzutreffen, also absichtlich verbreitete Falschinformationen.

Writing skills

S7 Textsorten und ihre Besonderheiten

1. Fiktionale Texte

Dialogue / Film script   Wenn du einen Dialog, z.B. für eine Filmszene, schreibst, fasse dich kurz und verwende echte mündliche Sprache, also *short forms*, *question tags*, verstärkende Ausdrücke usw. Gib bei den Regieanweisungen *(stage directions)* nur an, was man sehen oder darstellen kann. Gedanken kann man nicht sehen. Aber du kannst in den *stage directions* Hinweise auf die Gefühle einer Person geben, z.B. durch Anweisungen für Gesichtsausdrücke.

Fable / Tale   Klassische Fabeln *(fables)* sind kurze Erzählungen, in denen Tiere (oder Pflanzen) mit menschlichen Eigenschaften auftreten, um so der Leserschaft eine Lehre zu vermitteln. Ähnlich wird in traditionellen *tales* (Sagen / Volksmärchen) durch Fabelwesen oder magische Elemente häufig eine moralische Botschaft transportiert.

Sketch (comedy)   Ein Sketch ist eine kurze lustige Szene, die das Publikum zum Lachen bringen soll und in der Regel mit einer Pointe endet. Sketche können frei improvisiert werden oder wie bei einem Theaterstück auf einem schriftlichen Skript basieren.

Story   Wenn du Geschichten oder Bildergeschichten schreibst, schmücke sie aus und gestalte sie sprachlich abwechslungsreich. Meistens sind Geschichten im *past tense* geschrieben. Wenn du eine Geschichte vervollständigen sollst, muss dein Teil zum vorgegebenen Text passen. Außerdem sollten die Erzählperspektive und die Erzählzeit nicht wechseln.

Urban legend   Moderne Mythen (auch Großstadtlegenden genannt) sind unterhaltsame kurze Geschichten, die angeblich wahr sind und meist mündlich oder über soziale Medien verbreitet werden. Häufig enthalten sie merkwürdige oder mysteriöse Elemente und basieren auf einem angeblichen Tatsachenbericht: *"This happened to friend of a friend of mine ..."*

2. Sach- und Gebrauchstexte

Ads / Commercials   Werbung (gedruckt oder als Werbespot) möchte ihre Adressaten / Adressatinnen direkt ansprechen und von etwas (z.B. einem Produkt, einer Firma, einer Organisation) überzeugen. Dabei helfen u.a. folgende Elemente: ein Bild / Text / Sound, um Aufmerksamkeit zu erregen *(eye-/ear-catcher)*, ein griffiger Slogan, visuelle Gestaltung (Fotos, Farben, Logo), Soundgestaltung (Musik, Stimme des Sprechers / der Sprecherin) und die Angabe von Kontaktinformationen.

Argumentative essay   In einem *argumentative essay* beleuchtest du ein Thema näher. Dabei kannst du entweder versuchen, die Leser/-innen von einer Seite des Themas zu überzeugen *(persuasive essay)*, oder eine ausgewogene Pro- / Contra-Darstellung geben *(neutral essay)*. Formuliere in der Einleitung das Thema; du kannst auch kurz erklären, warum das Thema relevant ist oder welche Frage(n) dein Text beantworten soll. Ordne deine Argumente im Hauptteil sinnvoll an (→ **S8**). Fasse am Schluss deine Argumentation zusammen; du kannst auch deine eigene Meinung einbringen oder einen Ausblick auf die Zukunft geben.

Comment   In einem Kommentar gibst du deine Meinung zu einem meist umstrittenen Thema wieder. Nenne in der Einleitung das Thema und deine Meinung und versuche, das Interesse des Lesers / der Leserin zu wecken. Ordne deine Argumente im Hauptteil sinnvoll an (→ **S8**). Am Schluss fasst du deine Meinung zusammen; du kannst auch einen Ausblick auf die Zukunft geben oder Lösungsvorschläge machen.

E-mail / Letter / Postcard / Invitation   Achte auf die richtige Anrede, z.B. *Dear ...*, die Grußformel am Schluss, z.B. *Yours / Love / Best wishes / Sincerely*, und beachte die Höflichkeitsregeln. Bei formellen E-Mails oder Briefen verwendet man eher die Langformen, z.B. *I am* statt *I'm*. Denke bei einem Brief an die Angabe der Empfänger- und Absenderadresse und an das Datum.

Flyer   Ein Flyer sollte gut lesbar sein und alle wichtigen Informationen enthalten: *Who? What? When? Where? Why?* Formuliere außerdem einen ansprechenden Slogan.

Letter to the editor   Mit einem Leserbrief reagierst du auf einen Artikel in einer Zeitung oder Zeitschrift. In der Betreffzeile nennst du den Artikel (Titel, Autor/-in, Datum), die Anrede ist *Dear Sir or Madam*, und am Ende kommt keine Grußformel, nur dein Name und Wohnort. Fasse dich kurz, aber begründe deine Meinung mit überzeugenden Argumenten. Bleibe stets höflich und nutze formelle Sprache *(formal language)* → **S9**.

News report   Konzentriere dich bei einem Tatsachenbericht auf die Fakten und spare deine persönliche Meinung aus. Achte auf eine sachliche Sprache und vermeide emotionale Ausdrücke. Die Schlagzeile sollte direkt auf das Thema des Artikels hinweisen und das Interesse des Lesers / der Leserin wecken. In Zeitungsberichten werden häufig Passivformen verwendet.

Persuasive text   *Persuasive texts* sind Texte, die zu einem bestimmten Handeln auffordern, z.B. Werbetexte. Sie sollen den Leser/die Leserin direkt ansprechen und überzeugen. Dies gelingt z.B. mit rhetorischen Fragen, persönlichen Formulierungen und etwas Humor. Verbinde deine Sätze mit Konjunktionen und mache sie mit ausdrucksstarken Adjektiven interessant. Überlege dir für den Schluss einen besonders überzeugenden Satz, der im Gedächtnis bleibt.

Rating   Eine Bewertung gibt deine Meinung über z.B. einen Film oder ein Restaurant wieder. Sie ist keine vollständige Rezension. Der Fokus der Bewertung sollte daher auf deiner persönlichen Meinung liegen. Gehe auf Aspekte ein, die für dich ausschlaggebend und wichtig sind.

Reference article   Ein Artikel in einem Nachschlagewerk enthält die wichtigsten Informationen zu einem Begriff oder Thema. Überlege dir, was jemand, der von diesem Thema keine Ahnung hat, unbedingt wissen sollte, und lasse Detailinformationen, die nur für Experten/Expertinnen interessant sind, weg. Der Artikel beginnt mit dem Stichwort (= Nennung des Begriffs/Themas). Typische Beispiele im Internet sind z.B. Wikipedia-Artikel.

Report   Bei einem Bericht ist die Vollständigkeit und Verständlichkeit der sachlichen Informationen das Wichtigste. Er wird im *past tense* geschrieben.

Review   Eine Rezension bzw. Kritik bietet eine Entscheidungshilfe, ob es sich lohnt, z.B. eine bestimmte Veranstaltung zu besuchen oder ein Buch zu lesen. Zuerst werden kurz die wichtigsten Details beschrieben, dann wird eine mit Argumenten belegte Bewertung abgegeben.

Speech   Überlege zunächst, welches Ziel (oder welche Ziele) du mit einer Rede verfolgst: die Zuhörer/-innen zu informieren, aufzuklären, zu überzeugen, oder zum Handeln aufzufordern? Beginne mit einer höflichen Begrüßung und wecke das Interesse des Publikums, z.B. mit einer überraschenden Tatsache, einer provokativen Aussage oder einer Anekdote. Erläutere deine Ideen im Hauptteil und unterstütze sie mit Beispielen und Argumenten. Verwende Kontraste, Wiederholungen, rhetorische Fragen oder andere stilistische Mittel, um die Rede überzeugend zu gestalten und die Aufmerksamkeit des Publikums aufrecht zu erhalten. Das Ende der Rede sollte zur Zielstellung passen (z.B. Zusammenfassung oder Appell). Bedanke dich und lasse ggf. Fragen aus dem Publikum zu.

Wiki text   Wikis sind Webseiten mit Sammlungen von Beiträgen (Wiki-Texte). Wiki-Texte sind meist *reference articles* und definieren sich vor allem dadurch, dass sie von von mehreren Autoren/Autorinnen verfasst und bearbeitet werden.

3. Mischformen

Blog   Ein Blog ist eine Art Online-Tagebuch, in dem regelmäßig Beiträge veröffentlicht werden. Es gibt verschiedene Arten von Blogs, z.B. Reise- oder Musikblogs. Meist sind sie in der Ich-Perspektive geschrieben und vom Standpunkt des Bloggers/der Bloggerin geprägt.

Diary entry   Ein Tagebucheintrag erzählt und kommentiert vergangene und erwartete Ereignisse aus persönlicher Sicht und ist normalerweise nicht für Andere bestimmt. Verwende ausdrucksstarke Adjektive und Adverbien, um Gedanken und Gefühle zu beschreiben.

Travel literature   Reiseliteratur enthält neben der Schilderung einer persönlichen Reiseerfahrung und unterhaltenden Elementen auch Fakten über die Reise bzw. das Land. Dazu zählen u.a. Blogs, Reisetagebücher und -romane. Letztere können auch fiktive Elemente beinhalten.

S8 Einen eigenen Text schreiben

1. Die Planung deines Textes

Nimm dir für diese Phase ausreichend Zeit. Lies die Aufgabenstellung genau durch und über-lege, für wen dein Text bestimmt ist (Adressat/-in) und welchen Zweck er erfüllen soll. Vor dem Schreiben machst du dir am besten einen Plan *(outline)*.

Ein guter Text besteht normalerweise aus einem interessanten Titel und folgenden drei Teilen:

Einleitung *(introduction)*: Hier erfährt der Leser / die Leserin, worum es im Text geht. Du kannst auch eine Fragestellung einführen, die im Text erörtert werden soll.

Hauptteil *(main part)*: Der Hauptteil ist in mehrere Abschnitte gegliedert und beinhaltet die Details (Fakten, Argumente, Beispiele usw.) zu deinem Thema.

Schluss *(conclusion)*: Der Schlussteil kann eine Zusammenfassung von dem sein, was du im Hauptteil geschrieben hast, oder eine persönliche Äußerung.

Tipp für Erzähltexte *(fictional texts)*: Bevor du mit dem Schreiben beginnst, überlege, wo / wann die Geschichte spielt *(setting)*, was passiert *(plot)* und wer vorkommt *(characters)*.

Tipp für Sachtexte *(factual texts)*: Überlege, wie du deine Argumente im Hauptteil sinnvoll und logisch anordnen kannst, z. B.

a) Präsentiere zunächst alle Gegenargumente, dann alle Pro-Argumente; jeweils vom schwächsten zum stärksten *(con-con-con; pro-pro-pro)*.

b) Präsentiere in jedem Absatz ein Argument und das entsprechende Gegenargument *(pro-con, pro-con, pro-con)*.

2. Der erste Entwurf

Auf der Grundlage deiner Planung kannst du einen ersten Entwurf schreiben. Nutze die folgenden Tipps, um deinen Text möglichst flüssig und interessant zu gestalten:

– **Abwechslungsreiches Formulieren:** Verwende unterschiedliche Satzanfänge und vermei-de häufig benutzte Wörter (z. B. *amazing, fantastic, great, spectacular* statt *good*).

– **Stelle Zusammenhänge her,** indem du Konjunktionen *(although, if, …)*, Adverbien zur Strukturierung *(at first, therefore, …)* und kommentierende Adverbien *(obviously, …)* verwendest.

3. Die Überarbeitung

Es ist wichtig, dass du oder ein Mitschüler / eine Mitschülerin den Text noch einmal kritisch durchliest. Am hilfreichsten ist es, wenn du den Text mehrmals liest, jedes Mal mit einem anderen Schwerpunkt (siehe Checkliste rechts). Wenn du Feed-back von einer anderen Person bekommen hast, sieh es dir genau an und entscheide, was davon du für deinen Text übernehmen möchtest. Wenn du den Text eines Mitschü-lers / einer Mitschülerin liest, achte darauf, dass du bei deiner Kritik fair bleibst.

Checkliste
Inhalt:
– Alle wesentlichen Punkte enthalten?
– Zusammenhänge erkennbar / logisch?
– Passt die Sprachebene *(register)* zur Textsorte?
Rechtschreibung:
– Wörter richtig geschrieben?
– Am Satzanfang groß?
– Getrennt oder zusammen?
Grammatik:
– Richtige Zeitform, Satzbau, Pluralbildung usw.?

S9 Stil und Register

Achte stets darauf, dass Stil *(style)* und Sprachebene *(register)* zur Situation bzw. Textsorte passen.

	Merkmale	Textsorten	Beispiele
Formal language	höfliche bzw. neutrale Formulierungen, Langformen, längere Sätze und Satzgefüge, Passiv- und Partizipialkonstruktionen	*argumentative essay, comment, letter to the editor*	*Please **do not** interrupt.* │ ***Although** some **may** find talent shows entertaining, they can do real damage.*
Informal language	umgangssprachliche Formulierungen, Übertreibungen, Kurzformen, kurze Sätze, Auslassungen, Abkürzungen	*dialogue, film script*	***It's, like, super** exciting.* │ ***You** really mean that?* │ ***cos** (= because)* │ ***gonna** (= going to)* │ ***yep** (= yes)*

S10 Aufbau von Absätzen *(paragraph writing)*

Wenn du einen längeren Text schreibst, solltest du jeden Aspekt / jedes Argument in einem eigenen Absatz präsentieren. Ein Absatz ist meist so aufgebaut: Beginne mit einem *topic sentence*, d.h. einem Satz, der das zentrale Argument (z. B. eine These, Idee, Behauptung) nennt. Die folgenden Sätze veranschaulichen die Aussage des *topic sentence* mit Hilfe konkreter Beispiele.

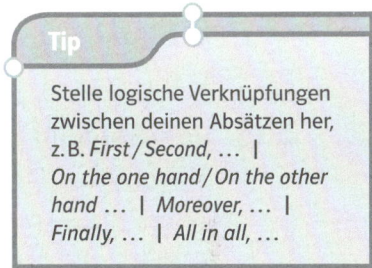

Tip

Stelle logische Verknüpfungen zwischen deinen Absätzen her, z. B. *First / Second, …* │ *On the one hand / On the other hand …* │ *Moreover, …* │ *Finally, …* │ *All in all, …*

S11 Texte analysieren

Bevor du mit dem Schreiben deiner Analyse beginnst, lies den Text gründlich durch und mache dir Notizen → **S5**. Die Analyse umfasst folgende drei Teile:

1. *Introduction:* Mache allgemeine Angaben zum Text (Textsorte, Titel, Autor/-in, Datum). Fasse die wichtigsten Punkte **(Sachtext)** bzw. den Inhalt **(Erzähltext)** kurz zusammen und erkläre, was der Autor / die Autorin mit dem Text beabsichtigt *(purpose)*. Wenn der Zweck des Textes nicht klar ist, kannst du auch eine begründete Vermutung abgeben oder sagen, ob der Text ein typisches Beispiel für sein Genre ist.
2. *Main part:* Untersuche, wie der Text erzählt wird und welche Wirkung dies auf den Leser / die Leserin hat. Achte bei **Sachtexten** vor allem auf Struktur, Argumentation, Sprache / Stil; und bei **Erzähltexten** auf Struktur, Erzählperspektive, Sprache / Stil, die Figuren und ihr Verhältnis zueinander (→ **S6**, **S9**, **S12**). Beginne für jeden neuen Aspekt einen neuen Abschnitt und belege deine Ergebnisse mit Zitaten aus dem Text (mit Fundstellen).
3. *Conclusion:* Fasse deine Ergebnisse zusammen. Gehe kurz darauf ein, ob der Text den beabsichtigten Zweck erfüllt oder nicht.

S12 Charakterisierung

Die Figuren und ihr Verhältnis zueinander tragen wesentlich dazu bei, ob dem Leser / der Leserin eine Geschichte, ein Film oder ein Theaterstück gefällt. Sind die Figuren witzig, mutig, hilfsbereit, gemein, …? (Auch negative oder böse Figuren können faszinierend sein!) Interessante Figuren sind meist vielschichtig, d.h. sie sind – wie im realen Leben – weder nur gut noch nur böse. Folge beim Schreiben einer Charakterisierung diesen Schritten:

1. Stelle die Figur (Name, Alter, Aussehen, …) und ihre Funktion / Rolle kurz vor.
2. Beschreibe die Eigenschaften und das Verhalten der Figur. Denke daran, dass dies im Text auf verschiedene Weise dargestellt sein kann:
   – Was sagen der Erzähler / die Erzählerin oder andere Personen über die Figur?
   – Was sagt, denkt und fühlt die Figur selbst? Wie verhält sie sich anderen gegenüber?
   – Verändern sich ihre Eigenschaften oder das Verhältnis zu anderen Figuren im Lauf der Geschichte? Wenn ja, wie?
   Beginne für jeden neuen Aspekt einen neuen Abschnitt und belege deine Ergebnisse mit Zitaten aus dem Text (mit Fundstellen).
3. Fasse die wichtigsten Aussagen zu der Figur nochmals kurz zusammen.

Listening skills

S13 Hörverstehen üben

Es ist immer sinnvoll, echte englischsprachige Texte anzuhören, z. B. Nachrichten, Podcasts oder Serien und Filme. Dabei ist es nicht schlimm, wenn du nicht jedes Wort verstehst. Dir wird außerdem auffallen, wie unterschiedlich die Aussprache je nach Herkunft des Sprechers / der Sprecherin sein kann. So gibt es neben Unterschieden zwischen britischem und amerikanischem Englisch auch innerhalb Großbritanniens und der USA verschiedene Dialekte oder regionale Akzente. Analog zum Leseverstehen (→ S5) können dir die folgenden Techniken helfen:

Listening for gist	Listening for detail
Welche Wörter / Themen kommen öfter vor und sind deshalb vermutlich besonders wichtig? Höre vor allem auf diese und fasse die wichtigsten Inhalte des Textes zusammen.	Nach welchen bestimmten Einzelheiten im Text wirst du gefragt? Höre besonders auf Wörter, die du in der Antwort erwartest, und die Informationen dazu.

Beim Hörverstehen hilft dir auch die Kenntnis von typischen Textsorten und Situationen. Überlege, worauf es beim Telefonieren, beim Dolmetschen, bei Präsentationen, Durchsagen, Radio- oder Fernsehsendungen ankommt und welche Themen jeweils zu erwarten sind. Achte beim Hören auf Geräusche sowie Stimme und Tonfall des Sprechers / der Sprecherin, auf Pausen und besonders betonte Wörter / Sätze. So kannst du Rückschlüsse auf die Stimmung der einzelnen Sprecher/-innen und der gesamten Situation ziehen. Bei einem Hörspiel spielen Geräusche und Musik eine wichtige Rolle, um Inhalt und Stimmung zu transportieren. In echten Gesprächssituationen können dir auch Gestik und Mimik das Verständnis erleichtern. Dies gilt ebenso für Filme (→ S19).

Speaking skills

S14 Gespräche führen

Mach dir vor einem Gespräch stets klar, um was für eine Situation es sich handelt (Formell oder informell? Kulturelle Unterschiede? Gesprächspartner älter oder jünger?) und passe deine Sprache entsprechend an.

1. Gespräch

Beginne freundlich, z. B. mit etwas, was euch beide verbindet (der Ort, die Situation usw.). Halte die Unterhaltung am Laufen. Wenn du etwas nicht sagen kannst, weil dir der nötige Wortschatz fehlt, versuche es zu umschreiben oder bitte deinen Gesprächspartner um Hilfe. Beende das **Gespräch** so freundlich, wie du es angefangen hast, und verabschiede dich. Vergiss nicht, dich zu bedanken, wenn du um Hilfe gebeten hast.

2. Dialog / Rollenspiel

Gib deinem **Dialogpartner**/deiner **Dialogpartnerin** immer das Gefühl, dass er/sie einbezogen wird. Dazu dienen *feedback phrases*, Nachfragen und *question tags* (*… you know.*/*… didn't you?*/*Guess what …!*).
Bei **Rollenspielen** musst du versuchen nachzufühlen, was die Person weiß, denkt und fühlt. Unterstütze deine Worte mit Mimik und Gestik.

3. Diskussion

In vielen Situationen des täglichen Lebens – im Klassenzimmer, mit Freunden, in der Familie – hast du es in **Diskussionen** mit unterschied-lichen Meinungen zu tun. Umso wichtiger ist es, Kompromisse zu finden. Die *Useful phrases* können dir helfen, typische Diskussionssituatio-nen zu meistern.

4. Debatte

Eine Debatte ist eine Sonderform der Diskus-sion, die bestimmten formalen Regeln folgt und häufig mit einer Abstimmung endet. Sowohl in Diskussionen als auch in Debatten hat auch der Moderator/die Moderatorin eine wichtige Rolle, indem er/sie dafür sorgt, dass die Regeln eingehalten werden und alle glei-chermaßen zu Wort kommen.

> **Useful phrases**
>
> **Asking for an opinion:** How do you feel about …? | What do you think about …?
> **Making a suggestion:** Why don't we …? | I've got an idea. Can we …? | If we did it this way, we could …
> **Agreeing:** Yes, we should do that. | I don't mind doing that.
> **Disagreeing:** You've got a point, but … | I don't think that's a good idea. It would be better to …
> **Finding a compromise:** Can we meet halfway? | If we did it this way, we could …
> **Moderator / Chairperson:** Would you please let X finish his/her statement? | Let's return to our original question. | We haven't heard X's opinion yet. | X, would you like to reply to this?

5. Interview

Überlege dir vor dem **Interview**, welche Fragen du zu deinem Gegenüber oder zum Thema stellen willst. Sei höflich, aber scheue dich nicht nachzufragen, wenn du etwas nicht sofort verstehst (*What was that you mentioned about …? Sorry, I didn't catch what you just said about …*). Achte bei den Fragen und Antworten auf die richtige Zeitform und das richtige Hilfsverb.

S15 Eine Präsentation vorbereiten und halten

Ob in der Schule oder später im Beruf: Eine gut vorbereitete und klar strukturierte Präsentation halten zu können, ist eine wichtige Fertigkeit.

Vorbereitung und Durchführung der Präsentation

1. Recherchiere Informationen zu deinem Thema (→ S3) und strukturiere sie, indem du z. B. eine Gliederung anlegst.
2. Überlege dir, mit welchem Material du deine Präsentation unterstützen willst. Gestalte dein Poster / deine Folie / dein Handout.
3. Bereite deine Präsentation vor, indem du nummerierte Karteikarten *(prompt cards)* anlegst, auf denen du dir die wichtigsten Punkte in Stichworten notierst.
4. Übe deine Präsentation zu Hause, aber lerne sie nicht auswendig. Stoppe die Zeit, die du brauchst, damit du bei deiner Präsentation nicht in Zeitnot gerätst.
5. Wenn du deine Präsentation hältst, achte darauf, dass du die Aufmerksamkeit aller Zuhörer / -innen hast. Sprich langsam und möglichst frei. Verwende deine *prompt cards* nur als Hilfestellung. Beende deine Präsentation mit einer kurzen Zusammenfassung der wichtigsten Punkte. Bedanke dich fürs Zuhören und frage nach, ob deine Zuhörer / -innen Fragen haben.

Useful phrases

- What I'm going to talk about is … | Today I'll talk about … | First I'd like to talk about … Then …
- On my poster you can see … | The mind map shows … | I've prepared a handout for you.
- That brings me to the end of my presentation. Thank you for listening / for your attention.
- I'll be happy to answer your questions now.

Handout

Ein Handout sollte nicht länger als eine Seite sein und die wichtigsten Punkte deiner Präsentation enthalten. Verwende dabei keinen ausformulierten Fließtext, sondern liste die wichtigsten Punkte stichwortartig auf. Vergiss nicht, die Quellen, die du für die Präsentation verwendet hast, anzugeben.

Digitale Tools

Wenn du deine Präsentation digital (z. B. durch Folien) unterstützen willst, können dir die folgenden Hinweise helfen:
- Mache dich mit den Grundfunktionen des Programms vertraut. Welche Möglichkeiten gibt es, um z. B. Bilder, Grafiken und Diagramme zu integrieren oder zu erstellen?
- Gib allgemeine Informationen (z. B. Titel, Seitenzahl, Name / Klasse) in der Kopf- oder Fußzeile an.
- Achte auf Lesbarkeit – packe nicht zu viel Inhalt auf eine Seite / Folie.
- Nutze Möglichkeiten der Formatierung (z. B. Schriftarten und -größen, Farben), um den Inhalt visuell zu unterstützen. Übertreibe dabei nicht – weniger ist mehr.
- Nutze die Rechtschreibprüfungsfunktion.

Mediation skills

S16 Bearbeitung von *Mediation*-Aufgaben

Mediation ist die Übertragung wichtiger Informationen aus einem gesprochenen oder geschriebenen Text in eine andere Sprache, z. B. aus dem Englischen ins Deutsche oder umgekehrt. Das machst du, wenn du bestimmte Aspekte aus einem Text für jemanden wiedergeben sollst, der die Sprache des Ausgangstexts nicht versteht. Gelegentlich kann es auch sein, dass du dolmetschen musst, also zwischen Gesprächspartnern vermittelst, die nicht dieselbe Sprache sprechen. Ganz wichtig: Es geht bei der *Mediation* niemals um eine wörtliche Übersetzung *(translation)*!

Lies dir die *Mediation*-Aufgabe gut durch und beachte besonders folgende Dinge:

Adressat / Adressatin:
Für wen ist die Information bestimmt?
→ Je nachdem, wer die Person ist und wie viel sie schon weiß, sprichst du sie unterschiedlich an.

Zweck:
Wozu benötigt die Person die Information?
→ Du musst nur die Informationen wiedergeben, die für den Adressaten / die Adressatin in der jeweiligen Situation wichtig sind. Alles andere – auch deine eigene Meinung – gehört nicht in den Mediation-Text. Es kann aber vorkommen, dass du Dinge zusätzlich erklären musst.

Ausgangstext

wichtige Info

Beispiel: Dein Ausgangstext ist die Infobroschüre eines Museums mit allen Öffnungszeiten und Eintrittspreisen. Wenn dein Gegenüber dich fragt, ob das Museum *heute* geöffnet ist, solltest du nicht sagen, wann es sonst noch geöffnet oder geschlossen ist. Will die Person den Eintrittspreis wissen, kommt es auf ihr Alter an und darauf, ob sie allein oder mit einer Gruppe unterwegs ist.

Einen schriftlichen Ausgangstext kannst du in Ruhe durchlesen und die wichtigen Informationen auswählen. Dabei helfen dir die Techniken zum Umgang mit Texten (→ **S5**) sowie zum Erschließen von neuen Wörtern (→ **S1**). Formuliere die entsprechenden Inhalte so, dass der Adressat / die Adressatin sie gut verstehen kann.

Bei einer Dolmetschaufgabe wird eine echte mündliche Gesprächssituation simuliert. Deshalb musst du schneller reagieren, um möglichst viel von dem sinngemäß wiederzugeben, was die Gesprächspartner zueinander sagen.

Wenn dir ein Wort in der Zielsprache nicht einfällt, umschreibe es mit anderen Worten *(paraphrasing)*. Beachte bei der schriftlichen und mündlichen Bearbeitung von *Mediation*-Aufgaben außerdem die Tipps unter *Writing* (→ **S7–S9**) und *Speaking* (→ **S14**, **S15**).

Useful phrases

- It's somebody / a person who …
- It's something that you use to …
- It's a place that / where …
- It's the same as … | It's the opposite of …

Dealing with visuals and films

S17 Bildbeschreibung

Wenn du aufgefordert wirst, ein Bild zu beschreiben, solltest du Folgendes beachten:

1. Benenne, um welche Art Bild es sich handelt, und, falls bekannt, wer es wann wozu angefertigt hat.
2. Beschreibe zuerst das Thema des Bildes und dann, wo sich was genau befindet und wie es aussieht.
3. Beschreibe ablaufende Vorgänge oder Handlungen stets im *present progressive*.
4. Wenn es gefragt ist, sage etwas über die Wirkung des Bildes und äußere ggf. Vermutungen darüber, was es ausdrücken soll und zu welchem Zweck es angefertigt wurde.

> **Useful phrases**
>
> **Describing pictures:**
> - At the top / bottom you can see …
> - In the foreground / background / middle / center / On the left / right there is / are …
> - In front of / Behind / Between / Next to …
> - The people in the photo are talking / having fun / celebrating / fighting …
>
> **Analysing pictures:**
> - The colours / … create an atmosphere of …
> - The picture is interesting / boring / exciting… because …
> - The photo shows … / represents …
> - The photo tries to show … but I think a photo with … would work better because …

Beim Beschreiben und Analysieren eines **Cartoons** ist es besonders wichtig, auf die Kombination von Bild und Text zu achten. Karikaturisten verwenden häufig Stilmittel wie Ironie *(irony)* und Übertreibung *(exaggeration)*, um ihre Aussage zu verdeutlichen.

background

behi[nd]

in th[e]
centr[e]

on th[e]
right

top left-hand / bottom left-hand corner

foreground

S18 Statistiken auswerten

Mit Diagrammen lässt sich eine Vielzahl von Informationen auf sehr kleinem Raum zusammenfassen. Häufig sind die folgenden Diagrammtypen, die jeweils einen anderen Schwerpunkt haben:

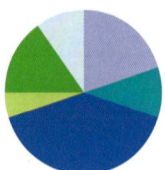

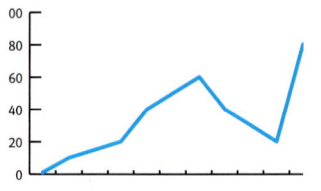

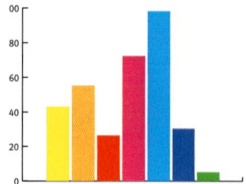

Mit einem Kuchendiagramm *(pie chart)* lassen sich Prozentzahlen darstellen, ausgehend vom gesamten Kreis (= 100 %).

Ein Kurvendiagramm *(line graph)* stellt eine Entwicklung über einen längeren Zeitraum hinweg dar.

Ein Säulen- oder Balkendiagramm *(bar graph)* nutzt du, um Zahlen direkt miteinander zu vergleichen.

Wenn du deine Auswertung eines Diagramms präsentieren sollst, gehe schrittweise vor:

1. Sage zunächst, um welche Art von Diagramm es sich handelt und was es darstellt. Vergiss nicht, die Quelle und das Jahr der Veröffentlichung zu nennen.
2. Beschreibe, was du aus dem Diagramm ablesen kannst.
3. Fasse die wichtigsten Aussagen des Diagramms in 1–2 Sätzen zusammen.

> **Useful phrases**
>
> – The table / bar graph / line graph / pie chart / … was published by … in …
> – It's about … / deals with …
> – The majority / minority of … | Half of … | Most of … | 30 percent of the people …
> – The number of … has (slightly / considerably) increased / grown / risen / decreased / fallen / hasn't changed.
> – The numbers / figures show / suggest that …
> – We can draw the conclusion that …

S19 Wichtige filmische Mittel

Um den Inhalt eines Films – d.h. das Setting *(setting)*, den Schauplatz *(location)*, die Handlung *(plot)* und die Figuren *(characters)* – zu verstehen, helfen dir die Techniken, die du vom Lese- und Hörverstehen kennst (→ **S5**, **S12**, **S13**). Achte zusätzlich auf die typischen filmischen Mittel:

– **Setting und Figuren:** Achte darauf, wie über Landschaften, Gebäude, Innenräume, Kleidung und Gegenstände der Handlungsort und die Handlungszeit dargestellt werden und ob diese Darstellung stimmig ist. Untersuche auch die Figuren des Films genau: Wie stellen die Schauspieler/-innen den Charakter der Personen dar, die sie verkörpern? Wie drücken sie Gefühle aus? Hier spielen vor allem Sprache, Mimik und Gestik eine wichtige Rolle, aber auch Kleidung, Frisuren und andere Requisiten.

– Ein Film erzählt eine Geschichte mit Worten, aber auch mit Bildern, Geräuschen, Licht, Farben und Musik. Diese **audiovisuellen Effekte** *(audio-visual effects)* schaffen eine ganz bestimmte Atmosphäre *(atmosphere)* und verstärken damit die Wirkung des Gesehenen. So wird z.B. eine Actionszene meist mit schneller, lauter Musik unterlegt, eine romantische Szene eher mit ruhiger, leiser Musik. Achte darauf, wie die Musik den Inhalt des Films unterstützt, also wann welche Musik ertönt und wann sie wechselt.

– Die **Kameraeinstellung** *(shot)* beeinflusst, wie wir Szenen wahrnehmen. Je nachdem, ob Personen oder Objekte als Nahaufnahme *(close-up)*, aus der mittleren Distanz *(medium shot)* oder als Totale *(long shot)* aufgenommen sind, hat eine Szene eine andere Wirkung.

Long shot

Medium shot

Close-up

– Ähnlich wie Erzähltexte haben Filme ganz spezifische Mittel, um **Spannung** *(suspense)* zu erzeugen. Dazu gehören Musik, Licht, Geräusche und natürlich die Gestik und Mimik der Schauspieler/-innen. Achte auch auf Andeutungen späterer Ereignisse oder Rückblenden.

Spannung kann außerdem über die Kamerabewegung *(camera movement)* erzeugt werden. So werden Überraschungs- oder Schockeffekte häufig durch schnelle Kamerabewegungen oder plötzliches Heranzoomen erzeugt.

– **Besetzung der Rollen** *(cast):* Ist die Darstellung der Schauspieler/-innen überzeugend?

Cooperative learning

S20 Ausgewählte Methoden der kooperativen Arbeit

1. Think – Pair – Share

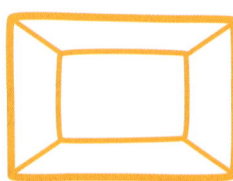

1. *Think:* Du sammelst still mögliche Lösungen zu der Aufgabe. Du kannst deine Ideen in Stichpunkten notieren.
2. *Pair:* Zusammen mit deinem Partner / deiner Partnerin besprichst du leise deine gesammelten Ideen.
3. *Share:* Teilt euren Mitschüler/-innen im Klassengespräch die Ergebnisse eurer Partnerarbeit mit.

Variante: *Placemat* in Vierergruppen

2. Milling around (Marktplatz)

Du gehst durch das Klassenzimmer, erfragst von deinen Mitschüler/-innen bestimmte Informationen und gibst auch selbst Auskunft. Versuche mit möglichst vielen Mitschüler/-innen zu sprechen und verschiedene Informationen zu sammeln. Ihr könnt auch ein Signal vereinbaren, zu dem ihr euren Gesprächspartner / eure Gesprächspartnerin wechselt.

3. Inside outside circle (Kugellager)

1. Bildet zwei Stuhlkreise, einen inneren und einen äußeren.
2. Setzt euch in den Stuhlkreisen so hin, dass immer ein Schüler / eine Schülerin des äußeren und des inneren Stuhlkreises sich gegenüber sitzen.
3. Stellt euch gegenseitig eure Fragen und beantwortet diese.
4. Rutscht im inneren oder äußeren Kreis nach dem Ende der Gesprächsrunde einen Platz weiter und beginnt ein neues Gespräch.

4. Bus stop (Lerntempoduett)

Sobald du deine Aufgabe fertig bearbeitet hast, gehst du zu einem vereinbarten Treffpunkt, dem *bus stop*. Dort wartest du auf den nächsten Mitschüler / die nächste Mitschülerin, der / die fertig ist, und zusammen besprecht und vergleicht ihr eure Lösungen. Anschließend verlasst ihr den *bus stop* und bearbeitet die nächste Aufgabe.

5. Gallery walk (Museumsgang)

1. *Group work:* In der Gruppe erarbeitet ihr ein Thema und haltet euer Ergebnis, z.B. auf einem Poster, fest. Die Ergebnisse werden dann ausgestellt, wie in einer Galerie.
2. *Gallery walk:* Es werden neue Gruppen gebildet. In jeder Gruppe ist ein Mitglied jeder Ausgangsgruppe. Jede Gruppe betrachtet die verschiedenen Ergebnisse der Gruppenarbeiten. Jeder präsentiert nun in der neuen Gruppe das Ergebnis seiner Ausgangsgruppe.

6. Balloon debate (Ballondebatte)

Stellt euch vor, ihr sitzt in einem Heißluftballon, der Luft verliert und abzustürzen droht. Damit wenigstens eine Person überleben kann, müssen alle anderen herausspringen. Dafür erläutert ihr nacheinander mit einem kurzen Redebeitrag, warum die Person / Figur, die ihr darstellt, „überleben" sollte. Die Zuschauer können jeweils Fragen zu eurer Person / Figur stellen. Am Ende stimmt das Publikum ab, wer „überlebt".

S21 Gemeinsame Projektarbeit

Wenn ihr gemeinsam, also kollaborativ, ein Projekt erarbeitet, können euch verschiedene Apps und digitale Tools helfen – von der ersten Ideensammlung bis zur fertigen Präsentation lassen sich viele Schritte online erledigen. Ein besonderer Vorteil ist, dass alle Gruppenmitglieder jederzeit Zugriff auf alle Informationen haben und sie ergänzen können. Verschiedene Arten von Tools, Apps oder Visualisierungsformen eignen sich für verschiedene Arbeitsschritte. Natürlich kann es sich je nach Thema oder Projektzeitraum auch anbieten, Arbeitsschritte analog auszuführen bzw. analoge und digitale Tools zu kombinieren.

Arbeitsschritt	Digitale Tools	Analoge Tools
1. Treffen organisieren und Aufgaben verteilen	Konferenztools / Chat-Apps / Checklist-Tools	Treffen direkt ausmachen / Liste mit Aufgaben führen
2. Ideensammlung	Schreibprogramme / Kollaborationsplattformen / Mindmapping-Tools	Papier und Stifte
3. Informationsbeschaffung	Suchmaschinen	Bücher / Zeitschriften
4. Schreibprozess	Kollaborative Schreibprogramme (gemeinsames Schreiben und Überarbeiten) / Storytelling-Tools zur Umsetzung kreativer Ideen	Themen werden aufgeteilt und einzeln bearbeitet, zur Korrektur weitergeben
5. Präsentation	Präsentationsprogramm / Video(-clips) / Audios / Interaktive Tafel / Beamer	Folien / Plakat / Flipchart / Stifte

Bei umfangreicheren Projekten empfiehlt es sich, zu Beginn klar festzulegen, wer welche Aufgaben übernimmt. Zusätzlich können folgende Rollen dabei helfen, das Projektziel konsequent zu verfolgen und die Arbeit rechtzeitig zum Abschluss zu bringen.

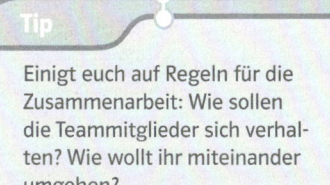

Tip

Einigt euch auf Regeln für die Zusammenarbeit: Wie sollen die Teammitglieder sich verhalten? Wie wollt ihr miteinander umgehen?

- **Zeitwächter/-in (*time keeper*):** Stellt die Einhaltung der vorgegebenen Arbeitszeit sicher, erstellt einen Zeitplan.
- **Protokollant/-in (*secretary*):** Hält Ideen und (Zwischen-)Ergebnisse fest.
- **Moderator/-in (*moderator*):** Achtet auf Einhaltung der Kommunikationsregeln.
- **Vortragende (*presenters*):** Visualisieren Ergebnisse, strukturieren die Präsentation, beantworten Verständnisfragen, bereiten Diskussionsfragen vor.

Grammar

Introduction

As you can see, the grammar section in this book is in English. This should not cause you any problems since you are now so familiar with the language and know all the grammatical terms.

What is also different from previous books is that this section not only provides grammar rules, it also contains all the grammar exercises in this book. There are no grammar exercises in the Units but references to the Grammar whenever there are some useful grammar examples in a text (→ G). They refer you to one or more paragraphs in the Grammar where you will find the most important rules and some exercises.

The Grammar section deals with a number of important areas of grammar that are often a source of mistakes for language learners. They are arranged according to their function: Talking about the past, Expressing conditions and consequences etc.

The exercises and rules will help you to revise these basic structures either in class or on your own. If you want to revise on your own, a good idea would be to look at recent English tests or homework that your teacher has corrected and make a list of your most common mistakes. If, for example, you often get conditional sentences wrong or find it difficult to differentiate between the different past tenses, you can turn to the relevant pages in the Grammar.

You will notice that parts A to F follow the same pattern, which is explained here:

Step 1: Test yourself

These exercises are fairly easy and straightforward, and they will enable you to see how well you know a particular structure and the way it works. You can check your answers on page 252.

If you have got any of the answers wrong or if you find that you are at all unsure, you should go on to look at the Basic rules and then try one or two of the Practice exercises.

If you don't have any difficulties with a particular grammar point, you can concentrate on a different one.

Step 2: Basic rules

These rules only cover the most essential grammar points. The rules are in simple English and the examples show you typical ways in which these structures are used. If you need more systematic or more detailed information on any of these structures, you should consult a grammar book.

Step 3: Practice

This part consists of a number of different communicative exercises, from relatively straightforward exercises at the beginning to more demanding ones later on. In some exercises you are asked to spot the mistake or explain your choice of grammatical structure, so it can be helpful to refer to the Basic rules again. In the more open and creative exercises you have the opportunity to bring in the structures you have revised in as natural a way as possible.

Grammatical terms

Grammatical term	Example	Paragraph
adjective	This is an **easy** exercise. That one looks **difficult**.	**G7**
adverb	**Actually**, you have to look at it more **closely**.	**G7**
adverbial	I did my homework **in the kitchen after lunch yesterday**.	**G7, G8**
aspect	I **read** the paper every day. I **'m reading** the paper just now.	**G1**
conditional sentences	It **would help** slowing down climate change **if we reduced** the number of flights.	**G6**
dynamic verb	He **was running** incredibly fast.	**G1**
future tenses	I **'m going to study** biotechnology, but I think it **won't be** easy.	**G5**
gerund constructions	**Growing up** means more responsibilities. **Instead of complaining**, we started to work.	**G10**
indirect speech	He **said** that he **needed** more time.	**G4**
-ing form or participle with a subject of its own	The teacher didn't mind **the students using** a dictionary. The reviews resulted in **the film being cut** differently for the German market. **All things considered**, it is difficult to reach a simple decision. **The rain having stopped**, we went outside.	**G12**
modal auxiliaries	**Are** we **supposed to** sit here? This **must** be the waiting room. Or **should** we stay outside?	**G3**
participle constructions	**Having arrived**, we first had to check in.	**G11**
passive	The wall **was built** after the village **had been founded**.	**G13**
past tense	I **rang** her yesterday. While I **was talking** to her on the telephone, she **arrived** at her office.	**G2, G4**
past perfect	We **had been watching** the film for a while when we realised that we **had seen** it before.	**G2, G4**
present perfect	My parents **have been married** for five years. They **have been living** in Manchester since they moved in together.	**G2**
present tense	I **get up** early every morning. My bus **leaves** at seven.	**G5**
relative clause	Mr Smith was the man **the witness had accused**. His sister, **who studied law**, helped him to write the letter.	**G9**
stative verb	We **have known** each other for a long time, and I really **like** him.	**G1**

A Talking about the past

Test yourself

Complete the dialogue between two friends with the correct verb forms.

Joe: Where (**1** you be)? I (**2** wait) for you for almost an hour. You said you (**3** be) here by 4:30. What (**4** happen)?

Lisa: I'm so sorry. I (**5** miss) the bus because I (**6** meet) Ron when I (**7** walk) to the bus stop. He (**8** stop) me and (**9** ask) me where I (**10** go).

Joe: Who (**11** be) Ron? How long (**12** you know) him?

Lisa: I (**13** get to know) him at the debating club three weeks ago. He (**14** only move) here from Glasgow and somebody (**15** must) show him around.

Joe: I (**16** see). (**17** You like) him?

Lisa: Oh Joe, you (**18** get) on my nerves! You (**19** not need) to be jealous!

Basic rules

G1 Aspect

It **has been raining** all day. Look, the boys **are playing** football!	Most English verbs are **dynamic** (e.g. *sing, walk, grow*). Use them in the **progressive** form to stress that an activity or event is or was in progress. Otherwise, use them in the **simple** form.
Do you **understand** what I mean? I **love** chocolate!	**Stative** verbs describe 'states': *know, belong, cost, be* etc. They are normally only used in the **simple** form.

❗ *For* and *since*
- *For* is used for a period of time: *I've known him **for** three years now.*
- *Since* is used for a point in time: *They've been playing **since** 4 o'clock.*

G2 Tenses referring to the past

Present perfect	
She **has** already **seen** the film three times. She **has switched** her phone off.	Use it to stress the result of an activity / event. Often with: *already, (not) yet, so far, ever, never.*
She **has been surfing** the internet for hours.	Use it for an activity / event that began in the past and has continued until now. Often with: *for, since.*

Past tense	
We **read** some Sherlock Holmes stories at school last year.	Use it for an activity / event that began and ended in the past. Often with: *last …, … ago, yesterday, when, in 2021 etc.*
The doorbell rang while I **was having** a shower.	Use it for an activity / event that was in progress in the past. Often with: *while.*
Past perfect	
When the McDonalds **had lost** the battle, their chief was taken prisoner.	Use it for an activity / event that happened before another activity / event in the past. Often with: *after, before, when.*
They **had been sleeping** for some hours when they were woken by a strange sound.	Use it for an activity / event that was in progress before another activity in the past. Often with: *for, since.*

G3   Modal auxiliaries referring to the past

It **could** happen any time. She **was able to** control the situation. They **weren't permitted to** speak. They **had to** keep calm. They **should have been allowed** to say what they think.	Use modal auxiliaries to add additional meaning to the main verb of a sentence, e.g. possibility, ability, permission or obligation. Most modal auxiliaries have substitute forms for referring to the past.

G4   Reported (indirect) speech

He said he **had checked** the conditions the day before and there **were** still some risks. He asked them **if** they **were** ready to cooperate. He said they **would** have to be careful during the following weeks. He asked them **to watch out**.	With an introductory verb in the past tense or past perfect, a backshift of the tenses in the reported sentence is necessary. For Yes / No questions, use *if* or *whether.* For requests and commands, use the infinitive with *to.*

❗ Remember to change **pronouns** and **adverbs / adverbials** in reported speech.

"I have checked"	⟶	He said he had checked
here, now	⟶	there, then
yesterday	⟶	the day before
two weeks ago	⟶	two weeks before
last year	⟶	the previous year

Practice

EXERCISE **1** A history quiz

Use the ideas to ask and answer questions.

1. where – Mary Queen of Scots – be brought up? (France)
2. why – she – return – to Scotland? (her French husband die)
3. how long – she – live – as a prisoner – when – she – finally – be executed? (19 years)
4. since when – Scotland – be united – with England? (1707)
5. when – Congress – abolish – slavery – in the USA? (1865)
6. what – Rosa Parks – do – on a bus in Montgomery on 1 December, 1955? (ride home)
7. why – she – be arrested? (refuse to give up her seat to a white person)
8. what – Martin Luther King Jr. – be remembered for? (be a famous civil rights leader)
9. when – Black people in the US – officially – get – the same rights as white people? (1968)

EXERCISE **2** An interview with a pop star

You have watched an interview with a pop star. Use indirect speech to report what she said.

1. I was a very lonely child because I grew up without any sisters or brothers.
2. So I spent a lot of time on my own.
3. I'm very grateful to my mum because she bought me a guitar for my 8th birthday.
4. I soon realised that I didn't want to go to college but to become a musician.
5. Mum never asked: Is this a good idea?
6. She has always believed in me.
7. It was hard at first, but I had a breakthrough hit three years ago.
8. Every radio station across the country has been playing my hits since then.
9. Last year I toured Australia and Japan, and my latest song has been in the US charts for 18 weeks.
10. I'm sure there will be a number one hit by me one day!

EXERCISE **3** The rivalry between Glasgow and Edinburgh

Decide whether the underlined forms are correct or not. Correct the mistakes.

In 2013, Scottish professor Robert Crawford **1** has published a book on the two biggest cities in Scotland, Glasgow and Edinburgh. He thinks that the rivalry between the two cities which **2** had been going on **3** since centuries **4** may have started when they **5** have disagreed over bread-baking in 1656. After the town council of Glasgow **6** criticised the quality of the bread Glaswegian bakers **7** were baking, two bakers from Edinburgh **8** were offering to bake better bread for Glasgow, claiming that their bread **9** was being better because Edinburgh standards **10** had been higher. Much **11** has been written about the differences between Glasgow and Edinburgh **12** since the 17th century, and there **13** was no other pair of cities in the UK which **14** can be compared to them because they **15** have been competing in all kinds of fields, unlike, for example, Oxford and Cambridge, whose rivalry **16** was limited to competition between their universities. According to Professor Crawford, one **17** must admit that both Glasgow and Edinburgh **18** had a lot to offer and Scotland **19** will be missing something if the rivalry **20** has ever stopped.

EXERCISE **2** Looking back at history

Talk about what would be different today if things had been different in the past.

Example: If Gutenberg hadn't invented a new printing technology, Martin Luther wouldn't have been able to publish his translation of the Bible.

1. Elizabeth I encouraged the work of explorers and scientists.
2. Spanish conquerors reintroduced horses to the American continent.
3. The Boston Tea Party started a revolution in the colonies on the East Coast.
4. Native Americans were driven from their land.
5. The Union Army won the American Civil War.
6. Suffragettes fought for the right to vote for women.
7. Alexander Fleming discovered that penicillin can kill bacteria.
8. The music Black people in the US made became very popular.

EXERCISE **3** Learning from mistakes

Students organised a charity project which has just ended with a big bazaar.
They are evaluating the project and planning the next one. Think of ideas and arguments to complete their statements. Use suitable verb forms.

Points of criticism and comments / ideas:
1. The team was too small. If more people …
2. Nobody was responsible for the communication between the teams. If somebody …
3. Roles and jobs in the team should have been assigned clearly. If everybody …
4. We didn't start advertising the bazaar early enough. If we …
5. When Maya was ill, nobody knew what to do. If there …
6. We didn't expect such a big demand for self-made cakes. If we …
7. We were left with a lot of old and damaged clothes that couldn't be sold. If we …

Ideas for the future
1. We need to get a better picture of what people want to buy. If we …
2. None of us has a driving licence. If …
3. We have learned that … if…
4. We know now that we … if … (give three ideas for improvement)

EXERCISE **4** Everything will be all right

Politicians are asked for their position on the issues below. Choose three of the issues and write what the politicians could say about them (about 120 words). Think of what went wrong in the past, what could be different and what conclusions they draw.

Example: In my opinion, … If we hadn't …, we wouldn't be in that situation now. If we want to reduce …, we'll have to put restrictions on some activities. There would be … if the taxes on … were higher.

| energy | mobility | taxes | environment | jobs | education | health | housing |

D Describing and commenting

Test yourself

a) *Use adjectives or adverbs to describe these people and their actions.*

1. **nice:** Bob is a `1` person. He looks `2` . He says things `3` . He acts `4` .
2. **hard:** Natalie is very ambitious. Her face is `5` . Her voice sounds `6` although she works `7` to make it sound less `8` . You will `9` ever catch her doing nothing.
3. **sad:** `10` , Amy's dog died yesterday. She told me because I asked her why she looked so `11` . That's why she's been looking out of the window so `12` for hours.

b) *Add the information from the second column to the sentence in the first column.*
Decide what kind of relative clause you need.

1. The guitarist plays extremely well.
2. Mr McGregor plays in the same band.
3. I talked to a man in the audience.
4. They started with a well-known song.

A. I saw him at the concert last week.
B. He is our English teacher.
C. His daughter is the lead singer.
D. That was a good idea.

Basic rules

G7 Adjective or adverb?

He's an **excellent** musician. That was the **greatest** concert he's ever played. It sounded **gigantic**.	Use adjectives to describe what someone or something is like.
The music began **quietly**, then it became **very** exciting, and it ended **quite dramatically**. **Fortunately**, we had the chance to see as well as hear the performance from here.	Use adverbs to describe the way something is done, to modify adjectives (very exciting) and other adverbs (quite dramatically). Use adverbs of comment to comment on a whole sentence.

🛑 Don't use **adjectives** to describe the way something is done. ~~He can talk good.~~

G8 Position of adverbs and adverbials

Front position	**After the war**, there had to be a new beginning. **Today**, communication is different because of the internet. **Obviously**, it's much quicker than a hundred years ago.	Use adverbs and adverbials of time and place (e.g. this morning, in London) in front position for emphasis. Use adverbs of comment in front position.

Mid position	We would **never** have expected it, but things were **slowly** beginning to change.	Use adverbs of frequency and adverbs of manner in mid position unless you want to emphasise them (→ **G15**).
End position	She's a lawyer and works very **hard**. She never leaves her office **in Edinburgh before 7 o'clock**.	Use adverbs of manner in end position (after verb and object). Use adverbs and adverbials of time and place in end position (place before time).

- Don't use **adverbs / adverbials** of time or place in mid position.
  ~~I had the day before done the shopping.~~
- Never put an **adverb / adverbial** between a verb and its object.
  ~~She loves really rock music.~~

G9 Relative clauses

Defining relative clauses	
Elvis Presley was one of the white people **who made rock 'n' roll popular**. Hip hop is the musical genre **that originated in urban Black communities in the 1970s and 80s**.	Use defining relative clauses to give information that is necessary to complete the meaning of the main clause. Use *who*, *that* and *whose* as relative pronouns for people. Use *which*, *that* and *whose* for things.
The blues developed out of music **(that) the slaves created** in the Southeast of the US.	You may leave out the relative pronoun if it is the object of the relative clause (= contact clause).
Non-defining relative clauses	
The Beatles, **who were among the first Europeans to play rock 'n' roll**, were a band from Liverpool. Hip hop, **which is the name of a musical genre as well as of a subculture**, was created in urban Black communities. The music industry has commercialised hip hop, **which means some artists have become very rich**.	Use non-defining relative clauses to add extra information which is not necessary to understand the meaning of the main clause. Never use *that* as a relative pronoun in non-defining relative clauses. Use *which* to comment on a whole main clause.

- Never add commas between main clause and defining relative clause.
- Always add commas – and a pause in speaking – between main clause and non-defining relative clause.

Practice

EXERCISE **1** Reflecting on self-esteem

Decide on an adjective or adverb that fits in the text.

I've played the guitar since I was a child. I don't think I'm a `1` player, but my parents say I play `2` `3`. `4`, I didn't believe them as they are my parents. Parents always think their child does everything `5` than other people's children. But I've been trying `6` to become a `7` player. I take lessons `8` and I practise every day – well, `9` every day. `10` year I started playing in a band, and we've just had our first gig. I had worked on my own solo for a song everyone knows, and it was `11` `12` to create something `13` `14` and to learn to play it, but `15` it sounded `16`: The audience `17` liked it and screamed for more! I'm so `18` now, I think I'm the `19` person in the world! I've `20` realised that my parents have been right in telling me to become `21` and to believe in my own strengths.

EXERCISE **2** The difficulties of climate policies

Change the sentences A–F into relative clauses and add them to the text in the right places. Add commas where necessary. Leave out the relative pronoun if possible.

Confronted with the global climate crisis, governments are looking for solutions `1` `2`. There may be some options `3`, but according to scientists like Eugene Wolff `4` they could only be achieved if the global community cooperated to an extent as yet unknown. People from different countries `5` would have to agree on a set of common goals `6`.

A He works for the influential Green Energy Institute in Wessex.
B It would secure a sufficient supply of energy for the needs of a growing world population.
C It sounds like trying the impossible.
D They control different resources and don't necessarily share the same beliefs or values
E They would give them top priority.
F They provide climate protection and prosperity at the same time.

EXERCISE **3** Should politics try to influence language?

Add the given words and clauses in the right places and decide when you need to change adjectives into adverbs.

(`1` **obvious**) One of the basic and most important functions of language is to represent the real world its speakers live in. (`2` **serious**) No one would doubt that it serves to describe people, animals and things, what they do and what happens to them. (`3` **furthermore | true**) It can even be used to describe what is not in the real world but what could be imagined, what could be or what people wish to come. (`4` **general**) Thus, it is agreed by linguists that language is not only influenced by reality, but there is also an impact of language on reality. (`5` **exciting**) This is where the matter gets. It is the chicken and egg problem.

(`6` **who fight against the discrimination of women or minorities | inferior | visible | actual**) Activists often argue that as long as language treats particular groups as or does not make them at all, there will be no change in the way these groups are treated in the real world. (**7** **recent | social | who accuse others of using racist or sexist language and want to see political action against what they consider problematic language use | who argue that language change cannot and should not be forced by politics**) Tensions have been building on media between people on the one hand and people on the other.

(**8** **abrupt**) It is true that, even with the best intentions, you cannot make language users change the way they speak or write, but language change has always happened and will always happen. (**9** **in fact | which have standardised language**) And there have been examples of state-controlled language institutions, especially written language, by prescribing rules to make communication easier.

(**10** **normal | slow | gradual**) Language change is a process which happens and over time. (**11** **that make us change our use of language much more quickly**) Yet there are sometimes events or developments in the real world, for example globalisation or digitalisation and the rise of the internet.

(**12** **moreover | historical | they represent**) Our reassessment of events has caused us to ban certain words from our vocabulary together with the concepts.

(**13** **fortunate | in which there is no general agreement on which terms may still be used**)

There is no arguing in some very clear cases, especially when it comes to addressing people of minority groups directly, as it is a matter of respect and politeness in personal interaction, but there are grey areas, and in which contexts. (**14** **original | historical**) For example, there is a controversy on whether texts and texts about events should be adapted to our new perspective or if they should not be touched.

(**15** **hurt | in which their ethnical group is referred to by a term that is not acceptable any longer but that was accepted at the time**) Although some people feel when they read older texts, it can be questioned whether it would not be easier for future generations to understand the difficult realities of the past and to learn about mistakes that were made in history if they were allowed to confront with the reality represented in the original language and compare it with the situation today.

(**16** **probable**) One possible solution could be to leave the texts uncensored and add a comment from a contemporary perspective.

E Linking ideas

Test yourself

Link the given ideas without using complete subordinate clauses.
Choose suitable linking words if necessary.

1. The charity bazaar was a wonderful event. (It was organised by our school.)
2. People donated things they didn't need any longer. (They helped us to raise a lot of money.)
3. We could give a big sum to the rainforest project. (We had got a lot of donations.)
4. We would love to do it again next year. (It was a lot of work.)

Basic rules

G10 Gerund constructions

He answered **without thinking** twice. **Instead of reading** the article herself, she asked me to summarise it. **Apart from waiting** for the rain to stop, we can't do much.	Use gerund constructions to link ideas if there are no corresponding subordinate clauses.

G11 Participle constructions

Participles shortening relative clauses	
The young man **playing the guitar** is my new boyfriend. = The young man **who is playing** the guitar is … All the songs **written by him** have become big hits. = All the songs **which / that were written by him** …	You can use participle constructions instead of relative clauses. Use present participles instead of active verb forms and past participles instead of passive verb forms.

Participles or gerunds shortening adverbial clauses	
Realising that his competitor was catching up, he started to run faster. = **When he realised** that his competitor was catching up, … **Having finished** breakfast, he put his plate in the dishwasher. = **When / After he had finished** breakfast, … She waved to us **while singing** and **dancing**. = She waved to us **while she was singing and dancing**. **Despite sending** several messages, he hadn't received an answer. = **Although he had sent** several messages, he hadn't …	You can use participle or gerund constructions instead of adverbial clauses.

❗ Don't use **participles** with no noun to refer to. ~~Walking in the park, the sun was shining.~~

G12 *-ing* forms with subjects of their own

She hates **people spreading** fake news. He doesn't mind **me / my borrowing** his tablet.	It isn't clear whether the *-ing* form in this kind of construction is a gerund or a participle.
His anger rising, he jumped up and ran outside. Wacken has become one of the largest heavy metal festivals **with about 80,000 fans getting together** every year.	This kind of construction is rather formal, unless it is introduced by *with*.

Practice

EXERCISE **1** A success story

Turn two sentences into one by linking the ideas with a participle or gerund construction.
There may be more than one solution.

1. His father died early. He grew up with his mother in relative poverty.
2. His mother recognised his potential. She worked hard to send him to school.
3. School was difficult for him at first. The other children bullied him.
4. But he didn't give up. He worked even harder.
5. He was a very good pupil. He was encouraged by his teachers.
6. He finished school. Then he got a scholarship at a good university.
7. He has written various successful books. He is internationally famous today.
8. He has written novels. He has also written poetry.

EXERCISE **2** Young people's problems and social media

Change these statements from an information brochure about young people's mental health problems using participle constructions.

1. When young people in Scotland were asked what they considered the biggest issue for teenagers at the moment, most of them named mental health.
2. If you look at statistics, teenagers today seem more likely to develop mental disorders than 30 years ago.
3. Surveys that have been conducted over the last couple of decades show that these problems have become worse since social media emerged.
4. About 30 percent of teenagers are worried about their bodies. This is a very alarming figure.
5. They want to be liked, so teenagers often go to extremes to fulfil what they think are general beauty standards.
6. Because they are convinced they are not beautiful enough, they start to change their behaviour.
7. Many of them want to shape their bodies, so they overdo workouts at the gym and develop serious eating disorders.
8. They compare themselves with others. They think they will never be good enough.
9. Some get depressed because of the constant pressure. This can be one of the consequences for them.
10. It may be the only solution to seek professional advice or even psychotherapy if they feel so bad that they hurt themselves or think of suicide.
11. Some parents are convinced that social media have created all these problems. They want to limit their children's use of the internet.
12. Some people put the blame on digitalisation because social media has made the issues more visible.
13. If you consider the spread of information on social media today, everyone is bound to be confronted with the problem.
14. However, there are some examples, like the body positivity movement. They show that social media may even help people overcome their problems.
15. Influencers who fight unhealthy beauty standards can also help.
16. If we look at all the facts, we will have to learn to live with the dangers of social media.

EXERCISE **3** **A yearbook contribution**

Write a short yearbook article (about 150 words) on a famous person who is connected with the topics you have dealt with in the current school year and who has impressed you (e.g. a Scottish inventor or scientist, a politician or a pop music artist). Include biographical facts (family, education etc.) and information on his/her achievements. State why you wrote about him/her.

F Focus on the passive

Test yourself

Shift the focus in these sentences by putting them in the passive.

1. The police arrested Rosa Parks in Montgomery in December 1955.
2. The bus driver had told her to give up her seat.
3. The driver had called the police.
4. After the incident, Black leaders organised a bus boycott to protest segregation.

Basic rules

G13 Active versus passive

The poor guy **is** always **made fun of** by his fellow students.	Use the passive if you want to emphasise that something happens to somebody / something or that something is done, but you don't know or don't want to mention who did it.
These giant stone circles **were constructed** thousands of years ago.	

Practice

EXERCISE **1** **A very special musical instrument**

Put the statements into the passive.

1. People usually associate the bagpipes with Scotland.
2. People have made lots of jokes about the Scots and their bagpipes.
3. But the Scots did not invent the bagpipes.
4. In Middle Eastern texts writers mentioned bagpipes more than 2,000 years ago.
5. Nero, the Roman Emperor, also played the bagpipes.
6. In the Middle Ages people played the bagpipes all over Europe.
7. People have mainly used them in folk music since the 19th century.
8. People are still playing different kinds of bagpipes in Europe, North Africa and Turkey.
9. But it's the Scottish bagpipes that people know all over the world.

EXERCISE **2** Tourism in Scotland

Put the marked sentences and clauses in this text about tourism in Scotland into the passive.

Scotland is a country that is popular with tourists. Most of them come from the UK, but international tourism is also an important factor in Scotland's economy. **1 Before 2020, international visitors spent about £2 billion in Scotland per year**.

Scotland has many attractions to offer: lively cities, vast open landscapes, historical sites, old traditions and friendly people. It is famous for its Celtic heritage, which is visible in the Western Highlands and Islands in particular. **2 A lot of people still speak Gaelic there**, a Celtic language that is related to Irish.

Among Scotland's main tourist attractions are Edinburgh and its castle, **3 which over 2 million people visited in 2019**. Glasgow has been equally popular, and **4 the Highlands have also attracted lots of travellers**. **5 The beautiful landscape fascinates visitors**. **6 Outdoor activities like hiking, mountain biking or water sports in the summer or skiing and snowboarding in the winter attract a lot of tourists**. Most of them are also keen on visiting Loch Ness, **7 where they might see Nessie, the famous monster**. **8 People will tell them that it still lives there**.

While they are in Scotland, some visitors will be interested to learn **9 how the Scots make whisky**. **10 They export more than one billion bottles of their famous 'water of life'**

every year. **11 Travel agents offer whisky tastings and guided tours of distilleries to visitors**.

Not only do tourists from abroad spend their holidays in Scotland, but also Queen Elizabeth. She usually stays in Balmoral Castle for three months in the summer, **12 which Sir William Drummond supposedly built in the 14th century**. **13 In 1852 Queen Victoria's husband Prince Albert bought it and made it a royal residence**. **14 So you may spot some members of the royal family there**.

If you are a sports fan, be sure to visit one of the highland games events **15 Scottish communities hold between May and September**. At these events, people compete in heavy sports disciplines like caber-tossing **16 while they also perform traditional music and dances in individual or group competitions**.

EXERCISE **3** A famous historical building

Choose a historical building in your country and write a short wiki article (about 100 words) about it. Use the passive whenever it is suitable. You may use the ideas in the box.

The … was built … | It looks … |
It served as … | People … | It used to … |
… was filmed there. | Today, … |
Since … | It's popular / famous … |
What is special about it is that … |
It may be …

Vocabulary

Im *Vocabulary* findest du alle wichtigen englischen Wörter und Redewendungen aus *Green Line 6* in der Reihenfolge, in der sie im Buch vorkommen.
Diese musst du lernen und anwenden können.
Zu den fakultativen Texten (Textteil in Spitzklammern) gibt es ein Zusatzangebot an Lernwortschatz.
Ob diese Vokabeln gelernt werden sollen, kann situationsabhängig entschieden werden.
Das *Vocabulary* ist in drei Spalten aufgeteilt:

- Links stehen die englischen Wörter und Sätze. Die Lautschrift in eckigen Klammern zeigt dir, wie du die Vokabeln aussprichst (siehe unten).
- In der Mitte steht die deutsche Übersetzung.
- Rechts findest du Beispielsätze, Erklärungen, Bilder oder Hinweise auf Besonderheiten.

Die **grün** gedruckten Wörter in den Kästen im *Vocabulary* sind ein Zusatzangebot. Du kannst sie verwenden, um über bestimmte Themen zu sprechen, musst sie aber nicht lernen.
Die Worterklärungen in den Fußnoten bei manchen Texten musst du nicht lernen.

Auf das *Vocabulary* folgt das **Dictionary (English – German)**. Falls du ein Wort nachschlagen musst, kannst du in dieser alphabetischen Wortliste (S. 201) nachsehen.

Englische Begriffe wie *e-mail*, *cool* oder *partner*, die auf Englisch und Deutsch gleich oder fast gleich geschrieben und ausgesprochen werden, stehen nicht im *Vocabulary*. Du kannst ihre Aussprache und Übersetzung aber im *Dictionary* nachschlagen.

Abkürzungen und Zeichen

5	In dieser Übung kommen die Wörter vor.	*infml*	*informal*	etw.	etwas
*	unregelmäßiges Verb (siehe Liste *Irregular verbs* im Anhang)	*sb*	*somebody*	jmd./jmds.	jemand/-es
		sth	*something*	jmdm./jmdn.	jemandem/-en
AE	*American English*	*pl/Pl.*	Plural	!	Achtung!
BE	*British English*	*sg/Sg.*	Singular	=	entspricht
Aus	*Australian English*	*ugs.*	umgangssprachlich	↔	ist das Gegenteil von
coll	*colloquial*	*Fr./Lat.*	verwandte Wörter in anderen Fremdsprachen	→	ist verwandt mit

Englische Laute

Konsonanten

[b]	**b**ed	[p]	**p**icture
[d]	**d**ay	[r]	**r**ed
[ð]	**th**e	[s]	**s**ix
[f]	**f**amily	[ʃ]	**sh**e
[g]	**g**o	[t]	**t**en
[ŋ]	morni**ng**	[tʃ]	**ch**air
[h]	**h**ouse	[v]	**v**ideo
[j]	**y**ou	[w]	**w**e, **o**ne
[k]	**c**an, mil**k**	[z]	ea**s**y
[l]	**l**etter	[ʒ]	revi**s**ion
[m]	**m**an	[dʒ]	**p**a**g**e
[n]	**n**o	[θ]	**th**ank you

Vokale

[ɑː]	c**ar**	[i]	happ**y**
[æ]	**a**pple	[iː]	t**ea**cher
[e]	p**e**n	[ɒ]	d**o**g
[ə]	**a**gain	[ɔː]	b**a**ll
[ɜː]	g**ir**l	[ʊ]	b**oo**k
[ʌ]	b**u**t	[u]	Jan**u**ary
[ɪ]	**i**t	[uː]	t**oo**, tw**o**

Diphthonge

[aɪ]	**I**, m**y**
[aʊ]	n**ow**, m**ou**se
[eɪ]	n**a**me, th**ey**
[eə]	th**ere**, p**air**
[ɪə]	h**ere**, id**ea**
[əʊ]	hell**o**
[ɔɪ]	b**oy**
[ʊə]	s**ure**

Zusätzliche Zeichen

[ː]	der vorangehende Laut ist lang, z. B. *you* [juː]
[‿]	der Bindebogen zeigt, dass zwei Wörter in der Aussprache verbunden werden
[']	die folgende Silbe trägt den Hauptakzent
[ˌ]	die folgende Silbe trägt den Nebenakzent

Der Aussprachestandard in *Green Line* ist *British English*. Dies gilt auch für die Lautschrift von Wörtern, die den Zusatz *AE* haben. Bei den Tonträgern und Filmsequenzen wird die jeweils passende Aussprache verwendet.

Across cultures 1 "Same same but different?"

	rainbow ['reɪnbəʊ]	Regenbogen	There are said to be seven colours in a *rainbow*.
	LGBTQIA+ [ˌeldʒiːbiːtiːkjuːaɪeɪˈplʌs]	Abkürzung für Lesbisch, Schwul, Bisexuell, Transgender, Queer / Questioning, Intersexuell, Asexuell / Aromantisch und andere Formen der sexuellen Identität und Orientierung	*LGBTQIA+* is an abbreviation of Lesbian, Gay, Bisexual, Transgender, Queer / Questioning, Intersex, Asexual / Aromantic and any other form of sexual identity and orientation.
1	similarity [ˌsɪmɪˈlærəti]	Ähnlichkeit; Gemeinsamkeit	*similarity* ↔ difference *similarity* → similar *Lat.* similis/-e
2	pidgin ['pɪdʒɪn]	Pidgin	A *pidgin* language consists of words and phrases of different languages.
	to simplify ['sɪmplɪfaɪ]	vereinfachen	! The suffix '-ify' at the end of verbs shows that something or someone is changed in some way: *to simplify*, to identify, to clarify, …
3	pluralistic [ˌplʊərəˈlɪstɪk]	pluralistisch; vielfältig	We live in a *pluralistic* society.
	mutual ['mjuːtʃuəl]	gegenseitig	A partnership should be based on *mutual* respect. *Fr.* mutuel/-le
	beneficial [ˌbenɪˈfɪʃl]	nützlich	*beneficial* → benefit *Lat.* beneficium *(nt)*
4	to proclaim [prəˈkleɪm]	verkünden; erklären; ausrufen	*to proclaim* = to publicly and officially tell people about sth important *to proclaim* = to declare
5	encounter [ɪnˈkaʊntə]	Begegnung; Zusammentreffen	An *encounter* is a meeting, especially an unplanned or unexpected one.
6	(song) lyrics *(pl)* [sɒŋ 'lɪrɪks]	Liedtext	Are the *lyrics* of songs important to you, or just the music?

Focus 1 Scottish history

1	to descend from [dɪˈsend frəm]	abstammen von; herstammen von	Most Americans are *descended from* immigrants.
	relative ['relətɪv]	Verwandte/-r	Aunts, uncles, cousins etc. are *relatives*.
	to pledge allegiance [ˌpledʒ əˈliːdʒns]	Treueschwur leisten	Every morning, American school children *pledge allegiance* to their flag.
	to pledge [pledʒ]	geloben	*to pledge* → a pledge
	exceptional [ɪkˈsepʃnl]	Ausnahme-; außergewöhnlich	*exceptional* → exception *Fr.* exceptionnel/-le
	bravery ['breɪvri]	Tapferkeit; Mut	*bravery* → brave
	loyalty *(no pl)* ['lɔəlti]	Treue; Loyalität	On July 4th, a lot of people show their *loyalty* to the US.
	surname ['sɜːneɪm]	Nachname	In Scotland many *surnames* start with 'Mac' which means 'son'.

Scot [skɒt]	Schotte / Schottin	*Scot* → Scotland, Scottish
weaver [ˈwiːvə]	Weber/-in	There aren't many *weavers* today because most textiles are made by machines.
2 to **chop** [tʃɒp]	hacken; klein schneiden	Please *chop* the vegetables for the soup.
heiress [ˈeəres]	Erbin	When a king dies, his heir or *heiress* becomes king or queen. *Lat.* heres *(m)*, *(f)*
alliance [əˈlaɪəns]	Allianz; Bündnis	Countries often form *alliances* to become stronger by working together. *Fr.* alliance *(f)*
rebel [ˈrebl]	Rebell/-in; Aufständische/-r	Robin Hood was a *rebel* who fought against the Sheriff of Nottingham.

History words

Time
- age / era / period: *the age / era / period of enlightenment, the Elizabethan / Victorian Age, the Middle Ages*
- prehistoric, ancient, medieval ⟷ modern, contemporary
- generation
- heyday   Höhepunkt, Blütezeit
- to date from *(the 1850s)* stammen aus
- to trace back *(to the 17th century)*

Relations
- ancestor, ancestry
- heir / heiress, heritage, inherit   erben, inheritance   Erbe
- origin, descent: *a person of noble descent*
- tradition
- to hand sth down   weitergeben

Aggression
- to assassinate   ermorden, assassination   Attentat
- to attack
- to conquer *(territories / a country)*, conqueror
- to defeat *(the enemy in a battle / an armed* bewaffnet *conflict / a war)*
- to destroy, destruction
- to execute, execution
- to imprison, imprisonment   verhaften, Inhaftierung

Development
- to abolish *(slavery / segregation)* abschaffen
- to build
- to develop
- to emerge   auftauchen
- to evolve   sich entwickeln
- to found / to establish *(a settlement / a colony)*
- to introduce *(new laws)*

Systems
- empire, kingdom, monarchy ⟷ republic: *The British Empire was the largest colonial empire in history.*
- colony, colonial, colonist, to colonise, colonialisation
- feudal system: gentry   niederer Adel, nobility   Adel, knight, lord / lady ⟷ peasant   Kleinbauer/-bäuerin, serf   Leibeigene/-r

- to invade *(a country)*, invasion
- to rebel [rɪˈbel], rebel [ˈrebl], rebellion [rɪˈbeljən]: *to rebel against the system, a rebel with a cause*
- to revolt *(against a government)* revoltieren, to revolutionise *(technology)* revolutionieren, revolution, revolutionary
- to riot   randalieren, riot, rioter

---

4 **contribution** [ˌkɒntrɪˈbjuːʃn]	Beitrag; Beteiligung	What's your *contribution* to the party? Food, music? *contribution* → to contribute
enlightenment [ɪnˈlaɪtnmənt]	Aufklärung; Erleuchtung	The Statue of Liberty's torch stands for *enlightenment*.
influential [ˌɪnfluˈenʃl]	einflussreich; maßgebend	Who is the most *influential* person at the moment? *influential* → influence
reason [ˈriːzn]	Vernunft; Verstand	*reason* ⟷ emotion *Fr.* raison *(f)*

philosopher [fɪˈlɒsəfə]	Philosoph/-in	*philosopher* → philosophy
economist [ɪˈkɒnəmɪst]	Betriebswirt/-in; Wirtschaftsexperte/-expertin	An *economist* studies the way in which economies work or studies developments within a particular economy. *economist* → economy
to **advance** [ədˈvɑːns]	voranbringen; vorantreiben	Scottish thinkers helped to *advance* science and philosophy in the 18th and 19th centuries.
engine [ˈendʒɪn]	Motor; Maschine	Almost all cars have the *engine* in front of the driver.
waterproof [ˈwɔːtəpruːf]	wasserdicht	You won't get wet if you wear *waterproof* clothing.
refrigerator [rɪˈfrɪdʒreɪtə]	Kühlschrank	The *refrigerator* was an important invention because it helped people to keep their food fresh.
balloon [bəˈluːn]	Ballon	After it was filled with hot air, the *balloon* rose slowly into the air. *Fr.* ballon *(m)*

Scottish enlightenment and industrialisation

Progress
- to achieve, achievement
- to advance
- to be acknowledged / praised
- to be based on (*reason / evidence*) Beweis, Beleg
- to challenge (*old ideas*)
- to develop (*further*)
- to discover, discovery
- to explore, explorer
- to have an impact on
- to influence, influence, influential
- to invent, inventor

Industrialisation
- innovation, innovative
- technology: steam engine
- machinery
- factory / mill Fabrik
- heavy industries: coal, iron Eisen, steel Stahl, shipbuilding
- labour
- workforce Arbeitskräfte
- working class
- working conditions

Unit 1 Scotland

Introduction

1	**oral** [ˈɔːrl]	mündlich	An *oral* exam is a test in which you have to show how good your speaking skills are.
2	**difficulty** [ˈdɪfɪklti]	Schwierigkeit	What *difficulties* do immigrants usually face? *difficulty* → difficult *Lat.* difficultas *(f)*
	inhabitant [ɪnˈhæbɪtnt]	Einwohner/-in; Bewohner/-in	All the people who live in a place are its *inhabitants*. *Fr.* habitant/-e *(m)/(f)*; *Lat.* habitare
4	to **dine** [daɪn]	zu Abend essen	Let's *dine* in a restaurant today. *to dine* → dinner
	to **sip** [sɪp]	nippen; schluckweise trinken	She enjoyed *sipping* her tea slowly.
	upside down [ˌʌpsaɪd ˈdaʊn]	verkehrt herum; auf dem Kopf stehend	My little brother doesn't know how to read. Yesterday he looked at a book *upside down*.
	pipe [paɪp]	Dudelsackpfeife	How many *pipes* do bagpipes have?

tartan ['tɑːtn]	Schottenkaro *(bestimmtes Muster eines Clans)*; karierter Schottenstoff	Different families have *tartans* of different colours, e.g. with a red, blue or green background.
glance [glɑːns]	Blick	They exchanged a meaningful *glance*. *glance* → to glance
proof [pruːf]	Beweis	She thinks Tom stole her mobile, but she has no *proof*. *proof* → to prove

Scottish traditions

Food and drink
- haggis — *gefüllter Schafsmagen*
- tatties (= potatoes)
- neeps (= turnips) — Steckrüben
- Irn Bru — *Softdrink mit Koffein*
- whisky

Culture
- Celtic myths
- bagpipes
- Highland dancing
- Royal Edinburgh Military Tattoo *Musikfestival*
- clans
- tartan
- kilt

Highland Games
- tossing the caber — Baumstammwerfen
- tug of war — Tauziehen
- stone put — Steinstoßen
- hammer throw — Hammerwerfen

Texts A

department [dɪˈpɑːtmənt]	Abteilung	The games *department* is the part of a shop that sells games.
to disintegrate [dɪˈsɪntɪgreɪt]	zerfallen; zerbrechen	*to disintegrate* = to fall into pieces *to disintegrate* ↔ to integrate
pile [paɪl]	Stapel; Haufen	There is always a *pile* of books on my desk. *pile* → to pile up
cottage [ˈkɒtɪdʒ]	Landhaus; Hütte	I spend my summers in a little *cottage* by the sea.
loch [lɒx; lɒk]	See *(in Schottland)*	! Careful with the pronunciation: The Scottish „ch" in *loch* is pronounced like the German „ch".
to tower [taʊə]	hoch aufragen	The castle *has towered* over the town for hundreds of years.
curtain [ˈkɜːtn]	Vorhang	*curtain* = a piece of material you can pull across a window, for example when it gets dark outside
isolated [ˈaɪsəleɪtɪd]	abgelegen; abgeschieden; isoliert	Many holiday cottages are in *isolated* areas. *isolated* → isolation *Fr.* isolé/-e
casual [ˈkæʒuəl]	zufällig; gelegentlich	I had a *casual* meeting with my teacher in town.
pub [pʌb]	Kneipe; Gasthaus	*pub* = a place where people can go and have drinks (especially beer, wine, whisky etc.) and talk to their friends
due to [ˈdjuː tə]	aufgrund; durch	The train is delayed *due to* technical problems. *due to* = because of
inexplicable [ˌɪnɪkˈsplɪkəbl]	unerklärlich	For some *inexplicable* reason he sold his fantastic house. *inexplicable* → to explain
to stock up [ˌstɒkˈʌp]	sich eindecken	We always *stock up* on wood before the winter comes.

	exposed [ɪkˈspəʊzd]	ungeschützt; exponiert	Our house is in a very *exposed* position on a hill. *Fr.* exposer, *Lat.* exponere
	gale [ɡeɪl]	Sturm; Orkan	The ship had to fight a heavy *gale*.
	to **reassure** [ˌriːəˈʃʊə]	beruhigen; beschwichtigen	After their accident, my parents *reassured* me that they were OK. *to reassure* → sure
	slot [slɒt]	Schlitz	Put your card or your money into the *slot*.
	burglar [ˈbɜːɡlə]	Einbrecher/-in	Most *burglars* break into houses when nobody is there.
	midge [mɪdʒ]	Mücke	The best thing in winter is that there are no *midges*.
	to **cope with** [ˈkəʊp wɪð]	bewältigen; fertig werden mit	She was unsure how to *cope with* her boyfriend leaving her.
	downside [ˈdaʊnsaɪd]	Kehrseite; Schattenseite	The *downside* of industrialisation is the destruction of nature.
	column [ˈkɒləm]	Spalte	Collect the pros and cons in a table with two *columns*. *Lat.* columna *(f)*
2	**myth** [mɪθ]	Mythos; Legende	*myth* = a story or version of the truth that is often still believed, even though it is not founded on facts
	enchanted [ɪnˈtʃɑːntɪd]	verzaubert	He felt like he was walking through an *enchanted* forest, it was so beautiful.
	to **inspire** [ɪnˈspaɪə]	inspirieren; anregen	*to inspire* = to give the idea for sth (e.g. a poem or a song)
	mythical creature [ˌmɪθɪkl ˈkriːtʃə]	Fabelwesen	Dragons are *mythical creatures*. *mythical* → myth
	fairy [ˈfeəri]	Fee	In Scotland, there are many tales about people being kidnapped by *fairies*. *fairy* → fairy tale
	stream [striːm]	Bach	They crossed the fast-moving *stream* on a wooden bridge.
	to **drip** [drɪp]	tropfen	Rain *was dripping* down his neck.
	shore [ʃɔː]	Ufer; Küste	They walked along the *shore* and watched the waves.
	despite [dɪˈspaɪt]	trotz	*Despite* feeling sick, she won the match.
	to **haunt** [hɔːnt]	spuken in; heimsuchen	A ghost *is haunting* the old castle. *to haunt* → haunted house
	mischievous [ˈmɪstʃɪvəs]	schelmisch; boshaft	A *mischievous* person likes playing tricks on other people.
	hump [hʌmp]	Buckel; Höcker	Some camels have only one *hump*.
	to **prove** [pruːv]	beweisen	*to prove* = to show definitely that sth is true *to prove* → proof
4	**remote** [rɪˈməʊt]	abgelegen; weit entfernt	It was an adventure to explore this *remote* mountain. *remote* = isolated
	bill [bɪl]	Rechnung	We'd like to pay. Could you bring us the *bill*, please?
	abandoned [əˈbændənd]	aufgegeben; verlassen	The *abandoned* building had to be pulled down. *Fr.* abandonné/e
	to **drag** [dræɡ]	schleifen; ziehen; schleppen	If you *drag* sth, you pull it along.
	content [kənˈtent]	zufrieden	I am very *content* with the test results. *Fr.* content/e
	to **flicker** [ˈflɪkə]	flackern; flimmern	I like it when things *flicker*, for example candles, fire, a light or the TV screen.

remains (pl) [rɪˈmeɪnz]	Überreste; Überbleibsel	In this picture you can see the *remains* of a Roman villa. *remains* → to remain
stick [stɪk]	Stock; Stange	Dogs love it when you throw *sticks* for them.
to **toss** [tɒs]	werfen; stoßen	Let's *toss* a coin to decide who is going to start.
to **stalk** [stɔːk]	stolzieren; marschieren	After the fight she *stalked* angrily out of the room.
doubt [daʊt]	Zweifel	Claire isn't sure about her decision. She has *doubts*. *Fr.* doute (f)
to **crouch** [kraʊtʃ]	hocken; sich niederkauern	The boy *crouched* under the table to hide from us.
butterfly [ˈbʌtəflaɪ]	Schmetterling	Some *butterfly* species can travel very long distances.
fancy [ˈfænsi]	schick; ausgefallen	1. The restaurant is very *fancy* and very expensive. 2. This dress has a *fancy* design.
provisions (pl) [prəˈvɪʒnz]	Vorräte	After the disaster the government sent *provisions* to the communities. *provision* → to provide *Fr.* provision (f)
corrugated [ˈkɒrəgeɪtɪd]	gewellt	*corrugated* iron = Wellblech
*to **lean** [liːn]	lehnen	I can *lean* back and forward, but I'm more comfortable leaning against the wall.
oak [əʊk]	Eiche	An *oak* is a tree that you find in the forest.
assortment (of) [əˈsɔːtmənt]	Sortiment (von); Auswahl (an)	The shop has a big *assortment* of sofas and chairs. *Fr.* assortiment (m)
cutlery (no pl) [ˈkʌtləri]	Besteck	*cutlery* = forks, knives and spoons
penknife [pennaɪf], **penknives** (pl) [pennaɪvz]	Taschenmesser	He took his *penknife* to slice an apple.
blunt [blʌnt]	stumpf	A *blunt* knife doesn't cut well. *blunt* ↔ sharp
to **mock** [mɒk]	spotten; höhnen	It is not nice to *mock* people because of their clothing.
hassle [ˈhæsl]	Schikane; Schwierigkeit	I don't think the project is worth the money or the *hassle*.
stove [stəʊv]	Ofen; Herd	I can't make dinner. The *stove* doesn't work.
tin [tɪn]	Dose; Büchse	The recipe calls for a *tin* of tomatoes.
fateful [ˈfeɪtfl]	schicksalhaft; verhängnisvoll	With deep sadness she remembered that *fateful* day in June.
to **row** [rəʊ]	rudern	You can *row* a small boat, but not a big ship.
to **associate sb / sth with sb / sth** [əˈsəʊʃieɪt ˌwɪθ]	jmdn. / etw. mit jmdm. / etw. in Verbindung bringen	People *associate* Italy *with* pizza and pasta, but it has so much more to offer than that. *Fr.* associer à / avec
simile [ˈsɪmɪli]	Vergleich	*simile* = an expression comparing one thing with another, always including the words "as" or "like"
metaphor [ˈmetəfə; metəfɔː]	Metapher	"All the world's a stage" is an example of Shakespeare's use of *metaphor*.
characterisation [ˌkærəktraɪˈzeɪʃn]	Beschreibung; Personenbe-schreibung; Charakterisierung	*characterisation* → characterise, character, characteristic

| 5 | **fence** [fens] | Zaun | There's a *fence* around the park. |
| | **counter** ['kaʊntə] | Theke; Tresen; Schalter | *counter* = the place in a shop, bank etc. where people are served |

Talking about literature

Character
- self-conscious befangen
- insecure
- nervous
- introverted introvertiert
- self-confident
- brave
- courageous mutig
- daring kühn
- outgoing
- open-minded aufgeschlossen
- mischievous
- affectionate liebevoll

Atmosphere
- dreary trostlos, düster
- dull trüb, düster
- spooky unheimlich
- (full of) suspense / tension
- casual zwanglos / relaxed
- cheerful heiter

Reactions
- to challenge
- to dare
- to sweat
- to tremble zittern
- to snap at sb
- to break down

Emotions
- concerned about
- haunted by geplagt
- worried
- anxious ängstlich
- frightened / scared
- irritated / annoyed
- angry
- furious / full of rage wütend
- upset
- confused
- desperate
- sad – depressed

- cheerful heiter
- happy
- overjoyed überglücklich
- confident
- untroubled unbeschwert
- calm

- relaxed
- content
- without fear
- excited
- thrilled aufgeregt

Texts B

1	**excess mortality** [ɪkˌses mɔːˈtæləti]	Übersterblichkeit; überdurchschnittlich hohe Sterblichkeitsrate	*Excess mortality* is significant in poor countries.
	housing ['haʊzɪŋ]	Unterkunft; Wohnungsbeschaffung	In big cities, *housing* has become very expensive. *housing* → a house
	to sadden ['sædn]	traurig machen; bekümmern	It *saddens* me to see that there are still so many wars going on in the world.
	majority [məˈdʒɒrəti]	Mehrheit; Mehrzahl	The *majority* of Americans live in cities. *Fr.* majorité *(f)*
	grim [grɪm]	entsetzlich; grausam	The family had to face the *grim* reality of having to leave their home.
	vibrant ['vaɪbrənt]	dynamisch; lebhaft; pulsierend	In this *vibrant* city, there are lots of music pubs, bars and theatres.
	bourgeois ['bɔːʒwɑː]	bürgerlich	People who describe others as '*bourgeois*' think of them as very conventional and middle-class.
	to detract [dɪˈtrækt]	mindern; schmälern	The fact that he wasn't a good pupil doesn't *detract* from his achievements as a scientist.
	appalling [əˈpɔːlɪŋ]	entsetzlich; schrecklich	Child labour in African mines is *appalling* and should be stopped.
	counterpoint ['kaʊntəˌpɔɪnt]	Kontrapunkt; Gegenbild	I can see no *counterpoint* to add to your arguments.
	to discourage [dɪˈskʌrɪdʒ]	abschrecken; entmutigen	People should be *discouraged* from bullying others. *to discourage* ↔ to encourage *Fr.* décourager

unprecedented [ʌnˈpresɪdentɪd]	beispiellos; noch nie da gewesen	An *unprecedented* number of young people demonstrated for climate change.
lopsided [ˌlɒpˈsaɪdɪd]	schief; nach einer Seite hängend	I cannot agree with you because I think that your presentation of the facts is *lopsided*.
to **deter** [dɪˈtɜː]	abschrecken; jdn davon abhalten etw. zu tun	During the Cold War, people believed that nations could *deter* others from attacking them by buying more and more horrible weapons.
coverage [ˈkʌvrɪdʒ]	Berichterstattung	The media *coverage* of the elections has been balanced so far.
Glaswegian [glæzˈwiːdʒn]	aus Glasgow	*Glaswegians* are often praised for their friendliness and hospitality. *Glaswegian* = from Glasgow

Talking about music

(Folk) Instruments
- bagpipes
- accordion Akkordeon
- harp Harfe
- fiddle (violin) Geige
- drums
- (bass) [beɪs] guitar
- banjo Banjo
- flute Flöte
- tin whistle Blechflöte
- piano
- synthesizer

Music words
- tune Melodie
- melody Melodie
- chord Akkord
- harmony
- rhythm
- high-pitched hoch ↔ low tone / voice
- verse
- line
- vocals
- voice

Describing effects
- a change in volume / dynamics
- to sing up ↔ to become quieter
- volume Lautstärke increases ↔ decreases
- voices soften leiser werden
- tempo / speed: to slow down ↔ to accelerate beschleunigen
- tension
- to hum summen / to sing / to whistle pfeifen

2 **holy** [ˈhəʊli]	heilig	The Bible contains stories of the *Holy* Spirit.
to **flow** [fləʊ]	fließen; strömen	Rivers *flow* into the sea.
cloth [klɒθ]	Stoff; Tuch; Gewebe	*cloth* → clothes
hose [həʊz]	Schlauch; Strumpf	I want to use the garden *hose* to water the plants.
furnace [ˈfɜːnɪs]	Hochofen; Schmelzofen	The *furnaces* were fired with coal.
iron [aɪən]	Eisen	There was a big *iron* gate in front of the house.
belly [ˈbeli]	Bauch	The dog rolled onto its back so we could stroke its *belly*.
mill [mɪl]	Fabrik	*mill* = a factory, especially one which produces with raw materials
sole [səʊl]	einzig; alleinig	*sole* = only *Fr.* seul/-e
reward [rɪˈwɔːd]	Belohnung; Preis	A *reward* of £100 has been offered to anybody who finds the stolen car.
dreary [ˈdrɪəri]	trostlos	Life seems *dreary* in the winter.
despair [dɪˈspeə]	Hoffnungslosigkeit; Verzweiflung	In times of *despair*, people often cry or pray to God. *Fr.* désespoir *(m)*
*to **come to one's mind** [ˌkʌm tə ˈmaɪnd]	in den Sinn kommen; einfallen	What *comes to your mind* when you think of the United States?

verse [vɜːs]	Vers; Strophe	Poems or songs are divided into *verses*.
vocals *(pl)* [ˈvəʊklz]	Gesang	The *vocals* were good, but the guitar was too loud.
dynamics *(no pl)* [daɪˈnæmɪks]	Dynamik	*Fr.* dynamique *(f)*
to interpret [ɪnˈtɜːprɪt]	interpretieren	I am not sure how to *interpret* his silence. *Fr.* interpréter; *Lat.* interpretari
3 fringe [frɪndʒ]	Rand-; Alternativ-	The Edinburgh *Fringe* Festival takes place every year.
exhibition [ˌeksɪˈbɪʃn]	Ausstellung; Vorführung	I love to go to art *exhibitions* in museums and galleries. *Fr.* exhibition *(f)*
fairly [ˈfeəli]	ziemlich; recht	We know our neighbours *fairly* well.
up-and-coming [ʌpəndˈkʌmɪŋ]	aufstrebend; vielversprechend	Many *up-and-coming* artists do shows at Glastonbury.
to flock [flɒk]	(scharenweise) strömen	After the concert, the crowd *flocked* outside.
to daunt [dɔːnt]	einschüchtern	The storm did not *daunt* the sailors.
to plunge in [ˌplʌndʒ ˈɪn]	sich hineinstürzen	The kids immediately *plunged* into the pool. *Fr.* plonger
to censor [ˈsensə]	zensieren	To *censor* a book (film, etc.) means to remove the parts that are considered to be offensive, immoral or a political threat.
venue [ˈvenjuː]	Austragungsort; Veranstaltungsort	The band's tour will cover all the important *venues*.
intriguing [ɪnˈtriːgɪŋ]	faszinierend	*intriguing* = fascinating
spread [spred]	Ausbreitung; Verbreitung; Spannweite	**!** Be careful with the pronunciation: '*Spread*' rhymes with 'bread' and 'head'. *spread* → to spread
to range (from … to …) [ˈreɪndʒ frəm tʊ]	sich erstrecken (von … bis …); reichen (von … bis …)	The topics we discussed *ranged* from soap operas to real philosophical questions.
basement [ˈbeɪsmənt]	Kellergeschoss; Untergeschoss	*basement* = the lowest floor of a building, below street level

Texts C

1 to invest [ɪnˈvest]	investieren	*to invest* = to put money in sth or to buy sth because you hope to make a profit *to invest* → investment
to pass away [ˌpɑːs əˈweɪ]	versterben; entschlafen	My mum *passed away* early, which was very hard for all of us.
welfare [ˈwelfeə]	Sozialhilfe	*welfare* = money and / or services you get from the state or an organisation when you are in need
mental health [ˌmentl ˈhelθ]	seelische Gesundheit	*mental* ↔ physical
housing [ˈhaʊzɪŋ]	Unterkunft; Wohnungsbeschaffung	In big cities, *housing* has become very expensive. *housing* → a house
fund [fʌnd]	Fonds	The city set up a *fund* to help the homeless.
initiative [ɪˈnɪʃətɪv]	Initiative; Aktion	I support the *initiative* against racism.
*to uphold [ʌpˈhəʊld]	aufrechterhalten; wahren	The company *upholds* strict hygiene standards, so you have to wash your hands regularly.

campaign [kæm'peɪn]	Kampagne; Aktion	The advertising *campaign* for our new product is very successful.
impartial [ɪm'pɑːʃl]	unparteiisch; unvoreingenommen	A good judge is *impartial* and fair.
2 crisis, crises *(pl)* ['kraɪsɪs; 'kraɪsiːz]	Krise	Europe has been in a *crisis* for some time. *Fr.* crise *(f)*
to loom [luːm]	sich abzeichnen	A financial crisis *is looming*.
eating disorder ['iːtɪŋ dɪˌsɔːdə]	Essstörung	If you worry too much about your weight, you may develop an *eating disorder*.
backlog ['bæklɒg]	Rückstand	We will need at least one assistant to work off this *backlog*.
ridiculous [rɪ'dɪkjələs]	lächerlich	The idea to run a marathon without preparation is *ridiculous*. *Fr.* ridicule; *Lat.* ridere
*to strike [straɪk]	treffen	The baseball player *struck* the ball hard.
exposure [ɪk'spəʊʒə]	Aussetzung; Ausgesetztsein	*exposure* → exposed
hazard ['hæzəd]	Gefahr; Risiko	The fire *hazard* is particularly high in California in the summer.
solar panel [ˌsəʊlə 'pænl]	Sonnenkollektor	*Solar panels* are mostly put on roofs. *Fr.* panneau solaire *(m)*
wind turbine ['wɪnd ˌtɜːbaɪn]	Windturbine	A lot of Scotland's electricity comes from *wind turbines*.
to reform [rɪ'fɔːm]	reformieren	Laws need to be *reformed* from time to time. *Fr.* réformer
graduate ['grædʒuət]	Hochschulabsolvent/-in	He is a *graduate* of physics. *graduate* = sb who has graduated from university or college
*to cast one's vote [ˌkɑːst wʌnz 'vəʊt]	die Stimme abgeben	What candidate did you *cast your vote* for?
to convict [kən'vɪkt]	verurteilen	The criminal *was convicted* of murder. *to convict* → convict
on remand [ɒn rɪ'mɑːnd]	in Untersuchungshaft	The police can keep someone prisoner *on remand* until their trial.
to prompt [prɒmt]	veranlassen; auffordern	The website *prompted* me to enter a new password.
proposition [ˌprɒpə'zɪʃn]	Aussage; These	*proposition* = statement
3 ambassador [æm'bæsədə]	Botschafter/-in	Who is Britain's *ambassador* to Germany? *Fr.* ambassadeur *(m)* / ambassadrice *(f)*
to champion ['tʃæmpiən]	eintreten für; unterstützen; verfechten	He passionately *championed* the poor.
to complement ['kɒmplɪmənt]	abrunden; ergänzen	The necklace *complements* her outfit.
councillor ['kaʊnslə]	Gemeinderat/-rätin; Stadtrat/-rätin	The town council consists of twenty *councillors*. *councillor* → council *Lat.* consilium *(n)*
to engage [ɪn'geɪdʒ]	faszinieren; begeistern	The storyteller *engaged* us with his adventure stories.

consultation [ˌkɒnsl'teɪʃn]	Beratung; Besprechung	Next week the Prime Minister will be in Florida for *consultations* with the American President. *Fr.* consultation *(f)*
to **showcase** ['ʃəʊkeɪs]	ausstellen	*to showcase* = to display

Media competence

1	**bilingual** [baɪ'lɪŋgwl]	zweisprachig	I speak English and German perfectly. I'm *bilingual*.
2	**abbreviation** [əˌbriː'vi'eɪʃn]	Abkürzung	'USA' is the *abbreviation* for 'United States of America'.
	part of speech [ˌpɑːt‿əv 'spiːtʃ]	Wortart; Wortklasse	Nouns, verbs, adjectives, adverbs etc. are different *parts of speech*.
	to **cross-check** [ˌkrɒs'tʃek]	die Gegenprobe machen; vergleichend überprüfen	You should always *cross-check* your results before presenting them.
	afterwards ['ɑːftəwədz]	danach; hinterher	I need to do my homework, but I can meet you *afterwards*.
	to **pronounce** [prə'naʊns]	aussprechen	! Be careful with the spelling: to pron**ou**nce [aʊ] – pron**u**nciation [ʌ]
	idiom ['ɪdiəm]	Redewendung; besondere Ausdrucksweise	*idiom* = a group of words that does not have the same meaning as the meanings of the individual words in the group
	Scots [skɒts]	Schottisch *(Dialekt)*	*Scots* → Scottish, Scotland
	etymology *(no pl)* [ˌetɪ'mɒlədʒi]	Etymologie	*etymology* = the study of the origin and history of words
	thesaurus [θɪ'sɔːrəs], **thesauri** [θɪ'sɔːraɪ] *(pl)*	Synonymwörterbuch	*thesaurus* = a type of dictionary in which words with similar meanings are arranged in groups
	to **type** [taɪp]	tippen	It's easier to read a text that has been *typed* than one that has been written by hand.
	inverted comma [ɪnˌvɜːtɪd 'kɒmə]	Anführungszeichen	Direct speech in dialogues is usually put in *inverted commas*.

Unit task

*to **get in touch (with)** [ˌget‿ɪn 'tʌtʃ]	kontaktieren; in Verbindung treten (mit)	*to get in touch (with)* = to make contact (with)
partnership ['pɑːtnəʃɪp]	Partnerschaft	To complete the project, a *partnership* between the business and our local politicians has been formed.
to **resolve** [rɪ'zɒlv]	lösen; klären	The two countries were able to *resolve* their conflict. *Lat.* solvere
copyright ['kɒpiraɪt]	Urheberrecht; Copyright	Fairy tales don't have a *copyright* because they are too old.
extracurricular [ˌekstrəkə'rɪkjələ]	außerhalb des Lehrplans	*Extracurricular* activities at school usually take place in the afternoon.
to **distribute** [dɪ'strɪbjuːt]	verteilen; aufteilen	*Fr.* distribuer; *Lat.* distribuere
workload ['wɜːkləʊd]	Arbeitspensum	I can easily deal with my *workload*.
artwork ['ɑːtwɜːk]	Illustrationen; Bebilderung	Every Indian tribe has its typical *artwork*.

correspondence [ˌkɒrɪˈspɒndəns]	Korrespondenz; Schriftwechsel	Business *correspondence* uses formal language. *Fr.* correspondance *(f)*
*to **meet** / **miss a deadline** [ˌmiːt / mɪs‿ə ˈdedlaɪn]	einen (Abgabe-)Termin einhalten / verpassen	Journalists have to be able to *meet a deadline*.
management [ˈmænɪdʒmənt]	Management; Verwaltung	*management* → to manage, manager

⟨ Texts D ⟩

1	**flagship project** [ˈflæɡʃɪp ˌprɒdʒekt]	Vorzeigeprojekt	This chocolate is the *flagship* product of this sweets company.
	to **sustain** [səˈsteɪn]	(am Leben) erhalten	There is not enough food in this house to *sustain* a mouse. *to sustain* → sustainable
	range [reɪndʒ]	Sortiment; Palette	*range* = group of products with the same brand name
	foundation [faʊnˈdeɪʃn]	Stiftung; Gründung	*foundation* → to found *Fr.* fondation *(f)*
	strategy [ˈstrætədʒi]	Strategie	What's our *strategy* for the match? ! Watch the spelling and the pronunciation. *Fr.* stratégie *(f)*
	hectare [ˈhekteə]	Hektar	*hectare* = 10,000 square metres
	Caledonian [ˌkæləˈdəʊniən]	schottisch	*Caledonian* = Scottish *Lat.* Caledonia
2	**rate** [reɪt]	Rate; Quote	*rate* = the level of sth (e.g. of recycling)
	enterprise [ˌentəˈpraɪz]	Unternehmen; Firma	*enterprise* = company *Fr.* entreprise *(f)*
	proposal [prəˈpəʊzl]	Vorschlag; Entwurf; Gesetzesvorlage	to make a *proposal* *proposal* → to propose *Lat.* proponere, propositum
3	**interviewee** [ˌɪntəvjuˈiː]	Befragte/-r; Interviewte/-r	The *interviewee* didn't want to answer some of the questions. *interviewee* ↔ interviewer *interviewee* → interviewer, to interview, interview

⟨ Texts E ⟩

croft [krɒft]	kleiner Bauernhof	People who work on small crofts in Scotland are called *crofters*.
crop [krɒp]	Getreide; Anbaupflanze; Feldfrucht	Some *crops* are better suited to dry conditions than others.
plough [plaʊ]	Pflug	A *plough* is an agricultural tool for turning the soil.
to **appreciate** [əˈpriːʃieɪt]	schätzen; anerkennen; würdigen	If you *appreciate* sth, you like it because you recognize its value. *Fr.* apprécier
in return [ɪn rɪˈtɜːn]	als Gegenleistung	*In return* for your cooperation we will give you a free gift.
cloak [kləʊk]	Mantel; Umhang	I've bought a long black *cloak*, which I'm going to wear at the Halloween party.
salt [sɔːlt]	Salz	Do you prefer rock *salt* or sea *salt*?

to **heal** [hiːl]	heilen	His broken heart will take a long time to *heal*.
patch [pætʃ]	Fleck; Stelle	There's a wet *patch* on the floor. What happend?
*to **bend over** [ˌbendˈəʊvə]	sich vorbeugen; sich beugen über	*to bend over* = to move the top part of the body towards the ground
chest [tʃest]	Kiste; Truhe	At the bottom of the *chest* I found some jewellery.
leather [ˈleðə]	Leder	I want to buy that *leather* jacket, but it's very expensive.
to **hum** [hʌm]	summen; brummen	*Humming* a tune can relax you.
tune [tjuːn]	Melodie; Ton	If you don't know the lyrics of the song, you can just hum along to the *tune*.
to **glisten** [ˈglɪsn]	glitzern	The calm sea *glistened* in the sunlight.
to **tense** [tens]	sich spannen; (sich) anspannen	He *tensed* a muscle to see if his training had had an effect. *to tense* ↔ to relax *to tense* → tension
furious [ˈfjʊəriəs]	wütend	*furious* = very, very angry *Fr.* furieux / furieuse; *Lat.* furiosus
to **rear up** [ˌrɪərˈʌp]	sich aufbäumen; sich aufrichten	The horse *reared up* and threw off its rider.
to **hiss** [hɪs]	zischen; fauchen	*Hissing* is the typical sound of snakes.
*to **lean back** [ˌliːn ˈbæk]	sich zurücklehnen	She *leaned back* in her chair and relaxed.
to **roar** [rɔː]	brüllen; dröhnen	The lions *have been roaring* all night.
bank [bæŋk]	Ufer	A river has two *banks*.
stable [ˈsteɪbl]	Stall	*stable* = a building in which horses are kept
*to **sow** [səʊ]	säen	Yesterday the field opposite *was sown* with corn.
as for ... [ˈæz fɔː]	was ... betrifft	*As for* me, I don't like dogs.
affectionate [əˈfekʃnət]	liebevoll; zärtlich	They seemed to be in love with each other and were openly *affectionate*.

Focus 2 Scottish identity

2	**distribution** [ˌdɪstrɪˈbjuːʃn]	Verteilung; Aufteilung	*distribution* → to distribute *Fr.* distribution (f)
	decline [dɪˈklaɪn]	Rückgang; Abnahme; Niedergang	The first signs of economic *decline* became visible.
3	**poet** [ˈpəʊɪt]	Dichter/-in	She is a famous *poet*. She writes beautiful poems. *Fr.* poète (m) (f); *Lat.* poeta (m)
	stanza [ˈstænzə]	Strophe	*stanza* = the basic unit in a poem (often four lines or more)
	poetry [ˈpəʊətri]	Poesie; Dichtkunst	*poetry* → poet, poem
4	**census** [ˈsensəs]	Zählung; Volkszählung	She was stopped in her car for a traffic *census*. *Fr.* recensement (m); *Lat.* census (m)
	force [fɔːs]	Kraft; Macht	The hero couldn't defeat the supernatural *forces*. *force* → to force sb to do sth

Writing essays and comments

Structuring and linking ideas

- First (of all), … / Second, … / Third, …
- To begin with / To start, …
- On the one hand, … on the other hand …
- Moreover/Furthermore, …
- Another reason is …
- However/In contrast, …
- Finally / Eventually / All in all / As a result / Consequently Folglich / At the end of the day, …

Expressing opinions / Convincing

- Have you ever wondered / imagined / thought about …?
- There are various reasons why …
- Studies show / have found that …
- This illustrates / underlines / emphasises …
- People advocating … often claim / argue that … befürworten
- Certainly, XY has a point. Yet / However / Nevertheless …
- Looking at (the issue) from this point of view, you have to admit that …
- Bearing … in mind, you can better understand why … berücksichtigen
- I strongly support / question / object to … ablehnen
- Therefore, you have to come to the conclusion that …

5	**graveyard** ['greɪvjɑːd]	Friedhof	*graveyard* = a place for graves, often next to a church
	suffragette [ˌsʌfrə'dʒet]	Frauenrechtlerin	The *suffragette* movement made voting possible for women. *Fr.* suffragette *(f)*
	rail [reɪl]	Schiene; Geländer	The train left the *rails* because there was something wrong with its wheels.
	devolution [ˌdiːvə'luːʃn]	Dezentralisierung; Delegierung	*devolution* = a transfer of authority from a central government to regional governments
	proportional [prə'pɔːʃnl]	Verhältnis-; Anteils-	*proportional* → proportion
	electoral system [ɪˌlektrl 'sɪstəm]	Wahlsystem	Proportional representation is a principle of the German *electoral system*.

Politics

The law

- constitution Verfassung
- act
- amendment Verfassungs-zusatz
- to propose vorschlagen / to introduce / to submit vorlegen a bill Gesetzentwurf
- to approve / to adopt / to pass verabschieden a bill / a law / legislation
- to oppose / to reject ablehnen / to veto ein Veto einlegen gegen a bill
- to implement einführen
- convention
- treaty

Elections

- candidate
- to stand for election / parliament (BE) / to run for presidency / president (AE) sich zur Wahl stellen, kandidieren (für)
- electoral system
- proportional representation (= proportional electoral system)
- first-past-the-post system Mehrheitswahlsystem
- suffrage Wahl-, Stimmrecht
- to vote / to cast a vote
- by secret / open ballot Wahl
- referendum

Administration

- federal state
  ↔ unitary state Einheitsstaat
- country – nation – province – region – county Landkreis – borough
- council, councillor
- mayor
- devolution
- tax, taxation Besteue-rung
- fiscal commission
- board of education Schulbehörde
- proposal Vorschlag, Gesetzesvorlage
- proposition

Politics

- policy
- interior or home affairs Innenpolitik ↔ external or foreign affairs Außenpolitik
- parliament
- minister (BE) / secretary (AE)
- foreign secretary (BE) / secretary of state (AE) Außen-minister/-in
- opponent Gegner/-in, opposition
- ambassador
- to negotiate ver-handeln, negotiation

6	**fiscal commission** [ˌfɪskl kəˈmɪʃn]	Finanzausschuss	The *fiscal commission* examines financial matters.
	loss [lɒs]	Verlust	*loss* → to lose

Across cultures 2 Folk and folk-inspired music

	folk music [ˈfəʊk ˌmjuːzɪk]	traditionelle Musik	Ireland is famous for its tradition of *folk music*.
2	**arrangement** [əˈreɪndʒmənt]	Arrangement; Orchestrierung	*arrangement* → to arrange *Fr.* arrangement *(m)*
	to incorporate [ɪnˈkɔːpreɪt]	einfügen; aufnehmen	The florists *had incorporated* paper butterflies in the flower bouquets.
	tune [tjuːn]	Melodie; Ton	If you don't know the lyrics of the song, you can just hum along to the *tune*.
	Oriental [ˌɔːriˈentl]	orientalisch	*Oriental* cuisine is underrated because not many people know it well.
	Latino [ləˈtiːnəʊ]	lateinamerikanisch	In the US, there is a strong *Latino* influence in states like California, Arizona or Florida.
	notable [ˈnəʊtəbl]	bedeutend; beachtlich	The organisation achieved some *notable* successes.
	alike [əˈlaɪk]	gleichermaßen; ähnlich	The brothers are like three peas in a pod, they all look *alike*.
3	***to be willing to do sth** [bi ˈwɪlɪŋ tə]	gewillt sein, etw. zu tun; bereit sein, etw. zu tun	How much *are* they *willing to* pay for the bike? *to be willing to do sth* = to be prepared to do sth
	fiddle [ˈfɪdl]	Geige	The *fiddle* is a musical instrument which is typically used in Irish folk music.
	upon [əˈpɒn]	auf	She put her hand *upon* his shoulder to calm him.
	stump [stʌmp]	Stumpf; Strunk	The tree was cut, now you can sit on its *stump*.
	sin [sɪn]	Sünde	According to Christian tradition, there are seven deadly *sins*.
	bow [bəʊ]	Bogen	You need a *bow* to play the fiddle.
	fingertip [ˈfɪŋgətɪp]	Fingerspitze	Hold the A string down with your *fingertip*.
	string [strɪŋ]	Saite	She bought a four-*string* fiddle to learn with.
	hiss [hɪs]	Zischen; Rauschen	*hiss* → to hiss
	to bow [baʊ]	beugen; verbeugen	He *bowed* before he left the stage. → to take a bow *(sich verbeugen)*
	***to beat** [biːt]	schlagen; besiegen	We're winning, come on, we can *beat* the other team!

Focus 3 Slavery and the Civil War

1	**enterprise** [ˌentəˈpraɪz]	Unternehmen; Firma	*enterprise* = company *Fr.* entreprise *(f)*
	sugarcane [ˈʃʊɡəkeɪŋ]	Zuckerrohr	Many slaves worked on plantations for cotton or *sugarcane*. *Fr.* canne à sucre *(f)*
	to **thrive** [θraɪv]	florieren; gedeihen; blühen	The company, which she founded five years ago, *is thriving*.
	to **enslave** [ɪnˈsleɪv]	versklaven	*to enslave* → slave, slavery
	to **question** [ˈkwestʃən]	fragen; hinterfragen; in Frage stellen	Our trainer always *questions* our motivation.
	theory [ˈθɪəri]	Theorie	His *theory* is very convincing. *Fr.* théorie *(f)*
	inferior [ɪnˈfɪəriə]	unterlegen; minderwertig	These recordings are of *inferior* quality. *inferior* ↔ superior
	raid [reɪd]	Angriff; Überfall	The rebels started a surprise *raid* on a military camp. *raid* = attack
	cargo, cargoes *(pl)* [ˈkɑːɡəʊ]	Ladung; Fracht	This ship's *cargo* was wine, fruit and coal.
	passage [ˈpæsɪdʒ]	Überfahrt; Passage	We arrived on the island after a 10-hour *passage* by ship.
	calculation [ˌkælkjəˈleɪʃn]	Berechnung; Kalkulation	*calculation* → to calculate
	proper [ˈprɒpə]	richtig; ordentlich; angemessen	For many in Britain, a *proper* English breakfast includes bacon and eggs, sausages, baked beans and tomatoes, with tea or coffee.
	beating [ˈbiːtɪŋ]	Prügel	*beating* → to beat
	voyage [ˈvɔɪɪdʒ]	Fahrt; Reise	*voyage* = journey *Fr.* voyage *(m)*
	demand [dɪˈmɑːnd]	Bedarf; Nachfrage	The *demand* for coal is down. *demand* → to demand
2	to **ban** [bæn]	verbannen; verbieten; ausschließen	He was *banned* from the party because he had publicly criticised its policies. to *ban* smoking in restaurants to *ban* = to forbid
	account [əˈkaʊnt]	Erzählung	I gave a detailed *account* of what had happened that night.
	brand [brænd]	Brandmal; Brandzeichen	Putting *brands* on animals is a controversial practice because it is very painful.
	initial [ɪˈnɪʃl]	Initiale; Anfangsbuchstabe	It was common that slaves got brands with their master's *initials*. *Lat.* initium *(nt)*
	*to **bear** [beə]	tragen; ertragen	She couldn't *bear* to see the cat in pain.
	barely [ˈbeəli]	kaum	We could *barely* hear his voice during the speech.
	*to **be attached to** [bi ˌəˈtætʃt tə]	hängen an	I'm so *attached to* my hometown that I can't imagine living anywhere else. *to be attached* → attachment
	cornmeal [ˈkɔːnmiːl]	Maismehl	Some famous biscuits are made with *cornmeal*.

dawn [dɔːn]	Morgendämmerung; Morgengrauen	I woke up at *dawn* although it was only five o'clock.
dusk [dʌsk]	Abenddämmerung; Sonnenuntergang	You must be home before *dusk*. *dusk* ↔ dawn
to **process** [ˈprəʊsəs]	verarbeiten; aufbereiten	The fruit *is processed* before export. *to process* → process
to **tend to sb / sth** [ˈtend tə]	sich um jdn. / etw. kümmern	My grandparents visit us from time to time to *tend to* the garden. *Lat.* tendere
to **boil** [bɔɪl]	kochen; sieden	The water *is boiling* now. Let's put the pasta in.
sticky [ˈstɪki]	klebrig	The child had *sticky* hands from eating honey.
overseer [ˈəʊvəˌsiːə]	Aufseher/-in; Vorarbeiter/-in	Enslaved people had to do what their *overseers* told them to do.
whip [wɪp]	Peitsche	*whip* = a piece of leather or rope, used for hitting people or animals
club [klʌb]	Schlagstock; Keule; Knüppel	Men with knives and *clubs* attacked his home.
poker [ˈpəʊkə]	Schürhaken	He moved the coals in the fire with a *poker*.
3 **Quaker** [ˈkweɪkə]	Quäker/-in *(Mitglied einer bestimmten christlichen Glaubensgemeinschaft)*	The religious society of the *Quakers* was founded in the 17th century.

Slavery

Slave trade
- to enslave, slave / enslaved person ↔ slaveholder / master / owner – overseer
- to buy / sell at auction
- to trade in sb / sth for sb / sth in Zahlung geben
- to bear / to be marked with a brand
- to gather / to amass *(wealth/power)* anhäufen

Living conditions
- cabin
- to work in the (cotton / tobacco) fields / on a (sugarcane) plantation
- horrible / inhuman conditions
- cruel treatment / atrocities Gräueltaten
- punishments: to whip – to shackle (mit Ketten) fesseln – to rape – to hang – to burn

Resistance
- equal – inferior ↔ superior
- anti-slavery / abolitionist (movement/activist)
- rebellion / revolt / uprising
- fugitive / runaway flüchtig
- to free / to enfranchise (Sklaven) freilassen
- freedman/freedwoman *(AE)* freigelassene/-r Sklave/Sklavin

5 to **preach** [priːtʃ]	predigen	The bishop *preached* to a huge crowd. *Fr.* prêcher
approach [əˈprəʊtʃ]	Herangehensweise; Vorgehensweise; Ansatz; Annäherung	We get the same results, but we have different *approaches*. *Fr.* approche *(f)*
equality [ɪˈkwɒləti]	Gleichberechtigung	*equality* = the same rights and responsibilities for everyone in a society or group *equality* → equal
playground [ˈpleɪɡraʊnd]	Schulhof; Pausenhof; Spielplatz	There is a *playground* at our school.
secession [sɪˈseʃn]	Abspaltung; Sezession	Being pro slavery was one reason for Texas's *secession* from Mexico in 1836.
*to **withdraw** [wɪðˈdrɔː]	(sich) zurückziehen	*to withdraw* = to remove or take away sth, to go away from a place

*to **split off** [ˌsplɪtˈɒf]	sich abtrennen; sich abspalten	The states that *split off* called themselves the Confederacy.
rival [ˈraɪvl]	Rivale / Rivalin; Konkurrent/-in	! Be careful with the pronunciation.
to **rape** [reɪp]	vergewaltigen	*rape* → rapist, to rape
to **enforce** [ɪnˈfɔːs]	durchsetzen	The police's job is to *enforce* the law.
bill [bɪl]	Gesetzentwurf; Gesetzesvorlage	A large part of the parliament didn't support the *bill*.
shall [ʃæl]	sollen	! '*Shall*' is used in formal conversations.
potential [pəˈtentʃl]	Potenzial	*potential* = ability or talent not yet in full use
knee [niː]	Knie	When he got down on his *knee*, she expected a marriage proposal.
intention [ɪnˈtenʃn]	Absicht; Intention	There's a saying that the road to hell is paved with good *intentions*.

Unit 2 Black in America

Introduction

memorial [məˈmɔːriəl]	Denkmal; Gedenkstätte; Denkschrift	There are thousands of Civil War *memorials* in the United States.
Hispanic [hɪˈspænɪk]	lateinamerikanisch; Latino / Latina; Hispano-Amerikaner/-in	He comes from Mexico, so he's *Hispanic*.
to **measure** [ˈmeʒə]	messen; abmessen	Let's *measure* this wardrobe to see if it fits into your room.
probability [ˌprɒbəˈbɪləti]	Wahrscheinlichkeit	In all *probability*, he will be elected mayor. *probability* → probable *(adj)* **Fr.** probabilité *(f)*
random [ˈrændəm]	zufällig; wahllos	I made a *random* choice of my nail polish colour.
2 **composition** [ˌkɒmpəˈzɪʃn]	Zusammensetzung	*composition* = the things or parts which make up a whole **Fr.** composition *(f)*; **Lat.** compositio *(f)*
sensitivity [ˌsensɪˈtɪvəti]	Empfindsamkeit; Sensibilität	*sensitivity* = the ability to understand other people's feelings *sensitivity* → sensitive
to **coin** [kɔɪn]	prägen *(einen Begriff / eine Münze)*	Shakespeare *coined* many expressions of the English language. *to coin* = to create (a word, a coin) *to coin* → coin
to **differentiate** [ˌdɪfˈrenʃieɪt]	unterscheiden	Some people can't *differentiate* between their imagination and the real world. *to differentiate* → difference, different
finding [ˈfaɪndɪŋ]	Ergebnis	The *findings* of the survey made the researchers happy. *finding* → to find
4 **repercussion** [ˌriːpəˈkʌʃn]	Auswirkung	She kept her mouth shut for fear of *repercussion*. *repercussion* = result or consequence of an action or event

Minorities in the US

- Black / Asian / White / Hispanic people / Native populations / … make up about (more / less than) 20 percent / half / a quarter / … of the population.
- The number of … has (slightly / considerably) increased / grown / risen / decreased / fallen / hasn't changed.
- The role of … in politics / education / the justice system Justizsystem / the economy is important / small / irrelevant.
- … have a great / small influence on …

- Discrimination is an issue for …
- … are often/rarely discriminated against because of stereotypes / their culture / language / religion / skin colour / …
- … (don't) have the same rights as …
- … suffer disproportionately from …

Texts A

1	**fictitious** [fɪkˈtɪʃəs]	fiktiv; erfunden; erdichtet	All the events in this film are *fictitious*. *fictitious* → fiction
	predominantly [prɪˈdɒmɪnəntli]	überwiegend	The districts north of the river are *predominantly* Black, but this is changing as more and more Hispanics move into the area.
	posh [pɒʃ]	vornehm; piekfein	I took my friend to a *posh* hotel for a cocktail.
	accidentally [ˌæksɪˈdentli]	versehentlich; aus Versehen	*accidentally* = by accident = you don't mean to do sth
	to **slip** [slɪp]	schlüpfen; gleiten (lassen)	! The German translations of verbs like 'to slip' or 'to drop' can be used with or without 'lassen'.
	ironic [ˌaɪˈrɒnɪk]	ironisch	I love writers with an *ironic* sense of humor. *ironic* → irony
	by default [ˌbaɪ dɪˈfɔːlt]	automatisch; standardmäßig; voreingestellt	The other team couldn't play so we won *by default*.
	familiar [fəˈmɪliə]	vertraut; bekannt	Things that you know well are *familiar* to you. ! familiar ≠ familiär *Fr.* familier / familière
	to **giggle** [ˈgɪgl]	kichern; lachen	*to giggle* = to laugh quietly or in a silly way, sometimes because you feel nervous
	*to **swear** [sweə]	schwören	Our teacher *swore* that he would do everything to help us.
	soap (*no pl*) [səʊp]	Seife	I'd like to wash my hands, but there's no *soap* in the bathroom.
	powder [ˈpaʊdə]	Puder; Pulver	Snow often looks like fine white *powder* on roofs. *Fr.* poudre (f)
	to **look a mess** [ˌlʊk ə ˈmes]	ungepflegt aussehen	I think I *look a mess* today!
	cancer [ˈkænsə]	Krebs (*Krankheit*)	A lot of money goes into *cancer* research. *Fr.* cancer (m)
	damn [dæm]	verdammt	People often say this when sth very annoying suddenly happens. *Lat.* damnare
	to **yell** [jel]	brüllen; laut schreien	Don't *yell* at me!
	apart [əˈpɑːt]	auseinander; getrennt	*apart* = separate in time, place or position
	to **mumble** [ˈmʌmbl]	murmeln; nuscheln	*to mumble* = to speak or say something, with the mouth partly closed, which can hardly be understood

to **pull over** [ˌpʊlˈəʊvə]	(heranfahren und) anhalten	I *pulled over* to answer the phone.
unarmed [ʌnˈɑːmd]	unbewaffnet	*unarmed* = not carrying weapons *unarmed* ↔ armed
coffin [ˈkɒfɪn]	Sarg	There were beautiful flowers on his *coffin*.
to **suspect sb / sth** [səˈspekt]	verdächtigen	*to suspect* = to think that sth (bad) is probably true or likely to happen, but without having definite proof
to **investigate** [ɪnˈvestɪgeɪt]	ermitteln; untersuchen; Nachforschungen anstellen; recherchieren	Police *are investigating* the cause of the accident. *to investigate* → investigation
to **recover** [rɪˈkʌvə]	zurückbekommen; wiedergewinnen; sicherstellen	It took her a long time to *recover* her strength after the flu.
to **pace** [peɪs]	hin und her gehen	She *paced* the room nervously.
to **rush** [rʌʃ]	hetzen; eilen	*to rush* = to hurry
lately [ˈleɪtli]	in letzter Zeit; kürzlich	His health hasn't been too good *lately*. *lately* = recently
thug [θʌg]	Gangster; Schläger; Verbrecher	*thug* = a tough and violent person, especially a criminal
to **mind one's own business** [ˌmaɪnd wʌnz ˌəʊn ˈbɪznɪs]	sich um die eigenen Angelegenheiten kümmern	*Mind your own business!*
to **swallow** [ˈswɒləʊ]	schlucken	Food that you don't like can seem hard to *swallow*.
2 **violence** *(no pl)* [ˈvaɪələns]	Gewalt	When there is *violence*, people try to hurt or even kill others. *violence* → violent *Fr.* violence *(f)*
prevention [prɪˈvenʃn]	Vorbeugung; Vermeidung; Verhütung	Schools hold workshops for crime *prevention* in some cities. *prevention* → to prevent sb from doing sth *Fr.* prévention *(f)*
bail [beɪl]	Kaution	His family couldn't pay the *bail*, so he had to stay in prison for the night. *bail* = a sum of money left with the court as security for a person's reappearance in court
*to **be located** [ˌbi ləʊˈkeɪtɪd]	gelegen sein; liegen	Where *is* the museum *located*? = Where exactly is the museum? *to be located* → location
3 to **reclaim** [rɪˈkleɪm]	zurückfordern; reklamieren; zurückgewinnen	I've come to *reclaim* my money. *Fr.* réclamer
self-empowerment [ˌselfɪmˈpaʊəmənt]	Selbstermächtigung	*self-empowerment* = the giving or delegation of power to oneself
to **originate** [əˈrɪdʒɪneɪt]	entstehen; seinen Anfang nehmen	The dish *originated* in North Africa. *to originate* → origin
intestine [ɪnˈtestɪn]	Darm; Eingeweide	Only few chefs cook *intestines* regularly. *Fr.* intestin *(m)*
to **nourish** [ˈnʌrɪʃ]	ernähren	The food the mother eats *nourishes* both her and her baby. *Fr.* nourrir
obesity [əˈbiːsəti]	Fettleibigkeit	Extreme consumption of sugar and fat leads to *obesity*. *obesity* → obese
4 **trendy** [ˈtrendi]	trendy; modisch	*trendy* → trend

rent [rent]	Miete	*rent* = the money you pay for sth you use, for example an apartment or a car **!** rent ≠ *Rente*
reputation [ˌrepjəˈteɪʃn]	Ruf	In the Middle Ages actors had a bad *reputation*. People often thought of them as thieves. **Fr.** réputation *(f)*
pep talk [ˈpep ˌtɔːk]	aufmunternde Worte; Motivationsgespräch	The coach gave a *pep talk* to the team before the game.
oppressive [əˈpresɪv]	unterdrückerisch; gewaltsam; repressiv	The new laws will be as *oppressive* as those they replace. *oppressive* → oppression, to oppress
napkin [ˈnæpkɪn]	Serviette	*napkin* = a piece of cloth or paper for wiping the mouth or protecting the clothes while eating
to crumble [ˈkrʌmbl]	zerfallen; zerbrechen; abbröckeln	*to crumble* = to fall apart
all of a sudden [ˌɔːl əv ə ˈsʌdn]	plötzlich; auf einmal	*all of a sudden* = suddenly
literacy *(no pl)* [ˈlɪtrəsi]	Lese- und Schreibfähigkeit; *hier:* Lese-	*literacy* = the ability to read and write
*to shrink [ʃrɪŋk]	einsinken; schrumpfen	*to shrink* = to get smaller

Describing neighbourhoods

Housing
- can / can't afford high rents
- (urban) ghetto
- low-income / middle-income / high-income / middle-class / working-class neighbourhoods / areas / families
- poor ↔ posh
- predominantly / exclusively Black / Hispanic / white
- gentrification *Aufwertung durch Luxussanierung*
- public housing *(AE)* / council housing *(BE)* sozialer Wohnungsbau

Problems
- disadvantage, to disadvantage
- education: (more / better) educational opportunities – (high / free of) tuition fees – affordable colleges erschwinglich
- lack of, to lack
- (small / minor / capital) crime
- drug trafficking Drogenhandel
- murder, to murder, murderer
- police brutality / killings / shootings
- prison / jail: to arrest – to incarcerate inhaftieren – to get a prison sentence (for) – to pay the / to be released on bail
- street gang – gang violence – gang war
- (extreme / domestic / street) violence häuslich

5 **sole** [səʊl]	Sohle	The *soles* of my favourite shoes need to be repaired.
prayer [preə]	Gebet	*prayer* = the activity of communicating with God *prayer* → to pray
pride [praɪd]	Stolz	to take *pride* in sth = to be proud of sth
faith [feɪθ]	Glaube; Vertrauen	1. She is an active member of the Muslim community and her *faith* is very important to her. 2. to have / put *faith* in sb / sth
steel [stiːl]	Stahl	*Steel* is used to make things like bridges, cars, knives and forks etc.
to yield [jiːld]	nachgeben; Vorfahrt gewähren	I finally *yielded* and accepted some cake.

to **guard** [gɑːd]	bewachen	Many Americans feel the US-Mexican border isn't *guarded* well enough. *to guard* → guard *Fr.* garder
rhyme scheme [ˈraɪm skiːm]	Reimschema	The *rhyme scheme* of the poem is ABBA.
repetition [ˌrepɪˈtɪʃn]	Wiederholung	*Repetitions* can be very boring. *repetition* → to repeat *Fr.* répétition (f); *Lat.* repetitio (f)
to **intensify** [ɪnˈtensɪfaɪ]	intensivieren; verstärken	When you *intensify* what you're doing, then you put more work into it. *Fr.* intensifier
reflective [rɪˈflektɪv]	nachdenklich	My brother is a quiet, *reflective* boy. *reflective* → to reflect
affectionate [əˈfekʃnət]	liebevoll; zärtlich	They seemed to be in love with each other and were openly *affectionate*.
prose [prəʊz]	Prosa	*Prose* is written language that is not poetry.

Texts B

1	**anxiety** [æŋˈzaɪəti]	Angst; Sorge	Full of *anxiety*, she didn't dare to go outside.
	Afro [ˈæfrəʊ]	Afrolook	She used to have an *Afro*.
	actual [ˈæktʃuəl]	tatsächlich; wirklich; eigentlich	She had written some notes, but she hadn't started the *actual* work.
	sum total [ˌsʌm ˈtəʊtl]	Summe; Gesamtheit	Good design is the *sum total* of modern technology and high-quality materials.
	contradictory [ˌkɒntrəˈdɪktri]	widersprüchlich	*contradictory* → contradiction, to contradict *Lat.* contradicere
	assumption [əˈsʌmpʃn]	Annahme; Voraussetzung	*assumption* → to assume *Fr.* assomption (f)
	brand [brænd]	Marke	*brand* = a particular product or line of products made by one company and sold under a special name
	commerce [ˈkɒmɜːs]	Handel	*commerce* = the activity of buying and selling goods, trade
	*to **mistake sb / sth for sb / sth** [mɪˈsteɪk fə]	jdn./etw. mit jdm./etw. verwechseln	My mum *is* often *mistaken* for my sister.
	proprietary [prəˈpraɪətri]	urheberrechtlich geschützt; eigen	My company uses *proprietary* software.
	observer [əbˈzɜːvə]	Beobachter/-in; Zuschauer/-in	When I see a bully hurting someone, I want to help and not be a silent *observer*. But at the same time I'm afraid that I could be hurt. *observer* → to observe
	discontent [ˌdɪskənˈtent]	Unzufriedenheit	The *discontent* of the people led to a revolution. *discontent* → content
	overt [əʊˈvɜːt]	offen; offenkundig	*overt* = in an open and obvious way *Fr.* ouvert/-e
	to **define** [dɪˈfaɪn]	definieren	Can you *define* what you mean by 'prosperity'? *to define* → definition

epic [ˈepɪk]	episch; gewaltig; unglaublich	*epic* = very large or grand
tragedy [ˈtrædʒədi]	Tragödie	*tragedy* ↔ comedy *Fr.* tragédie *(f)*; *Lat.* tragoedia *(f)*
ultimately [ˈʌltɪmətli]	schließlich; letztendlich	*ultimately* = finally, at last
courage [ˈkʌrɪdʒ]	Mut; Tapferkeit; Courage	❗ Be careful with the pronunciation. *Fr.* courage *(m)*
appropriation [əˌprəʊpriˈeɪʃn]	Aneignung; Verwendung	*appropriation* = the act of taking sth which isn't yours
peer group [ˈpɪə gruːp]	Gruppe von Gleichaltrigen	*peer* = a person of the same age
3 ladder [ˈlædə]	Leiter	Be careful! Don't fall off the *ladder*.
counterpart [ˈkaʊntəpaːt]	Gegenstück; Kollege / Kollegin	It is likely that his *counterpart* in the US will agree with him at this point.
shortage [ˈʃɔːtɪdʒ]	Knappheit; Mangel	If there's a *shortage* of sth, there isn't enough of it. *shortage* → short
to recruit [rɪˈkruːt]	rekrutieren; anwerben; einstellen	Soldiers *are recruited* to the army. *Fr.* recruter
*to seek [siːk]	suchen	Many people *are seeking* peace and happiness.
bathroom facilities [ˌbɑːθrʊm fəˈsɪlɪtiz]	Toiletten	The *bathroom facilities* are in a separate building.
to launch [lɔːnʃ]	starten; in Gang setzen	The company recently *launched* a new campaign. *to launch* = to start *to launch* → launch
to ensure [ɪnˈʃɔː]	sicherstellen; gewährleisten	Please *ensure* that all the doors are locked. *to ensure* → sure
to promote [prəˈməʊt]	fördern; befördern; voranbringen	The tax reduction *promoted* trade with other countries. *to promote* = to help sth to develop or increase *to promote* → promotion
to advocate [ˈædvəkeɪt]	befürworten; verteidigen; eintreten für	*to advocate* = to uphold or defend a cause or course of action
treatment [ˈtriːtmənt]	Behandlung	When I was in hospital, I didn't get the *treatment* I needed at first. I had a rare disease. *treatment* → to treat
manual [ˈmænjuəl]	händisch; manuell	*manual* work = work done with one's hands
to supervise [ˈsuːpəvaɪz]	beaufsichtigen; betreuen	*to supervise* = to watch sb or sth to make sure everything is done correctly *to supervise* → supervisor *Lat.* super + videre
to endure [ɪnˈdʒʊə]	ertragen; aushalten	He *had endured* years of pain and sleepless nights because of a disease.

🔗 Texts C

post- [pəʊst]	Nach-	We live in a *post*-colonial era. *post*- ↔ pre-
1 *to bring about [ˌbrɪŋ əˈbaʊt]	herbeiführen	The British Empire *brought about* a great many changes.

marriage ['mærɪdʒ]	Ehe; Heirat	*marriage* → to marry *Fr.* mariage *(m)*
chief executive officer (CEO) [ˌtʃiːfˌɪɡˌzekjətɪvˌˈɒfɪsə]	Vorstandvorsitzende/-r; Geschäftsführer/-in	The *chief executive* (officer) is the person in a company who has the most power and authority and is responsible for managing daily affairs.
momentous [məˈməntəs]	bedeutsam; weitreichend; folgenschwer	The president made a *momentous* decision concerning future visas. *Lat.* momentum *(nt)*
obligation [ˌɒblɪˈɡeɪʃn]	Verpflichtung	I feel the *obligation* to support my family and do whatever is possible.
multiple ['mʌltɪpl]	vielfältig; vielfach	There are *multiple* ways to be successful in life. *Fr.* multiple
to overlap [ˌəʊvəˈlæp]	(sich) überlappen	The pictures in the book *overlap*, which I think looks cool.
burden ['bɜːdn]	Last; Belastung	Having more responsibility at work feels like a *burden* to me.
*to **be bound to do sth** [bɪˈbaʊnd tə]	etw. tun müssen; nicht umhin-können, etw. zu tun; verpflichtet sein, etw. zu tun	Everybody *is bound to disappoint* some other person during their lives.
to what extent [tə ˌwɒt ɪkˈstent]	inwiefern; inwieweit	*To what extent* do you agree with the author?
2 **orator** ['ɒrətə]	Redner/-in	Barack Obama is said to be a very good *orator*. *orator* → oral *Lat.* orator *(m)*
standing *(no pl)* ['stændɪŋ]	Ansehen; Status	He has improved his country's *standing* abroad. *standing* = social or financial status or reputation
to accomplish [əˈkʌmplɪʃ]	vollbringen; erreichen; bewerkstelligen	If we all work together, I think we can *accomplish* our goal.
poll [pəʊl]	Umfrage	The latest opinion *poll* says that teenagers are worried about privacy. *poll* = survey
confidence ['kɒnfɪdns]	Vertrauen; Zuversicht	I lost my *confidence* in this government years ago. *confidence* → confident *Lat.* confidere
affair [əˈfeə]	Affäre; Angelegenheit	Keep out of my *affairs*!
implicitly [ɪmˈplɪsɪtli]	indirekt; implizit	She told us *implicitly* that she wasn't happy. *Fr.* implicitement
agenda [əˈdʒendə]	Vorhaben; Programm	The current political *agenda* is to stop climate change.
indicator ['ɪndɪkeɪtə]	Anzeichen; Hinweis	*indicator* = sign, symbol *indicator* → to indicate
well-being [ˌwelˈbiːɪŋ]	Wohlbefinden	The school is very concerned about the *well-being* of its pupils.
incarceration *(no pl)* [ɪnˌkɑːsrˈeɪʃn]	Inhaftierung	The *incarceration* rates among Black people in the USA are higher than among white people.
rate [reɪt]	Rate; Quote	*rate* = the level of sth (e.g. of incarceration or unemployment in a certain area)
outcome ['aʊtkʌm]	Ergebnis; Ausgang	*outcome* = result

to **fare** [feə]	ergehen	"How do you *fare?*" = "How are you?" in modern English.
expansion [ɪkˈspænʃn]	Expansion; Ausdehnung; Erweiterung	The *expansion* of private health insurance will profit many people.
failure [ˈfeɪljə]	Scheitern; Versagen	*failure* ↔ success *failure* → to fail
implausibility [ɪmˌplɔːzəˈbɪləti]	Unglaubwürdigkeit; Fadenscheinigkeit	*implausibility* → plausible
preparatory [prɪˈpærətri]	vorbereitend	For this project we will need a year's *preparatory* work. *preparatory* → to prepare, preparation
selective [sɪˈlektɪv]	anspruchsvoll; kritisch; wählerisch	Buyers get more and more *selective*. *selective* → to select
loan [ləʊn]	Darlehen; Kredit	*loan* = a sum of money you borrow, e.g. from a bank, and have to pay back
roughly [ˈrʌfli]	ungefähr; schätzungsweise	*roughly* = more or less *roughly* ↔ exactly
majority [məˈdʒɒrəti]	Mehrheit; Mehrzahl	The *majority* of Americans live in cities. *Fr.* majorité (f)
to **reject** [rɪˈdʒekt]	zurückweisen; ablehnen	The bill *was rejected* by the majority of Members of Congress. *to reject* = to refuse *to reject* ↔ to accept
3 to **kneel** [niːl]	knien	NFL players protested police brutality against African-Americans by *kneeling* during the US national anthem. *to kneel* → knee
anthem [ˈænθəm]	Hymne	National *anthems* are usually played at official celebrations.
league [liːg]	Liga	The new coach has already trained several other teams in this *league*. *Fr.* ligue (f)

Media competence

to **distinguish** [dɪˈstɪŋgwɪʃ]	unterscheiden; klar erkennen	You need to *distinguish* between England and the rest of the UK. **!** to *distinguish* between (= zwischen) / from (= von) *Fr.* distinguer
1 to **assess** [əˈses]	bewerten; beurteilen	Exams are not the only means of *assessing* a student's ability. *to assess* = to judge = to evaluate
2 **sensational** [senˈseɪʃnl]	sensationell; spektakulär	*sensational* = very exciting, or extremely good *Fr.* sensationnel/-le
capital letter [ˌkæpɪtl ˈletə]	Großbuchstabe	The 'B' in 'Brexit' is a *capital letter*, the 'e' in 'exit' isn't.
to **manipulate** [məˈnɪpjəleɪt]	manipulieren; beeinflussen	Statistics can be *manipulated* to make exaggerated claims. *Fr.* manipuler
to **verify** [ˈverɪfaɪ]	verifizieren; überprüfen	These numbers are surprisingly high and they'll have to be *verified*. *Fr.* vérifier
to **confirm** [kənˈfɜːm]	bestätigen; bekräftigen	Please *confirm* your reservation in writing by Friday.

dubious [ˈdjuːbɪəs]	dubios; zweifelhaft; fragwürdig	Police officers often speak with *dubious* characters. *dubious* → doubt *Lat.* dubius
imprint [ˈɪmprɪnt]	Impressum	You can find the name of the author and the publisher on the *imprint* of a book. *imprint* → to print
account [əˈkaʊnt]	Konto	Why is there never enough money in my bank *account*? to open / close a social media *account* *Fr.* compte *(m)*

Unit task

alliteration [ˌəlɪtəˈreɪʃn]	Alliteration; Stabreim	*alliteration* = the use, especially in poetry, of the same sound or sounds, especially consonants, at the beginning of several words that are close together
accordingly [əˈkɔːdɪŋli]	entsprechend	She's an expert in her field, and is paid *accordingly*.
vivid [ˈvɪvɪd]	lebendig; lebhaft	She was wearing a dress with a *vivid* pattern.
to **convey** [kənˈveɪ]	transportieren; ausdrücken; vermitteln	These adjectives *convey* the atmosphere to the reader. *to convey* = to make sth known
choppy [ˈtʃɒpi]	bewegt	We are passing through *choppy* waters.
to **recite** [rɪˈsaɪt]	vortragen; rezitieren	She *recited* the Pledge of Allegiance. *Fr.* réciter

⟨ Texts D ⟩

1 **opponent** [əˈpəʊnənt]	Gegner/-in; Widersacher/-in	A sports *opponent* will always try to win against you.
frustration [frʌsˈtreɪʃn]	Frust; Enttäuschung	After that awful Maths test I felt nothing but *frustration*.
to **tug** [tʌg]	ziehen; zupfen	*to tug* = to pull at sth quickly
daycare [ˈdeɪkeə]	Kita; Tagespflege	*daycare* = care or education provided during the day, especially for young children
setback [ˈsetbæk]	Rückschlag	The team suffered a major *setback*, but they have a positive attitude to improve.
to **arrange** [əˈreɪndʒ]	arrangieren; anordnen	*to arrange* = to plan, prepare for or organise something *to arrange* → arrangement *Fr.* arranger
chin [tʃɪn]	Kinn	He has dark eyes and a pointed *chin*.
to **handle** [ˈhændl]	umgehen mit	I can *handle* this problem on my own. *to handle* = to deal with
to **blink** [blɪŋk]	blinzeln; zwinkern	You've got something in your eye – try *blinking* a few times. *to blink* = to open and close your eyes quickly.
fist [fɪst]	Faust	He hit the table with his *fist*.
microphone [ˈmaɪkrəfəʊn]	Mikrofon	! *microphone* = mic
notebook [ˈnəʊtbʊk]	Heft; Notizbuch; Notebook (Computer)	*notebook* → to note down
to **shove** [ʃʌv]	schieben; drängen	You're next – there's no need to *shove*.

substance [ˈsʌbstns]	Substanz; Gehalt	1. Asbestos is a natural *substance* which is resistant to fire. 2. What is more important, *substance* or style? *Fr.* substance *(f)*
catchy [ˈkætʃi]	eingängig; einprägsam	If a song has a *catchy* tune, it's easy to remember.
buzz [bʌz]	Begeisterung; Kick	I love riding fast – it gives me a real *buzz*.
fame [feɪm]	Ruhm	She moved to Los Angeles in search of *fame* and fortune. *fame* → famous
fool [fuːl]	Trottel; Dummkopf	He always acts like a *fool* when he is in love.
ought to *(+ inf)* [ˈɔːt tə]	sollen	It's 10 p.m. That child *ought to* be in bed. *ought to* = should
terrific [təˈrɪfɪk]	ausgezeichnet; hervorragend	You look *terrific*!

Focus 4 Fight for your rights!

2 **amendment** [əˈmenmənt]	Abänderung (einer Gesetzes-vorlage); Zusatzartikel (zur Verfassung)	There was an *amendment* to the Act in 1972.
to **abolish** [əˈbɒlɪʃ]	aufheben; abschaffen	Apartheid *was abolished* in 1994. *to abolish* = to put an end to sth *Lat.* abolere
to **strengthen** [ˈstreŋθn]	stärken	! Some verbs are built by adding -(e)n to the adjective or noun: *strengthen*, widen, broaden, weaken, lessen, … *strengthen* → strength, strong
facilities *(pl)* [fəˈsɪlɪtiz]	Einrichtung; Anlage	Most hotel rooms have private bathroom *facilities*.
defiance *(no pl)* [dɪˈfaɪəns]	Auflehnung; Trotz	Running away was an act of *defiance* against his parents.
board of education [ˌbɔːd əv ˌedʒʊˈkeɪʃn]	Schulbehörde	*board of education* = a group of people who have been elected to organise the management of the local school system of a particular area
unconstitutional [ˌʌnkɒnstɪˈtjuːʃnl]	verfassungswidrig	Changing the law in this way would be *unconstitutional*.
white supremacist [ˌwaɪt suːˈpreməsɪst]	Anhänger/-in der Theorie von der Überlegenheit der Weißen	We want to limit the influence of *white supremacists*.
to **repress** [rɪˈpres]	unterdrücken	Some governments *repress* their people even today.
Jew [dʒuː]	Jude / Jüdin	The first immigrants to this part of London were *Jews*. *Jew* → Jewish
constitution [ˌkɒnstɪˈtjuːʃn]	Verfassung	Britain has no written *constitution*. *constitution* → constitutional *Fr.* constitution *(f)*; *Lat.* constituere
superior [suːˈpɪəriə]	überlegen; gehoben	They regard themselves as *superior* to other people. *superior* ↔ inferior
to **evoke sth** [ɪˈvəʊk]	etw. hervorrufen; etw. (herauf-)beschwören	That smell always *evokes* memories of my old school. *Fr.* évoquer; *Lat.* evocare
xenophobia *(no pl)* [ˌzenəˈfəʊbiə]	Fremdenhass; Xenophobie	*xenophobia* = extreme dislike or fear of strangers, their customs, their religions, etc.

enforcement [ɪnˈfɔːsmənt]	Erzwingung; zwangsweise Durchführung	It's not about new laws, but *enforcement* of the laws we have. *enforcement* → to enforce
to **pass** [pɑːs]	verabschieden *(Gesetze)*	A new law *was passed* in Congress yesterday.
stylistic devices [staɪˌlɪstɪk dɪˈvaɪsɪz]	Stilmittel	Talented writers make good use of *stylistic devices* in their texts.
3 to **digest** [daɪˈdʒest]	verdauen; auflösen	*Fr.* digérer
4 **curriculum** [kəˈrɪkjələm]	Lehrplan	*curriculum* = list of topics and learning goals in a school year
5 **ballot** [ˈbælət]	Wahl; geheime Abstimmung	They cast their votes in a secret *ballot*.
bullet [ˈbʊlɪt]	Kugel; Geschoss	He dodged the first *bullet* but got hit by the second one.
somewhat [ˈsʌmwɒt]	ein wenig; einigermaßen	1. We were *somewhat* tired after our long walk. 2. *Somewhat* to my surprise, I found the house empty.
minister [ˈmɪnɪstə]	Pfarrer/-in	*minister* = a religious leader in certain Christian churches
to **assassinate** [əˈsæsɪneɪt]	ermorden	Martin Luther King was *assassinated* in 1968. *Fr.* assassiner
to **convert** [kənˈvɜːt]	konvertieren; übertreten	She *converted* to Christianity.
to **symbolise** [ˈsɪmblaɪz]	symbolisieren	*to symbolise* → symbol *Fr.* symboliser
jail [dʒeɪl]	Gefängnis	*jail* = prison
persecution [ˌpɜːsɪˈkjuːʃn]	Verfolgung	Many of the first European settlers in North America had suffered religious *persecution* in their home countries.
redemptive [rɪˈdemtɪv]	heilend; erlösend	She experienced the *redemptive* power of friendship.
creed [kriːd]	Glauben; Glaubensbekenntnis; Kredo; Überzeugung	In our society there are people of every ethnicity and *creed*. *Fr.* croire; *Lat.* credere
*to **swing (at sb)** [swɪŋ]	(nach jdm.) schlagen	*to swing at sb* = to try to hit sb
pattern [ˈpætn]	Muster	*pattern* = the way in which sth is done or repeated / a design of lines, colours, shapes etc.
hypocrisy [hɪˈpɒkrəsi]	Heuchelei; Scheinheiligkeit	Just be honest with yourself and stop all this *hypocrisy*. *Fr.* hypocrisie *(f)*
rhetorical [rɪˈtɒrɪkl]	rhetorisch	Is this a *rhetorical* question?
aim [eɪm]	Ziel	What's the *aim* of your research? *aim* = goal
6 **incident** [ˈɪnsɪdnt]	Vorfall; Ereignis	The police asked witnesses about the *incident*. *Fr.* incident *(m)*
grassroots *(pl)* [ˈgrɑːsruːts]	Volk; Basis	'Black Lives Matter' started as a *grassroots* movement.
8 **beloved** [bɪˈlʌvɪd]	geliebt	Her *beloved* husband died last year. *beloved* → love, to love
humanity [hjuːˈmænəti]	Menschheit	*humanity* = all people *humanity* → human *Lat.* humanitas *(f)*

Civil rights movements

Problems

- discrimination – oppression Unterdrückung – persecution
- police brutality
- segregation
- to violate verletzen (rights / the constitution)
- (to be ruled) unconstitutional

Change

- to overcome überwinden (segregation)
- to bring about (change / reforms)
- to emancipate befreien
- empowerment
- (legal / racial / social) equality
- to strengthen

Forms of protest

- activism, activist
- boycott – demonstration – sit-in
- grassroots (movement)
- protest, to protest (against)
- to demonstrate solidarity

- to march, march
- resistance Widerstand, to resist arrest
- non-violence, non-violent (protest / resistance) / peaceful ↔ radical / militant

- to speak out about / against (injustice Ungerechtigkeit / inequality Ungleichheit)
- to stand up for your rights
- to struggle for civil rights

Across cultures 3 The Black roots of pop music

1	**occasion** [əˈkeɪʒn]	Gelegenheit; Anlass	The annual ball is a good *occasion* to get to know people. *Fr.* occasion (f)
	commercial [kəˈmɜːʃl]	kommerziell; profitorientiert	The movie was a *commercial* success, but the critics hated it. *commercial* → commerce
	numerous [ˈnjuːmrəs]	zahlreich	I met them on *numerous* occasions. *Fr.* nombreux / nombreuse
3	**big bang** [ˌbɪg ˈbæŋ]	Urknall; großer Knall	According to scientists, our universe began with a *big bang*.
	to **sanitise** [ˈsænɪtaɪz]	keimfrei machen; aufwerten	When rock 'n' roll was '*sanitised*', it became acceptable for a wider audience.
	subtext [ˈsʌbtekst]	versteckte Bedeutung	If something has a *subtext*, it has a hidden meaning.
	to **appropriate** [əˈprəʊprieɪt]	sich aneignen	Rock 'n' roll *was appropriated* by white people.

The development of Black music

In the **18th** and **19th** centuries, enslaved Black people created songs called **spirituals**, combining their African heritage with the experience of slavery in the South of the US. Spirituals were work songs, songs about slave life, biblical (biblisch) themes or freedom. They developed into **blues** and **gospel** music, and in the late 19th century Black people also took elements from European music and created a new genre called **ragtime**, which later evolved into **jazz**.

Since the **20th** century, a lot more genres have emerged: **jazz, rhythm and blues, rock 'n' roll, soul, funk, disco** and **hip hop** with lots of variations. Almost all kinds of modern pop music have evolved from these roots. They have been taken up and developed further in the entire world.

Focus 5   My generation?

1	**distinct** [dɪˈstɪŋkt]	unterschieden; klar; deutlich	There's a *distinct* smell of cigarettes in this room.
	mature [məˈtjʊə]	reif	Your behaviour isn't very *mature*. You're acting like a baby! *Lat.* maturus
	open-minded [ˈəʊpnˌmaɪndɪd]	offen; aufgeschlossen	*open-minded* = willing to consider new or different ideas *open-minded* ↔ narrow-minded
	overprotective [ˌəʊvəprəˈtektɪv]	überfürsorglich	It was difficult to train the *overprotective* dog. → to protect, protection
2	**contemporary** [kənˈtemprəri]	zeitgenössisch; zeitgemäß	*contemporary* = current *contemporary* ↔ old-fashioned, traditional *Fr.* contemporain/-e
	mindset [ˈmaɪndset]	Denkart; Mentalität	*mindset* = a person's way of thinking and their opinions
3	**sth as opposed to sth** [æzˌəˈpəʊzd tə]	etw. im Gegensatz zu etw.	The box is plastic, *as opposed to* this bowl, made of wood. *as opposed to* → opposite
	to **fade away** [ˌfeɪdˌəˈweɪ]	schwinden; zerrinnen; verblassen; sterben	*to fade away* = to slowly disappear, lose importance, become weaker, or die
	the end justifies the means [ðiˌend dʒʌstɪfaɪz ðə ˈmiːnz]	der Zweck heiligt die Mittel	*Does the end really justify the means?*
	stance [stæns]	Haltung	Politicians are trained to have a confident *stance*.
	substitute [ˈsʌbstɪtjuːt]	Ersatz; Ersatz-	Tofu can be used as a meat *substitute* in vegetarian recipes.

Growing up

• puberty / adolescence	Pubertät, Jugend, Entwicklungsjahre	to enter / to reach *puberty* / *adolescence*; to experience / undergo durchmachen puberty
• coming-of-age novel	Entwicklungsroman, Bildungsroman	*Coming-of-age* stories are a popular genre in literature as well as in films.
• distinct, distinctness	unterschieden, Unterschiedlichkeit	to be separate and *distinct* from your parents / other groups / people
• to define yourself	(sich) definieren, sich abgrenzen	*to define yourself* and the group you want to belong to
• to set yourself apart from	sich abheben von	*to set yourself apart from* mainstream culture
• mature, to mature, maturity	reif, reifen, Reife	Adolescence is the period in which people *mature*. At its end, they are supposed to reach physical / intellectual / emotional *maturity*.
• open-minded ↔ narrow-minded	aufgeschlossen ↔ engstirnig, spießig	Young people are said to be more *open-minded* than older people.

• drugs, dangerous substances
• addiction
  to become addicted
  to be addictive
	Drogen, gefährliche Substanzen
	Sucht, Abhängigkeit
	süchtig werden
	süchtig machen
		Some young people experiment with *drugs* because they want to expand erweitern their minds, which can be very dangerous because these *substances* may be highly *addictive*.

• idle, idleness • to reproach	faul, untätig, müßig vorwerfen	Some teenagers are *reproached* by their parents for being *idle*, but they just need time to grow up.

idle [aɪdl]	faul; träge; untätig	Actually, he's a very able student, he's just *idle*.
threat [θret]	Bedrohung; Gefahr	Nuclear weapons were a constant *threat* during the Cold War.
idle threat [ˌaɪdl ˈθret]	leere Drohung	You can't scare me with your *idle threats*.

Unit 3 Youth (and) culture

Introduction

1	consumerism [kənˈsjuːmərɪzm]	Konsum; Konsumdenken	I don't like Christmas and its extreme *consumerism*. *consumerism* → to consume, consumer
	to **emancipate oneself** [iˈmænsɪpeɪt wʌnˌself]	sich emanzipieren; sich unabhängig machen	At a certain point in history the middle classes *emancipated themselves* from the model provided by the aristocracy. *to emancipate* → emancipation *Fr.* émanciper
	*to **be absorbed by sth** [ˌbi ˌəbˈzɔːbd baɪ]	in etw. integriert werden; von etw. aufgesaugt werden	*to be absorbed* = to be appropriated
2	curator [kjʊəˈreɪtə]	Kurator/-in; Ausstellungsmacher/-in	*curator* = a person who is responsible for a museum, library, etc.
	aesthetical [iːsˈθetɪkl]	ästhetisch	Furniture that is both *aesthetical* and functional is rare. *Fr.* esthétique
	dissatisfaction [dɪsˌsætɪsˈfækʃn]	Unzufriedenheit	After everything had gone wrong, I had a feeling of *dissatisfaction*. *dissatisfaction* → satisfied
	to **emerge** [ɪˈmɜːdʒ]	auftauchen; entstehen	Due to the climate change, new species began to *emerge*. *to emerge* = to develop, to appear
	to **appreciate** [əˈpriːʃieɪt]	schätzen; anerkennen; würdigen	If you *appreciate* sth, you like it because you recognise its value. *Fr.* apprécier
	convention [kənˈvenʃn]	Konvention; Kongress; Tagung	Where are the Democrats holding their party *convention*?

Texts A

1	to **collide** [kəˈlaɪd]	kollidieren; zusammenstoßen	*to collide* = to hit something violently, especially when moving *to collide* → collision
	fundamental [ˌfʌndəˈmentl]	fundamental; grundlegend	There are *fundamental* differences between men and women. *Fr.* fondamental/e
	X-ray [ˈeksreɪ]	Röntgenstrahlen; Röntgenuntersuchung	She had an *X-ray* to see if her arm was broken.
	handcuffs *(pl)* [ˈhændkʌfs]	Handschellen	She was taken to the police station in *handcuffs*. a pair of *handcuffs*
	wrist [rɪst]	Handgelenk	*wrist* = the part of the body between the hand and the arm
	pad [pæd]	Schreibblock	*pad* = notebook

to edge one's way [ˈedʒ wʌnz ˌweɪ]	sich langsam bewegen	A long line of traffic *edged its way* forward. *to edge* → edge
social security [ˌsəʊʃl sɪˈkjʊərəti]	Sozialversicherung	*social security* = a system of payments made by the government to people who are ill, poor, or who have no job
stiff [stɪf]	steif	*stiff* ↔ soft
to pick [pɪk]	pflücken	Fruit tastes best when it's freshly *picked*.
to dial [daɪəl]	wählen *(Telefon)*; anrufen	In an emergency, *dial* 110 or 112.
blank [blæŋk]	ausdruckslos; leer	1. The robot's *blank* eyes on its *blank* face looked scary. 2. The students all got a *blank* sheet of paper to note down their answers.
lane [leɪn]	Fahrspur; Weg; Gasse	Eight-*lane* highways aren't uncommon in the US.
to handle [ˈhændl]	umgehen mit	I can *handle* this problem on my own. *to handle* = to deal with
poison [ˈpɔɪzn]	Gift	*poison* → to poison *Fr.* poison *(m)*
psychedelic [ˌsaɪkɪˈdelɪk]	psychedelisch; bewusstseins-verändernd	! You don't pronounce the 'p'. *Fr.* psychédélique
to disturb [dɪˈstɜːb]	stören	Don't *disturb* Grandpa. He's sleeping.
to suspend [səˈspend]	hängen; aufhängen	*to suspend* = to hang (up)
county [ˈkaʊnti]	(Land-)Kreis; Bezirk	Texas is divided into 254 *counties*.
medal [ˈmedl]	Medaille	The first three places in a race get a *medal* made of gold, silver or bronze. *Fr.* médaille *(f)*
reasoning [ˈriːznɪŋ]	Logik	I don't understand the *reasoning* behind her conclusion. *reasoning* → reason
to recall [riːˈkɔːl]	sich erinnern	*to recall* = to remember
faint [feɪnt]	schwach; leise	There's a *faint* smell of spring in the air.
dull [dʌl]	stumpf; dumpf	*dull* ↔ bright *dull* ↔ loud
scattered [ˈskætəd]	verstreut; verteilt	My family is *scattered* all over the world.
to pound [paʊnd]	laufen; trampeln	*to pound* = to walk with heavy steps
pale [peɪl]	bleich; blass	Are you sick? You look very *pale*. the *pale* moon
to contort [kənˈtɔːt]	verzerren; verziehen	His face *contorted* with pain.
volume [ˈvɒljuːm]	Lautstärke; Volumen	Could you turn the *volume* of the TV down, please? I'm trying to sleep. *Fr.* volume *(m)*
rehabilitation *(no pl)* [ˌriːhəˌbɪlɪˈteɪʃn]	Rehabilitation	*Rehabilitation* is the process of regaining your strength after an illness or injury. a *rehab* clinic ! *rehab* = Reha
matter-of-factly [ˌmætər əv ˈfæktli]	sachlich; nüchtern	He described it all very *matter-of-factly*, with no emotion.

recollection [ˌrekl'ekʃn]	Erinnerung	*recollection* = the ability to remember sth *recollection* = memory *recollection* → to recollect
grave [greɪv]	ernst	The policewoman looked *grave* when she told us about the accident.
decade ['dekeɪd; dɪ'keɪd]	Jahrzehnt	*decade* = a period of ten years *Fr.* décade *(f)*
to operate ['ɒpreɪt]	operieren	If it gets worse, they'll have to *operate*. *to operate* → operation *Fr.* opérer
property ['prɒpəti]	Eigentum; Grundbesitz; Besitz	This beach is private *property* – keep out! *property* = ownership
the Amish [ðɪˌ'ɑːmɪʃ]	die Amischen	*the Amish* = members of a religious group in the US who live in a simple traditional way that often involves farming and no modern technology
to maintain [meɪn'teɪn]	beibehalten; aufrechterhalten	The wind was so strong that it was hard to *maintain* the course for the ship. *to maintain sth* = to continue sth = to keep sth up *to maintain* ↔ to stop, to drop *Fr.* maintenir
2 **arcade** ['ɑːkeɪd]	Spielhalle; Passage	Everything you need you can find at the shopping *arcade* downtown.
obscure [əb'skjʊə]	unbekannt; obskur	1. A new *obscure* island in the Pacific has been found. 2. The group leader gave an *obscure* and confusing answer.
cushion ['kʊʃn]	Kissen	The new yellow *cushions* on the sofa are nice.
cardigan ['kɑːdɪgən]	kragenlose (Strick-)Jacke	Put on your red wool *cardigan* – it'll be nice and warm.
sweater ['swetə]	Pullover	A cotton *sweater* will keep you warm in winter.
slipper ['slɪpə]	Schuh; Pantoffel	*slipper* → to slip on
joy [dʒɔɪ]	Freude; Vergnügen	They felt great *joy*. = They were very happy. *Fr.* joie *(f)*
dumb [dʌm]	dumm; doof	*dumb* = another word for 'stupid' *(especially in AE)*
to hum [hʌm]	summen	What's that strange *humming* sound?
trumpet ['trʌmpɪt]	Trompete	Louis Armstrong was a famous *trumpet* player. *Fr.* trompette *(f)*
spooky ['spuːki]	unheimlich; sonderbar	*spooky* = strange and frightening
jungle ['dʒʌŋgl]	Dschungel	*jungle* = a tropical forest in which trees and plants grow very closely together
stereo ['steriəʊ]	Stereoanlage	We have a great *stereo* in our car.
where . . . is / are concerned [ˌweə ɪz/ɑː kən'sɜːnd]	was … betrifft; was … angeht	*Where* my studies *are concerned*, everything is going well.
to fold [fəʊld]	falten; klappen; verschränken	He *folded* his arms in front of his chest.
eyebrow ['aɪbraʊ]	Augenbraue	Your *eyebrows* are above your eyes.
*****to slide** [slaɪd]	gleiten (lassen); rutschen	He *slid* the LP back into its paper sleeve. *to slide* → slide

to **screw sb** [skruː]	jdn. reinlegen	Damn, we've been *screwed*! *to screw* = to cheat
*to **blow** [bləʊ]	zerstören; zerschlagen	*to blow* = to destroy
refusal [rɪˈfjuːzl]	Weigerung; Ablehnung	I was frustrated by his *refusal* to discuss the problem. *refusal* → to refuse (to do) sth

Texts B

1	**insufficient** [ˌɪnsəˈfɪʃnt]	ungenügend; unzureichend	I only got *insufficient* information beforehand, so I couldn't respond to all the questions in the meeting. *Fr.* insuffisant/e
	disunity *(no pl)* [dɪsˈjuːnɪti]	Uneinigkeit	We don't want to see *disunity* in the country.
	pregnancy [ˈpregnənsi]	Schwangerschaft	A lot of women feel sick in the mornings during their first months of *pregnancy*.
	addiction [əˈdɪkʃn]	Sucht; Abhängigkeit	Too many people die due to drug *addiction*. *addiction* → addicted
	*to **be apt to happen** [bi ˌæpt tə ˈhæpn]	möglicherweise passieren	The roof *is apt to leak* when it rains.
	to **file a claim** [ˌfaɪl ə ˈkleɪm]	einen Anspruch geltend machen; eine Forderung geltend machen	If you wish to *file a claim*, you should go to a lawyer.
	to **recount** [riːˈkaʊnt]	erzählen	I *recount* the story for those who didn't hear about it. *to recount* → account
	to **resist** [rɪˈzɪst]	widerstehen; sich widersetzen	*to resist* = to fight back, or to refuse to accept sth and try to prevent it from happening *Fr.* résister; *Lat.* resistere
	law suit [ˈlɔː ˌsuːt]	Gerichtsverfahren	*law suit* = a case in a court of law brought by one person or group against another
	odd [ɒd]	seltsam; komisch	That's *odd* – I'm sure I put my keys on the table, but they're not here. *odd* = strange
2	**regular** [ˈregjələ]	Stammgast	A *regular* is somebody who visits a bar, a pub or a restaurant regularly.
	blueprint [ˈbluːprɪnt]	Blaupause; Plan; Entwurf	Luckily, the architect found the mistake in the *blueprint* before the building began.
	ten-figure [ˈtenfɪgə]	zehnstellig	a *ten-figure* fortune = a billion or more *figure* = number
	to **accumulate** [əˈkjuːmjəleɪt]	anhäufen; ansammeln; aufbauen	Together, the couple *has accumulated* great wealth. *Fr.* accumuler
	conservative [kənˈsɜːvətɪv]	konservativ; zurückhaltend	1. People tend to be more and more *conservative* as they get older. 2. If I said there were three million unemployed, that would be a *conservative* estimate.
	to **total** [ˈtəʊtl]	sich belaufen auf	If you add 30, 50 and 20, it *totals* 100.
	steady [ˈstedi]	kontinuierlich; unaufhörlich	A *steady* beat of the drums is important in music bands.

to **encompass** [ɪnˈkʌmpəs]	umfassen; umspannen	The festival *encompasses* all forms of art. *to encompass* = to include different types of things
liquor [ˈlɪkə]	alkoholisches Getränk	*liquor* = alcoholic drinks
stake [steɪk]	Anteil	She has acquired *stakes* in five different enterprises.
notorious [nəˈtɔːriəs]	berüchtigt	The company is *notorious* for paying its bills late.
debut [ˈdeɪbjuː]	Debütalbum	They released their *debut* in 2017. *Fr.* début (m)
to **amass** [əˈmæs]	anhäufen; ansammeln	He *has amassed* a large fortune over the years. *to amass* → mass
reasonable [ˈriːznəbl]	vernünftig; angemessen	Tell him what happened, I'm sure he'll understand. He's a *reasonable* man. *Fr.* raisonable
crucially [ˈkruːʃli]	entscheidend; ausschlaggebend	Their work is *crucially* important.
to **model sth on sth** [ˈmɒdl ˌɒn]	als Vorlage für etw. benutzen	The architects *modelled* their plans *on* the boulevards of Paris. *to model* → model

Money and finances

rich / wealthy / prosperous ↔ poor / needy	reich, wohlhabend ↔ arm, bedürftig	stakeholder	Anteilseigner/-in, Teilhaber/-in
riches (pl only) / wealth / prosperity	Reichtum, Wohlstand	billionaire	Milliardär/-in
to boom – to flourish – to prosper	boomen, florieren, gedeihen	income, earnings (pl)	Einkommen, Einahmen, Verdienst
to accumulate / to amass wealth / a fortune	anhäufen	revenue [ˈrevnjuː]	Erträge
to have / hold / own stakes in a business / enterprise / firm	Anteile	tax, to tax, pretax	Steuer, besteuern, vor Steuern
to have / own / invest in / trade shares	Aktien	tax office the Inland Revenue (BE) / HM Revenue & Customs (BE) / the Internal Revenue Service (IRS) (AE)	Finanzamt
to earn interest (on)	Zinsen		

3	**misogynist** [mɪˈsɒdʒnɪst]	frauenfeindlich	The author has a *misogynist* attitude.
	persona, personae / personas (pl) [pəˈsəʊnə, pəˈsəʊniː]	Rolle; lyrisches Ich	At work he adopted the *persona* of a fearless hero.
	artistic licence [ɑːˌtɪstɪk ˈlaɪsns]	künstlerische Freiheit	*artistic licence* = the freedom of artists, writers, etc. to change the facts of the real world when producing art

Texts C

1	*to **be awake** [bi ̯əˈweɪk]	wach sein	I had to stay *awake* all night with the baby. In bed later, I lay *awake* thinking about life, which kept me *awake* even longer. Now I'm really tired. *to be awake* ↔ to be asleep

*to **be intent on doing sth** [bɪ ˌɪnˈtent ˌɒn]	fest entschlossen sein, etw. zu tun	He seems *intent on* upsetting everyone in the room! *to be intent on* → intention
credit *(no pl)* [ˈkredɪt]	Ansehen; Anerkennung; Ehre	She got no *credit* for solving the problem. Her boss took *credit* for it instead.
blame [bleɪm]	Schuld	He just put all the *blame* on me although he was to blame too! That wasn't fair.
to **edit** [ˈedɪt]	überarbeiten; bearbeiten	The teacher wasn't happy with my essay, so I had to *edit* it. *to edit* → editor
to **retouch** [ˌriːˈtʌtʃ]	retuschieren	Photographs do not lie, unless they are *retouched*. *Fr.* retoucher
to **homogenize** [həˈmɒdʒənaɪz]	homogenisieren; vereinheitlichen	*to homogenize* = to change sth so that all its parts or features become the same or very similar
to **alter** [ˈɔːltə]	ändern; verändern	He *altered* his appearance to escape the police. *to alter* = to change *Fr.* altérer
appearance [əˈpɪərns]	Erscheinung; Aussehen; Auftritt	1. There was nothing unusual about her *appearance*. 2. Madonna made a guest *appearance* at the concert. *appearance* → to appear
inadequate [ɪnˈædɪkwət]	unzureichend; inadäquat; unangemessen	The firm made an *inadequate* offer: They only wanted to pay half of the price.
precondition [ˌpriːkənˈdɪʃn]	Voraussetzung; Vorbedingung	*precondition* = sth which must happen before sth else can happen
to **enlarge** [ɪnˈlɑːdʒ]	vergrößern; erweitern	*to enlarge* = to become bigger or to make something bigger *to enlarge* → large
to **warrant** [ˈwɒrnt]	garantieren	The seller *warrants* that his products are high-quality.
homogenous [həˈmɒdʒənəs]	homogen; einheitlich	! Be careful with the spelling and pronunciation: homogenous [həˈmɒdʒənəs] homogeneous [ˌhɒməˈdʒiːniəs] *homogenous* → to homogenize

---

Digital tools and devices

Using your smartphone, tablet, display, touchscreen
- to tap and swipe wischen
- to charge a battery – a rechargeable wiederaufladbar battery
- to lock ↔ to unlock your SIM card
- SIM = subscriber identity module Teilnehmer-Identitätsmodul
- to switch on / to power save mode Betriebsart
- to change settings
- to install ↔ to deinstall apps / an operating system Betriebssystem
- to get (regular / automatic) updates / bugfixes Fehlerbehebung
- to upload ↔ to download files Dateien
- to make a purchase
- the amount is charged / credited to your account gutschreiben

Using a network
- there's no signal / my phone has got no reception Empfang
- to log / sign into a secure / open network
- internet security, firewall ↔ virus, Trojan horse Schadsoftware
- VPN = virtual private network
- to store speichern data in a cloud
- to import / to transfer / to read in data

4	haul boy / girl [ˈhɔːl bɔɪ/gɜːl]	Influencer/-in	*haul boy / girl* = influencer
	to **sneer** (at sb / sth) [ˈsnɪərˌət]	(über jdn. / etw.) spotten; jdn / etw. verhöhnen	"Is that the best you can do?" he *sneered*. *to sneer* = to speak in a way that shows you think the other person is stupid
	counter-argument [ˈkaʊntərˌɑːgjəmənt]	Gegenargument	*counter-argument* = an argument against another argument, idea, or suggestion
	to **storyboard** [ˈstɔːribɔːd]	ein Drehbuch schreiben	*to storyboard* → storyboard
	genuine [ˈdʒenjuɪn]	wirklich; echt	My shoes are made of *genuine* leather, they're not fake. *genuine* = true
	to **sign off** [ˌsaɪn ˈɒf]	aufhören; Schluss machen	As it's Friday, I think I'll *sign off* early today.
	like-minded [laɪkˈmaɪndɪd]	gleich gesinnt	She is a football fan who started a magazine for *like-minded* women.
	requirement [rɪˈkwaɪəmənt]	Anforderung	Previous experience is one of the *requirements* for the job. *requirement* → to require
	acolyte [ˈæklaɪt]	Gefolgsmann/-frau	To his *acolytes*, he is known simply as 'The Boss'.
	visible [ˈvɪzəbl]	sichtbar	The spot on her shirt was clearly *visible*. Hiding it was impossible. *Fr.* visible
	allegiance [əˈliːdʒns]	Loyalität; Ergebenheit	For many here, *allegiance* to their religious leader comes first. to pledge *allegiance*
	to **vary** [ˈveəri]	variieren; verschieden sein	The price for gas is not the same all the time. It *varies*. *to vary* → various, variety *Fr.* varier
	to **rebel** (against) [rɪˈbel əgenst]	rebellieren (gegen); sich auflehnen (gegen)	The people *rebelled against* the new government. *Fr.* se rebeller contre
	historian [hɪˈstɔːriən]	Historiker/-in	He knows everything about Columbus because he's a *historian*. *historian* → history, historical
	sort [sɔːt]	Sorte; Art	*a sort of* = a kind of
	transformative [ˌtrænsˈfɔːmətɪv]	umgestaltend; umformend; transformativ	Our minds go through a *transformative* process when we study. *transformative* → transformation, transform sth into sth
	straightforward [ˌstreɪtˈfɔːwəd]	einfach; unkompliziert; direkt	He asked me a *straightforward* question. *straightforward* = simple, easy, direct
	radical [ˈrædɪkl]	radikal; fundamental; total	Some *radical* ideas resulted in the American Revolution.
	blurred [blɜːd]	unscharf; verschwommen	After I had hit my head, everything was *blurred*.
	plenty of [ˈplenti əv]	eine Menge	*plenty of* food = lots of food
	self-conscious [ˌselfˈkɒnʃəs]	befangen; gehemmt	Stop staring – you make me *self-conscious*.
	non-committal [ˌnɒnkəˈmɪtl]	unverbindlich	The politician was typically *non-committal* when asked about further actions. *non-committal* → commitment
	to **dominate** [ˈdɒmɪneɪt]	dominieren; beherrschen	They work as a group – no one person is allowed to *dominate*. *Fr.* dominer

surveillance [sɜ:'veɪləns]	Überwachung; Beaufsichtigung	Due to public cameras, you are under *surveillance* in Britan most of the time. *Fr.* surveillance *(f)*
core [kɔ:]	Kern	Your behaviour is the *core* of the problem. If we can change the way you are acting, we could solve the problem.
aside [ə'saɪd]	beiseite	to leave / put *aside* Emotional arguments *aside*, here are the facts.

Media competence

1	**overwhelmed** [ˌəʊvə'welmd]	überwältigt	She was *overwhelmed* by the joy she felt.
	response [rɪ'spɒns]	Reaktion; Antwort	Her *response* to the film was very emotional. *Fr.* réponse *(f)*; *Lat.* respondere
2	**hate speech** ['heɪt spi:tʃ]	Hassrede; Hetzrede	*Hate speech* has become very common in the media.
3	**to implement** ['ɪmplɪment]	einführen; umsetzen; realisieren	The country had been slow to *implement* the new European laws. *Fr.* implémenter
	explicit language [ɪksplɪsɪt 'læŋgwɪdʒ]	obszöne Sprache; vulgäre Sprache	The main characters in the story are teenagers who drink, smoke and use *explicit language*.

Digital communication and cooperation

Activities

- to create / to maintain a blog / a vlog
- to post / to publish / to upload / to commit content to the internet
- to subscribe to / to use a messenger service / a streaming service / a dating service abonnieren

- to collaborate
- to contribute to a wiki
- to block / to disable / to unblock an account sperren, deaktivieren
- to mute a chat stummschalten
- to place classified ads Kleinanzeigen schalten

- to follow somebody
- fashion / lifestyle / fitness influencer – haul girl / boy
- unboxing Auspacken (vor laufender Kamera)
- to trend
- to crop / to edit pictures

Problems

- phishing Ausspionieren von Daten
- fake news

- copyright issues / violation Verletzung
- to control your privacy

- cyber bullying
- hate speech

Unit task

package ['pækɪdʒ]	Paket	*package* → to pack
noticeboard ['nəʊtɪsbɔ:d]	schwarzes Brett	I've put the list of things to do up on the *noticeboard*. *noticeboard* → to note
proof-reading ['pru:fri:dɪŋ]	Korrekturlesen	*proof-reading* = finding and correcting mistakes in a text before it is printed or put online

⟨ Texts D ⟩

1	**rage** [reɪdʒ]	Wut; Zorn	He felt so much *rage* that his face started to get red while he was screaming at us. *Fr.* rage *(f)*
	intent [ɪnˈtent]	Absicht; Vorsatz	*intent* = what sb wants to do *intent* → intention

⟨ Texts E ⟩

1	**reckless** [ˈrekləs]	unbesonnen; waghalsig; leichtsinnig	Going to India without preparation was a *reckless* decision.
	naked [ˈneɪkɪd]	nackt	! Be careful with the pronunciation: two syllables!
	dreadlocks *(pl)* [ˈdredlɒks]	Rastalocken	I wanted to have *dreadlocks* like Bob Marley.
	herbs *(pl)* [hɜːbz]	Kräuter; *hier:* Marihuana	1. *Herbs* are plants that people add to food to make it taste good. 2. The minister said he had smoked *herbs* once.
	to **straighten** [ˈstreɪtn]	geraderichten; zurechtrücken	The picture fell down while I was trying to *straighten* it. *to straighten* → straight
	to **smirk** [smɜːk]	grinsen	*to smirk* = to smile ironically, showing that you don't appreciate what sb says *to smirk* → smirk
	judgmental [dʒʌdʒˈmentl]	voreingenommen; beurteilend	! Both spellings are correct: judg**(e)**mental *judgmental* = very critical *judgmental* → to judge, judge
	to **cure** [kjʊə]	heilen; kurieren	Some people try hypnotism to *cure* themselves of addictions.
	humanitarian [hjuːˌmænɪˈteəriən]	Menschenfreund/-in	I like to think of myself as a *humanitarian*. *humanitarian* → human

⟨ Texts F ⟩

1	**button** [ˈbʌtn]	Knopf	Oh no! There's a *button* missing from my favourite shirt. *Fr.* bouton *(m)*
	anthropologist [ˌænθrəˈpɒlədʒɪst]	Anthropologe / Anthropologin	*Anthropologists* study humans, their culture and how they live together.
	soothing [ˈsuːðɪŋ]	beruhigend; schmerzlindernd	His voice had a *soothing* effect on me. I wasn't worried any longer.
	undercurrent [ˈʌndəkʌrnt]	Unterströmung; Unterton	He was a good writer, but I felt a slight *undercurrent* of racism in some of his texts.
	for instance [fərˌˈɪnstəns]	zum Beispiel	The company created a lot of popular video games, some complex simulation games, *for instance*.
	to **loiter** [ˈlɔɪtə]	herumhängen; herumlungern	She spent her afternoons *loitering* at the shopping mall with her friends.
	pointless [ˈpɔɪntləs]	sinnlos; zwecklos	Stop trying. It's *pointless*.
	cider [ˈsaɪdə]	Apfelwein	*Cider* is a drink made from apples and contains about as much alcohol as beer.

cutting-edge [ˌkʌtɪŋ ˈedʒ]	supermodern; Spitzen-	This new app is *cutting-edge* technology.
insight [ˈɪnsaɪt]	Einblick	The film offers an *insight* into post-war life.
seductive [sɪˈdʌktɪv]	verführerisch	Doing forbidden things is said to be *seductive*.
notion [ˈnəʊʃn]	Idee; Vorstellung	Some people have no *notion* of what it means to be poor.
escapist [ɪˈskeɪpɪst]	eskapistisch	*Escapist* literature offers you a world away from your everyday worries. *escapist* → to escape

Across cultures 4 The soundtrack to history

1	**opposition** [ˌɒpəˈzɪʃn]	Opposition; Widerstand	leader of the *opposition*, *opposition* to changes *Lat.* opponere, oppositum
	to expand [ɪkˈspænd]	(sich) ausdehnen; erweitern	The company wanted to *expand* and so they looked for more workers. *to expand* → expansion
	feudal [ˈfjuːdl]	feudal	In a *feudal* system people are not considered equal but depend on the economic and legal decisions of superiors.
	serf [sɜːf]	Leibeigene/-r	*serf* = a member of a low social class in medieval times who worked on the land and had to obey the person who owned that land *Lat.* servus/-a
	gentry [ˈdʒentri]	(niederer) Adel	*gentry* = people of high social class, especially in the past *Lat.* gens, gentis *(f)*
	abolition [ˌæbəˈlɪʃn]	Abschaffung	The *abolition* of slavery freed thousands of enslaved people. *abolition* → to abolish *Fr.* abolition *(f)*
	suffrage [ˈsʌfrɪdʒ]	Wahlrecht; Stimmrecht	New Zealand was the first country to grant women's *suffrage* in 1893. *suffrage* = the right to vote *suffrage* → suffragette
	extensive [ɪkˈstensɪv]	ausgiebig; ausführlich; ausgedehnt	We went for an *extensive* walk on the beach. *Lat.* extendere
	closure [ˈkləʊʒə]	Schließung; Stilllegung	Factory *closures* are the last option for the company. *closure* → to close
	hardship [ˈhɑːdʃɪp]	Not; Elend; Entbehrungen	Economic *hardship* too often leads to mental health problems. *hardship* → hard
	abuse [əˈbjuːs]	Missbrauch	Emotional *abuse* involves someone attempting to control a person's actions, isolating or frightening them.
	recession [rɪˈseʃn]	Rezession; Konjunkturrückgang	*recession* = a period of economic crisis *recession* ↔ boom *Lat.* recedere, recessum
2	**skeleton** [ˈskelɪtn]	Skelett	We went to see the dinosaur *skeletons* in the Natural History Museum. *Fr.* squelette *(m)*

3	**evidence** *(no pl)* [ˈevɪdns]	Beweis; Beleg; Beweismaterial	Is there any *evidence* he's a criminal? *Fr.* évidence *(f)*

Text smart

Poetry

	poetry [ˈpəʊətri]	Poesie; Dichtung; Lyrik	*poetry* → poet, poem
1	**occasion** [əˈkeɪʒn]	Gelegenheit; Anlass	The annual ball at the town hall is a good *occasion* to get to know people. *Fr.* occasion *(f)*
	to **recite** [rɪˈsaɪt]	vortragen; rezitieren	She *recited* the Pledge of Allegiance. *Fr.* réciter
	to **interpret** [ɪnˈtɜːprɪt]	interpretieren	I am not sure how to *interpret* his silence. *Fr.* interpréter; *Lat.* interpretari
	pattern [ˈpætn]	Muster	*pattern* = the way in which sth is done or repeated / a design of lines, colours, shapes etc.
	syllable [ˈsɪləbl]	Silbe	The word 'pattern' has two *syllables*.
	stanza [ˈstænzə]	Strophe	the basic unit in a poem (often four lines or more)
	metre [ˈmiːtə]	Versmaß	In the study of poetry, *metre* is the regular and rhythmic arrangement of syllables according to particular patterns.
	alliteration [əˌlɪtəˈreɪʃn]	Alliteration; Stabreim	*alliteration* = the use, especially in poetry, of the same sound or sounds, especially consonants, at the beginning of several words that are close together
	rhyme [raɪm]	Reim	Here's a *rhyme*: What's that? It's a cat.
	metaphor [ˈmetəfə]	Metapher	"All the world's a stage" is an example of Shakespeare's use of *metaphor*.
	simile [ˈsɪmɪli]	Vergleich	*simile* = an expression comparing one thing with another, always including the words "as" or "like"
2	**epic poem** [ˌepɪk ˈpəʊɪm]	Epos; erzählendes Gedicht	*epic poem* = a long narrative poem typically about the actions of unusual characters
	motion [ˈməʊʃn]	Bewegung	*motion* → to move *Lat.* movere, motum
3	to **enlarge** [ɪnˈlɑːdʒ]	vergrößern; erweitern	*to enlarge* = to become bigger or to make something bigger *to enlarge* → large
4	**row** [rəʊ]	Reihe	We've got really good seats in the front *row*.
	priest [priːst]	Priester; Pfarrer	Roman Catholic *priests* are not allowed to marry.
	to **tremble** [ˈtrembl]	zittern	He was so nervous! I could see his hands *trembling*. *Fr.* trembler; *Lat.* tremere
	to **twist** [twɪst]	verdrehen; verzerren; sich winden	If sth gets *twisted*, it moves into a strange shape.
	*to **seek** [siːk]	suchen	Many people *are seeking* peace and happiness in life.

nail [neɪl]	Nagel	My granny always said, "Keep your *nails* short and your hands clean."
kite [kaɪt]	Drachen	When it's windy, you can go outside and fly a *kite*.
*to **weep** [wiːp]	weinen; schluchzen	It's more formal to say '*to weep*' instead of 'to cry'.
spell [spel]	Zauber; Bann; Zauberspruch	Do you believe in *spells* and witches and things like that? I don't.
fist [fɪst]	Faust	He hit the table hard with his *fist*.

Drama

1 **tragedy** [ˈtrædʒədi]	Tragödie	*tragedy* ↔ comedy *Fr.* tragédie *(f)*
extra [ˈekstrə]	Statist/-in; Komparse / Komparsin	As an *extra*, you can get a feeling for what life as an actor is like. *extra* = a character in a film that doesn't speak *extra* ↔ protagonist
to **exit** [ˈeksɪt]	verlassen; aussteigen	I *exited* quickly before anyone could see me. *to exit* = to leave *to exit* → exit
2 *to **be torn** [bi ˈtɔːn]	hin und her gerissen sein	If you *are torn* between two or more things, you cannot decide which one to choose.
mercy *(no pl)* [ˈmɜːsi]	Mitleid; Erbarmen; Gnade	The gunmen showed no *mercy*, killing innocent men and women.
adviser [ədˈvaɪzə]	Ratgeber/-in	*adviser* → advice
indefinitely [ɪnˈdefɪnətli]	unbestimmt; unbegrenzt	*indefinitely* = without any limit of time or number
witch [wɪtʃ]	Hexe	In fairy stories, a *witch* is a woman, usually an old woman, who has evil magic powers.
the Scotch [ðə ˈskɒtʃ]	die Schotten	*Scots* → Scottish, Scotland
*to **split** [splɪt]	trennen; abspalten	They *split* the money in half.
shore [ʃɔː]	Ufer; Küste	They walked along the *shore* and watched the waves.
to **seize** [siːz]	ergreifen; packen	"Carpe diem" is Latin for "*seize* the day".
to **advance** [ədˈvɑːns]	vortreten	*to advance* = to move forward *Fr.* avancer
determination [dɪˌtɜːmɪˈneɪʃn]	Bestimmtheit; Entschlossenheit	There was an expression of *determination* on her face. *determination* → to be determined
subject [ˈsʌbdʒɪkt]	Untertan/-in	The king's *subjects* regarded him as a great and wise monarch. *Lat.* subiectus/-a
wise [waɪz]	weise	She had made a very *wise* decision.
to **trick** [trɪk]	täuschen; austricksen	Your friend is going to be upset when he finds out how you *tricked* him. *to trick* → trick

repetition [ˌrepɪˈtɪʃn]	Wiederholung	*Repetitions* can be very boring. *repetition* → to repeat *Fr.* répétition *(f)*; *Lat.* repetitio *(f)*
volume [ˈvɒljuːm]	Lautstärke; Volumen	Could you turn the *volume* of the TV down, please? I'm trying to sleep. *Fr.* volume *(m)*

Short film

1	**appearance** [əˈpɪərns]	Erscheinung; Aussehen; Auftritt	1. There was nothing unusual about her *appearance*. 2. Madonna made a guest *appearance* at the concert. *appearance* → to appear
	shot [ʃɒt]	Einstellung; Kameraeinstellung	*shot* → to shoot
	cast [kɑːst]	Besetzung; Ensemble	What a great *cast*! There were a lot of famous actors in the film.
	close-up [ˈkləʊsʌp]	Nahaufnahme	*close-up* = a photograph taken from a short distance that gives a very detailed picture
	facial expression [ˌfeɪʃl ɪkˈspreʃn]	Gesichtsausdruck	The *facial expression* of people sometimes tells you more than what they say. *Lat.* expressio *(f)*
	romance [rəˈmæns]	Liebesgeschichte; Liebesfilm	*romance* = a novel or film about a love affair
	supporting role [səˈpɔːtɪŋ ˌrəʊl]	Nebenrolle	*supporting role* = not the most important actor or part in a film or play
	turning point [ˈtɜːnɪŋ ˌpɔɪnt]	Wendepunkt	The dangerous situation was a *turning point* in the story. *turning point* = a point (usually in a story) when sth suddenly changes so that things start to happen differently *turning point* → to turn
	wide shot [ˈwaɪd ʃɒt]	Totale *(Kameraeinstellung)*	Let's use a *wide shot* for this scene so we can see everything that's going on. *wide shot* ↔ close-up
	glossary [ˈglɒsri]	Glossar; Stichwortverzeichnis	*glossary* = an alphabetical list, with meanings, of the words or phrases in a text that are difficult to understand
2	**the public** [ðə ˈpʌblɪk]	die Öffentlichkeit	Stars sometimes want to hide from *the public*. ! *in public* = in der Öffentlichkeit *Fr.* public *(m)*; *Lat.* publicum *(nt)*
4	**misery** *(no pl)* [ˈmɪzri]	Elend; Jammer; Not	We often see photos of people in *misery* in the news. *Lat.* miser, miserabilis
5	**fate** [feɪt]	Schicksal; Fügung; Vorsehung	*fate* = the things you can't control that will happen to you *fate* → fateful
	approach [əˈprəʊtʃ]	Herangehensweise; Vorgehensweise; Ansatz; Annäherung	We get the same results, but we have different *approaches*. *approach* = method, way, movement towards *Fr.* approche *(f)*
7	to **package** [ˈpækɪdʒ]	verpacken	*to package* = to put goods into boxes or containers to be sold
10	**surroundings** *(pl)* [səˈraʊndɪŋz]	Umgebung	*surroundings* = environment *surroundings* → to surround
	length [leŋθ]	Länge	*length* → long

Speech

1 **aim** [eɪm]	Ziel	What's the *aim* of your research? *aim* = goal
to **congratulate sb** [kən'grætʃʊleɪt]	jmdm. gratulieren	Everybody *congratulated* him on winning the competition. *to congratulate* → congratulation
2 to **doubt** [daʊt]	bezweifeln	If you *doubt* sth, you think it may not be true. *Fr.* douter; *Lat.* dubitare
Hispanic [hɪ'spænɪk]	lateinamerikanisch; Latino / Latina; Hispano-Amerikaner/-in	He comes from Mexico, so he's *Hispanic*.
cynical ['sɪnɪkl]	zynisch	My sister has a very *cynical* view of men.
*to **bend** [bend]	beugen; biegen	Make sure you *bend* your knees when you're picking up heavy objects.
defining [dɪ'faɪnɪŋ]	prägend; entscheidend	My marriage was a *defining* moment in life.
crisis, crises *(pl)* ['kraɪsɪs; 'kraɪsiːz]	Krise	Europe has been in a *crisis* for some time. *Fr.* crise *(f)*
preacher ['priːtʃə]	Prediger/-in	*preacher* = a person who gives a religious speech, often because it's their job
3 **rhetorical** [rɪ'tɒrɪkl]	rhetorisch	Is this a *rhetorical* question?
device [dɪ'vaɪs]	Stilmittel	Literary *devices* are used by writers to suggest there's a bigger picture or another meaning behind the story.
despair [dɪ'speə]	Hoffnungslosigkeit; Verzweiflung	In times of *despair*, people often cry or pray to God. *Fr.* désespoir *(m)*
to **witness** ['wɪtnəs]	miterleben	Did anyone *witness* the attack? *to witness* → witness
anaphora [ə'næfrə]	Anapher	An *anaphora* is the repetition of a word or a group of words at the beginnings of sentences or clauses that are close together.
alliteration [ˌəlɪtə'reɪʃn]	Alliteration; Stabreim	*alliteration* = the use, especially in poetry, of the same sound or sounds, especially consonants, at the beginning of several words that are close together
enumeration [ɪˌnjuːmr'eɪʃn]	Aufzählung	*enumeration* = the act of naming things separately, one by one
repetition [ˌrepɪ'tɪʃn]	Wiederholung	*Repetitions* can be very boring. *repetition* → to repeat *Fr.* répétition *(f)*; *Lat.* repetitio *(f)*
to **personalise** ['pɜːsnlaɪz]	persönlich gestalten; individualisieren	I *have personalised* my office with a few posters on the walls. *to personalise* → personal, person
4 **anecdote** ['ænɪkdəʊt]	Anekdote	My grandpa often tells amusing *anecdotes* about his years as a policeman.
tap water ['tæp ˌwɔːtə]	Leitungswasser	Some people think drinking mineral water is especially healthy, but others believe *tap water* is just as good.

Dictionary

In dieser alphabetischen Wortliste findest du das gesamte Vokabular von *Green Line* Band 1 bis 5. Namen stehen in einer extra Liste am Ende des ***Dictionary***. Einträge, die aus mehreren Wörtern bestehen, kannst du meist unter verschiedenen Stichwörtern nachschlagen. So ist z.B. *after all* unter *after* und unter *all* eingetragen. Die Fundstellen stehen immer hinter dem jeweiligen Wort und zeigen dir an, wo es zum ersten Mal vorkommt, z.B.:

abandoned [əˈbændənd] aufgegeben; verlassen **V U1**, 16 kommt zum ersten Mal vor in Band 5, Unit 1, Seite 16

to arrange [əˈreɪndʒ] arrangieren; anordnen ⟨**V U2**, 58⟩ kommt zum ersten Mal vor in Band 5, Unit 2, Seite 58.

U = Unit, **AC = Across cultures**, **F = Focus**, **TS = Text smart**

Die mit * gekennzeichneten Verben sind unregelmäßig. Die Vokabeln mit Fundstellen in Spitzklammern ⟨ ⟩ stellen ein fakultatives Zusatzangebot dar. Die Vokabeln mit **grünen** Fundstellen sind individueller Wortschatz.

A

a [ə] ein/-e **I**
 a bit [ə ˈbɪt] ein bisschen; ein wenig **I**
 a couple of [ə ˈkʌpl̩ əv] ein paar **I**
 a few [ə ˈfjuː] ein paar; wenige; einige **I**
 a hundred [ə ˈhʌndrəd; wʌn ˈhʌndrəd] einhundert; hundert **I**
 a little [ə ˈlɪtl̩] ein wenig; etwas **I**
 a lot [ə ˈlɒt] viel **I**
 a lot of [ə ˈlɒt əv] viel/-e; eine Menge **I**
 a total of [ə ˈtəʊtl̩ əv] insgesamt **III**
 a day [ə ˈdeɪ] pro Tag **III**
 a lot to learn [ə ˌlɒt tə ˈlɜːn] viel zu lernen **I**

A levels [ˈeɪ ˌlevlz] *britische Abiturprüfung* **IV**

a.m. [eɪˈem] vormittags *(Uhrzeit)* **I**

abandoned [əˈbændənd] aufgegeben; verlassen **V U1**, 16

abbreviation [əˌbriːviˈeɪʃn] Abkürzung **V U1**, 26

ability [əˈbɪləti] Fähigkeit; Begabung **II**

*to be able to (do sth) [biˈeɪbl̩ tə] fähig sein zu; können **II**

aboard [əˈbɔːd] an Bord **I**

to abolish [əˈbɒlɪʃ] aufheben; abschaffen **V F4**, 60

abolition [æbəˈlɪʃnɪst] Gegner/-in der Sklaverei **V F3**, 38

abolition [æbəˈlɪʃn] Abschaffung **V AC4**, 88

Aboriginal [æbəˈrɪdʒnl̩] von australischen Ureinwohnern abstammend; Ureinwohner/-in Australiens **IV**

about [əˈbaʊt] ungefähr; circa; etwa **I**

about [əˈbaʊt] über; von **I**
 *to be **about** to do sth [biˈaʊt tə] im Begriff sein, etw. zu tun **III**
 What **about** …? [ˈwɒtˌəbaʊt] Was ist mit …?; Wie wär's mit …? **I**
 What is … **about**? [ˌwɒtˌɪzˌəˈbaʊt] Worum geht es in/im …? **I**

above [əˈbʌv] oben **II**

above [əˈbʌv] über; oberhalb (von) **III**

abroad [əˈbrɔːd] im Ausland; ins Ausland **IV**

abrupt [əˈbrʌpt] abrupt **IV**

absolutely [ˌæbsəˈluːtli] absolut; völlig **III**

*to be absorbed by sth [biˌəbˈzɔːbd baɪ] in etw. integriert werden; von etw. aufgesaugt werden **V U3**, 68

abuse [əˈbjuːs] Missbrauch **V AC4**, 88

to accelerate [əkˈseləreɪt] beschleunigen; schneller werden **V U1**, 21

accent [ˈæksnt] Akzent **IV**

to accept [əkˈsept] akzeptieren; hinnehmen; annehmen **II**

acceptable [əkˈseptəbl̩] akzeptabel; annehmbar **III**

access (no pl) [ˈækses] Zugang; Zutritt **IV**

accessible [əkˈsesəbl̩] zugänglich **IV**

accident [ˈæksɪdnt] Unfall **II**

accidentally [ˌæksɪˈdentli] versehentlich; aus Versehen **V U2**, 42

to accomplish [əˈkʌmplɪʃ] vollbringen; erreichen; bewerkstelligen **V U2**, 52

according to [əˈkɔːdɪŋ tə] laut; gemäß **III**

accordingly [əˈkɔːdɪŋli] entsprechend **V U2**, 56

accordion [əˈkɔːdiən] Akkordeon **V U1**, 21

account [əˈkaʊnt] Erzählung **V F3**, 37; Konto **V U2**, 55

to account for [əˈkaʊnt fə] ausmachen; verantwortlich sein für **IV**

to accumulate [əˈkjuːmjəleɪt] anhäufen; ansammeln; aufbauen **V U3**, 76

accurate [ˈækjərət] akkurat; genau **IV**

to accuse (sb of sth) [əˈkjuːz] beschuldigen; anklagen **III**

to achieve [əˈtʃiːv] erreichen; erlangen **IV**

achievement [əˈtʃiːvmənt] Leistung; Errungenschaft **III**

to acknowledge [əkˈnɒlɪdʒ] anerkennen; einräumen **IV**

acolyte [ˈæklaɪt] Gefolgsmann/-frau **V U3**, 81

to acquire sth [əˈkwaɪə] etw. erwerben; sich etw. aneignen **IV**

across [əˈkrɒs] auf der anderen Seite von; über; hinüber; herüber; quer durch **I**

act [ækt] Gesetz **III**; Handlung; Aktion **IV**

to act [ækt] spielen *(Theater)* **I**; sich verhalten; handeln **III**
 acting a scene [ˌæktɪŋ ə ˈsiːn] eine Theaterszene spielen **I**

action [ˈækʃn] Handlung; Action; Aktion **I**

active [ˈæktɪv] aktiv **III**

activism [ˈæktɪvɪzm] Aktivismus **III**

activist [ˈæktɪvɪst] Aktivist/-in *(jmd., der sich für etw. engagiert)* **IV**

activity [ækˈtɪvəti] Aktivität **I**

actor [ˈæktə] Schauspieler/-in **III**

actual [ˈæktʃuəl] tatsächlich; wirklich; eigentlich **V U2**, 48

actually [ˈæktʃuəli] tatsächlich; wirklich; eigentlich **I**

classified ad [ˌklæsɪfaɪdˈæd] Kleinanzeige **V U3**, 83

AD (= Anno Domini) [eɪˈdiː] nach Christus **II**

to adapt to sth [əˈdæpt tə] sich etw. anpassen **IV**

film adaptation [ˌfɪlm ædæpˈteɪʃn] Verfilmung **IV**

to add [æd] hinzufügen; ergänzen **I**

addicted [əˈdɪktɪd] süchtig; abhängig **IV**

addiction [əˈdɪkʃn] Sucht; Abhängigkeit **V U3**, 75

*to be addictive [biˌəˈdɪktɪv] süchtig machen **V F5**, 67

addition [əˈdɪʃn] Zusatz; Ergänzung **IV**

additional [əˈdɪʃnl̩] zusätzlich **IV**

address [əˈdres] Adresse **I**

to address [əˈdres] ansprechen; sich wenden an **IV**

public administration (no pl) [ˌpʌblɪk ˌædmɪnɪˈstreɪʃn] öffentliche Verwaltung **IV**

to admire [ədˈmaɪə] bewundern **IV**

to admit [ədˈmɪt] zugeben **IV**

adobe (no pl) [əˈdəʊbi] Lehmziegel **III**

adolescence [ˌædlˈesns] Jugend; Pubertät; Entwicklungsjahre **V F5**, 67

to adopt [əˈdɒpt] annehmen; übernehmen; adoptieren **III**

adult [ˈædʌlt] Erwachsene/-r **II**

to advance [ədˈvɑːns] voranbringen; vorantreiben **V F1**, 11; vortreten **V TS**, 111

advantage [ədˈvɑːntɪdʒ] Vorteil **III**

adventure [ədˈventʃə] Abenteuer **II**

adventurous [ədˈventʃrəs] abenteuerlich; unternehmungslustig; wagemutig; experimentierfreudig **IV**

advert [ˈædvɜːt] Anzeige; Werbespot **III**

to **advertise** [ˈædvətaɪz] Werbung machen; werben; anpreisen; inserieren **IV**
advertisement [ədˈvɜːtɪsmənt] Anzeige; Werbespot **IV**
advice [ədˈvaɪs] Rat; Ratschlag **II**
adviser [ədˈvaɪzə] Ratgeber/-in **VTS**, 110
to **advocate** [ˈædvəkeɪt] befürworten; verteidigen; eintreten für **V U2**, 50
aesthetical [iːsˈθetɪkl] ästhetisch **V U3**, 69
affair [əˈfeə] Angelegenheit; Affäre **V U2**, 52
to **affect** [əˈfekt] beeinflussen; beeinträchtigen; betreffen **III**
affectionate [əˈfekʃnət] liebevoll; zärtlich **V U2**, 47
to **afford** [əˈfɔːd] sich leisten **II**
affordable [əˈfɔːdəbl] bezahlbar; erschwinglich **V U2**, 46
*to be **afraid** (of) [bɪ əˈfreɪd əv] (sich) fürchten; Angst haben (vor) **II**
I'm **afraid** … [aɪm əˈfreɪd] Leider … **III**
African [ˈæfrɪkən] Afrikaner/-in; afrikanisch **III**
  African-American [ˌæfrɪkənəˈmerɪkən] Afroamerikaner/-in; afroamerikanisch **II**
Afro [ˈæfrəʊ] Afrolook **V U2**, 48
after [ˈɑːftə] nach (zeitlich) **I**
  after all [ˌɑːftər ˈɔːl] doch; schließlich; immerhin **I**
  after that [ˌɑːftə ˈðæt] danach **I**
after [ˈɑːftə] nachdem **II**
afternoon [ˌɑːftəˈnuːn] Nachmittag **I**
afterwards [ˈɑːftəwədz] danach; hinterher **V U1**, 26
again [əˈgen] wieder; noch einmal; noch mal **I**
against [əˈgenst] gegen **II**
age [eɪdʒ] Alter; Zeitalter **II**
  Bronze **Age** [ˈbrɒnz ˌeɪdʒ] Bronzezeit (ca. 2200–800 v. Chr.) **II**
  Middle **Ages** [ˌmɪdl ˈeɪdʒɪz] Mittelalter **III**
  It took **ages**. [ɪt tʊk ˈeɪdʒɪz] Es dauerte ewig. **II**
agenda [əˈdʒendə] Vorhaben; Programm **V U2**, 52
travel **agent's** [ˈtrævl ˌeɪdʒnts] Reisebüro **II**
aggressive [əˈgresɪv] aggressiv **IV**
ago [əˈgəʊ] vor (zeitlich) **I**
  long **ago** [ˈlɒŋ əˌgəʊ] vor langer Zeit **II**
agony aunt [ˈægəni ˌɑːnt] Kummerkastentante **II**
to **agree** (on) [əˈgriː] sich einigen (auf) **II**
  to **agree** (with) [əˈgriː] einer Meinung sein (mit); zustimmen **II**
agreement [əˈgriːmənt] Abkommen; Vereinbarung **III**
agricultural [ˌægrɪˈkʌltʃrl] landwirtschaftlich **IV**
agriculture [ˈægrɪkʌltʃə] Landwirtschaft **IV**
ahead [əˈhed] vorn; nach vorn; voraus **III**
hearing **aid** [ˈhɪərɪŋ ˌeɪd] Hörgerät **II**
aim [eɪm] Ziel **V F4**, 62; **VTS**, 116

to **aim** to do sth [eɪm] etw. anstreben; abzielen auf etw. **IV**
air [eə] Luft **I**
  air ambulance [ˈeər ˌæmbjələns] Rettungshubschrauber **IV**
  air-conditioning [ˈeəkənˌdɪʃnɪŋ] Klimaanlage **III**
airline [ˈeəlaɪn] Fluggesellschaft **IV**
airport [ˈeəpɔːt] Flughafen **II**
alarm [əˈlɑːm] Alarm **IV**
alcohol (no pl) [ˈælkəhɒl] Alkohol **IV**
alien [ˈeɪliən] Außerirdische/-r; außerirdisches Wesen **I**
alike [əˈlaɪk] gleichermaßen; ähnlich **V AC2**, 34
alive [əˈlaɪv] lebend; am Leben; lebendig **III**
all [ɔːl] alle/-s; ganz **I**
  after **all** [ˌɑːftər ˈɔːl] doch; schließlich; immerhin **I**
  all around [ˌɔːl əˈraʊnd] überall; rundherum; rings umher **I**
  all by oneself [ˌɔːl baɪ wʌnˈself] ganz allein **II**
  all night [ˌɔːl ˈnaɪt] die ganze Nacht **I**
  all of a sudden [ˌɔːl əv ə ˈsʌdn] plötzlich; auf einmal **V U2**, 46
  all of us [ˈɔːl əvˌʌs] wir alle **II**
  all over [ˌɔːl ˈəʊvə] überall (in) **I**
  all right [ˌɔːl ˈraɪt] in Ordnung; alles klar **III**
  at **all** [ət ˈɔːl] überhaupt **I**
allegiance [əˈliːdʒns] Loyalität; Ergebenheit **V U3**, 81
  to pledge **allegiance** [ˌpledʒ əˈliːdʒns] Treueschwur leisten **V F1**, 10
bowling **alley** [ˈbəʊlɪŋ ˌæli] Bowlingbahn **I**
alliance [əˈlaɪəns] Allianz; Bündnis **V F1**, 10
alligator [ˈælɪgeɪtə] Alligator **I**
alliteration [əˌlɪtəˈreɪʃn] Alliteration; Stabreim **V U2**, 56; **VTS**, 108; **VTS**, 117
to **allow** [əˈlaʊ] erlauben; gestatten **III**
  *to be **allowed** to (do sth) [bɪ əˈlaʊd tə] dürfen **II**
allowance (AE) [əˈlaʊəns] Taschengeld **III**
all-rounder [ˌɔːlˈraʊndə] Allrounder; Alleskönner/-in; Multitalent **IV**
almost [ˈɔːlməʊst] fast; beinahe **I**
alone [əˈləʊn] allein; ohne fremde Hilfe **I**
  *to leave sb **alone** [ˌliːv əˈləʊn] jmdn. in Ruhe lassen **II**
  let **alone** [ˌlet əˈləʊn] geschweige denn **IV**
along [əˈlɒŋ] entlang **II**
  *to come **along** [ˌkʌm əˈlɒŋ] mitkommen **II**
alongside [əˌlɒŋˈsaɪd] neben; entlang **III**
aloud [əˈlaʊd] laut **IV**
alphabet [ˈælfəbet] Alphabet **I**
already [ɔːlˈredi] schon; bereits **I**
also [ˈɔːlsəʊ] auch **I**
to **alter** [ˈɔːltə] ändern; verändern **V U3**, 80

alternative [ɔːlˈtɜːnətɪv] Alternative **II**
although [ɔːlˈðəʊ] obwohl **I**
altogether [ˌɔːltəˈgeðə] insgesamt; gänzlich; ganz und gar **IV**
always [ˈɔːlweɪz] immer; ständig **I**
to **amass** [əˈmæs] anhäufen; ansammeln **V U3**, 76
amazed [əˈmeɪzd] erstaunt; verblüfft **III**
amazing [əˈmeɪzɪŋ] unglaublich; toll; erstaunlich **I**
ambassador [æmˈbæsədə] Botschafter/-in **V U1**, 25
ambition [æmˈbɪʃn] Ehrgeiz; Ambitionen **IV**
ambitious [æmˈbɪʃəs] ehrgeizig **II**
ambulance [ˈæmbjələns] Krankenwagen **III**
  air **ambulance** [ˈeər ˌæmbjələns] Rettungshubschrauber **IV**
amendment [əˈmenmənt] Abänderung (einer Gesetzesvorlage); Zusatzartikel (zur Verfassung) **V F4**, 60
American [əˈmerɪkən] amerikanisch; aus Amerika; Amerikaner/-in **I**
  African-**American** [ˌæfrɪkənəˈmerɪkən] Afroamerikaner/-in; afroamerikanisch **II**
  Cuban-**American** [ˌkjuːbənəˈmerɪkən] Amerikaner/-in kubanischer Abstammung **II**
  Native **American** [ˌneɪtɪv əˈmerɪkən] Ureinwohner/-in Amerikas; Indianer/-in; indianisch **I**
the **Amish** [ðiˈɑːmɪʃ] die Amischen **V U3**, 72
among [əˈmʌŋ] unter; inmitten **III**
amount (of) [əˈmaʊnt] Menge **IV**
amused [əˈmjuːz] amüsiert **IV**
an [ən] ein/-e **I**
to **analyse** [ˈænəlaɪz] analysieren **IV**
analysis [əˈnæləsɪs] Analyse; Untersuchung **IV**
anaphora [əˈnæfrə] Anapher **VTS**, 117
ancestor [ˈænsestə] Vorfahr/-in; Ahn/-in **III**
ancient [ˈeɪnʃnt] alt; altertümlich; antik **IV**
and [ænd; ənd] und **I**
anecdote [ˈænɪkdəʊt] Anekdote **VTS**, 117
anger (no pl) [ˈæŋgə] Zorn; Wut **II**
Anglo-Saxon [ˌæŋgləʊˈsæksn] Angelsachse; Angelsächsin; angelsächsisch **II**
angry [ˈæŋgri] wütend; zornig; verärgert; böse **I**
animal [ˈænɪməl] Tier **I**
  animal shelter [ˈænɪml ˌʃeltə] Tierheim **III**
ankle [ˈæŋkl] Fußgelenk; Fußknöchel **II**
  to twist your **ankle** [ˌtwɪst jɔːr ˈæŋkl] sich den Knöchel verrenken **II**
anniversary [ˌænɪˈvɜːsri] Jubiläum; Jahrestag **III**
to **announce** [əˈnaʊns] ankündigen; durchsagen **IV**
announcement [əˈnaʊnsmənt] Ankündigung; Durchsage **II**
annoying [əˈnɔɪɪŋ] ärgerlich; lästig **IV**

another [əˈnʌðə] ein/-e andere/-r/-s; noch ein/-e **I**

answer [ˈɑːnsə] Antwort **I**

to answer [ˈɑːnsə] antworten; beantworten **I**

to answer the phone [ˌɑːnsə ðə ˈfəʊn] einen Anruf entgegennehmen **I**

answering machine [ˈɑːnsrɪŋ məˌʃiːn] Anrufbeantworter **I**

anthem [ˈænθəm] Hymne **V U2**, 53

anthropologist [ˌænθrəˈpɒlədʒɪst] Anthropologe/Anthropologin ⟨**V U3**, 87⟩

anxiety [æŋˈzaɪəti] Angst; Sorge **V U2**, 48

anxious [ˈæŋkʃəs] besorgt; ängstlich **V U1**, 18

any [ˈeni] irgendein/-e/-er; irgendwelche **I**

not any longer [nɒtˌeni ˈlɒŋɡə] nicht mehr; (nicht) länger **I**

not any more [ˌnɒtˌeni ˈmɔː] nicht mehr **I**

not … any [nɒtˌeni] kein/-e/-en **I**

anybody [ˈeniˌbɒdi] jeder (beliebige); irgendjemand **I**

anyone [ˈeniwʌn] jeder (beliebige); irgendjemand **I**

anyone else [ˌeniwʌnˈels] jemand anderes **II**

anything [ˈeniθɪŋ] irgendetwas **I**; alles **III**

not … anything [nɒtˌeniθɪŋ] nichts **I**

Anything else? [eniθɪŋˈels] Sonst noch etwas? **I**

anyway [ˈeniweɪ] jedenfalls; trotzdem; sowieso **II**

anywhere [ˈeniweə] irgendwo; überall (egal, wo) **II**

apart [əˈpɑːt] auseinander; getrennt **V U2**, 43

apart from [əˈpɑːt frəm] abgesehen von; außer **III**

apartheid [əˈpɑːtaɪt] Apartheid **IV**

apartment (AE) [əˈpɑːtmənt] Apartment; Wohnung **III**

to apologise [əˈpɒlədʒaɪz] sich entschuldigen **III**

apology [əˈpɒlədʒi] Entschuldigung **III**

app [æp] App **II**

appalling [əˈpɔːlɪŋ] entsetzlich; schrecklich **V U1**, 20

apparently [əˈpærntli] anscheinend **III**

to appear [əˈpɪə] auftauchen; erscheinen **IV**

appearance [əˈpɪərns] Erscheinung; Aussehen; Auftritt **V U3**, 80; **VTS**, 112

apple [ˈæpl] Apfel **I**

applicant [ˈæplɪkənt] Bewerber/-in **IV**

application [ˌæplɪˈkeɪʃn] Bewerbung; Antrag **IV**

application letter [æplɪˈkeɪʃn ˌletə] Bewerbungsschreiben **IV**

to apply (for) [əˈplaɪ fə] sich bewerben (um); beantragen **IV**

to apply (to) [əˈplaɪ tə] gelten (für); zutreffen (auf) **IV**

to appoint sb [əˈpɔɪnt] jmdn. berufen; jmdn. ernennen **IV**

to appreciate [əˈpriːʃieɪt] schätzen; anerkennen; würdigen **V U3**, 69

approach [əˈprəʊtʃ] Herangehensweise; Vorgehensweise; Ansatz; Annäherung **V F3**, 38; **VTS**, 113

to appropriate [əˈprəʊprieɪt] sich aneignen **V AC3**, 65

appropriate [əˈprəʊpriət] angemessen **III**

appropriation [əˌprəʊpriˈeɪʃn] Aneignung; Verwendung **V U2**, 49

to approve [əˈpruːv] annehmen; zustimmen **III**

April [ˈeɪprl] April **I**

*to be apt to happen [biˌæpt tə ˈhæpn] möglicherweise passieren **V U3**, 75

aquarium [əˈkweəriəm] Aquarium **IV**

arcade [ɑːˈkeɪd] Spielhalle; Passage **V U3**, 73

architect [ˈɑːkɪtekt] Architekt/-in **III**

architecture [ˈɑːkɪtektʃə] Architektur **III**

Arctic [ˈɑːktɪk] arktisch **III**

area [ˈeəriə] Areal; Gebiet; Fläche **I**

run area [ˈrʌnˌeəriə] Gehege; Auslauf **III**

to argue [ˈɑːɡjuː] argumentieren; streiten **IV**

argument [ˈɑːɡjəmənt] Argument **II**; Auseinandersetzung; Streit **IV**

counter-argument [ˈkaʊntərˌɑːɡjəmənt] Gegenargument **V U3**, 81

argumentative essay [ɑːɡjəˌmentətɪvˈeseɪ] Erörterung **IV**

arm [ɑːm] Arm **I**

armchair [ˈɑːmtʃeə] Sessel **IV**

armed [ɑːmd] bewaffnet **V F1**, 10

army [ˈɑːmi] Armee **II**

around [əˈraʊnd] um … herum; umher **I**

all around [ˌɔːlˌəˈraʊnd] überall; rundherum; rings umher **I**

*to find one's way around [ˌfaɪnd wʌnzˌweɪ əˈraʊnd] sich zurechtfinden **III**

to turn around [ˌtɜːnˌ(ə)ˈraʊnd] (sich) umdrehen; wenden **III**

around [əˈraʊnd] ungefähr; etwa **III**

to arrange [əˈreɪndʒ] arrangieren; anordnen ⟨**V U2**, 58⟩

arrangement [əˈreɪndʒmənt] Arrangement; Orchestrierung **V AC2**, 34

to arrest [əˈrest] festnehmen; verhaften **III**

arrival [əˈraɪvl] Ankunft **III**

to arrive [əˈraɪv] ankommen **II**

Art [ɑːt] Kunstunterricht **I**

art [ɑːt] Kunst **I**

art print [ˈɑːt ˌprɪnt] Kunstdruck **IV**

article [ˈɑːtɪkl] Artikel; Bericht (in einer Zeitschrift, Zeitung) **II**

reference article [ˈrefrnsˌɑːtɪkl] Artikel in einem Nachschlagewerk **III**

artist [ˈɑːtɪst] Künstler/-in **III**

artistic [ɑːˈtɪstɪk] künstlerisch; kunstvoll **V U3**, 77

artistic licence [ɑːˌtɪstɪk ˈlaɪsns] künstlerische Freiheit **V U3**, 77

artwork [ˈɑːtwɜːk] Illustrationen; Bebilderung **V U1**, 27

as [æz; əz] wie **I**; als **III**

as if [əzˌˈɪf] als ob **III**

as well [əzˈwel] auch **III**

as … as [əz … əz] so … wie **I**

as [æz] während; indem **I**; da; weil **IV**

as early as [əzˌ'ɜːli əz] schon **IV**

as for … [ˈæz fɔː] was … betrifft ⟨**V U1**, 31⟩

as long as [əz ˈlɒŋˌəz] solange **II**

as soon as [əz ˈsuːnˌəz] sobald **II**

… as well as … [əzˈwelˌəz] sowie; und (auch) **III**

sth as opposed to sth [æzˌəˈpəʊzd tə] etw. im Gegensatz zu etw. **V F5**, 67

Asian [ˈeɪʃn] Asiate/Asiatin; asiatisch; aus Asien **IV**

aside [əˈsaɪd] beiseite **V U3**, 82

to ask [ɑːsk] fragen; bitten **I**

to ask for [ˈɑːsk fə] fragen nach; bitten um **I**

*to fall asleep [ˌfɔːlˌəˈsliːp] einschlafen **I**

aspect [ˈæspekt] Aspekt; Gesichtspunkt **III**

to assassinate [əˈsæsɪneɪt] ermorden **V F4**, 62

assassination [əˌsæsɪˈneɪʃn] Attentat; Ermordung **V F1**, 10

assembly [əˈsembli] Versammlung **III**; Morgenappell **IV**

to assess [əˈses] bewerten; beurteilen **V U2**, 55

to assign [əˈsaɪn] zuordnen; übertragen **IV**

assignment [əˈsaɪnmənt] Aufgabe; Auftrag; Mission **IV**

to assist [əˈsɪst] helfen; vorantreiben **IV**

assistant [əˈsɪstnt] Assistent/-in; Verkäufer/-in **II**

to associate [əˈsəʊʃieɪt] assoziieren; verbinden **IV**

to associate sb/sth with sb/sth [əˈsəʊʃieɪt ˌwɪθ] jmdn./etw. mit jmdm./etw. in Verbindung bringen **V U1**, 18

assortment (of) [əˈsɔːtmənt] Sortiment (von); Auswahl (an) **V U1**, 17

to assume [əˈsjuːm] annehmen **IV**

assumption [əˈsʌmpʃn] Annahme; Voraussetzung **V U2**, 48

astronaut [ˈæstrənɔːt] Astronaut/-in **IV**

at [æt; ət] in; auf; bei; an; um (bei Uhrzeitangaben) **I**

at all [ətˌˈɔːl] überhaupt **I**

at first [ət ˈfɜːst] zuerst; zunächst **II**

at home [ət ˈhəʊm] zu Hause; daheim **I**

at last [ət ˈlɑːst] endlich; schließlich **I**

at least [ət ˈliːst] mindestens; wenigstens **I**

at one's own risk [æt wʌnzˌəʊn ˈrɪsk] auf eigene Gefahr **III**

at the back of [ət ðə 'bæk ̩əv] hinten; am Ende; im hinteren Teil **I**

at the moment [ət ðə 'məʊmənt] im Moment; gerade **I**

at the same time [ət ðə ˌseɪm 'taɪm] zur selben Zeit; gleichzeitig **I**

at the seaside [ət ðə 'si:saɪd] am Meer **II**

at the weekend [ət ðə ˌwi:k'end] am Wochenende **I**

at the end of the day [æt ðiˌend ̩əv ðə 'deɪ] unterm Strich; letztendlich **IV**

athlete ['æθli:t] Sportler/-in **III**

atrocity [ə'trɒsəti] Gräueltat; Grausamkeit **V F3**, 38

*to be **attached** to [biˌə'tætʃt tə] hängen an **V F3**, 37

attachment [ə'tætʃmənt] Anhang **IV**

attack [ə'tæk] Angriff; Überfall **III**

to **attack** [ə'tæk] angreifen **II**

to **attend** [ə'tend] besuchen; an etw. teilnehmen **IV**

attention [ə'tenʃn] Aufmerksamkeit; Beachtung **II**

*to pay **attention** to [peɪˌə'tenʃn tə] beachten **II**

attic ['ætɪk] Dachboden **III**

attitude ['ætɪtju:d] Haltung; Einstellung **III**

to **attract** [ə'trækt] anziehen; auf sich ziehen **II**

attraction [ə'trækʃn] Attraktion; Sehenswürdigkeit **II**

attractive [ə'træktɪv] attraktiv **II**

auction ['ɔ:kʃn] Auktion; Versteigerung **V F3**, 38

audience ['ɔ:dɪəns] Publikum **II**

August ['ɔ:gəst] August **I**

aunt [ɑ:nt] Tante **I**

agony **aunt** ['ægəniˌɑ:nt] Kummerkastentante **I**

auntie (infml) ['ɑ:nti] Tantchen (ugs.) **III**

Aussie (coll) ['ɒzi] Australier/-in; australisch (ugs.) **IV**

Australian [ɒs'treɪlɪən] australisch; Australier/-in **III**

author ['ɔ:θə] Autor/-in **III**

autumn ['ɔ:təm] Herbst **I**

*to be **available** [biˌə'veɪləbl] zur Verfügung stehen; abkömmlich sein **IV**

average ['ævrɪdʒ] Durchschnitt; Durchschnitts- **III**

on **average** [ɒnˌ'ævrɪdʒ] durchschnittlich; im Durchschnitt **III**

to **avoid** (+ noun or -ing) [ə'vɔɪd] vermeiden; meiden; aus dem Weg gehen **III**

*to be **awake** [biˌə'weɪk] wach sein **V U3**, 79

award [ə'wɔ:d] Auszeichnung; Preis **II**

*to be **aware** of sth [biˌə'weər ̩əv] sich etw. bewusst sein **IV**

awareness [ə'weənəs] Bewusstsein; Sensibilisierung **IV**

away [ə'weɪ] weg **I**

*to do **away** with sth [du:ˌə'weɪ wɪð] etw. abschaffen; etw. loswerden **IV**

to fade **away** [ˌfeɪdˌə'weɪ] schwinden; zerrinnen; verblassen; sterben **V F5**, 67

far **away** [ˌfɑ:rˌə'weɪ] weit weg **II**

*to give **away** [ˌgɪvˌə'weɪ] verraten; preisgeben **IV**

right **away** [ˌraɪtˌə'weɪ] sofort; gleich **I**

*to run **away** [ˌrʌnˌə'weɪ] wegrennen **I**

*to throw **away** [ˌθrəʊˌə'weɪ] wegwerfen **I**

awesome ['ɔ:səm] super; spitze; beeindruckend **I**

awful ['ɔ:fl] schrecklich; furchtbar **I**

awkward ['ɔ:kwəd] peinlich; ungünstig; ungeschickt; unbeholfen **IV**

axe [æks] Axt **II**

B

baby ['beɪbi] Baby; Säugling **I**

*to **babysit** ['beɪbɪsɪt] babysitten **III**

bachelor's degree ['bætʃləz dɪˌgri:] Bachelor (niedrigster akademischer Grad) **IV**

back [bæk] Rücken; Rückseite **III**

at the **back** of [ət ðə 'bæk ̩əv] hinten; am Ende; im hinteren Teil **I**

*to go behind sb's **back** [gəʊ bɪˌhaɪnd səmbədiz 'bæk] jmdn. hintergehen **II**

to **back** down [ˌbæk 'daʊn] einen Rückzieher machen **IV**

back [bæk] zurück **I**; damals **IV**

back then [ˌbæk 'ðen] damals **III**

*to lean **back** [ˌli:n 'bæk] sich zurücklehnen 〈**V U1**, 31〉

to turn **back** [ˌtɜ:n 'bæk] umkehren; zurückgehen **III**

backache ['bækeɪk] Rückenschmerzen; Rückenweh **II**

backcountry (no pl) ['bækkʌntri] Hinterland **III**

background ['bækgraʊnd] Hintergrund **I**

backlog ['bæklɒg] Rückstand **V U1**, 24

backpack ['bækpæk] Rucksack **III**

backpacking ['bækpækɪŋ] Wandern; Rucksackreisen **II**

backwards ['bækwədz] rückwärts **II**

backyard [bæk'jɑ:d] Garten; Hinterhof **III**

bacon ['beɪkn] Schinkenspeck; Speck **I**

bad [bæd] schlecht; böse; schlimm (ugs.) **I**

bad luck [bæd 'lʌk] Pech; Unglück **I**

Too **bad**! [tu: 'bæd] Zu dumm!; Schade! **I**

badly-written [ˌbædli'rɪtn] schlecht geschrieben **IV**

badminton ['bædmɪntən] Badminton **I**

bag [bæg] Tasche; Tüte **I**; Sack **III**

mixed **bag** [ˌmɪkst 'bæg] buntes Allerlei; bunte Mischung **I**

bagpipes (pl) ['bægpaɪps] Dudelsack **V U1**, 13

bail [beɪl] Kaution **V U2**, 45

to **bake** [beɪk] backen **IV**

baked beans (pl) [ˌbeɪkt 'bi:nz] weiße Bohnen in Tomatensoße **I**

balance ['bæləns] Gleichgewicht **IV**

balcony ['bælkəni] Balkon **III**

ball [bɔ:l] Ball **I**

balloon [bə'lu:n] Ballon **V F1**, 11

ballot ['bælət] Wahl; geheime Abstimmung **V F4**, 62

to **ban** [bæn] verbannen; verbieten; ausschließen **V F3**, 37

banana [bə'nɑ:nə] Banane **I**

band [bænd] Band; Musikgruppe **II**

big **bang** [ˌbɪg 'bæŋ] Urknall; großer Knall **V AC3**, 65

Bang! [bæŋ] Peng! **II**

Bangladeshi [ˌbæŋglə'deʃi] Bangladescher/-in; bangladeschisch **IV**

banjo ['bændʒəʊ] Banjo **V U1**, 21

bank [bæŋk] Bank **III**; Ufer 〈**V U1**, 31〉

food **bank** ['fu:d ˌbæŋk] Tafel (Essensausgabe für sozial Schwächere) **III**

word **bank** ['wɜ:d ˌbæŋk] Wortsammlung **II**

banking ['bæŋkɪŋ] Banking; Bankwesen **IV**

banner ['bænə] Banner; Spruchband; Transparent **IV**

banquet ['bæŋkwɪt] Bankett **II**

snack **bar** ['snæk ˌbɑ:] Café; Imbissstube **I**

barbecue ['bɑ:bɪkju:] Grill; Grillparty **I**

barbie (Aus) (infml) (= barbecue) ['bɑ:bi] Grillparty **IV**

barely ['beəli] kaum **V F3**, 37

bargain ['bɑ:gɪn] Schnäppchen **I**

to **bark** [bɑ:k] bellen **I**

barn [bɑ:n] Scheune **IV**

barrel ['bærl] Fass; Tonne **I**

baseball ['beɪsbɔ:l] Baseball **I**

*to be **based** on [bi 'beɪst ɒn] basieren auf **IV**

basement ['beɪsmənt] Kellergeschoss; Untergeschoss **V U1**, 22

basic ['beɪsɪk] grundlegend; Grund- **II**

basically ['beɪsɪkli] eigentlich; grundsätzlich; im Grunde genommen **IV**

basketball ['bɑ:skɪtbɔ:l] Basketball **I**

bass [beɪs] Bass; Bassgitarre **V U1**, 21

bat [bæt] Fledermaus **II**

bath [bɑ:θ] Bad; Badewanne **I**

bathroom ['bɑ:θrʊm] Bad; Badezimmer **I**

bathroom facilities [ˌbɑ:θrʊm fə'sɪlɪtiz] Toiletten **V U2**, 50

battle ['bætl] Schlacht; Kampf **II**

bay [beɪ] Bucht **II**

BC (= before Christ) [bi:'si:] vor Christus **II**

*to **be** [bi:] sein **I**

*to **be** able to (do sth) [biˌ'eɪbl tə] fähig sein zu; können **II**

*to **be** about [biˌə'baʊt] gehen um; handeln von **I**

*to **be** about to do sth [biˌə'baʊt tə] im Begriff sein, etw. zu tun **III** *to **be** absorbed by sth [ˌbiˌəb'zɔːbd baɪ] in etw. integriert werden; von etw. aufgesaugt werden **V U3**, 68

*to **be** addictive [biˌə'dɪktɪv] süchtig machen **V F5**, 67

*to **be** afraid (of) [biˌə'freɪdˌəv] (sich) fürchten; Angst haben (vor) **II**

*to **be** allowed to (do sth) [biˌə'laʊd tə] dürfen **II**

*to **be** apt to happen [biˌæpt tə 'hæpn] möglicherweise passieren **V U3**, 75

*to **be** attached to [biˌə'tætʃt tə] hängen an **V F3**, 37

*to **be** available [bi ə'veɪləbl] zur Verfügung stehen; abkömmlich sein **IV**

*to **be** awake [biˌə'weɪk] wach sein **V U3**, 79

*to **be** aware of sth [biˌə'weərˌəv] sich etw. bewusst sein **IV**

*to **be** based on [ˌbi 'beɪstˌɒn] basieren auf **IV**

*to **be** born [bi 'bɔːn] geboren werden **II**

*to **be** bound to do sth [bi 'baʊnd tə] etw. tun müssen; nicht umhinkönnen; verpflichtet sein, etw. zu tun **V U2**, 51

*to **be** called [bi 'kɔːld] heißen; genannt werden **II**

*to **be** concerned about sth [bi kən'sɜːndˌə.baʊt] besorgt sein um etw.; sich um etw. Sorgen machen **II**

*to **be** connected (to/with) [bi kə'nektɪd] zusammenhängen (mit); in Zusammenhang stehen (mit) **II**

*to **be** crazy about [bi 'kreɪzi.əbaʊt] verrückt sein nach; abfahren auf **III**

*to **be** fearful of [bi 'fɪəfl] Angst haben vor **III**

*to **be** fed up (with) [bi fed 'ʌp wɪð] sauer sein (auf); die Nase voll haben (von) **II**

*to **be** gone [bi 'gɒn] verschwunden sein; weg sein **II**

*to **be** good at [bi 'gʊdˌət] gut sein in **I**

*to **be** grounded [bi 'graʊndɪd] Hausarrest haben **II**

*to **be** hard on sb [bi 'hɑːdˌɒn] streng mit jmdm. sein; mit jmdm. hart ins Gericht gehen **II**

*to **be** homesick [bi 'həʊmsɪk] Heimweh haben **III**

*to **be** in [biˌ'ɪn] dabei sein; mitmachen; in sein; angesagt sein **II**

*to **be** in progress [ˌbiˌɪn 'prəʊgres] ablaufen; im Gange sein **IV**

*to **be** in the way [biˌɪn ðə 'weɪ] im Weg sein/stehen **I**

*to **be** inhabited [biˌɪn'hæbɪtɪd] bewohnt sein **III**

*to **be** intent on doing sth [biˌɪn'tentˌɒn] fest entschlossen sein, etw. zu tun **V U3**, 79

*to **be** interested (in) [biˌ'ɪntrəstɪdˌɪn] interessiert sein (an); sich interessieren (für) **I**

*to **be** into [biˌ'ɪntə] mögen; stehen auf **I**

*to **be** involved (in) [biˌɪn'vɒlvdˌɪn] beteiligt sein (an); involviert sein (in); engagiert sein (für) **IV**

*to **be** jealous (of) [bi 'dʒeləs] eifersüchtig sein (auf); neidisch sein (auf) **I**

*to **be** late [bi 'leɪt] zu spät dran sein; zu spät kommen **I**

*to **be** likely [bi 'laɪkli] wahrscheinlich sein **III**

*to **be** located [ˌbi ləʊ'keɪtɪd] gelegen sein; liegen **V U2**, 45

*to **be** lucky [bi 'lʌki] Glück haben **I**

*to **be** made of [bi 'meɪdˌəv] bestehen aus **III**

*to **be** made up of [bi ˌmeɪd 'ʌpˌəv] bestehen aus **I**

*to **be** named after [bi 'neɪmdˌɑːftə] benannt sein nach **I**

*to **be** on [biˌ'ɒn] an sein; laufen **II**

*to **be** out [biˌ'aʊt] out sein **II**

*to **be** passionate about sth [bi 'pæʃnətˌə.baʊt] etw. leidenschaftlich gern tun; eine Leidenschaft für etw. haben; für etw. brennen **IV**

*to **be** prejudiced against sb/sth [bi 'predʒədɪstˌə.genst] voreingenommen sein gegenüber jmdm./etw. **IV**

*to **be** prepared [bi prɪ'peəd] bereit sein **III**

*to **be** right [bi 'raɪt] recht haben **I**

*to **be** said to (+ inf) [bi 'sed tə] gelten als **IV**

*to **be** scared (of) [bi 'skeədˌəv] Angst haben (vor) **I**

*to **be** set (in) [bi 'set ɪn] spielen (in); seinen Schauplatz haben (in) **IV**

*to **be** short of sth [biˌ'ʃɔːtˌəv] knapp sein an **IV**

*to **be** sorry [bi 'sɒri] leid tun **I**

*to **be** stuck [bi 'stʌk] festsitzen; feststecken; hängen bleiben **IV**

*to **be** supposed to (do) [bi sə'pəʊzd tə] (tun) sollen **III**

*to **be** surprised [bi sə'praɪzd] überrascht sein **I**

*to **be** suspended [bi sə'spendɪd] suspendiert werden; zeitweilig vom Unterricht ausgeschlossen werden **III**

*to **be** terrified (of sth) [bi 'terəfaɪdˌəv] (große) Angst (vor etw.) haben **III**

*to **be** tired of (+ noun or -ing) [bi 'taɪədˌəv] es müde sein (zu); es leid sein (zu); es satt haben (zu) **III**

*to **be** torn [bi 'tɔːn] hin und her gerissen sein **V TS**, 110

*to **be** trapped [bi 'træpt] eingeschlossen sein; in der Falle sitzen **III**

*to **be** unlucky [biˌʌn'lʌki] Pech haben **I**

*to **be** used to (+ -ing) [bi 'juːzd tə] gewöhnt sein an; gewohnt sein **III**

*to **be** willing to do sth [bi 'wɪlɪŋ tə] gewillt sein, etw. zu tun; bereit sein, etw. zu tun **V AC2**, 35

*to **be** worth [bi 'wɜːθ] wert sein **I**

*to **be** wrong [bi 'rɒŋ] unrecht haben; sich irren **I**

Here you **are**. [ˌhɪə juˌ'ɑː] Bitte schön. **I**

How **are** you? [ˌhaʊˌ'ɑː jə] Wie geht es dir?; Wie geht es euch?; Wie geht es Ihnen? **I**

How much **is/are** …? [ˌhaʊ 'mʌtʃˌɪz/ɑː] Wie viel (kostet/kosten) …? **I**

beach [biːtʃ] Strand **I**

bean [biːn] Bohne **I**
baked **beans** (pl) [ˌbeɪkt 'biːnz] weiße Bohnen in Tomatensoße **I**

bear [beə] Bär **II**
grizzly **bear** ['grɪzli ˌbeə] Grizzlybär **III**
polar **bear** ['pəʊlə ˌbeə] Eisbär **I**

*to **bear** [beə] tragen; ertragen **V F3**, 37
bearing in mind [ˌbeərɪŋ ɪn 'maɪnd] angesichts (der Tatsache, dass …); wenn man berücksichtigt **V F2**, 33

beard [bɪəd] Bart; Vollbart **IV**

*to **beat** [biːt] schlagen; besiegen **V AC2**, 35

beating ['biːtɪŋ] Prügel **V F3**, 36

beautiful ['bjuːtɪfl] schön; hübsch; wunderbar **II**

beauty ['bjuːti] Schönheit **III**

beaver ['biːvə] Biber **III**

because [bɪ'kɒz] weil; da **I**
because of [bɪ'kɒzˌəv] wegen **II**

*to **become** [bɪ'kʌm] werden **I**
*to **become** extinct [bɪˌkʌmˌɪk'stɪŋkt] aussterben **III**

bed [bed] Bett **I**

bedroom ['bedrʊm] Schlafzimmer **I**

bee [biː] Biene **I**

beef [biːf] Rindfleisch **II**

before [bɪ'fɔː] schon einmal; vorher; zuvor **II**

before [bɪ'fɔː] vor (zeitlich); bevor **I**

to **beg** (for) ['beg fə] betteln (um); anflehen **IV**

*to **begin** [bɪ'gɪn] beginnen; anfangen **II**

beginning [bɪ'gɪnɪŋ] Anfang; Beginn **I**

to **behave** [bɪ'heɪv] sich benehmen; sich verhalten **III**

behaviour (no pl) [bɪ'heɪvjə] Verhalten; Benehmen; Betragen **III**

behind [bɪ'haɪnd] hinter **I**

belief [bɪ'liːf] Glaube; Überzeugung **III**

believable [bɪ'liːvəbl] glaubwürdig **III**

to **believe** [bɪ'liːv] glauben **I**
I couldn't **believe** my eyes. [aɪ ˌkʊdnt bɪˌliːv maɪˌ'aɪz] Ich traute meinen Augen nicht. **II**

bell [bel] Glocke; Klingel **III**

belly ['beli] Bauch **V U1**, 21

to **belong** (to) [bɪ'lɒŋ (tə)] gehören (zu) **II**

beloved [bɪ'lʌvɪd] geliebt **V F4**, 63
below [bɪ'ləʊ] unterhalb; unten **I**
belt [belt] Gürtel **III**
bench [benʃ] Bank; Sitzbank **I**
*to **bend** [bend] beugen; biegen **VTS**, 116
  *to **bend** over [ˌbendˌəʊvə] sich vorbeugen; sich beugen über ⟨**V U1**, 30⟩
beneficial [ˌbenɪ'fɪʃl] nützlich **V AC1**, 8
benefit ['benɪfɪt] Vorteil; Nutzen; Unterstützung **IV**
beside [bɪ'saɪd] neben **IV**
besides [bɪ'saɪdz] neben **II**
best [best] beste/-r/-s; am besten; am
  liebsten **I**
  Best wishes [ˌbest 'wɪʃɪz] Viele Grüße;
  Herzliche Grüße **II**
*to **bet** [bet] wetten **II**
better ['betə] besser; lieber **I**
  You'd **better** ... (= You had better) [ˌjuːd
  'betə] Du solltest lieber ... **III**
between [bɪ'twiːn] zwischen **I**
to **beware** [bɪ'weə] sich in Acht nehmen **IV**
beyond [bi'ɒnd] jenseits; über ... hinaus **III**
bible ['baɪbl] Bibel **III**
biblical ['bɪblɪkl] biblisch **V AC3**, 65
bicycle ['baɪsɪkl] Fahrrad **II**
big [bɪg] groß **I**
  big bang [ˌbɪg 'bæn] Urknall; großer
  Knall **V AC3**, 65
bighorn sheep ['bɪghɔːn ˌʃiːp] Dickhornschaf **II**
bike [baɪk] Fahrrad **I**
mountain **biking** ['maʊntɪn ˌbaɪkɪn] Mountainbikefahren **I**
bilingual [baɪ'lɪŋgwl] zweisprachig **V U1**, 26
bill [bɪl] Rechnung **V U1**, 16; Gesetzentwurf;
  Gesetzesvorlage **V F3**, 39
  dollar **bill** ['dɒlə ˌbɪl] Dollarnote; Dollar-
  schein **I**
billion ['bɪliən] Milliarde **IV**
billionaire ['bɪliəneə] Milliardär/-in **IV**
biographical [ˌbaɪəʊ'græfɪkl] biografisch **III**
biography [baɪ'ɒgrəfi] Biografie **III**
biology [baɪ'ɒlədʒi] Biologie **II**
bird [bɜːd] Vogel **I**
birthday ['bɜːθdeɪ] Geburtstag **I**
biscuit ['bɪskɪt] Keks **I**
bishop ['bɪʃəp] Bischof **IV**
bison ['baɪsn], **bison** ['baɪsn] (pl) Bison;
  Büffel **III**
a **bit** [ə 'bɪt] ein bisschen; ein wenig **I**
bite [baɪt] Biss; Stich; Bissen **III**
*to **bite** [baɪt] beißen; stechen **II**
bitter ['bɪtə] bitter **IV**
black [blæk] schwarz **I**
  *to go **black** [ˌgəʊ 'blæk] schwarz
  werden **II**
blackish ['blækɪʃ] schwärzlich **III**
blackout ['blækaʊt] Stromausfall **IV**
blame [bleɪm] Schuld **V U3**, 79
to **blame** [bleɪm] die Schuld geben; beschuldigen **V U1**, 20

blank [blæŋk] ausdruckslos; leer **V U3**, 70
to **bleach** [bliːtʃ] bleichen **IV**
blind [blaɪnd] blind **IV**
to **blink** [blɪŋk] blinzeln; zwinkern
  ⟨**V U2**, 58⟩
blizzard ['blɪzəd] Schneesturm; Blizzard **II**
block [blɒk] Block; Häuserblock **IV**
to **block** [blɒk] blockieren; abblocken **II**
blog [blɒg] Blog; Internettagebuch **II**
blogger ['blɒgə] Blogger/-in **IV**
bloke (infml) [bləʊk] Typ (ugs.) **IV**
blond [blɒnd] blond **II**
blood [blʌd] Blut **III**
blossom ['blɒsəm] Blüte **II**
*to **blow** [bləʊ] zerstören; zerschlagen
  V U3, 74
  *to **blow** one's nose [ˌbləʊ ˌwʌnz 'nəʊz]
  sich die Nase putzen **III**
  *to **blow** out [ˌbləʊ ˌaʊt] ausblasen;
  auspusten **I**
blue [bluː] blau **I**
blueberry ['beri] Blaubeere; Heidelbeere **II**
blueprint ['bluːprɪnt] Blaupause; Plan;
  Entwurf **V U3**, 76
blunt [blʌnt] stumpf **V U1**, 17
blurred [blɜːd] unscharf; verschwommen
  V U3, 82
to **blush** [blʌʃ] erröten **IV**
board [bɔːd] Tafel **I**; Behörde; Amt **V F2**, 33
  board of education [ˌbɔːd əv ˌedʒʊ'keɪʃn]
  Schulbehörde **V F4**, 60
  on **board** [bɔːd] an Bord **III**
  tourist **board** ['tʊərɪst ˌbɔːd] Tourismuszentrale; Tourismusbehörde **II**
to **board** [bɔːd] an Bord gehen; besteigen
  II
boarding school ['bɔːdɪŋ ˌskuːl] Internat **IV**
boat [bəʊt] Boot **I**
boating lake ['bəʊtɪŋ ˌleɪk] See zum
  Rudern **I**
body ['bɒdi] Körper **II**; Leiche **III**
bodyguard ['bɒdigɑːd] Bodyguard **III**
to **boil** [bɔɪl] kochen; sieden **V F3**, 37
bold [bəʊld] fett; fett gedruckt **IV**
bomb shelter ['bɒm ˌʃeltə] Bunker; Luftschutzkeller **IV**
bond [bɒnd] Bindung **II**
bone [bəʊn] Knochen **IV**
bonfire ['bɒnfaə] Lagerfeuer; Freudenfeu-
  er **I**
book [bʊk] Buch **I**
  exercise **book** ['eksəsaɪz ˌbʊk] Übungsheft **I**
  to judge a **book** by its cover [ˌdʒʌdʒ ə
  ˌbʊk baɪ ɪts ˈkʌvə] jdn./etw. nach dem
  Äußeren beurteilen **IV**
to **book** [bʊk] buchen; reservieren **II**
bookkeeper ['bʊkiːpə] Buchhalter/-in **IV**
boom [buːm] Aufschwung; Boom **IV**
to **boom** [buːm] dröhnen **II**; florieren;
  boomen **III**
boomerang ['buːmræn] Bumerang **IV**

boost [buːst] Auftrieb **IV**
boot [buːt] Stiefel **II**; Kofferraum **III**
border ['bɔːdə] Grenze **III**
bored [bɔːd] gelangweilt **I**
boring ['bɔːrɪŋ] langweilig **I**
*to be **born** [bi 'bɔːn] geboren werden **II**
borough ['bʌrə] Bezirk; Stadtteil **IV**
to **borrow** ['bɒrəʊ] (sich) ausleihen **II**
boss [bɒs] Boss; Chef **III**
bossy ['bɒsi] herrisch; rechthaberisch **II**
both [bəʊθ] beide **I**
  both ... and ... ['bəʊθ ... ənd] sowohl ... als auch ... **IV**
to **bother** ['bɒðə] sich die Mühe machen **III**
bottle ['bɒtl] Flasche **I**
bottom ['bɒtəm] Boden; unterer Teil;
  Grund **I**
*to be **bound** to do sth [bi ˌbaʊnd tə] etw.
  tun müssen; nicht umhinkönnen; verpflichtet sein, etw. zu tun **V U2**, 51
bourgeois ['bɔːʒwɑː] bürgerlich **V U1**, 20
bow [bəʊ] Bogen **V AC2**, 35
to **bow** [baʊ] beugen; verbeugen **V AC2**, 35
bowl [bəʊl] Schale; Schälchen; Schüssel **I**
  to play **bowls** [ˌpleɪ 'bəʊlz] Bowling
  spielen **III**
bowling alley ['bəʊlɪŋ ˌæli] Bowlingbahn **I**
box [bɒks] Box; Kasten; Schachtel; Kiste **I**
  box jellyfish ['bɒks ˌdʒelifɪʃ] Würfelqualle
  IV
boy [bɔɪ] Junge; Bub **I**
  cabin **boy** ['kæbɪn ˌbɔɪ] Schiffsjunge **I**
boycott ['bɔɪkɒt] Boykott **IV**
to **boycott** ['bɔɪkɒt] boykottieren **IV**
bracelet ['breɪslət] Armband **I**
bracket ['brækɪt] Klammer **IV**
brain(s) [breɪn(z)] Gehirn; Verstand **IV**
brainstorming ['breɪnˌstɔːmɪŋ] Brainstorming (Sammlung von Ideen) **IV**
branches of government [ˌbrɑːnʃɪz əv
  'gʌvnmənt] Regierungszweig **IV**
brand [brænd] Brandmal; Brandzeichen
  V F3, 37; Marke **V U2**, 48
brave [breɪv] mutig; tapfer **I**
bravery ['breɪvri] Tapferkeit; Mut **V F1**, 10
bread [bred] Brot **I**
  bread roll ['bred ˌrəʊl] Brötchen **III**
breadbasket ['bred ˌbɑːskɪt] Brotkorb **II**
break [breɪk] Pause **I**
  lunch **break** ['lʌnʃbreɪk] Mittagspause **I**
*to **break** [breɪk] brechen; zerbrechen **I**
  *to **break** away (from) [ˌbreɪk əˈweɪ] sich
  trennen (von); sich lossagen (von) **III**
breakfast ['brekfəst] Frühstück **I**
  *to have **breakfast** [ˌhæv 'brekfəst]
  frühstücken **I**
breath [breθ] Atem; Atemzug **II**
  *to catch one's **breath** [ˌkætʃ wʌnz 'breθ]
  wieder zu Atem kommen **III**
  *to hold your **breath** [ˌhəʊld jə 'breθ] den
  Atem anhalten **II**

out of **breath** [ˌaʊt ˌəv ˈbreθ] außer Atem **III**

*to take a **breath** [ˌteɪk ə ˈbreθ] Luft holen; Atem holen **III**

to **breathe** [briːð] atmen **II**

breathtaking [ˈbreθˌteɪkɪŋ] atemberaubend **IV**

*to **breed** [briːd] züchten **IV**

bridge [brɪdʒ] Brücke **II**

brief [briːf] kurz **IV**

bright [braɪt] hell; leuchtend; strahlend **IV**

brilliant [ˈbrɪliənt] toll; prima; leuchtend **I**

*to **bring** [brɪŋ] bringen; mitbringen **I**

*to **bring** about [ˌbrɪŋ əˈbaʊt] herbeiführen **V U2**, 51

*to **bring** up [ˌbrɪŋ ˈʌp] großziehen; zur Sprache bringen **IV**

on the **brink** of [ˌɒn ðə ˈbrɪŋk ˌəv] am Rande von; kurz vor **III**

British [ˈbrɪtɪʃ] britisch; Brite/Britin **I**

Briton [ˈbrɪtn] Brite/Britin **III**

broad [brɔːd] breit **IV**

brochure [ˈbrəʊʃə] Broschüre; Prospekt **III**

broken [ˈbrəʊkn] gebrochen; kaputt **I**

Bronze Age [ˈbrɒnzˌeɪdʒ] Bronzezeit (ca. 2200–800 v. Chr.) **II**

brother [ˈbrʌðə] Bruder **I**

brown [braʊn] braun **I**

to **brush** [brʌʃ] bürsten; putzen **IV**

brutality [bruːˈtæləti] Brutalität **V U2**, 46

bubble [ˈbʌbl] Blase **IV**

Buddhist [ˈbʊdɪst] Buddhist/-in; buddhistisch **IV**

buffalo (sg or pl) [ˈbʌfləʊ] Büffel **III**

bugfix [ˈbʌgfɪks] Fehlerbehebung **V U3**, 80

*to **build** [bɪld] bauen **II**; aufbauen **III**

building [ˈbɪldɪŋ] Gebäude **I**

built-in closet [ˌbɪlt ɪn ˈklɒzɪt] Einbauschrank **III**

bullet [ˈbʊlɪt] Kugel; Geschoss **V F4**, 62

cyber **bully** [ˈsaɪbə ˈbʊli] jemand, der andere in sozialen Netzwerken belästigt/mobbt **II**

cyber **bullying** [ˈsaɪbə ˌbʊliɪŋ] Cybermobbing **III**

to **bump** into sb [ˌbʌmp ˈɪntə] jmdn. zufällig treffen; hier: jmdn. anrempeln **IV**

burden [ˈbɜːdn] Last; Belastung **V U2**, 51

burglar [ˈbɜːglə] Einbrecher/-in **V U1**, 14

burial [ˈberiəl] Begräbnis; Beerdigung **III**

*to **burn** [bɜːn] brennen; verbrennen **III**

to **bury** [ˈberi] begraben; beerdigen **IV**

bus [bʌs] Bus **I**

bus station [ˈbʌs ˌsteɪʃn] Busbahnhof **I**

double-decker **bus** [ˌdʌbl dekə ˈbʌs] Doppeldeckerbus **IV**

bush [bʊʃ] Busch (Buschlandschaft); Wildnis **III**

business [ˈbɪznɪs] Geschäft; Business **III**

business executive [ˈbɪznɪs ɪgˌzekjətɪv] Geschäftsführer/-in; Manager/-in; gehobene Führungskraft **IV**

to mind one's own **business** [ˌmaɪnd wʌnz ˌəʊn ˈbɪznɪs] sich um die eigenen Angelegenheiten kümmern **V U2**, 44

It's none of our **business**! [ɪts ˌnʌn əv aʊə ˈbɪznɪs] Das geht uns nichts an! **IV**

busy [ˈbɪzi] belebt; beschäftigt **I**

but [bʌt] aber **I**

not only … **but** (also) [nɒt ˌəʊnli … bʌt ˈɔːlsəʊ] nicht nur … sondern (auch) **IV**

butter [ˈbʌtə] Butter **I**

butterfly [ˈbʌtəflaɪ] Schmetterling **V U1**, 17

button [ˈbʌtn] Knopf ⟨**V U3**, 87⟩

*to **buy** [baɪ] kaufen **I**

*to **buy** time [ˌbaɪ ˈtaɪm] Zeit gewinnen **IV**

buyer [ˈbaɪə] Käufer/-in **I**

buzz [bʌz] Begeisterung; Kick ⟨**V U2**, 58⟩

by [baɪ] von; durch; bei; neben; an **II**; (spätestens) bis **III**; vorbei **IV**

all **by** oneself [ˌɔːl baɪ wʌnˈself] ganz allein **II**

by (+ gerund) [baɪ] indem **III**

by (bike) [baɪ] mit (dem Fahrrad) **I**

by default [ˌbaɪ dɪˈfɔːlt] automatisch; standardmäßig; voreingestellt **V U2**, 42

by mistake [baɪ mɪˈsteɪk] versehentlich **III**

by the way [ˌbaɪ ðə ˈweɪ] übrigens **II**

*to **go** by … [ˈgəʊ baɪ] fahren mit … **I**

Bye! [baɪ] Tschüss!; Servus! **I**

C

cab [kæb] Taxi **IV**

tossing the **caber** [ˌtɒsɪŋ ðə ˈkeɪbə] Baumstammwerfen **V U1**, 13

cabin [ˈkæbɪn] Kabine; Kajüte **II**

cabin boy [ˈkæbɪn ˌbɔɪ] Schiffsjunge **I**

log **cabin** [ˈlɒg ˌkæbɪn] Blockhütte **II**

cabinet [ˈkæbɪnət] Kabinett **IV**

cable [ˈkeɪbl] Kabel **IV**

cache [kæʃ] Cache **II**

cactus [ˈkæktəs], **cacti** (pl) [ˈkæktaɪ] Kaktus **II**

café [ˈkæfeɪ] Café **I**

cafeteria [ˌkæfəˈtɪəriə] Cafeteria **I**

cage [keɪdʒ] Käfig **IV**

cajón [kæˈhɒn] Cajón **II**

cake [keɪk] Kuchen; Torte **I**

calculation [ˌkælkjəˈleɪʃn] Berechnung; Kalkulation **V F3**, 36

Caledonian [ˌkæləˈdəʊniən] schottisch ⟨**V U1**, 28⟩

calendar [ˈkæləndə] Kalender **III**

Californian [ˌkælɪˈfɔːniən] kalifornisch; Kalifornier/-in **IV**

phone **call** [ˈfəʊn ˌkɔːl] Anruf; Telefonanruf **I**

to **call** [kɔːl] nennen; anrufen; rufen **I**

*to be **called** [bi ˈkɔːld] heißen; genannt werden **II**

caller [ˈkɔːlə] Anrufer/-in **I**

call-in [ˈkɔːlɪn] Sendung, bei der sich das Publikum telefonisch beteiligen kann **II**

to **calm** down [ˌkɑːm ˈdaʊn] sich beruhigen **I**

calm [kɑːm] ruhig; friedlich **II**

camel racing [ˈkæml ˌreɪsɪŋ] Kamelrennen **II**

camera [ˈkæmrə] Fotoapparat; Kamera **II**

camp [kæmp] Camp; Lager **II**

to **camp** [kæmp] campen; zelten **III**

campaign [kæmˈpeɪn] Kampagne; Aktion **V U1**, 23

camper [ˈkæmpə] Camper/-in **II**

campfire [ˈkæmpfaɪə] Lagerfeuer **II**

camping [ˈkæmpɪŋ] Camping; Zelten **I**

can [kæn] Dose; Büchse **II**

can [kæn; kən] können; dürfen **I**

Canadian [kəˈneɪdiən] kanadisch; Kanadier/-in **III**

to **cancel** [ˈkænsl] absagen; stornieren **IV**

cancer [ˈkænsə] Krebs (Krankheit) **V U2**, 42

candidate [ˈkændɪdət] Kandidat/-in; Bewerber/-in **IV**

candle [ˈkændl] Kerze **I**

candlelight (no pl) [ˈkændlaɪt] Kerzenlicht **II**

candy (AE) [ˈkændi] Süßigkeiten **I**

cannot [ˈkænɒt] kann nicht; können nicht **II**

canoe [kəˈnuː] Kanu **II**

canoeing [kəˈnuːɪŋ] Kanufahren **I**

canyon [ˈkænjən] Schlucht; Canyon **II**

per **capita** [pə ˈkæpɪtə] pro Kopf; Pro-Kopf-; pro Person **IV**

capital [ˈkæpɪtl] Hauptstadt **I**

capital [ˈkæpɪtl] Kapital- **V U2**, 46

capital letter Großbuchstabe **V U2**, 55

to **capsize** [kæpˈsaɪz] kentern **II**

captain [ˈkæptɪn] Kapitän/-in; Mannschaftsführer/-in **I**

caption [ˈkæpʃn] Bildunterschrift; Untertitel **II**

to **capture** [ˈkæptʃə] ergreifen; gefangen nehmen **III**

car [kɑː] Auto **I**

vintage **car** [ˌvɪntɪdʒ ˈkɑː] Oldtimer **III**

carbon [ˈkɑːbn] Kohlenstoff; Kohlenstoffdioxid **IV**

card [kɑːd] Karte; Spielkarte **I**

credit **card** [ˈkredɪt ˌkɑːd] Kreditkarte **II**

prompt **card** [ˈprɒmpt kɑːd] Stichwortkarte; Rollenkarte **II**

report **card** (AE) [rɪˈpɔːt ˌkɑːd] Zeugnis **II**

cardigan [ˈkɑːdɪgən] kragenlose (Strick-) Jacke **V U3**, 73

*to take **care** of [ˌteɪk ˈkeər ˌəv] sich kümmern um; sorgen für **III**

health **care** [ˈhelθ keə] Gesundheitsversorgung **IV**

social **care** [ˌsəʊʃl ˈkeə] Sozialfürsorge; Sozialdienstleistungen **IV** to **care** (about) ['keər‿ə‚baʊt] wichtig nehmen; sich kümmern (um); sich interessieren (für) **II**

I don't **care** [aɪ ‚daʊnt 'keə] es ist mir egal **II**

career [kə'rɪə] Beruf; Laufbahn; Karriere **III**

careful ['keəfl] vorsichtig; sorgfältig **II**

cargo, **cargoes** (pl) ['kɑ:gəʊ] Ladung; Fracht **V F3**, 36

caribou ['kærɪbu:] Karibu **III**

carpenter ['kɑ:pntə] Schreiner/-in; Zimmermann; Zimmerin **IV**

carpet ['kɑ:pɪt] Teppich **III**

carrot ['kærət] Karotte; Möhre **I**

to **carry** ['kæri] tragen **II**

cartoon [kɑ:'tu:n] Cartoon; Zeichentrickfilm **III**

case [keɪs] Fall **III**

to clear a **case** [‚klɪər‿ə 'keɪs] einen Fall klären **IV**

in **case** [ɪn 'keɪs] falls; für den Fall, dass … **IV**

cash [kæʃ] Bargeld **II**

casino [kə'si:nəʊ] Kasino; Spielkasino **III**

cast [kɑ:st] Besetzung; Ensemble **VTS**, 112

plaster **cast** ['plɑ:stə ‚kɑ:st] Gipsverband **III**

*to **cast** one's vote [‚kɑ:st wʌnz 'vəʊt] die Stimme abgeben **V U1**, 24

castle ['kɑ:sl] Schloss; Burg **I**

casual ['kæʒjuəl] zufällig; gelegentlich **V U1**, 14; informell; zwanglos; lässig **V U1**, 18

cat [kæt] Katze **I**

catastrophe [kə'tæstrəfi] Katastrophe **IV**

*to **catch** [kætʃ] fangen **II**; mitbekommen (ugs.); mitkriegen (ugs.) **IV**

*to **catch** a glimpse [‚kætʃ‿ə 'glɪms‿əv] einen (flüchtigen) Blick erhaschen von etw. **IV**

*to **catch** one's breath [‚kætʃ wʌnz 'breθ] wieder zu Atem kommen **III**

*to **catch** sb (+ -ing) [kætʃ] jmdn. erwischen, wie …; jmdn. ertappen, wie … **IV**

*to **catch** up with sb [‚kætʃ'ʌp wɪð] jmdn. einholen **III**

catchy ['kætʃi] eingängig; einprägsam ⟨**V U2**, 58⟩

category ['kætəgri] Kategorie; Klasse **III**

catering ['keɪtrɪŋ] Catering; Verpflegung **IV**

cathedral [kə'θi:drl] Kathedrale **III**

Catholic ['kæθlɪk] Katholik/-in; katholisch **III**

cattle (pl only) ['kætl] Vieh; Rindvieh **II**

*to get **caught** [get 'kɔ:t] erwischt werden; ertappt werden **III**

cause [kɔ:z] Grund; Ursache; Sache **IV**

to **cause** [kɔ:z] verursachen **II**

cave [keɪv] Höhle **II**

ceiling ['si:lɪŋ] Zimmerdecke; Decke **IV**

to **celebrate** ['seləbreɪt] feiern **I**

celebration [‚selə'breɪʃn] Feier **III**

celebrity [sə'lebrəti] Prominente/-r; berühmte Person **III**

cell phone (AE) ['sel fəʊn] Mobiltelefon; Handy **II**

degree Celsius (°C) [dɪgri: 'selsiəs] Grad Celsius **II**

Celt [kelt] Kelte/Keltin **II**

Celtic ['keltɪk; 'seltɪk] keltisch **II**

to **censor** ['sensə] zensieren **V U1**, 22

census ['sensəs] Zählung; Volkszählung **V F2**, 33

cent [sent] Cent (Währung) **I**

central ['sentrl] zentral; Zentral- **II**

centre ['sentə] Zentrum; Center **I**

community **centre** [kə'mju:nəti ‚sentə] Gemeindezentrum **I**

immigration detention **centre** [ɪmɪˌgreɪʃn dɪ'tenʃn ‚sentə] Auffanglager (für illegal Eingewanderte) **IV**

leisure **centre** ['leʒə ‚sentə] Freizeitzentrum **I**

tourist information **centre** [‚tʊərɪst‿ ɪnfə'meɪʃn ‚sentə] Touristeninformation **I**

century ['senʃri] Jahrhundert **II**

cereal (no pl) ['sɪəriəl] Frühstückszerealie; Getreideprodukt (z. B. Cornflakes oder Müsli) **I**

ceremony ['serɪməni] Zeremonie **IV**

certain ['sɜ:tn] bestimmt; sicher; gewiss **III**

chain [tʃeɪn] Kette **III**

chair [tʃeə] Stuhl; Sessel **I**

chairperson ['tʃeəˌpɜ:sn] Vorsitzende/-r; Vorsitz **IV**

challenge ['tʃælɪndʒ] Herausforderung **II**

to **challenge** ['tʃælɪndʒ] herausfordern **V F1**, 11

champagne [ʃæm'peɪn] Champagner; Sekt; Schaumwein **IV**

champion ['tʃæmpiən] Gewinner/-in; Sieger/-in; Champion **IV**

to **champion** ['tʃæmpiən] eintreten für; unterstützen; verfechten **V U1**, 25

championship ['tʃæmpiənʃɪp] Meisterschaft **III**

chance [tʃɑ:ns] Chance; Gelegenheit; Möglichkeit **II**

chancellor ['tʃɑ:nslər] Kanzler/-in **II**

change [tʃeɪndʒ] Änderung; Veränderung; Wechsel; Umstieg **II**

climate **change** ['klaɪmət ‚tʃeɪndʒ] Klimawandel **III**

to **change** [tʃeɪndʒ] wechseln; (sich) ändern; sich verwandeln; umsteigen **II**

to **change** one's mind [‚tʃeɪndʒ wʌnz 'maɪnd] seine Meinung ändern **III**

changing room ['tʃeɪndʒɪŋ ‚rʊm] Umkleideraum; Umkleidekabine **III**

chant [tʃɑ:nt] Sprechgesang **II**

chaos ['keɪɒs] Chaos; Durcheinander **III**

chaotic [keɪ'ɒtɪk] chaotisch **IV**

chapter ['tʃæptə] Kapitel **III**

character ['kærəktə] Charakter; Figur **I**

characterisation [‚kærəktraɪ'zeɪʃn] Beschreibung; Personenbeschreibung; Charakterisierung **V U1**, 18

characteristic [‚kærəktə'rɪstɪk] typisches Merkmal **IV**

congestion charge [kən'dʒestʃn ‚tʃɑ:dʒ] Citymaut **IV**

free of charge [‚fri:‿əv tʃɑ:dʒ] kostenlos; gebührenfrei **IV**

to **charge** [tʃɑ:dʒ] laden; aufladen **IV**

charity ['tʃærɪti] Wohltätigkeitsverein; wohltätige Zwecke; Wohlfahrt **I**

charity shop ['tʃærɪti ‚ʃɒp] Second-Hand-Laden **I**

lucky charm [‚lʌki 'tʃɑ:m] Glücksbringer; Talisman **I**

chart [tʃɑ:t] Tabelle; Diagramm **IV**

to **chase** [tʃeɪs] jagen; nachjagen **I**

chat [tʃæt] Chat **III**

video **chat** ['vɪdiəʊ ‚tʃæt] Videochat **I**

to **chat** [tʃæt] plaudern; chatten **I**

cheap [tʃi:p] billig; preiswert **I**

to **cheat** [tʃi:t] mogeln; betrügen **III**

cheat sheet ['tʃi:t ‚ʃi:t] Spickzettel **III**

to **check** [tʃek] überprüfen; prüfen; kontrollieren **I**

to **check** out [‚tʃek‿'aʊt] prüfen; abchecken (ugs.); auschecken **IV**

Check-in ['tʃekɪn] Einchecken **I**

checklist ['tʃeklɪst] Checkliste **IV**

checkout ['tʃekaʊt] Kasse **IV**

Check-out ['tʃekaʊt] Auschecken **I**

cheer [tʃɪə] Jubel; Hurraruf **III**

to **cheer** [tʃɪə] anfeuern; jubeln; zujubeln **II**

to **cheer** sb up [‚tʃɪər‿'ʌp] jmdn. aufheitern **IV**

cheerful ['tʃɪəfl] fröhlich; heiter **V U1**, 18

cheerleading ['tʃɪəli:dɪŋ] Cheerleading (Aktivitäten der Cheerleader) **III**

cheese [tʃi:z] Käse **III**

chef [ʃef] Koch/Köchin; Küchenchef/-in **IV**

chemical ['kemɪkl] Chemikalie **IV**

chest [tʃest] Brust; Brustkorb **III**; Kiste; Truhe ⟨**V U1**, 30⟩

chicken ['tʃɪkɪn] Huhn; Hähnchen **I**

chief [tʃi:f] Häuptling **III**

chief executive officer (CEO) [‚tʃi:f ɪgˌzekjətɪvˌ'ɒfɪsə] Vorstandvorsitzende/-r; Geschäftsführer/-in **V U2**, 51

chief justice [‚tʃi:f 'dʒʌstɪs] Oberster Richter/Oberste Richterin **IV**

child [tʃaɪld], **children** (pl) ['tʃɪldrən] Kind **I**

child labor (AE) [‚tʃaɪld 'leɪbə] Kinderarbeit **II**

only **child** ['əʊnli ‚tʃaɪld] Einzelkind **I**

childhood ['tʃaɪldhʊd] Kindheit **IV**

chili ['tʃɪli], **chilies** (pl) ['tʃɪliz] Chili; Chilischote **II**

to **chill** out [‚tʃɪl‿'aʊt] chillen **II**

chimney ['tʃɪmni] Kamin; Schornstein **II**

chin [tʃɪn] Kinn ⟨**V U2**, 58⟩

Chinese [tʃaɪˈniːz] Chinese/Chinesin; chinesisch; Chinesisch; aus China **IV**

chips (pl) (BE) [tʃɪps] Pommes frites **I**

chocolate [ˈtʃɒklət] Schokolade **I**

choice [tʃɔɪs] Wahl; Auswahl **IV**
 *to make a **choice** [ˌmeɪk ə ˈtʃɔɪs] eine Wahl treffen **IV**

choir [kwaɪə] Chor **III**

*to choose [tʃuːz] auswählen; wählen **I**

to chop [tʃɒp] hacken; klein schneiden **V F1**, 10

choppy [ˈtʃɒpi] bewegt **V U2**, 56

chord [kɔːd] Akkord **V U1**, 21

chore [tʃɔː] (lästige) Pflicht; Bürde **III**

Christian [ˈkrɪstʃn] Christ/-in **III**

Christian [ˈkrɪstʃn] christlich **I**

church [tʃɜːtʃ] Kirche **I**

cider [ˈsaɪdə] Apfelwein 〈**V U3**, 87〉

cinema [ˈsɪnəmə] Kino **I**

circle [ˈsɜːkl] Kreis; Ring **II**
 *to go round in **circles** [ɡəʊ ˌraʊnd ɪn ˈsɜːklz] sich im Kreis drehen; im Kreis gehen **III**

circus [ˈsɜːkəs] Zirkus **III**

citizen [ˈsɪtɪzn] Bürger/in **III**

city [ˈsɪti] Stadt; Großstadt **I**

civil rights (pl) [ˌsɪvl ˈraɪts] Bürgerrechte **IV**

civil war [ˌsɪvl ˈwɔː] Bürgerkrieg **II**

civilization [ˌsɪvɪlaɪˈzeɪʃn] Kultur; Zivilisation **III**

claim [kleɪm] Behauptung; Anspruch **IV**
 to file a **claim** [ˌfaɪl ə ˈkleɪm] einen Anspruch geltend machen; eine Forderung geltend machen **V U3**, 75

to claim [kleɪm] behaupten; beanspruchen **IV**

to clap [klæp] klatschen **I**
 Clap your hands. [ˌklæp jɔː ˈhændz] Klatsche/Klatscht in die Hände. **I**

class [klɑːs] Klasse; Schulklasse **I**; Unterricht **II**
 working **class** [ˌwɜːkɪŋ ˈklɑːs] Arbeiterklasse **IV**

classified ad [ˌklæsɪfaɪd ˈæd] Kleinanzeige **V U3**, 83

classmate [ˈklɑːsmeɪt] Klassenkamerad/-in; Mitschüler/-in **I**

classroom [ˈklɑːsrʊm] Klassenzimmer **I**

main clause [ˈmeɪn ˌklɔːz] Hauptsatz **III**

to clean [kliːn] säubern; reinigen **I**

clean [kliːn] sauber **III**

to clear a case [ˌklɪər ə ˈkeɪs] einen Fall klären **IV**

to clear out [ˌklɪərˈaʊt] ausräumen; entrümpeln **I**

clear [klɪə] klar; deutlich **I**

clever [ˈklevə] schlau; klug **I**

cliché [ˈkliːʃeɪ] Klischee **IV**

click [klɪk] Klicken; Klick **II**

cliff [klɪf] Klippe; Kliff **IV**

climate [ˈklaɪmət] Klima **III**

climate change [ˈklaɪmət ˌtʃeɪndʒ] Klimawandel **III**

climatic [klaɪˈmætɪk] klimatisch **IV**

to climb [klaɪm] klettern; besteigen; steigen **I**

climbing [ˈklaɪmɪŋ] Klettern; Bergsteigen **II**

*to cling (to sb/sth) [klɪŋ] sich an jmdm./etw. festhalten; sich an jmdm./etw. festklammern **IV**

cloak [kləʊk] Mantel; Umhang 〈**V U1**, 30〉

clock [klɒk] Uhr **I**
 o'**clock** [əˈklɒk] Uhr (Zeitangabe bei vollen Stunden) **I**

to close [kləʊz] schließen; zumachen **I**

close [kləʊs] eng; knapp; nahe **I**

closely [ˈkləʊsli] genau **IV**

closet [ˈklɒzɪt] Schrank; Wandschrank **III**
 built-in **closet** [ˌbɪltˌɪn ˈklɒzɪt] Einbauschrank **III**

closure [ˈkləʊʒə] Schließung; Stilllegung **V AC4**, 88

cloth [klɒθ] Stoff; Tuch; Gewebe **V U1**, 21

clothes (pl) [kləʊðz] Kleider; Kleidung **I**

clothing [ˈkləʊðɪŋ] Kleidung **III**
 clothing drive [ˈkləʊðɪŋ ˌdraɪv] Kleidersammlung **III**

cloud [klaʊd] Wolke **II**

clown [klaʊn] Clown **II**

club [klʌb] Klub; Verein; AG **I**; Schlagstock; Keule; Knüppel **V F3**, 37

clue [kluː] Hinweis; Spur **IV**

clumsy [ˈklʌmzi] ungeschickt; unbeholfen **IV**

cluster [ˈklʌstə] Bündel; Anhäufung **IV**

coach [kəʊtʃ] Trainer/-in **I**; Reisebus **II**

coal [kəʊl] Kohle **III**

coast [kəʊst] Küste **I**

coastal [ˈkəʊstl] Küsten- **IV**
 coastal path [ˌkəʊstl ˈpɑːθ] Küstenweg **II**

roller coaster [ˈrəʊlə ˌkəʊstə] Achterbahn **II**

coastline [ˈkəʊstlaɪn] Küste; Küstenverlauf **II**

coat [kəʊt] Mantel **III**

cocktail [ˈkɒkteɪl] Cocktail **IV**

cocoa [ˈkəʊkəʊ] Kakao **IV**

code [kəʊd] Code; Verschlüsselung **IV**
 dress **code** [ˈdres ˌkəʊd] Kleiderordnung; Bekleidungsvorschriften **II**

coeducation (no pl) [ˌkəʊedʒʊˈkeɪʃn] Koedukation (gemeinsames Lehren von Jungen und Mädchen) **IV**

coffee [ˈkɒfi] Kaffee **I**

coffin [ˈkɒfɪn] Sarg **V U2**, 43

coin [kɔɪn] Münze **I**

to coin [kɔɪn] prägen (einen Begriff/eine Münze) **V U2**, 40

coincidence [kəʊˈɪnsɪdns] Zufall **III**

coke [kəʊk] Cola **I**

cold [kəʊld] Erkältung **II**

cold [kəʊld] kalt **I**

to collapse [kəˈlæps] kollabieren; zusammenbrechen **IV**

colleague [ˈkɒliːɡ] Kollege/Kollegin **IV**

to collect [kəˈlekt] sammeln **I**

college [ˈkɒlɪdʒ] Universität (in den USA) **II**

to collide [kəˈlaɪd] kollidieren; zusammenstoßen **V U3**, 70

collocation [ˌkɒləˈkeɪʃn] Wortverbindung **IV**

colonial [kəˈləʊniəl] kolonial; Kolonial- **II**

colonialism [kəˈləʊniəlɪzm] Kolonialismus **IV**

colonist [ˈkɒlənɪst] Siedler/-in; Kolonist/-in **III**

to colonize [ˈkɒlənaɪz] kolonisieren; besiedeln **II**

colony [ˈkɒləni] Kolonie **II**
 penal **colony** [ˈpiːnl ˌkɒləni] Strafkolonie **IV**

colour [ˈkʌlə] Farbe **I**
 What **colour** is …? [ˌwɒt ˈkʌlər ɪz] Welche Farbe hat …? **I**

colourful [ˈkʌləfl] farbenfroh; bunt **I**

column [ˈkɒləm] Spalte **V U1**, 14

combination [ˌkɒmbɪˈneɪʃn] Kombination; Verbindung **III**

to combine [kəmˈbaɪn] kombinieren; verbinden **IV**

*to come [kʌm] kommen **I**
 *to **come** along [ˌkʌm əˈlɒŋ] mitkommen **II**
 *to **come** down [ˌkʌm ˈdaʊn] herunterkommen **I**
 *to **come** easily to sb [ˌkʌm ˈiːzɪli] jmdm. leichtfallen **II**
 *to **come** in [ˌkʌm ˈɪn] hereinkommen **II**
 *to **come** out [ˌkʌm ˈaʊt] sich outen **IV**
 *to **come** to one's mind [ˌkʌm tə wʌnz ˈmaɪnd] jmdm. in den Sinn kommen; jmdm. einfallen **V U1**, 21
 *to **come** true [ˌkʌm ˈtruː] wahr werden; in Erfüllung gehen **III**
 coming-of-age novel [ˌkʌmɪŋ əvˈeɪdʒ ˌnɒvl] Entwicklungsroman; Bildungsroman **V F5**, 67
 Come on! [ˌkʌm ˈɒn] Komm schon!; Komm jetzt! **I**

comedy [ˈkɒmədi] Komödie; Comedy- **III**

comfortable [ˈkʌmftəbl] komfortabel; bequem **III**

comforting [ˈkʌmfətɪŋ] tröstlich; ermutigend **IV**

comic [ˈkɒmɪk] Comicheft **II**

coming out [ˌkʌmɪŋˈaʊt] Coming-out **IV**

inverted comma [ɪnˌvɜːtɪd ˈkɒmə] Anführungszeichen **V U1**, 26

command [kəˈmɑːnd] Kommando; Befehl **IV**

comment [ˈkɒment] Kommentar **II**

to comment (on) [ˈkɒment(ˌɒn)] kommentieren **II**

commerce [ˈkɒmɜːs] Handel **V U2**, 48

commercial [kəˈmɜːʃl] kommerziell; profitorientiert **V AC3**, 64 fiscal **commission** [ˌfɪskl kəˈmɪʃn] Finanzausschuss **V F2**, 33

to **commit** [kəˌmɪt] übergeben; anvertrauen **V U3**, 83

   to **commit** a crime [kəˌmɪt əˈkraɪm] ein Verbrechen begehen **IV**

commitment [kəˈmɪtmənt] Bindung; Verpflichtung; Engagement **IV**

committee [kəˈmɪti] Komitee; Ausschuss **III**

common [ˈkɒmən] üblich; gewöhnlich; (weit) verbreitet; gebräuchlich **II**; gemeinsam **IV**

   *to have sth in **common** [ˌhæv ɪn ˈkɒmən] etw. gemeinsam haben **III**

to **communicate** [kəˈmjuːnɪkeɪt] kommunizieren; sich verständigen **I**

communication [kəˌmjuːnɪˈkeɪʃn] Kommunikation **III**

community [kəˈmjuːnəti] Gemeinde; Gemeinschaft **IV**

   community centre [kəˈmjuːnəti ˌsentə] Gemeindezentrum **I**

company [ˈkʌmpəni] Gesellschaft; Firma; Unternehmen **II**

comparable [ˈkɒmprəbl] vergleichbar **II**

to **compare** (with/to) [kəmˈpeə] vergleichen (mit) **I**

to **compete** (with/against) [kəmˈpiːt] konkurrieren (mit); sich messen (mit); in Wettbewerb treten (mit); antreten (gegen) **II**

competition [ˌkɒmpəˈtɪʃn] Wettbewerb; Turnier **I**

competitive [kəmˈpetɪtɪv] leistungsorientiert; konkurrierend **III**; Wettbewerbs-; konkurrenzfähig; wettbewerbsfähig **IV**

to **complain** [kəmˈpleɪn] sich beschweren; sich beklagen **II**

complaint [kəmˈpleɪnt] Beschwerde **III**

to **complement** [ˈkɒmplɪmənt] abrunden; ergänzen **V U1**, 25

to **complete** [kəmˈpliːt] vervollständigen **I**

complete [kəmˈpliːt] vollständig; komplett; völlig **III**

completely [kəmˈpliːtli] völlig **II**

complex [ˈkɒmpleks] komplexe/-r/-s **IV**

compliment [ˈkɒmplɪmənt] Kompliment **IV**

composition [ˌkɒmpəˈzɪʃn] Zusammensetzung **V U2**, 40

comprehensive school [kɒmprɪˈhensɪv ˌskuːl] Gesamtschule **IV**

compromise [ˈkɒmprəmaɪz] Kompromiss **II**

to **compromise** [ˈkɒmprəmaɪz] Kompromisse eingehen **II**

compulsory [kəmˈpʌlsri] verpflichtend; obligatorisch; vorgeschrieben **IV**

computing [ˌkəmˈpjuːtɪŋ] EDV **IV**

pros and **cons** [ˌprɒz ən ˈkɒnz] Argumente für und gegen etw. **II**

to **concentrate** [ˈkɒnsntreɪt] (sich) konzentrieren **II**

concept [ˈkɒnsept] Vorstellung; Idee; Konzept **IV**

*to be **concerned** about sth [bi kənˈsɜːnd əˌbaʊt] besorgt sein um etw.; sich um etw. Sorgen machen **IV**

where … is/are **concerned** [ˌweə … ɪz/ ɑː kənˈsɜːnd] was … betrifft; was … angeht **V U3**, 74

concert [ˈkɒnsət] Konzert **I**

concise [kənˈsaɪs] präzise; kurz; prägnant **IV**

to **conclude** [kənˈkluːd] enden; schließen; schlussfolgern **IV**

conclusion [kənˈkluːʒn] Schluss; Schlussfolgerung **III**

to **condemn** [kənˈdem] verurteilen; missbilligen **IV**

condition [kənˈdɪʃn] Kondition; Bedingung **III**

to **conduct** [kənˈdʌkt] durchführen; ausführen **IV**

confidence [ˈkɒnfɪdns] Vertrauen; Zuversicht **IV**

confident [ˈkɒnfɪdnt] selbstsicher; selbstbewusst **I**

to **confirm** [kənˈfɜːm] bestätigen; bekräftigen **IV**

conflict [ˈkɒnflɪkt] Konflikt; Auseinandersetzung **III**

to **confront** [kənˈfrʌnt] konfrontieren **IV**

confused [kənˈfjuːzd] verwirrt; wirr; konfus **III**

confusion [kənˈfjuːʒn] Verwirrung **IV**

congestion charge [kənˈdʒestʃn ˌtʃɑːdʒ] Citymaut **IV**

to **congratulate** sb [kənˈɡrætʃʊleɪt] jmdm. gratulieren **V TS**, 116

to **connect** (to) [kəˈnekt tə] verbinden (mit); vermitteln; anschließen **III**

*to be **connected** (to/with) [bi kəˈnektɪd] zusammenhängen (mit); in Zusammenhang stehen (mit) **II**

connection [kəˈnekʃn] Verbindung **IV**

to **conquer** [ˈkɒŋkə] erobern **III**

conscience [ˈkɒnʃns] Gewissen **IV**

   guilty **conscience** [ˌɡɪlti ˈkɒnʃns] schlechtes Gewissen; Schuldbewusstsein **IV**

consequence [ˈkɒnsɪkwəns] Konsequenz; Folge **III**

consequently [ˈkɒnsɪkwəntli] folglich; somit **V F2**, 33

conservation [ˌkɒnsəˈveɪʃn] Schutz; Erhaltung **IV**

conservative [kənˈsɜːvətɪv] konservativ **IV**; zurückhaltend **V U3**, 76

to **consider** [kənˈsɪdə] betrachten; erwägen **III**; berücksichtigen **IV**

considerable [kənˈsɪdrəbl] beträchtlich **III**

to **consist** of [kənˈsɪst əv] bestehen aus **III**

constant [ˈkɒnstənt] ständig; konstant; stetig; gleichmäßig **IV**

constituency [kənˈstɪtʃuensi] Wahlkreis; Wählerschaft eines Wahlkreises **IV**

constitution [ˌkɒnstɪˈtʃuːʃn] Verfassung **V F4**, 61

constitutional monarchy [ˌkɒnstɪˌtjuːʃnl ˈmɒnəki] konstitutionelle Monarchie **IV**

construction [kənˈstrʌkʃn] Konstruktion **III**; Bau; Baugewerbe **IV**

consultation [ˌkɒnslˈteɪʃn] Beratung; Besprechung **V U1**, 25

to **consume** [kənˈsjuːm] konsumieren; verbrauchen **IV**

consumerism [kənˈsjuːmərɪzm] Konsum; Konsumdenken **V U3**, 68

consumption [kənˈsʌmpʃn] Konsum; Verbrauch **IV**

contact [ˈkɒntækt] Kontakt **II**

to **contact** [ˈkɒntækt] sich in Verbindung setzen; kontaktieren **III**

to **contain** [kənˈteɪn] enthalten **IV**

to **contaminate** [kənˈtæmɪneɪt] kontaminieren; verseuchen **IV**

contemporary [kənˈtemprri] zeitgenössisch; zeitgemäß **V F5**, 66

content [ˈkɒntent] Inhalt **III**

content [kənˈtent] zufrieden **V U1**, 16

contest [ˈkɒntest] Wettkampf; Wettbewerb **I**

contestant [kənˈtestnt] Kandidat/-in **IV**

context [ˈkɒntekst] Kontext; Zusammenhang **II**

continent [ˈkɒntɪnənt] Kontinent **III**

to **continue** [kənˈtɪnjuː] fortfahren; andauern; weitergehen; weitermachen **III**

to **contort** [kənˈtɔːt] verzerren; verziehen **V U3**, 71

to **contradict** [ˌkɒntrəˈdɪkt] widersprechen **III**

contradictory [ˌkɒntrəˈdɪktri] widersprüchlich **V U2**, 48

on the **contrary** [ɒn ðə ˈkɒntrəri] im Gegenteil **IV**

contrast [ˈkɒntrɑːst] Kontrast; Unterschied; Gegensatz **III**

   in **contrast** [ɪn ˈkɒntrɑːst] im Gegensatz dazu; dagegen **III**

to **contrast** [kənˈtrɑːst] kontrastieren; gegenüberstellen **IV**

to **contribute** to [kənˈtrɪbjuːt tə] beitragen zu **IV**

contribution [ˌkɒntrɪˈbjuːʃn] Beitrag; Beteiligung **V F1**, 11

control [kənˈtrəʊl] Kontrolle **III**

to **control** [kənˈtrəʊl] kontrollieren; beherrschen; steuern **III**

controversial [ˌkɒntrəˈvɜːʃl] umstritten; kontrovers **III**

convenience [kənˈviːniəns] Komfort; Vorteil **IV**

convenient [kənˈviːniənt] bequem; zweckmäßig; passend; angenehm **IV**

convention [kən'venʃn] Konvention; Kongress; Tagung **V U3**, 69

conventional [kən'venʃnl] konventionell; herkömmlich; üblich **IV**

conversation [ˌkɒnvə'seɪʃn] Konversation; Gespräch; Unterhaltung **I**

to convert [kən'vɜːt] konvertieren; übertreten **V F4**, 62

to convey [kən'veɪ] transportieren; ausdrücken; vermitteln **V U2**, 56

convict ['kɒnvɪkt] Sträfling **IV**

to convict [kən'vɪkt] verurteilen **V U1**, 24

to convince [kən'vɪns] überzeugen **II**

convincing [kən'vɪnsɪŋ] überzeugend **IV**

to cook [kʊk] kochen **II**

cooker ['kʊkə] Herd **I**

cookie (AE) ['kʊki] Keks **I**

cooking ['kʊkɪŋ] Kochen **I**
Cooking Club ['kʊkɪŋ ˌklʌb] Koch-AG **I**

*to leave it to cool [ˌliːv ɪt tə 'kuːl] kalt stellen **I**

cool [kuːl] cool; super **I**; kühl **III**

cooperation [kəʊˌɒpə'reɪʃn] Zusammenarbeit; Kooperation **IV**

to cope with ['kəʊp wɪð] bewältigen; fertig werden mit **V U1**, 14

copper ['kɒpə] Kupfer **IV**

to copy ['kɒpi] abschreiben; kopieren **I**

copyright ['kɒpiraɪt] Urheberrecht; Copyright **V U1**, 27

coral reef [ˌkɒrəl 'riːf] Korallenriff **IV**

core [kɔː] Kern **V U3**, 82

corn [kɔːn] Korn; Mais; Getreide **I**

corner ['kɔːnə] Ecke **II**

Cornish ['kɔːnɪʃ] in Cornwall; kornisch **II**

cornmeal ['kɔːnmiːl] Maismehl **V F3**, 37

to correct [kə'rekt] korrigieren; verbessern; berichtigen **II**

correct [kə'rekt] richtig; korrekt **I**

correspondence [ˌkɒrɪ'spɒndəns] Korrespondenz; Schriftwechsel **V U1**, 27

corrugated ['kɒrəɡeɪtɪd] gewellt **V U1**, 17

cosmetics (pl) [kɒz'metɪks] Kosmetik **IV**

cost [kɒst] Preis; Kosten **IV**

*to cost [kɒst] kosten **I**

costume ['kɒstjuːm] Kostüm **I**

cottage ['kɒtɪdʒ] Landhaus; Hütte **V U1**, 14

cotton ['kɒtn] Baumwolle **I**

cougar ['kuːɡə] Puma; Berglöwe **II**

cough [kɒf] Husten **II**

could [kʊd] konnte/-n; könnte/-n **I**

council ['kaʊnsl] Rat; Ratsversammlung **III**
council housing [ˌkaʊnsl 'haʊzɪŋ] sozialer Wohnungsbau (brit.) **V U2**, 46
council of elders [ˌkaʊnsl əv 'eldəz] Ältestenrat **III**
student **council** [ˌstjuːdnt 'kaʊnsl] Schülerrat **IV**

councillor ['kaʊnslə] Gemeinderat/-rätin; Stadtrat/-rätin **V U1**, 25

counsellor ['kaʊnslə] Betreuer/-in; Berater/-in **IV**

to count (on) ['kaʊnt ɒn] zählen (auf) **I**

countdown ['kaʊntdaʊn] Countdown **IV**

counter ['kaʊntə] Theke; Tresen; Schalter **V U1**, 18

counter-argument ['kaʊntərˌɑːɡjəmənt] Gegenargument **V U3**, 81

counterpart ['kaʊntəpɑːt] Gegenstück; Kollege/Kollegin **V U2**, 50

counterpoint ['kaʊntəˌpɔɪnt] Kontrapunkt; Gegenbild **V U1**, 20

countless ['kaʊntləs] unzählige; viele **III**

country, countries (pl) ['kʌntri] Land **I**

countryside ['kʌntrisaɪd] Land; Landschaft **II**

county ['kaʊnti] Kreis; Bezirk **V U3**, 71

couple ['kʌpl] Paar **IV**
a **couple** of [ə 'kʌpl əv] ein paar **I**

courage ['kʌrɪdʒ] Mut; Tapferkeit; Courage **V U2**, 49

courageous [kə'reɪdʒəs] mutig **V U1**, 18

courier ['kʊriə] Kurier/-in **IV**

course [kɔːs] Kurs **IV**
of **course** [əv 'kɔːs] natürlich; selbstverständlich **I**

court [kɔːt] Spielfeld **II**; Hof; Gericht; Gerichtshof **III**

cousin ['kʌzn] Cousin/Cousine **I**

cover ['kʌvə] Cover; Titelblatt **II**
to judge a book by its **cover** [ˌdʒʌdʒ ə ˌbʊk baɪ ɪts 'kʌvə] jdn./etw. nach dem Äußeren beurteilen **I**

to cover ['kʌvə] abdecken; bedecken; zudecken **III**
covered wagon [ˌkʌvəd 'wæɡən] Planwagen **III**

coverage ['kʌvrɪdʒ] Berichterstattung **V U1**, 20

cow [kaʊ] Kuh **I**

cowboy ['kaʊbɔɪ] Cowboy; Rinderhirte **IV**

coyote [kə'jəʊti] Kojote; Präriewolf **II**

crack [kræk] Knacken; Krachen **III**

cracking ['krækɪŋ] knackend; brechend **III**

cramp [kræmp] Krampf **II**

cranberry ['krænbri] Cranberry (Preiselbeerart) **II**

to crash [kræʃ] aufschlagen; gegen etwas krachen; abstürzen **II**
to **crash** (into) [kræʃ] zusammenstoßen (mit) **III**

to crawl [krɔːl] kriechen; krabbeln **IV**

crazy ['kreɪzi] verrückt **I**
*to be **crazy** about [bi 'kreɪzi əbaʊt] verrückt sein nach; abfahren auf **III**
*to go **crazy** [ɡəʊ 'kreɪzi] ausflippen; durchdrehen; verrückt werden **II**

cream [kriːm] Creme; Sahne **I**
ice **cream** [ˌaɪs 'kriːm] Eis; Eiscreme **I**

to create [kri'eɪt] schaffen; erschaffen; erfinden **II**

creative [kri'eɪtɪv] kreativ **II**

creativity [ˌkriːeɪ'tɪvəti] Kreativität **IV**

creature ['kriːtʃə] Kreatur; Lebewesen; Geschöpf **IV**
mythical **creature** [ˌmɪθɪkl 'kriːtʃə] Fabelwesen **V U1**, 15

credit card ['kredɪt ˌkɑːd] Kreditkarte **II**

credit (no pl) ['kredɪt] Ansehen; Anerkennung; Ehre **V U3**, 79

to credit ['kredɪt] gutschreiben **V U3**, 80

creed [kriːd] Glauben; Glaubensbekenntnis; Kredo; Überzeugung **V F4**, 62

*to creep (up) [kriːp] schleichen; kriechen; sich anschleichen **IV**

crew [kruː] Crew; Besatzung; Mannschaft; Team **IV**

cricket ['krɪkɪt] Cricket **II**

crime [kraɪm] Verbrechen; Kriminalität **II**
to commit a **crime** [kəˌmɪt ə 'kraɪm] ein Verbrechen begehen **IV**
crime story ['kraɪm ˌstɔri] Krimi; Kriminalgeschichte **II**

criminal ['krɪmɪnəl] Kriminelle/-r; Verbrecher/-in **II**

crisis, crises (pl) ['kraɪsɪs; 'kraɪsiːz] Krise **V U1**, 24; **V TS**, 116

crisp (BE) [krɪsp] Kartoffelchip **I**

criterion [kraɪ'tɪəriən], criteria [kraɪ'tɪəriə] (pl) Kriterium; Merkmal **III**

critical ['krɪtɪkl] kritisch; entscheidend **IV**

criticism ['krɪtɪsɪzm] Kritik **IV**

to criticize (AE) ['krɪtɪsaɪz] kritisieren **II**

crocodile ['krɒkədaɪl] Krokodil **IV**

croft [krɒft] kleiner Bauernhof ⟨**V U1**, 29⟩

crop [krɒp] Getreide; Anbaupflanze; Feldfrucht ⟨**V U1**, 29⟩

to crop (a photo) [krɒp] (ein Foto) zurechtschneiden **III**

cross [krɒs] Kreuz **II**

to cross [krɒs] überqueren; kreuzen **II**
*to keep your fingers **crossed** [ˌkiːp jɔː ˌfɪŋɡəz 'krɒst] die Daumen drücken **I**

to cross-check [ˌkrɒs'tʃek] die Gegenprobe machen; vergleichend überprüfen **V U1**, 26

to crouch [kraʊtʃ] hocken; sich niederkauern **V U1**, 17

crowd [kraʊd] Menschenmenge **II**

crowded ['kraʊdɪd] überfüllt **III**

crown [kraʊn] Krone **II**

crucially ['kruːʃli] entscheidend; ausschlaggebend **V U3**, 76

cruel ['kruːəl] grausam **II**

to crumble ['krʌmbl] zerfallen; zerbrechen; abbröckeln **V U2**, 46

to cry [kraɪ] weinen; schreien; rufen **II**

CU (= See you) ['siː juː] Bis dann!; Bis … **I**

Cuban ['kjuːbən] Kubaner/-in; kubanisch **II**
Cuban-American [ˌkjuːbənə'merɪkən] Amerikaner/-in kubanischer Abstammung **II**

cultural ['kʌltʃrl] kulturell **III**

culture ['kʌltʃə] Kultur **I**

cup [kʌp] Tasse **III**

cupboard [ˈkʌbəd] Küchenschrank; Schrank **I**

curator [kjʊəˈreɪtə] Kurator/-in; Ausstellungsmacher/-in **V U3**, 69

to **cure** [kjʊə] heilen; kurieren ⟨**V U3**, 86⟩

curfew [ˈkɜːfjuː] Sperrstunde; Ausgangssperre **III**

curious [ˈkjʊəriəs] neugierig **IV**

currency [ˈkʌrnsi] Währung **IV**

current [ˈkʌrnt] Strömung **II**

rip **current** [ˈrɪp ˌkʌrnt] Brandungsrückströmung **IV**

currently [ˈkʌrntli] momentan; aktuell **IV**

curriculum [kəˈrɪkjələm] Lehrplan **V F4**, 62

curry [ˈkʌri] Curry (Gewürz oder Gericht) **I**

to **curse** [kɜːs] fluchen; verfluchen; verdammen **IV**

curtain [ˈkɜːtn] Vorhang **V U1**, 14

cushion [ˈkʊʃn] Kissen **V U3**, 73

custard [ˈkʌstəd] Vanillesoße; Vanillepudding **I**

custom [ˈkʌstəm] Gewohnheit; Brauch; Sitte **III**

customer [ˈkʌstəmə] Kunde/Kundin **IV**

*to **cut** [kʌt] schneiden; fällen **II**

*to **cut** down [ˌkʌt ˈdaʊn] fällen **III**

cute [kjuːt] niedlich; süß **I**

cutlery (no pl) [ˈkʌtləri] Besteck **V U1**, 17

cutting-edge [ˌkʌtɪŋ ˈedʒ] supermodern; Spitzen- ⟨**V U3**, 87⟩

CV (Curriculum Vitae) [ˌsiːˈviː: (kəˌrɪkjələm ˈviːtaɪ)] Lebenslauf **IV**

cyber bully [ˈsaɪbə ˈbʊli] jemand, der andere in sozialen Netzwerken belästigt/mobbt **II**

cyber bullying [ˈsaɪbə ˈbʊliɪŋ] Cybermobbing **III**

to **cycle** [ˈsaɪkl] Fahrrad fahren **III**

cycling [ˈsaɪklɪŋ] Radfahren **I**

cyclist [ˈsaɪklɪst] Radfahrer/-in **IV**

cynical [ˈsɪnɪkl] zynisch **VTS**, 116

D

dad [dæd] Papa **I**

daily [ˈdeɪli] täglich **IV**

dairy [ˈdeəri] Molkerei; Molkerei- **IV**

dam [dæm] Damm; Staumauer **III**

damage [ˈdæmɪdʒ] Schaden; Beschädigung **IV**

to **damage** [ˈdæmɪdʒ] beschädigen; schaden **III**

damn [dæm] verdammt **V U2**, 42

dance [dɑːns] Tanz; Tanzveranstaltung **II**

to **dance** [dɑːns] tanzen **I**

dancer [ˈdɑːnsə] Tänzer/-in **III**

danger [ˈdeɪndʒə] Gefahr **III**

dangerous [ˈdeɪndʒrəs] gefährlich **I**

to **dare** [deə] wagen **IV**

daring [ˈdeərɪŋ] kühn **V U1**, 18

dark [dɑːk] dunkel **III**

darling [ˈdɑːlɪŋ] Liebling **IV**

data (pl only) [ˈdeɪtə] Daten; Angaben **IV**

date [deɪt] Datum **I**

up to **date** [ˌʌptəˈdeɪt] auf dem Laufenden; modern; zeitgemäß; aktuell **III**

to **date** [deɪt] ausgehen mit **IV**

to **date** from [ˈdeɪt frəm] stammen aus; zurückgehen auf **V F1**, 10

daughter [ˈdɔːtə] Tochter **I**

to **daunt** [dɔːnt] einschüchtern **V U1**, 22

dawn [dɔːn] Morgendämmerung; Morgengrauen **V F3**, 37

day [deɪ] Tag **I**

G'**day**! (= Good day!) [gəˈdeɪ] Guten Tag.; Hallo.; Hi. (Begrüßung in Australien) **IV**

the **day** after tomorrow [ðə ˌdeɪˌɑːftə təˈmɒrəʊ] übermorgen **IV**

a **day** [ə ˈdeɪ] pro Tag **III**

at the end of the **day** [æt ðiˌendˌəv ðə ˈdeɪ] unterm Strich; letztendlich **IV**

daycare [ˈdeɪkeə] Kita; Tagespflege ⟨**V U2**, 57⟩

dead [ded] tot **II**

*to meet/miss a **deadline** [ˌmiːt/mɪsˌə ˈdedlaɪn] einen (Abgabe-)Termin einhalten/verpassen **V U1**, 27

deadly [ˈdedli] tödlich **III**

deaf [def] gehörlos; taub; schwerhörig **II**

*to **deal** (with) [diːl] sich befassen mit; umgehen mit **III**

Oh **dear**! [əʊ ˈdɪə] Oje! **II**

Dear … [dɪə] Liebe/-r … (Anrede in Briefen) **I**

Dear Sir or Madam [dɪə ˌsɜːrˌɔː ˈmædəm] Sehr geehrte Dame, sehr geehrter Herr **II**

death [deθ] Tod **III**

debate [dɪˈbeɪt] Debatte **IV**

debt [det] Schuld; Verschuldung; Verpflichtung **IV**

debut [ˈdeɪbjuː] Debütalbum **V U3**, 76

decade [ˈdekeɪd; dɪˈkeɪd] Jahrzehnt **V U3**, 72

December [dɪˈsembə] Dezember **I**

to **decide** [dɪˈsaɪd] (sich) entscheiden **I**

decision [dɪˈsɪʒn] Entscheidung **II**

*to make a **decision** [ˌmeɪkˌə dɪˈsɪʒn] eine Entscheidung treffen **II**

deck [dek] Deck **I**

declaration [ˌdekləˈreɪʃn] Erklärung; Aussage; Feststellung **III**

to **declare** [dɪˈkleə] erklären **III**

decline [dɪˈklaɪn] Rückgang; Abnahme; Niedergang **V F2**, 32

to **decorate** [ˈdekəreɪt] dekorieren; verzieren; schmücken **III**

decorations (pl) [ˌdekəˈreɪʃnz] Dekoration; Schmuck **III**

to **decrease** [dɪˈkriːs] abnehmen; reduzieren **IV**

to **dedicate** [ˈdedɪkeɪt] widmen **IV**

to **deduce** [dɪˈdjuːs] folgern; ableiten **IV**

deep [diːp] tief **II**

deep-fried [ˌdiːpˈfraɪd] frittiert **IV**

deer (sg or pl) [dɪə] Hirsch **III**

by **default** [ˌbaɪ dɪˈfɔːlt] automatisch; standardmäßig; voreingestellt **V U2**, 42

to **defeat** [dɪˈfiːt] besiegen **II**

to **defend** [dɪˈfend] verteidigen **IV**

defiance (no pl) [dɪˈfaɪəns] Auflehnung; Trotz **V F4**, 60

to **define** [dɪˈfaɪn] definieren **V U2**, 49

defining [dɪˈfaɪnɪŋ] prägend; entscheidend **VTS**, 116

definitely [ˈdefɪnətli] bestimmt; definitiv; eindeutig **III**

degree [dɪˈgriː] akademischer Grad; Hochschulabschluss **IV**

bachelor's **degree** [ˈbætʃləz dɪˌgriː] Bachelor (niedrigster akademischer Grad) **IV**

degree Celsius (°C) [ˌdɪgri: ˈselsiəs] Grad Celsius **II**

degree Fahrenheit (°F) [ˌdɪgri: ˈfærnhaɪt] Grad Fahrenheit **II**

master's **degree** [ˈmɑːstəz dɪˌgriː] Master (zweithöchster akademischer Grad); Magister; Magistra **IV**

to **deinstall** [ˌdiːɪnˈstɔːl] deinstallieren **V U3**, 80

to **delay** [dɪˈleɪ] verzögern; aufschieben **IV**

delayed [dɪˈleɪd] verspätet; verzögert **II**

to **delete** [dɪˈliːt] löschen **IV**

to **deliver** [dɪˈlɪvə] liefern **IV**

delivery [dɪˈlɪvri] Lieferung; Auslieferung; Zustellung **IV**

demand [dɪˈmɑːnd] Bedarf; Nachfrage **V F3**, 36

to **demand** [dɪˈmɑːnd] fordern; verlangen; fragen; wissen wollen **III**

democracy [dɪˈmɒkrəsi] Demokratie **II**

parliamentary **democracy** [pɑːləˌməntri dɪˈmɒkrəsi] parlamentarische Demokratie **IV**

democratic [ˌdeməˈkrætɪk] demokratisch **IV**

to **demonstrate** [ˈdemənstreɪt] demonstrieren **III**

demonstration [ˌdemənˈstreɪʃn] Demonstration **IV**

density [ˈdensɪti] Dichte **III**

dentist [ˈdentɪst] Zahnarzt/Zahnärztin **III**

to **deny** [dɪˈnaɪ] leugnen; abstreiten; verweigern **IV**

to **depart** [dɪˈpɑːt] abfahren; abfliegen **II**

department [dɪˈpɑːtmənt] Abteilung **V U1**, 14

to **depend** (on) [dɪˈpendˌ(ɒn)] abhängen von **II**

depressed [dɪˈprest] deprimiert; bedrückt **V U1**, 18

depression [dɪˈpreʃn] Depression; Niedergeschlagenheit **III**

to **descend** from [dɪˈsend frəm] abstammen von; herstammen von **V F1**, 10

descent [dɪˈsent] Abstammung **IV**
to describe [dɪˈskraɪb] beschreiben **I**
description [dɪˈskrɪpʃn] Beschreibung **III**
desert [ˈdezət] Wüste **II**
to deserve [dɪˈzɜːv] verdienen **III**
design [dɪˈzaɪn] Design; Gestaltung; Entwurf **III**
to design [dɪˈzaɪn] entwerfen; gestalten **III**
desire [dɪˈzaɪə] Wunsch; Sehnsucht; Verlangen **IV**
desk [desk] Schalter **II**; Schreibtisch; Pult **IV**
despair [dɪˈspeə] Hoffnungslosigkeit; Verzweiflung **V U1**, 21; **VTS**, 117
desperate [ˈdesprət] verzweifelt; hoffnungslos; ausweglos **IV**
despite [dɪˈspaɪt] trotz **V U1**, 15
dessert [dɪˈzɜːt] Dessert; Nachspeise **II**
destination [ˌdestɪˈneɪʃn] Ziel; Reiseziel **IV**
destiny [ˈdestɪni] Schicksal; Fügung; Vorsehung **IV**
to destroy [dɪˈstrɔɪ] zerstören **IV**
destruction [dɪˈstrʌkʃn] Zerstörung **III**
detail [ˈdiːteɪl] Detail; Einzelheit **IV**
detective [dɪˈtektɪv] Detektiv/-in **II**; Detektivgeschichte; Kriminalroman; Kriminalfilm; Krimi **III**
  private detective [ˌpraɪvət dɪˈtektɪv] Privatdetektiv/-in **II**
detention [dɪˈtenʃn] Nachsitzen; Haft; Verhaftung **III**
  immigration detention centre [ˌɪmɪˌɡreɪʃn dɪˈtenʃn ˌsentə] Auffanglager (für illegal Eingewanderte) **IV**
to deter [dɪˈtɜː] abschrecken; jdn davon abhalten etw. zu tun **V U1**, 20
detergent [dɪˈtɜːdʒnt] Waschmittel; Reinigungsmittel **IV**
determination [dɪˌtɜːmɪˈneɪʃn] Bestimmtheit; Entschlossenheit **VTS**, 111
to determine [dɪˈtɜːmɪn] bestimmen; ermitteln **IV**
determined [dɪˈtɜːmɪnd] (fest) entschlossen; entschieden; zielstrebig **IV**
to detract [dɪˈtrækt] mindern; schmälern **V U1**, 20
to develop [dɪˈveləp] entwickeln; sich entwickeln **II**
development [dɪˈveləpmənt] Entwicklung **III**
device [dɪˈvaɪs] Gerät; Vorrichtung **IV**; Stilmittel **V F4**, 61; **VTS**, 117
  stylistic device [staɪˌlɪstɪk dɪˈvaɪs] Stilmittel **V F4**, 61
devil [ˈdevl] Teufel **II**
devolution [ˌdiːvəˈluːʃn] Dezentralisierung; Delegierung **V F2**, 33
diagram [ˈdaɪəɡræm] Diagramm **II**
to dial [ˈdaɪəl] wählen (Telefon); anrufen **V U3**, 70
dialect [ˈdaɪəlekt] Dialekt **IV**
dialogue [ˈdaɪəlɒɡ] Dialog; Gespräch **I**

diamond [ˈdaɪəmənd] Diamant **IV**
diary [ˈdaɪəri] Tagebuch **II**
  diary entry [ˈdaɪəriˌentri] Tagebucheintrag **II**
dictionary [ˈdɪkʃnri] Wörterbuch **I**
didgeridoo [ˌdɪdʒriˈduː] Didgeridoo **IV**
to die [daɪ] sterben **II**
diet [ˈdaɪət] Ernährung; Diät **IV**
difference [ˈdɪfrəns] Unterschied **I**
  *to make a difference (to sth) [ˌmeɪk ə ˈdɪfrəns] etw. verändern; etw. bewegen **IV**
different [ˈdɪfrnt] anders; unterschiedlich; verschieden **I**
to differentiate [ˌdɪfˈrenʃieɪt] unterscheiden **V U2**, 40
difficult [ˈdɪfɪklt] schwierig **II**
difficulty [ˈdɪfɪklti] Schwierigkeit **V U1**, 12
*to dig [dɪɡ] graben **II**
to digest [daɪˈdʒest] verdauen; auflösen **V F4**, 61
digital [ˈdɪdʒɪtl] digital **III**
dilemma [daɪˈlemə] Dilemma; Zwickmühle **III**
to dine [daɪn] zu Abend essen **V U1**, 13
diner (AE) [ˈdaɪnə] einfaches Restaurant mit Theke und Tischen **II**
dinner [ˈdɪnə] Abendessen **I**
diploma [dɪˈpləʊmə] Diplom; Urkunde **IV**
direct [dɪˈrekt; daɪˈrekt] direkt **II**
direction [dɪˈrekʃn; daɪˈrekʃn] Richtung **III**
directly [dɪˈrektli; daɪˈrektli] direkt; ohne Umwege **II**
director [dɪˈrektə; daɪˈrektə] Regisseur/-in **III**
dirt [dɜːt] Schmutz; Dreck **III**
dirty [ˈdɜːti] dreckig; schmutzig **I**
disability [ˌdɪsəˈbɪləti] Behinderung; Unfähigkeit **IV**
to disable sth [dɪˈseɪbl] abschalten; blockieren **V U3**, 83
disadvantage [ˌdɪsədˈvɑːntɪdʒ] Nachteil **III**
to disadvantage [ˌdɪsədˈvɑːntɪdʒ] benachteiligen **V U2**, 46
to disagree (with) [ˌdɪsəˈɡriː] anderer Meinung sein; nicht einverstanden sein (mit) **II**
to disappear [ˌdɪsəˈpɪə] verschwinden **III**
disappointed [ˌdɪsəˈpɔɪntɪd] enttäuscht **I**
disappointing [ˌdɪsəˈpɔɪntɪŋ] enttäuschend **IV**
disaster [dɪˈzɑːstə] Desaster; Katastrophe; Unglück **II**
discontent [ˌdɪskənˈtent] Unzufriedenheit **V U2**, 48
to discourage [dɪˈskʌrɪdʒ] abschrecken; entmutigen **V U1**, 20
to discover [dɪˈskʌvə] entdecken **II**
discrimination [dɪˌskrɪmɪˈneɪʃn] Diskriminierung **IV**
to discuss [dɪˈskʌs] diskutieren **II**
discussion [dɪˈskʌʃn] Diskussion **II**

disease [dɪˈziːz] Krankheit **III**
disgusting [dɪsˈɡʌstɪŋ] abscheulich; ekelhaft **IV**
dishes (pl) [ˈdɪʃɪz] Geschirr **III**
  *to do the dishes [duː ðə ˈdɪʃɪz] den Abwasch machen **III**
dishwasher [ˈdɪʃˌwɒʃə] Spülmaschine **III**
to disintegrate [dɪˈsɪntɪɡreɪt] zerfallen; zerbrechen **V U1**, 14
likes and dislikes [ˌlaɪks ənˌˈdɪslaɪks] Vorlieben und Abneigungen **I**
to dislike [dɪˈslaɪk] nicht mögen **III**
to disobey [ˌdɪsəˈbeɪ] nicht gehorchen; ungehorsam sein **III**
eating disorder [ˈiːtɪŋ dɪˌsɔːdə] Essstörung **V U1**, 24
display [dɪˈspleɪ] Vorführung; Ausstellung; Schaukasten; Anzeige **II**; zeigen; ausstellen **IV**
disposal [dɪˈspəʊzl] Beseitigung; Entsorgung **IV**
disproportionately [ˌdɪsprəˈpɔːʃnətli] unverhältnismäßig; überproportional **V U2**, 41
disrespectful [ˌdɪsrɪˈspektfl] respektlos **IV**
dissatisfaction [dɪsˌsætɪsˈfækʃn] Unzufriedenheit **V U3**, 69
to dissolve [dɪˈzɒlv] (sich) auflösen **IV**
distance [ˈdɪstns] Distanz; Entfernung **III**
distant [ˈdɪstnt] entfernt; distanziert **IV**
distinct [dɪˈstɪŋkt] unterschieden; klar; deutlich **V F5**, 66
distinctness [dɪˈstɪŋktnəs] Unterschiedlichkeit **V F5**, 67
to distinguish [dɪˈstɪŋɡwɪʃ] unterscheiden; klar erkennen **V U2**, 55
to distract [dɪˈstrækt] ablenken **IV**
to distribute [dɪˈstrɪbjuːt] verteilen; aufteilen **V U1**, 27
distribution [ˌdɪstrɪˈbjuːʃn] Verteilung; Aufteilung **V F2**, 32
to disturb [dɪˈstɜːb] stören **V U3**, 71
disunity (no pl) [dɪsˈjuːnɪti] Uneinigkeit **V U3**, 75
diverse [daɪˈvɜːs] divers; verschieden **IV**
diversity [daɪˈvɜːsəti] Vielfalt; Verschiedenheit **IV**
to divide [dɪˈvaɪd] teilen; aufteilen **III**
diving [ˈdaɪvɪŋ] Tauchen **II**
to divorce [dɪˈvɔːs] sich scheiden lassen von **III**
dizzy [ˈdɪzi] schwindelig **III**
DJ [ˈdiːdʒeɪ] DJ; Discjockey **II**
*to do [duː] machen; tun **I**
  *to do away with sth [ˌduː əˈweɪ wɪð] etw. abschaffen; etw. loswerden **IV**
  *to do our hair [ˌduː aʊə ˈheə] uns frisieren; unsere Haare machen **I**
  *to do the dishes [ˌduː ðə ˈdɪʃɪz] den Abwasch machen **III**
  *to do without sth [ˌduː wɪðˈaʊt] ohne etw. auskommen **IV**

Don't worry! [ˌdəʊnt ˈwʌrɪ] Keine Sorge! **I**
dos and **don'ts** [ˌduːz ənd ˈdəʊnts] Ge-
und Verbote; was man tun und was man
nicht tun sollte **III**
We **did** it! [ˌwiː ˈdɪd ˌɪt] Wir haben es
geschafft! **II**
dock [dɒk] Dock **IV**
doctor [ˈdɒktə] Arzt/Ärztin **II**
document [ˈdɒkjəmənt] Dokument **III**
documentary [ˌdɒkjəˈmentrɪ] Dokumentar-
film; Dokumentation; Dokumentar- **III**
dog [dɒg] Hund **I**
dog-like [ˈdɒg laɪk] hundeartig **IV**
guide **dog** [ˈgaɪd ˌdɒg] Blindenhund **II**
hot **dog** [ˌhɒt ˈdɒg] Hot Dog *(Würstchen
im Brötchen)* **I**
to walk the **dog** [ˌwɔːk ðə ˈdɒg] den
Hund ausführen; mit dem Hund spazieren gehen **I**
I'm **dog**-tired. [ˌaɪm ˈdɒgˈtaɪəd] Ich bin
hundemüde. **I**
dogsled [ˈdɒgsled] Hundeschlitten **III**
dollar bill [ˈdɒlə ˌbɪl] Dollarnote; Dollar-
schein **I**
domestic [dəˈmestɪk] Haus-; Inlands-;
häuslich **V U2, 46**
dominance [ˈdɒmɪnəns] Dominanz **IV**
dominant [ˈdɒmɪnənt] dominant; domi-
nierend **IV**
to **dominate** [ˈdɒmɪneɪt] dominieren;
beherrschen **V U3, 82**
to **donate** [dəˈneɪt] spenden; stiften **III**
donation [dəˈneɪʃn] Spende; Schenkung;
Stiftung **III**
door [dɔː] Tür **I**
front **door** [ˌfrʌnt ˈdɔː] Haustür **II**
next **door** [ˌnekst ˈdɔː] (von) nebenan **III**
to **double** [ˈdʌbl] verdoppeln **III**
double-decker bus [ˌdʌbl dekə ˈbʌs] Doppeldeckerbus **IV**
doubt [daʊt] Zweifel **V U1, 17**
to **doubt** [daʊt] bezweifeln **V TS, 116**
dough [dəʊ] Teig **IV**
down [daʊn] entlang; herunter; hinunter
I; nieder **III**
*to come **down** [ˌkʌm ˈdaʊn] herunterkommen **I**
*to go **down** [ˌgəʊ ˈdaʊn] hinuntergehen;
nach unten gehen; entlanggehen **II**
to **hand sth down to sb** [ˌhænd ˈdaʊn]
etw. an jmdn. weitergeben; etw. an
jmdn. überliefern **V F1, 10**
to pull **down** [ˌpʊl ˈdaʊn] abreißen **III**
*to sit **down** [ˌsɪt ˈdaʊn] sich hinsetzen;
sich setzen **I**
to slow **down** [ˌsləʊ ˈdaʊn] langsamer
werden; bremsen **III**
upside **down** [ˌʌpsaɪd ˈdaʊn] verkehrt
herum; auf dem Kopf stehend **V U1, 13**
*to write **down** [ˌraɪt ˈdaʊn] aufschreiben **I**

to **download** [daʊnˈləʊd] herunterladen
(aus dem Internet) **II**
downside [ˈdaʊnsaɪd] Kehrseite; Schatten-
seite **V U1, 14**
downstairs [ˌdaʊnˈsteəz] nach unten; im
Untergeschoss; unten **II**
downtown *(AE)* [ˌdaʊnˈtaʊn] Stadtzentrum; im Stadtzentrum **III**
to **drag** [dræg] schleifen; ziehen; schlep-
pen **V U1, 16**
dragon [ˈdrægn] Drache **III**
drama [ˈdrɑːmə] Theater; Drama **I**
dramatic [drəˈmætɪk] dramatisch **II**
*to **draw** [drɔː] zeichnen **I**
*to **draw** sb into sth [drɔː ðə ˌriːdə ɪntə
ðə ˈstɔːrɪ/ækʃn] jmdn. in etw. hineinzie-
hen **III**
*to **draw** the line (at) [drɔː ðə ˈlaɪn] bei
etw. die Grenze ziehen **IV**
drawing [ˈdrɔːɪŋ] Zeichnung **I**
dreadlocks *(pl)* [ˈdredlɒks] Rastalocken
⟨**V U3, 86**⟩
dream [driːm] Traum **II**
*to **dream** [driːm] träumen **II**
dreary [ˈdrɪərɪ] trostlos **V U1, 21**
dress [dres] Kleid **I**
dress code [ˈdres ˌkəʊd] Kleiderordnung;
Bekleidungsvorschriften **II**
fancy **dress** [ˌfænsɪ ˈdres] Verkleidung;
Kostüm **II**
to **dress** [dres] (sich) kleiden **IV**
to **dress** up [ˌdres ˈʌp] sich verkleiden;
sich herausputzen; sich feinmachen **IV**
drink [drɪŋk] Getränk **I**
*to **drink** [drɪŋk] trinken **I**
to **drip** [drɪp] tropfen **V U1, 15**
drive [draɪv] Fahrt; Anfahrt; Autofahrt **II**
clothing **drive** [ˈkləʊðɪŋ ˌdraɪv] Kleidersammlung **II**
*to **drive** [draɪv] fahren **II**; treiben **III**
*to **drive** off [ˌdraɪv ˈɒf] wegfahren **III**
driving licence [ˈdraɪvɪŋ ˌlaɪsns] Führerschein **II**
driver [ˈdraɪvə] Fahrer/-in **III**
drizzle [ˈdrɪzl] Nieselregen **IV**
to **drop** [drɒp] fallen (lassen) **II**
to **drop** sb (off) [ˌdrɒp ˈɒf] jmdn. ab-
setzen; jmdn. aussteigen lassen **IV**
drought [draʊt] Dürre; Trockenheit **IV**
to **drown** [draʊn] ertrinken; ertränken **III**
drug [drʌg] Droge **III**
drug trafficking [ˈdrʌg ˌtræfɪkɪŋ] Drogenhandel **V U2, 46**
druid [ˈdruːɪd] Druide **III**
drum [drʌmz] Trommel **II**
dry [draɪ] trocken **II**
dubious [ˈdjuːbɪəs] dubios; zweifelhaft;
fragwürdig **V U2, 55**
duck [dʌk] Ente **III**
dude *(AE) (infml)* [duːd] Mann *(ugs.)*; Alter
(ugs.) **III**
due to [ˈdjuː tə] aufgrund; durch **V U1, 14**

dull [dʌl] trüb; düster **V U1, 18**; stumpf;
dumpf **V U3, 71**
dumb [dʌm] dumm; doof **V U3, 73**
during *(+ noun)* [ˈdjʊərɪŋ] während
(+ Nomen) **II**
dusk [dʌsk] Abenddämmerung; Sonnenuntergang **V F3, 37**
dust [dʌst] Staub **IV**
dusty [ˈdʌstɪ] staubig **IV**
the **Dutch** [ðə ˈdʌtʃ] das niederländische
Volk **IV**
Dutch [dʌtʃ] Niederländisch; niederländisch **IV**
duty [ˈdjuːtɪ] Pflicht **IV**
DVD [ˌdiːviːˈdiː] DVD **I**
to **dye** [daɪ] färben **I**
dynamics *(no pl)* [daɪˈnæmɪks] Dynamik
V U1, 21
dystopia [dɪsˈtəʊpɪə] Dystopie **IV**

E

e. g. *(= for example)* [ˌiːˈdʒiː] z. B. *(= zum
Beispiel)* **I**
each [iːtʃ] jede/-r/-s **I**
each other [ˌiːtʃ ˈʌðə] einander; sich; sich
gegenseitig **I**
each [iːtʃ] pro Person; pro Stück **I**
eagle [ˈiːgl] Adler **I**
ear [ɪə] Ohr **II**
early [ˈɜːlɪ] früh **I**
as **early** as [əzˈɜːli əz] schon **IV**
to **earn** [ɜːn] verdienen **I**
earth [ɜːθ] die Erde; Erde; Erdboden **II**
What on **earth** …? [ˌwɒt ˌɒn ˈɜːθ] Was
um alles in der Welt …? **II**
east [iːst] Osten; Ost- **I**
easy [ˈiːzɪ] einfach; leicht **I**
*to take it **easy** [ˌteɪk ɪt ˈiːzɪ] immer ruhig
bleiben; auf der faulen Haut liegen **II**
*to **eat** [iːt] essen; fressen **I**
eating disorder [ˈiːtɪŋ dɪˌsɔːdə] Essstörung **V U1, 24**
ecological [ˌiːkəˈlɒdʒɪkl] ökologisch **IV**
ecology [iːˈkɒlɒdʒɪ] Ökologie **IV**
economic [ˌiːkəˈnɒmɪk] ökonomisch; wirt-
schaftlich **IV**
economics [ˌiːkəˈnɒmɪks] Wirtschaft **IV**
economist [ɪˈkɒnəmɪst] Betriebswirt/-in;
Wirtschaftsexperte/-expertin **V F1, 11**
economy [ɪˈkɒnəmɪ] Ökonomie; Wirtschaft
III
edge [edʒ] Rand; Kante **IV**
to **edge** one's way [ˈedʒ wʌnz ˌweɪ] sich
langsam bewegen **V U3, 70**
to **edit** [ˈedɪt] überarbeiten; bearbeiten
V U3, 80
to **edit** out [ˌedɪt ˈaʊt] herausschneiden
III
editor [ˈedɪtə] Herausgeber/-in; Redakteur/
-in **IV**

letter to the **editor** [ˌletə tʊ ði ˈedɪtə] Leserbrief **IV**

to **educate** [ˈedʒʊkeɪt] erziehen; bilden **IV**

education *(no pl)* [edʒʊˈkeɪʃn] Erziehung; Bildung **III**

board of **education** [ˌbɔːd əv ˌedʒʊˈkeɪʃn] Schulbehörde **V F4**, 60

educational [ˌedʒʊˈkeɪʃnl] Bildungs-; lehrreich; erzieherisch **IV**

effect [ɪˈfekt] Effekt; Wirkung **III**

special **effect** [ˌspeʃl ɪˈfekt] Spezialeffekt **IV**

effective [ɪˈfektɪv] effektiv; wirkungsvoll **IV**

efficient [ɪˈfɪʃnt] effizient; leistungsfähig **IV**

effort [ˈefət] Bemühung; Mühe **IV**

egg [eg] Ei **I**

egoism [ˈiːgəʊɪzm] Egoismus **IV**

eight [eɪt] acht **I**

eighteen [ˌeɪˈtiːn] achtzehn **I**

eighty [ˈeɪti] achtzig **I**

not **either** [nɒt … ˈaɪðə; nɒt … ˈiːðə] auch nicht **I**

either … or … [ˈaɪðə/ˈiːðə … ɔː] entweder … oder … **II**

either [ˈaɪðə; ˈiːðə] beide / beides; eine/-r/ -s von beiden **IV**

council of **elders** [ˌkaʊnsl əv ˈeldəz] Ältestenrat **III**

the **elderly** [ði ˈeldəli] ältere Menschen; Senioren **IV**

to **elect** sb [ɪˈlekt] jmdn. wählen **II**

election [ɪˈlekʃn] Wahl **IV**

electoral system [ɪˌlektrl ˈsɪstəm] Wahlsystem **V F2**, 33

electric [ɪˈlektrɪk] elektrisch **III**

electrician [ˌelɪkˈtrɪʃn] Elektriker/-in **II**

electricity [ˌelɪkˈtrɪsəti] Elektrizität; Strom **II**

electrics [ɪˈlektrɪks] Elektrik **II**

electronic [ˌelekˈtrɒnɪk] elektronisch **I**

elegant [ˈelɪgnt] elegant **IV**

element [ˈelɪmənt] Element **III**

elementary school *(AE)* [elɪˈmentri ˌskuːl] Grundschule **IV**

elephant [ˈelɪfənt] Elefant **III**

elevator *(AE)* [ˈelɪveɪtə] Aufzug; Lift **III**

eleven [ɪˈlevn] elf **I**

elk *(AE)* [elk] Wapiti **IV**

else [els] andere/-r/-s; sonst noch **II**

Anything **else?** [ˌeniθɪŋ ˈels] Sonst noch etwas? **I**

what **else** [wɒt ˈels] was sonst; was noch **I**

e-mail [ˈiːmeɪl] E-Mail **I**

to **e-mail** [ˈiːmeɪl] mailen; per E-Mail schicken **II**

to **emancipate** [ɪˈmænsɪpeɪt] befreien **V F4**, 63

to **emancipate** oneself [ɪˈmænsɪpeɪt wʌnˌself] sich emanzipieren; sich unabhängig machen **V U3**, 68

to **embarrass** [ɪmˈbærəs] in Verlegenheit bringen **IV**

embarrassed [ɪmˈbærəst] verlegen **I**

embarrassing [ɪmˈbærəsɪŋ] peinlich **I**

to **emerge** [ɪˈmɜːdʒ] auftauchen; entstehen **V U3**, 65

emergency [ɪˈmɜːdʒnsi] Notfall; Notlage; Notfall- **IV**

to **emigrate** [ˈemɪgreɪt] emigrieren; auswandern **IV**

emission [ɪˈmɪʃn] Ausstoß; Emission **IV**

to **emit** [ɪˈmɪt] ausstoßen; absondern **IV**

emotion [ɪˈməʊʃn] Gefühl; Emotion **IV**

emotional [ɪˈməʊʃnl] emotional; Gefühls- **IV**

emperor [ˈemprə] Kaiser **II**

to **emphasise** [ˈemfəsaɪz] betonen **IV**

empire [ˈempaɪə] Reich; Kaiserreich **II**

to **employ** [ɪmˈplɔɪ] einstellen; anstellen; beschäftigen **IV**

employer [ɪmˈplɔɪə] Arbeitgeber/-in **IV**

employment [ɪmˈplɔɪmənt] Beschäftigung; Anstellung **IV**

to **empty** [ˈemti] leeren; ausräumen **III**

empty [ˈemti] leer **III**

emu [ˈiːmjuː] Emu **IV**

to **enable** sb to do sth [ɪˈneɪbl tə] jmdm. ermöglichen, etw. zu tun **IV**

enchanted [ɪnˈtʃɑːntɪd] verzaubert **V U1**, 15

enclosure [ɪnˈkləʊʒə] Anlage; Beilage **IV**

to **encompass** [ɪnˈkʌmpəs] umfassen; umspannen **V U3**, 76

encounter [ɪnˈkaʊntə] Begegnung; Zusammentreffen **V AC1**, 9

to **encourage** [ɪnˈkʌrɪdʒ] unterstützen; ermutigen **IV**

end [end] Ende; Schluss **I**

in the **end** [ˌɪn ði ˈend] schließlich; zum Schluss **I**

at the **end** of the day [æt ði ˌend əv ðə ˈdeɪ] unterm Strich; letztendlich **IV**

the **end** justifies the means [ði ˌend dʒʌstɪfaɪz ðə ˈmiːnz] der Zweck heiligt die Mittel **V F5**, 67

to **end** [end] enden; beenden **II**

to **end** up [ˌend ˈʌp] enden; landen **I**

ending [ˈendɪŋ] Ende; Schluss *(einer Geschichte)* **I**

happy **ending** [ˌhæpi ˈendɪŋ] Happy End **III**

endless [ˈendləs] endlos **IV**

to **endure** [ɪnˈdʒʊə] ertragen; aushalten **V U2**, 50

enemy [ˈenəmi] Feind/-in **III**

energy [ˈenədʒi] Energie; Kraft **IV**

to **enforce** [ɪnˈfɔːs] durchsetzen **V F3**, 39

enforcement [ɪnˈfɔːsmənt] Erzwingung; zwangsweise Durchführung **V F4**, 61

to **enfranchise** [ɪnˈfrænʃaɪz] befreien; freilassen **V F3**, 38

to **engage** [ɪnˈgeɪdʒ] faszinieren; begeistern **V U1**, 25

engine [ˈendʒɪn] Motor; Maschine **V F1**, 11

engineer [ˌendʒɪˈnɪə] Ingenieur/-in; Techniker/-in **III**

English [ˈɪŋglɪʃ] englisch; Englisch; aus England; Engländer/-in **I**

English-speaking [ˈɪŋglɪʃˌspiːkɪŋ] englischsprachig **I**

I'm **English**. [aɪm ˈɪŋglɪʃ] Ich bin Engländer/-in. **I**

to **enjoy** [ɪnˈdʒɔɪ] genießen; sich freuen an **I**

to **enjoy** oneself [ɪnˈdʒɔɪ] Spaß haben; sich amüsieren **II**

enjoyable [ɪnˈdʒɔɪəbl] reizend; angenehm; nett **IV**

to **enlarge** [ɪnˈlɑːdʒ] vergrößern; erweitern **V U3**, 80; **VTS**, 109

enlightenment [ɪnˈlaɪtnmənt] Aufklärung; Erleuchtung **V F1**, 11

enormous [ɪˈnɔːməs] enorm; gewaltig **IV**

enough [ɪˈnʌf] genug; genügend **I**

to **enslave** [ɪnˈsleɪv] versklaven **V F3**, 36

to **ensure** [ɪnˈʃɔː] sicherstellen; gewährleisten **V U2**, 50

to **enter** [ˈentə] hineingehen; betreten; eintreten; mitmachen **I**

enterprise [ˈentəpraɪz] Unternehmen; Firma **V F3**, 36

to **entertain** [ˌentəˈteɪn] unterhalten **IV**

entertainment *(no pl)* [ˌentəˈteɪnmənt] Unterhaltung **IV**

enthusiastic [ɪnˌθjuːziˈæstɪk] enthusiastisch; begeistert **IV**

entire [ɪnˈtaɪə] gesamt; ganz; komplett **IV**

entrance [ˈentrəns] Eingang; Eintritt **III**

entry [ˈentri] Eintrag **III**

diary **entry** [ˈdaɪəriˌentri] Tagebucheintrag **II**

enumeration [ɪˌnjuːmrˈeɪʃn] Aufzählung **VTS**, 117

environment [ɪnˈvaɪrnmənt] Umwelt; Umgebung **IV**

environmental [ɪnˌvaɪrnˈmentl] Umwelt-; die Umwelt betreffend; umweltbedingt **IV**

environmentalist [ɪnˌvaɪrnˈmentlɪst] Umweltschützer/-in **IV**

to **envy** [ˈenvi] beneiden **IV**

epic [ˈepɪk] episch; gewaltig; unglaublich **V U2**, 49

epic poem [ˌepɪk ˈpəʊɪm] Epos; erzählendes Gedicht **VTS**, 108

equal [ˈiːkwəl] gleich; gleichwertig **IV**

equality [ɪˈkwɒləti] Gleichberechtigung **V F3**, 38

equipment [ɪˈkwɪpmənt] Ausrüstung; Ausstattung **II**

er [ɜː] äh **I**

era [ˈɪərə] Ära; Zeitalter **III**

erosion [ɪˈrəʊʒn] Erosion; Abtragung **IV**

escalator [ˈeskəleɪtə] Rolltreppe **I**

to **escape** (from) [ɪˈskeɪp frəm] fliehen; entfliehen; flüchten; entkommen **III** escapist [ɪˈskeɪpɪst] eskapistisch ⟨V U3, 87⟩

especially [ɪˈspeʃli] besonders; vor allem III

essay [ˈeseɪ] Essay IV
argumentative essay [ɑːgjəˌmentətɪvˌ ˈeseɪ] Erörterung IV

essential [ɪˈsenʃl] essenziell; entscheidend IV

to establish [ɪˈstæblɪʃ] einrichten; gründen; herstellen IV

real estate [ˈrɪəlɪˌsteɪt] Grundbesitz; Immobilien IV

to estimate [ˈestɪmeɪt] schätzen IV

etc. (= et cetera) [ɪtˈsetrə] usw. (= und so weiter) II

ethnic [ˈeθnɪk] ethnisch; Volks- III

ethnicity [eθˈnɪsəti] ethnische Zugehörigkeit; Volkszugehörigkeit IV

etymology (no pl) [ˌetɪˈmɒlədʒi] Etymologie V U1, 26

euro [ˈjʊərəʊ] Euro (Währung) I

European [ˌjʊərəˈpiːən] Europäer/-in; europäisch; aus Europa II

even [ˈiːvn] sogar; selbst I
even so [ˌiːvn ˈsəʊ] trotzdem; selbst dann IV
even though [ˌiːvn ˈðəʊ] auch wenn; obwohl III
not even [ˌnɒtˈiːvn] nicht einmal; noch nicht einmal III

evening [ˈiːvnɪŋ] Abend I
in the evenings [ɪn ðiˌiːvnɪŋz] abends I

event [ɪˈvent] Ereignis; Veranstaltung I

eventually [ɪˈventʃuəli] schließlich; endlich; irgendwann IV

ever [ˈevə] jemals; überhaupt II
ever since [ˌevə ˈsɪns] seit; seitdem IV

every [ˈevri] jede/-r/-s I

everybody [ˈevribɒdi] jeder; alle II

everyday [ˈevrideɪ] alltäglich III

everyone [ˈevriwʌn] jeder; alle II

everything [ˈevriθɪŋ] alles I

everywhere [ˈevriweə] überall; überallhin I

evidence (no pl) [ˈevɪdns] Beweis; Beleg; Beweismaterial V AC4, 89

evil [ˈiːvl] böse; schlecht IV

to evoke sth [ɪˈvəʊk] etw. heraufbeschwören V F4, 61

to evolve [ɪˈvɒlv] sich entwickeln V F1, 10; V AC3, 65

exact [ɪgˈzækt] exakt; genau III

exaggerated [ɪgˈzædʒreɪtɪd] übertrieben II

exaggeration [ɪgˌzædʒrˈeɪʃn] Übertreibung IV

exam [ɪgˈzæm] Examen; Prüfung IV

to examine [ɪgˈzæmɪn] untersuchen; kontrollieren IV

example [ɪgˈzɑːmpl] Beispiel I
for example [fərˌɪgˈzɑːmpl] zum Beispiel II

excellent [ˈekslnt] exzellent; hervorragend III

except for [ɪkˈsept fə] bis auf; außer III

exceptional [ɪkˈsepʃnl] Ausnahme-; außergewöhnlich V F1, 10

excerpt [ˈeksɜːpt] Auszug III

excess mortality [ɪkˌses mɔːˈtæləti] Übersterblichkeit; überdurchschnittlich hohe Sterblichkeitsrate V U1, 20

exchange [ɪksˈtʃeɪndʒ] Austausch; Austausch- III
exchange student [ɪksˈtʃeɪndʒ ˌstjuːdnt] Austauschschüler/-in III

to exchange [ɪksˈtʃeɪndʒ] austauschen II

excited [ɪkˈsaɪtɪd] aufgeregt; begeistert I

excitedly [ɪkˈsaɪtɪdli] aufgeregt; begeistert II

excitement (no pl) [ɪkˈsaɪtmənt] Aufregung III

exciting [ɪkˈsaɪtɪŋ] spannend; aufregend I

exclusively [ɪksˈkluːsɪvli] ausschließlich V U2, 46

Excuse me … [ɪkˈskjuːz mi] Entschuldigung!; Entschuldigen Sie! I

to execute [ˈeksɪkjuːt] exekutieren; hinrichten V F1, 10

execution [ˌeksɪˈkjuːʃn] Exekution; Hinrichtung V F1, 10

(business) executive [ˈbɪznɪsˌɪgˌzekjətɪv] Geschäftsführer/-in; Manager/-in; gehobene Führungskraft IV

chief executive officer (CEO) [ˌtʃiːfˌɪgˌzekjətɪvˌˈɒfɪsə] Vorstandvorsitzende/-r; Geschäftsführer/-in V U2, 51

exercise [ˈeksəsaɪz] Übung; Aufgabe I; Bewegung; Training IV
exercise book [ˈeksəsaɪz ˌbʊk] Übungsheft I

exhausted [ɪgˈzɔːstɪd] erschöpft IV

exhausting [ɪgˈzɔːstɪŋ] anstrengend IV

exhibition [ˌeksɪˈbɪʃn] Ausstellung; Vorführung V U1, 22

to exist [ɪgˈzɪst] existieren; bestehen II

to exit [ˈeksɪt] verlassen; aussteigen V TS, 110

to expand [ɪkˈspænd] (sich) ausdehnen; erweitern V AC4, 88

expansion [ɪkˈspænʃn] Expansion; Ausdehnung; Erweiterung V U2, 52

to expect [ɪkˈspekt] erwarten III

*to meet sb's expectations [ˌmiːt sʌmbədizˌekspekˈteɪʃnz] jmds. Erwartungen erfüllen II

expedition [ˌekspɪˈdɪʃn] Expedition; Forschungsreise III

expensive [ɪkˈspensɪv] teuer I

experience [ɪkˈspɪəriəns] Erfahrung; Erlebnis III
work experience [ˈwɜːkˌɪkˌspɪəriəns] Praktikum; Schülerpraktikum IV

to experience [ɪkˈspɪəriəns] erfahren; erleben III

to experiment [ɪkˈsperɪmənt] experimentieren V F5, 67

expert [ˈekspɜːt] Experte/Expertin II

to explain [ɪkˈspleɪn] erklären I

explanation [ˌekspləˈneɪʃn] Erklärung; Erläuterung IV

explicit language [ɪkˈsplɪsɪt ˈlæŋgwɪdʒ] obszöne Sprache; vulgäre Sprache V U3, 83

to exploit sb/sth [ɪkˈsplɔɪt] jmdn./etw. ausbeuten; jmdn./etw. ausnutzen IV

exploitation [ˌeksplɔɪˈteɪʃn] Ausbeutung; Abbau IV

exploration [ˌekspləˈreɪʃn] Erforschung; Erkundung IV

to explore [ɪkˈsplɔː] auf Entdeckungsreise gehen; sich umschauen; erkunden; erforschen I

explorer [ɪkˈsplɔːrə] Entdecker/-in; Forscher/-in II

export [ˈekspɔːt] Export; Ausfuhr IV

to export [ɪkˈspɔːt] exportieren; ausführen IV

exposed [ɪkˈspəʊzd] ungeschützt; exponiert V U1, 14

exposure [ɪkˈspəʊʒə] Aussetzung; Ausgesetztsein V U1, 24

express [ɪkˈspres] Eilzug II

to express [ɪkˈspres] ausdrücken II

expression [ɪkˈspreʃn] Ausdruck; Wendung; Äußerung III
facial expression [ˌfeɪʃlɪkˈspreʃn] Gesichtsausdruck V TS, 112

extensive [ɪkˈstensɪv] ausgiebig; ausführlich; ausgedehnt V AC4, 88

to what extent [təˌwɒtɪkˈstent] inwiefern; inwieweit V U2, 51

external [ɪkˈstɜːnl] Außen- V F2, 33

*to become extinct [bɪˌkʌmˌɪkˈstɪŋkt] aussterben III

extinction (no pl) [ɪkˈstɪŋkʃn] Aussterben III

extra [ˈekstrə] Statist/-in; Komparse/Komparsin V TS, 110

extra [ˈekstrə] extra; zusätzlich I

extract [ˈekstrækt] Extrakt; Auszug; Exzerpt III

extracurricular [ˌekstrəkəˈrɪkjələ] außerhalb des Lehrplans V U1, 27

extreme [ɪkˈstriːm] Extrem III

extreme [ɪkˈstriːm] extrem; radikal; äußerste/-r/-s II

eye [aɪ] Auge I
to roll one's eyes [ˌrəʊl wʌnzˈaɪz] die Augen verdrehen I
I couldn't believe my eyes. [aɪˌkʊdnt bɪˌliːv maɪˈaɪz] Ich traute meinen Augen nicht. II

eyebrow [ˈaɪbraʊ] Augenbraue V U3, 74

eyewitness [ˈaɪwɪtnəs] Augenzeuge/Augenzeugin II

F

fabric (no pl) [ˈfæbrɪk] Stoff IV

face [feɪs] Gesicht I

face-to-**face** [ˌfeɪstə'feɪs] persönlich; von Angesicht zu Angesicht **II**

to **face** [feɪs] gegenüber stehen; konfrontiert werden mit; anblicken; sich zuwenden **III**

facial expression [ˌfeɪʃl̩ɪk'spreʃn] Gesichtsausdruck **VTS**, 112

facilities (pl) [fə'sɪlɪtiz] Einrichtung; Anlage **V F4**, 60

bathroom **facilities** [ˌbɑːθrʊm fə'sɪlɪtiz] Toiletten **V U2**, 50

fact [fækt] Fakt; Tatsache **I**

in **fact** [ɪn 'fækt] tatsächlich; eigentlich; genau genommen **III**

factor ['fæktə] Faktor; Gesichtspunkt; Einfluss **IV**

factory ['fæktri] Fabrik; Werk **IV**

factory farming ['fæktri ˌfɑːmɪŋ] Massentierhaltung **IV**

to **fade** away [ˌfeɪd ə'weɪ] schwinden; zerrinnen; verblassen; sterben **V F5**, 67

degree **Fahrenheit** (°F) [ˌdɪgriː 'færnhaɪt] Grad Fahrenheit **II**

to **fail** [feɪl] nicht bestehen **IV**

to **fail** sb [feɪl] jmdn. hängen lassen; jmdn. im Stich lassen; jmdn. enttäuschen **IV**

failure ['feɪljə] Scheitern; Versagen **V U2**, 52

faint [feɪnt] schwach; leise **V U3**, 71

fair [feə] Messe; Jahrmarkt **I**

fair [feə] gerecht; fair **I**

That's **fair** enough. [ˌðæts feər ɪ'nʌf] Das ist nur recht und billig. **IV**

fairly ['feəli] ziemlich; recht **V U1**, 22

fairy ['feəri] Fee **V U1**, 15

fairy tale ['feəri ˌteɪl] Märchen **IV**

faith [feɪθ] Glaube; Vertrauen **V U2**, 47

to **fake** [feɪk] vortäuschen; fälschen **III**

fake [feɪk] falsch; gefälscht **III**

fall (AE) [fɔːl] Herbst **IV**

*to **fall** [fɔːl] fallen; hinfallen **I**

*to **fall** asleep [ˌfɔːl ə'sliːp] einschlafen **I**

*to **fall** off [fɔːl 'ɒf] herunterfallen; hinunterfallen **I**

*to **fall** over [ˌfɔːl'əʊvə] hinfallen; umkippen **I**

falls (pl) [fɔːlz] Wasserfall **III**

false [fɔːls] falsch **III**

fame [feɪm] Ruhm (**V U2**, 58)

familiar [fə'mɪliə] vertraut; bekannt **V U2**, 42

family ['fæmli] Familie **I**

family tree ['fæmli ˌtriː] Stammbaum **I**

host **family** ['həʊst ˌfæmli] Gastfamilie **III**

famous ['feɪməs] berühmt **I**

fan [fæn] Fan; Anhänger/-in **II**; Ventilator **IV**

fancy ['fænsi] schick; ausgefallen **V U1**, 17

fancy dress [ˌfænsi 'dres] Verkleidung; Kostüm **II**

fantastic [fæn'tæstɪk] fantastisch; großartig **II**

fantasy ['fæntəsi] Fantasie; Traum- **I**; Fantasy **III**

fanzine [fæn'ziːn] Fanzeitschrift **II**

FAQ [ˌefeɪ'kjuː] Liste mit häufig gestellten Fragen **III**

far [fɑː] weit **II**

far away [ˌfɑːr ə'weɪ] weit weg **II**

so **far** [ˌsəʊ 'fɑː] bis jetzt **III**

far [fɑː] bei weitem; weitaus **IV**

to **fare** [feə] ergehen **V U2**, 52

farewell [ˌfeə'wel] Abschied; Abschieds- **IV**

farm [fɑːm] Farm; Bauernhof **I**

wind **farm** ['wɪnd pɑːk] Windpark **IV**

farmer ['fɑːmə] Farmer/-in; Landwirt/-in **II**

factory **farming** ['fæktri ˌfɑːmɪŋ] Massentierhaltung **IV**

farmland ['fɑːmlænd] Ackerland **II**

to **fascinate** ['fæsɪneɪt] faszinieren **III**

fashion ['fæʃn] Mode **IV**

fashionable ['fæʃnəbl̩] modisch; elegant **IV**

fast [fɑːst] schnell **I**

fast food [ˌfɑːst 'fuːd] Fastfood **III**

fat [fæt] fett; dick **IV**

fatal ['feɪtl̩] tödlich; verhängnisvoll **V U2**, 45

fate [feɪt] Schicksal; Fügung; Vorsehung **VTS**, 113

fateful ['feɪtfl̩] schicksalhaft; verhängnisvoll **V U1**, 17

father ['fɑːðə] Vater **I**

father-in-law [ˌfɑːðərɪn'lɔː] Schwiegervater **IV**

my **fault** [ˌmaɪ 'fɔːlt] meine Schuld **III**

flora and **fauna** [ˌflɔːrə ənd 'fɔːnə] Pflanzen- und Tierwelt **III**

favourite ['feɪvrɪt] Favorit/-in; Günstling **III**

favourite ['feɪvrɪt] Lieblings- **I**

My **favourite** … [maɪ 'feɪvrɪt] Mein/-e Lieblings… **I**

What's your **favourite** …? ['wɒts jə ˌfeɪvrɪt] Was ist dein/-e Lieblings…? **I**

fear [fɪə] Angst; Furcht; Befürchtung **II**

to **fear** [fɪə] (sich) fürchten **IV**

*to be **fearful** of [bi 'fɪəfl̩] Angst haben vor **III**

feast [fiːst] Festmahl **III**

feather ['feðə] Feder **II**

feature ['fiːtʃə] Eigenschaft; Merkmal **III**; Gesichtszug **II**

to **feature** ['fiːtʃə] eine Hauptrolle spielen; zeigen; aufweisen **IV**

February ['februri] Februar **I**

*to be **fed** up (with) [bi fed 'ʌp wɪð] sauer sein (auf); die Nase voll haben (von) **II**

fee [fiː] Gebühr; Abgabe **IV**

tuition **fee** [tjuː'ɪʃn ˌfiː] Studiengebühr; Schulgeld **IV**

*to **feed** [fiːd] füttern; ernähren **III**

feedback ['fiːdbæk] Feedback; Rückmeldung **I**

*to **feel** [fiːl] fühlen; sich fühlen; sich anfühlen **I**; meinen; das Gefühl haben **III**

*to **feel** left out [ˌfiːl left 'aʊt] sich ausgeschlossen fühlen **III**

*to **feel** like (+ noun or -ing) ['fiːl laɪk] Lust haben (auf/zu) **II**

*to **feel** sick [ˌfiːl 'sɪk] Übelkeit verspüren; sich schlecht fühlen **II**

feeling ['fiːlɪŋ] Gefühl **I**

fellow ['feləʊ] Mit-; Landsmann/Landsfrau **IV**

female ['fiːmeɪl] weiblich **II**

fence [fens] Zaun **V U1**, 18

fertile ['fɜːtaɪl] fruchtbar **IV**

festival ['festɪvl̩] Festival; Fest **I**

feudal ['fjuːdl̩] feudal **V AC4**, 88

fever ['fiːvə] Fieber **II**

few [fjuː] wenige **II**

a **few** [ə 'fjuː] ein paar; wenige; einige **I**

fiction (no pl) ['fɪkʃn] Erzählliteratur; Fiktion; Erfindung **III**

science **fiction** [ˌsaɪəns 'fɪkʃn] Science-Fiction (Zukunftsdichtung) **II**

fictional ['fɪkʃnl̩] fiktional; fiktiv; erdichtet **III**

fictitious [fɪk'tɪʃəs] fiktiv; erfunden; erdichtet **V U2**, 42

fiddle ['fɪdl̩] Geige **V AC2**, 35

field [fiːld] Feld; Wiese; Weide; Acker **I**

fifteen [ˌfɪf'tiːn] fünfzehn **I**

fifty ['fɪfti] fünfzig **I**

fight [faɪt] Kampf; Streit **I**

*to **fight** [faɪt] kämpfen; (sich) streiten **II**

figure ['fɪgə] Ziffer; Zahl **IV**

to **figure** ['fɪgə] sich vorstellen; glauben; schätzen **III**

to **figure** out [ˌfɪgər 'aʊt] herausfinden **III**

file [faɪl] Datei; Akte; Mappe **V U3**, 80

to **file** a claim [ˌfaɪl ə 'kleɪm] einen Anspruch geltend machen; eine Forderung geltend machen **V U3**, 75

to **fill** up [ˌfɪl 'ʌp] (sich) füllen **III**

film [fɪlm] Film **I**

film adaptation [ˌfɪlm ˌædæp'teɪʃn] Verfilmung **IV**

to **film** [fɪlm] filmen; drehen **IV**

final ['faɪnl̩] endgültig **II**; letzte/-r/-s **III**

finally ['faɪnli] schließlich; endlich; zum Schluss; letztlich **III**

financial [faɪ'nænʃl] finanziell; Finanz- **IV**

*to **find** [faɪnd] finden; herausfinden **I**

*to **find** one's way around [ˌfaɪnd wʌnz ˌweɪ ə'raʊnd] sich zurechtfinden **III**

*to **find** out [ˌfaɪnd 'aʊt] herausfinden **I**

Find the odd one out! [ˌfaɪnd ði ˌɒd wʌn ˌɒn 'aʊt] Finde das Element, das nicht in die Gruppe passt! **II**

finding ['faɪndɪŋ] Ergebnis **V U2**, 40

fine [faɪn] gut; in Ordnung; schön **I**

I'm **fine**. [ˌaɪm 'faɪn] Mir geht's gut. **I**

That's **fine** with me. [ˌðæts ˌfaɪn wɪð 'miː] Das ist in Ordnung für mich. **II**

finger ['fɪŋgə] Finger I
 *to keep your **fingers** crossed [ki:p jɔ: ˌfɪŋgəz 'krɔst] die Daumen drücken I
fingertip ['fɪŋgətɪp] Fingerspitze **V AC2**, 35
finish line ['fɪnɪʃ ˌlaɪn] Ziellinie II
to finish ['fɪnɪʃ] beenden; enden; fertigstellen; aufhören II
finished ['fɪnɪʃt] fertig I
fire [faɪə] Feuer; Kamin; Ofen II
firefighter ['faɪəˌfaɪtə] Feuerwehrmann/-frau III
firewall ['faɪəwɔ:l] Zugangsschutz (Internet) **V U3**, 80
fireworks (pl) ['faɪəwɜ:ks] Feuerwerk I
firm [fɜ:m] fest IV
first [fɜ:st] erste/-r/-s; zuerst; als Erstes I
 at **first** [ət 'fɜ:st] zuerst; zunächst II
 first language [ˌfɜ:st 'læŋgwɪdʒ] Muttersprache I
 first-past-the-post system [ˌfɜ:st pɑ:st ðə 'pəʊst 'sɪstəm] Mehrheitswahlsystem **V F2**, 33
 first-person narrator [ˌfɜ:st 'pɜ:sn nə'reɪtə] Ich-Erzähler/-in III
 in the **first** place [ɪn ðə 'fɜ:st ˌpleɪs] überhaupt erst; von vornherein IV
fiscal commission [ˌfɪskl kə'mɪʃn] Finanzausschuss **V F2**, 33
fish, fish (pl) [fɪʃ] Fisch I
to fish [fɪʃ] Fische fangen; angeln III
fishery ['fɪʃri] Fischfang; Fischerei IV
fishing ['fɪʃɪŋ] Angeln; Fischen; Fischerei I
fist [fɪst] Faust **VTS**, 109
 *to fit [fɪt] passen II
 to **fit** in [ˌfɪt 'ɪn] hineinpassen; sich einfügen II
 fitting room ['fɪtɪŋ ˌrʊm] Umkleidekabine II
 *to get **fit** [ˌget 'fɪt] in Form kommen; fit werden I
fitness ['fɪtnəs] Fitness IV
five [faɪv] fünf I
 five-hour ['faɪvaʊə] fünfstündig II
to fix [fɪks] reparieren; befestigen I
flag [flæg] Flagge; Fahne I
flagship project ['flægʃɪp ˌprɒdʒekt] Vorzeigeprojekt 〈**V U1**, 28〉
flame [fleɪm] Flamme II
flash [flæʃ] Blitz; Lichtblitz III
 flash flood [ˌflæʃ 'flʌd] Sturzflut III
flashback ['flæʃbæk] Rückblende; Flashback III
flashlight (AE) ['flæʃlaɪt] Taschenlampe II
flat [flæt] Wohnung I
flat [flæt] flach; platt III
flavor (AE) ['fleɪvə] Geschmack; Aroma III
flea market ['fli: ˌmɑ:kɪt] Flohmarkt I
flesh [fleʃ] Fleisch IV
flexible ['fleksɪbl] flexibel III
to flicker ['flɪkə] flackern; flimmern **V U1**, 16
flight [flaɪt] Flug II
float [fləʊt] Festzugswagen III

to flock [flɒk] (scharenweise) strömen **V U1**, 22
flood [flʌd] Flut; Hochwasser; Überschwemmung III
 flash **flood** [ˌflæʃ 'flʌd] Sturzflut III
floor [flɔ:] Fußboden I; Stockwerk III
flora and fauna [ˌflɔ:rə ənd 'fɔ:nə] Pflanzen- und Tierwelt III
to flourish ['flʌrɪʃ] florieren; gedeihen **V U3**, 76
to flow [fləʊ] fließen; strömen **V U1**, 21
flower ['flaʊə] Blume I
flute [flu:t] Flöte **V U1**, 21
 *to fly [flaɪ] fliegen II
flyer ['flaɪə] Flyer I
foam [fəʊm] Schaum; Gischt II
focus ['fəʊkəs] Blickpunkt; Schwerpunkt; Fokus III
 out of **focus** [ˌaʊt əv 'fəʊkəs] unscharf III
to focus (on) ['fəʊkəs ˌɒn] sich konzentrieren (auf) III
to fold [fəʊld] falten; klappen; verschränken **V U3**, 74
folder ['fəʊldə] Ordner; Mappe I
folk music ['fəʊk ˌmju:zɪk] traditionelle Musik **V AC2**, 34
folks (infml) (pl) [fəʊks] Leute IV
to follow ['fɒləʊ] folgen; hinterhergehen; befolgen II
the following [ðə 'fɒləʊɪŋ] folgende/-r/-s III
food [fu:d] Essen; Lebensmittel I; Futter III
 fast **food** [ˌfɑ:st 'fu:d] Fastfood III
 food bank ['fu:d ˌbæŋk] Tafel (Essensausgabe für sozial Schwächere) III
fool [fu:l] Trottel; Dummkopf 〈**V U2**, 58〉
foot [fʊt], feet (pl) [fi:t] Fuß I
footage ['fʊtɪdʒ] Filmmaterial IV
football ['fʊtbɔ:l] Fußball I
footprint ['fʊtprɪnt] Fußabdruck IV
for [fɔ:; fə] für I; wegen II
 for (+ Zeitraum) [fɔ:; fə] seit III
 for example [fər ɪg'zɑ:mpl] zum Beispiel II
 for instance [fər 'ɪnstəns] zum Beispiel 〈**V U3**, 87〉
 what for [ˌwɒt 'fɔ:] wozu III
 *to forbid [fə'bɪd] verbieten III
force [fɔ:s] Kraft; Macht **V F2**, 33
to force [fɔ:s] zwingen II
weather forecast [ˌwɛðə ˌfɔ:kɑ:st] Wettervorhersage II
foreign language [ˌfɒrɪn 'læŋgwɪdʒ] Fremdsprache II
forest ['fɒrɪst] Wald I
forestry ['fɒrestri] Forstwirtschaft III
forever [fə'revə] für immer; ewig II
 *to forget [fə'get] vergessen I
 *to forgive [fə'gɪv] vergeben; verzeihen II
fork [fɔ:k] Gabel III
form [fɔ:m] Form I; Formular II; Klasse; Jahrgangsstufe IV

to form [fɔ:m] formen; bilden II
formal ['fɔ:ml] formal; formell; förmlich III
former ['fɔ:mə] ehemalige/-r/-s; frühere/-r/-s III
fort [fɔ:t] Fort; Festung II
to venture forth (fml) [ˌventʃə 'fɔ:θ] sich vorwagen III
fortress ['fɔ:trəs] Festung III
fortunately ['fɔ:tʃnətli] zum Glück III
fortune ['fɔ:tʃu:n] Vermögen; Reichtum IV
forty ['fɔ:ti] vierzig I
forum ['fɔ:rəm] Forum II
forward ['fɔ:wəd] vorwärts IV
 to look **forward** to [ˌlʊk 'fɔ:wəd tə] sich freuen auf II
 *to put **forward** [ˌpʊt 'fɔ:wəd] vorbringen IV
fossil ['fɒsl] fossil IV
 fossil fuel ['fɒsl ˌfju:əl] fossiler Brennstoff IV
foster ['fɒstə] Pflege- IV
to found [faʊnd] gründen II
foundation [faʊn'deɪʃn] Stiftung; Gründung 〈**V U1**, 28〉
water fountain ['wɔ:tə ˌfaʊntɪn] Wasserspender III
four [fɔ:] vier I
fourteen [ˌfɔ:'ti:n] vierzehn I
lingua franca [ˌlɪŋgwə 'fræŋkə] Verkehrssprache IV
frankly ['fræŋkli] ehrlich gesagt; offen gestanden III
fraud [frɔ:d] Betrug IV
to free [fri:] befreien IV
free [fri:] frei; kostenlos I
 free of charge [ˌfri: əv 'tʃɑ:dʒ] kostenlos; gebührenfrei IV
 free time [ˌfri: 'taɪm] Freizeit I
 *to set **free** [set 'fri:] freilassen IV
freedman ['fri:dmæn] ehemaliger Sklave **V F3**, 38
freedom (no pl) ['fri:dəm] Freiheit; Unabhängigkeit I
freedwoman ['fri:dwʊmən] ehemalige Sklavin **V F3**, 38
freelance ['fri:lɑ:ns] freiberuflich IV
 *to freeze [fri:z] gefrieren; erstarren IV
freezer ['fri:zə] Tiefkühlschrank IV
French [frenʃ] Französisch I
French [frenʃ] französisch II
 the **French** (pl) [ðə 'frenʃ] die Franzosen I
frequent ['fri:kwənt] häufig IV
fresh [freʃ] frisch I
Friday ['fraɪdeɪ] Freitag I
fridge [frɪdʒ] Kühlschrank I
deep-fried [ˌdi:p'fraɪd] frittiert IV
friend [frend] Freund/-in I
 *to make **friends** [ˌmeɪk 'frendz] Freundschaft schließen I
 That's what **friends** are for. [ˌðæts wɒt 'frendz ɑ: ˌfɔ:] Dafür sind Freunde da. I
friendly ['frendli] freundlich; nett II

friendship ['frendʃɪp] Freundschaft III
fries (pl) (AE) [fraɪz] Pommes frites I
frightened ['fraɪtnd] verängstigt IV
fringe [frɪndʒ] Rand-; Alternativ- **V U1**, 22
from [frɒm; frəm] aus; von I
  from … to [frəm … tə] von … bis I
  Where … **from**? [ˌweə … 'frɒm] Wo-her …? I
front [frʌnt] Vorderseite; vorderer Bereich; Front-; Vorder- IV
  front door [ˌfrʌnt 'dɔ:] Haustür II
  front yard (AE) [ˌfrʌnt 'jɑ:d] Vorgarten III
  in **front** of [ɪn 'frʌnt əv] vor I
frontier [frʌn'tɪə] Grenze III
frost [frɒst] Frost IV
to **frown** [fraʊn] die Stirn runzeln IV
fruit [fru:t] Frucht; Obst I
frustration [frʌs'treɪʃn] Frust; Enttäu-schung ⟨**V U2**, 57⟩
fuel ['fju:əl] Treibstoff; Brennmaterial IV
  fossil **fuel** ['fɒsl ˌfju:əl] fossiler Brenn-stoff IV
fugitive ['fju:dʒətɪv] Flüchtige/-r **V F3**, 38
fulfilling [fʊl'fɪlɪŋ] erfüllend; befriedigend IV
full [fʊl] voll; ganz I
  full (of) [fʊl əv] voll (von) I
fun [fʌn] Freude; Spaß I
  *to have **fun** [ˌhæv 'fʌn] Spaß haben; sich amüsieren I
  It's **fun**. [ɪts 'fʌn] Es macht Spaß. I
fun [fʌn] lustig; witzig; fröhlich I
function ['fʌŋkʃn] Funktion II
to **function** ['fʌŋkʃn] funktionieren IV
fund [fʌnd] Fonds **V U1**, 23
fundamental [ˌfʌndə'mentl] fundamental; grundlegend **V U3**, 70
funeral ['fju:nrəl] Beerdigung; Begräbnis IV
funfair ['fʌnfeə] Jahrmarkt III
funny ['fʌni] lustig; witzig I; merkwürdig; komisch III
fur [fɜ:] Fell; Pelz III
furious ['fjʊəriəs] wütend **V U1**, 18; ⟨**V U1**, 31⟩
furnace ['fɜ:nɪs] Hochofen; Schmelzofen **V U1**, 21
furniture (singular noun with plural mean-ing) ['fɜ:nɪtʃə] Möbel IV
further ['fɜ:ðə] weiter (weg); wei-tere/-r/-s III
furthermore [ˌfɜ:ðə'mɔ:] überdies; außer-dem IV
future ['fju:tʃə] Zukunft III
future ['fju:tʃə] zukünftig II

G

gadget ['gædʒɪt] Gerät; technische Spie-lerei III
Gaelic ['geɪlɪk] gälisch; Gälisch II
to **gain** [geɪn] gewinnen; bekommen IV

gale [geɪl] Sturm; Orkan **V U1**, 14
game [geɪm] Spiel I
gang [gæŋ] Gang; Gruppe; Bande III
gap [gæp] Lücke; Spalt; Abstand III
  gap year ['gæp ˌjɪə] ein Jahr Auszeit (zwischen Schule und Ausbildung/Studium), das oft für einen freiwilligen ökologischen oder sozialen Dienst genutzt wird IV
garage ['gærɑ:ʒ] Garage I
garbage (AE) ['gɑ:bɪdʒ] Müll; Abfall III
garden ['gɑ:dn] Garten I
greenhouse gas [ˌgri:nhaʊz 'gæs] Treib-hausgas IV
gate [geɪt] Gate; Flugsteig; Ausgang II
to **gather** ['gæðə] sammeln; sich versam-meln IV
gatherer ['gæðərə] Sammler/-in IV
gay [geɪ] schwul; homosexuell; Schwuler; Homosexueller IV
GCSE (= General Certificate of Secondary Education) [ˌdʒi:si:es'i: (ˌdʒenrl sə.tɪfɪkət əv ˌsekəndri_edʒʊ'keɪʃn)] allg. Abschluss der weiterführenden Schulen in GB IV
geek [gi:k] Außenseiter/-in III
gender ['dʒendə] Geschlecht IV
  gender stereotyping ['dʒendə ˌsteriəʊtaɪpɪŋ] Einordnung nach Ge-schlechterklischees IV
general ['dʒenrl] General III
general ['dʒenrl] allgemein III
  in **general** [ɪn 'dʒenrl] im Allgemeinen IV
to **generate** ['dʒenreɪt] generieren; erzeu-gen IV
generation [ˌdʒenə'reɪʃn] Generation III
generic term [dʒe.nerɪk 'tɜ:m] Oberbegriff IV
genius ['dʒi:niəs] Genie II
genre ['ʒɑ:nrə] Gattung III
gentle ['dʒentl] sanft; behutsam IV
gentleman ['dʒentlmən], **gentlemen** ['dʒentlmen] (pl) Gentleman; feiner Herr III
gentrification [ˌdʒentrɪfɪ'keɪʃn] Aufwertung durch Luxussanierung **V U2**, 46
gentry ['dʒentri] (niederer) Adel **V F1**, 10; **V AC4**, 88
genuine ['dʒenjuɪn] wirklich; echt **V U3**, 81
geocaching ['dʒi:əʊˌkæʃɪŋ] Geocaching II
geographic [ˌdʒi:ə'græfɪk] geografisch IV
geography [dʒi'ɒgrəfi] Geografie; Erdkun-de IV
German ['dʒɜ:mən] deutsch; Deutsch; aus Deutschland; Deutsche/-r I
gesture ['dʒestʃə] Geste; Gebärde IV
*to **get** [get] bekommen; holen; bringen; besorgen; kaufen; werden I
  *to **get** around [get ə'raʊnd] hier: sich fortbewegen IV
  *to **get** caught [get 'kɔ:t] erwischt wer-den; ertappt werden III

  *to **get** fit [get 'fɪt] in Form kommen; fit werden I
  *to **get** hurt [get 'hɜ:t] verletzt werden II
  *to **get** in the way [ˌget ɪn ðə 'weɪ] stö-ren; im Weg stehen II
  *to **get** in touch (with) [get ɪn 'tʌtʃ] kontaktieren; in Verbindung treten (mit) **V U1**, 27
  *to **get** into [get 'ɪntə] einsteigen; hin-eingelangen I
  *to **get** into trouble [get ɪntə 'trʌbl] in Schwierigkeiten geraten III
  *to **get** lost [get 'lɒst] verloren gehen; sich verirren III
  *to **get** on (the bus) [get 'ɒn] einsteigen (in den Bus) II
  *to **get** on people's nerves [ˌget ɒn pi:plz 'nɜ:vz] jemandem auf die Nerven gehen I
  *to **get** organised [get 'ɔ:gənaɪzd] sich organisieren III
  *to **get** out of [get ˌaʊt əv] aussteigen; herauskommen aus II
  *to **get** over sth [get 'əʊvə] über etw. hinwegkommen; mit etw. fertigwerden III
  *to **get** sb to do sth [get sʌmbədi tə 'du: sʌmθɪŋ] jmdn. dazu bringen etw. zu tun IV
  *to **get** there ['get ðeə] hinkommen I
  *to **get** to ['get tə] kommen zu; kommen nach; erreichen I
  *to **get** to know [get tə 'nəʊ] kennen-lernen II
  *to **get** up [get 'ʌp] aufstehen (aus dem Bett) I
  *to **get** used to sth [get 'ju:zd tə] sich an etw. gewöhnen III
  *to **get** well [get 'wel] gesund werden II
Ghanaian [gɑ:'neɪən] ghanaisch; aus Ghana; Ghanaer/-in IV
ghost [gəʊst] Geist II
giant [dʒaɪənt] Riesen-; riesig IV
gig [gɪg] Auftritt; Gig III
gigantic [dʒaɪ'gæntɪk] gigantisch; riesig III
to **giggle** ['gɪgl] kichern; lachen **V U2**, 42
gila monster ['hi:lə ˌmɒnstə] Gilakrusten-echse III
girl [gɜ:l] Mädchen I
*to **give** [gɪv] geben; schenken I
  *to **give** away [gɪv ə'weɪ] verraten; preisgeben IV
  *to **give** sb a funny look [gɪv ə ˌfʌni 'lʊk] jmdn. schief anschauen III
  *to **give** thanks [gɪv 'θæŋks] danken III
  *to **give** up [gɪv 'ʌp] aufgeben III
glacier ['glæsiə] Gletscher III
glad [glæd] froh III
glance [glɑ:ns] Blick **V U1**, 13
to **glare** at ['gleər ət] zornig anstarren III
glass [glɑ:s] Glas I
glasses (pl) ['glɑ:sɪz] Brille II

Glaswegian [glæz'wiːdʒn] aus Glasgow **V U1**, 20

to **gleam** [gliːm] glänzen; schimmern **IV**

*to catch a **glimpse** [ˌkætʃˌə ˈglɪmsˌəv] einen (flüchtigen) Blick erhaschen von etw. **IV**

to **glisten** [ˈglɪsn] glitzern ⟨**V U1**, 31⟩

global [ˈgləʊbl] global; weltweit **IV**
global warming [ˌgləʊbl ˈwɔːmɪŋ] globale Erwärmung **IV**

glossary [ˈglɒsri] Glossar; Stichwortverzeichnis **VTS**, 112

glove [glʌv] Handschuh **I**

to **glow** [gləʊ] leuchten; glühen **IV**

*to **go** [gəʊ] gehen; fahren **I**; sagen **IV**
*to **go** behind sb's back [gəʊ bɪˌhaɪnd səmbədiz ˈbæk] jmdn. hintergehen **II**
*to **go** black [ˌgəʊ ˈblæk] schwarz werden **II**
*to **go** by ... [ˌgəʊ baɪ] fahren mit ... **I**
*to **go** crazy [gəʊ ˈkreɪzi] ausflippen; durchdrehen; verrückt werden **II**
*to **go** down [gəʊ ˈdaʊn] hinuntergehen; nach unten gehen; entlanggehen **II**
*to **go** for a walk [gəʊ fərˌə ˈwɔːk] spazieren gehen **II**
*to **go** on [ˌgəʊˌˈɒn] geschehen; weitergehen; weitermachen; weiterführen; fortfahren **II**
*to **go** out [ˌgəʊˌˈaʊt] ausgehen; hinausgehen **II**
*to **go** over to [ˌgəʊˌˈəʊvə tə] hinübergehen zu; zu jmdm. nach Hause gehen **II**
*to **go** round in circles [gəʊ ˌraʊnd ɪn ˈsɜːklz] sich im Kreis drehen; im Kreis gehen **III**
*to **go** shopping [ˌgəʊ ˈʃɒpɪŋ] einkaufen gehen **I**
*to **go** sightseeing [ˌgəʊ ˈsaɪtsiːɪŋ] eine Besichtigungstour machen **II**
*to **go** swimming [ˌgəʊ ˈswɪmɪŋ] schwimmen gehen **I**
*to **go** together [ˌgəʊ təˈgeðə] zueinander passen; zueinander gehören **I**
*to **go** with [ˈgəʊ wɪð] passen zu; gehören zu **I**
*to **go** wrong [ˌgəʊ ˈrɒŋ] schiefgehen **I**
*to let **go** (of) [ˌlet ˈgəʊ (əv)] loslassen **II**
What's **going** on? [wɒts ˌgəʊɪŋˌˈɒn] Was ist los?; Was geht ab? **II**

goal [gəʊl] Tor; Ziel **I**

goat [gəʊt] Ziege **IV**

god [gɒd] Gott **II**

gold [gəʊld] Gold **II**

golden [ˈgəʊldn] golden; Gold- **II**

golf [gɒlf] Golf **II**

*to be **gone** [bi ˈgɒn] verschwunden sein; weg sein **II**

gonna (= going to) (coll) [ˈgɒnə] wird/werden **III**

good [gʊd] gut **I**
*to be **good** at [bi ˈgʊdˌət] gut sein in **I**

G'day! (= Good day!) [gəˈdeɪ] Guten Tag.; Hallo.; Hi. (Begrüßung in Australien) **IV**

good luck [ˌgʊd ˈlʌk] viel Glück **III**

Good morning. [gʊd ˈmɔːnɪŋ] Guten Morgen. **I**

the **good** life [ðə ˈgʊd ˌlaɪf] das Dolce Vita **IV**

goodbye [gʊdˈbaɪ] auf Wiedersehen; servus **I**

goods (pl) [gʊdz] Güter; Waren **IV**

goose [guːs], **geese** (pl) [giːs] Gans **III**

to **govern** [ˈgʌvn] regieren; leiten **II**; regeln; verwalten **IV**

government [ˈgʌvnmənt] Regierung **I**
branches of **government** [ˌbrɑːnʃɪzˌəv ˈgʌvnmənt] Regierungszweig **IV**
head of **government** [ˌhedˌəv ˈgʌvnmənt] Regierungschef/-in **I**

governor [ˈgʌvnə] Gouverneur/-in **III**

governor-general [ˌgʌvnəˈdʒenrl] Generalgouverneur/-in **IV**

to **grab** [græb] greifen; ergreifen; schnappen **II**

grade (AE) [greɪd] Note; Klasse **II**

8th-**grader** (AE) [ˈeɪtθˌgreɪdə] Achtklässler/-in **III**

gradual [ˈgrædʒuəl] allmählich **IV**

graduate [ˈgrædʒuət] Hochschulabsolvent/-in **V U1**, 24

to **graduate** [ˈgrædjueɪt] einen Schul-/Hochschulabschluss machen; einen akademischen Grad erwerben **III**

grammar school [ˈgræmə ˌskuːl] Gymnasium **II**

grandad [ˈgrændæd] Opa **I**

grandchild [ˈgrænʃaɪld], **grandchildren** (pl) [ˈgrænˌʃɪldrn] Enkel/-in; Enkelkind **II**

grandma [ˈgrænmɑː] Oma **I**

grandpa (AE) [ˈgrænpɑː] Opa **II**

grandparents (pl) [ˈgrænˌpeərənts] Großeltern **I**

granny [ˈgræni] Oma **I**

to **grant** [grɑːnt] zusichern; gewähren **IV**

graph [grɑːf] Diagramm; Schaubild **IV**

graphic novel [ˌgræfɪk ˈnɒvl] Comicroman **III**

grass [grɑːs] Gras **III**

grassroots (pl) [ˈgrɑːsruːts] Volk; Basis **V F4**, 63

grateful [ˈgreɪtfl] dankbar **IV**

grave [greɪv] Grab **III**

grave [greɪv] ernst **V U3**, 72

graveyard [ˈgreɪvjɑːd] Friedhof **V F2**, 33

great [greɪt] großartig; toll; super; groß **I**
the **great** outdoors [ðə ˌgreɪtˌaʊtˈdɔːz] die freie Natur **II**
It's **great** for ... [ɪts ˈgreɪt fə] Es ist super zum/für ... **I**

greedy [ˈgriːdi] habgierig; raffsüchtig **IV**

Greek [griːk] Griechisch; griechisch; aus Griechenland **II**

green [griːn] grün **I**

greenhouse gas [ˌgriːnhaʊz ˈgæs] Treibhausgas **IV**

Greenwich Mean Time (= GMT) [ˌgrenɪdʒ ˈmiːn ˌtaɪm] westeuropäische Zeit **I**

to **greet** [griːt] begrüßen; grüßen **IV**

greeting [ˈgriːtɪŋ] Gruß **I**

grey [greɪ] grau **I**

grid [grɪd] Gitter; Tabelle; Raster **I**

grim [grɪm] entsetzlich; grausam **V U1**, 20

to **grin** [grɪn] grinsen **II**

grizzly bear [ˈgrɪzli ˌbeə] Grizzlybär **III**

groan [grəʊn] Stöhnen **IV**

ground [graʊnd] Boden; Erdboden **II**

*to be **grounded** [bi ˈgraʊndɪd] Hausarrest haben **II**

group [gruːp] Gruppe; Klasse **I**
peer **group** [ˈpɪə gruːp] Gruppe von Gleichaltrigen **V U2**, 49
tutor **group** [ˈtjuːtə ˌgruːp] Klasse (in einer englischen Schule) **I**

*to **grow** [grəʊ] anbauen; züchten **I**; wachsen **II**
*to **grow** up [grəʊ ˌʌp] aufwachsen; erwachsen werden **I**

growing [ˈgrəʊɪŋ] zunehmend; wachsend **III**

growth [grəʊθ] Wachstum **III**

to **grunt** [grʌnt] grunzen **II**

to **guard** [gɑːd] bewachen **V U2**, 47

guardian [ˈgɑːdiən] Hüter/-in; Wächter/-in **IV**

to **guess** [ges] raten; erraten; vermuten **I**

guest [gest] Gast **III**

guide [gaɪd] Führer/-in; Reiseführer (Buch) **III**
guide dog [ˈgaɪd ˌdɒg] Blindenhund **II**

guided tour [ˌgaɪdɪd ˈtʊə] geführte Tour; Führung **III**

guidebook [ˈgaɪdbʊk] Reiseführer **III**

guilty [ˈgɪlti] schuldig **IV**
guilty conscience [ˌgɪlti ˈkɒnʃns] schlechtes Gewissen; Schuldbewusstsein **IV**

guinea pig [ˈgɪni ˌpɪg] Meerschweinchen **I**

guitar [gɪˈtɑː] Gitarre **I**

gun [gʌn] Schusswaffe **III**

guy [gaɪ] Typ; Kerl; (Pl.) Leute **I**

gym [dʒɪm] Turnhalle; Fitnessstudio **III**

H

habit [ˈhæbɪt] Gewohnheit **IV**

haggis [ˈhægɪs] Haggis (schottisches Gericht aus in einem Schafsmagen gekochten Schafsinnereien und Haferschrot) **V U1**, 13

hair [heə] Haar; Haare **II**
*to do our **hair** [ˌduː ˌaʊə ˈheə] uns frisieren; unsere Haare machen **I**

hairbrush [ˈheəbrʌʃ] Haarbürste **III**

half [hɑːf], **halves** (pl) [hɑːvz] (of) die Hälfte **I**

half [hɑːf] halb **I**

half past [ˌhɑːf ˈpɑːst] halb (bei Uhrzeit-angaben) I

half-sister [ˈhɑːfˌsɪstə] Halbschwester I

*to meet **halfway** [ˌmiːt hɑːˈfweɪ] sich auf halbem Weg treffen II

hall [hɔːl] Flur; Diele; Korridor II; Halle; Saal III

hall pass [ˈhɔːl ˌpɑːs] Erlaubnis, sich während des Unterrichts auf dem Flur aufzuhalten III

hallway [ˈhɔːlweɪ] Flur; Diele; Korridor III

ham [hæm] Schinken I

hammer throw [ˈhæmə ˌθrəʊ] Hammer-werfen V U1, 13

hamster [ˈhæmstə] Hamster I

hand [hænd] Hand I

*to shake **hands** [ˌʃeɪk ˈhændz] Hände schütteln; sich die Hand geben III
Clap your **hands**. [ˌklæp jɔː ˈhændz] Klatsche/Klatscht in die Hände. I
On the one **hand** …, (but) on the other **hand** … [ɒn ðə ˈwʌn ˌhænd … (bʌt) ɒn ðiˈʌðə ˌhænd …] Einerseits …, (aber) andererseits … II

to **hand** sth down to sb [ˌhænd ˈdaʊn] etw. an jmdn. weitergeben; etw. an jmdn. überliefern V F1, 10

handcuffs (pl) [ˈhændkʌfs] Handschellen V U3, 70

to **handle** [ˈhændl] umgehen mit V U3, 71

handout [ˈhændaʊt] Arbeitsblatt; Informa-tionsblatt IV

handsome [ˈhænsəm] attraktiv; gut aus-sehend IV

*to **hang** on [ˌhæŋ ˈɒn] (einen Augenblick) warten II

*to **hang** out (with) (infml) [ˌhæŋ ˈaʊt wɪð] rumhängen (mit); sich herumtreiben (mit); sich treffen (mit) I

to **happen** [ˈhæpn] geschehen; passieren I
to **happen** to do sth [ˌhæpn tʊ ˈduː ˌsʌmθɪŋ] zufällig etw. tun III

happiness [ˈhæpɪnəs] Glück; Zufriedenheit; Fröhlichkeit III

happy [ˈhæpi] glücklich; froh; fröhlich I
happy ending [ˌhæpiˈendɪŋ] Happy End III

harassment [həˈræsmənt] Belästigung; Schikane IV

harbour [ˈhɑːbə] Hafen II

hard [hɑːd] hart; schwer; schwierig II; fest; stark IV
*to be **hard** on sb [bi ˈhɑːd ɒn] streng mit jmdm. sein; mit jmdm. hart ins Gericht gehen II
hard-working [ˌhɑːdˈwɜːkɪŋ] fleißig IV

to try **hard** [ˌtraɪ ˈhɑːd] sich anstrengen; sich Mühe geben II

hardly [ˈhɑːdli] kaum III

hardship [ˈhɑːdʃɪp] Not; Elend; Entbehrun-gen V AC4, 88

hardware [ˈhɑːdweə] Hardware III

to **harm** [hɑːm] Schaden anrichten; beschädigen IV

harmful [ˈhɑːmfl] schädlich IV

harmless [ˈhɑːmləs] harmlos; ungefährlich IV

harmony [ˈhɑːməni] Harmonie IV

harp [hɑːp] Harfe V U1, 21

harsh [hɑːʃ] rau; hart IV

harvest [ˈhɑːvɪst] Ernte III

to **harvest** [ˈhɑːvɪst] ernten IV

hashtag [ˈhæʃtæg] Hashtag IV

hassle [ˈhæsl] Schikane; Schwierigkeit V U1, 17

hat [hæt] Hut I

hate speech [ˈheɪt ˌspiːtʃ] Hassrede; Hetz-rede V U3, 83

to **hate** [heɪt] hassen; nicht mögen I

haul boy/girl [ˈhɔːl ˌbɔɪ/ɡɜːl] Influencer/-in V U3, 81

to **haunt** [hɔːnt] heimsuchen; spuken in IV

haunted [ˈhɔːntɪd] gequält; geplagt V U1, 18
haunted house [ˌhɔːntɪd ˈhaʊs] Geister-haus IV

*to **have** [hæv] haben I
*to **have** a look (at) [ˌhæv ə ˈlʊk] an-schauen II
*to **have** a point [ˌhæv ə ˈpɔɪnt] nicht ganz Unrecht haben II
*to **have** breakfast [ˌhæv ˈbrekfəst] frühstücken I
*to **have** fun [ˌhæv ˈfʌn] Spaß haben; sich amüsieren I
*to **have** got [ˌhæv ˈɡɒt] besitzen; haben I
*to **have** sth done [ˌhæv ˈdʌn] etw. machen lassen IV
*to **have** sth in common [ˌhæv ɪn ˈkɒmən] etw. gemeinsam haben III
*to **have** to [ˈhæv tə] müssen I

*to **have** (a sweet) [hæv] (ein Bonbon) nehmen; (ein Bonbon) essen I

Hawaiian [həˈwaɪən] Hawaiianer/-in; hawaiianisch IV

hazard [ˈhæzəd] Gefahr; Risiko V U1, 24

he [hiː] er I

head [hed] Kopf I
head of government [ˌhed əv ˈɡʌvnmənt] Regierungschef/-in II
head of state [ˌhed əv ˈsteɪt] Staatsober-haupt II
head teacher [ˌhed ˈtiːtʃə] Schulleiter/-in IV
With a very big **head**! [ˌwɪð ə ˌveri bɪɡ ˈhed] Und ein Angeber! II

to **head** (for/to) [ˈhed fə; ˈhed tə] zusteu-ern auf; sich auf den Weg machen nach/zu IV

headache (no pl) [ˈhedeɪk] Kopfschmerzen; Kopfweh II

headband [ˈhedbænd] Stirnband III

heading [ˈhedɪŋ] Überschrift; Titel I

headline [ˈhedlaɪn] Schlagzeile III

headphones (pl) [ˈhedfəʊnz] Kopfhörer II

to **heal** [hiːl] heilen ⟨V U1, 30⟩

health [helθ] Gesundheit II
health care [ˈhelθ keə] Gesundheitsver-sorgung IV
mental **health** [ˌmentl ˈhelθ] seelische Gesundheit V U1, 23

healthy [ˈhelθi] gesund I

*to **hear** [hɪə] hören I
*to **hear** sb (+ -ing) [hɪə] jmdn. etw. tun hören III
I **hear** … [aɪ ˈhɪə] Ich habe gehört, dass … I

hearing [ˈhɪərɪŋ] Hören II
hearing aid [ˈhɪərɪŋ ˌeɪd] Hörgerät II

heart [hɑːt] Herz II
*to learn … by **heart** [ˌlɜːn baɪ ˈhɑːt] auswendig lernen I

heat (no pl) [hiːt] Hitze; Wärme III

heating [ˈhiːtɪŋ] Heizung III

heatwave [ˈhiːtweɪv] Hitzewelle IV

heaven [ˈhevn] Himmel II

heavy [ˈhevi] schwer II

hectare [ˈhekteə] Hektar ⟨V U1, 28⟩

hedgehog [ˈhedʒhɒɡ] Igel III

heiress [ˈeəres] Erbin V F1, 10

helicopter [ˈhelɪkɒptə] Helikopter; Hub-schrauber II

hell [hel] Hölle II

Hello. [heˈləʊ] Hallo.; Grüß Gott.; Servus. I
*to say **hello** (to) [ˌseɪ heˈləʊ tə] grüßen; Grüße ausrichten (an) I

helmet [ˈhelmɪt] Helm III

help [help] Hilfe I

to **help** [help] helfen I
Help yourself. [ˈhelp jəself] Bediene dich.; Bedienen Sie sich. I
I can't **help** (+ -ing) [aɪ ˌkɑːnt ˈhelp] Ich kann nicht anders (als zu) … IV

helpful [ˈhelpfl] hilfsbereit; hilfreich I

helpless [ˈhelpləs] hilflos I

herbs (pl) [hɜːbz] Kräuter; hier: Marihuana ⟨V U3, 86⟩

here [hɪə] hier I
right **here** [ˌraɪt ˈhɪə] genau hier II
Here you are. [ˌhɪə juˈɑː] Bitte schön. I

hereditary [hɪˈredɪtri] mit ererbtem Titel; Erb-; angeboren IV

heritage [ˈherɪtɪdʒ] Erbe IV

hero [ˈhɪərəʊ], heroes [ˈhɪərəʊz] (pl) Held II

heroine [ˈherəʊɪn] Heldin II

hers [hɜːz] ihr/-es/-e/-er II

to **hesitate** [ˈhezɪteɪt] zögern; stocken IV

Hey! [heɪ] Hi.; He!; Hallo. I

heyday [ˈheɪdeɪ] Höhepunkt; Blütezeit V F1, 10

Hi. [haɪ] Hi.; Hallo. I

*to **hide** [haɪd] (sich) verstecken II

high [haɪ] hoch; groß I
high school [ˈhaɪ ˌskuːl] High School (weiterführende Schule in den USA, Oberstufe) II

highlight ['haɪlaɪt] Highlight; Höhepunkt **II**

high-pitched [ˌhaɪ'pɪtʃt] hoch **V U1**, 21

highway (AE) ['haɪweɪ] Landstraße; Bundesautobahn (amerik.); Highway **III**

hike [haɪk] Wanderung **II**

to hike [haɪk] wandern **II**

hiker ['haɪkə] Wanderer/Wanderin **II**

hiking ['haɪkɪŋ] Wandern **I**

hill [hɪl] Berg; Hügel **I**

himself [hɪm'self] er/sich (selbst); selber **I**

Hindu ['hɪndu:] Hindu; hinduistisch **IV**

hint [hɪnt] Hinweis; Andeutung; Tipp **IV**

hip [hɪp] hip; total in **IV**

his [hɪz] sein/-er/-e/-es **II**

Hispanic [hɪ'spænɪk] lateinamerikanisch; Latino/Latina; Hispano-Amerikaner/-in **V U2**, 41; **VTS**, 116

hiss [hɪs] Zischen; Rauschen **V AC2**, 35

to hiss [hɪs] zischen; fauchen ⟨**V U1**, 31⟩

historian [hɪ'stɔ:riən] Historiker/-in **V U3**, 81

historic [hɪ'stɒrɪk] historisch **IV**

historical [hɪ'stɒrɪkl] historisch; geschichtlich **I**

history ['hɪstri] Geschichte **II**
living **history** show [ˌlɪvɪŋ 'hɪstəri ˌʃəʊ] Show, in der historischer Alltag nachgespielt wird **II**

*to hit [hɪt] schlagen; treffen **I**

hoax [həʊks] Täuschung; Trick **IV**

hobby, hobbies (pl) ['hɒbi] Hobby **I**

hockey ['hɒki] Hockey **II**

*to hold [həʊld] halten; festhalten **I**; abhalten; durchführen **III**
*to **hold** on [həʊld ˌɒn] durchhalten **III**
*to **hold** onto [ˌhəʊld ˌɒntə] (sich) festhalten an **III**
*to **hold** your breath [ˌhəʊld jə 'breθ] den Atem anhalten **II**

hole [həʊl] Loch **II**

holiday ['hɒlədeɪ] Urlaub; Feiertag **I**
holidays (pl) ['hɒlədeɪz] Ferien **I**
public **holiday** ['pʌblɪk] gesetzlicher Feiertag **III**

holy ['həʊli] heilig **V U1**, 21

home [həʊm] Zuhause; Heim **I**
at **home** [ət 'həʊm] zu Hause; daheim **I**
home town ['həʊmtaʊn] Heimatstadt **I**
to pop **home** [ˌpɒp ˌ'həʊm] schnell zu Hause vorbeigehen **IV**

home [həʊm] nach Hause **I**

homeland ['həʊmlænd] Heimat; Heimatland **III**

homeless ['həʊmləs] obdachlos **III**
homeless shelter ['həʊmləs ˌʃeltə] Obdachlosenunterkunft **III**

the homeless [ðə 'həʊmləs] Obdachlose **IV**

homepage ['həʊmpeɪdʒ] Homepage **II**

homeschooling [ˌhəʊm'sku:lɪŋ] Unterricht zu Hause **III**

*to be homesick [bi 'həʊmsɪk] Heimweh haben **III**

homework ['həʊmwɜ:k] Hausaufgabe(n) **I**

to homogenize [hə'mɒdʒənaɪz] homogenisieren; vereinheitlichen **V U3**, 80

homogenous [hə'mɒdʒənəs] homogen; einheitlich **V U3**, 80

honest ['ɒnɪst] ehrlich **II**

honesty ['ɒnɪsti] Ehrlichkeit **IV**

honey ['hʌni] Honig **II**

to honor (AE) ['ɒnə] ehren; würdigen; auszeichnen **IV**

to hook [hʊk] hier: fesseln **III**

hope [həʊp] Hoffnung **II**

to hope [həʊp] hoffen **I**

hopeful ['həʊpfl] hoffnungsvoll **I**

hopefully ['həʊpfli] hoffentlich **IV**

horn [hɔ:n] Horn **III**

horrible ['hɒrəbl] schrecklich; furchtbar **II**

horrified ['hɒrɪfaɪd] entsetzt **I**

horror ['hɒrə] Horrorgeschichte; Horrorfilm; Horror **III**

horse [hɔ:s] Pferd **I**

hose [həʊz] Schlauch; Strumpf **V U1**, 21

hospital ['hɒspɪtl] Hospital; Krankenhaus **II**

hospitality [ˌhɒspɪ'tæləti] Gastfreundschaft **IV**

host [həʊst] Gastgeber/-in; Talkmaster/-in **IV**
host family ['həʊst ˌfæmli] Gastfamilie **III**

youth hostel ['ju:θ ˌhɒstl] Jugendherberge **II**

hot [hɒt] heiß **I**
hot dog [ˌhɒt 'dɒg] Hot Dog (Würstchen im Brötchen) **I**
hot pants ['hɒt pænts] Hotpants **II**

hotel [həʊ'tel] Hotel **I**

hour [aʊə] Stunde **II**
five-**hour** ['faɪvaʊə] fünfstündig **II**
rush **hour** ['rʌʃ aʊə] Hauptverkehrszeit **IV**

house [haʊs] Haus **I**
haunted **house** [ˌhɔ:ntɪd 'haʊs] Geisterhaus **IV**
to move (**house**) [mu:v (haʊs)] umziehen **I**

household ['haʊshəʊld] Haushalt **III**

housing ['haʊzɪŋ] Unterkunft; Wohnungsbeschaffung **V U1**, 20
council **housing** [ˌkaʊnsl 'haʊzɪŋ] sozialer Wohnungsbau (brit.) **V U2**, 46
public **housing** [ˌpʌblɪk 'haʊzɪŋ] sozialer Wohnungsbau (amerik.) **V U2**, 46

how [haʊ] wie **I**
How about (+ noun or gerund)? ['haʊ əbaʊt] Wie wäre es mit … ?; Wie ist es mit …? **I**
How are you doing? [ˌhaʊ ˌɑ: jə 'du:ɪŋ] Wie geht es dir/euch/Ihnen? **IV**
How are you? [ˌhaʊ ˌɑ: jə] Wie geht es dir?; Wie geht es euch?; Wie geht es Ihnen? **I**
How many …? [ˌhaʊ 'meni] Wie viele …? **I**

How much (is/are) …? [ˌhaʊ 'mʌtʃ ɪz/ɑ:] Wie viel (kostet/kosten) …? **I**
How old are you? [haʊ ˌəʊld ˌə ju:] Wie alt bist du?; Wie alt sind Sie? **I**
How to … ['haʊ tə] Wie man … **I**
This is **how** you do … ['ðɪs ɪz haʊ jʊ ˌdu:] So machst du … **I**

however [haʊ'evə] jedoch **III**

to hug [hʌg] umarmen **I**

huge [hju:dʒ] riesig; riesengroß; gewaltig **I**

to hum [hʌm] summen; brummen **V U3**, 73

human ['hju:mən] Mensch **III**

humanitarian [hju:ˌmænɪ'teəriən] Menschenfreund/-in ⟨**V U3**, 86⟩

humanity [hju:'mænəti] Menschheit **V F4**, 63

humid ['hju:mɪd] feucht **II**

humorous ['hju:mrəs] humorvoll; lustig **IV**

humour (no pl) ['hju:mə] Humor; Stimmung **III**

hump [hʌmp] Buckel; Höcker **V U1**, 15

hunger ['hʌŋgə] Hunger **III**

hungry ['hʌŋgri] hungrig **I**

to hunt [hʌnt] jagen **III**

hunter ['hʌntə] Jäger/-in **II**

hunting ['hʌntɪŋ] Jagen; Jagd **II**

hurricane ['hʌrɪkən] Hurrikan; Orkan; Wirbelsturm **II**

in a hurry [ˌɪn ə 'hʌri] in Eile **III**

to hurry ['hʌri] eilen; sich beeilen **I**

*to hurt [hɜ:t] verletzen; weh tun **I**
*to **get hurt** [ˌget 'hɜ:t] verletzt werden **II**

husband ['hʌzbənd] Ehemann **II**

hype [haɪp] Hype; Wirbel **IV**

hypocrisy [hɪ'pɒkrəsi] Heuchelei; Scheinheiligkeit **V F4**, 62

I

I [aɪ] ich **I**
I can't help (+ -ing) [aɪ ˌkɑ:nt 'help] Ich kann nicht anders (als zu) … **IV**
I couldn't believe my eyes. [aɪ ˌkʊdnt bɪˌli:v maɪˌ'aɪz] Ich traute meinen Augen nicht. **II**
I don't care [aɪ ˌdəʊnt 'keə] es ist mir egal **II**
I don't know! [aɪ ˌdəʊnt 'nəʊ] Ich weiß (es) nicht! **I**
I hear … [aɪ 'hɪə] Ich habe gehört, dass … **I**
I see your point. [aɪ si: jɔ: 'pɔɪnt] Ich verstehe, was du meinst. **III**
I see. [aɪ 'si:] Ich verstehe.; Aha!; Ach so! **I**
I'd like to … (= I would like to) [aɪd 'laɪk tə] Ich möchte …; Ich würde gern … **I**
I'd like you to … [aɪd 'laɪk jʊ tə] Ich möchte, dass du …; Ich möchte, dass Sie … **I**
I'd rather [aɪd 'rɑ:ðə] ich würde lieber **IV**
I'm afraid … [aɪmˌə'freɪd] Leider … **III**

I'm dog-tired. [ˌaɪm ˌdɒgˈtaɪəd] Ich bin hundemüde. I

I'm English. [aɪmˈɪŋglɪʃ] Ich bin Engländer/-in. I

I'm fine. [ˌaɪm ˈfaɪn] Mir geht's gut. I

I'm from … [ˌaɪm frɒm] Ich bin aus … I

I'm sorry! [ˌaɪm ˈsɒri] Tut mir leid! I

i.e. (= that is) [aɪˈiː (ðæt ˌɪz)] das heißt (Abk.: d.h.) IV

ice [aɪs] Eis I
  ice cream [ˌaɪs ˈkriːm] Eis; Eiscreme I
  ice rink [ˈaɪs ˌrɪŋk] Eisbahn; Schlittschuhbahn I

icon [ˈaɪkɒn] Ikone; Symbol IV

idea [aɪˈdɪə] Idee; Einfall I

ideal [aɪˈdɪəl] Ideal IV

identical [aɪˈdentɪkl] identisch; gleich IV

to identify [aɪˈdentɪfaɪ] aufzeigen; (sich) identifizieren IV
  to **identify** with [aɪˈdentɪfaɪ wɪð] sich identifizieren mit III

identity [aɪˈdentəti] Identität III
  subscriber **identity** module [səbˌskraɪbər aɪˈdentəti ˌmɒdjuːl] Teilnehmer-Identitätsmodul V U3, 80

idiom [ˈɪdiəm] Redewendung; besondere Ausdrucksweise V U1, 26

idiot [ˈɪdiət] Idiot/-in I

idle [aɪdl] faul; träge; untätig V F5, 67
  idle threat [ˌaɪdl ˈθret] leere Drohung V F5, 67

idleness [ˈaɪdlnəs] Faulheit; Trägheit; Müßiggang V F5, 67

if [ɪf] wenn; falls; ob I
  as **if** [əzˌˈɪf] als ob III

to ignore [ɪgˈnɔː] ignorieren; außer Acht lassen II

ill [ɪl] krank III

illegal [ɪˈliːgl] illegal; unrechtmäßig; rechtswidrig II

to illustrate [ˈɪləstreɪt] veranschaulichen; darstellen; illustrieren IV

image [ˈɪmɪdʒ] Bild; Image III

imagery [ˈɪmɪdʒri] Bilder; Bildsprache; Metaphorik IV

imagination [ɪˌmædʒɪˈneɪʃn] Fantasie; Vorstellungskraft II

to imagine [ɪˈmædʒɪn] sich (etwas) vorstellen I

immediately [ɪˈmiːdiətli] sofort; gleich IV

immigrant [ˈɪmɪgrənt] Immigrant/-in; Einwanderer/Einwanderin II

to immigrate [ˈɪmɪgreɪt] einwandern II

immigration [ˌɪmɪˈgreɪʃn] Immigration; Einwanderung; Einreise III
  immigration detention centre [ˌɪmɪˌgreɪʃn dɪˈtenʃn ˌsentə] Auffanglager (für illegal Eingewanderte) IV

impact [ˈɪmpækt] Auswirkung; Einfluss IV

impartial [ɪmˈpɑːʃl] unparteiisch; unvoreingenommen V U1, 23

impatient [ɪmˈpeɪʃnt] ungeduldig IV

implausibility [ɪmˌplɔːzəˈbɪləti] Unglaubwürdigkeit; Fadenscheinigkeit V U2, 53

to implement [ˈɪmplɪment] einführen; umsetzen; realisieren V U3, 83

implicitly [ɪmˈplɪsɪtli] indirekt; implizit V U2, 52

impolite [ˌɪmpəˈlaɪt] unhöflich III

importance [ɪmˈpɔːtns] Bedeutung; Wichtigkeit IV

important [ɪmˈpɔːtnt] wichtig I

impossible [ɪmˈpɒsəbl] unmöglich III

impressed [ɪmˈprest] beeindruckt II

impression [ɪmˈpreʃn] Impression; Eindruck III

impressive [ɪmˈpresɪv] beeindruckend IV

imprint [ˈɪmprɪnt] Impressum V U2, 55

to imprison [ɪmˈprɪzn] verhaften; inhaftieren V F1, 10

imprisonment [ɪmˈprɪznmənt] Verhaftung; Inhaftierung V F1, 10

to improve [ɪmˈpruːv] sich verbessern; verbessern I

in [ɪn] in; im; rein; herein I; aus; jede/-r/-s (zweite/dritte …); von IV
  *to be **in** [biˈˌɪn] in sein; angesagt sein II
  in a polite way [ɪnˌə pəˈlaɪt ˌweɪ] auf höfliche Art II
  in case [ɪn ˈkeɪs] falls; für den Fall, dass … IV
  in contrast [ɪn ˈkɒntrɑːst] im Gegensatz dazu; dagegen III
  in fact [ɪn ˈfækt] tatsächlich; eigentlich; genau genommen III
  in front of [ɪn ˈfrʌnt əv] vor I
  in general [ɪn ˈdʒenrl] im Allgemeinen IV
  in order to [ɪnˌˈɔːdə tə] um … zu; mit der Absicht, zu III
  in power [ɪn ˈpaʊə] an der Macht III
  in return [ɪn rɪˈtɜːn] als Gegenleistung ⟨V U1, 29⟩
  in sb's opinion [ɪn ˌsʌmbədizˌəˈpɪnjən] jmds. Meinung nach III
  in sb's shoes [ɪn ˌsʌmbədiz ˈʃuːz] an jmds. Stelle II
  in secret [ɪn ˈsiːkrət] heimlich II
  in spite of [ɪn ˈspaɪt əv] trotz III
  in the end [ɪn ðiˌˈend] schließlich; zum Schluss I
  in the evenings [ɪn ðiˌˈiːvnɪŋz] abends I
  in the first place [ɪn ðə ˈfɜːst ˌpleɪs] überhaupt erst; von vornherein IV
  in the middle (of) [ɪn ðə ˈmɪdl] in der Mitte (von); mitten in I
  in the mornings [ˌɪn ðə ˈmɔːnɪŋz] morgens; vormittags IV
  in the past [ˌɪn θə ˈpɑːst] früher; in der Vergangenheit II
  in the photo(s) [ˌɪn ðə ˈfəʊtəʊ(z)] auf dem Foto/den Fotos I
  in the street [ˌɪn ðə ˈstriːt] in der Straße; auf der Straße I

to trade sth **in** for sth [ˌtreɪdˈɪn] in Zahlung geben V F3, 38

inadequate [ɪnˈædɪkwət] unzureichend; inadäquat; unangemessen V U3, 80

to incarcerate [ɪnˌkɑːˈsreɪt] inhaftieren V U2, 46

incarceration (no pl) [ɪnˌkɑːsˈreɪʃn] Inhaftierung V U2, 52

inch [ɪnʃ] Zoll (Längenmaß, ca. 2,54 cm) III

incident [ˈɪnsɪdnt] Vorfall; Ereignis V F4, 63

to include [ɪnˈkluːd] einschließen; beinhalten II

including [ɪnˈkluːdɪŋ] einschließlich; inklusive III

inclusion [ɪnˈkluːʒn] Inklusion; Einbeziehung II

inclusive [ɪnˈkluːsɪv] inklusiv; einschließlich; umfassend II

incomplete [ˌɪnkəmˈpliːt] unvollständig III

to incorporate [ɪnˈkɔːpreɪt] berücksichtigen; integrieren IV; einfügen; aufnehmen V AC2, 34

increase [ˈɪnkriːs] Zunahme; Wachstum; Anstieg IV

to increase [ɪnˈkriːs] steigen; erhöhen; zunehmen; wachsen IV

increasingly [ɪnˈkriːsɪŋli] zunehmend IV

incredible [ɪnˈkredəbl] unglaublich IV

in-crowd [ˈɪnkraʊd] die Angesagten II

indeed [ɪnˈdiːd] in der Tat; tatsächlich; allerdings II

indefinitely [ɪnˈdefɪnətli] unbestimmt; unbegrenzt V TS, 110

independence (no pl) [ˌɪndɪˈpendəns] Unabhängigkeit III

independent [ˌɪndɪˈpendənt] unabhängig I

Indian [ˈɪndiən] Inder/-in; indisch I; Indianer/-in; indianisch II

to indicate [ˈɪndɪkeɪt] anzeigen; angeben IV

indicator [ˈɪndɪkeɪtə] Anzeichen; Hinweis V U2, 52

indigenous (fml) [ɪnˈdɪdʒɪnəs] einheimisch; heimisch II

indirect [ˌɪndɪˈrekt; ˌɪndaɪˈrekt] indirekt III

individual [ˌɪndɪˈvɪdʒuəl] Einzelperson; Einzelne/-r; Individuum IV

individual [ˌɪndɪˈvɪdʒuəl] individuell; einzeln II

indoors [ˌɪnˈdɔːz] drinnen; im Haus I

industrial [ɪnˈdʌstriəl] industriell; Industrie- II

industry [ˈɪndəstri] Industrie; Branche; Gewerbe II

inequality [ˌɪnɪˈkwɒləti] Ungleichheit V F4, 63

inexplicable [ˌɪnɪkˈsplɪkəbl] unerklärlich V U1, 14

inferior [ɪnˈfɪəriə] unterlegen; minderwertig V F3, 36

influence [ˈɪnfluəns] Einfluss II

to influence [ˈɪnfluəns] beeinflussen IV

influential [ˌɪnfluˈenʃl] einflussreich; maßgebend **V F1**, 11

to **inform** [ɪnˈfɔːm] informieren **IV**

informal [ɪnˈfɔːml] informell; zwanglos **III**

information (no pl) [ˌɪnfəˈmeɪʃn] Information; Informationen **I**

informative [ɪnˈfɔːmətɪv] informativ **IV**

ingredient [ɪnˈɡriːdiənt] Zutat **II**

inhabitant [ɪnˈhæbɪtnt] Einwohner/-in; Bewohner/-in **V U1**, 12

*to be **inhabited** [biˌɪnˈhæbɪtɪd] bewohnt sein **III**

to **inherit** [ɪnˈherɪt] erben **V F1**, 10

inheritance [ɪnˈherɪtns] Erbe; Erbschaft **V F1**, 10

inhuman [ɪnˈhjuːmən] unmenschlich **V F3**, 38

initial [ɪˈnɪʃl] Initiale; Anfangsbuchstabe **V F3**, 37

initially [ɪˈnɪʃli] zunächst; anfangs **IV**

initiative [ɪˈnɪʃətɪv] Initiative; Aktion **V U1**, 23

injury [ˈɪndʒəri] Verletzung **II**

injustice [ɪnˈdʒʌstɪs] Ungerechtigkeit **V F4**, 63

ink [ɪŋk] Tinte **IV**

inland revenue [ˌɪnlænd ˈrevnjuː] Finanzamt (brit.) **V U3**, 76

inline skating [ˈɪnlaɪn ˌskeɪtɪŋ] Inlineskatefahren **I**

inner [ˈɪnə] innere/-r/-s; Innen- **IV**

innocent [ˈɪnəsnt] unschuldig; Unschuldige/-r **IV**

input [ˈɪnpʊt] Beitrag; Input **IV**

insect [ˈɪnsekt] Insekt **II**

insecure [ˌɪnsɪˈkjʊə] unsicher **III**

inside [ɪnˈsaɪd] innen; im Innern; hinein; nach drinnen; in; drin **I**

insight [ˈɪnsaɪt] Einblick ⟨**V U3**, 87⟩

to **insist** (on) [ɪnˈsɪst] insistieren; bestehen auf **III**

to **inspire** [ɪnˈspaɪə] inspirieren; anregen **V U1**, 15

instead [ɪnˈsted] stattdessen **II**

instead of [ɪnˈsted ˌəv] statt; anstatt; an Stelle von **I**

institution [ˌɪnstɪˈtjuːʃn] Einrichtung; Organisation; Institution **IV**

to **instruct** [ɪnˈstrʌkt] anweisen; beauftragen **IV**

instruction [ɪnˈstrʌkʃn] Instruktion; Anweisung **I**

set of **instructions** [ˌset əv ɪnˈstrʌkʃnz] Anleitung **III**

instructor [ɪnˈstrʌktə] Lehrer/-in; Betreuer/-in **IV**

surf **instructor** [ˌsɜːf ɪnˈstrʌktə] Surflehrer/-in **IV**

instrument [ˈɪnstrəmənt] Instrument **II**

insufficient [ˌɪnsəˈfɪʃnt] ungenügend; unzureichend **V U3**, 75

insult [ˈɪnsʌlt] Beleidigung **IV**

insurance [ɪnˈʃʊərns] Versicherung **IV**

to **integrate** [ˈɪntɪɡreɪt] (sich) integrieren; (sich) einfügen; einbinden **IV**

intellectual [ˌɪntlˈektjuəl] intellektuell; geistig **II**

intelligent [ɪnˈtelɪdʒnt] intelligent; klug; vernünftig **III**

to **intend** [ɪnˈtend] beabsichtigen; intendieren **IV**

intense [ɪnˈtens] intensiv; heftig **IV**

to **intensify** [ɪnˈtensɪfaɪ] intensivieren; verstärken **V U2**, 47

intent [ɪnˈtent] Absicht; Vorsatz ⟨**V U3**, 85⟩

*to be **intent** on doing sth [biˌɪnˈtent ˌɒn] fest entschlossen sein, etw. zu tun **V U3**, 79

intention [ɪnˈtenʃn] Absicht; Intention **V F3**, 39

interaction [ˌɪntrˈækʃn] Interaktion **III**

interest [ˈɪntrəst] Interesse **II**

interest [ˈɪntrəst] Zinsen **V U3**, 76

*to be **interested** (in) [biˌɪntrəstɪd ˌɪn] interessiert sein (an); sich interessieren (für) **I**

interesting [ˈɪntrəstɪŋ] interessant **I**

interior [ɪnˈtɪəriə] Innen- **V F2**, 33

international [ˌɪntəˈnæʃnl] international **I**

internet [ˈɪntənet] Internet **I**

to **interpret** [ɪnˈtɜːprɪt] interpretieren **V U1**, 21; **VTS**, 108

to **interrupt** [ˌɪntəˈrʌpt] unterbrechen **II**

interruption [ˌɪntəˈrʌpʃn] Unterbrechung **IV**

interview [ˈɪntəvjuː] Interview; Befragung **I**

(job) **interview** [ˈdʒɒb ˌɪntəvjuː] Vorstellungsgespräch **IV**

to **interview** [ˈɪntəvjuː] interviewen; befragen **III**

interviewee [ˌɪntəvjuˈiː] Befragte/-r; Interviewte/-r ⟨**V U1**, 28⟩

interviewer [ˈɪntəvjuːə] Interviewer/-in; Befrager/-in **III**

intestine [ɪnˈtestɪn] Darm; Eingeweide **V U2**, 45

into [ˈɪntə] in; in … hinein **I**

*to be **into** [biˌɪntə] mögen; stehen auf **I**

intriguing [ɪnˈtriːɡɪn] faszinierend **V U1**, 22

to **introduce** [ˌɪntrəˈdjuːs] vorstellen; einführen; einleiten **II**

introduction [ˌɪntrəˈdʌkʃn] Einführung; Einleitung; Vorstellung **II**

introverted [ˌɪntrəʊˈvɜːtɪd] introvertiert **V U1**, 18

to **invade** [ɪnˈveɪd] einmarschieren (in); eindringen (in); überfallen **II**

invader [ɪnˈveɪdə] Eindringling; Angreifer/-in **III**

invasion [ɪnˈveɪʒn] Invasion; Einmarsch; Überfall **V F1**, 10

to **invent** [ɪnˈvent] erfinden **II**

invented [ɪnˈventɪd] erfunden **II**

invention [ɪnˈvenʃn] Erfindung **IV**

inventor [ɪnˈventə] Erfinder/-in **IV**

inverted comma [ɪnˌvɜːtɪd ˈkɒmə] Anführungszeichen **V U1**, 26

to **invest** [ɪnˈvest] investieren **V U1**, 23

to **investigate** [ɪnˈvestɪɡeɪt] ermitteln; untersuchen; Nachforschungen anstellen; recherchieren **V U2**, 43

investment [ɪnˈvesmənt] Einlage; Beteiligung; Investition **III**

invitation [ˌɪnvɪˈteɪʃn] Einladung **I**

to **invite** [ɪnˈvaɪt] einladen **I**

to **involve** [ɪnˈvɒlv] involvieren; einbeziehen; beteiligen **IV**

*to be **involved** (in) [biˌɪnˈvɒlvd ˌɪn] beteiligt sein (an); involviert sein (in); engagiert sein (für) **IV**

involvement [ɪnˈvɒlvmənt] Engagement; Beteiligung **IV**

Irish [ˈaɪrɪʃ] irisch; Irisch **II**

iron [aɪən] Eisen **V U1**, 21

ironic [aɪˈrɒnɪk] ironisch **V U2**, 42

irony [ˈaɪrəni] Ironie **IV**

irregular [ɪˈreɡjələ] unregelmäßig **II**

irrelevant [ɪˈreləvnt] irrelevant; nicht von Bedeutung **IV**

irresponsible [ˌɪrɪˈspɒnsəbl] unverantwortlich; leichtsinnig **IV**

to **irritate** [ˈɪrɪteɪt] verärgern; reizen **IV**

island [ˈaɪlənd] Insel **I**

Pacific **Islander** [pəˌsɪfɪk ˈaɪlændə] Bewohner/-in einer Pazifischen Insel **IV**

isolated [ˈaɪsəleɪtɪd] abgelegen; abgeschieden; isoliert **V U1**, 14

issue [ˈɪʃuː; ˈɪsjuː] Angelegenheit; Problem; Frage **III**

to **issue** [ˈɪʃuː; ˈɪsjuː] herausgeben; ausstellen **III**

it [ɪt] es **I**

It took ages. [ɪt tʊkˈeɪdʒɪz] Es dauerte ewig. **II**

It's fun. [ɪts ˈfʌn] Es macht Spaß. **I**

It's great for … [ɪts ˈɡreɪt fə] Es ist super zum/für … **I**

It's no use (+ gerund) [ɪts ˌnəʊ ˈjuːs] Es nützt nichts … **III**

It's none of our business! [ɪts ˌnʌn əv ˌaʊə ˈbɪznɪs] Das geht uns nichts an! **IV**

It's your turn. [ˌɪts ˈjɔː tɜːn] Du bist dran. **I**

It's …/They're … [ɪts/ðeə] Es kostet …/Sie kosten … **I**

IT (= Information Technology) [ˌaɪˈtiː] Informatik; Informationstechnik **II**

Italian [ɪˈtæliən] Italiener/-in; italienisch; Italienisch; aus Italien **IV**

item [ˈaɪtəm] Gegenstand; Objekt **IV**

its [ɪts] sein/-e; ihr/-e **I**

ivory (no pl) [ˈaɪvri] Elfenbein **III**

J

jacket ['dʒækɪt] Jacke **II**

jack-o'-lantern [ˌdʒækə'læntən] Kürbislaterne **II**

jail [dʒeɪl] Gefängnis **V F4**, 62

jam [dʒæm] Marmelade; Konfitüre **II**

January ['dʒænjuri] Januar **I**

Japanese [ˌdʒæpən'iːz] japanisch; Japanisch; Japaner/-in **IV**

*to be jealous (of) [bi 'dʒeləs] eifersüchtig sein (auf); neidisch sein (auf) **I**

jeans [dʒiːnz] Jeans **I**

jelly ['dʒeli] Tortenguss; Götterspeise; Wackelpudding; Gelee **I**

jellyfish ['dʒelifɪʃ] Qualle **IV**
   box jellyfish ['bɒks ˌdʒelifɪʃ] Würfelqualle **IV**

Jew [dʒuː] Jude/Jüdin **V F4**, 61

jewel ['dʒuːəl] Juwel; Edelstein **III**

jewellery ['dʒuːəlri] Schmuck **I**

Jewish ['dʒuːɪʃ] jüdisch **IV**

job [dʒɒb] Arbeit; Aufgabe; Job **I**
   (job) interview ['dʒɒb ˌɪntəvjuː] Vorstellungsgespräch **IV**

to join [dʒɔɪn] beitreten; sich anschließen; verbinden **I**

joke [dʒəʊk] Witz **I**

to joke [dʒəʊk] scherzen **II**

journalist ['dʒɜːnlɪst] Journalist/-in **IV**

journey ['dʒɜːni] Reise; Fahrt **II**

joy [dʒɔɪ] Freude; Vergnügen **V U3**, 73

judge [dʒʌdʒ] Juror/-in; Richter/-in **I**

to judge [dʒʌdʒ] beurteilen; bewerten **II**
   to judge a book by its cover [dʒʌdʒ ə ˌbʊk baɪ ɪts 'kʌvə] jdn./etw. nach dem Äußeren beurteilen **IV**

judgement ['dʒʌdʒmənt] Urteil; Beurteilung; Meinung **IV**

judgmental [dʒʌdʒ'mentl] voreingenommen; beurteilend ⟨**V U3**, 86⟩

juggling ['dʒʌglɪŋ] Jonglieren **II**

juice [dʒuːs] Saft **I**

July [dʒʊ'laɪ] Juli **I**

to jump [dʒʌmp] springen **I**
   to jump the queue [ˌdʒʌmp ðə 'kjuː] sich vordrängeln **I**

June [dʒuːn] Juni **I**

jungle ['dʒʌŋgl] Dschungel **V U3**, 73

jury ['dʒʊəri] Jury; Preisgericht **IV**

just [dʒʌst] gerade; nur; einfach **I**

justice ['dʒʌstɪs] Gerechtigkeit **III**
   chief justice [ˌtʃiːf 'dʒʌstɪs] Oberster Richter/Oberste Richterin **IV**

justice system ['dʒʌstɪs ˌsɪstəm] Justizsystem **V U2**, 41

to justify ['dʒʌstɪfaɪ] rechtfertigen; begründen **IV**
   the end justifies the means [ði ˌend dʒʌstɪfaɪz ðə 'miːnz] der Zweck heiligt die Mittel **V F5**, 67

K

Kansan ['kænzən] aus Kansas **V U2**, 53

kayaking ['kaɪækɪŋ] Kajakfahren **III**

*to keep [kiːp] halten; behalten; aufbewahren **II**
   *to keep (+ gerund) [kiːp] weiter tun; immer wieder tun **III**
   *to keep away from [ˌkiːp ə'weɪ frəm] (sich) fernhalten von; meiden **II**
   *to keep in mind [ˌkiːp ɪn 'maɪnd] beachten; im Gedächtnis behalten **IV**
   *to keep in touch [ˌkiːp ɪn 'tʌtʃ] in Kontakt bleiben **IV**
   *to keep out (of) [ˌkiːp 'aʊt əv] draußen bleiben; draußen halten **III**
   *to keep sb waiting [ˌkiːp 'weɪtɪŋ] jmdn. warten lassen **III**
   *to keep up [ˌkiːp ˌ'ʌp] aufrechterhalten **III**
   *to keep up (with) [ˌkiːp ˌ'ʌp (wɪð)] mithalten (mit); Schritt halten (mit) **II**
   *to keep your fingers crossed [kiːp jɔː ˌfɪŋgəz 'krɒst] die Daumen drücken **I**

ketchup ['ketʃʌp] Ketchup **III**

kettle ['ketl] Teekessel; Kessel; Wasserkocher **IV**

key [kiː] Schlüssel **III**
   key ring ['kiː ˌrɪŋ] Schlüsselbund; Schlüsselanhänger **III**
   key word ['kiː ˌwɜːd] Stichwort; Schlüsselbegriff **I**

key [kiː] besonders wichtig **II**

to kick [kɪk] schießen; treten **II**

kid [kɪd] Jugendliche/-r; Kind **II**

to kidnap ['kɪdnæp] kidnappen; entführen **IV**

to kill [kɪl] töten; umbringen **II**

killer ['kɪlə] Killer/-in **III**

kilogram (kg) ['kɪləgræm] Kilogramm **IV**

kilometre (km) ['kɪləˌmiːtə; kɪ'lɒmɪtə] Kilometer **II**
   kilometres per hour (km/h) [kɪˌlɒmɪtəz pər ˌ'aʊə] Stundenkilometer **III**

kind [kaɪnd] Art; Sorte **I**

kindergarten ['kɪndəˌgaːtn] Kindergarten **IV**

king [kɪŋ] König **I**

kiss [kɪs] Kuss **IV**

kitchen ['kɪtʃɪn] Küche **I**

kite [kaɪt] Drachen **V TS**, 109

kiwi ['kiːwiː] Kiwi (flugunfähiger Vogel); Kiwi (Frucht) **IV**

Kiwi (infml) ['kiːwiː] Neuseeländer/-in **IV**

knee [niː] Knie **V F3**, 39

to kneel [niːl] knien **V U2**, 53

knife [naɪf], knives [naɪvz] (pl) Messer **III**

knight [naɪt] Ritter **II**

knob [nɒb] Griff **II**

knock [nɒk] Klopfen; Schlag; Stoß **IV**

to knock [nɒk] stoßen; schlagen **IV**

*to know [nəʊ] kennen; wissen **I**

*to get to know [ˌget tə 'nəʊ] kennenlernen **II**

I don't know! [aɪ ˌdəʊnt 'nəʊ] Ich weiß (es) nicht! **I**

knowledge (no pl) ['nɒlɪdʒ] Wissen; Kenntnisse **IV**

koala [kəʊ'ɑːlə] Koala **III**

L

label ['leɪbl] Etikett; Beschriftung; Label; Marke **IV**

to label ['leɪbl] beschriften; etikettieren **IV**

child labor (AE) [ˌtʃaɪld 'leɪbə] Kinderarbeit **III**

laboratory [lə'bɒrətri] Labor **III**

lack of ['læk əv] Mangel an; Fehlen von **IV**

to lack [læk] fehlen; nicht haben **V U2**, 46

ladder ['lædə] Leiter **V U2**, 50

lady ['leɪdi] Lady; Dame; Frau **III**
   lady-in-waiting [ˌleɪdi ɪn 'weɪtɪŋ] Hofdame **III**

laid-back [leɪd'bæk] entspannt; locker **II**

lake [leɪk] See **I**
   boating lake ['bəʊtɪŋ ˌleɪk] See zum Rudern **I**

lamb [læm] Lamm; Lämmchen **I**
   roast lamb [ˌrəʊst 'læm] Lammbraten **III**

land [lænd] Land **I**

to land [lænd] landen **II**

landfill ['lænfɪl] Deponie **IV**

moon landing ['muːn ˌlændɪŋ] Mondlandung **IV**

landmark ['lænmɑːk] Wahrzeichen **IV**

landscape ['lænskeɪp] Landschaft **II**

lane [leɪn] Fahrspur; Weg; Gasse **V U3**, 71

language ['læŋgwɪdʒ] Sprache **I**
   explicit language [ɪksˌplɪsɪt 'læŋgwɪdʒ] obszöne Sprache; vulgäre Sprache **V U3**, 83
   first language [ˌfɜːst 'læŋgwɪdʒ] Muttersprache **I**
   foreign language [ˌfɒrɪn 'læŋgwɪdʒ] Fremdsprache **II**
   official language [əˌfɪʃl 'læŋgwɪdʒ] Amtssprache **I**

lantern ['læntən] Laterne **II**

laptop ['læptɒp] Laptop **II**

large [lɑːdʒ] groß **II**

lassi ['lʌsi] Lassi **I**

to last [lɑːst] dauern; andauern; anhalten **III**

last [lɑːst] letzte/-r/-s **I**
   at last [ət 'lɑːst] endlich; schließlich **I**
   last night [ˌlɑːst 'naɪt] gestern Abend; gestern Nacht **III**

lasting ['lɑːstɪŋ] bleibend; dauerhaft **III**

late [leɪt] spät; zu spät **I**
   *to be late [bi 'leɪt] zu spät dran sein; zu spät kommen **I**

lately ['leɪtli] in letzter Zeit; kürzlich **V U2**, 44

latest ['leɪtɪst] neueste/-r/-s I

Latin ['lætɪn] Latein I; lateinamerikanisch II; lateinisch IV

Latino [lə'ti:nəʊ] lateinamerikanisch V AC2, 34

laugh [lɑ:f] Lachen IV

to laugh [lɑ:f] lachen I
to laugh at sb ['lɑ:f ət] jmdn. auslachen III

laughter ['lɑ:ftə] Gelächter; Lachen IV

to launch [lɔ:nʃ] starten; in Gang setzen V U2, 50

law [lɔ:] Gesetz II; Recht III
law suit ['lɔ: ˌsu:t] Gerichtsverfahren V U3, 75

lawyer ['lɔɪə] Anwalt/Anwältin; Jurist/-in IV

*to lay [leɪ] legen IV
*to lay down [ˌleɪ 'daʊn] hinlegen III

layer (of) ['leɪə] Schicht (aus); Lage (aus) III

layout ['leɪaʊt] Layout; Anordnung III

lazy ['leɪzi] faul IV

*to lead [li:d] führen; anführen III

lead singer [li:d 'sɪŋə] Leadsänger/-in; Frontsänger/-in III

leader ['li:də] Führer/-in; Anführer/-in II

leaf [li:f], leaves [li:vz] (pl) Blatt III

leaflet ['li:flət] Broschüre; Informationsblatt; Prospekt IV

league [li:g] Liga V U2, 53

to leak (out) [ˌli:k ˈaʊt] auslaufen; durchsickern IV

*to lean [li:n] lehnen V U1, 17
*to lean back [ˌli:n 'bæk] sich zurücklehnen ⟨V U1, 31⟩

leap [li:p] Sprung; Satz IV

*to leap [li:p] springen IV

*to learn [lɜ:n] lernen I
*to learn … by heart [ˌlɜ:n baɪ 'hɑ:t] auswendig lernen I
a lot to learn [ə ˌlɒt tə 'lɜ:n] viel zu lernen I

learner ['lɜ:nə] Lernende/-r II

at least [ət 'li:st] mindestens; wenigstens I

leather ['leðə] Leder ⟨V U1, 30⟩

*to leave [li:v] lassen; verlassen; abfahren; losgehen I; überlassen II
*to leave a message [ˌli:v ə 'mesɪdʒ] eine Nachricht hinterlassen I
*to leave it to cool [ˈli:v ɪt tə 'ku:l] kalt stellen I
*to leave sb alone [ˌli:v ə'ləʊn] jmdn. in Ruhe lassen II

on the left [ɒn ðə 'left] auf der linken Seite; links I

left [left] übrig I

leg [leg] Bein II

legend ['ledʒənd] Legende; Sage II

legislation [ˌledʒɪ'sleɪʃn] Gesetze; Gesetzgebung IV

leisure ['leʒə] Freizeit; Freizeit- I

leisure centre ['leʒə ˌsentə] Freizeitzentrum I

lemonade [ˌlemə'neɪd] Limonade I

*to lend (to) ['lend tə] leihen; verleihen II

length [leŋθ] Länge V TS, 115

lesbian ['lezbiən] lesbisch; Lesbe IV

less [les] weniger II

lesson ['lesn] Unterrichtsstunde; Schulstunde; Unterricht I

*to let [let] lassen I
*to let go (of) [ˌlet 'gəʊ (əv)] loslassen II
let alone [ˌlet ə'ləʊn] geschweige denn IV
Let's … [lets] Lass/Lasst uns … I

letter ['letə] Buchstabe I; Brief II
application letter [ˌæplɪ'keɪʃn ˌletə] Bewerbungsschreiben IV
letter to the editor [ˌletə tʊ ðiˌ'edɪtə] Leserbrief III

level ['levl] Niveau; Level III

LGBTQIA+ [ˌeldʒi:bi:ti:kju:aɪeɪ'plʌs] Abkürzung für Lesbisch, Schwul, Bisexuell, Transgender, Queer/Questioning, Intersexuell, Asexuell/Aromantisch und andere Formen der sexuellen Identität und Orientierung V AC1, 8

liberty ['lɪbəti] Freiheit III

library ['laɪbri] Bibliothek; Bücherei II

artistic licence [ɑ:ˌtɪstɪk 'laɪsns] künstlerische Freiheit V U3, 77

driving licence [ˌdraɪvɪŋ ˌlaɪsns] Führerschein II

lie [laɪ] Lüge III

to lie [laɪ] lügen II

*to lie [laɪ] liegen II
*to lie down [laɪ 'daʊn] sich hinlegen II

life [laɪf], lives [laɪvz] (pl) Leben I
the good life [ðə ˌgʊd ˌlaɪf] das Dolce Vita IV

lifeboat ['laɪfbəʊt] Rettungsboot I

lifebuoy ['laɪfbɔɪ] Rettungsring I

lifeguard ['laɪfgɑ:d] Rettungsschwimmer/-in IV

lifestyle ['laɪfstaɪl] Lebensstil; Lifestyle III

lift [lɪft] Lift; Fahrstuhl II

to lift [lɪft] heben; anheben; sich heben II

light [laɪt] Licht; Lampe II

lightning (no pl) ['laɪtnɪŋ] Blitz II

likes and dislikes [ˌlaɪks ən'dɪslaɪks] Vorlieben und Abneigungen I

to like [laɪk] mögen; gern haben I
would like [wʊd 'laɪk] würde/-st/-n/-t gern; hätte/-st/-n/-t gern I
I'd like to … (= I would like to) [aɪd 'laɪk tə] Ich möchte …; Ich würde gern … I
I'd like you to … [aɪd 'laɪk jʊ tə] Ich möchte, dass du …; Ich möchte, dass Sie … I

like [laɪk] wie; als ob I
dog-like ['dɒg laɪk] hundeartig IV
like-minded [laɪk'maɪndɪd] gleich gesinnt V U3, 81

like that [laɪk 'ðæt] so I

like this [laɪk 'ðɪs] so I

likely ['laɪkli] wahrscheinlich III
*to be likely [bi 'laɪkli] wahrscheinlich sein III

limit ['lɪmɪt] Limit; Grenze IV

to limit (to) ['lɪmɪt tə] limitieren (auf); begrenzen (auf); beschränken (auf) IV

line [laɪn] Linie; Zeile I
*to draw the line (at) [ˌdrɔ: ðə 'laɪn] bei etw. die Grenze ziehen IV
finish line ['fɪnɪʃ ˌlaɪn] Ziellinie II
*to stand in line (AE) [ˌstænd ɪn 'laɪn] anstehen; Schlange stehen; (sich) anstellen III
time line ['taɪm ˌlaɪn] Zeitstrahl I

to line up [laɪnˈʌp] (sich) aufstellen; sich anstellen (amerik.) III

lingua franca [ˌlɪŋgwə 'fræŋkə] Verkehrssprache III

link [lɪŋk] Link; Verbindung II

to link [lɪŋk] verbinden II
linking word ['lɪŋkɪŋ ˌwɜ:d] Verbindungswort II

lip [lɪp] Lippe III

liquor ['lɪkə] alkoholisches Getränk V U3, 76

list [lɪst] Liste I

to list [lɪst] auflisten; nennen IV

to listen (to) ['lɪsn] zuhören; anhören I
to listen for ['lɪsn fə] horchen auf I

listener ['lɪsənə] Zuhörer/-in II

listening ['lɪsnɪŋ] Hören I

liter (l) (AE) ['li:tə] Liter IV

literacy (no pl) ['lɪtrəsi] Lese- und Schreibfähigkeit; Lese- V U2, 46

literal ['lɪtrl] wörtlich; buchstäblich IV

literature ['lɪtrətʃə] Literatur IV

to litter ['lɪtə] verschmutzen; verunreinigen; Müll herumliegen lassen III

little ['lɪtl] klein I

little ['lɪtl] wenig II
a little [ə 'lɪtl] ein wenig; etwas I

to live [lɪv] wohnen; leben I
living history show [ˌlɪvɪŋ 'hɪstəri ˌʃəʊ] Show, in der historischer Alltag nachgespielt wird II

live [laɪv] live III

lively ['laɪvli] lebendig III

living ['lɪvɪŋ] Lebensweise II
living room ['lɪvɪŋ rʊm] Wohnzimmer I
standard of living [ˌstændəd əv 'lɪvɪŋ] Lebensstandard IV

lizard ['lɪzəd] Echse; Eidechse III

load [ləʊd] Ladung; Last IV

to load [ləʊd] einräumen; laden III

loan [ləʊn] Darlehen; Kredit IV

lobby ['lɒbi] Lobby; Eingangshalle III

lobster ['lɒbstə] Hummer II

local ['ləʊkl] Ortsansässige/-r; Einheimische/-r IV

local ['ləʊkl] örtlich; lokal II

*to be **located** [ˌbi ləʊˈkeɪtɪd] gelegen sein; liegen **V U2**, 45

location [ləʊˈkeɪʃn] Lage; Standort; Handlungsort **III**

loch [lɒx; lɒk] See *(in Schottland)* **V U1**, 14

locked [lɒkt] abgeschlossen **III**

locker [ˈlɒkə] Schließfach; Spind **I**

loft [lɒft] Dachboden **I**

log cabin [ˈlɒɡ ˌkæbɪn] Blockhütte **II**

logic [ˈlɒdʒɪk] Logik **II**

logical [ˈlɒdʒɪkl] logisch **III**

logistics *(pl)* [lɒˈdʒɪstɪks] Logistik **IV**

logo [ˈləʊɡəʊ] Logo; Firmenzeichen **IV**

to **loiter** [ˈlɔɪtə] herumhängen; herumlungern ⟨**V U3**, 87⟩

LOL *(= laughing out loud)* [lɒl] LOL **I**

Londoner [ˈlʌndənə] Londoner/-in **I**

lonely [ˈləʊnli] einsam **I**

long [lɒŋ] lang **I**
　as **long** as [əz ˈlɒŋ ˌəz] solange **II**
　long ago [ˈlɒŋ ˌəˌɡəʊ] vor langer Zeit **II**
　no **longer** [ˌnəʊ ˈlɒŋɡə] nicht länger; nicht mehr **IV**
　not any **longer** [nɒt ˌeni ˈlɒŋɡə] nicht mehr; (nicht) länger **II**

look [lʊk] Blick **I**
　*to give sb a funny **look** [ˌɡɪv ə ˌfʌni ˈlʊk] jmdn. schief anschauen **III**
　*to have a **look** (at) [ˌhæv ə ə ˈlʊk] anschauen **II**
　*to take a **look** at [teɪk ə ˈlʊk ˌæt] einen Blick werfen auf **II**

to **look** [lʊk] schauen; sehen; aussehen **I**
　to **look** a mess [ˌlʊk ə ˈmes] ungepflegt aussehen **V U2**, 42
　to **look** after [ˌlʊk ˈɑːftə] aufpassen auf; hüten; sich kümmern um **I**
　to **look** at [ˈlʊk ˌət] anschauen; ansehen **I**
　to **look** for [ˈlʊk fɔː] suchen nach **I**
　to **look** forward to [ˌlʊk ˈfɔːwəd tə] sich freuen auf **II**
　to **look** out for [ˌlʊk ˈaʊt fə] Ausschau halten nach; sich in Acht nehmen vor; aufpassen auf **II**
　to **look** up [ˌlʊk ˈʌp] nachschlagen; nachschauen **I**

to **loom** [luːm] sich abzeichnen **V U1**, 24

lopsided [ˌlɒpˈsaɪdɪd] schief; nach einer Seite hängend **V U1**, 20

lord [lɔːd] Lord; Herr **III**

*to **lose** [luːz] verlieren **II**

loser [ˈluːzə] Verlierer/-in; Loser/-in **II**

loss [lɒs] Verlust **V F2**, 33

lost [lɒst] verloren **I**
　*to get **lost** [ˌɡet ˈlɒst] verloren gehen; sich verirren **III**

a **lot** [ə ˈlɒt] viel **I**
　a **lot** of [ə ˈlɒt ˌəv] viel/-e; eine Menge **I**
　lots (of) [ˈlɒts ˌəv] viel/-e; jede Menge **I**

loud [laʊd] laut **I**
　*to read out **loud** [ˌriːd ˌaʊt ˈlaʊd] laut vorlesen **II**

love [lʌv] Liebe **III**

Love … [lʌv] Liebe Grüße *(am Briefende)*; Herzliche Grüße *(am Briefende)* **I**

to **love** [lʌv] lieben; gern mögen **I**
　would **love** [wʊd ˈlʌv] würde/-st/-n/-t sehr gern; hätte/-st/-n/-t sehr gern **I**

lovely [ˈlʌvli] schön; hübsch **IV**

low [ləʊ] niedrig **IV**

to **lower** one's voice [ˈləʊə wʌnz ˈvɔɪs] die Stimme senken **IV**

loyal [ˈlɔɪəl] loyal; treu **II**

loyalty *(no pl)* [ˈlɔəlti] Treue; Loyalität **V F1**, 10

luck [lʌk] Glück **II**
　bad **luck** [ˌbæd ˈlʌk] Pech; Unglück **I**
　good **luck** [ˌɡʊd ˈlʌk] viel Glück **III**

luckily [ˈlʌkɪli] glücklicherweise **III**

lucky … [ˈlʌki] … der/die Glückliche **I**
　*to be **lucky** [bi ˈlʌki] Glück haben **I**
　lucky charm [ˌlʌki ˈtʃɑːm] Glücksbringer; Talisman **I**

luggage *(no pl)* [ˈlʌɡɪdʒ] Gepäck **II**

lunar [ˈluːnə] Mond- **IV**

lunch [lʌnʃ] Mittagessen **I**
　lunch break [ˈlʌnʃbreɪk] Mittagspause **I**

lunchtime [ˈlʌnʃtaɪm] Mittagszeit; Mittagspause **III**

(song) **lyrics** *(pl)* [sɒŋ ˈlɪrɪks] Liedtext **V AC1**, 9

M

machine [məˈʃiːn] Automat; Maschine; Apparat; Gerät **I**
　answering **machine** [ˈɑːnsrɪŋ məˌʃiːn] Anrufbeantworter **I**
　washing **machine** [ˈwɒʃɪŋ məˌʃiːn] Waschmaschine **II**

machinery [məˈʃiːnri] Maschinen **IV**

mad [mæd] verrückt; wütend **I**

Dear Sir or **Madam** [dɪə ˌsɜːr ɔː ˈmædəm] Sehr geehrte Dame, sehr geehrter Herr **II**

magazine [ˌmæɡəˈziːn] Zeitschrift **I**

magic [ˈmædʒɪk] Magie; Zauberei **II**
　to work **magic** (on) [ˌwɜːk ˈmædʒɪk] Zauber ausüben (auf) **III**

magical [ˈmædʒɪkl] magisch; Zauber- **II**

to **mail** [ˈiːmeɪl] mailen; per E-Mail schicken **II**

main [meɪn] Haupt- **I**
　main clause [ˈmeɪn ˌklɔːz] Hauptsatz **III**

the **mainland** *(no pl)* [ˈmeɪnlænd] Festland **III**

mainly [ˈmeɪnli] hauptsächlich; in erster Linie; vorwiegend **IV**

mainstream [ˈmeɪnstriːm] Masse; Durchschnitt; Massen-; Durchschnitts- **IV**

to **maintain** [meɪnˈteɪn] beibehalten; aufrechterhalten **V U3**, 72

majority [məˈdʒɒrəti] Mehrheit; Mehrzahl **IV**

*to **make** [meɪk] machen; tun; bilden; *hier:* ergeben **I**
　*to be **made** of [bi ˈmeɪd ˌəv] bestehen aus **III**
　*to be **made** up of [bi ˌmeɪd ˈʌp ˌəv] bestehen aus **I**
　*to **make** a choice [ˌmeɪk ə ˈtʃɔɪs] eine Wahl treffen **IV**
　*to **make** a decision [ˌmeɪk ə dɪˈsɪʒn] eine Entscheidung treffen **II**
　*to **make** a difference (to sth) [ˌmeɪk ə ˈdɪfrəns] etw. verändern; etw. bewegen **IV**
　*to **make** a team [ˌmeɪk ə ˈtiːm] sich für ein Team qualifizieren **III**
　*to **make** a wish [ˌmeɪk ə ˈwɪʃ] sich etwas wünschen **I**
　*to **make** friends [ˌmeɪk ˈfrendz] Freundschaft schließen **I**
　*to **make** it [ˈmeɪk ˌɪt] es schaffen **II**
　*to **make** money [ˌmeɪk ˈmʌni] Geld verdienen **I**
　*to **make** notes [ˌmeɪk ˈnəʊts] Notizen machen **I**
　*to **make** one's point [ˌmeɪk wʌnz ˈpɔɪnt] seinen Standpunkt deutlich machen; auf etwas hinauswollen; ein Argument anbringen **IV**
　*to **make** sb do sth [ˌmeɪk sʌmbədi ˈduː ˌsʌmθɪŋ] jmdn. veranlassen etw. zu tun **II**
　*to **make** sure [ˌmeɪk ˈʃɔː] sich versichern **II**
　*to **make** trouble [ˌmeɪk ˈtrʌbl] Ärger machen; in Schwierigkeiten bringen **I**

male [meɪl] männlich **IV**

mall [mɔːl] Einkaufszentrum **I**

man [mæn], **men** *(pl)* [men] Mann **I**

to **manage** (to do sth) [ˈmænɪdʒ] schaffen (etw. zu tun) **IV**

management [ˈmænɪdʒmənt] Management; Verwaltung **V U1**, 27

manager [ˈmænɪdʒə] Manager/-in **IV**

manga [ˈmæŋɡə] Manga *(japanischer Comic)* **I**

mango [ˈmæŋɡəʊ] Mango **I**

to **manipulate** [məˈnɪpjəleɪt] manipulieren; beeinflussen **V U2**, 55

manual [ˈmænjuəl] händisch; manuell **V U2**, 50

many [ˈmeni] viele **I**

Maori [ˈmaʊri] Maori **IV**

map [mæp] Stadtplan; Landkarte **I**
　mind **map** [ˈmaɪnd mæp] Wörternetz *(eine Art Schaubild)* **I**

maple [ˈmeɪpl] Ahorn **III**
　maple syrup [ˌmeɪpl ˈsɪrəp] Ahornsirup **II**

maracas [məˈrækəz] Rumba-Rasseln **II**

marathon [ˈmærəθn] Marathon **II**

March [mɑːtʃ] März **I**

march [mɑːtʃ] Marsch; Kundgebung **III**

to **march** [mɑːtʃ] marschieren **III**

mark *(BE)* [mɑːk] Note **IV**

to **mark** [mɑːk] markieren; kennzeichnen III

market ['mɑːkɪt] Markt I
flea **market** ['fliː ˌmɑːkɪt] Flohmarkt I

marmalade ['mɑːməleɪd] Marmelade aus Zitrusfrüchten III

marriage ['mærɪdʒ] Ehe; Heirat **V U2**, 51

to **marry** ['mæri] heiraten III

mass [mæs] Masse; Massen- III

massive ['mæsɪv] riesig; massiv IV

Master ['mɑːstə] Herr (histor. Anrede) III
master's degree ['mɑːstəz dɪˌɡriː] Master (zweithöchster akademischer Grad); Magister; Magistra IV

to **master** ['mɑːstə] meistern; beherrschen IV

match [mætʃ] Spiel; Match I

to **match** [mætʃ] zuordnen; passen zu; entsprechen I

mate [meɪt] Schiffsoffizier; Maat I; Partner/-in IV

mate (infml) [meɪt] Kumpel IV

material [mə'tɪəriəl] Material II

materialistic [məˌtɪəriə'lɪstɪk] materialistisch IV

Math (AE) (infml) [mæθ] Mathematik; Mathe III

Maths (infml) [mæθs] Mathematik; Mathe I

matter ['mætə] Angelegenheit; Frage IV
no **matter** [nəʊ 'mætə] egal; ganz gleich IV
What's the **matter**? [wɒts ðə 'mætə] Was ist los?; Was hast du? II

to **matter** ['mætə] von Bedeutung sein; etw. ausmachen II

matter-of-factly [ˌmætər əv 'fæktli] sachlich; nüchtern **V U3**, 71

to **mature** [mə'tjʊə] reifen **V F5**, 67

mature [mə'tjʊə] reif **V F5**, 66

maturity [mə'tjʊərəti] Reife **V F5**, 67

May [meɪ] Mai I

may [meɪ] (vielleicht) können; dürfen II

maybe ['meɪbi] vielleicht I

mayor ['meə] Bürgermeister/-in IV

maze [meɪz] Labyrinth; Gewirr IV

me [miː] ich; mich; mir I
Me too. [ˌmiː 'tuː] Ich auch. I

meal [miːl] Mahlzeit; Essen II
ready **meal** [ˌredi 'miːl] Fertiggericht I

*to **mean** [miːn] bedeuten I; meinen III
*to **mean** to [miːn] wollen III

mean [miːn] gemein III

meaning ['miːnɪŋ] Bedeutung; Sinn I

meaningful ['miːnɪŋfl] aussagekräftig; bedeutsam; wichtig IV

means, means (pl) [miːnz; miːnz] Mittel IV
means of transport (sg or pl) [ˌmiːnz əv 'trænspɔːt] Transportmittel; Verkehrsmittel III

the end justifies the **means** [ðiː ˌend dʒʌstɪfaɪz ðə 'miːnz] der Zweck heiligt die Mittel **V F5**, 67

meanwhile [ˌmiːn'waɪl] unterdessen; inzwischen IV

measure ['meʒə] Maßnahme IV

to **measure** ['meʒə] messen; abmessen **V U2**, 41

meat (no pl) [miːt] Fleisch II

mechanic [mə'kænɪk] Mechaniker/-in; Kfz-Mechaniker/-in IV

medal ['medl] Medaille **V U3**, 71

media ['miːdiə] Medien II
social **media** [ˌsəʊʃl 'miːdiə] soziale Netzwerke III

mediating Vermitteln; Schlichten II

mediation [ˌmiːdi'eɪʃn] Sprachmittlung I

medicine (no pl) ['medsn] Medizin; Medikamente II

medieval [ˌmedi'iːvl] mittelalterlich II

medium, media (pl) ['miːdiəm; 'miːdiə] Medium, Medien (Pl.) IV

*to **meet** [miːt] treffen; sich treffen I; erfüllen; entsprechen III
*to **meet** halfway [ˌmiːt hɑː'fweɪ] sich auf halbem Weg treffen II
*to **meet** sb's expectations [ˌmiːt sʌmbədiz ˌekspek'teɪʃnz] jmds. Erwartungen erfüllen IV
*to **meet** up [ˌmiːt 'ʌp] sich treffen III
*to **meet**/miss a deadline [ˌmiːt/mɪs ə 'dedlaɪn] einen (Abgabe-)Termin einhalten/verpassen **V U1**, 27

meeting ['miːtɪŋ] Meeting; Treffen; Besprechung IV
meeting point ['miːtɪŋ ˌpɔɪnt] Treffpunkt III

melody ['melədi] Melodie **V U1**, 21

to **melt** [melt] schmelzen II

member ['membə] Mitglied II

membership ['membəʃɪp] Mitgliedschaft IV

memorial [mə'mɔːriəl] Denkmal; Gedenkstätte; Denkschrift **V U2**, 40

memory ['memri] Erinnerung; Gedächtnis III

mental health [ˌmentl 'helθ] seelische Gesundheit **V U1**, 23

to **mention** ['menʃn] erwähnen II

mercy (no pl) ['mɜːsi] Mitleid; Erbarmen; Gnade **VTS**, 110

mess [mes] Unordnung; Durcheinander; Schweinerei **V U2**, 42
to look a **mess** [ˌlʊk ə 'mes] ungepflegt aussehen **V U2**, 42

to **mess** sth up (infml) [ˌmes 'ʌp] etw. vergeigen (ugs.) IV

message ['mesɪdʒ] Botschaft; Nachricht I
*to leave a **message** [ˌliːv ə 'mesɪdʒ] eine Nachricht hinterlassen I

*to take a **message** [ˌteɪk ə 'mesɪdʒ] eine Nachricht entgegennehmen; jmdm. etw. ausrichten I
text (**message**) ['tekst ˌmesɪdʒ] SMS; Kurznachricht I

messy ['mesi] unordentlich III

metal ['metl] Metall II

metaphor ['metəfə; 'metəfɔː] Metapher **V U1**, 18; **VTS**, 108

meter (AE) ['miːtə] Meter II

method ['meθəd] Methode IV

metre ['miːtə] Versmaß **VTS**, 108

Mexican ['meksɪkən] mexikanisch; Mexikanisch; aus Mexiko; Mexikaner/-in III

microphone ['maɪkrəfəʊn] Mikrofon (**V U2**, 58)

middle ['mɪdl] Mitte I
in the **middle** (of) [ɪn ðə 'mɪdl] in der Mitte (von); mitten in I
Middle Ages [ˌmɪdl 'eɪdʒɪz] Mittelalter III
middle school (AE) ['mɪdl ˌskuːl] Mittelschule (weiterführende Schule in den USA, Mittelstufe) II

midge [mɪdʒ] Mücke **V U1**, 14

midnight ['mɪdnaɪt] Mitternacht I

might [maɪt] könnte/-n (vielleicht) II

mile [maɪl] Meile (brit. und amerikan. Längenmaß) I
miles per hour (mph) [ˌmaɪlz pər 'aʊə] Meilen pro Stunde III

militant ['mɪlɪtnt] militant; aggressiv **V F4**, 63

milk [mɪlk] Milch I

mill [mɪl] Mühle IV; Fabrik **V U1**, 21

to **mill** around [ˌmɪl ə'raʊnd] umherlaufen IV

million ['mɪljən] Million I
I've done this a **million** times before. [aɪv dʌn ðɪs ə ˌmɪljən taɪmz bɪ'fɔː] Ich habe das schon eine Million Mal gemacht. II

mind [maɪnd] Geist; Verstand; Kopf III
bearing in **mind** [ˌbeərɪŋ ɪn 'maɪnd] angesichts (der Tatsache, dass …); wenn man berücksichtigt **V F2**, 33
to change one's **mind** [ˌtʃeɪndʒ wʌnz 'maɪnd] seine Meinung ändern III
*to come to one's **mind** [ˌkʌm tə wʌnz 'maɪnd] jmdm. in den Sinn kommen; jmdm. einfallen **V U1**, 21
*to keep in **mind** [ˌkiːp ɪn 'maɪnd] beachten; im Gedächtnis behalten IV
mind map ['maɪnd mæp] Wörternetz (eine Art Schaubild) I

to **mind** sth [maɪnd] auf etw. aufpassen III
to **mind** one's own business [ˌmaɪnd wʌnz əʊn 'bɪznɪs] sich um die eigenen Angelegenheiten kümmern **V U2**, 44
I don't **mind** … (+ -ing) [aɪ dəʊnt 'maɪnd] Ich habe nichts dagegen (zu) …; Mir macht es nichts aus (zu) … II

mindset ['maɪndset] Denkart; Mentalität **V F5**, 66

mine [maɪn] Mine **II**

mine [maɪn] mein/-er/-e/-es **II**

miner ['maɪnə] Bergarbeiter/-in **III**

mineral ['mɪnrl] Mineral **III**

mini [mɪni] Mini- **II**

mining ['maɪnɪŋ] Bergbau **II**

minister ['mɪnɪstə] Pfarrer/-in **V F4**, 62

minority [maɪ'nɒrəti] Minderheit **IV**

minute ['mɪnɪt] Minute **I**

miracle ['mɪrəkl] Wunder; Wunder- **IV**

mirror ['mɪrə] Spiegel **III**

mischievous ['mɪstʃɪvəs] schelmisch; boshaft **V U1**, 15

misery (no pl) ['mɪzri] Elend; Jammer; Not **V TS**, 113

misogynist [mɪ'sɒdʒnɪst] frauenfeindlich **V U3**, 77

Miss [mɪs] Fräulein (Anrede) **IV**

to miss [mɪs] verpassen; versäumen; vermissen **II**

*to meet/**miss** a deadline [ˌmi:t/mɪs ə 'dedlaɪn] einen (Abgabe-)Termin einhalten/verpassen **V U1**, 27

missing ['mɪsɪŋ] fehlend; verschwunden **II**

mission ['mɪʃn] Mission; Auftrag **IV**

mist [mɪst] Nebel; Dunst **III**

mistake [mɪ'steɪk] Fehler **I**

by **mistake** [baɪ mɪ'steɪk] versehentlich **III**

*to **mistake** sb/sth for sb/sth [mɪ'steɪk fə] jdn./etw. mit jdm./etw. verwechseln **V U2**, 48

Mistress ['mɪstrəs] Frau (histor. Anrede) **III**

misunderstood [ˌmɪsʌndə'stʊd] missverstanden **II**

mix [mɪks] Mix **II**

to mix [mɪks] mixen; mischen; vermischen **II**

to **mix** up [ˌmɪks ˌʌp] vermischen; durcheinanderbringen **III**

mixed bag [ˌmɪkst 'bæg] buntes Allerlei; bunte Mischung **I**

mobile ['məʊbaɪl] Handy; Mobiltelefon **II**

mobility [mə'bɪləti] Mobilität **IV**

moccasin ['mɒkəsɪn] Mokassin **III**

to mock [mɒk] spotten; höhnen **V U1**, 17

mode [məʊd] Modus; Betriebsart **V U3**, 80

model ['mɒdl] Modell; Tonmodell; Model **I**

role **model** ['rəʊl ˌmɒdl] Vorbild **IV**

to **model** sth on sth ['mɒdl ɒn] als Vorlage für etw. benutzen **V U3**, 76

moderator ['mɒdreɪtə] Moderator/-in **IV**

modern ['mɒdn] modern **II**

module ['mɒdju:l] Modul; Element **IV**

subscriber identity **module** [səbˌskraɪbər aɪ'dentəti ˌmɒdju:l] Teilnehmer-Identitätsmodul **V U3**, 80

moment ['məʊmənt] Moment; Augenblick **I**

at the **moment** [ət ðə 'məʊmənt] im Moment; gerade **I**

momentous [mə'məntəs] bedeutsam; weitreichend; folgenschwer **V U2**, 51

mommy (AE) ['mɑ:mi] Mama; Mami; Mutti **II**

monarch ['mɒnək] Monarch/-in **II**

constitutional **monarchy** [kɒnstɪˌtju:ʃnl 'mɒnəki] konstitutionelle Monarchie **IV**

Monday ['mʌndeɪ] Montag **I**

on **Mondays** [ɒn 'mʌndeɪz] montags **I**

money ['mʌni] Geld **I**

*to make **money** [ˌmeɪk 'mʌni] Geld verdienen **I**

pocket **money** ['pɒkɪt ˌmʌni] Taschengeld **I**

to raise **money** [ˌreɪz 'mʌni] Geld sammeln **II**

monster ['mɒnstə] Monster; Ungeheuer **I**

month [mʌnθ] Monat **I**

monument ['mɒnjəmənt] Monument; Denkmal **I**

mood [mu:d] Stimmung; Laune **IV**

moon [mu:n] Mond **I**

moon landing ['mu:n ˌlændɪŋ] Mondlandung **IV**

moonlight ['mu:nlaɪt] Mondlicht **III**

moose, **moose** (pl) [mu:s] Elch **II**

moral ['mɒrl] moralisch **IV**

more [mɔ:] mehr; weitere **I**

more and more ['mɔ:r ˌən mɔ:] immer mehr **III**

no **more** [ˌnəʊ 'mɔ:] nicht mehr **III**

not any **more** [ˌnɒt eni 'mɔ:] nicht mehr **I**

more … than ['mɔ: ðən] mehr … als **I**

moreover [mɔ:r'əʊvə] überdies; außerdem **III**

morning ['mɔ:nɪŋ] Morgen; Vormittag **I**

in the **mornings** [ˌɪn ðə 'mɔ:nɪŋz] morgens; vormittags **I**

Good **morning.** [ˌgʊd 'mɔ:nɪŋ] Guten Morgen.; Grüß Gott. **I**

excess **mortality** [ɪkˌses mɔ:'tæləti] Übersterblichkeit; überdurchschnittlich hohe Sterblichkeitsrate **V U1**, 20

mosaic [mə'zeɪɪk] Mosaik **III**

(the) **most** [ðə 'məʊst] der/die/das meiste; die meisten **I**

(the) **most** [ðə 'məʊst] am meisten **II**

at (the) **most** [ət ðə 'məʊst] höchstens **III**

mostly ['məʊstli] meistens; größtenteils; hauptsächlich **III**

mother ['mʌðə] Mutter **I**

motion ['məʊʃn] Bewegung **V TS**, 108

to motivate ['məʊtɪveɪt] motivieren **II**

motivation [ˌməʊtɪ'veɪʃn] Motivation; Beweggründe **IV**

mountain ['maʊntɪn] Berg **I**

mountain biking ['maʊntɪn ˌbaɪkɪŋ] Mountainbikefahren **I**

mountain range [ˌmaʊntɪn 'reɪndʒ] Bergkette **II**

mountainboarding ['maʊntɪnˌbɔ:dɪŋ] Mountainboardfahren **II**

to mourn [mɔ:n] trauern **IV**

mouse [maʊs], **mice** (pl) [maɪs] Maus, Mäuse **I**

mouth [maʊθ] Mund **I**

move [mu:v] Bewegung; Zug **IV**

to move [mu:v] (sich) bewegen **I**

to **move** (house) [mu:v (haʊs)] umziehen **I**

movement ['mu:vmənt] Bewegung **IV**

movie ['mu:vi] Film **I**

movie theater (AE) [ˌmu:vi 'θɪətə] Kino (amerik.) **I**

Mr ['mɪstə] Herr (Anrede) **I**

Mrs ['mɪsɪz] Frau (Anrede) **I**

Ms [mɪz] Frau (Anrede) **IV**

much [mʌtʃ] viel **I**

much [mʌtʃ] sehr **II**

very **much** [ˌveri 'mʌtʃ] sehr **I**

mud [mʌd] Schlamm **II**

muesli ['mju:zli] Müsli **III**

mug [mʌg] Becher **III**

multi- [ˌmʌlti] viel-; multi- **IV**

multicultural [ˌmʌlti'kʌltʃrl] multikulturell **III**

multiple ['mʌltɪpl] vielfältig; vielfach **V U2**, 51

mum [mʌm] Mama **I**

to mumble ['mʌmbl] murmeln; nuscheln **V U2**, 43

murder ['mɜ:də] Mord **III**

to murder ['mɜ:də] ermorden; umbringen **V U2**, 46

murderer ['mɜ:dərə] Mörder; Mörderin **V U2**, 46

muscle ['mʌsl] Muskel **IV**

museum [mju:'zi:əm] Museum **I**

music ['mju:zɪk] Musik **I**

folk **music** ['fəʊk ˌmju:zɪk] traditionelle Musik **V AC2**, 34

musical ['mju:zɪkl] musikalisch; Musik- **III**

musician [mju:'zɪʃn] Musiker/-in **II**

musketeer [ˌmʌskə'tɪə] Musketier (Soldat) **III**

Muslim ['mʊzlɪm] Muslim/-in; muslimisch **IV**

must [mʌst] müssen **I**

mustn't ['mʌsnt] nicht dürfen **I**

to mute [mju:t] stummschalten **V U3**, 83

mutual ['mju:tʃuəl] gegenseitig **V AC1**, 8

my [maɪ] mein/-e **I**

My name is … [maɪ 'neɪm ˌɪz] Ich heiße … **I**

mysterious [mɪ'stɪərɪəs] mysteriös; geheimnisvoll **II**

mystery ['mɪstri] Mysterium; Rätsel; Geheimnis **III**

myth [mɪθ] Mythos; Legende **V U1**, 15

mythical creature [ˌmɪθɪkl 'kri:tʃə] Fabelwesen **V U1**, 15

N

nail [neɪl] Nagel **VTS**, 109
naked ['neɪkɪd] nackt ⟨**V U3**, 86⟩
name [neɪm] Name **I**
name day ['neɪm ˌdeɪ] Namenstag **I**
My name is … [maɪ 'neɪm ˌɪz] Ich
heiße … **I**
What's your name? [wɒts jə 'neɪm] Wie
heißt du?; Wie heißen Sie? **I**
to name [neɪm] nennen; benennen **I**
*to be named after [bɪ 'neɪmd ˌɑ:ftə]
benannt sein nach **I**
nap [næp] Nickerchen **II**
napkin ['næpkɪn] Serviette **V U2**, 46
narrative ['nærətɪv] Erzähl-; erzählerisch **III**
narrator [nə'reɪtə] Erzähler/-in **IV**
first-person narrator [ˌfɜ:st ˌpɜ:sn
nə'reɪtə] Ich-Erzähler/-in **IV**
third-person narrator [θɜ:d ˌpɜ:sn
nə'reɪtə] Erzähler/-in, der/die in der 3.
Person erzählt **III**
narrow ['nærəʊ] eng; schmal **III**
narrow-minded [ˌnærəʊ'maɪndɪd] eng-
stirnig **V F5**, 67
nasty ['nɑ:sti] garstig; gemein **II**
nation ['neɪʃn] Nation **III**
national ['næʃnl] national; landesweit **I**
national park [ˌnæʃnl 'pɑ:k] Nationalpark; Naturpark **I**
nationality [ˌnæʃn'æləti] Nationalität;
Staatsangehörigkeit **II**
native ['neɪtɪv] einheimisch; eingeboren **III**
Native American [ˌneɪtɪv ə'merɪkən]
Ureinwohner/-in Amerikas; Indianer/-in;
indianisch **I**
native speaker [ˌneɪtɪv 'spi:kə] Mutter-
sprachler/-in **IV**
Native Studies (pl) ['neɪtɪv ˌstʌdiz] Studi-
enfach, das sich mit Ureinwohnern und
ihrer Kultur befasst **III**
natural ['nætʃrl] natürlich; Natur- **III**
nature ['neɪtʃə] Natur **II**
near [nɪə] nahe; in der Nähe von **I**
nearby [ˌnɪə'baɪ] in der Nähe **IV**
nearly ['nɪəli] fast; annähernd **II**
necessary ['nesəsri] nötig; notwendig;
erforderlich **II**
neck [nek] Hals; Nacken; Genick **IV**
necklace ['nekləs] Halskette **III**
need [ni:d] Bedürfnis **II**
(There's) no need to … [ˌðeəz nəʊ 'ni:d
tə] Es gibt keinen Grund zu … **III**
to need [ni:d] brauchen; benötigen **I**
to need (to do) [ni:d] (tun) müssen **I**
needn't ['ni:dnt] nicht brauchen; nicht
müssen **I**
needle ['ni:dl] Nadel **IV**
needy ['ni:di] bedürftig **V U3**, 76

negative ['negətɪv] negativ; verneint **I**
neglected [nɪ'glektɪd] vernachlässigt **IV**
to negotiate [nɪ'gəʊʃieɪt] verhandeln
V F2, 33
negotiation [nɪˌgəʊʃi'eɪʃn] Verhandlung
V F2, 33
neighborhood (AE) ['neɪbəhʊd] Nachbar-
schaft **III**
neighbour (BE) ['neɪbə] Nachbar/-in **I**
neither … nor … ['naɪðə/'ni:ðə … nɔ:]
weder … noch … **IV**
neither ['naɪðə; 'ni:ðə] keine/-r/-s (von
beiden) **IV**
nerd [nɜ:d] Nerd (Person, die intelligent,
aber sozial unbeholfen ist) **IV**
*to get on people's nerves [ˌget ɒn pi:plz
'nɜ:vz] jemandem auf die Nerven
gehen **I**
nervous ['nɜ:vəs] nervös; aufgeregt **I**
net [net] Netz **II**
netball ['netbɔ:l] Korbball **I**
social network [ˌsəʊʃl 'netwɜ:k] soziales
Netzwerk **II**
virtual private network [ˌvɜ:tʃʊəl praɪvət
'netwɜ:k] sichere Netzwerkverbindung
V U3, 80
neutral ['nju:trl] neutral **III**
never ['nevə] nie; niemals **I**
nevertheless [ˌnevəðə'les] trotzdem; dennoch; nichtsdestoweniger **IV**
new [nju:] neu **I**
newcomer ['nju:ˌkʌmə] Neuling; Neuan-
kömmling **IV**
news (sg) [nju:z] Nachrichten; Neuig-
keiten **I**
news report ['nju:z rɪˌpɔ:t] Tatsachenbericht; Nachrichtenbeitrag; Meldung **III**
newspaper ['nju:sˌpeɪpə] Zeitung **III**
next [nekst] nächste/-r/-s; der/die
Nächste(n) **I**
next door [nekst 'dɔ:] (von) nebenan **III**
next to ['nekst tə] neben **I**
next [nekst] als Nächstes **I**
NGO (non-governmental organisation)
[ˌendʒi:'əʊ] Nichtregierungsorganisation
IV
nice [naɪs] nett; schön; lieb **I**
Nice to meet you. [naɪs tə 'mi:t ju:] Nett,
dich/euch/Sie kennenzulernen. **II**
nickname ['nɪkneɪm] Spitzname **II**
night [naɪt] Nacht **I**
all night [ɔ:l 'naɪt] die ganze Nacht **I**
last night [lɑ:st 'naɪt] gestern Abend;
gestern Nacht **III**
nightmare ['naɪtmeə] Alptraum **III**
nine [naɪn] neun **I**
nineteen [ˌnaɪn'ti:n] neunzehn **I**
ninety ['naɪnti] neunzig **I**
no [nəʊ] kein/-e **I**
no longer [nəʊ 'lɒŋgə] nicht länger;
nicht mehr **IV**

no matter [nəʊ 'mætə] egal; ganz gleich
IV
no more [nəʊ 'mɔ:] nicht mehr **III**
no one ['nəʊ wʌn] niemand **I**
no sooner [nəʊ 'su:nə] kaum **IV**
no way [nəʊ 'weɪ] auf keinen Fall;
keineswegs **IV**
no wonder [nəʊ 'wʌndə] kein Wunder **II**
No worries. (Aus) [ˌnəʊ 'wʌriz] Kein
Problem.; Gern geschehen. **IV**
no [nəʊ] nein **I**
nobility [nə'bɪləti] Adel **V F1**, 10
nobleman ['nəʊblmən], noblemen (pl)
['nəʊblmən] Adliger **III**
nobody ['nəʊbədi] niemand **I**
nod [nɒd] Nicken **IV**
to nod [nɒd] nicken **IV**
noise [nɔɪz] Lärm; Geräusch **II**
noisy ['nɔɪzi] laut **II**
to nominate ['nɒmɪneɪt] nominieren;
ernennen **IV**
non- [nɒn] nicht- **III**
non-committal [ˌnɒnkə'mɪtl] unverbind-
lich **V U3**, 82
none [nʌn] keine/-r/-s **IV**
It's none of our business! [ɪts ˌnʌn əv
aʊə 'bɪznɪs] Das geht uns nichts an! **IV**
nonviolent [nɒn'vaɪələnt] gewaltlos **IV**
neither … nor … ['naɪðə/'ni:ðə … nɔ:]
weder … noch … **IV**
normal ['nɔ:ml] normal **I**
normally ['nɔ:mli] normalerweise **III**
Norman ['nɔ:mən] Normanne/Normannin;
normannisch **II**
north [nɔ:θ] Norden; Nord- **I**
north [nɔ:θ] nördlich; im Norden **I**
nose [nəʊz] Nase **II**
*to blow one's nose [ˌbləʊ wʌnz 'nəʊz]
sich die Nase putzen **III**
not [nɒt] nicht **I**
not any more [nɒt eni 'mɔ:] nicht mehr **I**
not either [nɒt … 'aɪðə; nɒt … 'i:ðə]
auch nicht **I**
not even [nɒt ˌ'i:vn] nicht einmal; noch
nicht einmal **III**
not only … but (also) [nɒt ˌəʊnli … bʌt
'ɔ:lsəʊ] nicht nur … sondern (auch) **IV**
not … any [nɒt eni] kein/-e/-en **I**
not … anything [ˌnɒt 'eniθɪŋ] nichts **I**
not … until [nɒt ən'tɪl] nicht bevor; erst
wenn **I**
not … yet [nɒt 'jet] noch nicht **II**
notable ['nəʊtəbl] bedeutend; beachtlich
V AC2, 34
note [nəʊt] Notiz; Anmerkung **I**
*to make notes [ˌmeɪk 'nəʊts] Notizen
machen **I**
*to take notes [teɪk 'nəʊts] sich Notizen
machen **I**
to note [nəʊt] notieren **II**
notebook ['nəʊtbʊk] Heft; Notizbuch;
Notebook (Computer) ⟨**V U2**, 58⟩

nothing ['nʌθɪŋ] nichts **I**
  There's **nothing** more exciting than …
  [ðeəz ˌnʌθɪŋ mɔːˌrˌɪkˈsaɪtɪŋ ðən] Es gibt
  nichts Spannenderes als … **I**
to **notice** ['nəʊtɪs] bemerken; wahrnehmen **I**
noticeboard ['nəʊtɪsbɔːd] schwarzes Brett
  V U3, 84
notion ['nəʊʃn] Idee; Vorstellung 〈**V U3**, 87〉
notorious [nəˈtɔːriəs] berüchtigt **V U3**, 76
to **nourish** ['nʌrɪʃ] ernähren **V U2**, 45
novel ['nɒvl] Roman **III**
  coming-of-age **novel** [ˌkʌmɪŋˌəvˈeɪdʒ
  ˌnɒvl] Entwicklungsroman; Bildungsroman **V F5**, 67
  graphic **novel** [ˌɡræfɪk ˈnɒvl] Comicroman **III**
November [nəˈvembə] November **I**
now [naʊ] jetzt; nun **I**
  right **now** [ˌraɪt ˈnaʊ] jetzt gleich; sofort;
  gerade **II**
nowadays ['naʊədeɪz] heutzutage **IV**
nowhere ['nəʊweə] nirgendwo; nirgend-
  wohin **II**
number ['nʌmbə] Zahl; Nummer **I**
numerous ['njuːmrəs] zahlreich **V AC3**, 64
nun [nʌn] Nonne **IV**
nurse [nɜːs] Krankenschwester; Kranken-
  pfleger **III**
nursery school ['nɜːsri ˌskuːl] Vorschule;
  Kindergarten **IV**
nut [nʌt] Nuss **I**

O

o'clock [əˈklɒk] Uhr (Zeitangabe bei vollen
  Stunden) **I**
oak [əʊk] Eiche **V U1**, 17
obesity [əˈbiːsəti] Fettleibigkeit **V U2**, 45
to **obey** [əˈbeɪ] gehorchen **III**
object ['ɒbdʒɪkt] Gegenstand **II**
to **object** [əbˈdʒekt] ablehnen; Einspruch
  erheben **V F2**, 33
objective [əbˈdʒektɪv] objektiv **IV**
obligation [ˌɒblɪˈɡeɪʃn] Verpflichtung
  V U2, 51
obscure [əbˈskjʊə] unbekannt; obskur
  V U3, 73
observer [əbˈzɜːvə] Beobachter/-in;
  Zuschauer/-in **V U2**, 48
obvious ['ɒbviəs] offensichtlich **III**
occasion [əˈkeɪʒn] Gelegenheit; Anlass
  V AC3, 64; **VTS**, 108
occupation [ˌɒkjəˈpeɪʃn] Beruf; Beschäftigung **IV**
ocean ['əʊʃn] Ozean **II**
October [ɒkˈtəʊbə] Oktober **I**
odd [ɒd] seltsam; komisch **V U3**, 75
  Find the **odd** one out! [ˌfaɪnd ðiˌˌɒd
  wʌˌnˌ ˈaʊt] Finde das Element, das nicht
  in die Gruppe passt! **II**
of [ɒv; əv] von **I**

of course [əv ˈkɔːs] natürlich; selbstverständlich **I**
off [ɒf] (von …) weg/ab/herunter **III**
  off to ['ɒf tə] auf nach **II**
  *to show **off** [ˌʃəʊ ˈɒf] angeben **II**
  to sign **off** [ˌsaɪn ˈɒf] aufhören; Schluss
  machen **V U3**, 81
  *to take **off** [ˌteɪk ˈɒf] abnehmen; herunternehmen; ausziehen **II**
  to turn **off** [ˌtɜːnˌ ˈɒf] abschalten; ausschalten **II**
to **offend** [əˈfend] beleidigen; verletzen **IV**
special **offer** [ˌspeʃl ˈɒfə] Sonderangebot **I**
to **offer** ['ɒfə] anbieten **II**
office ['ɒfɪs] Büro **I**
  tax **office** ['tæksˌɒfɪs] Finanzamt **V U3**, 76
  term of **office** [ˌtɜːmˌəv ˈɒfɪs] Amtszeit **IV**
  ticket **office** ['tɪkɪt ˌɒfɪs] Kartenschalter
  III
chief executive **officer** (CEO) [ˌtʃiːf
  ɪɡˌzekjuːtɪv ˈɒfɪsə] Vorstandvorsitzende/-r;
  Geschäftsführer/-in **V U2**, 51
police **officer** [pəˈliːsˌ ˌɒfɪsə] Polizeibeam-
  ter/Polizeibeamtin; Polizist/-in **II**
official [əˈfɪʃl] Schiedsrichter/-in **II**
official [əˈfɪʃl] offiziell **III**
  official language [əˌfɪʃl ˈlæŋɡwɪdʒ]
  Amtssprache **I**
offline ['ɒflaɪn] offline **II**
often ['ɒfn] oft; häufig **I**
oh [əʊ] null (bei Telefonnummern und
  Uhrzeitangaben) **I**
Oh! [əʊ] O! **I**
  Oh dear! [əʊ ˈdɪə] Oje! **II**
oil [ɔɪl] Öl **I**
oily ['ɔɪli] ölig **IV**
ointment ['ɔɪntmənt] Salbe **II**
OK [əʊˈkeɪ] o.k.; in Ordnung **I**
old [əʊld] alt **I**
  11-year-**old** [ɪˈlevnˌjɪərəʊld] 11-Jähri-
  ge/-r **II**
  How **old** are you? [haʊ ˈəʊldˌə ˈjuː] Wie
  alt bist du?; Wie alt sind Sie? **I**
old-fashioned [ˌəʊldˈfæʃnd] altmodisch **III**
on [ɒn] weiter **IV**
on [ɒn] auf; an; am; in; im **I**
  *to be **on** [biˌ ˈɒn] an sein; laufen **II**
  on average [ɒnˈ ˌævrɪdʒ] durchschnittlich; im Durchschnitt **III**
  on Mondays [ɒn ˈmʌndeɪz] montags **I**
  on remand [ɒn rɪˈmɑːnd] in Untersuchungshaft **V U1**, 24
  on the brink of [ˌɒn ðə ˈbrɪŋkˌəv] am
  Rande von; kurz vor **III**
  on the contrary [ˌɒn ðə ˈkɒntrəri] im
  Gegenteil **IV**
  on the left [ɒn ðə ˈleft] auf der linken
  Seite; links **I**
  on the right [ɒn ðə ˈraɪt] auf der rechten
  Seite; rechts **I**
  on time [ɒn ˈtaɪm] pünktlich **II**
  on top [ɒn ˈtɒp] oben; obendrauf **I**

on your own [ɒn jərˌˈəʊn] allein; für
  dich **I**
  *to put **on** [ˌpʊt ˈɒn] anziehen; auftragen
  II
  Come **on**! [ˌkʌm ˈɒn] Komm schon!;
  Komm jetzt! **I**
once [wʌns] einmal; einst **II**
once [wʌns] sobald; als **IV**
one [wʌn] eins **I**
  one hundred [ə ˈhʌndrəd; wʌn ˈhʌndrəd]
  einhundert; hundert **I**
  one-sided [ˌwʌnˈsaɪdɪd] einseitig **IV**
  twenty-**one** [ˌtwentiˈwʌn] einundzwanzig **I**
one [wʌn], **ones** [wʌnz] (pl) eine/-r/-s **II**
onion ['ʌnjən] Zwiebel **III**
online [ɒnˈlaɪn] online **I**
only ['əʊnli] einzige/-r/-s **II**
  only child ['əʊnli ˌtʃaɪld] Einzelkind **I**
only ['əʊnli] erst; bloß; nur **I**
  not **only** … but (also) [nɒtˌəʊnli … bʌt
  ˈɔːlsəʊ] nicht nur … sondern (auch) **IV**
onto ['ɒntə] auf **II**
Oops! [uːps] Hoppla!; Huch! **I**
opal ['əʊpl] Opal **IV**
to **open** ['əʊpn] öffnen; aufmachen **I**; er-
  öffnen **III**
  to **open** to ['əʊpn tə] führen zu/in **III**
open ['əʊpn] offen; geöffnet; aufgeschla-
  gen **I**
  open-minded ['əʊpnˌmaɪndɪd] offen;
  aufgeschlossen **V F5**, 66
opening ['əʊpnɪŋ] Öffnung **III**
opera ['ɒprə] Oper **IV**
to **operate** ['ɒpreɪt] operieren **V U3**, 72
  operating system ['ɒpreɪtɪŋ ˌsɪstəm]
  Betriebssystem **V U3**, 80
opinion [əˈpɪnjən] Meinung **II**
  in sb's **opinion** [ɪn ˌsʌmbədizˌəˈpɪnjən]
  jmds. Meinung nach **II**
opponent [əˈpəʊnənt] Gegner/-in; Wider-
  sacher/-in **V F2**, 33; 〈**V U2**, 57〉
opportunity [ˌɒpəˈtjuːnəti] Chance; Gelegenheit; Möglichkeit **IV**
sth as **opposed** to sth [æzˌəˈpəʊzd tə] etw.
  im Gegensatz zu etw. **V F5**, 67
opposite ['ɒpəzɪt] Gegenteil **II**
opposite ['ɒpəzɪt] gegenüber; gegenüber-
  liegend; entgegengesetzt **II**
opposition [ˌɒpəˈzɪʃn] Opposition; Widerstand **V AC4**, 88
to **oppress** [əˈpres] unterdrücken **IV**
oppression [əˈpreʃn] Unterdrückung
  V F4, 63
oppressive [əˈpresɪv] unterdrückerisch;
  gewaltsam; repressiv **V U2**, 46
option ['ɒpʃn] Möglichkeit; Wahl; Option **III**
or [ɔː] oder **I**
  either … **or** … ['aɪðə/'iːðə … ɔː] entweder … oder … **II**
oral ['ɔːrl] mündlich **V U1**, 12
orange ['ɒrɪndʒ] Orange **I**

orange ['ɒrɪndʒ] orange **I**

orator ['ɒrətə] Redner/-in **V U2**, 52

order ['ɔ:də] Reihenfolge; Ordnung **I**; Befehl **III**

in **order** to [ɪn ˈɔ:də tə] um … zu; mit der Absicht, zu **III**

to order ['ɔ:də] bestellen **III**

ordinary ['ɔ:dnri] gewöhnlich; normal **IV**

organic [ɔ:'gænɪk] biologisch (angebaut) **IV**

organisation [ˌɔ:gənaɪ'zeɪʃn] Organisation **II**

to organise ['ɔ:gənaɪz] organisieren **I**

*to get organised [ˌget ˈɔ:gənaɪzd] sich organisieren **III**

organiser ['ɔ:gənaɪzə] Organisator/-in **III**

Oriental [ˌɔ:ri'entl] orientalisch **V AC2**, 34

orientation [ˌɔ:riən'teɪʃn] Orientierung; Orientierungs- **III**

origin ['ɒrɪdʒɪn] Ursprung; Herkunft; Abstammung **II**

original [ə'rɪdʒnl] Original **III**

original [ə'rɪdʒnl] original; ursprünglich **III**

to originate [ə'rɪdʒɪneɪt] entstehen; seinen Anfang nehmen **V U2**, 45

orphanage ['ɔ:fnɪdʒ] Waisenhaus **IV**

other ['ʌðə] anders; andere/-r/-s; weitere **I**

each other [ˌi:tʃ 'ʌðə] einander; sich; sich gegenseitig **I**

the others [ði ˈʌðəz] die anderen **I**

otherwise ['ʌðəwaɪz] sonst **III**

Ouch! [aʊtʃ] Aua! **II**

ought to (+ inf) ['ɔ:t tə] sollen ⟨**V U2**, 58⟩

our [aʊə; ɑ:] unser/-e **I**

ours unser/-er/-e/-es **II**

out [aʊt] außerhalb; heraus; hinaus; nach draußen **I**

*to be out [bi ˈaʊt] out sein **II**

to clear out [klɪər ˈaʊt] ausräumen; entrümpeln **I**

*to come out [kʌm ˈaʊt] sich outen **IV**

*to hang out (with) (infml) [ˌhæŋ ˈaʊt wɪð] rumhängen (mit); sich herumtreiben (mit); sich treffen (mit) **I**

out of ['aʊt əv] aus … heraus **II**; von **III**

out of breath [ˌaʊt əv 'breθ] außer Atem **III**

out of focus [ˌaʊt əv 'fəʊkəs] unscharf **III**

to pick out [pɪk ˈaʊt] aussuchen; auswählen; heraushören; herausfiltern; herauslesen **I**

*to run out [ˌrʌn ˈaʊt] ausgehen **IV**

the outback [ði 'aʊtbæk] Outback (australisches Hinterland) **IV**

outcome ['aʊtkʌm] Ergebnis; Ausgang **V U2**, 52

outdated [ˌaʊt'deɪtɪd] veraltet; überholt **IV**

outdoor ['aʊtdɔ:] Freiluft-; Outdoor- **II**

the great outdoors [ðə ˌgreɪt ˌaʊt'dɔ:z] die freie Natur **II**

outdoors [ˌaʊt'dɔ:z] draußen; im Freien **I**

outfit ['aʊtfɪt] Outfit; Kleidung **I**

outgoing [ˌaʊt'gəʊɪŋ] kontaktfreudig **IV**

outlaw ['aʊtlɔ:] Geächtete/-r; Gesetzlose/-r **II**

outline ['aʊtlaɪn] Skizze; Umriss **IV**

outside [ˌaʊt'saɪd] nach draußen; draußen; außerhalb (von) **I**

outstanding [ˌaʊt'stændɪŋ] außergewöhnlich; herausragend **IV**

over ['əʊvə] hinüber; über **I**; vorüber; vorbei **II**

*to bend over [ˌbend ˈəʊvə] sich vorbeugen; sich beugen über ⟨**V U1**, 30⟩

*to go over to [ˌgəʊ ˈəʊvə tə] hinübergehen zu; zu jmdm. nach Hause gehen **II**

over the top (infml) [ˌəʊvə ðə 'tɒp] übertrieben; überzogen **IV**

over there [ˌəʊvə 'ðeə] da drüben; dort drüben **I**

to turn over [ˌtɜ:n ˈəʊvə] umdrehen; umkippen **II**

overall [ˌəʊvər'ɔ:l] insgesamt **IV**

overboard ['əʊvəˌbɔ:d] über Bord **III**

*to overcome [ˌəʊvə'kʌm] überwinden **V F4**, 63

*to overhear [ˌəʊvə'hɪə] belauschen; zufällig mit anhören **IV**

overjoyed [ˌəʊvə'dʒɔɪd] überglücklich **V U1**, 18

to overlap [ˌəʊvə'læp] (sich) überlappen **V U2**, 51

overnight [ˌəʊvə'naɪt] über Nacht **II**

overprotective [ˌəʊvəprə'tektɪv] überfürsorglich **V F5**, 66

to overreact [ˌəʊvəri'ækt] überreagieren **II**

overseas [ˌəʊvə'si:z] in Übersee; im Ausland **IV**

overseer ['əʊvəˌsi:ə] Aufseher/-in; Vorarbeiter/-in **V F3**, 37

overt [əʊ'vɜ:t] offen; offenkundig **V U2**, 49

overview ['əʊvəvju:] Überblick **IV**

overweight [ˌəʊvə'weɪt] übergewichtig **IV**

overwhelmed [ˌəʊvə'welmd] überwältigt **V U3**, 83

to own [əʊn] besitzen **IV**

own [əʊn] eigene/-r/-s **I**

on your own [ˌɒn jər ˈəʊn] allein; für dich **I**

owner ['əʊnə] Besitzer/-in **IV**

P

p.m. [ˌpi:'em] nachmittags (Uhrzeit); abends (Uhrzeit) **I**

to pace [peɪs] hin und her gehen **V U2**, 43

Pacific Islander [pəˌsɪfɪk ˈaɪlændə] Bewohner/-in einer Pazifischen Insel **IV**

to pack [pæk] packen; einpacken **III**

package ['pækɪdʒ] Paket **V U3**, 84

to package ['pækɪdʒ] verpacken **V TS**, 114

packaging ['pækɪdʒɪŋ] Verpackung; Verpackungsmaterial **IV**

packet ['pækɪt] Päckchen; Paket; Packung **I**

pad [pæd] Schreibblock **V U3**, 70

to paddle ['pædl] paddeln **II**

page [peɪdʒ] Seite **I**

pain [peɪn] Schmerz **II**

to paint [peɪnt] anmalen; malen **I**

painting ['peɪntɪŋ] Malerei; Gemälde **IV**

pair [peə] Paar **I**

palace ['pæləs] Palast **III**

pale [peɪl] bleich; blass **V U3**, 71

palm tree ['pɑ:m ˌtri:] Palme **II**

pancake ['pænkeɪk] Pfannkuchen **I**

solar panel [ˌsəʊlə 'pænl] Sonnenkollektor **V U1**, 24

to panic ['pænɪk] panisch werden **III**

panther ['pænθə] Panther; Puma **II**

pants (pl) (AE) [pænts] Hosen **II**

hot pants ['hɒt pænts] Hotpants **II**

paper ['peɪpə] Papier **I**; Zeitung **IV**

parade [pə'reɪd] Parade; Umzug **II**

paradise ['pærədaɪs] Paradies **II**

paragraph ['pærəgrɑ:f] Paragraf; Absatz **III**

parcel ['pɑ:sl] Paket; Päckchen **IV**

parents (pl) ['peərənts] Eltern **I**

park [pɑ:k] Park **I**

national park [ˌnæʃnl 'pɑ:k] Nationalpark; Naturpark **I**

theme park ['θi:m ˌpɑ:k] Vergnügungspark (meist mit einem bestimmten Thema); Themenpark **I**

parliament ['pɑ:ləmənt] Parlament **II**

parliamentary democracy [pɑ:ləˌmentri dɪ'mɒkrəsi] parlamentarische Demokratie **IV**

parrot ['pærət] Papagei **IV**

part [pɑ:t] Teil; Stadtteil **I**

part of speech [ˌpɑ:t əv 'spi:tʃ] Wortart; Wortklasse **V U1**, 26

*to take part (in) [teɪk 'pɑ:t (ɪn)] teilnehmen (an) **II**

to part [pɑ:t] trennen; sich teilen; auseinandergehen **IV**

partially sighted [ˌpɑ:ʃli 'saɪtɪd] sehbehindert; teilsichtig **II**

participant [pɑ:'tɪsɪpnt] Teilnehmer/-in **IV**

to participate [pɑ:'tɪsɪpeɪt] teilnehmen **IV**

participation [pɑ:ˌtɪsɪ'peɪʃn] Mitwirkung; Beteiligung; Teilnahme **IV**

particular [pə'tɪkjələ] bestimmte/-r/-s **III**; besonders **IV**

partly ['pɑ:tli] teilweise **IV**

partner ['pɑ:tnə] Partner/-in **I**

partnership ['pɑ:tnəʃɪp] Partnerschaft **V U1**, 27

party ['pɑ:ti] Party; Feier **I**; Partei **IV**

pass [pɑ:s] Ausweis; Pass **II**

hall pass ['hɔ:l ˌpɑ:s] Erlaubnis, sich während des Unterrichts auf dem Flur aufzuhalten **III**

to pass [pɑ:s] zupassen; zuspielen **II**; durchgehen; vorbeigehen (an); passieren **III**; bestehen **IV**; verabschieden (Gesetze) **V F4**, 61

to **pass** (on) [pɑːsˈɒn] weitergeben **IV**
to **pass** away [ˌpɑːs əˈweɪ] versterben; entschlafen **V U1**, 23
passage [ˈpæsɪdʒ] Überfahrt; Passage **V F3**, 36
passenger [ˈpæsndʒə] Passagier/-in; Fahrgast **II**
passion [ˈpæʃn] Passion; Leidenschaft **IV**
passionate [ˈpæʃnət] leidenschaftlich **IV**
*to be **passionate** about sth [bi ˈpæʃnət əˌbaʊt] etw. leidenschaftlich gern tun; eine Leidenschaft für etw. haben; für etw. brennen **IV**
passport [ˈpɑːspɔːt] Pass; Reisepass **II**
past [pɑːst] Vergangenheit **II**
in the **past** [ɪn ðə ˈpɑːst] früher; in der Vergangenheit **II**
past [pɑːst] vergangen; letzte/-r/-s **III**
past [pɑːst] nach (bei Uhrzeitangaben) **I**; vorbei (an); vorüber (an) **II**
half **past** [ˌhɑːf ˈpɑːst] halb (bei Uhrzeitangaben) **I**
quarter **past**/to [ˈkwɔːtə pɑːst/tə] Viertel nach/vor **I**
pasta [ˈpæstə] Pasta; Nudeln **I**
patch [pætʃ] Fleck; Stelle ⟨**V U1**, 30⟩
path [pɑːθ] Pfad; Weg **II**
coastal **path** [ˌkəʊstl ˈpɑːθ] Küstenweg **II**
pathetic [pəˈθetɪk] erbärmlich; armselig **IV**
patient [ˈpeɪʃnt] geduldig **IV**
pattern [ˈpætn] Muster **V F4**, 62; **VTS**, 108
pay [peɪ] Lohn; Gehalt **IV**
*to **pay** (for) [peɪ] bezahlen **I**
*to **pay** attention to [ˌpeɪ əˈtenʃn tə] beachten **II**
payment [ˈpeɪmənt] Bezahlung; Lohn; Zahlung **IV**
PC (= personal computer) [piːˈsiː] PC **II**
PE (Physical Education) [piːˈiː] Sportunterricht **I**
peace [piːs] Frieden **II**
peaceful [ˈpiːsfl] friedlich **IV**
peak [piːk] Gipfel; Spitze **II**
peak [piːk] Haupt-; Spitzen- **III**
peasant [ˈpeznt] Kleinbauer/-bäuerin **V F1**, 10
pedestrian [pɪˈdestriən] Fußgänger/-in; Fußgänger- **IV**
pedestrian zone [pɪˈdestriən zəʊn] Fußgängerzone **IV**
peer [pɪə] Mitglied des britischen Oberhauses **IV**
peer group [ˈpɪə gruːp] Gruppe von Gleichaltrigen **V U2**, 49
pen [pen] Füller **I**
penal colony [ˈpiːnl ˌkɒləni] Strafkolonie **IV**
pencil [ˈpensl] Bleistift; Buntstift **I**
pencil-case [ˈpensl ˌkeɪs] Federmäppchen; Mäppchen **I**
penknife [ˈpenaɪf], **penknives** (pl) [penaɪvz] Taschenmesser **V U1**, 17

penny [ˈpeni], **pence** (pl) [pens] Penny (brit. Währungseinheit) **I**
people [ˈpiːpl] Volk **III**
people (pl) [ˈpiːpl] Leute; Menschen **I**
people skills (pl) [ˈpiːpl ˌskɪlz] soziale Kompetenz **IV**
pep talk [ˈpep ˌtɔːk] aufmunternde Worte; Motivationsgespräch **V U2**, 46
per [pɜː; pə] pro **II**
per capita [pə ˈkæpɪtə] pro Kopf; Pro-Kopf-; pro Person **IV**
percent, **percent** (pl) [pəˈsent] Prozent **III**
percentage [pəˈsentɪdʒ] Prozentsatz **IV**
perception [pəˈsepʃn] Wahrnehmung **IV**
percussion [pəˈkʌʃn] Percussion; Schlaginstrumente **II**
perfect [ˈpɜːfɪkt] perfekt; vollkommen **II**
perfection [pəˈfekʃn] Perfektion; Vollkommenheit **IV**
to **perform** [pəˈfɔːm] durchführen; verrichten **IV**
performance [pəˈfɔːməns] Aufführung; Vorstellung; Leistung **IV**
performer [pəˈfɔːmə] Darsteller/-in; Künstler/-in **III**
perhaps [pəˈhæps] vielleicht **III**
period [ˈpɪəriəd] Periode; Zeitspanne **III**
period (AE) [ˈpɪəriəd] Stunde; Unterrichtsstunde **III**
permanent [ˈpɜːmnənt] permanent; dauerhaft **III**
permission [pəˈmɪʃn] Erlaubnis; Genehmigung **IV**
to **permit** [pəˈmɪt] erlauben; genehmigen **IV**
persecution [ˌpɜːsɪˈkjuːʃn] Verfolgung **V F4**, 62
person [ˈpɜːsn], **people** (pl) [ˈpiːpl] Person; Mensch **I**
persona, **personae** (pl) [pəˈsəʊnə, pəˈsəʊniː] Rolle; lyrisches Ich **V U3**, 77
personal [ˈpɜːsnl] persönlich **II**
to **personalise** [ˈpɜːsnlaɪz] persönlich gestalten; individualisieren **VTS**, 117
personality [ˌpɜːsnˈæləti] Persönlichkeit **II**
personnel services (pl) [pɜːsnˈel ˌsɜːvɪsɪz] Personaldienstleistungen **IV**
perspective [pəˈspektɪv] Perspektive; Blickwinkel **II**
to **persuade** [pəˈsweɪd] überreden **III**
persuasive [pəˈsweɪsɪv] überzeugend **III**
pet [pet] Haustier **I**
petition [pəˈtɪʃn] Petition; Gesuch; Unterschriftenliste **IV**
petrol (BE) [ˈpetrl] Benzin **IV**
phase [feɪz] Phase **IV**
philosopher [fɪˈlɒsəfə] Philosoph/-in **V F1**, 11
phishing [ˈfɪʃɪŋ] Ausspionieren (von Daten zu kriminellen Zwecken) **V U3**, 83
phone [fəʊn] Telefon; Handy **I**

to answer the **phone** [ˌɑːnsə ðə ˈfəʊn] einen Anruf entgegennehmen **I**
cell **phone** (AE) [ˈsel fəʊn] Mobiltelefon; Handy **II**
phone call [ˈfəʊn ˌkɔːl] Anruf; Telefonanruf **I**
photo [ˈfəʊtəʊ] Foto; Fotografie **I**
in the **photo**(s) [ɪn ðə ˈfəʊtəʊ(z)] auf dem Foto/den Fotos **I**
photo shoot [ˈfəʊtəʊ ˌʃuːt] Fotoshooting; Fotoaufnahmen **III**
photo story [ˈfəʊtəʊ ˌstɔːri] Fotostory; Bildgeschichte **I**
*to take **photos** [ˌteɪk ˈfəʊtəʊz] fotografieren; Fotos machen **I**
to **photobomb** [ˈfəʊtəʊbɒm] ins Foto laufen **III**
photographer [fəˈtɒgrəfə] Fotograf/-in **III**
phrase [freɪz] Redewendung; Ausdruck; Satz **I**
physical [ˈfɪzɪkl] physisch; körperlich **II**
to **pick** [pɪk] pflücken **V U3**, 70
to **pick** out [pɪk ˈaʊt] aussuchen; auswählen; heraushören; herausfiltern; herauslesen **IV**
to **pick** up [pɪk ˈʌp] aufheben; abholen **II**
pickup [ˈpɪkʌp] Pickup; Kleintransporter **III**
picnic [ˈpɪknɪk] Picknick **I**
picture [ˈpɪktʃə] Bild; Foto **I**
pidgin [ˈpɪdʒɪn] Pidgin **V AC1**, 8
pie [paɪ] Kuchen; Pastete **I**
piece [piːs] Stück **I**
pier [pɪə] Pier; Hafendamm **I**
piercing [ˈpɪəsɪŋ] Piercing **II**
pig [pɪg] Schwein **I**
guinea **pig** [ˈgɪni ˌpɪg] Meerschweinchen **I**
pile [paɪl] Stapel; Haufen **V U1**, 14
Pilgrim [ˈpɪlgrɪm] Pilger/-in **II**; Pilger/-in (Person, die 1620 aus religiösen Gründen nach Amerika auswanderte) **III**
pill [pɪl] Pille; Tablette **I**
pilot [ˈpaɪlət] Pilot/-in **IV**
pine [paɪn] Kiefer; Pinie **IV**
pink [pɪŋk] pink; rosa **I**
pioneer [ˌpaɪəˈnɪə] Pionier/-in **III**
pipe [paɪp] Rohr; Rohrleitung **II**; Pfeife **III**; Dudelsackpfeife **V U1**, 13
pit [pɪt] Grube; Bergwerk **III**
pitch [pɪtʃ] Spielfeld; Platz **II**
pizza [ˈpiːtsə] Pizza **I**
place [pleɪs] Ort; Stelle; Platz **I**
in the first **place** [ɪn ðə ˈfɜːst ˌpleɪs] überhaupt erst; von vornherein **IV**
*to take **place** [ˌteɪk ˈpleɪs] stattfinden **I**
to **place** [pleɪs] unterbringen **IV**; platzieren; schalten **V U3**, 83
placemat [ˈpleɪsmæt] Placemat; Platzdeckchen **III**
plain [pleɪn] Ebene **IV**
plain [pleɪn] klar; schlicht; einfach; deutlich **IV**

plan [plæn] Plan; Entwurf **I**

to **plan** [plæn] planen **I**

plane [pleɪn] Flugzeug **II**

planet ['plænɪt] Planet **II**

planner ['plænə] Handbuch; Kalender **I**

plant [plɑːnt] Pflanze **II**

to **plant** [plɑːnt] pflanzen; anpflanzen **III**

plantation [plænˈteɪʃn] Plantage **IV**

plaster cast ['plɑːstə ˌkɑːst] Gipsverband **III**

plastic ['plæstɪk] Plastik; Kunststoff; Plastik- **IV**

plastic surgery (no pl) [ˌplæstɪk 'sɜːdʒəri] Schönheitschirurgie **IV**

plate [pleɪt] Teller **III**

platform ['plætfɔːm] Plattform; Bahnsteig **II**

play [pleɪ] Theaterstück **III**

role **play** ['rəʊl ˌpleɪ] Rollenspiel **I**

to **play** [pleɪ] spielen **I**

to **play** a trick (on) [ˌpleɪ ə 'trɪk ˌɒn] einen Streich spielen **I**

to **play** bowls [ˌpleɪ 'bəʊlz] Bowling spielen **III**

player ['pleɪə] Spieler/-in; Mitspieler/-in **II**

playground ['pleɪgraʊnd] Schulhof; Pausenhof; Spielplatz **V F3**, 39

Please. [pliːz] Bitte. **I**

pleased [pliːzd] erfreut; zufrieden **IV**

pleasure ['pleʒə] Freude; Vergnügen **IV**

to **pledge** [pledʒ] geloben **V F1**, 10

to **pledge** allegiance [ˌpledʒ əˈliːdʒns] Treueschwur leisten **V F1**, 10

plenty of ['plenti ˌəv] eine Menge **V U3**, 82

plot [plɒt] Handlung **III**

plough [plaʊ] Pflug ⟨**V U1**, 29⟩

plum [plʌm] Pflaume **I**

plumber ['plʌmə] Installateur/-in; Klempner/-in **II**

plumbing ['plʌmɪŋ] Sanitärarbeit **II**

to **plunge in** [ˌplʌndʒ 'ɪn] sich hineinstürzen **V U1**, 22

pluralistic [ˌplʊərə'lɪstɪk] pluralistisch; vielfältig **V AC1**, 8

poaching (no pl) ['pəʊtʃɪŋ] Wilderei **III**

pocket ['pɒkɪt] Tasche; Hosentasche **III**

pocket money ['pɒkɪt ˌmʌni] Taschengeld **I**

podcast ['pɒdkɑːst] Podcast **III**

poem ['pəʊɪm] Gedicht **I**

epic **poem** [ˌepɪk 'pəʊɪm] Epos; erzählendes Gedicht **V TS**, 108

poet ['pəʊɪt] Dichter/-in **V F2**, 32

poetry ['pəʊətri] Poesie; Dichtkunst **V F2**, 32; Dichtung; Lyrik **V TS**, 108

point [pɔɪnt] Punkt; Komma (bei Zahlenangaben) **I**; Argument; Standpunkt **IV**

*to have a **point** [ˌhæv ə 'pɔɪnt] nicht ganz Unrecht haben **II**

*to make one's **point** [ˌmeɪk wʌnz 'pɔɪnt] seinen Standpunkt deutlich machen; auf etwas hinauswollen; ein Argument anbringen **IV**

meeting **point** ['miːtɪŋ ˌpɔɪnt] Treffpunkt **III**

point of view [ˌpɔɪnt əv 'vjuː] Standpunkt; Ansicht; Perspektive **II**

to the **point** [tə ðə 'pɔɪnt] prägnant; treffend **IV**

I see your **point**. [aɪ ˌsiː jɔː 'pɔɪnt] Ich verstehe, was du meinst. **III**

to **point** [pɔɪnt] zeigen **I**

to **point** out sth [ˌpɔɪnt 'aʊt] hinweisen auf etw.; etw. aufzeigen **IV**

pointless ['pɔɪntləs] sinnlos; zwecklos ⟨**V U3**, 87⟩

poison ['pɔɪzn] Gift **V U3**, 71

to **poison** ['pɔɪzn] vergiften **IV**

poker ['pəʊkə] Schürhaken **V F3**, 37

polar bear ['pəʊlə ˌbeə] Eisbär **I**

police [pə'liːs] Polizei **II**

police officer [pə'liːs ˌɒfɪsə] Polizeibeamter/Polizeibeamtin; Polizist/-in **II**

policy ['pɒləsi] Politik; politische Linie **IV**

polite [pə'laɪt] höflich **I**

in a **polite** way [ɪn ˌə pə'laɪt ˌweɪ] auf höfliche Art **II**

politeness [pə'laɪtnəs] Höflichkeit **III**

political [pə'lɪtɪkl] politisch **II**

politician [ˌpɒlɪ'tɪʃn] Politiker/-in **IV**

politics (pl) ['pɒlətɪks] Politik **III**

poll [pəʊl] Umfrage **V U2**, 52

to **pollute** [pə'luːt] verschmutzen; verunreinigen **IV**

pollution [pə'luːʃn] Verschmutzung **IV**

pony ['pəʊni] Pony **I**

pony trekking ['pəʊni ˌtrekɪŋ] Ponyreiten im Gelände **II**

swimming **pool** ['swɪmɪŋ ˌpuːl] Swimmingpool; Schwimmbecken **III**

the **poor** [ðə 'pʊə] die Armen **II**

poor [pɔː; pʊə] arm **I**; schlecht **IV**

to **pop** home [ˌpɒp 'həʊm] schnell zu Hause vorbeigehen **IV**

the Pope [ðə 'pəʊp] der Papst **III**

popular ['pɒpjələ] beliebt; populär **I**

population [ˌpɒpjə'leɪʃn] Bevölkerung; Population **III**

porch (AE) [pɔːtʃ] Veranda **III**

porcupine ['pɔːkjəpaɪn] Baumstachler **II**

pork [pɔːk] Schweinefleisch **II**

port [pɔːt] Hafen; Hafenstadt **III**

posh [pɒʃ] vornehm; piekfein **V U2**, 42

position [pə'zɪʃn] Stelle; Position **IV**

positive ['pɒzətɪv] positiv **I**

possibility [ˌpɒsə'bɪləti] Möglichkeit **II**

possible ['pɒsəbl] möglich **I**

post [pəʊst] Post (Eintrag im Internet) **I**

trading **post** ['treɪdɪŋ ˌpəʊst] Handelsposten **III**

to **post** [pəʊst] online stellen; posten **II**

post- [pəʊst] Nach- **V U2**, 51

postcard ['pəʊskɑːd] Postkarte **I**

poster ['pəʊstə] Poster **I**

potato [pə'teɪtəʊ], potatoes [pə'teɪtəʊz] (pl) Kartoffel **III**

sweet **potatoes** (pl) ['swiːt pəˌteɪtəʊz] Süßkartoffeln **II**

potential [pə'tentʃl] Potenzial **V F3**, 39

pound [paʊnd] Pfund (Maßeinheit) **III**

pound (£) [paʊnd] Pfund (brit. Währungseinheit) **I**

to **pound** [paʊnd] laufen; trampeln **V U3**, 71

to **pour** [pɔː] einschenken; eingießen; schütten **I**

poverty ['pɒvəti] Armut **IV**

powder ['paʊdə] Puder; Pulver **V U2**, 42

power [paʊə] Kraft; Macht; Stärke **II**; Strom; Elektrizität; Energie **III**

in **power** [ɪn 'paʊə] an der Macht **II**

power cut ['paʊə ˌkʌt] Stromausfall **II**

power station ['paʊə ˌsteɪʃn] Kraftwerk **IV**

powerful ['paʊəfl] stark; mächtig **II**

practical ['præktɪkl] praktisch **II**

practice ['præktɪs] Training; Übung **II**

to **practise** ['præktɪs] üben; trainieren **I**

prairie ['preəri] Prärie **III**

to **praise** [preɪz] loben; preisen **IV**

to **pray** [preɪ] beten **II**

to **preach** [priːtʃ] predigen **V F3**, 38

preacher ['priːtʃə] Prediger/-in **V TS**, 116

precious ['preʃəs] wertvoll; kostbar **IV**

precise [prɪ'saɪs] genau; präzise **III**

precondition [ˌpriːkən'dɪʃn] Voraussetzung; Vorbedingung **V U3**, 80

predator ['predətə] Raubtier **IV**

to **predict** [prɪ'dɪkt] vorhersagen; voraussagen **IV**

prediction [prɪ'dɪkʃn] Vorhersage; Voraussage **II**

predominantly [prɪ'dɒmɪnəntli] überwiegend **V U2**, 42

to **prefer** [prɪ'fɜː] vorziehen **III**

preference ['prefrns] Vorliebe **III**

pregnancy ['pregnənsi] Schwangerschaft **V U3**, 75

prehistoric [ˌpriːhɪ'stɒrɪk] vorgeschichtlich; prähistorisch **II**

prejudice ['predʒədɪs] Vorurteil **IV**

*to be prejudiced against sb/sth [bi 'predʒədɪst əˌgenst] voreingenommen sein gegenüber jmdm./etw. **IV**

preparation [ˌprepr'eɪʃn] Vorbereitung **IV**

preparatory [prɪ'pærətri] vorbereitend **V U2**, 53

to **prepare** [prɪ'peə] vorbereiten; zubereiten **I**

*to be prepared [bi prɪ'peəd] bereit sein **III**

prescription [prɪ'skrɪpʃn] Rezept (für Arzneimittel) **II**

present ['preznt] Geschenk **I**

present ['preznt] Gegenwart; Präsens **III**

to **present** [prɪ'zent] präsentieren; vorstellen **I**

to **present** sb with sth [prɪˈzent wɪð] jmdm. etw. darbieten; jmdm. etw. präsentieren; jmdm. etw. schenken **IV**

presentation [ˌprezn̩ˈteɪʃn] Präsentation; Vortrag **I**

presenter [prɪˈzentə] Moderator/-in **II**

to **preserve** [prɪˈzɜːv] bewahren; erhalten **IV**

president [ˈprezɪdnt] Präsident/-in **I**

presidential [ˌprezɪˈdenʃl] Präsidenten-; Präsidentschafts- **IV**

to **press** [pres] drücken; pressen **II**

pressure [ˈpreʃə] Druck **IV**

pretax [ˈpriːtæks] vor Steuern **V U3**, 76

to **pretend** [prɪˈtend] vorgeben; vortäuschen; so tun, als ob … **II**

pretty [ˈprɪti] hübsch **II**

pretty [ˈprɪti] ziemlich; ganz schön **II**

to **prevent** [prɪˈvent] verhindern; abhalten **IV**

prevention [prɪˈvenʃn] Vorbeugung; Vermeidung; Verhütung **V U2**, 45

previous [ˈpriːviəs] früher; vorherig; vorhergehend **IV**

price [praɪs] Preis **I**

pride [praɪd] Stolz **V U2**, 47

priest [priːst] Priester; Pfarrer **V TS**, 109

primary school [ˈpraɪmri ˌskuːl] Grundschule **IV**

prime minister [ˌpraɪm ˈmɪnɪstə] Premierminister/-in **II**

primitive [ˈprɪmɪtɪv] primitiv **III**

prince [prɪns] Prinz **III**

principal (AE) [ˈprɪnsɪpl] Schulleiter/-in **III**

print [prɪnt] Druck; Abdruck **IV**
art **print** [ˈɑːt ˌprɪnt] Kunstdruck **IV**

to **print** [prɪnt] drucken **IV**

print [prɪnt] gedruckt; Druck- **II**

prison [ˈprɪzn] Gefängnis **III**

prisoner [ˈprɪznə] Gefangene/-r **II**

privacy [ˈprɪvəsi] Privatsphäre **IV**

private [ˈpraɪvɪt] privat **III**
private detective [ˈpraɪvət dɪˈtektɪv] Privatdetektiv/-in **II**

prize [praɪz] Preis; Gewinn **I**

pro [prəʊ] Profi; Profi- **III**
pros and cons [ˌprəʊz ən ˈkɒnz] Argumente für und gegen etw. **II**

probability [ˌprɒbəˈbɪləti] Wahrscheinlichkeit **V U2**, 41

probably [ˈprɒbəbli] wahrscheinlich **II**

problem [ˈprɒbləm] Problem; Schwierigkeit **I**

problematic [ˌprɒbləˈmætɪk] problematisch; schwierig **IV**

process [ˈprəʊses] Prozess; Verlauf **IV**

to **process** [ˈprəʊses] verarbeiten; aufbereiten **V F3**, 37

to **proclaim** [prəˈkleɪm] verkünden; erklären; ausrufen **V AC1**, 9

to **produce** [prəˈdjuːs] herstellen; produzieren **I**; hervorbringen; zur Welt bringen **III**

producer [prəˈdjuːsə] Produzent/-in **III**

product [ˈprɒdʌkt] Produkt; Erzeugnis **III**

production [prəˈdʌkʃn] Produktion; Inszenierung **III**

profession [prəˈfeʃn] Beruf **IV**

professional [prəˈfeʃnl] professionell **II**; Berufs- **IV**

professor [prəˈfesə] Professor/-in **III**

profile [ˈprəʊfaɪl] Profil; Porträt **II**

to **profit** [ˈprɒfɪt] profitieren **IV**

profitable [ˈprɒfɪtəbl] profitabel; gewinnbringend **IV**

programme [ˈprəʊgræm] Programm; Sendung **II**

to **programme** [ˈprəʊgræm] programmieren **IV**

progress [ˈprəʊgres] Fortschritt **IV**
*to be in **progress** [ˌbi ɪn ˈprəʊgres] ablaufen; im Gange sein **IV**

to **prohibit** (sb from doing) [prəˈhɪbɪt] jmdm. untersagen (etw. zu tun); jmdm. verbieten (etw. zu tun) **IV**

project [ˈprɒdʒekt] Projekt **I**
flagship **project** [ˈflæɡʃɪp ˌprɒdʒekt] Vorzeigeprojekt ⟨**V U1**, 28⟩

promise [ˈprɒmɪs] Versprechen **II**

to **promise** [ˈprɒmɪs] versprechen **II**

to **promote** [prəˈməʊt] fördern; befördern; voranbringen **V U2**, 50

prompt card [ˈprɒmpt kɑːd] Stichwortkarte; Rollenkarte **III**

to **prompt** [prɒmt] veranlassen; auffordern **V U1**, 24

to **pronounce** [prəˈnaʊns] aussprechen **V U1**, 26

pronunciation [prəˌnʌnsiˈeɪʃn] Aussprache **I**

proof [pruːf] Beweis **V U1**, 13
proof-reading [ˈpruːfriːdɪŋ] Korrekturlesen **V U3**, 84

prop [prɒp] Requisite **II**

proper [ˈprɒpə] richtig; ordentlich; angemessen **V F3**, 36

property [ˈprɒpəti] Eigentum; Grundbesitz; Besitz **V U3**, 72

proportion [prəˈpɔːʃn] Anteil; Verhältnis **IV**

proportional [prəˈpɔːʃnl] proportional; Verhältniswahl- **IV**; Verhältnis-; Anteils- **V F2**, 33

proposal [prəˈpəʊzl] Vorschlag; Entwurf; Gesetzesvorlage ⟨**V U1**, 28⟩; **V F2**, 33

to **propose** [prəˈpəʊz] vorschlagen **V F2**, 33

proposition [ˌprɒpəˈzɪʃn] Aussage; These **V U1**, 24

proprietary [prəˈpraɪətri] urheberrechtlich geschützt; eigen **V U2**, 48

prose [prəʊz] Prosa **V U2**, 47

to **prosper** [ˈprɒspə] florieren; gedeihen **V U3**, 76

prosperity [prɒsˈperəti] Wohlstand; Erfolg **V U3**, 76

prosperous [ˈprɒsprəs] wohlhabend; blühend; erfolgreich **V U3**, 76

to **protect** [prəˈtekt] beschützen; schützen **II**

protection [prəˈtekʃn] Schutz **II**

protest [ˈprəʊtest] Protest **III**

to **protest** [prəˈtest] protestieren **III**

protester [prəˈtestə] Protestierende/-r; Demonstrant/-in **III**

proud (of) [ˈpraʊd əv] stolz (auf) **I**

to **prove** [pruːv] beweisen **V U1**, 15

to **provide** [prəˈvaɪd] liefern; bereit stellen **IV**

province [ˈprɒvɪns] Provinz **III**

provincial [prəˈvɪnʃl] Provinz-; provinziell **III**

provisions (pl) [prəˈvɪʒnz] Vorräte **V U1**, 17

provocative [prəˈvɒkətɪv] provokativ; provozierend **IV**

to **provoke** [prəˈvəʊk] provozieren; hervorrufen **IV**

psychedelic [ˌsaɪkɪˈdelɪk] psychedelisch; bewusstseinsverändernd **V U3**, 71

psychological [ˌsaɪklˈɒdʒɪkl] psychologisch; psychisch **III**

psychologist [ˌsaɪˈkɒlədʒɪst] Psychologe/Psychologin **III**

pub [pʌb] Kneipe; Gasthaus **V U1**, 14

puberty [ˈpjuːbəti] Pubertät **V F5**, 67

the **public** [ðə ˈpʌblɪk] die Öffentlichkeit **V TS**, 112

public [ˈpʌblɪk] öffentlich **IV**
public administration (no pl) [ˌpʌblɪk ədˌmɪnɪˈstreɪʃn] öffentliche Verwaltung **IV**
public holiday [ˈpʌblɪk] gesetzlicher Feiertag **III**
public housing [ˌpʌblɪk ˈhaʊzɪŋ] sozialer Wohnungsbau (amerik.) **V U2**, 46
public school [ˌpʌblɪk ˈskuːl] Privatschule (brit.); staatliche Schule (amerik.) **III**

to **publish** [ˈpʌblɪʃ] veröffentlichen; publizieren; verlegen **III**

puck [pʌk] Puck (Eishockey) **III**

pudding [ˈpʊdɪŋ] Pudding; Nachtisch **I**

puffin [ˈpʌfɪn] Papageientaucher **III**

to **pull** [pʊl] ziehen **I**
to **pull** down [pʊl ˈdaʊn] abreißen **III**
to **pull** over [pʊl ˈəʊvə] (heranfahren und) anhalten **V U2**, 43

pullover [ˈpʊləʊvə] Pullover **I**

pumpkin [ˈpʌmpkɪn] Kürbis **II**

punctual [ˈpʌŋktʃuəl] pünktlich **III**

to **punish** [ˈpʌnɪʃ] bestrafen **III**

punishment [ˈpʌnɪʃmənt] Strafe **III**

purchase (fml) [ˈpɜːtʃəs] Kauf; Erwerb **III**

purple [ˈpɜːpl] violett; lila **I**

purpose [ˈpɜːpəs] Ziel; Absicht; Zweck **IV**

purse [pɜːs] Geldbeutel **IV**

to **push** [pʊʃ] stoßen; schieben; schubsen **I**
to **push** oneself [ˈpʊʃ wʌnˌself] sich alles abverlangen; sich Mühe geben **II**

to **push** sb [pʊʃ] jmdn. drängen **II**

pushy ['pʊʃi] aufdringlich; penetrant; aggressiv **II**

stone **put** ['stəʊn pʊt] Steinstoßen **V U1**, 13

*to **put** [pʊt] setzen; stellen; legen **I**

*to **put** forward [ˌpʊt ˈfɔːwəd] vorbringen **IV**

*to **put** on [pʊt ˈɒn] anziehen; auftragen **II**

*to **put** sth right [pʊt] etw. richtigstellen **II**

*to **put** through [ˌpʊt ˈθruː] verbinden **I**

puzzle ['pʌzl] Rätsel **I**

puzzled ['pʌzld] verwirrt; verdutzt **IV**

Q

Quaker ['kweɪkə] Quäker/-in **V F3**, 38

qualification [ˌkwɒlɪfɪˈkeɪʃn] Qualifikation; Befähigung; Abschluss; Schulabschluss **IV**

quality ['kwɒləti] Qualität; Eigenschaft **I**

quantity ['kwɒntiti] Menge; Quantität **IV**

quarter ['kwɔːtə] Viertel **III**

quarter past/to ['kwɔːtə pɑːst/tə] Viertel nach/vor **I**

queen [kwiːn] Königin **I**

question ['kwestʃən] Frage **I**

to **question** ['kwestʃən] fragen; hinterfragen; in Frage stellen **V F3**, 36

queue [kjuː] Schlange; Warteschlange **I**

to jump the **queue** [ˌdʒʌmp ðə ˈkjuː] sich vordrängeln **I**

quick [kwɪk] schnell **I**

quiet [kwaɪət] still; ruhig; leise **I**

quill [kwɪl] Federkiel **III**

quite [kwaɪt] ziemlich; ganz; völlig **III**

quiz [kwɪz] Quiz; Rätsel **I**

quotation [kwəˈteɪʃn] Zitat; Belegstelle **IV**

quote [kwəʊt] Zitat **IV**

R

rabbit ['ræbɪt] Kaninchen **I**

race [reɪs] Wettlauf; Rennen **I**; Volksgruppe; Rasse *(in Bezug auf Menschen im Deutschen nicht zu verwenden)* **IV**

racial ['reɪʃl] Rassen- *(nur im historischen Kontext in Bezug auf Menschen zu verwenden)* **IV**

camel **racing** ['kæml ˌreɪsɪŋ] Kamelrennen **II**

racism ['reɪsɪzm] Rassismus **IV**

racquet ['rækɪt] Schläger **II**

radical ['rædɪkl] radikal; fundamental; total **V U3**, 82

radio ['reɪdiəʊ] Radio **II**

raffle ['ræfl] Tombola **I**

rafting ['rɑːftɪŋ] Schlauchbootfahren **I**

rage [reɪdʒ] Wut; Zorn **V U1**, 18; ⟨**V U3**, 85⟩

raid [reɪd] Angriff; Überfall **V F3**, 36

rail [reɪl] Schiene; Geländer **V F2**, 33

railway ['reɪlweɪ] Eisenbahn **IV**

rain [reɪn] Regen **II**

to **rain** [reɪn] regnen **II**

rainbow ['reɪnbəʊ] Regenbogen **V AC1**, 8

raindrop ['reɪndrɒp] Regentropfen **III**

rainforest ['reɪnˌfɒrɪst] Regenwald **IV**

rainy ['reɪni] regnerisch **II**

to **raise** [reɪz] anheben; erhöhen; *(Kinder)* aufziehen **II**

to **raise** money [ˌreɪz ˈmʌni] Geld sammeln **II**

ranch [rɑːnʃ; rænʃ] Ranch **III**

random ['rændəm] zufällig; wahllos **V U2**, 41

range [reɪndʒ] Sortiment; Palette ⟨**V U1**, 28⟩
mountain **range** [ˌmaʊntɪn ˈreɪndʒ] Bergkette **II**

to **range** (from … to …) ['reɪndʒ frəm tʊ] sich erstrecken (von … bis …); reichen (von … bis …) **V U1**, 22

ranger *(AE)* ['reɪndʒə] Ranger **III**

rap [ræp] Rap **I**

to **rap** [ræp] rappen **I**

to **rape** [reɪp] vergewaltigen **V F3**, 39

rare [reə] rar; selten **IV**

rat [ræt] Ratte **I**

rate [reɪt] Rate; Quote **V U2**, 52

to **rate** [reɪt] bewerten; einstufen **III**

rather ['rɑːðə] eher; eigentlich **IV**
I'd **rather** [aɪd ˈrɑːðə] ich würde lieber **IV**

rating ['reɪtɪŋ] Bewertung; Einstufung **IV**

ration ['ræʃn] Ration **IV**

rattlesnake ['rætlsneɪk] Klapperschlange **III**

raw [rɔː] roh; Roh-; unbehandelt **IV**

to **reach** [riːʃ] erreichen; dran kommen **II**
to **reach** (for) ['riːtʃ fə] greifen (nach) **III**

to **react** [riˈækt] reagieren **II**

reaction [riˈækʃn] Reaktion **II**

*to **read** [riːd] lesen **I**

*to **read** out loud [ˌriːd aʊt ˈlaʊd] laut vorlesen **II**

reader ['riːdə] Leser/-in **II**

reading ['riːdɪŋ] Lesen **I**

ready ['redi] fertig; bereit **I**
ready meal [ˌredi ˈmiːl] Fertiggericht **I**

real [rɪəl] echt; richtig; wirklich **I**
real estate ['rɪəl ɪˌsteɪt] Grundbesitz; Immobilien **IV**

to **realise** ['rɪəlaɪz] erkennen; realisieren **III**

realism ['rɪəlɪzm] Realismus; Realitätssinn **IV**

realistic [ˌrɪəˈlɪstɪk] realistisch **II**

reality [riˈæləti] Realität; Wirklichkeit **IV**

really ['rɪəli] wirklich **I**

to **rear** up [rɪər ˈʌp] sich aufbäumen; sich aufrichten ⟨**V U1**, 31⟩

reason ['riːzn] Grund **II**; Vernunft; Verstand **V F1**, 11

reasonable ['riːznəbl] vernünftig; angemessen **V U3**, 76

reasoning ['riːznɪŋ] Logik **V U3**, 71

to **reassure** [ˌriːəˈʃʊə] beruhigen; beschwichtigen **V U1**, 14

rebel ['rebl] Rebell/-in; Aufständische/-r **V F1**, 10

to **rebel** (against) [rɪˈbel əˌgenst] rebellieren (gegen); sich auflehnen (gegen) **V U3**, 81

rebellion [rɪˈbeliən] Rebellion **III**

*to **rebuild** [ˌriːˈbɪld] wieder aufbauen **III**

to **recall** [riːˈkɔːl] sich erinnern **V U3**, 71

to **receive** [rɪˈsiːv] empfangen; erhalten; bekommen **II**

recent ['riːsnt] kürzlich; neueste/-r/-s; letzte/-r/-s **IV**

reception [rɪˈsepʃn] Empfang **V U3**, 80

recession [rɪˈseʃn] Rezession; Konjunkturrückgang **V AC4**, 88

rechargeable [ˌriːˈtʃɑːdʒəbl] wieder aufladbar **V U3**, 80

recipe ['resɪpi] Rezept **III**

to **recite** [rɪˈsaɪt] vortragen; rezitieren **V U2**, 56; **V TS**, 108

['rekləs] leichtsinnig ⟨**V U3**, 86⟩

to **reclaim** [rɪˈkleɪm] zurückfordern; reklamieren; zurückgewinnen **V U2**, 45

recognition [ˌrekəgˈnɪʃn] Anerkennung; Erkennung **IV**

to **recognize** *(AE)* ['rekəgnaɪz] erkennen; anerkennen **III**

recollection [ˌreklˈekʃn] Erinnerung **V U3**, 72

to **recommend** [ˌrekəˈmend] empfehlen **IV**

recommendation [ˌrekəmenˈdeɪʃn] Empfehlung **IV**

record ['rekɔːd] Rekord **III**

to **record** [rɪˈkɔːd] aufnehmen; aufzeichnen **II**

recording [rɪˈkɔːdɪŋ] Aufnahme; Aufzeichnung **I**

recording studio [rɪˈkɔːdɪŋ ˌstjuːdiəʊ] Aufnahmestudio; Tonstudio **I**

to **recount** [riːˈkaʊnt] erzählen **V U3**, 75

to **recover** [rɪˈkʌvə] zurückbekommen; wiedergewinnen; sicherstellen **V U2**, 43

recreation [ˌrekriˈeɪʃn] Freizeitbeschäftigung; Erholung **IV**

to **recruit** [rɪˈkruːt] rekrutieren; anwerben; einstellen **V U2**, 50

to **recycle** [ˌriːˈsaɪkl] recyceln; wiederverwenden **IV**

recycling [ˌriːˈsaɪklɪŋ] Recycling; Wiederaufbereitung **I**

red [red] rot **I**

redemptive [rɪˈdemtɪv] heilend; erlösend **V F4**, 62

*to **redo** [ˌriːˈduː] noch einmal machen **I**

to **reduce** [rɪˈdjuːs] reduzieren; vermindern; verringern **IV**

reduction [rɪˈdʌkʃn] Reduzierung; Verminderung **IV**

coral **reef** [ˌkɒrəl ˈriːf] Korallenriff **IV**

to **reef** the sails [ˌriːf ðə ˈseɪlz] die Segel einholen **I** to **refer** to [rɪ'fɜː tə] sich beziehen auf **III**

reference ['refrns] Referenz; Referenz-schreiben; Bezugnahme; Erwähnung **IV**

reference article ['refrns ˌɑːtɪkl] Artikel in einem Nachschlagewerk **III**

referendum [ˌrefr'endəm] Referendum; Volksentscheid **IV**

reflective [rɪ'flektɪv] nachdenklich **V U2**, 47

to **reform** [rɪ'fɔːm] reformieren **V U1**, 24

refrigerator [rɪ'frɪdʒreɪtə] Kühlschrank **V F1**, 11

refugee [ˌrefjʊ'dʒiː] Geflüchtete/-r **IV**

to **refund** [ˌriː'fʌnd] zurückerstatten **III**

refusal [rɪ'fjuːzl] Weigerung; Ablehnung **V U3**, 74

to **refuse** [rɪ'fjuːz] ablehnen; sich weigern; zurückweisen **IV**

to **regard** [rɪ'gɑːd] betrachten **IV**

regarding [rɪ'gɑːdɪŋ] im Hinblick auf **IV**

region ['riːdʒn] Region; Gegend **II**

regional ['riːdʒnl] regional **IV**

register ['redʒɪstə] Sprachebene; Register **III**

regret [rɪ'gret] Bedauern; Reue **IV**

regular ['regjələ] Stammgast **V U3**, 76

regular ['regjələ] regelmäßig; gleichmäßig **II**

to **regulate** ['regjəleɪt] regeln; regulieren **IV**

rehabilitation (no pl) [ˌriːhə'bɪlɪ'teɪʃn] Rehabilitation **V U3**, 71

to **rehearse** [rɪ'hɜːs] proben **III**

reign [reɪn] Herrschaft; Regierungszeit **III**

to **reign** [reɪn] herrschen; regieren **III**

to **reintroduce** [ˌriːɪntrə'djuːs] wieder einführen; wieder ansiedeln **III**

to **reject** [rɪ'dʒekt] zurückweisen; ablehnen **V U2**, 53

related [rɪ'leɪtɪd] verwandt; bezogen **I**

relation [rɪ'leɪʃnz] Verhältnis; Beziehung **III**

relationship [rɪ'leɪʃnʃɪp] Beziehung **II**

relative ['relətɪv] Verwandte/-r **V F1**, 10

to **relax** [rɪ'læks] sich entspannen; sich ausruhen; sich beruhigen **II**

release [rɪ'liːs] Freistellung; Entlassung **IV**

to **release** [rɪ'liːs] hier: freilassen **III**; herausbringen; veröffentlichen **IV**

relevant ['reləvnt] relevant; von Bedeutung **IV**

reliable [rɪ'laɪəbl] verlässlich; zuverlässig; vertrauenswürdig **IV**

relief [rɪ'liːf] Erleichterung **IV**

religion [rɪ'lɪdʒn] Religion **III**

religious [rɪ'lɪdʒəs] religiös; gläubig **I**

to **remain** [rɪ'meɪn] bleiben **III**

remains (pl) [rɪ'meɪnz] Überreste; Überbleibsel **V U1**, 16

on **remand** [ɒn rɪ'mɑːnd] in Untersuchungshaft **V U1**, 24

to **remember** [rɪ'membə] sich erinnern (an); sich merken; denken an **I**

to **remind** (sb of sth/sb) [rɪ'maɪnd] (jmdn. an etw./jmdn.) erinnern **III**

remote [rɪ'məʊt] abgelegen; weit entfernt **V U1**, 16

to **remove** [rɪ'muːv] entfernen **III**

to **rename** [ˌriː'neɪm] umbenennen **III**

renewable [rɪ'njuːəbl] erneuerbar; verlängerbar **IV**

to **renovate** ['renəveɪt] renovieren **IV**

rent [rent] Miete **V U2**, 46

to **rent out** [ˌrent ˈaʊt] vermieten **III**

to **repair** [rɪ'peə] reparieren **III**

to **repeat** [rɪ'piːt] wiederholen **I**

repercussion [ˌriːpə'kʌʃn] Auswirkung **V U2**, 41

to **replace** (by/with) [rɪ'pleɪs] ersetzen (durch) **IV**

to **replay** [ˌriː'pleɪ] erneut spielen; erneut abspielen **II**

reply [rɪ'plaɪ] Antwort; Erwiderung; Entgegnung **I**

to **reply** (to) [rɪ'plaɪ] antworten (auf); erwidern; entgegnen **I**

report [rɪ'pɔːt] Bericht; Meldung **II**

news **report** ['njuːz rɪˌpɔːt] Tatsachenbericht; Nachrichtenbeitrag; Meldung **III**

report card (AE) [rɪ'pɔːt ˌkɑːd] Zeugnis **II**

to **report** [rɪ'pɔːt] berichten; wiedergeben **III**

reporter [rɪ'pɔːtə] Reporter/-in **II**

to **represent** [ˌreprɪ'zent] repräsentieren; darstellen; stehen für **III**

representative [ˌreprɪ'zentətɪv] Repräsentant/-in; Stellvertreter/-in **IV**

to **repress** [rɪ'pres] unterdrücken **V F4**, 61

to **reproach** sb for sth [rɪ'prəʊtʃ] vorwerfen **V F5**, 67

republic [rɪ'pʌblɪk] Republik **III**

republican [rɪ'pʌblɪkən] republikanisch; Republikaner/-in **IV**

reputation [ˌrepjə'teɪʃn] Ruf **V U2**, 46

request [rɪ'kwest] Anfrage; Nachfrage **IV**

to **require** [rɪ'kwaɪə] benötigen; erfordern **IV**

requirement [rɪ'kwaɪəmənt] Anforderung **V U3**, 81

*to **reread** [ˌriː'riːd] noch einmal lesen **II**

rescue ['reskjuː] Rettung **II**

to **rescue** ['reskjuː] retten **III**

research (no pl) [rɪ'sɜːtʃ] Recherche; Forschung; Untersuchung **III**

to **resent** sb/sth [rɪ'zent] sich ärgern über jmdn./etw.; jmdm. etw. übelnehmen **IV**

reserve [rɪ'zɜːv] Reserve; Vorrat **III**

reserved [rɪ'zɜːvd] reserviert; zurückhaltend; vorbehalten **III**

to **resettle** [ˌriː'setl] sich neu niederlassen; umsiedeln **III**

resident ['rezɪdnt] Bewohner/-in; Einwohner/-in **IV**

residential school (CE) [ˌrezɪ'dentʃl ˌskuːl] staatliches Internat für Kinder der Ureinwohner Kanadas **III**

to **resist** [rɪ'zɪst] widerstehen; sich widersetzen **V U3**, 75

resistance [rɪ'zɪstns] Widerstand **V F4**, 63

to **resolve** [rɪ'zɒlv] lösen; klären **V U1**, 27

resource [rɪ'zɔːs] Ressource **III**

respect [rɪ'spekt] Respekt **III**

respectful [rɪ'spektfl] respektvoll **IV**

response [rɪ'spɒns] Reaktion; Antwort **V U3**, 83

responsibility [rɪˌspɒnsə'bɪləti] Verantwortung **II**; Aufgabe **IV**

responsible [rɪs'pɒnsəbl] verantwortlich; verantwortungsvoll **IV**

rest [rest] Rast; Ruhe **III**

the **rest** [rest] der Rest **II**

restaurant ['restrɒnt] Restaurant; Gaststätte **I**

to **restrict** [rɪ'strɪkt] begrenzen; beschränken **IV**

restriction [rɪ'strɪkʃn] Einschränkung; Beschränkung **IV**

restrictive [rɪ'strɪktɪv] beschränkend; einengend **IV**

restroom (AE) ['restrʊm] Toilette **III**

result [rɪ'zʌlt] Ergebnis; Resultat **II**

to **result** in sth [rɪ'zʌlt ɪn] etw. ergeben; in etw. resultieren **IV**

retail ['riːteɪl] Einzelhandel **IV**

*to **retell** [ˌriː'tel] nacherzählen; nochmals erzählen **I**

retired [rɪ'taəd] pensioniert; im Ruhestand **II**

to **retouch** [riː'tʌtʃ] retuschieren **V U3**, 80

return [rɪ'tɜːn] Hin- und Rückfahrkarte **II**

in **return** [ɪn rɪ'tɜːn] als Gegenleistung ⟨**V U1**, 29⟩

to **return** [rɪ'tɜːn] zurückkehren; zurückfahren **III**

reunion [rɪ'juːnjən] Treffen; Zusammenkunft **IV**

to **reuse** [ˌriː'juːz] wieder verwenden **II**

to **reveal** [rɪ'viːl] offenbaren; aufdecken **IV**

revenge [rɪ'vendʒ] Rache; Revanche **III**

*to take **revenge** [ˌteɪk rɪ'vendʒ] (sich) rächen **III**

revenue ['revnjuː] Erlös; Einnahmen **V U3**, 76

inland **revenue** [ˌɪnlænd 'revnjuː] Finanzamt (brit.) **V U3**, 76

review [rɪ'vjuː] Kritik; Rezension **III**

revolt [rɪ'vəʊlt] Revolte; Aufstand **V F3**, 38

to **revolt** [rɪ'vəʊlt] revoltieren; sich auflehnen (gegen) **V F1**, 10

revolution [ˌrevl'uːʃn] Revolution **IV**

revolutionary [ˌrevl'uːʃnri] revolutionär **III**

to **revolutionise** [ˌrevl'uːʃnaɪz] revolutionieren **V F1**, 10

reward [rɪ'wɔːd] Belohnung; Preis **V U1**, 21

rewarding [rɪ'wɔːdɪŋ] lohnend; bereichernd **IV**

*to **rewrite** [ˌriː'raɪt] umschreiben; neu schreiben **II** rhetorical [rɪ'tɒrɪkl] rhetorisch **V F4**, 62; **V TS**, 117

rhino ['raɪnəʊ] Rhinozeros; Nashorn **III**

rhyme [raɪm] Reim **V U2**, 47; **V TS**, 108
  rhyme scheme ['raɪm ski:m] Reimschema **V U2**, 47

rhythm ['rɪðm] Rhythmus **I**

the rich [ðə 'rɪtʃ] die Reichen **II**

rich [rɪtʃ] reich **II**; reichhaltig **IV**

riches (pl) ['rɪtʃɪz] Reichtümer **V U3**, 76

ride [raɪd] Fahrt; Ritt; Fahrgeschäft **II**

*to ride [raɪd] fahren; reiten **I**

rider ['raɪdə] Reiter/-in **II**

ridiculous [rɪ'dɪkjələs] lächerlich **V U1**, 24

riding ['raɪdɪŋ] Reiten **II**

rifle ['raɪfl] Gewehr **III**

rigging ['rɪgɪŋ] Takelage **I**

right [raɪt] Recht **II**
  civil **rights** (pl) [sɪvl 'raɪts] Bürgerrechte **IV**

right [raɪt] richtig; korrekt **I**
  all **right** [ɔːl 'raɪt] in Ordnung; alles klar **III**
  *to be **right** [bi 'raɪt] recht haben **I**
  on the **right** [ɒn ðə 'raɪt] auf der rechten Seite; rechts **I**
  *to put sth **right** [pʊt] etw. richtigstellen **II**
  right away [raɪt ə'weɪ] sofort; gleich **I**
  right here [raɪt 'hɪə] genau hier **II**
  right now [raɪt 'naʊ] jetzt gleich; sofort; gerade **II**

right [raɪt] direkt; genau; gerade **IV**

ring [rɪŋ] Ring **III**
  key **ring** ['ki: rɪŋ] Schlüsselbund; Schlüsselanhänger **III**

*to ring [rɪŋ] klingeln; läuten **I**

ice rink ['aɪs rɪŋk] Eisbahn; Schlittschuhbahn **I**

riot [raɪət] Aufruhr; Aufstand **IV**

to riot [raɪət] randalieren; Krawall machen **V F1**, 10

rioter [raɪətə] Randalierer/-in; Aufständische/-r **V F1**, 10

rip current ['rɪp kʌrnt] Brandungsrückströmung **IV**

rise [raɪz] Anstieg; Zunahme; Aufstieg **IV**

*to rise [raɪz] steigen; sich erheben **III**

risk [rɪsk] Risiko; Gefahr **III**
  at one's own **risk** [æt wʌnz əʊn 'rɪsk] auf eigene Gefahr **III**
  *to take a **risk** [teɪk ə 'rɪsk] ein Risiko eingehen **III**

to risk [rɪsk] riskieren **IV**

rival ['raɪvl] Rivale/Rivalin; Konkurrent/-in **V F3**, 39

river ['rɪvə] Fluss **I**

road [rəʊd] Straße **II**

to roar [rɔː] brüllen; dröhnen ⟨**V U1**, 31⟩

roast [rəʊst] Braten **IV**

roast lamb [rəʊst 'læm] Lammbraten **III**
  roast turkey [rəʊst 'tɜːki] Putenbraten **II**

to roast [rəʊst] anbraten; rösten **IV**

robber ['rɒbə] Räuber/-in **II**

rock [rɒk] Fels; Stein **I**

rodeo [rə'deɪəʊ; 'rəʊdɪəʊ] Rodeo **I**

role [rəʊl] Rolle **I**
  role model ['rəʊl mɒdl] Vorbild **IV**
  role play ['rəʊl pleɪ] Rollenspiel **I**
  supporting **role** [sə'pɔːtɪŋ rəʊl] Nebenrolle **V TS**, 112
  to swap **roles** [swɒp 'rəʊlz] Rollen tauschen **I**

bread roll ['bred rəʊl] Brötchen **III**

to roll [rəʊl] rollen **II**
  to **roll** one's eyes [rəʊl wʌnz 'aɪz] die Augen verdrehen **III**

roller coaster ['rəʊlə kəʊstə] Achterbahn **II**

Roman ['rəʊmən] Römer/-in; römisch **II**

romance [rə'mæns] Liebesgeschichte; Liebesfilm **V TS**, 112

romantic [rə'mæntɪk] romantisch **IV**

roof [ru:f] Dach **II**

room [ru:m; rʊm] Zimmer; Raum **I**
  changing **room** ['tʃeɪndʒɪŋ rʊm] Umkleideraum; Umkleidekabine **III**
  fitting **room** ['fitɪŋ rʊm] Umkleidekabine **II**
  living **room** ['lɪvɪŋ rʊm] Wohnzimmer **I**

roommate ['ru:mmeɪt] Zimmergenosse/Zimmergenossin **I**

rope [rəʊp] Seil **III**

rough [rʌf] rau; grob; uneben; holprig **IV**

roughly ['rʌfli] ungefähr; schätzungsweise **V U2**, 53

round [raʊnd] rund **II**
  the **Round** Table [ðə raʊnd 'teɪbl] die Tafelrunde **II**

*to go round in circles [gəʊ raʊnd ɪn 'sɜːklz] sich im Kreis drehen; im Kreis gehen **II**

to turn round [tɜːn (ə)'raʊnd] (sich) umdrehen; wenden **I**

route [ru:t] Strecke; Route **III**

row [rəʊ] Reihe **V TS**, 109

to row [rəʊ] rudern **V U1**, 17

royal ['rɔɪəl] königlich **I**

to rub [rʌb] reiben; scheuern **IV**

rubber ['rʌbə] Radiergummi **I**

rubbish ['rʌbɪʃ] Müll; Gerümpel **I**

rude [ru:d] unhöflich; unverschämt **I**

rug [rʌg] Vorleger; Teppich **III**

rugby ['rʌgbi] Rugby **II**

ruin [ru:ɪn] Ruine; Trümmer **III**

to ruin ['ru:ɪn] ruinieren; zerstören **II**

rule [ru:l] Regel **I**; Herrschaft **II**

to rule [ru:l] herrschen; regieren **II**

ruler ['ru:lə] Lineal **I**

rumour ['ru:mə] Gerücht **IV**

run [rʌn] Rennen; Lauf **II**
  run area ['rʌn eəriə] Gehege; Auslauf **III**

*to run [rʌn] rennen; laufen **I**; betreiben; leiten; führen **II**

*to run away [rʌn ə'weɪ] wegrennen **I**

*to run out [rʌn 'aʊt] ausgehen **IV**

runaway ['rʌnəweɪ] Ausreißer/-in; Entlaufene/-r **II**

runner ['rʌnə] Läufer/-in **II**

running ['rʌnɪŋ] Laufen; Rennen **II**

running water [rʌnɪŋ 'wɔːtə] fließendes Wasser **II**

rural ['rʊərl] ländlich **II**

rush hour ['rʌʃ aʊə] Hauptverkehrszeit **IV**

to rush [rʌʃ] hetzen; eilen **V U2**, 43

S

sacred ['seɪkrɪd] heilig **III**

sad [sæd] traurig **I**

to sadden ['sædn] traurig machen; bekümmern **V U1**, 20

safari [sə'fɑːri] Safari **IV**

safe [seɪf] sicher; ungefährlich **II**

safety ['seɪfti] Sicherheit **II**

saguaro [sə'weərəʊ] Saguaro **III**

to reef the sails [ri:f ðə 'seɪlz] die Segel einholen **I**

to sail [seɪl] segeln; umsegeln **II**

sailboat ['seɪlbəʊt] Segelboot **II**

sailor ['seɪlə] Seemann; Matrose **I**

salad ['sæləd] Salat **I**

sales [seɪlz] Vertrieb; Verkauf **IV**

salt [sɔːlt] Salz ⟨**V U1**, 30⟩

the same [ðə 'seɪm] der-/die-/dasselbe; der/die/das gleiche **I**
  same-sex [seɪm'seks] gleichgeschlechtlich **IV**
  Same to you. [seɪm tə 'ju:] Danke, gleichfalls. **I**

the same [ðə 'seɪm] der-/die-/dasselbe; der/die/das gleiche **I**

sand [sænd] Sand **II**

sandal ['sændl] Sandale **III**

sandwich ['sænwɪdʒ] Sandwich; belegtes Brot **I**

to sanitise ['sænɪtaɪz] keimfrei machen; aufwerten **V AC3**, 65

satellite ['sætlaɪt] Satellit **IV**

satisfied ['sætɪsfaɪd] zufrieden; befriedigt **IV**

Saturday ['sætədeɪ] Samstag **I**

sauce [sɔːs] Soße **II**

sausage ['sɒsɪdʒ] Wurst; Bratwurst **III**

to save [seɪv] retten; bergen **I**; sparen; aufheben **II**

sax [sæks] Saxofon **I**

Saxon ['sæksn] Sachse/Sächsin; sächsisch **II**

saxophone ['sæksəfəʊn] Saxofon **I**

*to say [seɪ] sagen; aufsagen; sprechen **I**
  *to be **said** to (+ inf) [bi 'sed tə] gelten als **IV**
  *to **say** hello (to) [seɪ hel'əʊ tə] grüßen; Grüße ausrichten (an) **I**

saying ['seɪɪŋ] Redensart; Sprichwort **II**

scandal ['skændl] Skandal **IV**

scar [skɑ:] Narbe **IV**

to **scare** sb [skeə] jmdm. Angst machen; jmdn. erschrecken **III**

*to be **scared** (of) [bi 'skeəd‿əv] Angst haben (vor) **I**

scary ['skeəri] unheimlich; gruselig; beängstigend **II**

scattered ['skætəd] verstreut; verteilt **V U3**, 71

scene [si:n] Szene **I**; Schauplatz **II**
   acting a **scene** [ˌæktɪŋ‿ə 'si:n] eine Theaterszene spielen **I**

scenery ['si:nri] Landschaft **III**

schedule ['ʃedju:l] (BE); ['skedʒu:l] (AE) Stundenplan (amerik.); Fahrplan; Terminkalender **III**

rhyme **scheme** ['raɪm ski:m] Reimschema **V U2**, 47

scholarship ['skɒləʃɪp] Stipendium **III**

school [sku:l] Schule **I**
   boarding **school** ['bɔ:dɪŋ ˌsku:l] Internat **IV**
   comprehensive **school** [kɒmprɪ'hensɪv ˌsku:l] Gesamtschule **IV**
   elementary **school** (AE) [elɪ'mentri ˌsku:l] Grundschule **IV**
   grammar **school** ['græmə ˌsku:l] Gymnasium **II**
   high **school** ['haɪ ˌsku:l] High School (weiterführende Schule in den USA, Oberstufe) **II**
   middle **school** (AE) ['mɪdl ˌsku:l] Mittelschule (weiterführende Schule in den USA, Mittelstufe) **II**
   nursery **school** ['nɜ:sri ˌsku:l] Vorschule; Kindergarten **IV**
   primary **school** ['praɪmri ˌsku:l] Grundschule **IV**
   public **school** [ˌpʌblɪk 'sku:l] Privatschule (brit.); staatliche Schule (amerik.) **III**
   residential **school** (CE) [ˌrezɪ'dentʃl ˌsku:l] staatliches Internat für Kinder der Ureinwohner Kanadas **III**
   secondary **school** ['sekəndri ˌsku:l] weiterführende Schule **IV**
   vocational **school** [və'keɪʃnl ˌsku:l] Berufsschule **IV**

schoolbag ['sku:lbæg] Schultasche **I**

schooling ['sku:lɪŋ] Schulbildung **II**

Science [saɪəns] Naturwissenschaften **I**

science [saɪəns] Wissenschaft; Naturwissenschaft **IV**
   science fiction [ˌsaɪəns 'fɪkʃn] Science-Fiction (Zukunftsdichtung) **II**

scientific [ˌsaɪən'tɪfɪk] wissenschaftlich; naturwissenschaftlich **IV**

scientist ['saɪəntɪst] Wissenschaftler/-in **IV**

scissors (pl only) ['sɪzəz] Schere **IV**

to **scoop** [sku:p] schöpfen; schaufeln **II**

score [skɔ:] Punktestand; Spielstand **II**

to **score** [skɔ:] punkten; ein Tor schießen **III**

scorpion ['skɔ:piən] Skorpion **III**

Scot [skɒt] Schotte/Schottin **V F1**, 10

the **Scotch** [ðə 'skɒtʃ] die Schotten **V TS**, 110

Scots [skɒts] Schottisch (Dialekt) **V U1**, 26

Scotsman ['skɒtsmən]/**Scotswoman** ['skɒtswʊmən], **Scotsmen** (pl) ['skɒtsmen]/**Scotswomen** (pl) ['skɒtswɪmɪn] Schotte/Schottin **IV**

Scottish ['skɒtɪʃ] schottisch **II**

scout [skaʊt] Talentsucher/-in **III**

to **scratch** [skrætʃ] kratzen; kritzeln **III**

to **scream** [skri:m] schreien; kreischen **III**

screen [skri:n] Bildschirm **IV**

to **screw** sb [skru:] jdn. reinlegen **V U3**, 74

script [skrɪpt] Drehbuch; Skript **III**

sculpture ['skʌlptʃə] Skulptur **III**

sea [si:] Meer **I**

seafood ['si:fu:d] Meeresfrüchte **II**

seal [si:l] Seehund; Robbe **III**

search [sɜ:tʃ] Suche; Such- **I**

to **search** (for) ['sɜ:tʃ fə] suchen (nach); durchsuchen **III**

seashell ['si:ʃel] Muschel **IV**

seasick ['si:sɪk] seekrank **III**

at the **seaside** [ət ðə 'si:saɪd] am Meer **II**

season ['si:zn] Saison; Jahreszeit **II**

seasonal ['si:znl] saisonal; jahreszeitlich bedingt **IV**

seat [si:t] Sitz; Sitzplatz **IV**

secession [sɪ'seʃn] Abspaltung; Sezession **V F3**, 39

second ['seknd] Sekunde **I**

second ['seknd] zweite/-r/-s **I**

secondary school ['sekəndri ˌsku:l] weiterführende Schule **IV**

in **secret** [ɪn 'si:krət] heimlich **II**

secret ['si:krət] geheim **II**

secretary ['sekrətri] Sekretär/-in **IV**; Minister/in **V F2**, 33

section ['sekʃn] Abschnitt; Paragraf **II**

sector ['sektə] Sektor **IV**

to **secure** [sɪ'kjʊə] sichern **III**

security [sɪ'kjʊərəti] Sicherheit; Schutz; Wachdienst; Wach-; Sicherheits- **IV**
   social **security** [ˌsəʊʃl sɪ'kjʊərəti] Sozialversicherung **V U3**, 70

seductive [sɪ'dʌktɪv] verführerisch ⟨**V U3**, 87⟩

*to **see** [si:] sehen **I**
   *to **see** sb (+ -ing) [si:] jmdn. etw. tun sehen **III**
   I **see** your point. [aɪ ˌsi: jɔ: 'pɔɪnt] Ich verstehe, was du meinst. **III**
   I **see**. [aɪ 'si:] Ich verstehe.; Aha!; Ach so! **I**
   See you! ['si: jə] Bis dann!; Bis ... **I**
   Wait and **see**! [ˌweɪt‿ənd 'si:] Warte ab! **I**

*to **seek** [si:k] suchen **V U2**, 50; **V TS**, 109

to **seem** [si:m] scheinen **III**

segregation [ˌsegrɪ'geɪʃn] Segregation; Trennung; Rassentrennung **IV**

to **seize** [si:z] ergreifen; packen **V TS**, 111

to **select** [sɪ'lekt] auswählen; aussuchen **IV**

selective [sɪ'lektɪv] anspruchsvoll; kritisch; wählerisch **V U2**, 53

self [self], **selves** [selvz] (pl) das Selbst **II**
   self-conscious [ˌself'kɒnʃəs] befangen; gehemmt **V U3**, 82
   self-critical ['self ˌkrɪtɪkl] selbstkritisch **II**
   self-empowerment [ˌselfɪm'paʊəmənt] Selbstermächtigung **V U2**, 45
   self-esteem [ˌselfɪ'sti:m] Selbstwertgefühl; Selbstachtung **III**
   self-evaluation [ˌselfɪˌvæljʊ'eɪʃn] Selbsteinschätzung **I**

selfie ['selfi] Selfie **II**

selfish ['selfɪʃ] selbstsüchtig; egoistisch **IV**

selfishness ['selfɪʃnəs] Selbstsucht **IV**

*to **sell** [sel] verkaufen **I**

seller ['selə] Verkäufer/-in (auf einem Flohmarkt) **I**

senator ['senətə] Senator/-in **IV**

*to **send** [send] schicken; senden **I**
   *to **send** off [send ˌɒf] abschicken **II**

senior ['si:niə] leitend; älter **IV**

sensational [sen'seɪʃnl] sensationell; spektakulär **V U2**, 55

sense [sens] Sinn **II**

sensible ['sensɪbl] vernünftig **IV**

sensitive ['sensɪtɪv] sensibel; empfindsam; heikel **IV**

sensitivity [ˌsensɪ'tɪvəti] Empfindsamkeit; Sensibilität **V U2**, 40

sentence ['sentəns] Satz **I**; Strafe; Strafmaß; Urteil **IV**

to **separate** ['sepreɪt] (sich) trennen **IV**

separate ['seprət] separat; getrennt; verschieden **I**

September [sep'tembə] September **I**

sequence ['si:kwəns] Abfolge; Reihenfolge **III**

serf [sɜ:f] Leibeigene/-r **V AC4**, 88

series (sg or pl) ['sɪəri:z] Serie **III**

*to take sth **seriously** [teɪk 'sɪəriəsli] ernst nehmen **II**

serious ['sɪəriəs] ernsthaft; ernst **I**

seriousness (no pl) ['sɪəriəsnəs] Ernst; Ernsthaftigkeit **IV**

to **serve** [sɜ:v] dienen; servieren; bedienen **III**

service ['sɜ:vɪs] Service; Dienstleistung; Dienst; Verbindung(Zug, Bus) **IV**
   personnel **services** (pl) [pɜ:sn'el ˌsɜ:vɪsɪz] Personaldienstleistungen **IV**

session ['seʃn] Sitzung; Stunde **IV**

set [set] Umgebung; Rahmen **II**; Aufnahmeort; Drehort **III**
   set of instructions [ˌset‿əv ɪn'strʌkʃnz] Anleitung **III**

*to **set** [set] setzen; aufstellen **IV**

*to be **set** (in) [bi 'set ɪn] spielen (in); seinen Schauplatz haben (in) **IV**

*to **set** free [set 'friː] freilassen **IV**

*to **set** oneself apart (from) [ˌset wʌnˌself əˈpɑːt frəm] sich abheben(von) **V F5**, 67

*to **set** the table [ˌset ðə ˈteɪbl] den Tisch decken **III**

*to **set** up [ˌset ˈʌp] einrichten; aufbauen **I**

setback [ˈsetbæk] Rückschlag ⟨**V U2**, 57⟩

setting [ˈsetɪŋ] Schauplatz; Rahmen **III**

to **settle** [ˈsetl] besiedeln; sich niederlassen **III**

settlement [ˈsetlmənt] Siedlung **III**

settler [ˈsetlə] Siedler/-in **II**

seven [ˈsevn] sieben **I**

seventeen [ˌsevnˈtiːn] siebzehn **I**

seventy [ˈsevnti] siebzig **I**

several [ˈsevrl] einige; mehrere; verschiedene **II**

*to **sew** [səʊ] nähen **IV**

sex [seks] Geschlecht; Sexualität **III**

sexual [ˈsekʃʊəl] sexuell **IV**

to **shackle** [ˈʃækl] mit Ketten fesseln **V F3**, 38

shadow [ˈʃædəʊ] Schatten **III**

shake [ʃeɪk] Shake; Milchshake **II**

*to **shake** [ʃeɪk] schütteln **III**

*to **shake** hands [ˌʃeɪk ˈhændz] Hände schütteln; sich die Hand geben **III**

shaky [ˈʃeɪki] zitternd; bebend **IV**

shall [ʃæl] sollen **V F3**, 39

shallow [ˈʃæləʊ] oberflächlich; seicht; flach **IV**

shame [ʃeɪm] Scham; Schande; Schmach **IV**

What a **shame**! [ˌwɒt ə ˈʃeɪm] Wie schade! **I**

shape [ʃeɪp] Form **I**

to **shape** [ʃeɪp] formen **III**

share [ʃeə] Anteil **IV**

to **share** [ʃeə] teilen **I**

shark [ʃɑːk] Hai **IV**

sharp [ʃɑːp] scharf; schneidend **III**

she [ʃiː] sie **I**

sheep, sheep (pl) [ʃiːp] Schaf **I**

bighorn **sheep** [ˈbɪɡhɔːn ˌʃiːp] Dickhornschaf **II**

sheet [ʃiːt] Blatt **IV**

cheat **sheet** [ˈtʃiːt ˌʃiːt] Spickzettel **III**

shelf [ʃelf], **shelves** (pl) [ʃelvz] Regal; Regalbrett **III**

shelter [ˈʃeltə] Obdach; Schutz; Schutzhütte **III**

animal **shelter** [ˈænɪml ˌʃeltə] Tierheim **III**

bomb **shelter** [ˈbɒm ˌʃeltə] Bunker; Luftschutzkeller **IV**

homeless **shelter** [ˈhəʊmləs ˌʃeltə] Obdachlosenunterkunft **III**

shhh [ʃ] psst **II**

shield [ʃiːld] Schild **II**

to **shift** [ʃɪft] hin- und herrutschen **IV**

*to **shine** [ʃaɪn] scheinen; glänzen **II**

ship [ʃɪp] Schiff **I**

to **ship** [ʃɪp] mitbringen; importieren **IV**

shipping [ˈʃɪpɪŋ] Versand; Transport (von Gütern) **IV**

shirt [ʃɜːt] Hemd; Shirt **I**

shock [ʃɒk] Schock **II**

shocked [ʃɒkt] schockiert; geschockt **I**

shoe [ʃuː] Schuh **I**

in sb's **shoes** [ɪn ˌsʌmbədɪz ˈʃuːz] an jmds. Stelle **II**

photo **shoot** [ˈfəʊtəʊ ˌʃuːt] Fotoshooting; Fotoaufnahmen **III**

*to **shoot** (at) [ʃuːt] schießen (auf) **III**

shop [ʃɒp] Geschäft; Laden **I**

charity **shop** [ˈtʃærɪti ˌʃɒp] Second-Hand-Laden **I**

to **shop** [ʃɒp] einkaufen; shoppen **III**

*to go **shopping** [ˌɡəʊ ˈʃɒpɪŋ] einkaufen gehen **I**

shore [ʃɔː] Ufer; Küste **V U1**, 15; **V TS**, 110

short [ʃɔːt] kurz **I**

*to be **short** of sth [bi ˌʃɔːt əv] knapp sein an **IV**

shortage [ˈʃɔːtɪdʒ] Knappheit; Mangel **V U2**, 50

shot [ʃɒt] Aufnahme **III**

wide **shot** [ˈwaɪd ˌʃɒt] Totale (Kameraeinstellung) **V TS**, 112

should [ʃʊd] sollte; solltest; sollten; solltet **I**

shoulder [ˈʃəʊldə] Schulter **II**

to **shout** [ʃaʊt] schreien; rufen **I**

to **shove** [ʃʌv] schieben; drängen ⟨**V U2**, 58⟩

shovel [ˈʃʌvl] Schaufel **II**

show [ʃəʊ] Show; Schau; Aufführung **II**

living history **show** [ˌlɪvɪŋ ˈhɪstəri ˌʃəʊ] Show, in der historischer Alltag nachgespielt wird **II**

talent **show** [ˈtælənt ˌʃəʊ] Talentwettbewerb **I**

*to **show** [ʃəʊ] zeigen **I**

*to **show** off [ˌʃəʊ ˈɒf] angeben **II**

to **showcase** [ˈʃəʊkeɪs] ausstellen **V U1**, 25

shower [ˈʃaʊə] Dusche **I**

show-off [ˈʃəʊ ɒf] Angeber/-in **I**

*to **shrink** [ʃrɪŋk] einsinken; schrumpfen **V U2**, 46

shrub [ʃrʌb] Strauch; Busch **IV**

to **shrug** (one's shoulders) [ʃrʌɡ] mit den Schultern zucken **III**

to **shuffle** [ˈʃʌfl] mischen **II**

shut [ʃʌt] zu; geschlossen **IV**

shutter [ˈʃʌtə] Fensterladen **IV**

shy [ʃaɪ] schüchtern **III**

sick [sɪk] krank; unwohl **II**

*to feel **sick** [ˌfiːl ˈsɪk] Übelkeit verspüren; sich schlecht fühlen **II**

side [saɪd] Seite **II**

sigh [saɪ] Seufzer **IV**

to **sigh** [saɪ] seufzen **IV**

sight [saɪt] Sehenswürdigkeit; Anblick **I**

sighting [ˈsaɪtɪŋ] Sichtung **IV**

*to go **sightseeing** [ˌɡəʊ ˈsaɪtsiːɪŋ] eine Besichtigungstour machen **II**

sign [saɪn] Zeichen; Schild **II**

to **sign** [saɪn] unterzeichnen; unterschreiben **II**

to **sign** off [ˌsaɪn ˈɒf] aufhören; Schluss machen **V U3**, 81

signal [ˈsɪɡnl] Signal; Empfang **III**

signature [ˈsɪɡnətʃə] Unterschrift **IV**

significant [sɪɡˈnɪfɪkənt] signifikant; bedeutend; wesentlich **IV**

silence (no pl) [ˈsaɪləns] Stille; Schweigen; Ruhe **III**

silent [ˈsaɪlənt] still; ruhig; schweigsam; stumm **III**

silly [ˈsɪli] Dummkopf **II**

silly [ˈsɪli] dumm; doof; albern **I**

silver [ˈsɪlvə] Silber **II**

similar [ˈsɪmɪlə] ähnlich **II**

simile [ˈsɪmɪli] Vergleich **V U1**, 18; **V TS**, 108

simple [ˈsɪmpl] einfach; simpel **III**

to **simplify** [ˈsɪmplɪfaɪ] vereinfachen **V AC1**, 8

sin [sɪn] Sünde **V AC2**, 35

since [sɪns] da **IV**

ever **since** [ˌevə ˈsɪns] seit; seitdem **IV**

since (+ Zeitpunkt) [sɪns] seit; seitdem **III**

Sincerely, . . . [sɪnˈsɪəli] Mit freundlichen Grüßen **I**

*to **sing** [sɪŋ] singen **I**

singer [ˈsɪŋə] Sänger/-in **II**

lead **singer** [ˈliːd ˌsɪŋə] Leadsänger/-in; Frontsänger/-in **III**

single [ˈsɪŋɡl] einfache Fahrkarte **II**

single [ˈsɪŋɡl] einzeln; einzig; alleinstehend **IV**

*to **sink** [sɪŋk] sinken **IV**

to **sip** [sɪp] nippen; schluckweise trinken **V U1**, 13

Dear **Sir** or Madam [dɪə ˌsɜːr ɔː ˈmædəm] Sehr geehrte Dame, sehr geehrter Herr **II**

sister [ˈsɪstə] Schwester **I**

half-**sister** [ˈhɑːfˌsɪstə] Halbschwester **I**

*to **sit** [sɪt] sitzen **I**

Sit! [sɪt] Sitz! (Befehl für Hunde) **I**

*to **sit** down [ˌsɪt ˈdaʊn] sich hinsetzen; sich setzen **I**

sit-in [ˈsɪtɪn] Sitzstreik **IV**

sitcom [ˈsɪtkɒm] Sitcom; Situationskomödie **IV**

site [saɪt] Website **II**; Ort; Gelände; Schauplatz **III**

situation [ˌsɪtjuˈeɪʃn] Situation **I**

six [sɪks] sechs **I**

sixteen [ˌsɪkˈstiːn] sechzehn **I**

sixty [ˈsɪksti] sechzig **I**

size [saɪz] Größe; Kleidergröße **I**

to **skate** [skeɪt] Inlineskates fahren; Schlittschuh laufen **I** (inline) **skating** ['ɪnlaɪn ˌskeɪtɪŋ] Inline-skatefahren **I**

skateboard ['skeɪtbɔːd] Skateboard **I**

skateboarding ['skeɪtbɔːdɪŋ] Skateboard-fahren **I**

skates *(pl)* [skeɪts] Inlineskates; Rollschuhe; Schlittschuhe **I**

skeleton ['skelɪtn] Skelett **V AC4**, 89

ski [skiː] Ski **III**

skiing ['skiːɪŋ] Skifahren **I**

skill [skɪl] Fertigkeit; Geschick **I**
people **skills** *(pl)* ['piːpl ˌskɪlz] soziale Kompetenz **IV**

skin [skɪn] Haut; Fell **II**

skinny ['skɪni] dünn; mager **IV**

to **skip** [skɪp] auslassen; schwänzen **III**

skirt [skɜːt] Rock **II**

sky [skaɪ] Himmel **II**

skyline ['skaɪlaɪn] Skyline **III**

skyscraper ['skaɪskreɪpə] Wolkenkratzer **I**

slate [sleɪt] Schiefer **III**

slave [sleɪv] Sklave/Sklavin **II**

slavery ['sleɪvri] Sklaverei **II**

*to **sleep** [sliːp] schlafen **I**

sleepover ['sliːpˌəʊvə] Übernachtung **I**

sleeve [sliːv] Ärmel **II**

to **slice** [slaɪs] in Scheiben schneiden **I**

slide [slaɪd] Rutschbahn **I**
water **slide** ['wɔːtə ˌslaɪd] Wasserrutsche **I**

*to **slide** [slaɪd] gleiten (lassen); rutschen **V U3**, 74

slight [slaɪt] leicht; gering **IV**

to **slip** [slɪp] schlüpfen; gleiten (lassen) **V U2**, 42

slipper ['slɪpə] Schuh; Pantoffel **V U3**, 73

slippery ['slɪpri] rutschig; glitschig **IV**

slogan ['sləʊgən] Slogan; Werbespruch **II**

slot [slɒt] Schlitz **V U1**, 14

to **slow** down [sləʊ 'daʊn] langsamer werden; bremsen **III**

slow [sləʊ] langsam **II**

slum [slʌm] Slum; Elendsviertel **IV**

small [smɔːl] klein **I**

smart [smɑːt] schlau; klug; intelligent **II**

smartphone ['smɑːtfəʊn] Smartphone **II**

to **smash** [smæʃ] schlagen; zerschmettern **II**

smell [smel] Geruch; Duft; Gestank **III**

*to **smell** [smel] riechen; duften **II**

smile [smaɪl] Lächeln **I**

to **smile** [smaɪl] lächeln **I**

to **smirk** [smɜːk] grinsen ⟨**V U3**, 86⟩

smoke [sməʊk] Rauch **III**

smoky ['sməʊki] verraucht; rauchig **III**

smooth [smuːð] glatt; weich; geschmeidig **IV**

smuggler ['smʌglə] Schmuggler/-in **III**

smuggling ['smʌglɪŋ] Schmuggel **III**

snack [snæk] Snack; Imbiss **I**
snack bar ['snæk ˌbɑː] Café; Imbissstube **I**

snake [sneɪk] Schlange **III**

to **snap** (at sb) ['snæp ˌət] anfahren; anschnauzen *(ugs.)* **III**

sneaker *(AE)* ['sniːkə] Turnschuh **II**

to **sneer** (at sb/sth) ['snɪər ˌət] (über jdn./etw.) spotten; jdn/etw. verhöhnen **V U3**, 81

to **snore** [snɔː] schnarchen **I**

snow [snəʊ] Schnee **II**
snow tire *(AE)* ['snəʊ ˌtaɪə] Winterreifen **IV**

so [səʊ] so; also **I**; es; das **III**
so (that) [səʊ 'ðət] damit; sodass **II**
so far [səʊ 'fɑː] bis jetzt **III**

to **soak** up [səʊk 'ʌp] aufsaugen **III**

soap *(no pl)* [səʊp] Seife **V U2**, 42

soccer *(AE)* ['sɒkə] Fußball **I**

social ['səʊʃl] sozial; gesellschaftlich **II**
social care [ˌsəʊʃl 'keə] Sozialfürsorge; Sozialdienstleistungen **IV**
social media [ˌsəʊʃl 'miːdiə] soziale Netzwerke **III**
social network [ˌsəʊʃl 'netwɜːk] soziales Netzwerk **II**
social security [ˌsəʊʃl sɪ'kjʊərəti] Sozialversicherung **V U3**, 70

society [sə'saɪəti] Verein; Gesellschaft **II**

sock [sɒk] Socke **II**

sofa ['səʊfə] Sofa; Couch **I**

soft [sɒft] weich; sanft **III**

to **soften** ['sɒftn] weich werden; leiser werden **V U1**, 21

soil [sɔɪl] Erde; Boden **IV**

solar energy [ˌsəʊlə 'pænl] Sonnenkollektor **V U1**, 24

soldier ['səʊldʒə] Soldat/-in **II**

sole [səʊl] Sohle **V U2**, 47

sole [səʊl] einzig; alleinig **V U1**, 21

solidarity [ˌsɒlɪ'dærəti] Solidarität; Zusammenhalt **IV**

solo ['səʊləʊ] Solo **III**

solution [sə'luːʃn] Lösung **I**

to **solve** [sɒlv] lösen **II**

some [sʌm; səm] einige; ein paar; etwas **I**; irgendein/-e **III**

somebody ['sʌmbədi] jemand **I**

somehow ['sʌmhaʊ] irgendwie **III**

someone ['sʌmwʌn] jemand **I**

something ['sʌmθɪŋ] etwas **I**

sometimes ['sʌmtaɪmz] manchmal **I**

somewhat ['sʌmwɒt] ein wenig; einigermaßen **V F4**, 62

somewhere ['sʌmweə] irgendwo; irgendwohin **II**

son [sʌn] Sohn **II**

song [sɒŋ] Song; Lied **I**

soon [suːn] bald **II**
as **soon** as [əz 'suːn ˌəz] sobald **II**
no **sooner** [nəʊ 'suːnə] kaum **IV**

soothing ['suːðɪŋ] beruhigend; schmerzlindernd ⟨**V U3**, 87⟩

Sorry! ['sɒri] Entschuldigung!; Tut mir leid! **I**
*to be **sorry** [bi 'sɒri] leid tun **I**
I'm **sorry**! [ˌaɪm 'sɒri] Tut mir leid! **I**

sort [sɔːt] Sorte; Art **V U3**, 82

soul [səʊl] Seele **II**

souling ['səʊlɪŋ] Souling *(mittelalterlicher Brauch, bei dem man durch Gabe von Broten seine Seele zu retten hoffte)* **II**

sound [saʊnd] Ton; Geräusch; Klang **I**

to **sound** [saʊnd] klingen **I**

soup [suːp] Suppe **III**

source [sɔːs] Quelle **III**

south [saʊθ] Süden; Süd- **I**

souvenir [ˌsuːvn'ɪə] Souvenir; Andenken **III**

sovereign ['sɒvrɪn] Herrscher/-in; Souverän/-in **IV**

*to **sow** [səʊ] säen ⟨**V U1**, 31⟩

space [speɪs] Raum; Weltraum **I**; Fläche; Platz; Ort **III**

spaceship ['speɪsʃɪp] Raumschiff **II**

Spanish ['spænɪʃ] spanisch; Spanisch; Spanier/-in **II**

*to **speak** [spiːk] sprechen **I**
*to **speak** out (about sth) [spiːk 'aʊt] seine Meinung (über etw.) deutlich vertreten; sich (zu etw.) äußern **IV**

speaker ['spiːkə] Redner/-in; Sprecher/-in **I**
native **speaker** [ˌneɪtɪv 'spiːkə] Muttersprachler/-in **IV**

speaking ['spiːkɪŋ] Sprechen **I**

spear [spɪə] Speer **II**

special ['speʃl] besonders; speziell **I**
special effect [speʃl ɪ'fekt] Spezialeffekt **IV**
special offer [speʃl 'ɒfə] Sonderangebot **I**

speciality *(BE)* [ˌspeʃi'æləti] Spezialität; Besonderheit **IV**

specialty *(AE)* ['speʃlti] Spezialität; Besonderheit **II**

species, species *(pl)* ['spiːʃiːz] Art; Spezies **III**

specific [spə'sɪfɪk] spezifisch; speziell **III**

spectacular [spek'tækjələ] spektakulär **III**

speech [spiːtʃ] Rede **II**
hate **speech** ['heɪt ˌspiːtʃ] Hassrede; Hetzrede **V U3**, 83
part of **speech** [ˌpɑːt əv 'spiːtʃ] Wortart; Wortklasse **V U1**, 26
speech bubble ['spiːtʃ ˌbʌbl] Sprechblase **I**

speed [spiːd] Geschwindigkeit **III**

spell [spel] Zauber; Bann; Zauberspruch **VTS**, 109

*to **spell** [spel] buchstabieren **I**

spelling ['spelɪŋ] Rechtschreibung **I**

*to **spend** [spend] ausgeben *(Geld)* **I**; verbringen *(Zeit)* **II**

spicy ['spaɪsi] würzig; pikant **III**

spider ['spaɪdə] Spinne **IV**

*to spin [spɪn] spinnen; (sich) schnell drehen **IV**

spirit ['spɪrɪt] Geist; Stimmung **III**

spirituality [ˌspɪrɪtʃuˈæləti] Spiritualität **IV**

*to spit [spɪt] spucken **III**

in spite of [ɪn ˈspaɪt əv] trotz **III**

to splash [splæʃ] spritzen; platschen; planschen **II**

*to split [splɪt] trennen; abspalten **VTS**, 110

*to split off [ˌsplɪt ˈɒf] sich abtrennen; sich abspalten **VF3**, 39

sponge [spʌndʒ] Rühr-; Biskuit- **I**

spontaneous [spɒnˈteɪniəs] spontan **IV**

spooky ['spuːki] gespenstisch **IV**; unheimlich; sonderbar **VU3**, 73

spoon [spuːn] Löffel **III**

sport [spɔːt] Sport; Sportart **I**

sporty ['spɔːti] sportlich **IV**

spot [spɒt] Fleck; Ort **III**

to spot [spɒt] entdecken; erkennen **III**

spread [spred] Ausbreitung; Verbreitung; Spannweite **VU1**, 22

*to spread [spred] (sich) verbreiten **III**

spring [sprɪŋ] Frühling **I**

to spy on [ˈspaɪ ɒn] nachspionieren; bespitzeln **IV**

square [skweə] Quadrat; Quadrat- **III**; Platz **IV**

squirrel ['skwɪrəl] Eichhörnchen **I**

stable ['steɪbl] Stall ⟨**VU1**, 31⟩

to stack [stæk] stapeln **IV**

stadium ['steɪdiəm] Stadion **I**

staff [stɑːf] Personal; Mitarbeiter **IV**

stage [steɪdʒ] Bühne **II**

to stage [steɪdʒ] inszenieren; aufführen **IV**

staircase ['steəkeɪs] Treppenhaus; Treppenaufgang **III**

stairs (pl) [steəz] Treppe **III**

stake [steɪk] Anteil **VU3**, 76

stakeholder ['steɪkhəʊldə] Anteilseigner/-in; Teilhaber/-in **VU3**, 76

to stalk [stɔːk] stolzieren; marschieren **VU1**, 17

stall [stɔːl] Stand; Bude **IV**

stamp [stæmp] Stempel **III**

stance [stæns] Haltung **VF5**, 67

*to stand [stænd] stehen **I**

to stand for election [ˌstænd fər ɪˈlekʃn] kandidieren; sich zur Wahl stellen **VF2**, 33

*to stand in line (AE) [ˌstænd ɪn ˈlaɪn] anstehen; Schlange stehen; (sich) anstellen **III**

*to stand out (from) [ˌstænd ˈaʊt] sich abheben (von); herausragen (aus) **IV**

*to stand up [ˌstænd ˈʌp] aufstehen (von einer Sitzgelegenheit) **I**

*to stand up for sb/sth [ˌstænd ˈʌp fə] jmdn./etw. verteidigen; für jmdn./etw. einstehen **IV**

standard of living [ˈstændəd əv ˈlɪvɪŋ] Lebensstandard **IV**

to standardize (AE) ['stændədaɪz] standardisieren; vereinheitlichen **IV**

standing (no pl) ['stændɪŋ] Ansehen; Status **VU2**, 52

stanza ['stænzə] Strophe **VF2**, 32; **VTS**, 108

star [stɑː] Star; Stern **I**

to stare [steə] starren; anstarren **I**

start [stɑːt] Anfang; Start **III**

to start [stɑːt] anfangen; beginnen; starten **I**

to start with [tə ˈstɑːt wɪθ] zunächst einmal **III**

state [steɪt] Staat; Bundesstaat; Land **I**; Zustand **IV**

head of state [ˌhed əv ˈsteɪt] Staatsoberhaupt **II**

unitary state [ˌjuːnɪtri ˈsteɪt] Einheitsstaat **VF2**, 33

to state [steɪt] feststellen; aussagen; darstellen **IV**

statement ['steɪtmənt] Aussage; Behauptung; Erklärung **II**

station ['steɪʃn] Haltestelle; Bahnhof; Station **I**; Sender **II**

bus station [ˈbʌs ˌsteɪʃn] Busbahnhof **I**

power station [ˈpaʊə ˌsteɪʃn] Kraftwerk **IV**

statistics (pl) [stəˈtɪstɪks] Statistik **IV**

statue ['stætʃuː] Statue; Standbild **II**

stay [steɪ] Aufenthalt **II**

to stay [steɪ] bleiben **I**; übernachten **II**

to stay in touch (with) [ˌsteɪ ɪn ˈtʌtʃ wɪð] in Kontakt bleiben (mit) **II**

to stay up [ˌsteɪ ˈʌp] aufbleiben **I**

steady ['stedi] kontinuierlich; unaufhörlich **VU3**, 76

steak [steɪk] Steak **I**

*to steal [stiːl] stehlen **I**

steel [stiːl] Stahl **VU2**, 47

steep [stiːp] steil **II**

step [step] Stufe; Schritt **I**

step-by-step [ˌstepbaɪˈstep] Schritt-für-Schritt- **II**

to step [step] treten; steigen **III**

stepmum ['stepmʌm] Stiefmutter **I**

stereo ['steriəʊ] Stereoanlage **VU3**, 74

stereotype ['steriəʊtaɪp] Klischee; Stereotyp **IV**

gender stereotyping [ˈdʒendə ˌsteriəʊtaɪpɪŋ] Einordnung nach Geschlechterklischees **IV**

stick [stɪk] Schläger (Hockey) **III**; Stock; Stange **VU1**, 16

sticky ['stɪki] klebrig **VF3**, 37

stiff [stɪf] steif **VU3**, 70

still [stɪl] Standbild **III**

still [stɪl] still **I**

still [stɪl] noch; immer noch **I**; dennoch **II**

*to sting [stɪŋ] stechen **IV**

to stock up [ˌstɒk ˈʌp] sich eindecken **VU1**, 14

stomach ['stʌmək] Magen; Bauch **II**

stomachache ['stʌməkeɪk] Bauchschmerzen; Bauchweh **II**

stone [stəʊn] Stein **II**

stone put ['stəʊn pʊt] Steinstoßen **VU1**, 13

stop [stɒp] Haltestelle; Halt **II**

to stop [stɒp] aufhören (mit); anhalten; stoppen **I**

Stop it! ['stɒp ɪt] Mach/Macht das aus!; Hör/Hört auf! **I**

store (AE) [stɔː] Laden; Geschäft **III**

to store [stɔː] speichern **VU3**, 80

storm [stɔːm] Sturm **I**

stormy ['stɔːmi] stürmisch **II**

story, stories (pl) ['stɔːri] Story; Geschichte; Erzählung **I**

crime story ['kraɪm ˌstɔri] Krimi; Kriminalgeschichte **II**

photo story ['fəʊtəʊ ˌstɔːri] Fotostory; Bildgeschichte **I**

to storyboard ['stɔːrɪbɔːd] ein Drehbuch schreiben **VU3**, 81

stove [stəʊv] Ofen; Herd **VU1**, 17

straight [streɪt] gerade; direkt; geradewegs **II**

straight (infml) [streɪt] heterosexuell **IV**

straight on [streɪt ˈɒn] geradeaus **II**

to straighten ['streɪtn] geraderichten; zurechtrücken ⟨**VU3**, 86⟩

straightforward [ˌstreɪtˈfɔːwəd] einfach; unkompliziert; direkt **VU3**, 82

strange [streɪndʒ] fremd; seltsam; merkwürdig **I**

stranger ['streɪndʒə] Fremde/-r **III**

strategy ['strætədʒi] Strategie ⟨**VU1**, 28⟩

straw (no pl) [strɔː] Stroh **III**

strawberry, strawberries (pl) ['strɔːbri] Erdbeere **I**

stream [striːm] Bach **VU1**, 15

streaming ['striːmɪŋ] Streaming **IV**

street [striːt] Straße (in der Stadt) **I**

in the street [ɪn ðə ˈstriːt] in der Straße; auf der Straße **I**

strength [streŋθ] Stärke; Kraft **IV**

to strengthen ['streŋθn] stärken **VF4**, 60

stress [stres] Stress **III**

to stress [stres] betonen; hervorheben **III**

to stretch [stretʃ] sich erstrecken; strecken; dehnen **IV**

stretcher ['stretʃə] Tragbahre **III**

strict [strɪkt] streng; strikt **II**

strike [straɪk] Streik **II**

*to strike [straɪk] schlagen; zuschlagen **IV**; treffen **VU1**, 24

striking ['straɪkɪŋ] bemerkenswert; auffallend **III**

string [strɪŋ] Saite **VAC2**, 35

stripe [straɪp] Streifen **III**

*to strive (for/to) [straɪv] anstreben; streben; sich bemühen (um) **IV**

to stroke [strəʊk] streicheln **IV**

strong [strɒŋ] stark **I**

structure ['strʌktʃə] Struktur; Aufbau; Gliederung **IV**

to structure ['strʌktʃə] strukturieren; gliedern **III**

stubborn ['stʌbən] eigensinnig; störrisch **II**

*to be stuck [bi 'stʌk] festsitzen; feststecken; hängen bleiben **II**

student ['stjuːdnt] Schüler/-in; Student/-in **I**

  exchange student [ɪksˈtʃeɪndʒ ˌstjuːdnt] Austauschschüler/-in **III**

  student council [ˌstjuːdnt ˈkaʊnsl] Schülerrat **IV**

studies (pl) ['stʌdiz] Studium; Lernen; Arbeit für die Schule **IV**

studio ['stjuːdiəʊ] Studio; Atelier **IV**

  recording studio [rɪˈkɔːdɪŋ ˌstjuːdiəʊ] Aufnahmestudio; Tonstudio **I**

study ['stʌdi] Studie; Untersuchung **IV**

to study ['stʌdi] studieren; lernen **II**

stuff [stʌf] Zeug **I**

stump [stʌmp] Stumpf; Strunk **V AC2**, 35

stunt [stʌnt] Stunt; Trick **IV**

stupid ['stjuːpɪd] dumm; blöd **II**

style [staɪl] Stil **II**

stylistic [staɪˈlɪstɪk] Stil-; stilistisch **V F4**, 61

  stylistic devices [staɪˌlɪstɪk dɪˈvaɪsɪz] Stilmittel **V F4**, 61

subject ['sʌbdʒɪkt] Schulfach; Thema **II**; Untertan/-in **V TS**, 111

to submit [səbˈmɪt] einreichen; vorlegen **V F2**, 33

to subscribe (to) [səbˈskraɪb] abonnieren; teilnehmen (an) **V U3**, 83

subscriber identity module [səbˌskraɪbər aɪˈdentəti ˌmɒdjuːl] Teilnehmer-Identitätsmodul **V U3**, 80

substance ['sʌbstns] Substanz; Gehalt ⟨**V U2**, 58⟩; **V F5**, 67

subtext ['sʌbtekst] versteckte Bedeutung **V AC3**, 65

suburb ['sʌbɜːb] Vorort **III**

suburban [səˈbɜːbn] Vorstadt- **III**

to succeed (in) [səkˈsiːd ɪn] Erfolg haben (in/bei/mit); gelingen **IV**

success [səkˈses] Erfolg **II**

successful [səkˈsesfl] erfolgreich **II**

such [sʌtʃ] solch; solche/-r/-s **III**

  such as [ˈsʌtʃ əz] (solche) wie; wie (zum Beispiel) **I**

to suck [sʌk] lutschen; saugen **IV**

  It sucks. (slang) [ɪt ˈsʌks] Das ist zum Kotzen. (ugs.) **III**

all of a sudden [ˌɔːl əv ə ˈsʌdn] plötzlich; auf einmal **V U2**, 46

suddenly ['sʌdnli] plötzlich; auf einmal **I**

to suffer (from) ['sʌfə frəm] leiden (unter) **IV**

suffrage ['sʌfrɪdʒ] Stimmrecht; Wahlrecht **V F2**, 33

suffrage ['sʌfrɪdʒ] Wahlrecht; Stimmrecht **V AC4**, 88

suffragette [ˌsʌfrəˈdʒet] Frauenrechtlerin **V F2**, 33

sugar ['ʃʊɡə] Zucker **III**

sugarcane ['ʃʊɡəkeɪn] Zuckerrohr **V F3**, 36

to suggest [səˈdʒest] vorschlagen **II**; andeuten; nahelegen **IV**

suggestion [səˈdʒestʃn] Vorschlag; Anregung **III**

suicide ['suːɪsaɪd] Selbstmord; Suizid **III**

suit [suːt] Anzug; Kostüm **IV**

  law suit ['lɔː ˌsuːt] Gerichtsverfahren **V U3**, 75

to suit sb [suːt] (zu) jmdm. passen; jmdm. stehen **IV**

suitable ['suːtəbl] geeignet; passend **III**

suited ['suːtɪd] geeignet; passend **III**

sum total [ˌsʌm ˈtəʊtl] Summe; Gesamtheit **V U2**, 48

to sum up [ˌsʌm ˈʌp] zusammenfassen **II**

to summarise ['sʌmraɪz] zusammenfassen **IV**

summary ['sʌmri] Zusammenfassung **III**

summer ['sʌmə] Sommer **I**

summit ['sʌmɪt] Gipfel; Berggipfel **IV**

sun [sʌn] Sonne **II**

Sunday ['sʌndeɪ] Sonntag **I**

sunglasses (pl) ['sʌnˌɡlɑːsɪz] Sonnenbrille **IV**

sunlight ['sʌnlaɪt] Sonnenlicht **III**

sunny ['sʌni] sonnig **II**

sunscreen ['sʌnskriːn] Sonnencreme **II**

sunset ['sʌnset] Sonnenuntergang **IV**

sunshine ['sʌnʃaɪn] Sonnenschein **II**

superhero ['suːpəˌhɪərəʊ] Superheld **III**

superior [suːˈpɪəriə] überlegen; gehoben **V F4**, 61

supermarket ['suːpəˌmɑːkɪt] Supermarkt **I**

to supervise ['suːpəvaɪz] beaufsichtigen; betreuen **V U2**, 50

supply [səˈplaɪ] Vorrat; Versorgung; Zufuhr **IV**

to supply [səˈplaɪ] versorgen **II**

support (no pl) [səˈpɔːt] Unterstützung; Hilfe **III**

to support [səˈpɔːt] unterstützen **III**

  supporting role [səˈpɔːtɪŋ ˌrəʊl] Nebenrolle **V TS**, 112

to suppose [səˈpəʊz] vermuten; annehmen **IV**

  *to be supposed to (do) [bi səˈpəʊzd tə] (tun) sollen **III**

white supremacist [ˌwaɪt suːˈpreməsɪst] Anhänger/-in der Theorie von der Überlegenheit der Weißen **V F4**, 61

sure [ʃʊə; ʃɔː] sicher **I**

  *to make sure [ˌmeɪk ˈʃɔː] sich versichern **II**

surf instructor [ˈsɜːf ɪnˈstrʌktə] Surflehrer/-in **IV**

surface ['sɜːfɪs] Oberfläche **IV**

surfing ['sɜːfɪŋ] Surfen **I**

surgery ['sɜːdʒri] Arztpraxis; Praxis; Praxisräume **I**

  plastic surgery (no pl) [ˌplæstɪk ˈsɜːdʒəri] Schönheitschirurgie **IV**

surname ['sɜːneɪm] Nachname **V F1**, 10

surprise [səˈpraɪz] Überraschung **I**

to surprise [səˈpraɪz] überraschen **II**

*to be surprised [bi səˈpraɪzd] überrascht sein **I**

surprising [səˈpraɪzɪŋ] überraschend **III**

to surround [səˈraʊnd] umgeben; umringen **IV**

surroundings (pl) [səˈraʊndɪŋz] Umgebung **V TS**, 115

surveillance [sɜːˈveɪləns] Überwachung; Beaufsichtigung **V U3**, 82

survey ['sɜːveɪ] Umfrage; Studie **I**

to survive [səˈvaɪv] überleben **II**

to suspect sb/sth [səˈspekt] verdächtigen **V U2**, 43

to suspend [səˈspend] hängen; aufhängen **V U3**, 71

*to be suspended [bi səˈspendɪd] suspendiert werden; zeitweilig vom Unterricht ausgeschlossen werden **III**

suspense [səˈspens] Spannung **III**

to sustain [səˈsteɪn] (am Leben) erhalten ⟨**V U1**, 28⟩

sustainability [səˌsteɪnəˈbɪləti] Nachhaltigkeit **IV**

sustainable [səˈsteɪnəbl] nachhaltig **IV**

to swallow ['swɒləʊ] schlucken **V U2**, 44

to swap roles [ˌswɒp ˈrəʊlz] Rollen tauschen **I**

*to swear [sweə] schwören **V U2**, 42

sweat [swet] Schweiß **IV**

to sweat [swet] schwitzen **IV**

sweater ['swetə] Pullover **V U3**, 73

sweatshop ['swetʃɒp] Ausbeuterbetrieb **III**

*to sweep [swiːp] fegen; wegspülen **IV**

sweet [swiːt] süß **I**

  sweet potatoes (pl) ['swiːt pəˌteɪtəʊz] Süßkartoffeln **II**

sweets (pl) [swiːts] Süßigkeiten; Bonbons **I**

*to swim [swɪm] schwimmen **I**

swimmer ['swɪmə] Schwimmer/-in **II**

swimming ['swɪmɪŋ] Schwimmen **I**

  *to go swimming [ˌɡəʊ ˈswɪmɪŋ] schwimmen gehen **I**

  swimming pool ['swɪmɪŋ ˌpuːl] Swimmingpool; Schwimmbecken **III**

*to swing (at sb) [swɪŋ] (nach jdm.) schlagen **V F4**, 62

to swipe [swaɪp] wischen **V U3**, 80

Swiss [swɪs] Schweizer; schweizerisch **IV**

to switch off [ˌswɪtʃ ˈɒf] ausschalten **III**

sword [sɔːd] Schwert **III**

syllable ['sɪləbl] Silbe **V TS**, 108

symbol ['sɪmbl] Symbol **I**

symbolic [sɪmˈbɒlɪk] symbolisch **IV**

to symbolise ['sɪmblaɪz] symbolisieren **V F4**, 62

symptom ['sɪmtəm] Symptom; Merkmal **IV**
synonym ['sɪnənɪm] Synonym **IV**
synthesizer ['sɪnθəˌsaɪzə] Synthesizer **V U1**, 21
syrup ['sɪrəp] Sirup **III**
   maple **syrup** [ˌmeɪpl 'sɪrəp] Ahornsirup **II**
system ['sɪstəm] System **II**
   electoral **system** [ɪˌlektrl 'sɪstəm] Wahlsystem **V F2**, 33
   justice **system** ['dʒʌstɪs ˌsɪstəm] Justizsystem **V U2**, 41
   operating **system** ['ɒpreɪtɪŋ ˌsɪstəm] Betriebssystem **V U3**, 80

T

table ['teɪbl] Tisch **I**
   *to **set** the **table** [ˌset ðə 'teɪbl] den Tisch decken **III**
   the Round **Table** [ðə ˌraʊnd 'teɪbl] die Tafelrunde **II**
tablet ['tæblət] Tablet **II**
tail [teɪl] Schwanz; Schweif **I**
*to **take** [teɪk] nehmen; mitnehmen; wegnehmen; bringen; mitbringen **I**; dauern; (Zeit) brauchen **II**
   *to **take** a breath [ˌteɪk ə 'breθ] Luft holen; Atem holen **III**
   *to **take** a look at [ˌteɪk ə 'lʊk æt] einen Blick werfen auf **II**
   *to **take** a message [ˌteɪk ə 'mesɪdʒ] eine Nachricht entgegennehmen; jmdm. etw. ausrichten **I**
   *to **take** a risk [ˌteɪk ə 'rɪsk] ein Risiko eingehen **II**
   *to **take** care of [teɪk 'keər ˌəv] sich kümmern um; sorgen für **III**
   *to **take** it easy [ˌteɪk ɪt ˌi:zi] immer ruhig bleiben; auf der faulen Haut liegen **II**
   *to **take** notes [ˌteɪk 'nəʊts] sich Notizen machen **I**
   *to **take** off [teɪk ˌɒf] abnehmen; herunternehmen; ausziehen **II**
   *to **take** out [ˌteɪk 'aʊt] herausnehmen **I**
   *to **take** part (in) [ˌteɪk 'pɑːt (ɪn)] teilnehmen (an) **II**
   *to **take** photos [ˌteɪk 'fəʊtəʊz] fotografieren; Fotos machen **I**
   *to **take** place [teɪk 'pleɪs] stattfinden **I**
   *to **take** revenge [teɪk rɪ'vendʒ] (sich) rächen **III**
   *to **take** sth seriously [teɪk 'sɪərɪəsli] ernst nehmen **II**
   *to **take** sth the wrong way [ˌteɪk ðə rɒŋ 'weɪ] etw. falsch auffassen; etw. in den falschen Hals bekommen **IV**
   It **took** ages. [ɪt tʊk ˌeɪdʒɪz] Es dauerte ewig. **II**
   Take turns. [teɪk 'tɜːnz] Wechselt euch ab. **I**
take-off ['teɪk ˌɒf] Start; Abheben **II**
tale [teɪl] Geschichte; Erzählung **IV**

fairy **tale** ['feəri ˌteɪl] Märchen **IV**
talent ['tælənt] Talent **I**
   talent show ['tælənt ˌʃəʊ] Talentwettbewerb **I**
talk [tɔːk] Vortrag; Rede **II**; Gespräch; Unterhaltung **I**
   pep **talk** ['pep ˌtɔːk] aufmunternde Worte; Motivationsgespräch **V U2**, 46
to **talk** [tɔːk] sprechen; reden **I**
   to **talk** about ['tɔːk ˌəbaʊt] sprechen über; erzählen von **I**
   to **talk** to ['tɔːk tə] reden mit **I**
tall [tɔːl] groß; hoch **I**
tap water ['tæp ˌwɔːtə] Leitungswasser **V TS**, 117
to **tap** [tæp] antippen **II**
tarantula [tə'ræntjələ] Tarantel (*Spinnenart*) **III**
target ['tɑːgɪt] Ziel; Ziel- **IV**
tartan ['tɑːtn] Schottenkaro (*bestimmtes Muster eines Clans*); karierter Schottenstoff **V U1**, 13
task [tɑːsk] Aufgabe; Auftrag **I**
taste [teɪst] Geschmack **II**
to **taste** [teɪst] schmecken; probieren **III**
tasty ['teɪsti] lecker; schmackhaft **III**
neep (*Scot*) [niːp] Steckrübe **V U1**, 13
tattie (*Scot*) ['tæti] Kartoffel **V U1**, 13
tattoo [tæt'uː] Tattoo; Tätowierung **IV**
tax [tæks] Steuer; Abgabe **III**
   tax office ['tæks ˌɒfɪs] Finanzamt **V U3**, 76
to **tax** [tæks] besteuern **V U3**, 76
taxation [tæk'seɪʃn] Besteuerung **V F2**, 33
taxi ['tæksi] Taxi **IV**
tea [tiː] Tee **I**
*to **teach** [tiːtʃ] unterrichten; lehren; beibringen **I**
   *to **teach** somebody a lesson [ˌtiːtʃ ə 'lesn] jmdm. eine Lehre/Lektion erteilen **IV**
teacher ['tiːtʃə] Lehrer/-in **I**
   head **teacher** [ˌhed 'tiːtʃə] Schulleiter/-in **IV**
team [tiːm] Team; Gruppe **I**
   *to **make** a **team** [ˌmeɪk ə 'tiːm] sich für ein Team qualifizieren **III**
tear [tɪə] Träne **II**
to **tease** sb [tiːz] jmdn. aufziehen; jmdn. hänseln; jmdn. ärgern **I**
technical ['teknɪkl] technisch; handwerklich; fachlich **I**
technique [tek'niːk] Methode; Technik **III**
technological [ˌteknə'lɒdʒɪkl] technologisch; technisch **IV**
technology [tek'nɒlədʒi] Technologie **I**
teen [tiːn] Teenager; Jugendliche/-r **II**; Jugend- **III**
teenager ['tiːnˌeɪdʒə] Teenager; Jugendliche/-r **I**
telephone ['telɪfəʊn] Telefon **I**
*to **tell** [tel] erzählen; sagen; mitteilen; erkennen; wissen **I**

   *to **tell** sb to do sth [ˌtel sʌmbədi tə 'duː sʌmθɪŋ] jmdm. sagen, was er tun soll **II**
temperate ['temprət] gemäßigt **IV**
temperature ['temprətʃə] Temperatur **II**
temporary ['temprəri] vorübergehend; temporär **IV**
ten [ten] zehn **I**
   ten-figure ['tenfɪgə] zehnstellig **V U3**, 76
to **tend** to ['tend tə] neigen zu; tendieren zu **IV**
to **tend** to sb/sth ['tend tə] sich um jdn./etw. kümmern **V F3**, 37
tennis ['tenɪs] Tennis **I**
tense [tens] Zeit; Zeitform (*grammatisch*) **III**
to **tense** [tens] sich spannen; (sich) anspannen (**V U1**, 31)
tension ['tenʃn] Spannung **IV**
tent [tent] Zelt **II**
term [tɜːm] Trimester; Semester; Halbjahr **III**; Begriff **IV**
   generic **term** [dʒeˌnerɪk 'tɜːm] Oberbegriff **IV**
   term of office [ˌtɜːm əv 'ɒfɪs] Amtszeit **IV**
terrace ['terɪs] Terrasse **IV**
terrible ['terəbl] schrecklich; schlimm; furchtbar **II**
terrific [tə'rɪfɪk] ausgezeichnet; hervorragend (**V U2**, 59)
*to be **terrified** (of sth) [bi 'terəfaɪd ˌəv] (große) Angst (vor etw.) haben **III**
territory ['terɪtri] Gebiet; Revier; Territorium **III**
test [test] Test; Klassenarbeit; Prüfung **I**
testimonial [ˌtestɪ'məʊniəl] Erfahrungsbericht **IV**
text [tekst] Text **I**
   text (message) ['tekst ˌmesɪdʒ] SMS; Kurznachricht **I**
to **text** [tekst] eine SMS schicken **II**
textile ['tekstaɪl] textil; Textil- **IV**
than [ðæn] als (bei Vergleichen) **II**
   more … **than** ['mɔː ðən] mehr … als **I**
*to give **thanks** [ˌgɪv 'θæŋks] danken **III**
to **thank** [θæŋk] danken **II**
   Thank you. ['θæŋk ju] Danke. **I**
thankful ['θæŋkfl] dankbar **I**
Thanks. [θæŋks] Danke. **I**
that (+ adj) [ðæt] so **III**
that [ðæt; ðət] dass **I**
that [ðæt] das; jenes **I**
   after **that** [ˌɑːftə 'ðæt] danach **I**
   i. e. (= **that** is) [aɪˈiː (ðæt ˌɪz)] das heißt (Abk.: d.h.) **IV**
   like **that** [laɪk 'ðæt] so **I**
   That was close! [ðæt wəz 'kləʊs] Das war knapp! **I**
   That's fair enough. [ˌðæts feər ɪ'nʌf] Das ist nur recht und billig. **IV**
   That's fine with me. [ˌðæts ˌfaɪn wɪð 'miː] Das ist in Ordnung für mich. **II**

That's what friends are for. [ˌðæts wɒt ˈfrendz ɑː ˌfɔː] Dafür sind Freunde da. I

that's why [ˌðæts ˈwaɪ] deshalb II

That's … [ˌðæts] Das macht … I

the [ðə; ðɪ] der; die *(auch Pl.)*; das I

the others [ðɪ ˈʌðəz] die anderen I

the rest [rest] der Rest II

the same [ðə ˈseɪm] der-/die-/dasselbe; der/die/das gleiche I

the … the … + *comparative form* [ðə … ðə] je … desto … + *Komparativ* II

movie **theater** *(AE)* [ˌmuːvi ˈθɪətə] Kino *(amerik.)* I

theatre [ˈθɪətə] Theater I

their [ðeə] ihr/-e *(Pl.)* I

theirs ihre/-er/-es II

them [ðem] sie *(Pl.)*; ihnen I

theme [θiːm] Thema; Motto I

theme park [ˈθiːm ˌpɑːk] Vergnügungspark *(meist mit einem bestimmten Thema)*; Themenpark II

themselves [ðemˈselvz] sich selbst *(3. P. Pl.)* II

then [ðen] dann; danach I

back then [ˌbæk ˈðen] damals III

theory [ˈθɪəri] Theorie V F3, 36

there [ðeə] da; dort; dahin; dorthin I

over **there** [ˌəʊvə ˈðeə] da drüben; dort drüben I

there is/are [ðər ˈɪz/ˈɑː] da ist/sind; es gibt I

There's nothing more exciting than … [ˌðeəz ˌnʌθɪŋ mɔː ɪkˈsaɪtɪŋ ðən] Es gibt nichts Spannenderes als … I

therefore [ˈðeəfɔː] deshalb; deswegen; daher; somit III

thesaurus [θɪˈsɔːrəs], **thesauri** [θɪˈsɔːraɪ] *(pl)* Synonymwörterbuch V U1, 26

these [ðiːz] diese (hier) I

they [ðeɪ] sie *(Pl.)* I; man III

It's …/**They**'re … [ɪts/ðeə] Es kostet …/Sie kosten … I

thick [θɪk] dick *(nicht für Personen)* III

thief [θiːf], **thieves** *(pl)* [θiːvz] Dieb/-in IV

thin [θɪn] dünn III

thing [θɪŋ] Ding; Sache I

*to **think** [θɪŋk] denken; nachdenken; glauben I

*to **think** of [ˈθɪŋk ˌəv] halten von; denken über I; denken an III

third [θɜːd] Drittel III

third [θɜːd] dritte/-r/-s I

third-person narrator [ˌθɜːd ˈpɜːsn nəˈreɪtə] Erzähler/-in, der/die in der 3. Person erzählt III

thirsty [ˈθɜːsti] durstig III

thirteen [ˌθɜːˈtiːn] dreizehn I

thirty [ˈθɜːti] dreißig I

this *(+ adj)* [ðɪs] so III

this [ðɪs] dies; diese/-r/-s I

This is how you (do) … [ˈðɪs ɪz haʊ jʊ ˌduː] So machst du … I

those [ðəʊz] diese dort; jene I

though [ðəʊ] doch; jedoch; obwohl III

even **though** [ˌiːvn ˈðəʊ] auch wenn; obwohl III

thought [θɔːt] Gedanke III

thousands of [ˈθaʊzndz əv] Tausende (von) I

threat [θret] Bedrohung; Gefahr V F5, 67

idle **threat** [ˌaɪdl ˈθret] leere Drohung V F5, 67

to **threaten** [ˈθretn] drohen; bedrohen III

three [θriː] drei I

three and a half times [θriː ˌənd ə ˈhɑːf taɪmz] dreieinhalbmal II

thrilled [θrɪld] aufgeregt; außer sich vor Freude V U1, 18

to **thrive** [θraɪv] florieren; gedeihen; blühen V F3, 36

throat [θrəʊt] Rachen; Kehle; Hals IV

throne [θrəʊn] Thron II

through [θruː] durch I

throughout [θruːˈaʊt] während; überall in IV

hammer **throw** [ˈhæmə ˌθrəʊ] Hammerwerfen V U1, 13

*to **throw** (at) [θrəʊ] werfen (nach) I

*to **throw** away [θrəʊ əˈweɪ] wegwerfen I

thug [θʌg] Gangster; Schläger; Verbrecher V U2, 44

thumb [θʌm] Daumen III

thunder *(no pl)* [ˈθʌndə] Donner II

thunderstorm [ˈθʌndəstɔːm] Gewitter III

Thursday [ˈθɜːzdeɪ] Donnerstag I

thus [ðʌs] dadurch; deshalb IV

ticket [ˈtɪkɪt] Los; Ticket; Eintrittskarte I; Fahrschein II

ticket office [ˈtɪkɪt ˌɒfɪs] Kartenschalter III

tide [taɪd] Ebbe und Flut IV

to **tidy** *(a room)* [ˈtaɪdi] aufräumen; in Ordnung bringen I

tidy [ˈtaɪdi] sauber; ordentlich II

to **tie** (to) [ˈtaɪ tə] binden (an); fesseln (an) II

tight [taɪt] eng IV

till [tɪl] bis I

time [taɪm] Zeit; Mal I

at the same **time** [ət ðə ˌseɪm ˈtaɪm] zur selben Zeit; gleichzeitig I

*to buy **time** [ˌbaɪ ˈtaɪm] Zeit gewinnen IV

free **time** [ˌfriː ˈtaɪm] Freizeit I

on **time** [ɒn ˈtaɪm] pünktlich II

three and a half **times** [θriː ˌənd ə ˈhɑːf taɪmz] dreieinhalbmal II

time line [ˈtaɪm ˌlaɪn] Zeitstrahl I

Time to get up! [ˌtaɪm tə ˌget ˈʌp] Es ist Zeit aufzustehen! I

What **time**? [wɒt ˈtaɪm] Um wie viel Uhr? I

What's the **time**? [ˌwɒts ðə ˈtaɪm] Wie spät ist es?; Wie viel Uhr ist es? I

Your **time** is up. [jɔː ˌtaɪm ˌɪz ˈʌp] Deine/Eure Zeit ist um. IV

timetable [ˈtaɪmˌteɪbl] Stundenplan; Fahrplan I

tin [tɪn] Zinn II; Dose; Büchse V U1, 17

tin whistle [ˌtɪn ˈwɪsl] Blechflöte V U1, 21

tinned [tɪnd] Dosen-; aus der Dose I

tiny [ˈtaɪni] klein; winzig IV

tip [tɪp] Tipp; Ratschlag I

on **tiptoe** [ɒn ˈtɪptəʊ] auf Zehenspitzen IV

to **tiptoe** [ˈtɪptəʊ] auf Zehenspitzen gehen II

tire *(AE)* [taɪə] Reifen IV

snow **tire** *(AE)* [ˈsnəʊ ˌtaɪə] Winterreifen IV

tired [taɪəd] müde I

*to be **tired** of *(+ noun or -ing)* [bi ˈtaɪəd əv] es müde sein (zu); es leid sein (zu); es satt haben (zu) III

title [ˈtaɪtl] Titel; Überschrift I

to [tʊ; tə] zu; nach; auf; in; vor *(bei Uhrzeitangaben)* I

from … **to** [frəm … tə] von … bis I

quarter past/**to** [ˈkwɔːtə pɑːst/tə] Viertel nach/vor I

to the point [tə ðə ˈpɔɪnt] prägnant; treffend IV

toast [təʊst] Toast I

toaster [ˈtəʊstə] Toaster IV

tobacco *(no pl)* [təˈbækəʊ] Tabak III

today [təˈdeɪ] heute I

toe [təʊ] Zeh III

together [təˈgeðə] zusammen; miteinander; gemeinsam I

toilet [ˈtɔɪlət] Toilette I

tolerance [ˈtɒlrns] Toleranz IV

tolerant [ˈtɒlrnt] tolerant IV

to **tolerate** [ˈtɒlreɪt] tolerieren; dulden IV

tomato, **tomatoes** *(pl)* [təˈmɑːtəʊ] Tomate II

tomorrow [təˈmɒrəʊ] morgen I

ton [tʌn] Tonne IV

tongue [tʌŋ] Zunge III

tongue twister [ˈtʌŋ ˌtwɪstə] Zungenbrecher III

tonight [təˈnaɪt] heute Abend; heute Nacht III

too [tuː] auch; zu I

Me **too**. [ˌmiː ˈtuː] Ich auch. I

Too bad! [ˌtuː ˈbæd] Zu dumm!; Schade! I

You **too**? [juː ˈtuː] Du auch? II

tool [tuːl] Werkzeug; Gerät II

tooth [tuːθ], **teeth** *(pl)* [tiːθ] Zahn IV

toothbrush [ˈtuːθbrʌʃ] Zahnbürste IV

top [tɒp] Spitze; oberer Teil; oberes Ende I

on **top** [ɒn ˈtɒp] oben; obendrauf I

over the **top** *(infml)* [ˌəʊvə ðə ˈtɒp] übertrieben; überzogen IV

topic [ˈtɒpɪk] Thema II

torch [tɔːtʃ] Fackel; Taschenlampe II

*to be **torn** [bi 'tɔːn] hin und her gerissen sein **VTS**, 110

to **toss** [tɒs] werfen; stoßen **V U1**, 16
tossing the caber ['tɒsɪŋ ðə 'keɪbə] Baumstammwerfen **V U1**, 13

a **total** of [ə 'təʊtl̩ əv] insgesamt **III**

to **total** ['təʊtl̩] sich belaufen auf **V U3**, 76

total ['təʊtl̩] total; gesamt; vollständig **III**
sum **total** [ˌsʌm 'təʊtl̩] Summe; Gesamtheit **V U2**, 48

totally ['təʊtli] völlig; total **III**

*to get in **touch** (with) [ˌget ɪn 'tʌtʃ] kontaktieren; in Verbindung treten (mit) **V U1**, 27

*to keep in **touch** [ˌkiːp ɪn 'tʌtʃ] in Kontakt bleiben **III**

to stay in **touch** (with) [ˌsteɪ ɪn 'tʌtʃ wɪð] in Kontakt bleiben (mit) **II**

to **touch** [tʌtʃ] berühren; antippen **II**

tough [tʌf] hart; rau; zäh **III**

tour [tʊə] Tour; Fahrt; Rundgang **II**
guided **tour** [ˌgaɪdɪd 'tʊə] geführte Tour; Führung **III**

tourism ['tʊərɪzm] Tourismus **II**

tourist ['tʊərɪst] Tourist/-in **I**
tourist board ['tʊərɪst ˌbɔːd] Tourismuszentrale; Tourismusbehörde **II**
tourist information centre [ˌtʊərɪst ɪnfə'meɪʃn ˌsentə] Touristeninformation **I**

towards [tə'wɔːds] in Richtung **II**

tower [taʊə] Turm **III**

to **tower** [taʊə] hoch aufragen **V U1**, 14

town [taʊn] Stadt **I**
home **town** ['həʊmtaʊn] Heimatstadt **I**

toy [tɔɪ] Spielzeug **I**

to **trace** back [ˌtreɪs 'bæk] zurückverfolgen **IV**

track [træk] Spur; Fährte; Pfad; Bahn **II**

trade [treɪd] Handel **III**

to **trade** [treɪd] Handel treiben **II**
to **trade** sth in for sth [ˌtreɪd 'ɪn] in Zahlung geben **V F3**, 38

trader ['treɪdə] Händler/-in **III**

trading ['treɪdɪŋ] Handel **III**
trading post ['treɪdɪŋ ˌpəʊst] Handelsposten **III**

tradition [trə'dɪʃn] Tradition **I**

traditional [trə'dɪʃnl̩] traditionell **II**

traffic ['træfɪk] Verkehr **III**

drug **trafficking** ['drʌg ˌtræfɪkɪŋ] Drogenhandel **V U2**, 46

tragedy ['trædʒədi] Tragödie **V U2**, 49; **VTS**, 110

trail [treɪl] Weg; Pfad; Spur **II**

train [treɪn] Zug **I**

to **train** [treɪn] trainieren **I**

trainer ['treɪnə] Trainer/-in **II**

training ['treɪnɪŋ] Training **II**

to **trample** (on) ['træmpl̩] zertrampeln; herumtrampeln **IV**

trampoline ['træmpiːn] Trampolin **II**

transfer ['trænsfɜː] Transfer **IV**

to **transfer** [træns'fɜː] übertragen; transferieren **IV**

transformative [ˌtræns'fɔːmətɪv] umgestaltend; umformend; transformativ **V U3**, 82

transition [træn'zɪʃn] Übergang **IV**

to **translate** [trænz'leɪt] übersetzen **I**

translation [trænz'leɪʃn] Übersetzung **I**

transport ['trænspɔːt] Verkehrsmittel; Transport **II**
means of **transport** (sg or pl) [ˌmiːnz əv 'trænspɔːt] Transportmittel; Verkehrsmittel **III**

to **transport** [træn'spɔːt] transportieren; befördern **IV**

transportation (AE) [ˌtrænspɔː'teɪʃn] Transport **IV**

*to be **trapped** [bi 'træpt] eingeschlossen sein; in der Falle sitzen **III**

trash (AE) [træʃ] Abfall; Müll **II**

trauma, **traumas**/**traumata** (pl) ['trɔːmə; 'trɔːmətə] Trauma; seelischer Schock **IV**

travel ['trævl̩] (das) Reisen; Reise **II**
travel agent's ['trævl̩ ˌeɪdʒnts] Reisebüro **II**

to **travel** ['trævl̩] fahren; reisen **II**

treasure ['treʒə] Schatz **II**

treat [triːt] besondere Freude; Belohnung **II**; Leckerei **III**

to **treat** [triːt] behandeln **III**

treatment ['triːtmənt] Behandlung **V U2**, 50

treaty ['triːti] Vertrag **III**

tree [triː] Baum **I**
family **tree** ['fæmli ˌtriː] Stammbaum **I**
palm **tree** ['pɑːm ˌtriː] Palme **II**

pony **trekking** ['pəʊni ˌtrekɪŋ] Ponyreiten im Gelände **II**

to **tremble** ['trembl̩] zittern **VTS**, 109

trend [trend] Trend; Entwicklung; Richtung **IV**

trendy ['trendi] trendy; modisch **V U2**, 46

trial [traɪəl] Qualifikation **II**

tribe [traɪb] Stamm; Volksstamm **II**

trick [trɪk] Trick; Streich **I**
trick-or-treating [ˌtrɪk ɔː 'triːtɪŋ] Süßes oder Saures (Spiel zu Halloween, bei dem Kinder von Tür zu Tür gehen und um Süßigkeiten bitten) **II**
to play a **trick** (on) [ˌpleɪ ə 'trɪk ɒn] einen Streich spielen **I**

to **trick** [trɪk] täuschen; austricksen **VTS**, 111

tricky ['trɪki] schwierig; kompliziert **IV**

trifle ['traɪfl̩] Trifle (englischer Nachtisch) **I**

trip [trɪp] Trip; Reise; Ausflug; Fahrt **I**

to **trip** (over) [ˌtrɪp 'əʊvə] stolpern (über) **I**

Trojan horse [ˌtrəʊdʒn 'hɔːs] trojanisches Pferd (Schadsoftware) **V U3**, 80

trolley ['trɒli] Karren; Einkaufswagen **IV**

trouble ['trʌbl̩] Ärger; Probleme; Schwierigkeiten **II**

*to get into **trouble** [ˌget ɪntə 'trʌbl̩] in Schwierigkeiten geraten **III**

*to make **trouble** [ˌmeɪk 'trʌbl̩] Ärger machen; in Schwierigkeiten bringen **I**

troublemaker ['trʌbl̩ˌmeɪkə] Unruhestifter/-in **III**

trousers (pl) ['traʊzəz] Hose **II**

truck (AE) [trʌk] Truck; Lastwagen **III**

true [truː] wahr **II**
*to come **true** [ˌkʌm 'truː] wahr werden; in Erfüllung gehen **III**

trumpet ['trʌmpɪt] Trompete **V U3**, 73

trust [trʌst] Vertrauen **II**

to **trust** [trʌst] vertrauen **II**

truth [truːθ] Wahrheit **III**

to **try** [traɪ] versuchen; probieren **I**
to **try** hard [ˌtraɪ 'hɑːd] sich anstrengen; sich Mühe geben **II**
to **try** on [ˌtraɪ 'ɒn] anprobieren **II**
to **try** out [ˌtraɪ 'aʊt] ausprobieren **III**
to **try** out for [ˌtraɪ 'aʊt fə] am Auswahlverfahren teilnehmen **III**

tryout ['traɪaʊt] Aufnahmetest (für eine Mannschaft) **III**

T-shirt ['tiːʃɜːt] T-Shirt **I**

the **Tube** [tjuːb] U-Bahn (in London) **II**

Tudor ['tjuːdə] Tudor- **III**

Tuesday ['tjuːzdeɪ] Dienstag **I**

tug of war [ˌtʌg əf 'wɔː] Tauziehen **V U1**, 13

to **tug** [tʌg] ziehen; zupfen ⟨**V U2**, 57⟩

tuition fee [tjuˈɪʃn ˌfiː] Studiengebühr; Schulgeld **IV**

tundra (no pl) ['tʌndrə] Tundra **III**

tune [tjuːn] Melodie; Ton **V AC2**, 34

tunnel ['tʌnl̩] Tunnel **I**

wind **turbine** ['wɪnd ˌtɜːbaɪn] Windturbine **V U1**, 24

roast **turkey** [ˌrəʊst 'tɜːki] Putenbraten **II**

turn [tɜːn] Wendung; Drehung **I**
It's your **turn**. [ˌɪts 'jɔː tɜːn] Du bist dran. **I**
Take **turns**. [ˌteɪk 'tɜːnz] Wechselt euch ab. **I**
Your **turn**. ['jɔː tɜːn] Du bist dran. **I**

to **turn** [tɜːn] drehen; (sich) umdrehen; einbiegen; abbiegen **II**; werden **IV**
to **turn** (a)round [ˌtɜːn (ə)'raʊnd] (sich) umdrehen; wenden **I**
to **turn** back [ˌtɜːn 'bæk] umkehren; zurückgehen **III**
to **turn** into [ˌtɜːn 'ɪntə] ändern in; umwandeln in **III**
to **turn** off [ˌtɜːn 'ɒf] abschalten; ausschalten **II**
to **turn** on [ˌtɜːn 'ɒn] einschalten **II**
to **turn** out (to be) [ˌtɜːn 'aʊt] sich herausstellen (als) **III**
to **turn** over [ˌtɜːn 'əʊvə] umdrehen; umkippen **II**
to **turn** to ['tɜːn tə] sich wenden an; sich zuwenden **II**

turtle ['tɜːtl̩] Schildkröte **IV**

tusk [tʌsk] Stoßzahn **III**

tutor ['tjuːtə] Klassenlehrer/-in **I**
  tutor group ['tjuːtə ˌgruːp] Klasse *(in einer englischen Schule)* **I**
tutorial [tjuːˈtɔːriəl] Anleitung; Tutorial **IV**
TV *(= television)* [tiːˈviː: (ˈtelɪvɪʒn)] Fernsehen; Fernseher **I**
  to watch **TV** [ˌwɒtʃ tiːˈviː] fernsehen **I**
twelve [twelv] zwölf **I**
twenty ['twenti] zwanzig **I**
  twenty-one [ˌtwentiˈwʌn] einundzwanzig **I**
twice [twaɪs] zweimal **III**
twin [twɪn] Zwilling; Zwillings- **II**
to **twist** [twɪst] verdrehen; verzerren; sich winden **VTS**, 109
  to **twist** your ankle [ˌtwɪst jɔːrˈæŋkl] sich den Knöchel verrenken **II**
two [tuː] zwei **I**
  the **two** of them [ðə ˈtuːˌəv ðəm] beide **II**
type [taɪp] Typ; Art; Sorte **III**
to **type** [taɪp] tippen **VU1**, 26
typical ['tɪpɪkl] typisch **I**

U

u *(= you)* [juː:; jə] du; Sie; ihr **I**
UFO [juːefˈəʊ] UFO **II**
ultimately ['ʌltɪmətli] schließlich; letztendlich **VU2**, 49
unarmed [ʌnˈɑːmd] unbewaffnet **VU2**, 43
unattended [ˌʌnəˈtendɪd] unbeaufsichtigt **II**
unboxing [ʌnˈbɒksɪŋ] Auspacken *(neuer Produkte vor laufender Kamera)* **VU3**, 83
uncle ['ʌŋkl] Onkel **I**
uncomfortable [ʌnˈkʌmftəbl] unwohl; unbehaglich; unbequem **III**
unconstitutional [ˌʌnkɒnstɪˈtjuːʃnl] verfassungswidrig **VF4**, 60
uncool [ʌnˈkuːl] nicht cool **II**
to **uncover** [ʌnˈkʌvə] aufdecken; frei legen **II**
under ['ʌndə] unter **I**
undercurrent ['ʌndəkʌrnt] Unterströmung; Unterton ⟨**VU3**, 87⟩
underestimated [ˌʌndəˈestɪmeɪtɪd] unterschätzt **IV**
*to **undergo** [ˌʌndəˈgəʊ] sich etw. unterziehen; durchmachen **VF5**, 67
Underground ['ʌndəgraʊnd] U-Bahn **IV**
underground [ˌʌndəˈgraʊnd] unter der Erde; unter die Erde **III**
to **underline** [ˌʌndəˈlaɪn] unterstreichen **IV**
*to **understand** [ˌʌndəˈstænd] verstehen **I**
understandable [ˌʌndəˈstændəbl] verständlich **II**
understanding [ˌʌndəˈstændɪŋ] Verständnis **II**
unemployed [ˌʌnɪmˈplɔɪd] arbeitslos **IV**
unemployment [ˌʌnɪmˈplɔɪmənt] Arbeitslosigkeit **IV**
unexpected [ˌʌnɪkˈspektɪd] unerwartet **III**

unfair [ʌnˈfeə] unfair **I**
unfortunately [ʌnˈfɔːtʃnətli] leider; unglücklicherweise **III**
unhappy [ʌnˈhæpi] unglücklich **I**
unhealthy [ʌnˈhelθi] ungesund **III**
uniform ['juːnɪfɔːm] Uniform **I**
uninhabitable [ˌʌnɪnˈhæbɪtəbl] unbewohnbar **IV**
unique [juːˈniːk] einzigartig **IV**
unit ['juːnɪt] Lektion; Kapitel; Einheit **I**
unitary state [juːnɪtri ˈsteɪt] Einheitsstaat **VF2**, 33
universal [juːnɪˈvɜːsl] allgemein; universell **IV**
university [juːnɪˈvɜːsəti] Universität **III**
unkind [ʌnˈkaɪnd] unfreundlich; gemein **III**
unless [ənˈles] es sei denn, (dass) …; wenn nicht **IV**
unlike [ʌnˈlaɪk] anders als; im Gegensatz zu **IV**
unlikely [ʌnˈlaɪkli] unwahrscheinlich **III**
to **unlock** [ʌnˈlɒk] entsperren **VU3**, 80
*to be **unlucky** [biˌʌnˈlʌki] Pech haben **I**
unnecessary [ʌnˈnesəsri] unnötig **III**
to **unpack** [ʌnˈpæk] auspacken **III**
unprecedented [ʌnˈpresɪdentɪd] beispiellos; noch nie da gewesen **VU1**, 20
unpredictable [ˌʌnprɪˈdɪktəbl] unvorhersehbar **IV**
unrealistic [ˌʌnrɪəˈlɪstɪk] unrealistisch **III**
unsure [ʌnˈʃʊə] unsicher **I**
until [ʌnˈtɪl] bis **II**
  not … **until** [ˌnɒtˌənˈtɪl] nicht bevor; erst wenn **II**
untroubled [ʌnˈtrʌbld] unbeschwert; sorglos **VU1**, 18
unusual [ʌnˈjuːʒl] ungewöhnlich **II**
to **unwrap** [ʌnˈræp] auswickeln; auspacken **IV**
up [ʌp] hinauf; (nach) oben **I**
  to end **up** [ˌendˌʌp] enden; landen **I**
  *to get **up** [ˌgetˌʌp] aufstehen *(aus dem Bett)* **I**
  *to give **up** [ˌgɪvˌʌp] aufgeben **III**
  *to keep **up** [ˌkiːpˌʌp] aufrechterhalten **III**
  to look **up** [ˌlʊkˌʌp] nachschlagen; nachschauen **I**
  to rear **up** [ˌrɪərˌʌp] sich aufbäumen; sich aufrichten ⟨**VU1**, 31⟩
  up to date [ˌʌptəˈdeɪt] auf dem Laufenden; modern; zeitgemäß; aktuell **III**
  What's **up**? *(infml)* [ˌwɒtsˌʌp] Was ist los? **III**
  Your time is **up**. [jɔː ˌtaɪmˌɪzˌʌp] Deine/Eure Zeit ist um. **IV**
up to [ˌʌp tə] bis zu **I**
up-and-coming [ˌʌpəndˈkʌmɪŋ] aufstrebend; vielversprechend **VU1**, 22
*to **uphold** [ʌpˈhəʊld] aufrechterhalten; wahren **VU1**, 23
upon [əˈpɒn] auf **VAC2**, 35

upright ['ʌpraɪt] aufrecht **IV**
uprising ['ʌpˌraɪzɪŋ] Aufstand **VF3**, 38
*to **upset** [ʌpˈset] aus der Fassung bringen; aufregen **III**
upset [ʌpˈset] aufgebracht; bestürzt **I**
upside down [ˌʌpsaɪd ˈdaʊn] verkehrt herum; auf dem Kopf stehend **VU1**, 13
upstairs [ʌpˈsteəz] nach oben; im Obergeschoss; oben **II**
urban ['ɜːbn] städtisch; Stadt- **III**
urbanised ['ɜːbnaɪzd] verstädtert; urbanisiert **IV**
us [ʌs] uns **I**
usage ['juːsɪdʒ] Gebrauch; Nutzung **III**
use [juːs] Verwendung; Gebrauch; Nutzen **IV**
  It's no **use** *(+ gerund)* [ɪts ˌnəʊ ˈjuːs] Es nützt nichts … **III**
to **use** [juːz] benutzen; verwenden; gebrauchen **I**
  *to be **used** to *(+ -ing)* [bi ˈjuːzd tə] gewöhnt sein an; gewohnt sein **III**
  *to get **used** to sth [ˌget ˈjuːzd tə] sich an etw. gewöhnen **III**
  used to *(+ infinitive)* ['juːst tə] pflegte(n) zu; tat(en) früher **IV**
useful ['juːsfl] nützlich; hilfreich **I**
usual ['juːʒl] üblich **II**
usually ['juːʒli] normalerweise; gewöhnlich; meistens **I**
utopia [juːˈtəʊpiə] Utopie **IV**

V

v [viː] gegen **IV**
v. [viː] gegen **IV**
vacation *(AE)* [vəˈkeɪʃn] Ferien; Urlaub **I**
to **vacuum** ['vækjuːm] staubsaugen **III**
valid ['vælɪd] gültig **IV**
valley ['væli] Tal **IV**
valuable ['væljuəbl] wertvoll **III**
value ['væljuː] Wert **III**
variety (of) [vəˈraɪətiˌəv] Vielzahl (an); Vielfalt (von) **IV**
various ['veəriəs] verschieden; verschiedenartig **IV**
to **vary** ['veəri] variieren; verschieden sein **VU3**, 81
vast [vɑːst] riesig; enorm; unermesslich **III**
vegan ['viːgən] vegan; Veganer/-in **IV**
vegetable ['vedʒtəbl] Gemüse **II**
vegetarian [ˌvedʒɪˈteəriən] Vegetarier/-in **III**
vegetarian [ˌvedʒɪˈteəriən] vegetarisch **IV**
venom *(no pl)* ['venəm] Gift **III**
venomous ['venəməs] giftig **III**
to **venture** forth *(fml)* [ˌventʃə ˈfɔːθ] sich vorwagen **IV**
venue ['venjuː] Austragungsort; Veranstaltungsort **VU1**, 22
to **verify** ['verɪfaɪ] verifizieren; überprüfen **VU2**, 55
verse [vɜːs] Vers; Strophe **VU1**, 21

version ['vɜːʃn] Version **IV**
versus ['vɜːsəs] gegen **IV**
very ['veri] sehr **I**
 very much [ˌveri 'mʌtʃ] sehr **I**
vet [vet] Tierarzt/Tierärztin **I**
vibrant ['vaɪbrənt] dynamisch; lebhaft; pulsierend **V U1**, 20
victim ['vɪktɪm] Opfer **IV**
Victorian [vɪk'tɔːriən] viktorianisch; Viktorianer/-in **III**
video ['vɪdiəʊ] Video **II**
 video chat ['vɪdiəʊ ˌtʃæt] Videochat **I**
view [vjuː] Aussicht; Blick **III**; Ansicht; Einstellung; Standpunkt **IV**
 point of **view** [ˌpɔɪnt əv 'vjuː] Standpunkt; Ansicht; Perspektive **II**
viewing ['vjuːɪŋ] Hör-/Sehverstehen **I**
village ['vɪlɪdʒ] Dorf **I**
villain ['vɪlən] Bösewicht **II**
vintage car ['vɪntɪdʒ 'kɑː] Oldtimer **III**
to **violate** ['vaɪəleɪt] verletzen **V F4**, 63
violation [vaɪə'leɪʃn] Verletzung **V U3**, 83
violence (no pl) ['vaɪəlns] Gewalt **V U2**, 45
violent ['vaɪələnt] gewaltsam; gewalttätig; brutal **III**
violin [ˌvaɪə'lɪn] Violine; Geige **V U1**, 21
virtual private network ['vɜːtʃuəl praɪvət 'netwɜːk] sichere Netzwerkverbindung **V U3**, 80
virtually ['vɜːtʃuəli] praktisch; so gut wie **IV**
virus ['vaɪrəs] Virus (Schadsoftware) **V U3**, 80
visa ['viːzə], **visas** ['viːzəz] (pl) Visum, Visa; Einreisebewilligung **IV**
visible ['vɪzəbl] sichtbar **V U3**, 81
visit ['vɪzɪt] Besuch **I**
to **visit** ['vɪzɪt] besichtigen; besuchen **I**
visitor ['vɪzɪtə] Besucher/-in **I**
visual ['vɪʒuəl] Bild **IV**
vivid ['vɪvɪd] lebendig; lebhaft **V U2**, 56
vlog [vlɒg] Vlog; Videoblog **III**
vocabulary [və'kæbjələri] Vokabular; Wortschatz **I**
vocals (pl) ['vəʊklz] Gesang **V U1**, 21
vocational school [və'keɪʃnl ˌskuːl] Berufsschule **IV**
voice [vɔɪs] Stimme **I**; Mitsprache **IV**
 to lower one's **voice** [ˌləʊə wʌnz 'vɔɪs] die Stimme senken **IV**
volleyball ['vɒlibɔːl] Volleyball **I**
volume ['vɒljuːm] Lautstärke; Volumen **V U3**, 71; **V TS**, 111
volunteer [ˌvɒlən'tɪə] Freiwillige/-r; Ehrenamtliche/-r **IV**
to **volunteer** [ˌvɒlən'tɪə] sich freiwillig melden; eine ehrenamtliche Tätigkeit übernehmen **III**
*to cast one's **vote** [ˌkɑːst wʌnz 'vəʊt] die Stimme abgeben **V U1**, 24
vote [vəʊt] Abstimmung; Stimme; Wahl **IV**
to **vote** [vəʊt] abstimmen; wählen **II**
voyage ['vɔɪɪdʒ] Fahrt; Reise **V F3**, 36

vs ['vɜːsəs] gegen **IV**
vs. ['vɜːsəs] gegen **IV**

W

wage [weɪdʒ] Lohn **IV**
covered **wagon** [ˌkʌvəd 'wægən] Planwagen **III**
to **wait** (for) [weɪt] warten (auf) **I**
 *to keep sb **waiting** [ˌkiːp 'weɪtɪŋ] jmdn. warten lassen **III**
 Wait and see! [ˌweɪt ənd 'siː] Warte ab! **I**
*to **wake** up [weɪk ˌʌp] aufwachen; aufwecken **II**
walk [wɔːk] Gang **IV**
 *to go for a **walk** [ˌgəʊ fər ə 'wɔːk] spazieren gehen **II**
to **walk** [wɔːk] gehen; laufen **I**
 to **walk** the dog [wɔːk ðə 'dɒg] den Hund ausführen; mit dem Hund spazieren gehen **I**
wall [wɔːl] Wand; Mauer **I**
to **want** (to) ['wɒnt tə] wollen; mögen **I**
 to **want** somebody to do something [wɒnt sʌmbədi tə 'duː sʌmθɪŋ] wollen, dass jemand etwas tut **I**
war [wɔː] Krieg **II**
 civil **war** [ˌsɪvl 'wɔː] Bürgerkrieg **II**
 tug of **war** [ˌtʌg əf 'wɔː] Tauziehen **V U1**, 13
wardrobe ['wɔːdrəʊb] Kleiderschrank **I**
warehouse ['weəhaʊs] Lager; Lagerhalle; Depot **IV**
warehousing ['weəhaʊzɪŋ] Lagerhaltung **IV**
to **warm** up [ˌwɔːm ˌʌp] aufwärmen; sich aufwärmen **I**
warm [wɔːm] warm **II**
global **warming** [ˌgləʊbl 'wɔːmɪŋ] globale Erwärmung **IV**
warm-up ['wɔːm ˌʌp] Aufwärmübung **IV**
to **warn** [wɔːn] warnen **III**
warning ['wɔːnɪŋ] Warnung **III**
warpath ['wɔːpɑːθ] Kriegspfad **III**
to **warrant** ['wɒrnt] garantieren **V U3**, 80
warrior ['wɒriə] Krieger **II**
to **wash** [wɒʃ] waschen; sich waschen **I**
washing machine ['wɒʃɪŋ məˌʃiːn] Waschmaschine **II**
waste [weɪst] Verschwendung **II**; Abfall; Müll **IV**
to **waste** [weɪst] verschwenden **II**
watch [wɒtʃ] Armbanduhr **I**
to **watch** [wɒtʃ] beobachten; (sich) ansehen; zuschauen **I**
 to **watch** TV [wɒtʃ tiːˈviː] fernsehen **I**
water ['wɔːtə] Wasser **I**
 running **water** [ˌrʌnɪŋ 'wɔːtə] fließendes Wasser **II**
 tap **water** ['tæp ˌwɔːtə] Leitungswasser **V TS**, 117

water fountain ['wɔːtə ˌfaʊntɪn] Wasserspender **III**
water slide ['wɔːtə ˌslaɪd] Wasserrutsche **I**
waterfront ['wɔːtəfrʌnt] Hafenviertel; Ufer **IV**
waterproof ['wɔːtəpruːf] wasserdicht **V F1**, 11
watery ['wɔːtri] wässrig; dünn **III**
wave [weɪv] Welle **I**
to **wave** [weɪv] winken; schwenken **III**
way [weɪ] Weg; Art und Weise **I**
 *to be in the **way** [bi ɪn ðə 'weɪ] im Weg sein/stehen **I**
 by the **way** [ˌbaɪ ðə 'weɪ] übrigens **II**
 to edge one's **way** ['edʒ wʌnz ˌweɪ] sich langsam bewegen **V U3**, 70
 *to find one's **way** around [ˌfaɪnd wʌnz ˌweɪ ə'raʊnd] sich zurechtfinden **III**
 *to get in the **way** [get ɪn ðə 'weɪ] stören; im Weg stehen **II**
 in a polite **way** [ɪn ə pə'laɪt ˌweɪ] auf höfliche Art **II**
 no **way** [nəʊ 'weɪ] auf keinen Fall; keineswegs **III**
 *to take sth the wrong **way** [ˌteɪk ðə rɒŋ 'weɪ] etw. falsch auffassen; etw. in den falschen Hals bekommen **IV**
way [weɪ] weit; lange **IV**
we [wiː; wi] wir **I**
weak [wiːk] schwach **III**
weakness ['wiːknəs] Schwäche **IV**
wealth [welθ] Reichtum; Vermögen **IV**
wealthy ['welθi] wohlhabend; reich **IV**
weapon ['wepən] Waffe **III**
*to **wear** [weə] anhaben; tragen (Kleidung) **I**
weary ['wɪəri] müde; überdrüssig **IV**
weather ['weðə] Wetter **I**
 weather forecast ['weðə ˌfɔːkɑːst] Wettervorhersage **I**
weaver ['wiːvə] Weber/-in **V F1**, 10
website ['websaɪt] Website; Internetauftritt **I**
wedding ['wedɪŋ] Hochzeit **I**
Wednesday ['wenzdeɪ] Mittwoch **I**
week [wiːk] Woche **I**
weekend [ˌwiːk'end] Wochenende **I**
 at the **weekend** [ət ðə ˌwiːk'end] am Wochenende **I**
weekly ['wiːkli] wöchentlich **IV**
*to **weep** [wiːp] weinen; schluchzen **V TS**, 109
to **weigh** [weɪ] wiegen **III**
weight [weɪt] Gewicht **III**
weird [wɪəd] merkwürdig; seltsam; sonderbar **II**
Welcome! ['welkəm] Willkommen! **I**
to **welcome** ['welkəm] willkommen heißen **II**
You're **welcome.** [jɔː 'welkəm] Bitte schön.; Nichts zu danken.; Gern geschehen. **I**

welfare ['welfeə] Sozialhilfe **V U1**, 23

well [wel] Brunnen; Quelle **IV**

well [wel] gut **II**

  as well [əz 'wel] auch **III**

  *to get **well** [ˌget 'wel] gesund werden **II**

  well-being [ˌwel'biːɪŋ] Wohlbefinden **V U2**, 52

  well-written [ˌwel'rɪtn] gut geschrieben **IV**

  … as **well** as … [əz 'wel ˌəz] sowie; und (auch) **III**

well [wel] tja; nun **I**

Welsh [welʃ] walisisch; Walisisch; Waliser/-in **II**

west [west] Westen; West- **I**

wet [wet] nass **I**

whale [weɪl] Wal **III**

to what extent [tə ˌwɒt ɪk'stent] inwiefern; inwieweit **V U2**, 51

what [wɒt] was **I**

  what a … ['wɒt ˌə] was für ein/-e …; welch ein/-e … **I**

  What a shame! [ˌwɒt ə 'ʃeɪm] Wie schade! **I**

  What about … ? ['wɒt ˌəbaʊt] Was ist mit …?; Wie wär's mit …? **I**

  What colour is …? [ˌwɒt 'kʌlər ɪz] Welche Farbe hat …? **I**

  what else [ˌwɒt 'els] was sonst; was noch **I**

  what for [ˌwɒt 'fɔː] wozu **III**

  What is … about? [ˌwɒt ɪz əˈbaʊt] Worum geht es in/im …? **I**

  What is … like? [ˌwɒt ɪz … 'laɪk] Wie ist …? **II**

  what it's like [ˌwɒt ˌɪts 'laɪk] wie das ist **II**

  What on earth …? [ˌwɒtː ɒn 'ɜːθ] Was um alles in der Welt …? **II**

  What time? [ˌwɒt 'taɪm] Um wie viel Uhr? **I**

  what to … ['wɒt tə] was man … **I**

  What's your name? [ˌwɒts jə 'neɪm] Wie heißt du?; Wie heißen Sie? **I**

  What's going on? [wɒts ˌgəʊɪŋ ɒn] Was ist los?; Was geht ab? **II**

  What's the matter? [ˌwɒts ðə 'mætə] Was ist los?; Was hast du? **II**

  What's the time? [ˌwɒts ðə 'taɪm] Wie spät ist es?; Wie viel Uhr ist es? **I**

  What's up? (infml) [ˌwɒts 'ʌp] Was ist los? **II**

  What's wrong? [ˌwɒts 'rɒŋ] Was ist los?; Was stimmt nicht? **III**

  … **what** to do. ['wɒt tə duː] … was ich tun soll. **II**

what … [wɒt] welche/-r/-s …; was für ein … **I**

whatever [wɒt'evə] wie auch immer; egal (was/welche) **III**

wheat [wiːt] Weizen **I**

wheel [wiːl] Rad; Steuerrad; Steuer **I**

wheelchair ['wiːltʃeə] Rollstuhl **I**

when [wen] wenn; wann; als **I**

whenever [wen'evə] wann immer; jedes Mal, wenn; so oft **II**

where [weə] wo; wohin **I**

  Where … from? [ˌweə … 'frɒm] Woher …? **I**

  where … is/are concerned [ˌweə … ɪz/ɑː kən'sɜːnd] was … betrifft; was … angeht **V U3**, 74

whereas [weə'ræz] während; wohingegen **IV**

whether ['weðə] ob **III**

which [wɪtʃ] welche/-r/-s **I**

a while [ə 'waɪl] eine Weile **III**

while [waɪl] während **I**

whip [wɪp] Peitsche **V F3**, 37

to whip [wɪp] (Sahne) schlagen **I**

whisky ['wɪski] Whisky **V U1**, 13

to whisper ['wɪspə] flüstern **I**

tin whistle [ˌtɪn 'wɪsl] Blechflöte **V U1**, 21

to whistle ['wɪsl] pfeifen **V U1**, 21

white [waɪt] weiß **I**

  white supremacist [ˌwaɪt suː'preməsɪst] Anhänger/-in der Theorie von der Überlegenheit der Weißen **V F4**, 61

who [huː] wer; wem; wen **I**

  Who … for? [ˌhuː 'fɔː] Für wen …? **I**

  Who's in? [huːz 'ɪn] Wer macht mit?; Wer ist dabei? **II**

whoa [wəʊ] ho; langsam **II**

whole [həʊl] ganz **I**

whoosh [wʊʃ] wusch **I**

whose [huːz] wessen **I**; dessen (Relativpronomen); deren (Relativpronomen) **II**

why [waɪ] warum **I**

  that's **why** [ðæts 'waɪ] deshalb **II**

wide [waɪd] weit; breit; ausgedehnt **II**

  wide shot [ˌwaɪd 'ʃɒt] Totale (Kameraeinstellung) **V TS**, 112

  wide-open [ˌwaɪd 'əʊpn] weit und flach **III**

widespread ['waɪdspred] weit verbreitet **IV**

wife [waɪf], wives [waɪvz] (pl) Ehefrau **II**

wifi ['waɪfaɪ] WLAN **IV**

wig [wɪg] Perücke **III**

wiki ['wɪkɪ] Wiki (Website mit Sammlung von Beiträgen, die von den Nutzern verändert werden können) **IV**

wild [waɪld] wild **II**

wilderness ['wɪldənəs] Wildnis **II**

wildlife ['waɪldlaɪf] Tierwelt (in freier Wildbahn) **III**

*to be **willing** to do sth [bi 'wɪlɪŋ tə] gewillt sein, etw. zu tun; bereit sein, etw. zu tun **V AC2**, 35

willingly ['wɪlɪŋli] gern; freiwillig **IV**

*to win [wɪn] gewinnen; siegen **I**

wind [wɪnd] Wind **II**

  wind farm ['wɪnd pɑːk] Windpark **IV**

  wind turbine ['wɪnd ˌtɜːbaɪn] Windturbine **V U1**, 24

window ['wɪndəʊ] Fenster **I**

windsurfing ['wɪndsɜːfɪŋ] Windsurfen **II**

windy ['wɪndi] windig **II**

wine [waɪn] Wein **I**

wing [wɪŋ] Flügel **IV**

winner ['wɪnə] Gewinner/-in; Sieger/-in **II**

winter ['wɪntə] Winter **I**

to wipe [waɪp] wischen; abwischen; abtrocknen **III**

wisdom (no pl) ['wɪzdəm] Weisheit; Klugheit **IV**

wise [waɪz] weise **V TS**, 111

wish [wɪʃ] Wunsch **I**

  *to make a **wish** [ˌmeɪk ə 'wɪʃ] sich etwas wünschen **I**

  Best **wishes** [ˌbest 'wɪʃɪz] Viele Grüße; Herzliche Grüße **II**

to wish [wɪʃ] (sich) wünschen **III**

witch [wɪtʃ] Hexe **V TS**, 110

with [wɪð] mit; bei **I**

*to withdraw [wɪð'drɔː] (sich) zurückziehen **V F3**, 39

within [wɪ'ðɪn] innerhalb **III**

without [wɪ'ðaʊt] ohne **I**

  *to do **without** sth [ˌduː wɪð'aʊt] ohne etw. auskommen **IV**

witness ['wɪtnəs] Zeuge/Zeugin **II**

to witness ['wɪtnəs] miterleben **V TS**, 117

wizard ['wɪzəd] Zauberer **II**

wolf [wʊlf], wolves (pl) [wʊlvz] Wolf **III**

woman ['wʊmən], women (pl) ['wɪmɪn] Frau **I**

no wonder [ˌnəʊ 'wʌndə] kein Wunder **II**

to wonder ['wʌndə] sich Gedanken machen; sich fragen **III**

wonderful ['wʌndəfl] wunderbar **I**

wood [wʊd] Holz **III**

wooden ['wʊdn] hölzern; aus Holz **II**

woods [wʊdz] Wald; Wäldchen **III**

wool [wʊl] Wolle **IV**

word [wɜːd] Wort **I**

  key **word** ['kiː ˌwɜːd] Stichwort; Schlüsselbegriff **I**

  linking **word** ['lɪŋkɪŋ ˌwɜːd] Verbindungswort **II**

  word bank ['wɜːd ˌbæŋk] Wortsammlung **II**

  Word power ['wɜːd ˌpaʊə] die Kraft der Wörter (Wortschatzübung) **I**

work [wɜːk] Arbeit **I**

  work experience ['wɜːk ɪkˌspɪərɪəns] Praktikum; Schülerpraktikum **IV**

to work [wɜːk] arbeiten **I**; funktionieren **II**

  to **work** magic (on) [ˌwɜːk' mædʒɪk] Zauber ausüben (auf) **III**

  working class [ˌwɜːkɪŋ 'klɑːs] Arbeiterklasse **IV**

worker ['wɜːkə] Arbeiter/-in; Mitarbeiter/-in **III**

workforce ['wɜːkfɔːs] Arbeitskräfte; Belegschaft **V F1**, 11

workload ['wɜːkləʊd] Arbeitspensum **V U1**, 27

worksheet ['wɜːkʃiːt] Arbeitsblatt **IV**
workshop ['wɜːkʃɒp] Workshop **I**
world [wɜːld] Erde; Welt **I**
worm [wɜːm] Wurm **I**
worried ['wʌrid] beunruhigt; besorgt **I**
No worries. (Aus) [ˌnaʊ 'wʌriz] Kein Problem.; Gern geschehen. **IV**
to worry ['wʌri] sich Sorgen machen **I**
   to worry sb ['wʌri] jmdn. beunruhigen **II**
   Don't worry! [ˌdaʊnt 'wʌri] Keine Sorge! **I**
to worship ['wɜːʃip] verehren; anbeten **III**
*to be worth [bi 'wɜːθ] wert sein **I**
would [wʊd] würde-/st/-n/-t **II**
   would like [wʊd 'laɪk] würde-/st/-n/-t gern; hätte-/st/-n/-t gern **I**
   would love [wʊd 'lʌv] würde-/st/-n/-t sehr gern; hätte-/st/-n/-t sehr gern **I**
wounded ['wuːndɪd] verwundet; verletzt **III**
Wow! [waʊ] Wow! **I**
wrist [rɪst] Handgelenk **V U3**, 70
*to write [raɪt] schreiben **I**
   *to write down [raɪt 'daʊn] aufschreiben **I**
writer ['raɪtə] Autor/-in; Verfasser/-in; Schriftsteller/-in **II**
writing ['raɪtɪŋ] Schreiben **I**
wrong [rɒŋ] falsch **I**
   *to be wrong [bi 'rɒŋ] unrecht haben; sich irren **I**
   *to go wrong [ˌgəʊ 'rɒŋ] schiefgehen **I**
   What's wrong? [ˌwɒts 'rɒŋ] Was ist los?; Was stimmt nicht? **III**

X

xenophobia (no pl) [ˌzenə'fəʊbiə] Fremdenhass; Xenophobie **V F4**, 61
XOXO [ˌhʌgz ˌən 'kɪsɪz] Umarmungen und Küsse (am Ende von E-Mails und SMS) **I**
X-ray ['eksreɪ] Röntgenstrahlen; Röntgenuntersuchung **V U3**, 70

Y

yard (AE) [jaːd] Garten **I**
   front yard (AE) [ˌfrʌnt 'jaːd] Vorgarten **III**
to yawn [jɔːn] gähnen **II**
yeah (infml) [jeə] ja **I**
year [jɪə] Jahr; Schuljahr **I**
   gap year ['gæp ˌjɪə] ein Jahr Auszeit (zwischen Schule und Ausbildung/Studium), das oft für einen freiwilligen ökologischen oder sozialen Dienst genutzt wird **IV**
   11-year-old [ɪ'levnˌjɪərəʊld] 11-Jährige/-r **II**
yearbook ['jɪəbʊk] Jahrbuch **I**
to yell [jel] brüllen; laut schreien **V U2**, 42
yellow ['jeləʊ] gelb **I**
yes [jes] ja **I**
yesterday ['jestədeɪ] gestern **I**
yet [jet] schon; noch **II**

not … yet [nɒt 'jet] noch nicht **II**
to yield [jiːld] nachgeben; Vorfahrt gewähren **V U2**, 47
yoghurt ['jɒgət] Joghurt **I**
you [juː; jə] du; ihr; Sie **I**
   You too? [juː 'tuː] Du auch? **I**
   You'd better … (= You had better) [juːd 'betə] Du solltest lieber … **III**
   You're welcome. [jɔː 'welkəm] Bitte schön.; Nichts zu danken.; Gern geschehen. **I**
young [jʌŋ] jung **I**
your [jɔː; jə] dein/-e; euer/eure; Ihr/-e **I**
   What's your name? [ˌwɒts jə 'neɪm] Wie heißt du?; Wie heißen Sie? **I**
   Your turn. ['jɔː tɜːn] Du bist dran. **I**
yours [jɔːz] dein/-er/-e/-es; eure/-r/-s; Ihr/-er/-e/-es **II**
Yours … [jɔːz] Viele Grüße … (am Ende von Briefen und Mails) **II**
yourself [jɔː'self] du/dir/dich/Sie/sich (selbst); selber **I**
   Help yourself. ['help jəself] Bediene dich.; Bedienen Sie sich. **I**
yourselves [jɔː'selvz] ihr/euch/Sie/sich (selbst); selber **II**
youth [juːθ] Jugend **I**
   youth hostel ['juːθ ˌhɒstl] Jugendherberge **II**
yummy ['jʌmi] lecker **I**

Z

zero ['zɪərəʊ] null **I**
zipline ['zɪplaɪn] Seilrutsche **II**
to zipline ['zɪplaɪn] mit der Seilrutsche fahren **II**
pedestrian zone [pɪ'destriən zəʊn] Fußgängerzone **IV**
zoo [zuː] Zoo; Tierpark **I**
to zoom in (on) [zuːmˌ'ɪn] heranzoomen (auf) **III**

Place names

Aberdeen [ˌæbə'diːn] **V U1**, 12
Atlanta [ət'læntə] **V U2**, 41
Crieff [kriːf] **V U1**, 13
Falkirk ['fælkɜːk] 〈**V U1**, 29〉
Fife [faɪf] **V U1**, 21
Glasgow ['glɑːzgəʊ] **V U1**, 12
the Hamptons [ðə 'hæmptənz] Region im US-Bundesstaat New York **V U3**, 76
Harlem ['hɑːləm] Stadtteil von New York City **V U2**, 47
Honolulu [ˌhɒnə'luːluː] **V U2**, 53
Inverness [ˌɪnvə'nes] **V U1**, 12
Manchester ['mæntʃɪstə] **V U1**, 14
Memphis ['memfɪs] Stadt in Tennessee **V F4**, 62
Montgomery [mɒnt'gɒmri] Stadt in Alabama **V F4**, 62

Oakland ['əʊklənd] Stadt in Kalifornien **V U3**, 75
Omaha ['əʊməhɑː] Stadt in Nebraska **V U3**, 76
Pearl Harbor [ˌpɜːl 'hɑːbə] Stadt auf Hawaii **V TS**, 116
Selma ['selmə] Stadt in Alabama **V F4**, 61
Sheffield ['ʃefiːld] 〈**V U1**, 28〉
Thurso ['θɜːsəʊ] 〈**V U1**, 28〉
Tribeca [traɪ'biːkə] Stadtteil von New York City **V U3**, 76

Geographical names

Alabama [ˌælə'bæmə] **V F4**, 61
Ben Cruachan [ˌben 'kruːxən] Berg in Schottland **V U1**, 14
Brittany ['brɪtni] Bretagne **V AC2**, 34
Caithness [keɪθ'nes] 〈**V U1**, 28〉
the Falklands [ðə 'fɔːkləndz] die Falklandinseln **V AC4**, 89
Galicia [gə'lɪsiə] Galizien **V AC2**, 34
Illinois [ˌɪlɪ'nɔɪ] **V U2**, 52
Kenya ['kenjə] Kenia **V U2**, 53
Loch Morag/Loch Morar [ˌlɒx 'mɔːrə] See in Schottland **V U1**, 15
Molendinar Burn [ˌməʊlən'daɪnə ˌbɜːn] **V U1**, 21
Namibia [nə'mɪbiə] **V U3**, 72
Nebraska [nə'bræskə] **V U3**, 76
Portugal ['pɔːtʃəgl] Portugal **V F3**, 36
River Clyde [ˌrɪvə 'klaɪd] **V U1**, 21
South Carolina [ˌsaʊθ kær'laɪnə] **V F3**, 39
Sussex ['sʌseks] Grafschaft im Süden Englands, rund um die Stadt Brighton **V U3**, 81
Tennessee [ˌtenə'siː] **V F4**, 62
Wisconsin [wɪ'skɒnsɪn] **V U3**, 77

Other names

Affordable Care Act [ə,fɔːdəbl 'keərˌækt] Bundesgesetz der USA, das den Zugang zur Krankenversicherung regelt **V U2**, 52
American Recovery and Reinvestment Act [əˌmerɪkən rɪˌkʌvriˌənd ˌriːɪn'vestmənt ˌækt] Amerikanisches Aufschwungs- und Reinvestitionsgesetz, ein Konjunkturprogramm **V U2**, 52
Berkshire-Hathaway [ˌbɜːkʃə'hæðəweɪ] US-amerikanische Holdinggesellschaft **V U3**, 76
Confederacy [kən,fedrəsi] Konföderierte Staaten **V F3**, 39
Foucault pendulum [ˌfuːkəʊ 'pendjələm] Foucault'sches Pendel **V U3**, 71
glaistig ['glɑːʃtɪg] schottisches Fabelwesen **V U1**, 12
goths [gɒθs] Anhänger einer Subkultur der 1980er und 1990er Jahre, die aus dem Punk- und New-Wave-Umfeld hervorging **V U3**, 81

Harvard Law Review [ˌhɑːvəd lɔː rɪˈvjuː] *rechtswissenschaftliche Zeitschrift* **V U2**, 53

HM Revenue & Customs [ˌeɪtʃ em ˌrevnjuː ən ˈkʌstəmz] Finanz- und Zollbehörde *(brit.)* **V U3**, 76

Internal Revenue Service [ˌɪntɜːnl ˈrevnjuː ˌsɜːvɪs] Finanzamt *(amerik.)* **V U3**, 76

Irn Bru [ˌaɪən ˈbruː] Irn Bru *(koffeinhaltiger Softdrink)* **V U1**, 13

Jim Crow laws [ˌdʒɪm ˈkraʊ ˌlɔːz] *Gesetze nach 1865, die der schwarzen Bevölkerung die neu erlangten Rechte wieder nehmen wollten* **V F4**, 60

Ku Klux Klan [ˌkuː klʌks ˈklæn] *rassistischer Geheimbund zur Unterdrückung der Schwarzen* **V F4**, 61

Medicaid [ˈmedɪkeɪd] *Gesundheitsfürsorgeprogramm für Bedürftige* **V U2**, 52

Military Tattoo [ˌmɪlɪtri tætˈuː] *Musikparade/Musikfestival des Militärs* **V U1**, 13

Milky Way [ˌmɪlki ˈweɪ] Milchstraße **V TS**, 109

mods [mɒdz] *Anhänger einer Subkultur der frühen und mittleren 1960er Jahre und Ende der 1970er bis Anfang der 1980er Jahre* **V U3**, 81

National Association for the Advancement of Colored People (NAACP) [ˌnæʃnl əsəʊsɪˌeɪʃn fə ðɪ ədˌvɑːnsmənt əv ˌkʌləd ˈpiːpl] *Nationale Organisation für die Förderung farbiger Menschen* **V F4**, 60

NHS (National Health Service) [ˌeneɪtʃˈes] *Staatliches Gesundheitssystem in Großbritannien* **V U1**, 24

Peace Corps [ˈpiːs ˌkɔː] **V U3**, 72

soulboys [ˈsəʊlbɔɪz] *Anhänger einer Subkultur der späten 1970er Jahre bis Anfang der 1980er Jahre, Fans der amerikanischen Soul- und Funk-Musik* **V U3**, 81

Union [ˈjuːnjən] Nordstaaten **V F3**, 39

Famous names

Dr. Martin Luther King Jr. [ˌdɒktə ˌmɑːtɪn ˌluːθə ˌkɪŋ ˈdʒuːniə] **V F4**, 61

Malcolm X [ˌmælkəmˈeks] **V F4**, 62

the Virgin Queen [ðə ˌvɜːdʒɪn ˈkwiːn] *die jungfräuliche Königin (Elizabeth I. wurde so genannt, weil sie nie heiratete.)* **V TS**, 111;

Grammar solutions

A Talking about the past

Test yourself
1 were you / have you been; 2 have / 've been waiting; 3 would be; 4 happened / has happened; 5 missed; 6 met; 7 was walking; 8 stopped; 9 asked; 10 was going; 11 is / 's; 12 have you known; 13 got to know; 14 had only moved; 15 had to; 16 see; 17 Do you like; 18 are / 're getting; 19 don't need

Practice
1 A history quiz
1. Where was Mary Queen of Scots brought up? (She was brought up in France.)
2. Why did she return to Scotland? (She returned because her French husband died.)
3. How long had she lived / been living as a prisoner when she was finally executed? (She had lived / been living as a prisoner for 19 years.)
4. Since when has Scotland been united with England? (Scotland and England have been united since 1707.)
5. When did Congress abolish slavery in the USA? (Congress abolished slavery in 1865.)
6. What was Rosa Parks doing on a bus in Montgomery on 1 December 1955? (She was riding home.)
7. Why was she arrested? (Because she refused to give up her seat to a white person.)
8. What is Martin Luther King Jr. remembered for? (He was a famous civil rights leader.)
9. When did Black people in the US officially get the same rights as white people? (They officially got the same rights in 1968.)

2 An interview with a pop star
1. She said (that) she had been a very lonely child because she had grown up without any sisters or brothers.
2. She noted that she had spent a lot of time on her own.
3. She said (that) she was very grateful to her mum because she had bought her a guitar for her 8th birthday.
4. She claimed (that) she had soon realised that she didn't want to go to college but become a musician.
5. She stated (that) her mum had never asked if / whether that was a good idea.
6. She said (that) her mum had always believed in her.
7. She claimed (that) it had been hard at first, but she had had a breakthrough hit three years before.
8. She said (that) every radio station across the country had been playing her hits since then.
9. She stated (that) the previous year / the year before she had toured Australia and Japan, and (that) her latest song had been in the US charts for 18 weeks.
10. She said (that) she was sure there would be a number one hit by her one day.

3 The rivalry between Glasgow and Edinburgh
1 published; 2 has been going on; 3 for; 4 correct; 5 disagreed; 6 had criticised / criticised; 7 correct; 8 offered; 9 was; 10 were; 11 correct; 12 correct; 13 has been; 14 could be compared / correct; 15 correct; 16 has been limited; 17 correct; 18 have; 19 would be; 20 ever stopped

4 Our holiday in Scotland
1 had to decide; 2 were going to go; 3 wasn't easy; 4 have; 5 were we going to find / did we find; 6 did we want; 7 had just gotten / had just got; 8 we didn't want; 9 could we imagine; 10 told / had told; 11 would be; 12 hadn't been; 13 started; 14 could say / was allowed to say; 15 wanted; 16 loves; 17 suggested; 18 could / would be able to relax and read; 19 wished; 20 wasn't; 21 am / 'm; 22 like; 23 chose; 24 had been arguing; 25 came up; 26 thought; 27 would be; 28 had to be; 29 offered; 30 agreed; 31 are; 32 had finished; 33 had gotten / had got; 34 needed; 35 drove; 36 had booked; 37 arrived; 38 was; 39 had planned; 40 included; 41 had already booked; 42 had not agreed; 43 had hardly slept; 44 talked; 45 were waiting; 46 will send; 47 did; 48 was definitely; 49 have ever had

5 The story behind the cartoon
Lösungsvorschlag: **Cartoon 1:** The characters are Josh and Brian. Josh is an American friend of Brian's who is visiting him in Scotland. It's Josh's first time in Scotland, so he wants to see the landscape of the Highlands that he read about. Brian and Josh pack some things into their backpacks and start walking along the road. It doesn't take long before it starts to rain. Josh had been told that it often is cold, dark and rainy in Scotland, but he didn't expect this weather because he is used to warm, sunny weather during that season. Brian isn't happy with the weather either that day. The two turn around and walk home to have a hot cup of tea and some biscuits to warm up. Then they go to the local pub for dinner and decide to go hiking again on a nicer day.

Cartoon 2: The characters are Mr and Mrs Chance, who are a married couple on holiday in Scotland. They came to Edinburgh to see some acts at the Fringe Festival. Mr Chance had searched the internet for cheap tickets beforehand and had found two discounted tickets; he couldn't believe his luck and happily told his wife. Now, having arrived at the address printed on their tickets, however, Mrs Chance understands why the tickets were so cheap: Mr Chance had unfortunately misread the event title and they had bought tickets for a refrigerator sale. She commented on this but could already see how sorry he was for the mistake. Instead of being angry, Mrs Chance takes out her mobile phone and purchases two new tickets online and pays for a taxi to the real Fringe Festival event location. They love it there and enjoy the rest of their holiday. The mistake becomes a story they laugh about and tell all their friends back home.

B Talking about the future

Test yourself
1 are you doing / are you going to do; 2 will be; 3 'm meeting / 'm going to meet; 4 will have; 5 'm going / will be going / 'm going to go; 6 'll ring; 7 's going to rain; 8 leaves

Practice
1 Plans and preparations
1 'm going to take (intention); 2 is going to start (certain to happen) / starts (timetable (university calendar)); 3 will be (general prediction); 4 am going to go (intention); 5 are you going to do (intention / plan); 6 'll have to (spontaneous decision); 7 'm going to buy (intention); 8 Will you come (spontaneous

decision); **9** 'll come (spontaneous decision); **10** 'll be (promise); **11** 'm going to send (intention); **12** leaves (schedule); **13** won't be able to (general prediction); **14** won't be (prediction); **15** 'll be able to (prediction); **16** 'm going to get (intention / plan) / am getting (agreement / appointment); **17** 'll have to ask (spontaneous decision); **18** 'll be (general prediction); **19** 'm going to be (intention / plan); **20** 'm meeting (agreement / appointment); **21** 'll be able to (general prediction); **22** 'll be allowed to go (prediction); **23** 'm going to tell him (plan / intention); **24** 're going to be (intention) / 'll be (prediction); **25** 'll be able to convince (general prediction); **26** 're going to need (certain to happen) / 'll need (prediction); **27** 'll ask (spontaneous decision) / 'm going to ask (plan); **28** is flying (appointment) / is going to fly (plan); **29** 'll lend (prediction)

2 Applying for a job
Lösungsvorschlag:

Dear Sir or Madam,

I would like to apply for the position as a garden help at your hotel. I will graduate school in the summer and am going to start an apprenticeship as a gardener and florist at a local gardening shop in autumn. I've already done an internship with a florist last year and love growing vegetables in my own garden, that's why I believe I will be able to support the team planting trees and growing vegetables. Because I am 175 cm tall, I can reach high branches, and I have often helped my parents cut the hedges in our garden, so I will be able to cut your hedges and grass too. I love working outdoors and thus believe I'm suited for the job on offer.

I look forward to answering any questions you might have. Please find my CV attached.

Best regards, (name)

C Talking about conditions and consequences

Test yourself
A: If you eat too much, you gain weight.
B: If you eat too much, you will gain weight.
C: If you ate too much, you would gain weight.
D: If you had eaten too much, you would have gained weight.

Practice
1 Giving advice
Lösungsvorschlag:
1. If you want to go to your book club, you'll have to leave now. / If you want to catch your bus, you'll have to hurry up.
2. If you hadn't seen the advertisement, you wouldn't want to buy the watch. / If you hadn't spent all your money on a new smartphone, you would be able to buy the watch.
3. If you help our older neighbours with their shopping, you'll / you may be able to earn some extra money.
4. If you had asked me for help earlier, your boss wouldn't have seen your holiday photos.
5. If you don't stand still, you'll fall down the ladder.
6. If you had studied harder, you would be better at Spanish.

2 Looking back at history
Lösungsvorschlag:
1. If Elizabeth I hadn't encouraged the work of explorers and

scientists, England wouldn't have had as many discoveries in medicine or at sea.
2. If Spanish conquerors hadn't reintroduced horses to the American continent, Native Americans wouldn't have been able to tame them.
3. If the Boston Tea Party hadn't happened, America would have been dependent on Britain for a longer time / the US might not exist today.
4. If Native Americans hadn't been driven from their land, the US would have had less problems with racism / they would still be able to live the traditional way.
5. If the Union Army hadn't won the Civil War, the enslaved people wouldn't have been freed.
6. If the suffragettes hadn't fought for women's voting rights, women wouldn't have been able to make decisions for themselves in the twentieth century / there would be no gender equality today.
7. If penicillin hadn't been discovered, a lot more people would have died.
8. If the music that Black people made hadn't become popular, hip hop wouldn't have spread around the world.

3 Learning from mistakes
Lösungsvorschlag:
Points of criticism:
1. If more people had helped, we would have been able to collect more items.
2. If somebody had taken responsibility for the communication between teams, the teams would have had someone to go to with questions.
3. If everybody had been assigned one role or job, the bazaar would have been less chaotic.
4. If we had started advertising earlier, we would have had more guests.
5. If there had been at least two people on each job, it wouldn't have mattered if one person was ill.
6. If we had expected such a big demand for self-made cakes, we would have had more cakes made.
7. If we had only accepted clean and suitable clothes, we wouldn't have been left with so many old and damaged ones.

Ideas for the future:
1. If we have a better picture of what people want to buy, we will make more profit.
2. If we ask adults with a car to collect the donations, we will have less manual labour.
3. We learned that guests loved the food stalls. If we sell a greater variety of cakes and coffee, we will make more money.
4. We know now that we need more space. If we have the bazaar in our gym, there will be more space for people to walk around.

4 Everything will be all right
Lösungsvorschlag: In my opinion, factories use too much energy. If we hadn't allowed them to use fossil fuels, we wouldn't be in that situation now. If we want to reduce our CO_2 footprint, we'll have to put restrictions on some activities. There would be more interest in renewable energy if the taxes on fossil fuels were higher.

D Describing and commenting

Test yourself

a) 1 nice; 2 nice; 3 nicely; 4 nicely; 5 hard; 6 hard; 7 hard; 8 hard; 9 hardly; 10 Sadly; 11 sad; 12 sadly

b) 1. The guitarist, who / that I saw at the concert last week, plays extremely well.
2. Mr McGregor, who is our English teacher, plays in the same band.
3. I talked to a man in the audience whose daughter is the lead singer.
4. They started with a well-known song, which was a good idea.

Practice

1 Reflecting on self-esteem

1 good; 2 very; 3 well; 4 Obviously; 5 better; 6 hard; 7 better; 8 regularly / weekly; 9 nearly / almost; 10 Last; 11 really / very; 12 exciting / hard / difficult; 13 very / really / completely; 14 original / unique / new; 15 luckily / fortunately / actually / finally; 16 good / great / fantastic; 17 really; 18 glad / happy / proud; 19 happiest; 20 just / now / finally / eventually; 21 self-confident

2 The difficulties of climate policies

Confronted with the global climate crisis, governments are looking for solutions **(1F) that / which** provide climate protection and prosperity at the same time, **(2C) which** sounds like trying the impossible. There may be some options **(3B) that / which** would secure a sufficient supply of energy for the needs of a growing world population, but according to scientists like Eugene Wolff **(4A), who** works for the influential Green energy Institute in Wessex, they could only be achieved if the global community cooperated to an extent as yet unknown. People from different countries **(5D) who** control different resources and don't necessarily share the same beliefs or values would have to agree on a set of common goals **(6E) that / which** they would give top priority.

3 Should politics try to influence language?

1. **Obviously**, one …
2. No one would **seriously** doubt …
3. **Furthermore**, it can even be used to describe what is not **true / truly** in the real world but …
4. **Thus**, it is **generally** agreed …
5. This is where the matter gets **exciting**.
6. Activists often argue that as long as language treats particular groups **who fight against the discrimination of women or minorities** as **inferior** or does not make them **visible** at all, there …
7. **Recently**, tensions have been building on **social** media between people **who accuse others of using racist or sexist language and want to see political action against what they consider problematic language use** on the one hand and people **who argue that language change cannot and should not be forced by politics** on the other.
8. It is true that, even with the best intentions, you cannot make language users **abruptly** change …
9. And **in fact** there have been examples of state-controlled language institutions **which have standardised language**, especially …

10. **Normally**, language change is a **slow** process which happens **gradually** and over time.
11. Yet there are sometimes events or developments in the real world **that make us change our use of language much more quickly**, for example …
12. **Moreover**, our reassessment of **historical** events has caused us to ban certain words from our vocabulary together with the concepts **they represent**.
13. **Fortunately**, there is no … but there are grey areas **in which there is no general agreement on which terms may still be used**, and in which contexts.
14. For example, there is a controversy on whether **original** texts and texts about **historical** events …
15. Although some people feel **hurt** when they read older texts **in which their ethnical group is referred to by a term that is not acceptable any longer but that was accepted at the time**, it can …
16. One possible solution (**probably**) could (**probably**) be …

E Linking ideas

Test yourself

1. The charity bazaar **organised by our school** was a wonderful event.
2. People donated things they didn't need any longer, **(thus) helping us to raise a lot of money.**
3. **Having gotten / got a lot of donations**, we could give a big sum to the rainforest project.
4. We would love to do it again next year **despite it being a lot of work**.

Practice

1 A success story

Lösungsvorschlag:
1. (With) His father having died early, he grew up with his mother in relative poverty.
2. Recognising his potential, his mother worked hard to send him to school.
3. (With) The other children bullying him, school was difficult for him at first.
4. Instead of giving up, he worked even harder.
5. Being a very good pupil, he was encouraged by his teachers.
6. After finishing / Having finished school, he got a scholarship at a good university.
7. Having written various successful books, he is famous internationally today.
8. Apart from witing novels, he has also written poetry.

2 Young people's problems and social media

Lösungsvorschlag:
1. Being asked what they considered the biggest issues for teenagers at the moment, most young people in Scotland named mental health.
2. Looking at statistics, teenagers today seem more likely to develop mental disorders than 30 years ago.
3. Having been conducted over the last couple of decades, surveys show that these problems have become worse since social media emerged.
4. About 30 percent is an alarming figure for teenagers being

worried about their bodies. / About 30 percent of teenagers being worried about their bodies is an alarming figure.

5. Wanting to be liked, teenagers often go to extremes to fulfil what they think are general beauty standards.
6. Convinced they are not beautiful enough, they start to change their behaviour.
7. Wanting to shape their bodies, they overdo workouts at the gym and develop serious eating disorders.
8. Comparing themselves with others, they think they will never be good enough.
9. Getting depressed because of the constant pressure can be one of the consequences for them.
10. Seeking professional advice or even psychotherapy may be the only solution if they feel so bad that they hurt themselves or think of suicide.
11. Convinced that social media have created all these problems, parents want to limit their children's use of the internet.
12. (With) Social media having made the issues more visible, some people put the blame on digitalisation.
13. Considering the spread of information on social media today, everyone is bound to be confronted with the problem.
14. However, there are examples like the body positivity movement, showing that social media may even help people overcome their problems.
15. Influencers fighting unhealthy beauty standards can also help.
16. Looking at all the facts, we will have to learn to live with the dangers of social media.

3   A yearbook contribution
Lösungsvorschlag:
Williamina Fleming, born in 1857, was an astronomer who invented a system to categorise stars and discovered hundreds of new stars and astrological phenomena. Williamina, being originally from Dundee in Scotland, had already become a teacher at her school at only 14. She moved to Boston with her husband at 21 years of age. Her husband having left her and their baby, she found work as a household help. Noticing how clever she was, her employer gave her an assistant job at the observatory, where she did research and published her findings. I see her as a feminist because Williamina later wrote an article describing what she and other women at the observatory did, trying to motivate other women to get a job in astronomy. She died of a lung infection in 1911.
I wrote about Williamina Fleming because she is one of few well-known Scottish women who have influenced world history.

F Focus on the passive

Test yourself
1. Rosa Parks was arrested (by the police) in Montgomery in December 1955.
2. She had been told (by the bus driver) to give up her seat.
3. The police had been called (by the driver).
4. After the incident, a bus boycott was organised (by Black leaders) to protest segregation.

Practice
1   A very special musical instrument
1. Bagpipes are usually associated with Scotland.
2. Lots of jokes about the Scots and their bagpipes have been made.
3. But the bagpipes were not invented by the Scots.
4. Bagpipes were mentioned in Middle Eastern texts more than 2,000 years ago.
5. The bagpipes were also played by Nero, the Roman Emperor.
6. The bagpipes were played all over Europe in the Middle Ages.
7. They have mainly been used in folk music since the 19th century.
8. Different kinds of bagpipes are still being played in Europe, North Africa and Turkey.
9. But it's the Scottish bagpipes that are known (by people) all over the world.

2   Tourism in Scotland
1. Before 2020, about £2 billion were spent by international visitors in Scotland per year.
2. Gaelic is still spoken by a lot of people there,
3. which was visited by over 2 million people in 2019.
4. lots of travellers have also been attracted by the Highlands.
5. Visitors are fascinated by the beautiful landscape.
6. A lot of tourists are attracted by outdoor activities like hiking, mountain biking or water sports in the summer or skiing and snowboarding in the winter.
7. where Nessie, the famous monster, might be seen.
8. They will be told that it still lives there.
9. how whisky is made (by the Scots).
10. More than one billion bottles of their famous 'water of life' are exported every year.
11. Visitors are offered whisky tastings and guided tours of distilleries.
12. which supposedly was built in the 14th century by Sir William Drummond.
13. It was bought by Queen Victoria's husband Prince Albert in 1852 and was made a royal residence.
14. Some members of the royal family may be spotted there.
15. held (by Scottish communities) between May and September.
16. while traditional music and dances are performed in individual or group competitions.

3   A famous historical building
Lösungsvorschlag:
The Brandenburger Tor was built following the order of King Friedrich Wilhelm II between 1788 and 1791. Having been built in neoclassical style, it is the last of formerly 18 city gates. It serves as the end of the boulevard 'Unter den Linden'. The Brandenburger Tor is known as a national symbol of Germany. Standing on what used to be the border of East and West Germany, it can be seen in many historical films. What is special about it is that it has been printed on the German 50-cent coin as well as the old 5 DM bank note and different stamps.

infinitive	simple past	past participle	German
be [biː]	was [wɒz]/were [wɜː]	been [biːn]	sein
bear [beə]	bore [bɔː]	borne / AE: born [bɔːn]	tragen
beat [biːt]	beat [biːt]	beaten ['biːtn] / AE: beat [biːt]	schlagen
become [bɪ'kʌm]	became [bɪ'keɪm]	become [bɪ'kʌm]	werden
begin [bɪ'gɪn]	began [bɪ'gæn]	begun [bɪ'gʌn]	beginnen, anfangen
bend [bend]	bent [bent]	bent [bent]	biegen, beugen
bet [bet]	bet [bet]/betted ['betɪd]	bet [bet]/betted ['betɪd]	wetten
bite [baɪt]	bit [bɪt]	bitten ['bɪtn]	beißen
blow [bləʊ]	blew [bluː]	blown [bləʊn]	blasen, pusten
break [breɪk]	broke [brəʊk]	broken ['brəʊkn]	(zer-)brechen, kaputt machen
breed [briːd]	bred [bred]	bred [bred]	züchten, sich vermehren
bring [brɪŋ]	brought [brɔːt]	brought [brɔːt]	(mit-)bringen
build [bɪld]	built [bɪlt]	built [bɪlt]	bauen
burn [bɜːn]	burnt [bɜːnt]/burned [bɜːnd]	burnt [bɜːnt]/burned [bɜːnd]	brennen
burst [bɜːst]	burst [bɜːst]/bursted ['bɜːstɪd]	burst [bɜːst]/bursted ['bɜːstɪd]	bersten, platzen
buy [baɪ]	bought [bɔːt]	bought [bɔːt]	kaufen
cast [kɑːst]	cast [kɑːst]	cast [kɑːst]	werfen
catch [kætʃ]	caught [kɔːt]	caught [kɔːt]	fangen
choose [tʃuːz]	chose [tʃəʊz]	chosen ['tʃəʊzn]	(aus-)wählen
come [kʌm]	came [keɪm]	come [kʌm]	kommen
cost [kɒst]	cost [kɒst]	cost [kɒst]	kosten
cling [klɪŋ]	clang [klæŋ]	clung [klʌŋ]	kleben, klammern
creep [kriːp]	crept [krept]	crept [krept]	schleichen
cut [kʌt]	cut [kʌt]	cut [kʌt]	schneiden
deal [diːl]	dealt [delt]	dealt [delt]	(be-)handeln
dig [dɪg]	dug [dʌg]	dug [dʌg]	graben
do [duː]	did [dɪd]	done [dʌn]	machen, tun
draw [drɔː]	drew [druː]	drawn [drɔːn]	zeichnen, ziehen
dream [driːm]	dreamt [dremt]/dreamed [driːmd]	dreamt [dremt]/dreamed [driːmd]	träumen
drink [drɪŋk]	drank [dræŋk]	drunk [drʌŋk]	trinken
drive [draɪv]	drove [drəʊv]	driven ['drɪvn]	fahren, treiben
eat [iːt]	ate [et/eɪt]	eaten ['iːtn]	essen
fall [fɔːl]	fell [fel]	fallen ['fɔːlən]	fallen
feed [fiːd]	fed [fed]	fed [fed]	füttern, ernähren
feel [fiːl]	felt [felt]	felt [felt]	fühlen
fight [faɪt]	fought [fɔːt]	fought [fɔːt]	kämpfen, (sich) streiten
find [faɪnd]	found [faʊnd]	found [faʊnd]	finden
fit [fɪt]	fit [fɪt]/fitted ['fɪtɪd]	fit [fɪt]/fitted ['fɪtɪd]	passen
fly [flaɪ]	flew [fluː]	flown [fləʊn]	fliegen
forbid [fə'bɪd]	forbade [fə'bæd]	forbidden [fə'bɪdn]	verbieten
forget [fə'get]	forgot [fə'gɒt]	forgotten [fə'gɒtn]	vergessen
forgive [fə'gɪv]	forgave [fə'geɪv]	forgiven [fə'gɪvn]	vergeben, verzeihen
freeze [friːz]	froze [frəʊz]	frozen ['frəʊzn]	gefrieren, erstarren
get [get]	got [gɒt]	got [gɒt]/AE: gotten ['gɒtn]	bekommen, erhalten
give [gɪv]	gave [geɪv]	given ['gɪvn]	geben
go [gəʊ]	went [went]	gone [gɒn]	gehen, fahren
grow [grəʊ]	grew [gruː]	grown [grəʊn]	wachsen, anbauen, züchten
hang [hæŋ]	hung [hʌŋ]	hung [hʌŋ]	hängen
have [hæv]	had [hæd]	had [hæd]	haben
hear [hɪə]	heard [hɜːd]	heard [hɜːd]	hören
hide [haɪd]	hid [hɪd]	hidden ['hɪdn]	(sich) verstecken
hit [hɪt]	hit [hɪt]	hit [hɪt]	schlagen, treffen
hold [həʊld]	held [held]	held [held]	halten
hurt [hɜːt]	hurt [hɜːt]	hurt [hɜːt]	verletzen, sich weh tun
keep [kiːp]	kept [kept]	kept [kept]	(auf-)bewahren, behalten
know [nəʊ]	knew [njuː]	known [nəʊn]	kennen, wissen
lay [leɪ]	laid [leɪd]	laid [leɪd]	legen
lead [liːd]	led [led]	led [led]	führen
lean [liːn]	leant [lent]/leaned [liːnd]	leant [lent]/leaned [liːnd]	lehnen, beugen
leap [liːp]	leapt [lept]/leaped [liːpt]	leapt [lept]/leaped [liːpt]	springen
learn [lɜːn]	learnt [lɜːnt]/learned [lɜːnd]	learnt [lɜːnt]/learned [lɜːnd]	lernen
leave [liːv]	left [left]	left [left]	(ver-)lassen
lend [lend]	lent [lent]	lent [lent]	leihen

infinitive	simple past	past participle	German
let [let]	let [let]	let [let]	lassen
lie [laɪ]	lay [leɪ]	lain [leɪn]	liegen
lose [luːz]	lost [lɒst]	lost [lɒst]	verlieren
make [meɪk]	made [meɪd]	made [meɪd]	machen, tun
mean [miːn]	meant [ment]	meant [ment]	bedeuten, meinen
meet [miːt]	met [met]	met [met]	treffen
pay [peɪ]	paid [peɪd]	paid [peɪd]	(be-)zahlen
put [pʊt]	put [pʊt]	put [pʊt]	legen, setzen, stellen
read [riːd]	read [red]	read [red]	lesen
ride [raɪd]	rode [rəʊd]	ridden ['rɪdn]	fahren, reiten
ring [rɪŋ]	rang [ræŋ]	rung [rʌŋ]	klingeln, läuten
rise [raɪz]	rose [rəʊz]	risen ['rɪzn]	aufsteigen, sich erheben
run [rʌn]	ran [ræn]	run [rʌn]	laufen, rennen
say [seɪ]	said [sed]	said [sed]	sagen
see [siː]	saw [sɔː]	seen [siːn]	sehen
seek [siːk]	sought [sɔːt]	sought [sɔːt]	suchen
sell [sel]	sold [səʊld]	sold [səʊld]	verkaufen
send [send]	sent [sent]	sent [sent]	senden, verschicken
set [set]	set [set]	set [set]	setzen, einrichten
sew [səʊ]	sewed [səʊd]	sewn [səʊn]/sewed [səʊd]	nähen
shake [ʃeɪk]	shook [ʃʊk]	shaken ['ʃeɪkn]	schütteln
shine [ʃaɪn]	shone [ʃɒn]	shone [ʃɒn]	scheinen
shoot [ʃuːt]	shot [ʃɒt]	shot [ʃɒt]	schießen
show [ʃəʊ]	showed [ʃəʊd]	shown [ʃəʊn]	zeigen
shrink [ʃrɪŋk]	shrank [ʃræŋk]	shrunk [ʃræŋk]	schrumpfen, weichen
sing [sɪŋ]	sang [sæŋ]	sung [sʌŋ]	singen
sink [sɪŋk]	sank [sæŋk]	sunk [sʌŋk]	sinken
sit [sɪt]	sat [sæt]	sat [sæt]	sitzen
sleep [sliːp]	slept [slept]	slept [slept]	schlafen
slide [slaɪd]	slid [slɪd]	slid [slɪd]	rutschen
smell [smel]	smelt [smelt]/smelled [smeld]	smelt [smelt]/smelled [smeld]	riechen, duften
sow [səʊ]	sowed [səʊd]	sown [səʊn]/sowed [səʊd]	säen
speak [spiːk]	spoke [spəʊk]	spoken ['spəʊkn]	sprechen
speed [spiːd]	sped [sped]/speeded ['spiːdɪd]	sped [sped]/speeded ['spiːdɪd]	sausen, rasen
spell [spel]	spelt [spelt]/spelled [speld]	spelt [spelt]/spelled [speld]	buchstabieren
spend [spend]	spent [spent]	spent [spent]	ausgeben, verbringen
spin [spɪn]	span [spæn]/spun [spʌn]	spun [spʌn]	drehen, spinnen
spit [spɪt]	spat [spæt]	spat [spæt]	spucken
split [splɪt]	split [splɪt]	split [splɪt]	spalten, teilen
spread [spred]	spread [spred]	spread [spred]	(sich) verbreiten
stand [stænd]	stood [stʊd]	stood [stʊd]	stehen
steal [stiːl]	stole [stəʊl]	stolen ['stəʊlən]	stehlen
stick [stɪk]	stuck [stʌk]	stuck [stʌk]	kleben, stecken
sting [stɪŋ]	stung [stʌŋ]	stung [stʌŋ]	stechen
strike [straɪk]	struck [strʌk]	struck [strʌk]	schlagen, zuschlagen
strive [straɪv]	strove [strəʊv]/strived [straɪvd]	striven [strɪvn]/strived [straɪvd]	streben, sich bemühen
swear [sweə]	swore [swɔː]	sworn [swɔːn]	schwören, fluchen
sweep [swiːp]	swept [swept]	swept [swept]	fegen
swell [swel]	swelled [sweld]	swollen ['swəʊlən]/swelled [sweld]	anschwellen, anwachsen
swim [swɪm]	swam [swæm]	swum [swʌm]	schwimmen
swing [swɪŋ]	swung [swʌŋ]	swung [swʌŋ]	schwingen
take [teɪk]	took [tʊk]	taken ['teɪkn]	nehmen
teach [tiːtʃ]	taught [tɔːt]	taught [tɔːt]	unterrichten, lehren, beibringen
tell [tel]	told [təʊld]	told [təʊld]	erzählen
think [θɪŋk]	thought [θɔːt]	thought [θɔːt]	(nach-)denken, glauben
throw [θrəʊ]	threw [θruː]	thrown [θrəʊn]	werfen
understand [ˌʌndə'stænd]	understood [ˌʌndə'stʊd]	understood [ˌʌndə'stʊd]	verstehen
upset [ʌp'set]	upset [ʌp'set]	upset [ʌp'set]	aufregen
wake [weɪk]	woke [wəʊk]	woken ['wəʊkn]	wecken, aufwachen
wear [weə]	wore [wɔː]	worn [wɔːn]	anhaben, tragen
weep [wiːp]	wept [wept]	wept [wept]	weinen
win [wɪn]	won [wʌn]	won [wʌn]	gewinnen, siegen
write [raɪt]	wrote [rəʊt]	written ['rɪtn]	schreiben

Robert II was the first king from the **House of Stewart** (later **Stuart**). His descendants were kings and queens in Scotland from 1371, and of England and Great Britain from 1603, to 1714. The Stuart dynasty ended with the death of Queen Anne, when her husband George of Hanover took the throne. Claims to the throne by exiled Stuart descendants weren't successful.

James VI, Mary Stuart's son, King of England and Lord of Ireland, became **James VI & I** when he succeeded to the English throne after Elizabeth I died with no children. This historic move is known as the **Union of the Crowns** because the independent states England and Scotland were governed by the same person after centuries of fighting.

Hadrian's Wall, near today's Scottish-English border

The **Romans** built **Hadrian's Wall** and the **Antonine Wall**. One of the reasons was failed attempts to conquer Scotland, others include keeping Scots and Romans separate and controlling trade and the movement of people.

Henry VIII, king of England, led England to **Protestantism** because he wanted to divorce his wife and the pope wouldn't allow it. This led to the **Scottish Reformation**: Most of the Scottish Lowlands also broke with the pope and became Protestant. The Highlands remained mostly Catholic.

The **Glorious Revolution** made it possible to end royal absolutism and for the first time form a **parliament** in the UK thanks to its first Bill of Rights. The last absolute monarch, James VII & II, a Catholic, found exile in France. The UK has been a constitutional monarchy since.

122–154   800   1297–1320   1371   1560   1567   1603   1688–1689   1689–1746

The **Vikings** arrived in the west of Scotland.

In ongoing fights between Scotland and England, Scottish warriors, led by William Wallace and Andrew Moray in the **Battle of Stirling Bridge** (1297) and Scotland's king **Robert the Bruce** in the **Battle of Bannockburn** (1314), defeated the English army. In 1320 Scottish nobles declared Scotland an independent sovereign state in a letter to the pope known as the **Declaration of Arbroath**.

Mary Stuart, Queen of Scots, was forced to abdicate after being suspected of murdering her second husband. She fled to England but was kept prisoner because of ongoing conflicts with her relative Queen Elizabeth I of England, who finally had Mary executed in 1587.

The **Jacobite uprisings** were a series of attacks on the new Protestant government, mainly by Highlanders who supported the exiled Stuart king James VII & II (Latin: Jacobus) and his descendants after the Glorious Revolution. They ended unsuccessfully in the **Battle of Culloden** (1746).

The **Highland Clearances** banned wearing traditional tartan clothes and took away the clan chiefs' right of making their own laws, eventually destroying traditional clan life as people moved away.

The Edinburgh Agreement states that a **referendum on Scottish independence** can be held once in a generation and will be respected by the Scottish and British government. The 2014 referendum was unsuccessful, even though 45% voted for Scotland to be an independent country.

With the **Acts of Union**, a single parliament of the United Kingdom of Great Britain was created to bring Scotland closer to Britain.

End of the **slate industry** in Scotland and closure of the around 80 quarries.

2014

19th century

Late 1800s–1960s

1997

1706–1707

1720s–1820s

1746–1850s

The **Scottish Enlightenment**, which declared the principle of reason over religion, and the **Industrial Revolution** turned Scotland into a modern intellectual, commercial, and industrial centre.

Masses of people worked on small plots of land known as **crofts**, which they cultivated and rented. Most of them were very poor and relied on the potato harvest for food. In 1846 and following years the potato crops died. The government reacted to the **Highland Potato Famine** by advising people to emigrate to Canada and Australia. About a third of the western Scottish Highlander population **emigrated** between 1841 and 1861.

Successfully cloning the first mammal, **Dolly the Sheep**, the Roslin Institute made headlines internationally.

Slaves on a plantation, end of the 18th century

The **Emancipation Proclamation**, issued by Abraham Lincoln (US president 1861–1865), declared all enslaved people free. It is celebrated on **Juneteenth** (June 19th) – the day the proclamation arrived in Texas in 1865.

During the 18th century, the system of **slavery** spread quickly through the American colonies, resulting in around 6–7 million African people being transported to the Americas. Revolts, such as the **Stono Rebellion** and **Nat Turner's Rebellion**, were quickly put down and new laws further restricted enslaved people's lives, making them even harder.

The 13th, 14th, and 15th Amendments to the US Constitution supported racial justice: They abolished slavery, granted equal protection, made all people born in the US citizens, and gave every male citizen the right to vote regardless of "race, color, or previous condition of servitude".

1877–1954

18th century

1790s–1831

1861–1865

1863

1865

1865–1870

16th century

FREE!

colored

The southern states passed new laws requiring the racial segregation of white and African-American people, which came to be known as **Jim Crow laws.** They detailed when, where, and how Black people could work, took away voting rights, controlled where Black people could live and even allowed taking their children away to work for others.

While Black people lived on the continent as early as the 14th century, European powers brought the **first enslaved Africans** to the New World in the 16th century, using them as cheap labour force for their colonies.

The South was a slave-holding, agricultural society; the North was more industrialized. Because of these differences, the southern states wanted to be separate, and a terrible **Civil War** followed.
The victory of the North saved the unity of the US and freed all slaves.

The **Ku Klux Klan (KKK)** was founded as a white supremacist group terrorising Black Americans, e.g. by burning down houses and lynching people. A third wave of the KKK has been active in the US since the 1950s.

Free Black people and different groups of white settlers (e.g. Quakers), who opposed slavery on religious or moral grounds, developed the **Underground Railway**, a network of safe houses that helped slaves escape from southern plantations.

After **Rosa Parks** had refused to give up her seat on a bus in Montgomery, Alabama, where racial segregation was enforced strictly, the Black community boycotted the Montgomery buses for over a year. Parks went to court to fight bus segregation, which was finally ruled unconstitutional.

Malcolm X, another influential leader of the civil rights movement, was shot to death. Unlike Martin Luther King, Jr., he was in favour of Blacks defending themselves against white aggression, if necessary, with violence.

Barack Obama became the first African-American president in US history. This was a huge milestone in race relations for the entire country.

YES, WE CAN!

In January 2021 **Kamala Harris** became the first female and first Black vice president of the United States.

1950s–1960s · **1955** · **1963** · **1964** · **1965** · **2009–2017** · **2013** · **2021**

Rosa Parks and Martin Luther King Jr., among others, protested against the unfair treatment of African-Americans in the **civil rights movement** of the 1950s and 1960s. Eventually, protests grew so strong that the policy of segregation finally came to an end. But this didn't yet mean the end of race problems in the US.

The **Civil Rights Act** ensures legal protection for all citizens against discrimination on the basis of race, religion, sex or national origin.

Martin Luther King, Jr. held his speech "I have a Dream" after the non-violent **March on Washington**. He called for voting rights, equal employment opportunities for Black Americans and an end to racial segregation.

After the shooting of 17-year-old Trayvon Martin in 2012, the **Black Lives Matter** movement was founded. The hashtag #BlackLivesMatter spread widely as a series of deaths of Black Americans at the hand of police officers led to protests all over the US.

Bildquellen

2.1 ShutterStock.com RF, New York (hedgehog94); **2.2** ShutterStock.com RF, New York (Rawpixel.com); **2.3** Alamy stock photo, Abingdon (World History Archive); **3.1** stock.adobe.com, Dublin (Alexey Fedorenko); **3.2** Alamy stock photo, Abingdon (Monica Wells); **3.3** Getty Images Plus, München (Gannet77); **4.1** Alamy stock photo, Abingdon (Marjorie Kamys Cotera/Bob Daemmrich Photography); **4.2** ShutterStock.com RF, New York (Agave Photo Studio); **4.3** stock.adobe.com, Dublin (Hakan Ozturk); **4.4** ShutterStock.com RF, New York (Jacob Lund); **5.1** Alamy stock photo, Abingdon (Paul Carstairs); **5.2** ShutterStock.com RF, New York (Leonard Zhukovsky); **5.3** Getty Images, München (JEWEL SAMAD/AFP); **5.4** Alamy stock photo, Abingdon (Kristin Cato); **6.1** Getty Images Plus, München (pacifica); **6.2** ShutterStock.com RF, New York (TotemArt); **6.3** ShutterStock.com RF, New York (GrooveZ); **6.4** Isabelle Sieb, London; **7.1** ShutterStock.com RF, New York (Axel Bueckert); **7.2** ShutterStock.com RF, New York (Prostock-studio); **7.3** ShutterStock.com RF, New York (Josie Elias); **8.1** ShutterStock.com RF, New York (StunningArt); **8.2** Getty Images, München (Beáta Angyalosi / EyeEm); **8.3** ShutterStock.com RF, New York (Rawpixel.com); **8.4** ShutterStock.com RF, New York (hedgehog94); **9.1** Getty Images Plus, München (saiko3p); **9.2** Alamy stock photo, Abingdon (Justin Kase z12z); **9.3** Alamy stock photo, Abingdon (Kayte Deioma); **9.4** ShutterStock.com RF, New York (Jacob Lund); **10.1** Alamy stock photo, Abingdon (Keith Corrigan); **10.2** stock.adobe.com, Dublin (mmmg); **11.1** Alamy stock photo, Abingdon (World History Archive); **11.2** Alamy stock photo, Abingdon (Old Books Images); **12.1** stock.adobe.com, Dublin (Alexey Fedorenko); **12.2** ShutterStock.com RF, New York (Barbara Ash); **13.1** Alamy stock photo, Abingdon (MB Media Solutions); **13.2** Alamy stock photo, Abingdon (Monica Wells); **15.1** ShutterStock.com RF, New York (Lubomira08); **15.2** ShutterStock.com RF, New York (Narongsak Nagadhana); **16.1** Kramer, Peer, Düsseldorf; **17.1** Kramer, Peer, Düsseldorf; **19.1** Alamy stock photo, Abingdon (Mike Saint); **19.2** stock.adobe.com, Dublin (Duncan Andison); **19.3** Getty Images Plus, München (Ashley Cooper); **19.4** Alamy stock photo, Abingdon (PhotoXpress/ZUMAPRESS.com); **20.1** ShutterStock.com RF, New York (richardjohnson); **21.1** ShutterStock.com RF, New York (DrimaFilm); **22.1** Alamy stock photo, Abingdon (Arch White); **23.1** stock.adobe.com, Dublin (mmmg); **25.1** Alamy stock photo, Abingdon (Iain Masterton); **26.1** ShutterStock.com RF, New York (garagestock); **29.1** ShutterStock.com RF, New York (Kamira); **32.1** Getty Images Plus, München (Gannet77); **32.2** ShutterStock.com RF, New York (GRSI); **32.3** ShutterStock.com RF, New York (Complexli); **32.4** iStockphoto, Calgary, Alberta (ene); **32.5** Alamy stock photo, Abingdon (Jack Barr); **32.6** Ohlms, Ute, Braunschweig; **32.7** ShutterStock.com RF, New York (Everett Collection); **33.1** stock.adobe.com, Dublin (mmmg); **34.1** Alamy stock photo, Abingdon (Stephen Power); **34.2** Alamy stock photo, Abingdon (Susie Kearley); **35.1** Getty Images Plus/Microstock, München (Planet Flem); **36.1** ShutterStock.com RF, New York (Puwadol Jaturawutthichai); **36.2** ShutterStock.com RF, New York (fat_69); **37.1** Alamy stock photo, Abingdon (Michael Brooks); **38.1** Getty Images Plus, München (Keith Lance); **38.2** CartoonStock Ltd, Bath (Leo Cullum); **40.1** Alamy stock photo, Abingdon (Marjorie Kamys Cotera/Bob Daemmrich Photography); **40.2** ShutterStock.com RF, New York (Agave Photo Studio); **41.1** ShutterStock.com RF, New York (Phil Pasquini); **41.2** Getty Images Plus, München (HRAUN); **41.3** nach: US Census Bureau/2020; **42.1** Alamy stock photo, Abingdon (AF archive); **44.1** Alamy stock photo, Abingdon (AA Film Archive); **45.1** ShutterStock.com RF, New York (granata1111); **45.2** ShutterStock.com RF, New York (Elena Veselova); **45.3** stock.adobe.com, Dublin (koss13); **46.1** ShutterStock.com RF, New York (Drazen Zigic); **47.1** stock.adobe.com, Dublin (Hakan Ozturk); **49.1** Getty Images, München (Charles Sykes/Bravo/NBCU Photo Bank); **50.1** Alamy stock photo, Abingdon (Levantine Films/Entertainment Pictures/ZUMAPRESS.com); **51.1** ShutterStock.com RF, New York (Daniel Hernandez-Salazar); **52.1** Alamy stock photo, Abingdon (ZUMA Press, Inc.); **53.1** Alamy stock photo, Abingdon (UPI); **56.1** Getty Images, München (Jennifer E. Pottheiser/NBAE); **58.1** Kramer, Peer, Düsseldorf; **59.1** Kramer, Peer, Düsseldorf; **60.1** Alamy stock photo, Abingdon (Alpha Historica); **60.2** Getty Images, München (Pacific Press / Kontributor); **61.1** akg-images, Berlin (WHA / World History Archive); **62.1** Alamy stock photo, Abingdon (Historic Collection); **62.2** Picture-Alliance, Frankfurt/M. (AP Images); **63.1** Getty Images, München (Gary W. Green/Orlando Sentinel/Tribune News Service); **63.2** ShutterStock.com RF, New York (Jacob Lund); **64.1** Alamy stock photo, Abingdon (Pictorial Press Ltd); **65.1** Alamy stock photo, Abingdon (PictureLux / The Hollywood Archive); **66.1** Alamy stock photo, Abingdon (Keystone Press); **66.2** Alamy stock photo, Abingdon (Trinity Mirror / Mirrorpix); **66.3** Alamy stock photo, Abingdon (Paul Carstairs); **66.4** ShutterStock.com

RF, New York (Gorodenkoff); **67.1** Alamy stock photo, Abingdon (Pictorial Press Ltd); **68.1** stock.adobe.com, Dublin (Jacob Lund); **69.1** ShutterStock.com RF, New York (Leonard Zhukovsky); **69.2** ShutterStock.com RF, New York (JJFarq); **69.3** Getty Images, München (JEWEL SAMAD/AFP); **69.4** Getty Images, München (Peathegee Inc); **70.1** Kramer, Peer, Düsseldorf; **71.1** Kramer, Peer, Düsseldorf; **75.1** Alamy stock photo, Abingdon (Pat Johnson/MediaPunch); **76.1** Getty Images, München (Johnny Nunez/WireImage); **77.1** ShutterStock.com RF, New York (hurricanehank); **77.2** ShutterStock.com RF, New York (Black Creator 24); **79.1** CartoonStock Ltd, Bath (Len Hawkins); **79.2** CartoonStock Ltd, Bath (Chris Wildt); **80.1** stock.adobe.com, Dublin (alexandru verinciuc); **81.1** Getty Images, München (PYMCA/Universal Images Group); **81.2** ShutterStock.com RF, New York (Sergey Goruppa); **81.3** ShutterStock.com RF, New York (oneinchpunch); **83.1** Alamy stock photo, Abingdon (Kristin Cato); **84.1** Getty Images, München (Gie Knaeps); **84.2** Alamy stock photo, Abingdon (BSIP SA); **85.1** ShutterStock.com RF, New York (TanyaCPhotography); **85.2** Getty Images, München (Gary Reyes/Oakland Tribune Staff Archives/MediaNews Group/Bay Area News); **88.1** Alamy stock photo, Abingdon (Jeff Morgan 01); **88.2** Alamy stock photo, Abingdon (Alain Le Garsmeur „The Troubles" Archive); **89.1** Alamy stock photo, Abingdon (Granger Historical Picture Archive); **89.2** Getty Images Plus, München (pacifica); **89.3** Getty Images, München (Cultura); **89.4** Alamy stock photo, Abingdon (Pictorial Press Ltd); **89.5** ShutterStock.com RF, New York (TotemArt); **89.6** Alamy stock photo, Abingdon (The Photo Access); **89.7** ShutterStock.com RF, New York (Rawpixel.com); **93.1** Oser, Liliane, Hamburg; **93.2** Oser, Liliane, Hamburg; **95.1** Alamy stock photo, Abingdon (Doreen Kennedy); **97.1** Getty Images Plus, München (E+ / sanjeri); **97.2** ShutterStock.com RF, New York (GrooveZ); **98.1** ShutterStock.com RF, New York (Rawpixel.com); **100.1** Kramer, Peer, Düsseldorf; **101.1** Kramer, Peer, Düsseldorf; **104.1** Alamy stock photo, Abingdon (Pacific Press Media Production Corp.); **105.1** Getty Images, München (Andrew D. Bernstein/NBAE); **105.2** Getty Images, München (John W. McDonough /Sports Illustrated); **108.1** ShutterStock.com RF, New York (titoOnz); **109.1** ShutterStock.com RF, New York (PRESSLAB); **111.1** ShutterStock.com RF, New York (Axel Bueckert); **112.1** Isabelle Sieb, London; **113.1** Isabelle Sieb, London; **113.2** Isabelle Sieb, London; **113.3** Isabelle Sieb, London; **114.1** Isabelle Sieb, London; **114.2** Isabelle Sieb, London; **115.1** Isabelle Sieb, London;

115.2 Isabelle Sieb, London; **115.3** Isabelle Sieb, London; **115.4** Isabelle Sieb, London; **115.5** Isabelle Sieb, London; **115.6** Picture-Alliance, Frankfurt/M. (The Advertising Archives); **116.1** CartoonStock Ltd, Bath (Chris Wildt); **118.1** ShutterStock.com RF, New York (Andrewshots); **123.1** ShutterStock.com RF, New York (LightField Studios); **132.1** ShutterStock.com RF, New York (wavebreakmedia); **134.1** Kramer, Peer, Düsseldorf; **134.2** Ernst Klett Verlag GmbH, Stuttgart; **134.3** Ernst Klett Verlag GmbH, Stuttgart; **134.4** Ernst Klett Verlag GmbH, Stuttgart; **135.1** Kramer, Peer, Düsseldorf; **135.2** Kramer, Peer, Düsseldorf; **135.3** Kramer, Peer, Düsseldorf; **138.1** ShutterStock.com RF, New York (Prostock-studio); **138.2** ShutterStock.com RF, New York (fizkes); **143.1** CartoonStock Ltd, Bath (Barker, Jim); **143.2** CartoonStock Ltd, Bath (Clive Goddard); **145.1** Alamy stock photo, Abingdon (Ian Lamond); **145.2** ShutterStock.com RF, New York (David Tadevosian); **145.3** ShutterStock.com RF, New York (ESB Professional); **151.1** ShutterStock.com RF, New York (Josie Elias); **155.1** ShutterStock.com RF, New York (JASPERIMAGE); **155.2** ShutterStock.com RF, New York (JASPERIMAGE); **155.3** ShutterStock.com RF, New York (Massimo Todaro); **159.1** ShutterStock.com RF, New York (The Mumus); **160.1** ShutterStock.com RF, New York (CKP1001); **160.2** ShutterStock.com RF, New York (patrimonio designs ltd); **163.1** Barman, Adrienne, Grandson; **163.2** Barman, Adrienne, Grandson; **164.1** ShutterStock.com RF, New York (Naty_Lee); **185.1** iStockphoto, Calgary, Alberta (Josie Desmarais); **192.1** ShutterStock.com RF, New York (mayrum); **258.1** Alamy stock photo, Abingdon (John Michaels); **258.2** Alamy stock photo, Abingdon (Old Books Images); **258.3** Alamy stock photo, Abingdon (Andy Thompson); **259.1** Alamy stock photo, Abingdon (Mark Bourdillon); **259.2** Picture-Alliance, Frankfurt/M. (Reuters/Jeff J Mitchell); **260.1** Alamy stock photo, Abingdon (The Print Collector/Heritage Images); **260.2** By D. Van Nostrand - Moore, Frank, ed. Portrait Gallery of the War. New York: D. Van Nostrand, 1865., Public Domain, https://commons.wikimedia.org/w/index.php?curid=405570; **260.3** Alamy stock photo, Abingdon (Glasshouse Images); **261.1** Alamy stock photo, Abingdon (Science History Images); **261.2** ShutterStock.com RF, New York (BiksuTong); **261.3** REX/Shutterstock, Berlin (Natasha Quarmby); **261.4** Picture-Alliance, Frankfurt/M. (ipol code); **265.1** Dekelver, Christian, Weinstadt; **266–267.1** Dekelver, Christian, Weinstadt

Textquellen

13 © 2003, Carol Ann Duffy; **14** Flic Everett © Telegraph Media Group Limited 2016; **16–18** From: Sea Change, © 2019 Silvia Hehir; **18** From: Sea Change, © 2019 Silvia Hehir; **19** © 2022, SWR Südwestrundfunk; **20** Gavin Moffat © 2021 Guardian News & Media Ltd.; **21** Song: The Dear Green Place Texter: Pincock, Douglas / Reid, Alan / McNeill, B. / Russell, Alistair McKenzie, Verlag/Subverlag: KINMOR MUSIC; **22** 2020, City of Edinburgh Council; **23** 2020, Scottish Youth Parliament; **24** Mary McCool, BBC Scotland news, 28 April 2021; **25** Year of young people 2018, Scottish Government; **29–31** From: Scottish Myths and Legends, Daniel Allison, © 2020 by House of Legends.; **32** Robert Burns †1796; **35** Song: The devil went down Georgia Texter: Crain, John Thomas Jr / Daniels, Charlie / Marshall, James W / Gregorio, Joel di / Edwards, Fred Laroy / Hayward, Charles Fred, Verlag/Subverlag: Songs of Universal Inc./ Universal/MCA Music Publishing GmbH, Berlin; **38–39** From: Stamped: Racism, Antiracism, and You: A Remix of the National Book Award-winning Stamped from the Beginning © 2020 Ibram X. Kendi and Jason Reynolds; **41.1 (Zitat)** Thomas Jefferson †1826; **41.2 (Zitat)** From: Still Life With Woodpecker © 1980 by Tom Robbins; **41.3 (Zitat)** From: Rainbow in the Cloud: The Wisdom and Spirit of Maya Angelou © 2014 by The Estate of Maya Angelou; **42–44** From: The hate u give © 2017 Angie Thomas; **46** From: This Side of Home, © 2015, Renée Watson; **47** Langston Hughes: The Heart of Harlem from The Collected Works of Langston Hughes, Volume 2, Copyright © 2001 by Ramona Bass and Arnold Rampersad, Administrators of the Estate of Langston Hughes; **48–49** Justin Simien, CNN – Cable News Network, February 25, 2014; **51** From the New York Times © 2021 The New York Times Company. All rights reserved. Used under license.; **52.1** Nahal Toosi, Politico Magazine, July 09, 2016; **52.2** Randall Kennedy, Politico Magazine, July/August 2014; **53** Dorothy A. Brown, CNN, 19.01.2017; **54** From: Was weiße Menschen nicht über Rassismus hören wollen aber wissen sollten © 2019 Alice Hasters; **55.1 (Zitat)** © 2021 Guardian News & Media Ltd.; **55.2 (Zitat)** Jon Lockett, The Sun, 12 July 2021; **57–59** From: On the Come Up, © 2019 Angie Thomas; **63** From: Stamped: Racism, Antiracism, and You: A Remix of the National Book Award-winning Stamped from the Beginning © 2020 Ibram X. Kendi and Jason Reynolds; **67.1** Song: My Generation Texter: Townshend, Peter, Verlag/ Subverlag: Fabulous Music LTD. für D/A/CH Essex Musikvertrieb GmbH, Hamburg; **67.2** Song: Your generation Texter: Broad, William Michael Albert / James, Anthony Eric, Verlag/Subverlag: Boneidol Music/BMG Monarch/BMG Rights Management GmbH, Berlin; **68.1 (Zitat)** Attributed to Vivienne Westwood; **68.2 (Zitat)** Tupac Shakur; **68.3 (Zitat)** Autor(en): unbekannt; **70–72** From: Schooled, © 2008 Gordon Korman; **73–74** From: Hairstyles of the Damned © 2004 Joe Meno; **75** On The Line With … 2PAC SHAKUR, The Lost Interview … by Davey D; **76** From Forbes. © 2019 Forbes. All rights reserved. Used under license.; **77–78** „Die Überbetonung von Männlichkeit verweist immer auf einen Bruch", aus SPIEGEL.de, von Jurek Skobala, am 07.03.2020.; **79** Song: Video killed the radio star Texter: Woolley, Bruce Martin / Horn, Trevor Ch. / Downes, Geoffrey, Verlag/Subverlag: Carlin Music Corp. / Island Music Ltd. Universal Music Publ. GmbH, Berlin Musikverlag Intersong GmbH & Co. KG, Hamburg; **80** From HuffPost. © 2019 BuzzFeed. All rights reserved. Used under license.; **81–82** Alexis Petridis, © 2014 Guardian News & Media Ltd.; **83** Monica Anderson, Jiang Jingjing, Pew Research Center, 28th November 2018; **85.1** From: The Rose that Grew from Concrete, © 1999 Tupac Shakur; **85.2** From: The Rose that Grew from Concrete, © 1999 Tupac Shakur; **86** From: Let Me Hear a Rhyme, © 2019 Tiffany D Jackson; **87** Keza MacDonald ©2021 Guardian News & Media Ltd.; **94** Langston Hughes: The Heart of Harlem from The Collected Works of Langston Hughes, Volume 2, Copyright © 2001 by Ramona Bass and Arnold Rampersad, Administrators of the Estate of Langston Hughes; **95** dpa, 2020; **99** ZEIT ONLINE, Fabian Held, 4. März 2021; **100–103** From: Sea Change, © 2019 Silvia Hehir; **104.1** © 2018 Cortney Lamar Charleston; **104.2** „I, too" by Langston Hughes © 1994 Estate of Langston Hughes.; **104.3** © 1994 Ethelbert Miller; **105** © 2015 Kobe Bryant; **106–107** From: Fat kid rules the world © 2004 K. L. Going; **108.A** © 2017 Carol Ann Duffy; **109.B** © 1985 Carol Ann Duffy; **109.C** © 2017 Carol Ann Duffy; **110–111** © 2013 Liz Lochhead; **116** Victory Speech, Barack Obama, 05.11.2008; **119.1** Wörterbuchauszug PONS Schülerwörterbuch ISBN 978-3-12-517539-6, S. 423 („mean"); **119.2** Wörterbuchauszug PONS Schülerwörterbuch ISBN 978-3-12-517539-6, S. 966 („bis"); **120** decline: Cambridge Advanced Learner's Dictionary, Fourth Edition, Cambridge University Press

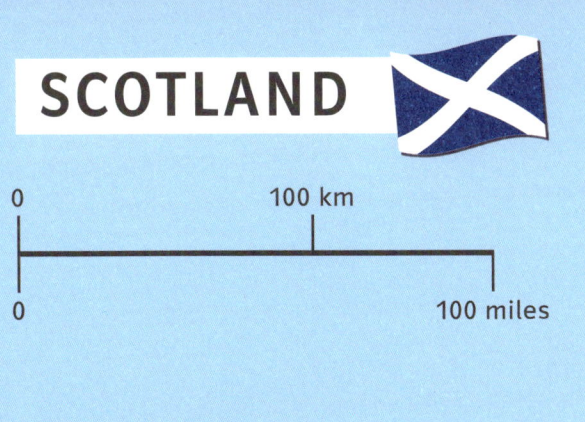

SCOTLAND

0   100 km

0   100 miles

Atlantic Ocean

SHETLAND
ISLANDS

ORKNEY
ISLANDS

Thurso

OUTER
HEBRIDES

ISLE OF
SKYE

H i g h l a n d s

Inverness

Loch Ness

▲ *Ben Nevis*

INNER
HEBRIDES

Aberdeen

North Sea

Dundee

Glasgow

Edinburgh

L o w l a n d s

NORTHERN
IRELAND

Belfast

ENGLAND

Newcastle

Areas in which at
least 25% of the
population speak

Scots

Gaelic

CANADA

ALASKA
Denali▲

CANADA

Juneau

Seattle
WASHINGTON
Portland

OREGON

IDAHO

R
o
c
k
y

MONTANA

NORTH DAKOTA

SOUTH DAKOTA

WYOMING

M
o
u
n
t
a
i
n
s

NEBRASKA

Sacramento
San Francisco

Salt Lake City

NEVADA

UTAH

CALIFORNIA

COLORADO

Denver

KANSAS

Las Vegas

Los Angeles

San Diego

ARIZONA

Albuquerque

OKLAHO

NEW MEXICO

Phoenix

Pacific Ocean

Tucson

TEXAS

Honolulu

San Antonio

Au

Ho

HAWAII

MEXICO